# MUSIC

*in the New World*

# MUSIC
## in the New World

### CHARLES HAMM
Dartmouth College

**W · W · Norton and Company**
New York   London

Copyright © 1983 by Recorded Anthology of American Music, Inc.
All rights reserved.
Published simultaneously in Canada by George J. McLeod Limited, Toronto.
Printed in the United States of America.

The text of this book is composed in Aster.
Manufacturing by The Maple-Vail Book Manufacturing Group.
Book design by Bernard Klein.

Library of Congress Cataloging in Publication Data

Hamm, Charles.
Music in the New World.

Bibliography: p.
Discography: p.
Includes index.
1. Music—United States—History and criticism.
I. Title.
ML200.H17          781.773          82–6481

ISBN 0-393-95193-6                          AACR2

W. W. Norton & Company, Inc. 500 Fifth Avenue, New York, N.Y. 10110
W. W. Norton & Company, Ltd. 37 Great Russell Street, London WC2B 3NU

2 3 4 5 6 7 8 9 0

*This book is dedicated to my wife Marilyse,*
*who helped in so many ways.*

# CONTENTS

# INTRODUCTION

This seemed to be a propitious time to undertake a book on the history of music in the United States, for two reasons.

First, the past decade has produced important and numerous resources for a study of American music, partly as a result of the celebration of our country's Bicentennial. Printed and recorded materials covering an immense stylistic range of music have appeared in profusion, materials which were not available to the authors of the several excellent books on American music presently in print.[1]

The most ambitious and comprehensive project has been *New World Records*, Recorded Anthology of American Music, Inc., executed under the direction of its president, Herman Krawitz. Funded by the Rockefeller Foundation, New World was originally planned as a set of 100 phonograph discs ranging over the entire 200-year history of our music since the Revolution. These were distributed,

---

[1]Gilbert Chase's *America's Music from the Pilgrims to the Present* (New York: McGraw-Hill, 1966, rev. 2nd ed.) set new standards of scope, scholarship and writing style against which every subsequent history of American music has had to be measured; every student and scholar of the subject is indebted to this landmark book, in countless ways. H. Wiley Hitchcock's *Music in the United States: A Historical Introduction* (Englewood Cliffs; Prentice-Hall, 1969) is both an excellent text for a one-term course in American music and an intelligent, comprehensive summary of the musical history of our country. Wilfrid Mellers's *Music in a New Found Land* (New York: Alfred A. Knopf, 1965) is a brilliant, quirky, fascinating, opinionated, highly articulate view of American music stressing the music itself, devoted largely to the twentieth century and concerning itself more with jazz and other vernacular music than any book to that point.

as gifts from the Foundation, to libraries and educational institutions here and abroad. As a result of the wide and favorable critical acclaim accorded the project, New World Records, Inc. decided to bring out additional discs, as a commercial venture; several dozen have already appeared, or are projected for the near future.

The present book has been planned to take full advantage of this unprecedented Recorded Anthology of American music. References to pieces included in the set have been woven into every chapter, and certain chapters are in fact based largely on music available on *New World Records*.[2] Footnotes throughout the text refer the reader to such pieces.

The Bicentennial also yielded a 15-disc set devoted to traditional and vernacular music, *Folk Music in America*, brought out by the Library of Congress under the general editorship of Richard K. Spottswood; wherever appropriate, I have referred to pieces in this collection. I have also made similar use of several older recorded anthologies of American music, and listed the contents of these in my discography: Harry Smith's superb 6-disc *Anthology of American Folk Music* (1952) and the extensive and useful *Music in America* (1958–72), the work of Karl Krueger. I have also made frequent reference to pieces included in the excellent *Smithsonian Collection of Classic Jazz* (1973), selected and annotated by Martin Williams; unfortunately, the equally important *Smithsonian Collection of Classic Country Music* (1981), compiled by Bill Malone, appeared after I had finished this book. But there is considerable overlap between pieces I chose for discussion or mention in my chapter on country-western music and those chosen by Malone for his anthology, and the reader can match these up without difficulty.

Equally impressive have been a number of books, monographs and editions of music. *Music in American Life*, brought out by the University of Illinois Press, is a continuing series concerned with vernacular and popular music; *Earlier American Music* is a series of facsimile scores of important compositions by Americans, under the general editorship of H. Wiley Hitchcock; the Institute for Studies in American Music, based at Brooklyn College, has brought out a number of useful monographs; *Recent Researches in American Music* is devoted to modern editions of American pieces from the eighteenth and nineteenth centuries; *Bibliographies in American Music* is yet another series devoted to American topics. I have made use of all these new resources whenever possible, and have listed the individual titles of each series at the beginning of my bibliog-

---

[2] For a comprehensive index to the first 100 discs, see Elizabeth A. Davis, *Index to the New World Recorded Anthology of American Music* (New York: W. W. Norton & Company, 1981).

raphy. Each is an ongoing venture, with new titles appearing regularly; unfortunately, some items now in print were not yet available as I wrote these words.

A second circumstance making this a favorable time to write a book on the history of music in the United States is the fact that virtually every genre of American music is presently on a stylistic plateau. For a book which sets out to take a broad historical view of the development of music over a wide time span, it is a convenience if the present state of the art is relatively calm, simplifying discussions of genres which are still part of our musical life. Inevitably we will reach another period of radical experimentation; when this happens, my own interest will be in once again writing about the present rather than the past. The late 1970s and early '80s have been a good time to look backwards.

I have taken as a basic premise my conviction that a historical study of American music must be concerned with both written and unwritten music, that popular and vernacular genres must be considered at least as carefully as the various forms of classical music.

The present book is both a history of music in America and a history of American music. Virtually every kind of music considered in the following pages has gone through three distinct phases: it was brought to the New World from elsewhere; in a second stage, new works were created here which resemble this imported music; finally, pieces gradually emerged with stylistic elements differing from those of the first two stages, usually as a result of acculturation of two or more national, racial, or ethnic groups in the New World. It makes little sense to separate these three; thus most of my chapters begin with a discussion of the musical life generated in America by a certain type of imported music, then progress to a consideration of pieces generated in this environment.

Beyond that, I have nothing to say as introduction. The book speaks for itself.

*Norwich, Vermont, 1978–81*

# ACKNOWLEDGEMENTS

This book could not have come into being without assistance from many sources.

A generous grant from the Rockefeller Foundation relieved me of most of the pressures of academic life while I wrote the first ten chapters and planned most of the remainder. Dartmouth College made funds available for much of the typing and bibliographical work, through several grants from the Committee on Research. The Recorded Anthology of American Music, Inc., furnished me with a full set of the 100 discs of *New World Records,* and also the written materials prepared by dozens of scholars for the accompanying liner notes; Elizabeth Ostrow, Vice President and Director of Artists and Repertoire, was particularly helpful in seeing that I had what I needed.

Dale Cockrell worked closely with me the first year, as a research associate, helping in countless ways: preparing an index of all pieces on these discs, at a time when such an index had not been published: locating and organizing material; assembling masses of bibliographical information; assisting with footnotes and music examples; reading first drafts of chapters as they were finished and offering criticisms and suggestions; typing second drafts from quite rough copy. As invaluable as all of these things proved to be, I appreciated even more his enthusiasm for the project, and for American music; his willingness to serve as a sounding board for ideas; and his availability for discussions on American music over a protracted period of time, even after his official connection with the project had ended and he had taken a teaching post at Middlebury College. It is fair to say that many parts of this book were shaped by the two of us together.

Donna Lee Norvell-Race was an excellent typist, but much more than that. Being a musician and a writer herself, she was willing and able to work from rough and heavily hand-edited copy, and do discreet and excellent editing herself at this stage of the book. She also gave supportive feedback at every stage; without her talents and enthusiasm, the book would have taken much longer to be completed.

My editor, Claire Brook, was closely involved in the project from its inception to the end; her constant assistance, encouragement, support, and advice helped keep me going for the three years necessary to bring the book to completion.

The staffs of both Paddock Music Library and Baker Library at Dartmouth College were unfailingly helpful and patient in assisting me to locate and use the many hundreds of books, scores, and periodicals needed for my research. I would like to thank Pat Fisken, Cindy Pawlek, Amy Nickerson, and Sue Marcoulier in particular for their cheerful and sustained assistance.

Marley McMullen and my wife Marilyse gave substantial and greatly appreciated help with footnotes and preliminary proofing. My son Chris took over a large share of the work on bibliography and music examples in the final frantic stages; I couldn't have made it through the final weeks without him. Carol Elliott, administrative associate of the Department of Music at Dartmouth, was masterfully diplomatic in helping to shield me from unnecessary distractions when I was most pressed.

And my two cats, Junior and Mao, were never far away while I worked, and afforded useful models of relaxation and calm when I was under the most pressure.

# MUSIC
## *in the New World*

# 1

## The Music of the Native American

We are the Ancient People;
  Our father is the Sun;
Our mother, the Earth, where the mountains tower
  And the rivers seaward run;
The stars are the children of the sky,
  The red men, of the plain;
And ages over us both had rolled
  Before you crossed the main;
For we are the Ancient People,
Born with the wind and rain.

—Edna Dean Proctor,
*The Song of the Ancient People*

Like all people now inhabiting the United States of America, the American Indians were immigrants to this land.

There is no important scholarly disagreement with the theory that these people first came to North America from Asia, across a land bridge then connecting Siberia with Alaska, and that over a period of many centuries they spread throughout the two Americas. Anthropologists classify them as Asiatics, or Mongoloids, along with the Japanese, Chinese, Burmese, Tibetans, Siamese, Malays, and Lapps.

Supporting the idea that man came to the Americas from elsewhere is the widely accepted theory that man is descended from other forms, and that all evidence for early man has been discovered in Africa and Asia. The anthropoid apes, the species most closely related to man, are all found in the Old World—the gorilla and chimpanzee in Africa, the gibbon and orangutan in Asia. Hundreds of fossil remains of "missing links"—intermediate between the apes and man—have been found in Asia and Africa, none in the Americas. Even the more fanciful theories of the origin of the American Indian—that he is a descendent of the Lost Tribe of Israel, that he came here from the legendary lost continents of Atlantis or Mu—have him arriving from elsewhere. At the moment, the universally accepted theory of his origin is that

> Man evolved from brute ancestry in the Old World and migrated to the New World only after he had become modern physically and a member of the single species of modern man called *Homo sapiens*, wise man.[1]

Until recently it was believed that the Indians first came to America some fifteen to twenty thousand years ago, with the earliest recovered remains of their culture dating from about eleven thousand years ago. More recent discoveries have changed this date radically. A bone from the foreleg of a caribou, fashioned into a toothed hide scraper, found in 1973 near the Old Crow River in Yukon Territory, has been radiocarbon-dated as twenty-seven thousand years old. This date coincides well with recent geological research suggesting that the land bridge between Siberia and Alaska, at a spot where today the two continents are separated by only fifty-six miles of water broken by several islands, was above sea level at just this time, for a period of about ten thousand years. There is also evidence that an ice-free corridor extended southward from Alaska (the "Alaskan Refuge") during this same time, giving the migrating people easy access to Canada and the United States.[2]

The earliest remains of man discovered in the Americas suggest a type rather less Mongoloid than the modern Chinese or Japanese, or the present-day Eskimo. The first immigration occurred when the physical characteristics differentiating the Mongoloid from other races of man were less marked than they are today. As a generalization, the less Mongoloid the features of a given tribe or group of American Indians, the longer they have been in America.

[1] Harold E. Driver, *Indians of North America*, 2nd rev. ed. (Chicago: University of Chicago Press, 1970), p. 1.

[2] These matters are summarized in Robert F. Spencer, Jesse D. Jennings, et al., *The Native Americans: Ethnology and Backgrounds of the North American Indians*, 2nd ed. (New York: Harper & Row, 1977), pp. 2–12.

The difficulties in reconstructing a history of Native American culture are formidable. A first obstacle is that these were nonliterate people, with no written documentation of their history. The earliest written accounts and descriptions of their life date from the arrival of Europeans in the late fifteenth century, leaving some thirty or forty thousand years of their history unrecorded. The historian must depend on the findings and theories of anthropology and archeology, on legends and other oral history of modern-day Indians, and on comparisons with other cultures, ancient and modern.

Equally staggering is the diversity among Native Americans of the historical era. Though all are descended from Asian immigrants, certain tribes and larger groups have been isolated from others for many centuries. Furthermore, there were historical and cultural changes in Asia itself from the time of the first American emigrés to the last; thus later immigrants were quite different culturally from those who had come earlier. Modern scholars recognize more than six hundred distinct tribes or societies among the Native Americans of the United States and Canada, and it has been estimated that some two thousand different languages, all mutually unintelligible, were spoken in North and South America when the white man arrived.[3] Even tribes living in close proximity often could not understand one another's language.

Despite this cultural and historical complexity, it is possible to define certain general characteristics of American Indian life and culture, if one takes a broad enough view. These common points come most sharply into focus in a comparison with European culture at the time of the discovery of America, and other cultures in the world studied by these Europeans.

When the Native Americans came to the New World, they were a nomadic people subsisting primarily by hunting and fishing. Their culture was comparable to that of the Late Paleolithic or the Early Neolithic periods of European history: they fashioned tools and weapons from wood, stone, and animal bones; they made clothing and other objects from animal skins; they knew the art of weaving; they made utensils and certain nonfunctional objects from clay. They were omniverous, varying their diet of meat and fish with wild fruits, berries, and grains. At some point they learned to cultivate wild corn, or maize; in the view of some scholars, this was

[3] Driver, p. 555. The essay "American Indians" by Edward H. Spicer (found in the *Harvard Encyclopedia of American Ethnic Groups*, Stephan Thernstrom, ed., Cambridge: Harvard University Press/Belknap Press, 1980) puts the number of tribes in the 1600s at somewhat over 200.

"the most remarkable development in agricultural history."[4] Other plants were eventually cultivated, but there was no significant domestication of animals. No written languages were developed north of Mexico. Some tribes learned to build permanent dwelling places, singly or in clusters; others were still nomadic when discovered by the European.

It has been estimated that no more than one million Native Americans inhabited what is now the United States when the white man came to this land. The Indian was in constant contact with the natural world—the animals, birds, plants, waters, terrain. He depended on this world for his food, clothing, shelter, and medicine. Though he took what he needed, he was never wantonly destructive; the Indian "existed in perfect ecological balance with the forest, the plain, the desert, the waters, and the animal life."[5] This may have been partly a function of underpopulation, but it was also a matter of attitude. Eastern (Asian) religion and philosophy tend to emphasize adaptation to one's environment, building with what is given, living in harmony with the world. Builders and architects of the East—the Japanese, for example—use indigenous materials for their structures, taking advantage of existing terrain and vegetation, and strive for buildings in harmony with the environment; the West tends to conceive of a structure in the abstract, then to change or even destroy whatever happens to be on the site, to make way for what has been planned. These contrasting attitudes were apparent from the first contact between the European and the Indian:

> To the Indian it seemed that these Europeans hated everything in nature—the living forests and their birds and beasts, the grassy glades, the water, the soil, and the air itself.[6]

And in the words of an Indian:

> The white men were many and we could not hold our own against them. We were like deer. They were like grizzly bears. We were contented to let things remain as the Great Spirit made them. They were not, and would change the rivers and mountains if they did not suit them.[7]

Given his close contact with the natural world and his dependence upon it, the American Indian based his religion, his art, and

---

[4] John Collier, *Indians of the Americas* (New York: W. W. Norton & Company, 1947), p. 33.

[5] Collier, p. 172.

[6] Dee Brown, *Bury My Heart at Wounded Knee* (New York: Holt, Rinehart & Winston, 1971), p. 7.

[7] Chief Joseph of the Nez Percé, as quoted in Brown, p. 304.

his life-view on what he observed and experienced there. A sympathetic observer of the ways of the Indian wrote, early in the nineteenth century:

> Among all savage nations, so long as the human mind remains unenlightened by literature and science, the darkness which rests upon it is favorable to the workings of the imagination. The lofty mountains, the cataract rushing with its mighty volume of waters, the flood, the lake convulsed by the tremendous storm, the tornado's fury, the whirlwind's force, the thunder's awful voice, and the zigzag vivid lightning's flash, agitate the savage mind with the most awful and sublime emotions. These are contrasted in his mind, with the peaceful, wide-spread prairie, the gentle river, moving noiselessly along within its banks, the placid lake, unruffled by a breath of air, and the clear sky without a cloud in view. Ignorant of all secondary causes, the savage looks only to the GRAT (sic) FIRST CAUSE, as the only and immediate Author of all things, and all events, and his soul is filled with dread, awe, and wonder.[8]

The difficulties in dealing with the music of the Native American are as great as those in studying his culture and history in general. The same problems pertain—the immense time span of the Indians' residence in America, the isolation of tribes and larger groups from one another, the enormous diversity.

There is an additional problem with music, which exists in sound, not in physical form as do the plastic arts. Some cultures devised ways of recording music on paper, through a set of symbols called musical notation, but the Native Americans did not; thus there is absolutely no physical trace of what Indian music was like during the centuries before the European came to the New World. The problem was put more poetically by a writer early in this century:

> The voices that greeted the sunrise of the race have died away without an echo. A bit of broken pottery, a bone-awl, an arrowhead, a grave-mound, mute testimonies these of the art, the industry, the life, the death of man in the long ago. And of his thoughts? The lips of the past are closed forever on the mystery . . .[9]

Our only knowledge of music of the Indian before the fifteenth century is based on various sorts of indirect evidence: the legends and tales of the Indians themselves; a study of Indian music today,

---

[8] Caleb Atwater, *The Writings of Caleb Atwater* (Columbus: Published by the Author, printed by Scott and Wright, 1833), p. 303.

[9] Natalie Curtis, *The Indians' Book* (New York and London: Harper and Brothers Publishers, 1907), p. xxix.

with extrapolation backwards; comparison with the music of people in various parts of the world today who seem to be at stages of cultural development comparable to that of the prehistoric Indian.

With the arrival of the European in the New World, more concrete evidence becomes available. Whether or not the white man understood the Native American, he found him interesting, and from the earliest contact there are numerous written documents—logs, letters, journals, books—describing and discussing his physical appearance, his habits, his dress, his rituals and ceremonies, his music.

> For their musicke they use a thicke cane, on which they pipe as on a Recorder. For their warres, they have a great deepe platter of wood. They cover the mouth thereof with a skin, at each corner they tie a walnut, which meeting on the backside neere the bottome, with a small rope they twitch them togither till it be so tought and stiffe, that they may beat upon it as upon a drumme. But their chiefe instruments are Rattels made of small gourds or Pumpion shels. Of these they have Base, Tenor, Countertenor, Meane and Trible. These mingled with their voices sometimes 20 or 30 togither, make such a terrible noise as would rather affright then delight any man.[10]

Since few of the early explorers and settlers were trained musicians, their accounts were of a general, nontechnical nature—sometimes telling us as much about the biases and cultural limitations of the person writing the account as about what he heard.

The first attempts to deal with this music by recording it in European musical notation date from the seventeenth and eighteenth centuries. An account of a calumet dance (a ceremonial, usually intertribal, dance popular in the eastern United States and Canada) written by Marquette in 1674 includes a transcription into Western notation of a "calumet song";[11] William Beresford offered a single Indian melody in musical notation as part of his *A Voyage Around the World; but More Particularly to the Northwest Coast of America*, published in 1789.

Serious scholarly study of the music of the Native American began with a dissertation at Leipzig University by Theodore Baker, *Über die Musik der Nordamerikanischen Wilden*, completed in 1880 and published in 1882 by the Leipzig publishing house Breitkopf

---

[10] Captain John Smith, *Works: 1608–1631* (Birmingham, England: n.p., 1884), p. 73.

[11] David Crawford, *"The Jesuit Relations and Allied Documents*, Early Sources for an Ethnography of Music among American Indians," in *Ethnomusicology* XI/2 (May, 1967), pp. 202–3.

& Härtel. Transcription of Indian songs into Western notation for purposes of structural and style analysis was an important part of the study. Alice C. Fletcher was the most industrious early American scholar of Indian music; her study of the music of the Omaha tribe, published in 1893, was the first of numerous monographs.[12] Natalie Curtis published in 1907 the most comprehensive collection of transcriptions of Indian songs to appear to that point; in collecting material for *The Indians' Book,* she visited tribes from the east coast to California, observing their rituals and taking down their song.

The recording of Indian music on the phonograph was first done successfully by Jesse Walter Fewkes, with songs of the Passamaquoddy tribe in Maine. Benjamin Ives Gilman made use of Fewkes's phonograph recordings of songs of the Zuñi tribe for his monograph on their music; and Frances Densmore, for many years at the Bureau of American Ethnology of the Smithsonian Institution in Washington, recorded and analyzed hundreds of Indian songs. These discs were the foundation for a continuing collection of phonograph records of Indian music at the Smithsonian, which, with important additions in recent years by Willard Rhodes, has grown to be the largest and most important one in the world.

As the twentieth century developed, more scholars were drawn to the music of the American Indian, and their research methods became more sophisticated as phonographic equipment improved, the tape recorder was introduced, various electrical devices made it easier to detect pitch variations, and techniques from other disciplines—most notably anthropology—were borrowed and adapted.

As with Indian life and culture in general, certain characteristics are practically universal among the music of the Native Americans in all parts of North America:

—Two or more notes are almost never sounded together in a planned, systematic way. Indian music is sung by a single voice, or by a number of voices together in unison. The only exceptions are the occasional use of sustained or drone notes against the melody, or ostinato patterns by a chorus against the melody of a leading singer, found mostly in the west and northwest regions of the United States and Canada,[13] and the overlapping of solo and chorus parts in the music of some eastern Indians.[14]

---

[12] Alice Cunningham Fletcher, *A Study of Omaha Indian Music* (Cambridge: Peabody Museum of American Archeology and Ethnology, 1893).

[13] An example is found on NW 246, s2/1: Women's Brush Dance of the Yurok Indians.

[14] Cf. NW 246, s1/5: the Gar Dance of the Creeks.

—The only instruments are idiophones (rattles, sticks and pieces of wood beaten together), membraphones (drums with skin heads), and aerophones (whistles and flutes). The first two are used almost exclusively to accompany dancing and singing, sometimes setting and maintaining the basic pulse for the singers, sometimes having a rhythmic shape of their own so that two planes of rhythmic activity occur simultaneously. Flutes and whistles are used to give signals, to play tunes alone, or to play in unison with a solo singer. Aerophones never play in groups of two or more, nor are they used to accompany group singing. There is no such thing as an independent instrumental piece, played by a group of instruments without voice(s).

—Indian music is built up from one or several brief melodic phrases or fragments, repeated over and over. A section or portion of a ceremony or dance may come to an end and be succeeded by another, which will have its own brief melodic phrase or phrases repeated until still another section begins. The shape and duration of a piece of Indian music is usually dependent on the ceremony or ritual of which it is a part, rather than abstract musical considerations, and the music is static, stating and repeating a musical idea with little change or progression until a section is over.

—Many pieces of Indian music are based on scales of three, four, five, or six notes.

—Though many Indian songs have texts that are semantically meaningful and depend for at least part of their effect on the comprehension of the words and their sense, many others have apparently meaningless syllables, words from other Indian languages, words and phrases that may have once been meaningful but are so no longer.

These general characteristics define Indian music of today, but there is evidence that they hold for the entire period of contact between the European and the Indian as well. A recent scholar has described responsorial singing, accompanied by drums and rattles, among the Seneca Indians on their reservation in Salamanca, New York:

> The vocal style is partly unison and partly responsorial. The leader begins, the chorus echoes the first phrase, and then they sing in unison, with a nasal, sometimes pulsating quality, until the refrain. Then the sustained notes on "yo he" and the halved drumbeat signal the change in the dance step. The leader sings "yo yo" in a pulsating voice, and the chorus answers "hi ha" on a slightly higher pitch (less than a semitone higher). After this refrain has been sung eight or nine times, the "yo he" signal is sung again, and the song and dance resume as in the beginning.

This form repeats five times, with some variations in pitch (in Nos. 1 and 3) and incomplete repetitions of the song (in Nos. 2 and 5).[15]

Captain John Smith did not have the technical vocabulary to describe what he saw and heard in such detail; but certainly a ceremony he observed among Indians inhabiting the eastern part of Virginia, in the early sixteen hundreds, had music similar in many ways, including responsorial singing:

> The faces of all their Priests are painted as ugly as they can devise. In their hands, they had every one his Rattell, some base, some smaller. Their devotion was most in songs which the chiefe Priest beginneth and the rest followed him: sometimes he maketh invocations with broken sentences, by starts and strange passions, and at every pause, the rest give a short groane.[16]

And a century later, another writer reports something quite similar among the Hurons, another eastern tribe:

> The Savages generally sing one after the other, at their feasts. While one is yelling or singing as loud as he can, the others reply by a deep respiration, uttering this sound only from the depths of their chests, "Ho, ho, ho,"—striking with their spoons or with sticks on their bark plates, or on some other object.[17]

Writer after writer has commented on the repetitious nature of Indian music, and its dependence on scales with a small number of notes:

> When we entered the cabin of this Savage, we found a Fire lighted, near which a Man beat (singing at the same time) upon a Kind of Drum: Another shook, without ceasing his *Chichikoué*, and sang also. This lasted two Hours, till we were quite tired of it; for they always said the same thing, or rather they formed Sounds that were but half articulate, without any Variation. We begged of the Master of the Cabin to put an End to this.[18]
>
> Their songs, whether of war or devotion, harvest or hunting, consisted of but few words and scanty intonations, repeated in the most monotonous way.[19]

---

[15] Joyce Heth, liner notes for NW 246.
[16] Smith, p. 76.
[17] Crawford, p. 205.
[18] Father Charlevoix, *Letters to the Dutchess of Lesdiguieres: Giving an Account of a Voyage to Canada, and Travels through that vast Country, and Louisiana, to the Gulf of Mexico* (London: R. Goadby, 1763), pp. 148–49.
[19] Charles C. Jones, Jr., *Antiquities of the Southern Indians, Particularly of the Georgia Tribes* (New York: D. Appleton and Company, 1873), p. 92.

. . . it is difficult to believe, that the music of the savages was but two or three notes which are repeated continually. This makes their feasts very tiresome to a European after he has seen them once, because they last a long time, and you hear the same thing.[20]

These samples could be multiplied many times; and what they report can be verified with the first transcriptions of Indian music in Western notation, which show melodies of a limited number of notes repeated over and over, and from the earliest phonograph recordings of Indian songs, which reveal the same characteristics.

A Comanche dance-song, from Baker's *Über die Musik der nord-amerikanischen Wilden*, p. 72

Kwakiutl cradle-song, from Curtis's *The Indians' Book*, p. 302

The music of the Native American is equally remote from that of Europe in its role in culture—how it is conceived, what it is intended to do.

American Indian music is inextricably linked with ceremony or ritual. Music accompanied dance, religious rite, tribal ceremony and celebration, healing rituals, games, even personal and private rituals and rites. It did not exist apart from such occasions, but was an integral and inseparable part of them, as were also dance or ritualized body movement, costume, mask, and ceremonial trappings such as fire and tobacco.

Songs were not thought of as having been composed, at least by an individual. Some ceremonial music was "traditional," having been the property of a tribe for as long as anyone could remember. Other songs were associated with individuals, such as medicine men; here, too, the songs were thought of as having always existed

[20] John McIntosh, *The Origin of the North American Indians* (New York: Sheldon, Blakeman & Company, 1858), p. 158.

Buffalo Dance of the Mandans, a 19th century lithograph by Karl Bodmer. (Rare Books and Manuscripts Division, the New York Public Library, Astor, Lenox and Tilden Foundations)

or, when a "new" song was appropriate for a given circumstance, as having been given to an individual by the gods, most often in a dream:

> He (a Huron medicine man) had a dream, in which he saw himself present at one of those dances or festivals, and handling fire like the others, and he heard at the same time a song, which he was astonished to know perfectly on awakening. At the first feast of this kind which was made, he began to sing his song, and behold, by degrees he felt himself becoming frenzied, he took the burning embers and the hot stones with his hands and with his teeth from the midst of the live coals, he plunged his bare arm to the bottom of the boiling kettles, and all without any injury or pain; in a word, he was master of his trade.[21]

Music was viewed as having god-given magical properties, and the purpose of singing or playing music was to invoke this magic, to set it in operation for the benefit of the person(s) making the music and/or other participants and onlookers.

The famous Sun Dance of the Sioux was one of several ceremonies among this tribe in which participants were subjected to pain and even multilation with no apparent suffering because of the invocation—through music, dance, and ceremony—of magical

[21] Crawford, p. 200.

powers. As this "greatest of all Indian ceremonies"—intended to give thanks to "the great giver of light and heat, who makes the snows melt, the grass and trees grow, and brings warmth to our bodies"—was recounted by an observer,[22] the "master of ceremonies" began the climactic ceremony by announcing:

> Lakotas, Lakotas, Lakotas, to-day you will witness the valor of our people! Those of you who have come from afar off can return, when this ordeal is over, and tell those who could not come of the strong hearts of our warriors. You can tell them of the valor of our braves. You can tell them that the prayers to our Great Creator have been heard, and will be answered.[23]

Eleven chosen young warriors began to dance around a tall pole erected at the center of the ritual grounds, with other members of the tribe dancing in a larger circle around them—all this, of course, accompanied by the appropriate music.

After three days and nights of dancing, "during which time the dancers neither ate, drank, slept, nor smoked," prominent warriors of the tribe made slits in the skin of the chests, backs, and thighs of the eleven young warriors, passed lariats through these slits, and attached the other ends to the central pole. In the words of another observer of a similar ceremony:

> The unflinching fortitude, with which every one of them bore this part of the torture surpassed credulity; each one as the knife was passed through his flesh sustained an unchangeable countenance; and several of them, seeing me making sketches, beckoned me to look at their faces, which I watched through all this horrid operation, without being able to detect anything but the pleasantest smiles as they looked me in the eye, while I could hear the knife rip through the flesh, and feel enough of it myself, to start involuntary and uncontrollable tears over my cheeks.[24]

The dance around the pole was continued, now with the eleven young warriors pulling against the lariats until they ripped through their skin, and when all were free the ceremony came to an end. The eleven young men, "with lacerated bodies but stout hearts, were recognized as heroes for a time, and braves forever."[25] From

---

[22] J. Lee Humfreville, *Twenty Years Among Our Hostile Indians* (New York: Hunter & Company, 1899), pp. 325–33.

[23] Humfreville, p. 327.

[24] George Catlin, *Letters and Notes on the Manners, Customs, and Condition of the North American Indian* (New York: Wiley and Putnam, 1841), p. 171.

[25] Humfreville, pp. 330–31.

the Indians' point of view, the three days of singing and dancing had invoked protection against pain, from the gods. Music was the means of transfering this magic, from the gods to the participants.

This ceremony was outlawed by the American government in the late nineteenth century. There are no recordings of the music of the Sun Dance; but music of a similar style (though to a secular, part English, text) accompanied the Rabbit Dance done by Northern Plains Indians.[26]

I cannot resist a personal note here. On Easter Sunday, 1978, in Durban, South Africa, I witnessed a ceremony among members of a Buddhist sect of the Indian community. After hours of ritual—including music—needles were thrust through the skin of the face and back of many participants, daggers were put through the cheeks and tongues of others, some men had slits cut in the skin of their chests and backs from which were hung fruits and other objects, others put on shoes of nails, and still others had slits cut in the skin of their backs through which thin ropes were passed and then attached to small altars, which were dragged behind them during a processional to a temple some distance away. As the culmination of the ceremony, all participants walked through a thirty-foot-long trench of glowing coals. All this was accomplished without the slightest sign of pain, or a single drop of blood.

Similar to the Sun Dance, though less dramatic, is the Eagle Dance of the Arapaho.[27] A successful hunt for the giant bird is followed by a four-day ceremony of dancing, singing, and ritual; the purpose is to persuade the gods to transfer the attributes of the bird—its swiftness, fearlessness, tenacity—to members of the tribe. The feathers were afterwards distributed and worn, not as mere ornament, but as a token of what each individual had gained from the hunt and the ceremony.

"Hlin Biyin," the "Song of the Horse," is sung by the Navajo to insure that the tribe will have beautiful and strong horses, like those of Johano-Ai, the Sun-God. The legend tells that:

Johano-Ai starts each day from his hogan, in the east, and rides across the skies to his hogan in the west, carrying the shining golden disk, the sun. He has five horses—a horse of turquoise, a horse of white shell, a horse of pearl shell, a horse of red shell, and a horse of coal. When the skies are blue and the weather is fair, Johano-Ai is riding his turquoise horse or his horse of white shell or of pearl; but when the heavens are dark with storm, he has mounted the red horse, or the horse of coal. . . .

Johano-Ai pastures his herds on flower-blossoms and gives them to

[26] NW 246, s1/4.
[27] NW 246, s1/2.

drink of the mingled waters. . . . When the horse of the sun-god goes, he raises, not dust, but "pitistshi," glittering grains of mineral such as are used in religious ceremonies; and when he rolls, and shakes himself, it is a shining pitistshi that flies from him. When he runs, the sacred pollen offered to the sun-god is all about him, like dust, so that he looks like a mist; for the Navajos sometimes say that the mist on the horizon is the pollen that has been offered to the gods.[28]

It is in the context of this legend that the Navajos sing their song of the horse:

Navajo "Hlin Biyin," from Curtis's *The Indians' Book,* p. 372

The Turtle Dance is the most important ceremony of the entire year at the Pueblo of San Juan in New Mexico, held at the winter solstice, a day taken to be the end of one year and the beginning of another. Since the turtle is thought by the Indians to be the first hibernating animal to revive in the new year, it is taken as a symbol of this occasion. The participants in the dance wear rattles made of turtle shells on their legs, and carry a branch from an evergreen tree in one hand and a rattle made from a gourd in the other. Songs accompanying the dance are "new," in keeping with the spirit of the ceremony; actually, they are pieced together in a different way each year from a store of traditional songs. Their texts emphasize "renewal and regeneration and the continuing process of creation. In their frequent mention of lakes, rainwater, fog rainbows, and mist cream, they express a concern for fertility."[29]

The Creek Indians depended on the gar for food and used its scales, teeth, and bones for both practical and ceremonial purposes; their Gar Dance[30] is part of a ceremony honoring this fish while invoking good fortune from the gods for their fishing. The Brush Dance, among the Yuroks of northern California, was originally performed to cure an ailing member of the tribe.[31] Gambling

[28] Curtis, pp. 360–61.
[29] Four extended songs from this ceremony are available on NW 301.
[30] NW 246, s1/5.
[31] NW 246, s2/1.

The Turtle Dance as performed by the Pueblo Indians of San Juan, New Mexico. (Photograph by Harvey Caplin)

songs, found among Indians in all parts of North America, were sung before and during gambling to bring luck in the game; Indians do not allow the texts of these (and many other) songs to be written down, for fear they will lose their magical properties. Young males sing love songs, not to attract a young woman by their beauty and poetical content, but privately, to invoke the magic transmitted by the song.[32] Indian women may sing while weaving—not work songs to accompany physical activity, but songs to imbue the basket with magic, insuring that someone will be attracted to the product and buy it.[33]

Thus, music functions not as a means whereby a composer communicates something to an audience, but rather as a medium whereby the performers or participants are put in touch with the gods or the forces of nature, to draw the strength, skill, or assistance needed for a certain task or situation.

For the Native American, music was not rational, but a matter of faith; not personalized, but a gift from the gods; not specialized,

[32] NW 297, s1/1.
[33] NW 297, s1/6.

but one component in ceremonies involving large groups of people; not communicative, but a means of getting in touch with higher and more powerful beings and forces. As one writer put it:

> ... song was not simply self-expression. It was a magic which called upon the powers of Nature and constrained them to man's will. ... Magic will be worked if the description is vivid and if the singing or the recitation is done, as it should be, at the right time and with the right behavior, on behalf of all the people.
>
> Such a magic spell is never consciously composed: it is "given" by the supernatural powers. A man who desired a song did not put his mind on words and tunes: he put it on pleasing the supernaturals. He must be a good hunter or a good warrior. Perhaps they would "like his ways" and one day, in a natural sleep, he would hear singing. So does the Papago interpret the trancelike state of the artist who derives his material from the unconscious. "He hears a song and he knows it is the hawk singing to him or the great white birds that fly from the ocean." Perhaps the clouds sing, or the wind, or the feathery red rain spider, swinging on its invisible rope.
>
> The honored men are singers. The man who has fought for his people gets no honor from that fact, but only from the attendant fact that he was able to "receive"—or compose, shall we say—a song. ... What of a society which puts no premium whatever on aggressiveness and where the practical man is valued only if he is also a poet? What of a society where the misfit, wandering hopelessly misunderstood on the outskirts of life, is not the artist, but the unimaginative young businessman? [34]

Columbus wrote that the first Indians he encountered were "so tractable, so peaceful," and that "they love their neighbors as themselves; and their discourse is ever sweet and gentle, and accompanied with a smile; and though it is true that they are naked, yet their manners are decorous and praiseworthy." Despite this, his next thought was that the Indians should be "made to work, sow and do all that is necessary and to *adopt our ways.*" [35]

Time and again the first reaction to the Indian was virtually the same:

> The hospitality of these Indians [the Mohawks] is no less remarkable than their other virtues. As soon as any stranger comes among them, they are sure to offer him victuals; if a number arrive, one of their best

[34] Ruth Murray Underhill, *Singing for Power: The Song Magic of the Papago Indians of Southern Arizona* (Berkeley: University of California Press, 1938), pp. 5–8, passim.
[35] As quoted in Brown, pp. 1 and 2.

houses is cleaned for their accommodation, and not infrequently they are accommodated with female society while they remain.[36]

The white man's treatment of these people was equally predictable.

It is no less curious than lamentable to observe the uniform and withering persecution which the Indians have laboured under from their earliest acquaintance with white men to the present day. Whatever dissimilarity may have existed in the characteristics, political and moral, of the various nations of Europe, they seem to have resembled each other in this one thing, namely, inextinguishable, unsparing oppression of the North American Indians. Dutch, French, English, and even those who, in one sense, may be termed their own countrymen, the citizens of the United States, have all agreed in keeping no faith with the original inhabitants of this vast continent. No: their dominions were too fertile in sources of wealth, for them to expect any thing like fair-dealing from their refined invaders, who first flattered and cajoled them, and then rewarded their hospitality with the sword and the cannon.[37]

Or, as the Indians themselves put it:

Where today are the Pequot? Where are the Narragansett, the Mohican, the Pokanoket, and many other once powerful tribes of our people? They have vanished before the avarice and the oppression of the White Man, as snow before a summer sun.[38]

It never occurred to the European that he might learn from the Indian and his ways; to him, these people were "savages." Captain John Smith wrote:

But their chiefe God they worship is the Divell. Him they call *Oke* and serve him more of feare than love. They say they have conference with him and fashion themselves as neare to his shape as they can imagine. In their Temples, they have his image evill favouredly carved, and then painted and adorned with chaines, copper, and beades; and covered with a skin, in such manner as the deformity may well suit with such a God. . . . And in this lamentable ignorance doe these poore soules sacrifice themselves to the Divell, not knowing their Creator.[39]

---

[36] James Buchanan, *Sketches of the History, Manners & Customs of the North American Indians, with a Plan for Their Melioration* (New York: William Borradaile, 1824), p. 110.

[37] Buchanan, p. 107.

[38] Tecumseh of the Shawnees, as quoted in Brown, p. 1.

[39] Smith, pp. 73, 79.

And to good Christians among the white men, this meant that their task was to bring religious "enlightenment" to these poor creatures, for:

> I saw enough to cause my heart to swell with deep and conflicting emotions in beholding the depth of heathen superstition into which this people have fallen. Forgetting the true and living God, they have substituted in His stead a mass of fantastic objects, before which their wild orgies are solemnly and devoutly performed.[40]

It would probably be a misreading of history to suggest that Christianity was the chief force behind the white man's treatment of the Native American; he would not have adopted this religion had it not fitted his character. At the very least, though, Christianity was often invoked as rationalization for various brutal and barbaric acts against the "heathens" of the New World.

This is not the place to recount in detail the treatment of the American Indian at the hands of the European; it has been done effectively elsewhere.[41] For the purposes of the present book, it is sufficient to observe that the European correctly saw the music of the Indian as an inseparable part of his religious rites and ceremonies, and thus as something to be replaced or exterminated. The missionaries, who came to America close on the heels of the early explorers and settlers, used music as one means of converting the "heathens" to Christianity, and of keeping them in the fold. Indians were taught to sing psalms and hymns in the style of the white man. These were sometimes translated into their own language, but there was no serious attempt to adapt their own music to Christian purposes. The fact that some Indians learned to sing simple sacred music in the European style was seen by the white man as a great and hopeful step, an indication that they could be civilized:

> The Christian Indians sang again this evening, their hymns being made more strikingly sweet by the yelling and whooping of the wild Indians by whom they were surrounded. What a contrast! The woods made vocal on the one hand by Christian music, and startled on the other by the wild yells of the uncivilized! And yet both proceeding from the same race.[42]

[40] Thomas C. Battey, *The Life and Adventures of a Quaker Among the Indians* (Boston: Lee and Shepard, 1875), pp. 182–83.
[41] Cf. Brown.
[42] Thomas L. M'Kenney, *Memoirs, Official and Personal, with Sketches of Travels among the Northern and Southern Indians* (New York: Paine and Burgess, 1846), pp. 83–84.

This same attitude was expressed in a lengthy essay entitled "Attempts Recently Made to Lead the Indian Tribes to Admit Teachers of Christianity among Them; with Observations thereon, and Hints to Missionaries," by James Buchanan, who bore the title of "His Brittanic Majesty's Consul for the State of New-York." Buchanan saw as the only hope for the American Indian a complete break from his "savage" ways, and he gave high priority to the building of permanent structures, among them a place for the teaching of European music:

> . . . connected with a school, there should always be associated a smith's forge, a wheelwright's, and a carpenter's shop, and facilities for such other trades as may appear essential; to which should be added a school of music, wherein should be taught such simple wind, and other instruments as are most attractive; this instruction should be the reward of industry and obedience in those Indians who should acquire a knowledge of any of the approved trades.
> . . . the operations should begin in a fertile place, in the neighbourhood of such of the tribe as might desire an establishment of this nature; making the pleasures of music, or the possession of manufactures, the reward for devoting themselves to industry. . . .[43]

The general uprooting and destruction of Indian life and culture was mirrored by the fate of Indian music. While it has not been altogether lost, it has been seriously impoverished in the past two centuries. Entire tribes have vanished, their music with them. The pressures and attractions of the white man's world have led many Native Americans to reject their own culture and to enter the mainstream of American life. And various events and movements have brought different tribes into contact with one another, with a consequent blurring of cultural identities. Several tribes have often been forced to live together on the same reservation; the Peyote cult became a powerful intertribal force, particularly in the Southwest, with music and ritual compounded from various tribal sources; the Ghost Dance movement of the late nineteenth century, part of a last attempt to resist the white man in the Great Plains region, was likewise intertribal in its membership and music; and for more than a century a literature of pan-Indian songs and dances has grown up around the institution of the pow-wow, a gathering of all Indians in a given area for the purposes of entertainment and unity. Each of these movements has brought its own intertribal music, but the quantity and variety of this has been no match for the lost tribal music.

[43] Buchanan, pp. 150, 404.

By the beginning of the twentieth century, the destruction wrought on the Indian and his ways had become so severe as to threaten the loss of any trace of the culture of the Native American. In the belief that this was indeed happening, Natalie Curtis undertook the collection of Indian legends, oral history, and songs; she wrote in the Introduction to her *The Indians' Book:*

> The olden days were gone; the buffalo had vanished from the plains; even so would there soon be lost forever the songs and stories of the Indian. But there was a way to save them to the life and memory of their children, and that was to write them even as the white man writes. The white friend had come to be the pencil in the hand of the Indian.[44]

But there has been hope for the Indian, at times, as the twentieth century has unfolded. President Theodore Roosevelt, after a visit to the Hopis, called their culture "as precious as anything existing in the United States." Shortly after Franklin D. Roosevelt assumed the presidency in 1933, he appointed as new Indian Commissioner John Collier, who wrote of the Native Americans:

> The deep cause of our world agony is that we have lost that passion and reverence for human personality and for the web of life and the earth which the American Indians have tended as a central, sacred fire since before the Stone Age. . . . They had and have this power for living which our modern world has lost—as world-view and self-view, as tradition and institution, as practical philosophy dominating their societies and as an art supreme among all the arts.[45]

Since the end of World War II, the Native Americans, like so many other ethnic and racial groups within the United States, have become increasingly aware of their own culture and heritage, and of the necessity for preserving it. Active and militant Indians have spoken out strongly against the continuing erosion of their way of life, and of the desirability of maintaining it in the face of the complexities of the present age. On the other hand, many white, European-descended Americans have questioned their own cultural heritage. They have sought alternatives to the Judeo-Christian attitudes and ethics that have spawned so many of the best ideas and actions, and works of art, of the Western world—but have also been at the root of much of the aggressive, destructive nature of this particular era of man's history. The last several decades have seen an increasing interest on the part of Americans, the majority of them young, in the attitudes, philosophies, and religions of the

[44] Curtis, p. xxi.
[45] Collier, pp. 15–17.

East. Zen Buddhism has been widely studied; Indian gurus have imparted their wisdom. Meditation, vegetarianism, pacifism, sitar music, and the chanting of mantras have become increasingly familiar phenomena in American life of the last third of the twentieth century. If these trends continue, the time may yet come when white Americans will be able to respond to and understand the deeper qualities of the music of the Native American.

The history of music in America, as will be detailed in the following chapters, is the story of music from various cultures brought to the New World, where various stylistic mixtures produced music unlike that of any other part of the earth—and therefore distinctly American.

But the music of the Native American has played little part in this story, to the present. Not only did the European ignore the music of the American Indian, the Indian also largely ignored the music of the white man, except when it was forced on him as part of religious conversion. To the extent that the Indian has preserved his native music, it seems to be largely untouched by the styles and sounds of European and African music.

There have been scattered attempts to merge European and Indian music. From late in the eighteenth century to the present, European and American composers have attempted, with varying degrees of success, to weave Indian melodies into their composition.[46] And from time to time, Indians respond to one type of music or another springing out of the white man's culture: country-western music enjoys some popularity among Indians now living in the American West, for instance. Mostly, Indian music has been one thing and all other music in America has been something else.

The explanation seems obvious. Immigrants to the New World since the voyage of Columbus in 1492 have come from the West, from Europe and Africa. Arriving in the New World, they confronted a people, long established on this continent, who had come from the East. The history of America since its "discovery" by Columbus suggests repeatedly that cultural differences between East and West were so profound as to inhibit interaction between the peoples who arrived in the New World from opposite directions.

Thus the music of the Native American will play almost no role in the story to follow.

[46] NW 299, s1/3 is an early attempt at this, a piece called "Alknomook, or the Death Song of the Cherokee Indians"; and NW 213 contains a number of instrumental and vocal works from the early twentieth century in which Indian songs have been used as the basic thematic material.

# 2

## Psalms, Hymns, and Spiritual Songs in the Colonies

North America was explored and settled by people from many European nations. The English, under Captain John Smith, established themselves at Jamestown, Virginia, in 1607 and eventually made Williamsburg (settled in 1633) the center of their colony; the French, under Samuel de Champlain, were at Quebec in 1608; the Pilgrims came to Plymouth Rock in 1620; the Dutch had settled at Albany by 1624, and the Dutch West India Company purchased Manhattan Island from the Indians in 1626, to establish the colony of New Amsterdam; and the first of the Puritans set sail for what was to become the Massachusetts Bay Colony in late 1629.

By the early eighteenth century, a string of English colonies extended along the Atlantic Coast from Maine to Georgia. When they united against the tyranny of England and declared themselves a new nation, their language was English, and religious, educational, legal, cultural, and social institutions were patterned after those of England.

Thus the early history of music among the European settlers in the region that was to become the United States must begin with music imported from the British Isles, which only gradually took on a different character in the New World.

The band of some one hundred Pilgrims who landed at Plymouth Rock in December of 1620 had come from the congregation established in Leyden, Holland, after the Brownist church in London had been forced to flee the country with its pastor, Francis Johnson. A Separatist branch of the English Puritan movement, they shared the belief that salvation could be gained only by each individual, through his or her actions and way of life, and that the Holy Bible was the guide to a proper religious life. The church and its clergy existed solely to interpret the teachings of Christianity, as laid out in this book.

When the Pilgrims set out from Leyden for the New World in July of 1620, it was with the sound of psalm singing in their ears:

> They that stayed at Leyden feasted us that were to go at our pastor's house, being large; where we refreshed ourselves, after tears, with singing of Psalms, making joyful melody in our hearts as well as with the voice, there being many of our congregation very expert in music; and indeed it was the sweetest melody that ever mine ears heard.[1]

Though there are no similar passages describing their arrival, it is reasonable to assume that psalms were sung as soon as possible after their safe landing, and throughout the remainder of the seventeenth century, in their churches and homes.

Calvin believed that song used in Christian worship should be taken directly from the Bible, from the Book of Psalms and the biblical canticles. Henry Ainsworth (1570–1623), a member of the Leyden congregation, published a psalter in 1612 entitled *The Book of Psalmes: Englished both in Prose and Metre*. The first verses of Psalm 100 will serve as a sample of his work:

> 1. Show to Jehovah, al the earth.
> 2. Serv ye Jehovah with gladnes:
>    Before him come with singing-merth.
> 3. Know, that Jehovah he God is:
>
>    Its he that made us, and not Wee;
>    his folk, and sheep of his feeding.
> 4. O with confession enter yee
>    his gates, his courtyards with praising:

The Bible contains no musical notation. Ainsworth addressed himself to this problem in his preface:

> Tunes for the Psalms I find none set of God; so that each people is to use the most grave, decent and comfortable manner of singing that they know. ... The singing-notes, therefore, I have taken from our former Englished Psalms, when they will fit the measure of the verse. And for

[1] Edward Winslow, "Hypocrisie Unmasked," quoted in Waldo Selden Pratt, *The Music of the Pilgrims: A Description of the Psalm-book brought to Plymouth in 1620* (Boston: Oliver Ditson Company, 1921), p. 6.

the other long verses I have also taken (for the most part) the gravest and easiest tunes of the French and Dutch Psalmes.

There are forty-eight tunes printed in Ainsworth's psalter; nine are duplicates, thus there are thirty-nine different melodies. As was the case with all English psalmody of the time, each psalm was set in one of several "meters," defined by the number of lines in the verse and the number of syllables in these lines. Psalm 100, quoted above, is in Long Meter (L.M.), with a four-line verse, each line of eight syllables. Any psalm in L.M. could be sung to any long-meter tune, with its four phrases each containing eight notes of music. Thus Psalm 100 could be sung to the tune given it by Ainsworth, the venerable "Old Hundred":

Psalm 100, to the "Old Hundred" tune (Ainsworth)

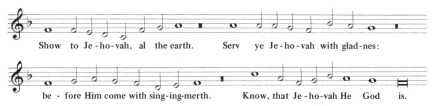

And also, at least theoretically, to any of the other L.M. tunes in the collection:

Psalm 100, to "Psalm 66" tune (Ainsworth)

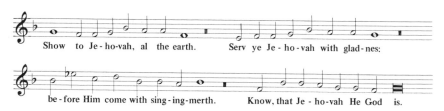

The larger group of Puritans who settled the Massachusetts Bay Colony a decade later sailed from England itself. They were equally devoted to psalm singing, though the psalter they favored was a different one, commonly referred to as "Sternhold and Hopkins," which later came to be known as the "Old version."

The history of this book was a bit more complicated than that of Ainsworth's psalter. Thomas Sternhold (d. 1549) published a metrical version of nineteen psalms—without music—in 1549; another edition of the same year contained thirty-seven such psalms, with

a supplement of seven additional ones by John Hopkins (d. 1570).
An edition of 1553 added seven psalms by Whittingham, for a total
of fifty-one. These were unpretentious verses, intended to be utilitarian.

> Sternhold did not write his verses as literature; they were sacred bal-
> lads for the people, and made no more pretence to literature than the
> secular ballad upon which he founded them.[2]

Sternhold and Hopkins displayed a strong preference for Common
Meter (8.6.8.6.), also known as the Ballad Meter because of its frequent use in secular ballads of the day.

King Edward's death in 1553 put a temporary halt to metrical
English psalmody; the policies of Queen Mary Tudor, his succes-
sor, forced English religious reformers to flee to Geneva, where they
became familiar with Calvin's psalter, first published in 1539. While
in Geneva, in 1556, these exiles published a new edition of the
Sternhold and Hopkins psalter, the first to include music. With
Queen Elizabeth's accession to the throne in 1558, and the return
of a liberal attitude toward Protestantism, they returned to
England, where "in the year of grace 1559, began the public use of
English metrical psalmody."[3] In 1562, a complete English psalter,
containing all 150 psalms, was printed by John Day; though there
were twelve contributors, the psalter continued to be known as
"Sternhold and Hopkins," after the man who published the first
metrical psalms in English (Sternhold) and the man who contributed the largest number of psalms, fifty-six (Hopkins). This
became the standard English psalter, not only among the Puritans
but for all Protestants; more than six hundred different editions
appeared, from the first in 1562 to the last in 1828. It was usually
bound with the Book of Common Prayer, and in addition to its use
in public services, it was also "very met to be used of all sortes of
people privately for their solace and comfort." Next to the Bible
itself, it was the most widely used book of religious text for several
centuries. The first verses of Psalm 100 will serve as a sample of its
style, and as a contrast with Ainsworth's versification (see above):

> All people that on earth do dwel
>   sing to the Lord with chearful voice:
> Him serve with feare, his prayse forth tell,
>   come ye before him and rejoyce.

[2] S. Lothrop Thorndike, "The Psalmodies of Plymouth and Massachusetts Bay,"
*Publications of the Colonial Society of Massachusetts*, I (1895), pp. 228ff.
[3] Thorndike, p. 233.

The Lord ye know is God indeed:
    without our aide he did us make:
We are his flocke he doth us feed,
    and for his sheep he doth us take.

Though this psalm is in Long Meter (8.8.8.8.) as in Ainsworth's psalter, Sternhold and Hopkins used Common Meter (8.6.8.6.) to the virtual exclusion of all others: 128 of the 150 psalms are versified in this meter.

The Puritans brought to America a collection of ninety-seven four-part harmonizations of psalm tunes by some of the leading English composers of the day—John Dowland, Thomas Morley, Thomas Tompkins, Thomas Tallis—compiled and published in London in 1621 by Thomas Ravenscroft, and titled *The Whole Booke of Psalms.* The collection came to be "universally received as the musical exponent of the Sternhold and Hopkins Psalms,"[4] and appears to have been the source for psalm tunes sung in the Massachusetts Bay Colony for the first decades of its existence. Later in the century, a collection by John Playford, also entitled the *Whole Book of Psalms* (London, 1667 and thereafter), enjoyed some currency; it contained simpler, three-voice versions of many of the tunes found in Ravenscroft.

But the Puritans did not depend for long on imported psalms. Dissatisfied with the clumsiness and inaccuracy of certain of the psalms in Sternhold and Hopkins, some thirty clergymen of the colony, led by Richard Mather, Thomas Weld, and John Eliot, prepared a more faithful and idiomatic translation. The fruits of their work appeared in 1640, printed in Cambridge, Massachusetts, on a press brought from England in 1638, as *The Whole Booke of Psalmes Faithfully Translated into English Metre*—the first book of any sort printed in British North America.

> If therefore the verses are not always so smooth and elegant as some may desire or expect; let them consider that Gods Altar needs not our pollishings: for wee have respected rather a plaine translation, than to smooth our verses with the sweetness of any paraphrase, and soe have attended Conscience rather than Elegance, fidelity rather than poetry, in translating the hebrew words into english language, and Davids poetry into english meetre; that soe wee may sing in Sion the Lords songs of prayse according to his own will; untill hee take us from hence, and wipe away all our tears, & bid us enter into our masters joye to sing eternall Halleluiahs.[5]

[4] Thorndike, p. 235.
[5] Preface to the 1st ed. (Cambridge, 1640).

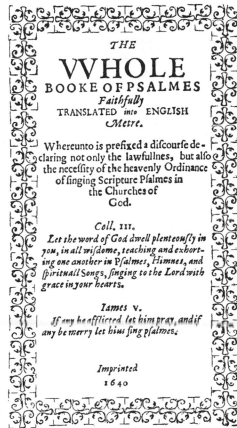

Title page of the *Bay Psalm Book*.

The first edition of 1700 copies was quickly dispersed through-out the Bay Colony, and adopted by virtually every congregation. Soon known as the *Bay Psalm Book*, though never designated as such on the title page, it went through seventy editions (the last in 1773), and also became popular in England (eighteen editions, until 1754) and Scotland (twenty-two editions, until 1759). The "American" version of Psalm 100 began:

1. Make yee a joyfull sounding noyse
   unto Jehovah, all the earth:
2. Serve yee Jehovah with gladness:
   before his presence come with mirth.

3. Know, that Jehovah he is God,
   who hath us formed it is hee,
   & not our selves: his owne people
   & sheepe of his pastures are wee.

No tunes were printed with the collection; the user is referred to those "as they are collected, out of our chief musicians, by *Tho. Ravenscroft*" (his 1621 collection mentioned above). The preference for psalms in Common Meter is almost as striking as in Sternhold and Hopkins: 112 psalms in the *Bay Psalm Book* are in this meter. Another twenty-nine are in Short Meter (6.6.8.6.) or Long Meter (8.8.8.8.). In all, only six meters are used, as compared to seventeen in Sternhold and Hopkins.

A third edition, in 1651, was largely revised by Henry Dunster and Richard Lyon. The translations were made even more colloquial, alternate versions of certain of the psalms were added, and thirty-six metrical biblical texts not taken from the Book of Psalms were included. The *Bay Psalm Book* remained virtually unchanged after this revision for almost a century. Some sense of its poetic style may be seen in Psalm 100:

> Shout to Jehovah all the earth.
> With joyfulness the Lord serve ye:
> Before his presence come with mirth.
> Know, that Jehovah God, is he.
>
> It's he that made us and not we,
> His folk his pastures sheep also
> Into his gates with thanks come ye
> With praises to his Court-yards go.

The differences between this first American psalter and its English predecessors may seem slight, from a distance of three and a half centuries. But they are in a language closer to that spoken by members of the congregations, rather than that of the college-trained translators of earlier English psalters.

The *Bay Psalm Book* eventually became the most widely used psalter, even among the Pilgrims. The Salem colony voted to discontinue the use of Ainsworth and the tunes associated with it at a meeting held May 4, 1667, because of "the difficulty of the tunes, and that we could not sing them so well as formerly."[6] Even at Plymouth, there was growing dissatisfaction with the psalm translations and tunes that had served the colony for so long. The Plymouth Church Records for May 17, 1685 record that:

... the Elders stayed the church & propounded to them, a mention to sing Psalme, 130: in another Translation, because in M^r Ainsworths which wee sang, the Tune was soe defficult as few could follow it; the

[6] George Hood, *A History of Music in New England* (Boston: Wilkins, Carter and Company, 1846), p. 53.

church consented thereunto, & on May, 24: sang, Ps:130: in the Translation used by the churches in the Bay.[7]

And a few years later:

> June 19 (1692): the Pastor stayed the church after meeting & pro-
> pounded that seeing many of the Psalmes in m[r] Ainsworths Translation
> which wee now sung, had such difficult tunes that none in the chh could
> set, that the chh would consider of some way of accomodation that wee
> might sing all the Psalmes & left it to their consideration.
>
> August, 7, at the conclusion of the sacrament, the Pastor called upon
> the chh to expresse their Judgements about this motion; the vote was
> this. when the tunes are difficult in Translation wee use, wee will sing
> the Psalmes now used in our neighbor-ches in the Bay; not one brother
> opposed this conclusion; the sabbath following, Aug:14: wee began to
> sing the Psalmes in course according to the vote of the chh.[8]

There was no corresponding attempt to create American tunes.
When a selection of psalm tunes was first printed in America, in
the ninth edition of the *Bay Psalm Book* (Boston: B. Green and V.
Allen, 1698), they were taken from several editions of John Playford's *A Brief Introduction to the Skill of Musick*, first published in
London in 1654. The eleven-page supplement of thirteen two-part
settings of psalm tunes appended to this edition of the *Bay Psalm
Book* was the first music of any sort printed in the colonies, but its
impact was slight, judging from the fact that most later editions of
the *Bay Psalm Book* contained texts only.

It is tempting, given music printed so neatly and apparently
unequivocally by Ainsworth, Ravenscroft, and Playford, to assume
that we can recreate the sound of seventeenth-century psalm singing in Massachusetts by singing the music today, as written down.
And indeed this has been often done, in live performance and on
recordings.[9] But there is evidence that the music sounded quite
different from the way it was fixed in musical notation.

One of the most informative discussions of psalm singing in seventeenth-century New England was written by the Rev. John Cotton (1584–1652), who came to Massachusetts in 1633 after a twenty-
one year ministry at Boston, England. His *Singing of Psalmes a
Gospel-Ordinance* (1647) was not only a resounding defense of the
singing of psalms, based on quotations from the Bible, but also the
clearest statement in English of the Calvinist doctrine of psalm

---

[7] Plymouth Church Records: 1620–1859, *Publications of the Choral Society of Massachusetts*, XXII. (Boston: John Wilson and Son, 1920), p. 257.
[8] Plymouth Church Records: 1620–1859, p. 171.
[9] For instance, Haydn Society 2068 contains a collection of psalms from the Ainsworth Psalter; MIA 96 (see p. 704) has pieces from the *Bay Psalm Book*.

singing: music exists in worship only as a medium for words; this music should be simple, so as not to interfere with the message of the text; sacred music should have a different character from secular. He also discusses practical matters of psalm singing, including the practice of "lining out," which grew up on both sides of the Atlantic. An even earlier description and justification is found in the *Ordinance* of 1644:

> That the whole congregation may join herein, every one that can read is to have a psalm-book, and all others, not disabled by age or otherwise, are to be exhorted to learn to read. But for the present, where many in the congregation cannot read, it is convenient that the minister, or some fit person appointed by him and the other ruling officers, do read the psalm line by line before the singing thereof.[10]

The reference here is to the reading of the text before the psalm is sung, but many other accounts make it clear that the leader or "preceptor" was also usually responsible for *singing* the psalm, line by line, with the congregation singing each phrase after him. Samuel Sewall (1652–1730), for many years preceptor at the Old South Church in Boston, recorded in his diary the various occasions on which he "set" the tunes, often mentioning the specific tune to which a psalm was sung:

> Sabbath, Oct. 22 (1691). Capt. Frary's voice failing him in his own Essay, by reason of his Palsie, he calls to me to set the Tune, which accordingly I doe; 17, 18, 19, 20, verses 68th Psalm, Windsor Tune; After the Lord's Supper, 6, 7, 8, 9, verses 16th Low-Dutch.[11]

A similar practice was followed in devotionals in private homes:

> Monday, Dec. 21, 1691. I went with Mr. Addington and his wife to Muddy-River, to the house of Joshua Gardner, where came Mr. Walter and his wife, Mr. Denison and wife, Sir Ruggles and Mrs. Weld the Mother. Had a very good Dinner. Mr. Walter crav'd a Blessing, Mr. Denison return'd Thanks, mentioning the sad Providence that befell them last January, and God's present smiles in their new House and children; Mr. Walter pray'd that God would double their Mercies. Sung the 23. Ps. and 18th v. 51. Mr. Walter desired me to set the Tune, which I did; St. David's.[12]

It is a simple matter to fit together the *Bay Psalm Book* version of Psalm 23 and "St. David's" tune:

[10] Percy A. Scholes, *The Puritans and Music in England and New England* (London: Oxford University Press, 1934), p. 265.
[11] Samuel Sewall, *The Diary of Samuel Sewall, 1674–1729*, ed. by M. Halsey Thomas (New York: Farrar, Strauss and Giroux, 1973), p. 283.
[12] Sewall, p. 285.

Psalm 23, to "St. David's" tune (*Bay Psalm Book*)

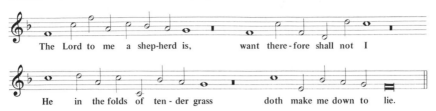

How it sounded as set by Sewall and echoed by the others assembled with him that day is another matter.

Lining out was an expediency, adopted because the majority of the colonists were musically illiterate. The congregation did not merely echo each musical phrase; various members changed the music to fit their own musical tastes and abilities. The result was often heterophony—several voices singing the same melody, but varying it individually—or perhaps even a type of oral polyphony—different voices deliberately singing different notes, to create some sort of chordal effect. Accounts of such singing are legion:

> I have often wonder'd that the Spirit of Singing, and the great care taken to regulate it in our Congregations throughout the Country, has not been attended with some Endeavours after the Removal of that indecent, unwarrantable, and unedifying way of *reading the Psalm Line by Line*. ... I have but one thing more to observe, and that is, that the same Person who sets the Tune, and guides the Congregation in Singing, commonly reads the Psalm, which is a Task to few are capable of performing well, that in Singing two or three Staves, the Congregation falls from a cheerful Pitch to downright *Grumbling*, and then some to relieve themselves mount an Eighth above the rest, others perhaps a Fourth or Fifth, by which Means the Singing appears to be rather a confused Noise, made up of *Reading, Squecking* and *Grumbling*, than a decent and orderly Part of God's Worship.[13]

> I have observed in many Places, one Man is upon this Note, while another is a Note before him, which produces something so hideous and disorderly, as is beyond Expression bad. ... Much time is taken up in shaking out these Turns and Quavers; and besides, no two Men in the Congregation quaver alike, or together; which sounds in the Ears of a good Judge, like *Five Hundred* different Tunes roared out at the same time, whose perpetual interferings with one another, perplexed Jars, and unmeasured Periods, would make a Man wonder ...[14]

---

[13] Jeoffrey Chanticleer, "To Old Master Janus," *The New-England Courant*, February, 17–24, 1724.

[14] Thomas Walter, *The Grounds and Rules of Musick Explained: Or, An Introduction to the Art of Singing by Note* (Boston: Printed by J. Franklin for Samuel Gerrish, 1721), pp. 4–5.

If in the same Congregation at the same time, when a Psalm is nam'd by the Minister, some should sing it in *one Tune*, and some in *another;* or some should greatly raise, and others as evidently lower their Voice, or some draw out their Voice on the *same Syllable twice so long as others,* what Discord, Jarring and Confusion would this make?[15]

Sewall reported occasional confusion as to what psalm tune was being sung:

Febr. 2 (1718). Lord's Day. In the Morning I set York Tune, and in the 2[d] going over, the Gallery carried it irresistibly to St. David's which discouraged me very much.[16]

Moreover, the tunes themselves began to deviate from their notated versions, as even preceptors depended more and more on oral transmission of the tunes.

For to compare small things with great, our *Psalmway* has suffered the like Inconvenience which our *Faith* has laboured under, in case it had been committed and trusted to the uncertain and doubtful Conveyance of *Oral Tradition.* . . . Yes, I have my self heard (for Instance) *Oxford* Tune sung in *three* Churches (which I purposely forbear to mention) with as much difference as there can possibly be between *York* and *Oxford,* or any two other different Tunes.[17]

The Rules of Singing not being taught or learnt, every one sang as best pleased himself, and every *Leading-Singer* would take the Liberty of raising any *Note* of the *Tune,* or lowering it, as best pleas'd his Ear, and add such *Turns* and *Flourishes* as were grateful to him. . . . One *Clerk* or *Chorister* would alter the *Tunes* a little in his Day, the next, a little in his, and so one after another, till in *Fifty* or *Sixty* Years it caus'd a *Considerable Alteration.* . . . Your *Usual Way* of Singing is handed down by *Tradition* only, and whatsoever is only so conveyed down to us, it is a thousand to one if it not be miserably corrupted in *Three* or *Fourscore* Years Time.[18]

What had begun as a written tradition of psalmody had been transformed into an oral tradition. Tunes so transmitted were subject to modification in the process; and any semblance of proper part singing, as written down in the collections of Ravenscroft and Playford, had given way to a responsorial, heterophonic practice.

---

[15] Cotton Mather (?), *A Pacificatory Letter about Psalmody* (Boston: Printed by J. Franklin for Benjamin Eliot, 1724), p. 6.

[16] Sewall, p. 881.

[17] Walter, p. 3.

[18] Thomas Symmes, *The Reasonableness of Regular Singing, or, Singing by Note* (Boston: Printed by B. Green for Samuel Gerrish, 1720), pp. 8–9.

Oral traditions which transform a written tradition have often been condemned:

> The dark age of music had come, for the sturdy psalm-singing founders had long since gone and their psalm-droning successors, utterly without instruction, singing by ear, if at all, catching garbled tunes as best they could from a quavering voice, added their own embellishments, which resulted in a jargon in which the loudest or most cutting voice triumphed.[19]
>
> The cultivation of music was neglected, until in the latter part of the seventeenth century, the congregations throughout New England were rarely able to sing more than three or four tunes. . . . Every melody was "tortured and twisted" . . . until their psalms were uttered in a medley of confused and disorderly noises, rather than a decorous song.[20]

An alternate view is that psalm singing, in moving from a written to an oral tradition and taking on a different character in the process, had become American music: it had become something different from what had been transplanted from England, shaped by the realities of life in the New World.

The problem, of course, is that this "American" variation of psalm singing has long since disappeared from New England, and our only source of information about it would appear to be such contemporary accounts as those quoted above. But just as there is at least enough of the oral-tradition music of the American Indian still extant, enough to enable us to conjecture what this music might have been like in the centuries before it was recorded in music notation and on discs and tape, one can find oral-tradition sacred music in America today descended from seventeenth-century practice. In certain isolated areas of the Appalachian region, and also in rural areas of the Southeast, sacred music is still "lined out": the minister or some member of the congregation sings each line of a hymn or sacred song, and the congregation—most of it musically illiterate—sings each phrase after him. Recordings have been made, and even today, live performances can be heard in which the sound is close to descriptions of psalm singing in the seventeenth and early eighteenth centuries in New England: various members of the congregation embellish tunes according to individual taste and memory, producing a sort of heterophony; these are long and drawn out, much more so than what is sung by the leader; the tunes themselves have been changed over the years,

---

[19] William Arms Fisher, *Ye Olde New-England Psalm-Tunes: 1620–1820* (Boston and New York: Oliver Ditson Company, 1930), p. iv.
[20] Hood, p. 140.

so they no longer resemble those normally associated with a given set of words.[21]

This is not to suggest that Southern practice descended from the New England psalm singing discussed above. Few people in these regions are descended from families who migrated from the New England colonies to the South and what was then the West; rather their forefathers came directly from the British Isles to Virginia or the Carolinas, and worked their way inland from there. But even though written commentary on psalm singing in the more southerly colonies is almost completely lacking, and there was no publication of psalm texts and tunes in these regions, the same texts and tunes were brought from England and the practice of psalmody apparently developed in the same ways as in New England. Furthermore, lining out was practiced in seventeenth-century England and Scotland, and similar comments and complaints about congregational singing abound in British church literature of the late seventeenth and early eighteenth centuries. Thus English and Scotch immigrants to the southern colonies arriving as late as the eighteenth century could have brought with them a psalm-singing tradition of lining out and heterophonic congregational response similar to that which developed in the North. What we can hear even today in the South is a close relative of early New England psalmody, if not a direct descendant of it.

The first two decades of the eighteenth century brought stirrings of dissatisfaction with the state of psalm singing in New England. Ministers—mostly in Boston—began speaking from the pulpit on the subject of how the "proper" tradition of psalm singing had been lost, and of the necessity of returning to it. The quarrel was with the "Usual Way" of singing, i.e., the oral tradition that had taken over throughout the region; what was being urged was a return to "Regular Singing," by which was meant singing from musical notation.

The first lengthy, published document addressing itself to this matter was brought out in Boston in 1720 by the Rev. Thomas Symmes, who had graduated from Harvard College in 1698. Entitled *The Reasonableness of Regular Singing or, Singing by Note*, this essay laid out its thesis in the lengthy subtitle: "To Revive the True and Ancient Mode of Singing Psalm-Tunes, according to the Pattern in our *New-England* Psalm-Books; the Knowledge and Practice of which is greatly decay'd in most Congregations." Symmes

[21] Cf. NW 294, *The Gospel Ship: Baptist Hymns and White Spirituals from the Southern Mountains*, for examples of such sacred pieces as *Amazing Grace* (s1/2) sung in this style.

set himself the task of proving "That *Singing by or according to Note*, is to be preferred to the *Usual Way of Singing*," writing in the "plainest, most easy and popular Way I can, (for 'tis for the sake of common People I write)." His chief arguments:

1. *"Singing by Note* is the most *Ancient* way of Singing, and claims the preference to the other on that Account." He argues that "Regular Singing" was the first type of singing done in New England, as attested by preserved psalm books, the memory of the oldest members of the congregation, and the fact that it was "known and approv'd of in our *College*, for many Years after its first Founding."
2. *"Singing by Note* is the most *Melodious* . . . because when *Tunes* are Sung exactly by *Note*, in the several parts of them, there is such a perfect *Harmony* between the *Notes* and *Turning* of the Voice, in which true *Melody* consists, as cannot be in the *Usual Way*." His reference here is both to the singing of the melody in its "proper" form, and to the three- or four-part harmony that was written in some psalm books, but is absent in the "Usual Way" of singing.
3. *"Singing by Note, is the most Rational Way*, Therefore it is the *most excellent*." He explained that the "Confusion and Disorder" resulting when "every Man follow(s) his own *Fancy*, and leaving the *Rule*" is "very contrary to Him, who is not the *Author of Confusion*, but the GOD of Order."
4. "Singing with *Skill* or by *Note*, which is the same thing, is most agreable to the General Instructions which we have in the Scripture."[22]

This last point, supported by copious quotation from the Bible, is intended to be the clinching argument, given the Puritan belief that the word of God is to be found only in the Scriptures.

Sermons and essays supporting the same view poured from the pulpits and presses of New England in the following decade. Cotton Mather's *The Accomplished Singer* (Boston, 1721) laid out "Instructions, First, How the Piety of Singing with a True Devotion, may be obtained and expressed; the Glorious GOD after an Uncommon manner Glorified in it, and His PEOPLE Edified. and then, HOW the MELODY OF REGULAR SINGING, and the SKILL of doing it, according to the RULES of it, may be easily arrived unto." The Rev. Josiah Dwight, pastor of the Church of Christ in Woodstock, published in 1725 (Boston) *"An Essay to Silence the Outcry* That has been made in some Places against *Regular Singing."* The Rev. Nathaniel Chauncey published *Regular Singing Defended* (New London, 1728), in which he proves this to be "the only TRUE WAY of Singing the SONGS of the LORD; By Arguments both from Reason and Scripture"; the title page quotes 2

---

[22] Symmes, pp. 5–12, passim.

Corinthians, 13:8: "We can do nothing against the Truth, but for the Truth."

Of a more practical nature were two publications of 1721 offering elementary, step-by-step instruction in learning to sing from musical notation, complete with selections of psalm tunes. Probably the first of these to appear was *An Introduction to the Singing of Psalm-Tunes* by the Rev. John Tufts (1689–1750), who served as minister in Newbury from 1714 to 1738. The first edition, of which no copies have been recovered,[23] was described in the *Boston NewsLetter* for January 2–9, 1721:

> A Small Book containing 20 Psalm Tunes, with Directions how to Sing them, contrived in the most easy Method ever yet Invented, for the Ease of Learners, whereby even Children, or People of the meanest Capacities, may come to Sing them by Rule.

A brief, nine-page set of instructions lays out the basic elements of musical notation; pitch is explained in terms of the four-syllable solmization system popular in England in the seventeenth century and described as early as 1597 in Thomas Morley's *Plaine and Easie Introduction to Practicall Musicke.* The thirty-seven three-part settings of psalm tunes which follow are notated on a five-line staff, but letters indicating the solmization syllables associated with each note—*f*(a), *s*(ol), *l*(a), or *m*(i)—are placed on the staff, in place of noteheads.

*The Grounds and Rules of Musick Explained,* published in Boston in 1721, was the work of Rev. Thomas Walter (1696–1725) of Roxbury. His book, subtitled "An Introduction to the Art of Singing by Note. Fitted to the meanest Capacities," has a much more extensive preface, including a description of and attack on the Usual Way of singing ("miserably tortured, and twisted, and quavered, in some Churches, into a horrid Medly of confused and disorderly Noises."), and instructions for singing by note cribbed from several seventeenth-century English sources. Twenty-four three-part settings of psalm tunes follow, notated in the normal fashion of the day, without solmization syllables.

Reflecting the trend away from singing by note, the eleventh (1705) through the twenty-fourth (1732) editions of the *Bay Psalm Book* had included tune supplements with single-line melodies only, rather than three- or four-part harmonizations. But the twenty-fifth (1737) and twenty-sixth (1742) editions contained supplements of thirty-nine harmonized psalm tunes—evidence that the campaign to restore singing by note was bearing fruit. These,

---

[23] The first surviving edition is the fifth, of 1726 (Boston).

together with the pieces included in Tufts and Walter, gave a repertory of some sixty-seven harmonized psalm tunes printed in the northern colonies by the mid-eighteenth century.

The singing school was the institution through which music literacy was promulgated. Thomas Symmes wrote:

> Would it not greatly tend to the promoting (of) Singing Psalms, if Singing Schools were promoted; Would not this be a Conforming to Scripture Pattern? Have we not as much need of them as GOD's People of *Singing*, any more than that of *Reading?* or to attain it without the use of suitable means, any more than they of Old, when *Miracles, Inspirations,* &c. were common? Where would be the *Difficulty,* or what the *Disadvantages,* if People that want *Skill* in *Singing,* would procure a *Skilfull Person* to *Instruct* them, and meet *Two* or *Three* Evenings in the Week from *Five* or *Six* a Clock, to *Eight,* and spend the Time in Learning to Sing?[24]

Such singing schools were already being held, in Boston—where one is mentioned as early as 1714—and in such neighboring towns as Cambridge, Andover, and Dorchester. Soon these schools had spread to other New England colonies, and to the middle and southern colonies as well.

Organized usually among members of the congregation of a church, these schools were conducted by a "singing master." The "scholars" were instructed in the rudiments of music notation— the staff, the names of notes and their location on the staff, the several clefs ("cliffs"), scales, intervals, sharps and flats, solmization, the various meters (times), and the application of all these in the singing of scales and simple melodies. Tuft's or Walter's book was often used; scholars were expected to purchase copies, and the culmination of such schooling came when the class would undertake the singing of various psalm tunes in the collection, first in unison and then in three-part harmony.

The church-led crusade against musical illiteracy resulted in remarkable improvement in the singing at some churches. Samuel Sewall, no longer "setting" the psalm tunes himself, wrote in his diary in the early 1720s, "House was full, and the Singing extraordinarily Excellent, such as has hardly been heard before in Boston,"[25] and Cotton Mather (1663–1728) wrote to a friend in London, in 1723:

> A mighty Spirit came Lately upon abundance of our people, to Reform their singing which was degenerated in our Assemblies to an Irregularity, which made a Jar in the ears of the more curious and skilful singers.

[24] Symmes, p. 20.

Our Ministers generally Encouraged the people, to accomplish themselves for a Regular singing, and a more beautiful Psalmody.[26]

But many people continued to feel that the Usual Way was the best. Cotton Mather wrote, in 1723, that the opposition to the introduction of Regular Singing was particularly intense in smaller towns and rural areas:

Tho' in the more polite city of Boston this design [Regular Singing]met with general acceptance, in the country, where they have more of the *rustic,* some numbers of elder and angry people bore zealous testimonies against these wicked innovations, and this bringing in of popery. Their zeal transported some of them so far . . . that they would not only use the most approbrious terms, and call the singing of these Christians a worshipping of the devil, but also they would run out of the meeting-house at the beginning of the exercise.[27]

"Essays to bring it [Regular Singing] in have been withstood and oppos'd; and great Heats, Animosities, Contentions, have been occasion'd among Christians hereby," wrote the anonymous author of *A Pacificatory Letter about Psalmody* (Boston, 1724).

Such opposition prompted another flood of sermons and essays defending and justifying the introduction of Regular Singing. Typical was a sermon preached at Framingham by the Rev. Josiah Dwight, pastor of the Church of Christ at Woodstock. After a detailed scriptural defense of the new practice, the Rev. Dwight spoke to the congregation more on its own terms, responding to various of their objections:

*Quest.* Is it equal, that the Elderly, should yield, to be turned out of the old way of Singing, to gratify the Youngerly, who urge on a Regulation the most.
*Ans.* It is not to yield to man but to God, to fall in with a more advantageous way of performing his worship.
*Quest.* Were our Fathers to blame for Singing God's Praises in that way that is now censur'd for it's defects.
*Ans.* Persons are accepted of God, if with a good and honest heart, they Sing, Pray or Read God's Word as well as they can. But to do these *brokenly,* when they might do them more *accurately* is a disrespect & dishonour to God, & therefore censurable.

*Quest.* Can you desire us to be reconciled to the new way of Singing, when it brings in so much disturbance with it?

[25] Sewall, III, p. 285.
[26] Kenneth Silverman, *Selected Letters of Cotton Mather* (Baton Rouge: Louisiana State University Press, 1971), p. 376.
[27] Silverman, p. 376.

*Ans.* I must needs ask leave here to plead, that the blame is mislay'd; and the wrong horse Saddled.

A foundation was laid, however, which bore fruit in the next generation. Three new collections appeared in the colonies in the 1750s: an untitled tune supplement to accompany a new version of the psalms by John Barnard (Boston, 1752); William Dawson's *Youths Entertaining Amusement* (Philadelphia, 1754); and another untitled tune supplement (Boston, 1755), compiled and engraved by Thomas Johnston. And the decade of the 1760s saw three more new American collections:

*Urania* (Philadelphia, 1761), by James Lyon
*Collection of the Best Psalm Tunes* (Boston, 1764), by Josiah Flagg
*Sixteen Anthems* (Boston, 1766), by Flagg
and also American editions of several large British collections:
*Royal Melody Complete* (Boston, 1767 and afterwards), by William Tans'ur (1706–1783); first edition in London, 1755
*Universal Psalmodist* (Newburyport, 1769 and afterwards), by Aaron Williams (1731–1776); first edition in London, 1763
Taken together, these publications of the 1760s added more than three hundred tunes to those already printed in the colonies, more than quadrupling the tune repertory in little over a decade. Also, some of these new pieces were in much more complex musical style than the simple three- and four-part harmonizations of psalm tunes printed before mid-century.

Protestant music in England was in a period of great change in the first half of the eighteenth century.[28] There was, first of all, a serious and eventually successful challenge to the Sternhold and Hopkins version of the psalms. Nahum Tate (1652–1715) and Nicholas Brady (1659–1726) brought out their *New Version of the Psalms of David, fitted to the tunes used in churches* in 1696, in London. By 1708 it had reached a sixth edition, with a supplement of seventy-five psalm tunes set in two parts, and though it never completely replaced the Old Version (which was in print as late as 1828), it quickly surpassed it in popularity. The New Version of Psalm 100 will serve to illustrate the quite different, more modern style of this translation:

> With one consent let all the Earth
> to God their chearful Voices raise;
> Glad Homage pay with awful Mirth,
> And sing before him Songs of praise:

[28] For the best and most complete discussion of these matters, cf. Nicholas Temperley, *The Music of the English Parish Church* (Cambridge: Cambridge University Press, 1979).

Convinc'd that he is God alone,
From whom both we and all proceed,
We, whom he chuses for his own,
The Flock that he vouchsafes to feed.

Musical style in British psalmody also changed. Settings by such composers as Tans'ur, William Knapp (1698–1768), and John Arnold (c. 1720–1792) were usually for four voices, with more variety of rhythmic movement than found in homorhythmic psalm settings of the seventeenth century. Solo and duet passages for the various voices, and even occasional passages of contrapuntal writing, demanded far greater ability, training, and experience than had been previously required.

An anthem (Psalm 47), by William Tans'ur

In the colonies, the New Version was accepted more slowly than in England, because of the great popularity of the American (*Bay*

*Psalm Book*) version of the psalms. Nevertheless, certain churches—chiefly Baptist and Episcopalian—adopted Tate and Brady, and others used it together with older versions. And though the introduction and spread of "singing by note" proceeded more slowly in the colonies than in the British Isles, by the time of the American Revolution some churches in America boasted singers who could perform church music as complex and difficult as that written and sung in England.

In the second half of the eighteenth century, the contest between the Old Version and the New Version of the psalms was largely laid to rest by the overwhelming popularity of yet another rhymed, metrical version of the psalms, this one by Isaac Watts (1674–1748). *The Psalms of David Imitated* (London, 1719) fell somewhere between a strict translation and a paraphrase; its appeal was in a more immediate and accessible language, a more contemporary orientation, and in Watt's considerable skill as a poet. His version of Psalm 100 reads:

> Ye nations round the earth, rejoice
> Before the Lord, your sovereign King;
> Serve him with cheerful heart and voice,
> With all your tongues his glory sing.
>
> The Lord is God; 'tis He alone
> Doth life, and breath, and being give;
> We are his work, and not our own;
> The sheep that on his pastures live.

The congregation at Plymouth, the oldest and one of the most conservative in the colonies, reflected the attitudes of the American colonies concerning the several versions:

Feb[r] 13th (1770). The Brethren met, in Number 23. (it being a very rainy Day) and after some considerable Discourse upon the Affair—The Question was put seperately to Each Member, whither they were for exchanging the *Old Version* for any other—& it appeared that *twelve* of y[e] Brethren were for continuing y[e] *Old Version* & Eleven for *Tate & Brady*. The Pastor afterwards signify'd his Choice for *Tate & Brady*. So that there being a Tie, the Matter remained yet undetermin'd. It was manifest, in the Course of y[e] Conversation, that several of y[e] Brethren rather prefer[d] *Dr Watts's*, but as this was more particularly obnoxious to some others of y[e] Brethren, they were willing to condescend to vote for *Tate & Brady*.[29]

[29] Plymouth Church Records: 1620–1859, pp. 332–33. The "Old Version" here refers to the *Bay Psalm Book*.

The matter was resolved the following year with the adoption of the New Version. But the triumph of Tate & Brady was short-lived:

> On March 21, 1786 At a very full meeting of s^d Precinct, the Vote was called, which of the two versions they will use, & *Voted*, that *Doct^r Watts's Version* . . . be sung in future, in our public Worship, viz, 17 Votes for Tate & Brady, & 38 for Doct^r Watts's, to which the rest amicably agreed.[30]

Watts contributed much more than a new version of the psalms, however. Convinced that the restriction of texts sung in public worship to only psalms and biblical canticles was unfortunate, since "many of them (are) foreign to the State of the New-Testament, and widely different from the present Circumstances of Christians," he published, in 1707, a collection of *Hymns and Spiritual Songs*, newly composed religious poems reflecting current Christian attitudes. These were not the first "original" (i.e., nonbiblical) devotional texts introduced into the public worship of British and American Protestant churches; but their immediate and immense popularity led to the singing of more and more "hymns & spiritual songs" in public and private worship as the eighteenth century unfolded. Several examples, chosen from hymns particularly popular in America, demonstrate the vividness, simplicity, and intensity of Watts's language:

> Hark! from the tombs a doleful sound;
>   Mine ears, attend the cry.
> "Yes living men, come view the ground
>   Where you must shortly lie."
>
> "Princes, this clay must be your bed,
>   In spite of all your towers;
> The tall, the wise, the reverend head
>   Must lie as low as ours!"
>
> Great God! is this our certain doom?
>   And are we still secure?
> Still walking downward to the tomb,
>   And yet prepare no more!
> Grant us the power of quickening grace
>   To fit our souls to fly;
> Then, when we drop this dying flesh,
>   We'll rise above the sky.
>
>
> Salvation, oh! the joyful sound,
>   Tis pleasure to our ears;

---

[30] Plymouth Church Records: 1620–1859, p. 366.

A sovreign balm for ev'ry wound.
A cordial for our fears.
Salvation! let the echo fly
The spacious world around,
While all the armies of the sky
Conspire to raise the sound.

When I can read my title clear,
    To mansions in the skies,
I'll bid farewell to every fear,
    And wipe my weeping eyes.
Should earth against my soul engage,
    And hellish darts be hurled,
Then I can smile at Satan's rage,
    And face a frowning world.

Broad is the road that leads to death,
And thousands walk together there;
But wisdome shews a narrow'r path,
With here and there a traveler.
The fearful soul that tires and faints,
And walks the ways of God no more,
Is but esteem'd almost a saint,
And makes his own destruction sure.

Watts's poems appealed to all classes of Americans, for two centuries: literate, urban New Englanders; the more common folk in villages and towns; rural, nonliterate settlers in the more remote areas of the South and West; and African slaves. He was a religious poet, rather than a translator and versifier, whose creations will be encountered time and again in ensuing chapters of the present book.

This account of church music in the colonies has concentrated on New England, and more particularly Boston and its surrounding towns, for purely practical reasons: most of the published documents pertaining to this story, and also the majority of the collections of sacred texts and tunes brought out in America, are from this region. But the same story unfolded in other British colonies. The same translations of the psalms were used; there was the same trend to singing in the Usual Way, or the practice of lining out psalms, in the seventeenth and early eighteenth centuries; singing by note was reintroduced in the singing schools of Virginia and elsewhere; by the time of the Revolution, churches in many

A Pennsylvania church service in the early 1800's. From a drawing by Lewis Miller.

cities and larger towns boasted singers able to cope with the more difficult music of Tans'ur and his English contemporaries.

The great psalm-singing controversy of the 1720s was in essence a confrontation between literate, urban people who preferred literal performances from musical notation, and rural, nonliterate folk who were quite content with oral-tradition music.

This pattern was to be repeated, time and time again, in later chapters of the history of music in America.

# 3

## Anglo-American Music in Oral Tradition

From the earliest settlement of the American colonies by English-speaking people, many of the immigrants from the British Isles were from laboring, farming, and servant classes. They were a different breed from the colonists whose activity in psalmody and hymnody was detailed in the previous chapter, or from the more cultured elements who laid the foundations for concert and operatic life in America.

They arrived in a steady stream from England, Ireland, and Scotland, from the early seventeenth century until well past the midpoint of the nineteenth. They came as indentured servants, as escapees from poverty and famine, as laborers brought over by the boatload at various times when there was a demand for unskilled labor in the New World, as criminals sent away from the British Isles to relieve their home country of the responsibility of caring for them, as refugees from the political tides rolling against them.

The conditions under which they crossed the Atlantic were often scarcely better than those of the slave ships bringing Africans to the New World. Once here, they met the same patterns of prejudice they had known in Britain; the Irish, in particular, were subjected to the scorn and hatred they had endured for so long from the English. Coming from families descended from the peasantry of the Middle Ages and Renaissance, it was difficult for them to take advantage of the potential for upward mobility in America. They continued to be laborers and farmers in their new environment, and tended to drift away from urban areas, settling on land undesired by anyone else—the hills and mountains of Virginia, North Carolina, Vermont, and New Hampshire, or the rocky and sandy soil elsewhere unsuitable to large-scale farming. They eked out livings as farmers and sometimes developed into carpenters, masons, blacksmiths, and the like.

When the Revolution began, they appeared as militia, scouts, and sharpshooters, experienced in unconvential warfare from their constant skirmishes with American Indians on the fringes of the expanding country. After the war, they were among the first to push westward, as guides, Indian fighters, hunters and trappers, and early settlers in the rugged country of Kentucky and Tennessee. Here, too, whenever new territory became too thickly settled, they moved on—to more remote pockets of this country, further to the south, westward into what is now Ohio, Indiana, and Illinois, eventually across the Mississippi into Missouri, Kansas, Arkansas, and Texas.

The most distinctive aspect of this subculture was the fact that its roots were in nonliterate layers of British life, and many of these people remained nonliterate in America into the twentieth century. Much of the music they brought to the New World, and nourished and developed here, was shaped by the fact that neither musical pitches nor song texts were written down.

Of the several types of vocal music they brought to the New World, the oldest and most distinctive was the ballad. Many hundreds of these were in circulation among the uneducated people of the British Isles at the time of their emigration to America. Some dealt with identifiable historical events. "The Battle of Harlaw" (Child 163)[1] narrates some details of a battle fought just north of Aberdeen on July 24, 1411; "Durham Field" (Child 159) tells of an encounter between the English and the Scots in 1346. Others are suspected of having originated in historical fact, though the precise identification of the incident is no longer certain. "The Gypsy Laddie" (Child 200), also known as "Gypsy Davy" and "The Wraggle Taggle Gypsies," tells of a gypsy enticing a noble lady to leave her home and husband; the lord pursues them and a number of gypsies are killed in the ensuing battle. It may have originated in the early seventeenth century, when a gypsy named Johnny Faa and a number of his followers were put to death when they remained in Britain, defying the laws exiling them from England and Scotland.

Others deal with persons and events poised somewhere between

[1] Ballads will be identified by the number assigned them in Francis James Child, *The English and Scottish Popular Ballads*, 5 vols. (Boston and New York: Houghton, Mifflin Company, 1882–98).

history and legend; several dozen ballads are concerned with events in the life of Robin Hood, for instance.[2]

But the vast majority are populated with characters whose exact identity has been lost in the mists of time. "The Twa Sisters" (Child 10) narrates the story of a girl pushed into the water of a mill stream by her older sister; the miller sees her drowning, but refuses to save her. Though such an incident may well have happened, there is no longer any way to link this ballad with a specific event.

The tales are frequently grisly. Two schoolboys quarrel on their way home, in "The Twa Brothers" (Child 49), and the elder stabs the younger to death with a penknife.[3] "Earl Brand" (Child 7) is the story of a young woman who elopes with her lover, against the wishes of her family; her father and brothers pursue the pair, are killed when ambushed by the lover, but the latter is mortally wounded in the fight and goes to the home of his mother to die.[4] "Edward" (Child 13) is another tale of fratricide; "Lord Randall" (Child 12) is poisoned by his lover; a sailor persuades a young woman to leave her husband and young child in "The Daemon Lover" (Child 243), but she is drowned at sea.

Many ballads introduce elements of the supernatural. "The Cruel Mother" (Child 20) kills her illegitimate twins with a knife, then is haunted by visions of them. William, in "Fair Margaret and Sweet William" (Child 74), marries another woman, dreams of Margaret lying in her bed in a pool of blood, and goes to her house to find that she has indeed killed herself. The mother in "The Wife of Usher's Well" (Child 79) grieves for her three sons, dead in a foreign land, until they appear to her as apparitions. A young woman mourns on the grave of her dead lover, in "The Unquiet Grave" (Child 78), until he speaks to her from his coffin.

Some are humorous, as "The Farmer's Curst Wife" (Child 278), in which the devil takes a scolding wife off to hell but quickly brings her back again.[5] Some are romantic tales of lovers who find happiness in spite of the obstacles of class difference ("The Bailiff's Daughter of Islington," Child 105) or lengthy separations ("Young Beichan," Child 53). A few, such as "The Cherry Tree Carol" (Child 54), are religious.

The function of these ballads is complex. Certainly they served as entertainment, in a culture possessing no written literature and with little access to the various forms of public amusement:

[2] One of these, "Robin Hood and the Peddler" (Child 132), may be found on NW 291, s1 / 3.

[3] Cf. NW 239, s1 / 3.

[4] Cf. the version titled "Sweet William" on NW 245, s1 / 3.

[5] NW 239, s1 / 2.

[They] represent the distilled essence of all those qualities which we call romantic. Their stories usually take place in the indefinite past, often in the Middle Ages, among people of high rank or fame. Castles and bowers, gold and silver, minstrels and harpers, kings and queens, high sheriffs and outlaws, fair ladies and wicked stepmothers—all help to transport the listener far from his prosaic surroundings into a world molded in many ways nearer to the heart's desire. The frequent use of the supernatural and the vestiges of half-forgotten beliefs add further to the charm of the old balladry. . . . It is not the events alone that move us, or the romantic characters, or the dreamlike setting, but the happy blending of them all in a simple story-song, often crude by artistic standards yet perfect in its lasting power to cast a spell.[6]

But they struck at a deeper level also. They share with fairy tales and certain other forms of orally transmitted literature the function of serving as guides to morality, illustrating what is and what is not permissible behavior, dramatizing what might happen to a person who commits a forbidden act. The false knight in "Lady Isabel and the Elf Knight" (Child 4) has lured a number of young women to their deaths, but is done in himself by one of his intended victims. The sister who has pushed her younger sibling into the millstream, and the miller who refuses to pull her out, are both put to death in some versions of "The Twa Sisters." Though Lady Margaret had provocation for murdering her unfaithful lover in "Young Hunting," her pet bird refuses to have anything to do with her, for fear she will kill him also, and in some versions of the ballad she is burned in a bonfire as punishment for her crime.

  Other transgressions are likewise punished. Though the incest in "The Bonny Hind" (Child 50) is unintentional—the brother and sister do not recognize one another until after he has "taen her by the milk-white hand, and softly laid her down"—this forbidden act leads swiftly to tragedy:

> She's putten her hand down by her spare,
> And out she's taen a knife,
> And she has putn't in her heart's bluid,
> And taen away her life.[7]

Adultery is punished decisively in "Little Musgrave and Lady Barnard" (Child 81); the husband first kills the young man who has "kept his wife from the cold" while he was away, and then:

  [6] G. Malcolm Laws, Jr., *American Balladry from British Broadsides* (Philadelphia: The American Folklore Society, 1957), pp. 78–79.
  [7] Francis James Child, *English and Scottish Popular Ballads* (Boston and New York: Houghton, Mifflin Company, 1904), p. 93.

> He took his lady by the hair of the head,
> And he drug her over the plain;
> He drew his sword, and one mighty blow,
> He split her head in twain, Oh,
> He split her head in twain.[8]

"Lord Lovel" (Child 75) abandons his sweetheart for a life of adventure, returns to find that she has died of grief, and soon perishes himself, from sorrow and remorse. A similar fate overtakes the hardhearted "Bonny Barbara Allan" (Child 84)[9] after she has abandoned her dying lover.

Sometimes the message is made even more explicit in a final stanza, laying out the moral to be drawn from the tale. Some versions of "The Cruel Mother" end this saga of seduction, infanticide, and punishment with the admonition:

> Young ladies all, of beauty bright,
> Take warning by her last good-night.[10]

Formally, most ballads are cast in four-line stanzas, with lines alternating between four and three stresses and a rhyme between the second and fourth lines:

> Well met, well met, my own true love,
> Well met, well met, says he;
> I've just returned from the salt, salt sea,
> And it's all for love of thee.
>
> I could have married the king's daughter fair;
> You might as well, said she,
> For now I'm married to a house carpenter,
> And a nice young man is he.[11]

("The Daemon Lover," Child 243)

This pattern may be broken by repetition of the last line:

> It rained a mist, it rained a mist,
> It rained all over the town;
> And two little boys came home from school

---

[8] Bertrand Harris Bronson, *The Traditional Tunes of the Child Ballads*, II (Princeton: Princeton University Press, 1959), p. 274, as sung by John Rittenhouse of Mannington, West Virginia.

[9] NW 223, s1 / 5.

[10] Child, 1904 ed., p. 39.

[11] Arthur Kyle Davis, Jr., *Traditional Ballads of Virginia* (Cambridge: Harvard University Press, 1929), p. 449.

To toss their balls around, around,
To toss their balls around.[12]

("Sir Hugh, or the Jew's Daughter,"
Child 155)

Refrain lines, usually consisting of nonsense syllables, may be introduced:

There was an old man lived under the hill,
Sing tiro rattle-ing day,
If he ain't moved away he's living there still,
Sing tiro rattle-ing day.

This old man went out to his plow,
Sing tiro rattle-ing day,
To see the old devil fly over his mow,
Sing tiro rattle-ing day.[13]

("The Farmer's Curst Wife," Child 278)

The four- (or five-) phrase tune to which the first stanza is sung is repeated, without significant change, for each verse.

These ballads, traditionally sung by a single unaccompanied voice, were performed at home for the benefit of family and friends, or sometimes in places of public amusement. Some, such as "Lord Lovel," are generally associated with a single tune, but most of them seem to have been sung to a variety of tunes, and it is not uncommon for the same tune to be used for different texts. The tradition of one body of texts and another of tunes, which may be matched up in various combinations, is similar to that of early Protestant psalmody, where a given text could be sung to any tune that matched it metrically.

The ballad singer assumes the role of journalist, delivering a story in a detached manner, uninvolved in the suspense and passions of the unfolding tale:

During the performance the eyes are closed, the head upraised, and a rigid expression of countenance maintained until the song is finished. A short pause follows the conclusion, and then the singer relaxes his attitude and repeats in his ordinary voice the last line of the song, or its title.[14]

[12] Davis, p. 404.
[13] Davis, p. 509.
[14] Cecìl J. Sharp, *English Folk Song: Some Conclusions*, 4th rev. ed. (Belmont, Ca.: Wadsworth Publishing Company, 1965), p. 134.

Though these songs were the creation and property of nonliterate people of the British Isles, their texts came to be of considerable interest to certain members of the literate and cultured classes in the eighteenth and nineteenth centuries. Various scholars, gentlemen of leisure, writers, and even clerics began listening to ballads and writing them down, as examples of "unconscious art" touched by no school of writing or criticism. Bishop Thomas Percy brought out a three-volume set of *Reliques of Ancient English Poetry* in London between 1765 and 1775, containing texts he had taken down himself, or gotten from others. David Herd edited similar collections, including *The Ancient and Modern Scots Songs, Heroic Ballads, etc.* (Edinburgh, 1769); Joseph Ritson brought out others, between 1783 and 1795; and Sir Walter *Scott's Minstrelsy of the Scottish Border* came out in 1802–1803.

In retrospect, we can see that these men were not interested in making a precise or scholarly transcription of what they heard among the "folk." As an early American reviewer of their efforts put it:

> Unfortunately, all of them were more or less poets on their own account, and saw no reason for omitting to improve a barbarous composition with a smooth line, now and then, or neglecting to fill up any gap as fancy suggested. Almost all of them, from Scott down, had a secret or avowed contempt for the "rude" compositions which they reproduced, and considered that a great part of the value of these was to set off as a foil the immense progress which had been made by their own "polished age," as they chose to term it.[15]

Ballads sometimes reached print in another way, as broadsides. As early as the sixteenth century, these large single sheets with proclamations, notices of public events, news items, and the like were widely hawked on the streets of London and other English cities and towns. Ballad texts, sold for a penny, were usually among the items offered for sale; the street seller was often a singer, who would call attention to his wares by singing some of the ballads he had for sale. Such ballad peddlars would make their way to the country also, visiting markets, fairs, and village festivities. Many of the ballad texts disseminated in this way were topical, the work of writers and journalists with a flair for turning out easily assimilated popular poetry; these were among the forerunners of popular song of the eighteenth and nineteenth centuries. Others, however, were traditional ballads, perhaps polished and altered to

[15] *Atlantic Monthly*, LI (March, 1883), p. 405.

fit the literary taste of the day, but nevertheless valuable documents for the history of the ballad in the British Isles.

Late in the nineteenth century, an American scholar, Francis James Child (1825–96), set himself the task of collecting and comparing "every obtainable version of every extant English or Scottish ballad, with the fullest possible discussion of related songs or stories in the 'popular' literature of all nations."[16] The fruit of this undertaking was the five-volume *The English and Scottish Popular Ballads* (1882–98), containing the texts of 305 ballads. Most were offered in multiple versions, each prefaced with a discussion of antecedents or similar ballads in other European cultures. Collectively, this group of 305 has been known ever since as the "Child ballads."

Child had virtually no interest in the tunes to which these ballads were sung. But the appearance of his monumental work stimulated and aided scholars who were interested in music. A group of younger Englishmen, centered around Cecil J. Sharp (1859–1924), was just beginning to study the oral tradition music of the British Isles. Their work was done in the field, locating persons who knew "folk" songs and ballads and writing down tunes and texts from their singing. Among the pieces collected and recorded were more than a hundred of Child's ballads, still very much part of the living song tradition of Britain. Sharp eventually published the fruits of his work in such collections as *Folk Songs from Somerset* (5 volumes, 1905–9) and *English Folk Songs* (1920).

Sharp was also responsible for calling general attention to the fact that British ballads and songs were still very much alive in America. At the urging of Mrs. Olive Dame Campbell, whose husband was director of the Southern Highland Division of the Russell Sage Foundation, and who had begun collecting traditional songs and ballads in the Southern Appalachian Mountains herself in 1908, Sharp came to that region in 1916. His first reaction was one of amazement at the isolation from the modern world:

> There are but few roads—most of them little better than mountain tracks—and practically no railroads. Indeed, so remote and shut off from outside influence were, until quite recently, these sequestered mountain valleys that the inhabitants have for a hundred years or more been completely isolated and cut off from all traffic with the rest of the world.[17]

Even more fascinating for him were the people inhabiting this country:

[16] Child, 1882–98 ed., I, p. xxvii.
[17] Cecil J. Sharp, *English Folk Songs from the Southern Appalachians* (London: Oxford University Press, 1932), I, p. xxii.

Their speech is English, not American, and, from the number of expressions they use which have long been obsolete elsewhere, and the old-fashioned way in which they pronounce many of their words, it is clear that they are talking the language of a past day. . . . A few of those we met were able to read and write, but the majority were illiterate. They are, however, good talkers, using an abundant vocabulary racily and often picturesquely. Although uneducated, in the sense in which that term is usually understood, they possess that elemental wisdom, abundant knowledge, and intuitive understanding which those only who live in constant touch with Nature and face to face with reality seem to be able to acquire.[18]

Most astonishing was their music:

Instead . . . of having to confine my attention to the aged, as in England, where no one under the age of seventy ordinarily possesses the folk-song tradition, I discovered that I could get what I wanted from pretty nearly every one I met, young and old. In fact, I found myself for the first time in my life in a community in which singing was as common and almost as universal a practice as speaking. . . . The only secular music . . . is that which his British forefathers brought with them from their native country and has since survived by oral tradition. . . . These mountain valleys are in fact far less affected by modern musical influences than the most remote and secluded English village.[19]

During forty-six weeks spent in North Carolina, Kentucky, Virginia, Tennessee, and West Virginia, Sharp recorded 1,612 tunes. Three hundred twenty-three of these, including forty-two from the collection of Mrs. Campbell, were published in 1917 as *English Folk Songs from the Southern Appalachians;* a two-volume set brought out in 1932 under the same title contained 968 tunes.

As was the case with all music brought by immigrants to the New World, these ballads were imported in precisely the form in which they had been known in the Old. There was nothing American about them at first. But Sharp's collection gives evidence that both texts and music had been altered in the course of their oral transmission over a period of a hundred years or more.

European visitors to America, from as early as the beginning of the nineteenth century, observed that the new American nation had taken on a character of its own. One difference had to do with language: though English was the national tongue, and most Americans at that time were of British origin, so many peculiarities of pronunciation, vocabulary, syntax, and word usage had

[18] Sharp, *English Folk Songs from the Southern Appalachians*, I, pp. xxii–xxiii.
[19] Sharp, *English Folk Songs from the Southern Appalachians*, I, pp. xxv–xxvi.

developed as to make the language a dialect of English—amusing, infuriating, and at times almost unintelligible to English visitors. Frederick Marryat (1792–1848), an English sailor and novelist, addressed himself to this matter after a visit to America in 1837:

> It is remarkable how very debased the language has become in a short period in America. There are few provincial dialects in England much less intelligible than the following. A Yankee girl, who wished to hire herself out, was asked if she had any followers or sweethearts? After a little hesitation, she replied, "Well, now, can't exactly say; I bees a sorter courted and a sorter not; reckon more a sorter yes than a sorter no." In many points the Americans have to a certain degree obtained that equality which they profess; and, as respects their language, it certainly is the case. If their lower classes are more intelligible than ours, it is equally true that the higher classes do not speak the language so purely or so classically as it is spoken among the well educated English.[20]

He then proceeds to quote examples of the "American" language that struck him as ridiculous, typical, and revealing of the sort of country he had found himself in. Some samples:

> "Have you ever been at Paris?" "No; but I should *admire* to go."
> "I were thinking of Sal myself, for I feel lonesome, and when I am thrown in my store promiscious alone, I can tell you I have the blues, the worst kind, no mistake."
> "When she came to meeting, with her yellow hat and feathers, wasn't she in full blast?"
> "Well, how he contrived to fork into her young affections, I can't tell; but I've a mind to put my whole team on, and see if I can't run him off the road."
> "That's my sister, stranger; and I flatter myself that she shows the nastiest ankle in all Kentuck."
> "Well, I don't go much to theatricals, that's a fact; but I do think he piled the agony up a little too high in that last scene."[21]

The same transformation of the language can be seen in ballad texts. For instance, "The Maid Freed from the Gallows," (Child 95), which begins as follows in a typical English version:

> O hangman hold thy hand,
> And stay it for a while,

[20] Captain C. B. Marryat, *A Diary in America, With Remarks on its Institutions* (New York: D. Appleton & Company, 1839), p. 146.
[21] Marryat, pp. 147–51, passim.

> For I fancy I see my father a-coming
> All cross the yonder stile.
>
> O father, have you got my gold
> And can you set me free,
> Or are you come to see me hung
> All on the gallows tree.[22]

has become, in an American version collected by Sharp in Kentucky:

> Slack, man, slack, man, slack up your rope,
> O slack it for just awhile;
> I looked over yonder and I saw Pa coming,
> He's walked through many a long mile.
>
> Say, Pa, say, Pa, have you brought me any gold,
> Any gold to pay on my fine?
> Or have you come over for to see me hung,
> Hung on the gallows line?[23]

Musically, these transplanted British ballads took on equally distinctive forms in America. Most of the English tunes Sharp and his contemporaries collected were based on seven-note diatonic scales, often modal in character, with melodic contours often unfolding gradually, rising to climaxes, and subsiding from these. The following, to which "Young Beichan" (Child 53) was swung to Sharp in 1909 by an elderly gentleman at Snowshill, Gloucestershire, is typical:

"Lord Bateman (Young Beichan)," from Karpeles, *Cecil Sharp's Collection of English Folk Songs*, I, p. 46

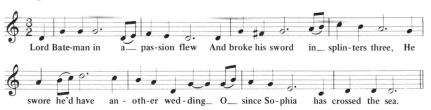

Tunes from the Southern mountains tended to be pentatonic (based on a five-note scale) and were often built of brief fragments. Sharp notated the following tune for "Young Beichan" in Kentucky:

[22] Maud Karpeles, ed., *Cecil Sharp's Collection of English Folk Songs*, I (London: Oxford University Press, 1974), pp. 118–19.
[23] Sharp, *English Folk Songs from the Southern Appalachians*, I, p. 211.

"Young Beichan," from Sharp, *English Folk Songs from the Southern Appalachians*, I, p. 79

1. There was a man who lived in Eng-land And he was of some high de-gree; He be-came un-eas-y,—dis-con-tent-ed, Some fair— land, some land to see.

His provisional explanation was that such American tunes had been brought over from the north of England and Scotland, where pentatonic melodies are more common than in the areas of England where most of his research took place. Whatever the cause, an indigenous tune tradition for the singing of Child ballads existed in the Southern highlands and—as will be seen later—permeated other music of this region also.

American scholars had begun collecting oral-tradition ballads and songs before Sharp's visit, and the 1920s, '30s, and '40s saw numerous publications of pieces collected in New England,[24] other parts of the South,[25] and the Midwest.[26] With each of these publications, a picture came more sharply into focus of the preservation of oral-tradition British balladry in every part of America settled by nonliterate immigrants from the British Isles. It also became apparent that such oral-tradition ballads and songs survived even when the people who had brought them here and nourished them became literate.

The 305 ballads in Child's collection by no means exhausted the oral-tradition ballad literature of the British Isles; hundreds of others were in wide circulation, and many were brought to America. Typical is "Fair Fannie Moore,"[27] a tale of a young woman who marries a shepherd rather than her high-born suitor; the latter stabs her to death in a fit of jealous passion, and her distraught husband wanders aimlessly until he dies and is buried by the side of his

[24] Phillips Barry *et al.*, *British Ballads from Maine* (New Haven: n.p., 1929), and Helen Hartness Flanders and George Brown, *Vermont Folk Songs and Ballads* (Brattleboro: n.p., 1931).

[25] Arthur Kyle Davis, Jr., *Traditional Ballads of Virginia* (Cambridge: Harvard University Press, 1929); John Harrington Cox, *Folk-Songs of the South* (Cambridge: n.p., 1925); Reed Smith, *South Carolina Ballads* (Cambridge: n.p., 1928); and Arthur P. Hudson and George Herzog, *Folk Tunes from Mississippi* (New York: n.p., 1937).

[26] Mary O. Eddy, *Ballads and Songs from Ohio* (New York: n.p., 1939); George Korson, *Pennsylvania Songs and Legends* (Philadelphia: n.p., 1949); and Vance Randolph, *Ozark Folksongs* (Columbia: The State Historical Society of Missouri, 1946–50).

[27] NW 239, s1 / 7.

bride. It resembles many of the Child ballads in subject matter and language, and its popularity in oral tradition was great, judging from the number of times it has been included in British and American collections.

Apparently Child excluded ballads known to have been disseminated widely as broadsides, or suspected of having originated as a broadside. Many scholars of the nineteenth century had put forward the notion that folk poetry and music came into being by some process of "collective creation"; a broadside ballad, the product of the pen of a single individual, was therefore not "folk" art. But most scholars now accept the notion that oral-tradition ballads must have begun life as the creation of a single individual; they become "folk songs" if they are "subjected to the processes of oral tradition for a reasonable period of time."[28]

"Late One Evening" is another example of a ballad not included in Child's collection, perhaps because it can be traced to a British broadside.[29] It is also a tale of passion and murder: a young woman is in love with a man from a lower class; to prevent a marriage, two of her brothers take the lover hunting and murder him. The victim appears to the young woman in a dream, covered with blood; she finds the corpse; her brothers flee when confronted with her knowledge of their act, and eventually they are both killed. Known in Britain under such titles as "The Merchant's Daughter," "In Bruton Town," and "The Bramble Briar," it was brought to America and has been found in Virginia, North Carolina, Kentucky, West Virginia, Indiana, Tennessee, Ohio, Michigan, and Missouri. As sung by Barry Sutterfield of Marshall, Arkansas, in 1962, its language has become Americanized:

> A-late that evening as they were 'turning,
> Their sister inquired of her own true love,
> Saying he'd got lost in a game of huntin'
> And there were said no more of him.

> She went to bed and dreamed of her lover
> A-comin' to her bedside alone,
> Sayin', "They have killed me and treated me cruel,
> They've wallowed me in a gore of blood."[30]

And the music to which this melancholy tale is sung has likewise taken on an American character, with a tendency to pentatonicism

[28] Arthur Kyle Davis, Jr., *Folk-Songs of Virginia: A Descriptive Index and Classification* (Durham: Duke University Press, 1949), p. xii.
[29] Laws, pp. 196–97.
[30] NW 223; s1 / 6.

and the mannerism of "feathering," a vocal technique in which the voice scoops upwards at the end of a phrase.

Almost 300 ballads of this sort, excluded by Child, have been collected and traced to broadsides.[31] There are, in addition, some 200 more found only in America, and thus assumed to be native to this country.[32] These tales of murders and other crimes, true and false lovers, disasters, tragedies, and other adventures in the lives of sailors, lumberjacks, cowboys, soldiers, and even common citizens are the New World's contribution to oral-tradition balladry. Many are based on identifiable incidents, recent enough not to have been obscured by the changes inevitable in oral transmission. The ballad "Henry Green," for instance, narrates the story of a young man hanged in Rensselaer County, New York, in 1845, for poisoning his wife after becoming infatuated with another woman:

> Come listen to my tragedy,
> Good people, young and old;
> I'll tell you of a story
> 'Twill make your blood run cold.
>
> Concerning a fair damsel,
> Miss Wyatt was her name,
> She was murdered by her husband
> And he hung for the same.[33]

As a ballad, this story quickly spread across the eastern part of America; it has been recovered from as far north as Maine and New Brunswick, and as far south as Virginia.

"The Johnstown Flood"[34] is an account of the great disaster of May, 1889, one of the worst floods in American history. "The Dreadnaught"[35] is the tale of a voyage between London and New York, in the mid-nineteenth century. "The Jam at Gerry's Rock"[36] tells of the death of a young lumberman named Monroe when a log jam breaks; his sweetheart soon dies of grief. The incident on which it was based probably took place in Maine, sometime after the middle of the nineteenth century. More recent is "Lily Schull,"[37]

---

[31] Cf. Laws, *American Balladry from British Broadsides*.

[32] Cf. G. Malcolm Laws, Jr., *Native American Balladry* (Philadelphia: The American Folklore Society, 1959). Subsequent references to American ballads will use the numbering system established in this book.

[33] Laws, *Native American Balladry*, p. 192.

[34] Laws, *Native American Balladry*, p. 212. Recorded on NW 239, s2 / 8.

[35] Laws, *Native American Balladry*, p. 167. Recorded on NW 239, s2 / 3.

[36] Laws, *Native American Balladry*, p. 143. Recorded on NW 239, s1 / 8.

[37] NW 245, s1 / 5.

based on the murder of one Lillie Shaw by her jealous lover, Finley Preston, in Tennessee in 1903, and his subsequent hanging for the crime.

The three categories—Child ballads, ballads from British broadsides, and native American ballads—by no means encompass the entire repertory of Anglo-American oral-tradition song. Sharp and other scholars collected many vocal pieces that presented only a fragment of a narrative, or did not tell a story at all. Sharp called these simply "songs," explaining that their poetical structure is often different from that of the ballad, that they were shorter, and that they often dropped the detached, journalistic pose of the ballad: often cast in the first person, they became "far more intense and more heavily charged with sentiment."[38] There are no clues to their age, since they never mention historical events, and did not attract the attention of poets and scholars of the eighteenth and nineteenth centuries.

An English song of this sort is "Seventeen Come Sunday;" as collected in Gloucestershire in 1921, it has the modal character and melodic contour of so many oral-tradition English ballads:

"Seventeen Come Sunday," from Karpeles, *Cecil Sharp's Collection of English Folk Songs*, I, p. 423

In subsequent verses, the young woman invites her new acquaintance to come to her house late that evening, after her mother is asleep. In some versions the two are eventually married, in some they are not, in many others it simply is not clear what happens after that evening.

After being brought to America, the song gradually took on a somewhat different character. The text assimilated aspects of the local dialect, the tunes to which it was sung in the Southern Appa-

[38] Sharp, *English Folk Songs from the Southern Appalachians*, I, p. xxix.

lachians assumed the pervasive pentatonic nature of music of this region. The following version was collected in Virginia in 1918:

"Seventeen Come Sunday," from Sharp, *English Folk Songs from the Southern Appalachians*, II, p. 157

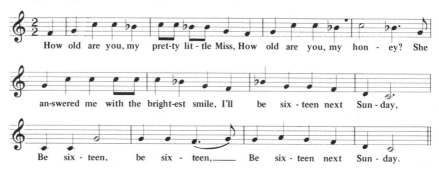

Among the songs collected in America that appear to be indigenous is "Sweet Wine." Though its first stanza is reminiscent of the beginnings of many British oral-tradition songs,

> As I rode out one cold winter night,
> A-drinking of sweet wine,
> A-thinking of that pretty little miss,
> That miss I left behind.

and its final verse is a paraphrase of similar verses scattered through a number of English songs,

> Do you see yonder little dove,
> A-flying from pine to pine,
> A-mourning for his own lost love,
> Just as I am mourning for mine?[39]

the sequence of verses does not match any song yet recovered in the British Isles. Even more than that, the character imparted to this fragment of a tale by its music—pentatonic, vocally embellished, sung with a pure, nasal, clear, high, and thin vocal timbre (the "mountain whine" or "high mountain sound," it has been called)—makes it totally unlike any thing heard in Britain.

Songs from parts of America other than the South tend to be closer to British models, either because they have been passed on with less distortion, or because they were brought here from the British Isles more recently and have thus had less time to be transformed. For instance, there is remarkably little difference between

[39] NW 223, s1 / 4.

the first verse of "The Keys of Canterbury," as sung in Warehorne, Kent, in 1908, and "My Man John," as sung in 1977 in Norwell, Massachusetts:[40]

> O madam, I will buy you a fine silken gown,
> Four and twenty yards, for to draggle on the ground
> If you will walk with me, with me,
> If you will walk with me.

> Madam, I will give you a gown of silk and lace,
> And ribbons fair to deck the hair that curls about your face
> If you will be my joy, my pride, and my dear,
> If you will take a walk with me anywhere.

The two proceed in similar fashion, verse by verse, until the end—when the suitor makes the young woman an offer she can't refuse:

> Madam, I will give you the keys to my heart,
> If you will keep them in your own and we will never part,
> If you will be my bride, my pride, and my dear,
> If you will take a walk with me anywhere.

> O madam, I will give you the keys of my heart,
> We'll get married and never, never part
> If you will be my joy and sweet and onerly dear
> And walk along with me anywhere.

The tunes to which the two versions are sung have a great deal in common, though they are by no means identical: they are based on a major, seven-note scale, and both proceed with obvious reference to an underlying series of harmonic, tonal chords. Putting it in a slightly different way, both tunes have the character of eighteenth- or nineteenth-century harmonically based music, rather than the nonharmonic shape of most tunes from the Southern Appalachian region, or many traditional Scottish and Irish melodies.

At the other extreme are songs of such completely American character, in both text and music, that they must have been created here.

"If You Want to Go A-courting," from Sharp, *English Folk Songs from the Southern Appalachians*, II, p. 6

If you want to go a-court-ing, I'll   tell you where to go,   Just down yon - der,

---

[40] Karpeles, ed., I, pp. 485–86. Recorded on NW 239, s1/4.

just down be-low. The old man, old wom-an gone from the home, And the

girls all mad with their heads not combed,And the girls all_ mad with their heads not combed.

In addition to entertaining and instructing grown-ups, oral-tradition Anglo-American songs are often sung for children, or sung by them to accompany song-games. Some are made up of fragments of narrative interspersed with refrain of nonsense syllables;[41] others, such as the extremely persistent "Frog Went A-Courting," originated as topical songs or ballads but proved to be irresistible to children as nonsense songs;[42] some came from the allegorical animal tales once popular with the English peasantry (as in so many other repressed cultures) as a way of commenting on conditions of their life and caricaturing members of the ruling classes;[43] some are cast as cumulative songs, so easy for children to respond to and sing themselves.[44]

Another group might be called private devotional songs, with religious or moralizing texts.[45] All this music was virtually invisible to the literate and cultured classes of America, until the twentieth century. An American reviewer of Child's first volume of ballad texts could come up with no more than several inconclusive references to the ballad tradition of this country, then lamented, "so nearly has this lore perished that it must always remain uncertain how large a measure of the ancient ballad poetry Puritans brought with them to American shores."[46] And the author of one of the earliest attempts at a history of music in America, an immigrant to the New World himself, was totally unaware of the existence of oral-tradition music here and consequently passed one of the most wrong-headed judgments ever committed to print:

The people's song is not to be found among the American people. The American farmer, mechanic, journeyman, stage-driver, shepherd, etc., does not sing,—unless he happens to belong to a church-choir or a singing-society; hence, the American landscape is silent and monotonous; it seems inanimate, and imparts a melancholy impression, though Nature has fashioned it beautifully. The sympathetic, refreshing, cheering,

[41] For an example, Cf. "Chick-a-li-lee-lo" on NW 245, s1 / 1.
[42] NW 291, s1 / 1.
[43] Cf. "Old Mother Hippletoe" on NW 291, s1 / 1.
[44] Cf. "My Little Rooster" on NW 291, s1 / 3.
[45] Cf. "I am a Poor Wayfaring Stranger" on NW 294, s2 / 5.
[46] *Atlantic Monthly*, LI (March, 1883), pp. 406–7.

enlivening tones of the human voice are totally absent; the emotional life of the human being impressing his footprint upon the land he cultivates seems to be repressed within his bosom, or non-existent. The serious, industrious inhabitant of this beautiful land does not express his joys and sorrows in sound; but for the bleating of sheep, the lowing of cattle, the barking of dogs, the crowing of cocks, the singing of birds,—the woods, the pastures, the farmyard, would be silent and gloomy.[47]

Cecil Sharp, who encountered the same situation in England, suggests an explanation: "His (the peasant's) songs are his own, the creations of his own class; he is proud of them. . . . His instinct tells him that they are very different from the songs of educated people . . . and fear of ridicule makes him secretive."[48] Realizing that at least part of the problem must lie with the attitudes of the upper classes, he adds:

> The clergyman of the village is usually present at the annual Club feast, and very often at the Harvest Home, and folk singing is very much in evidence on these festive occasions. But the songs that he then hears are sung with rough voices and without accompaniment, and, thus disguised, he dismisses them as crude, archaic music, quite unworthy of his serious attention.[49]

It remained for the twentieth century to develop attitudes that would begin to bridge the gap between the music of literate and nonliterate people.

These same people also brought to the New World a body of instrumental music, the story of which—to a point—closely parallels that of their ballads and songs.

Communal, social dancing was part of peasant life in the British Isles for many centuries. Serving as recreation or as part of the celebration of such events as weddings, it took place in open-air locations and also in taverns and other places of public amusement. When the mass emigration to America began, in the seventeenth and eighteenth centuries, the fiddle was the usual accompanying instrument, having replaced the hornpipe and tabor of earlier days.[50]

---

[47] Frédéric Louis Ritter, *Music in America* (New York: Charles Scribner's Sons, 1883), p. 385.

[48] Sharp, *English Folk Songs: Some Conclusions*, p. 131.

[49] Sharp, *English Folk Songs: Some Conclusions*, p. 132.

[50] Typical pictorial evidence of the use of the fiddle to accompany dancing in the British Isles may be seen in George S. Emmerson, *A Social History of Scottish Dance* (Montreal and London: McGill-Queen's University Press, 1972). Plate 20 shows several couples dancing in a tavern, to the music of a fiddle played by a man seated on an elevated platform. Plate 30, an engraving by Wrightson of an Irish wedding, shows a similar scene, again in a tavern.

That such dancing and music were brought to America is known both from contemporary accounts and from survivals into the twentieth century. There is substantial evidence of the practice of dancing to fiddle music, from the eighteenth century onward:

> May 31, 1794. The observation of the holydays at Election is an abuse in this part of the Country. Not only on our return yesterday, did we observe crowds around the new Tavern at the entrance of the Town, but even at this day, we saw at Perkins' on the neck, persons of all discriptions, dancing to a fiddle, drinking, playing with pennies, &c. It is proper such excesses should be checked.[51]

> As the boats were laid to for the night in an eddy [on the Ohio River], a part of the crew could give them headway on starting in the morning, while the others struck up a tune on their fiddles, and commenced their day's work with music to scare the devil away and secure good luck. The boatmen, as a class, were masters of the fiddle, and the music, heard through the distance from these boats, was more sweet and animating than any I have heard since. When the boats stopped for the night at or near a settlement, a dance was got up, if possible, which all the boatmen would attend.[52]

And Cecil Sharp quickly discovered that the people of the Southern Appalachian region had preserved dances of British origin, as well as the ballads he was seeking:

> In the course of our travels in the Southern Appalachian Mountains in search of traditional songs and ballads, we had often heard of a dance, called the Running Set, but, as our informants had invariably led us to believe that it was a rough, uncouth dance, remarkable only as an exhibition of agility and physical endurance, we had made no special effort to see it. When at last we did see it performed at one of the social gatherings at the Pine Mountain Settlement School it made a profound impression upon us. We realized at once that we had stumbled upon a most interesting form of the English Country-dance which, so far as we knew, had not been hitherto recorded. . . . It was danced after dark, on the porch of one of the largest houses of the Pine Mountain School, with only one dim lantern to light up the scene. But the moon streamed fitfully in lighting up the mountain peaks in the background and, casting its mysterious light over the proceedings, seemed to exaggerate the

---

[51] William Bentley, *The Diary of William Bentley, D.D., Pastor of East Church, Salem, Massachusetts* (Salem: Essex Institute, 1905–14), II, p. 92.

[52] From "Western Keelboatmen," *American Pioneer*, Vol. II. 1843, pp. 272–73 as quoted in Harry R. Stevens, "Folk Music on the Midwestern Frontier, 1788–1825," *Ohio State Archaeological and Historical Quarterly*, Vol. 57, No. 2. April, 1948, pp. 126–46.

Dancing to fiddle music at a Kentucky wedding in the late 1700's. Engraving by Howard Pyle.

wildness and the break-neck speed of the dancers as they whirled through the mazes of the dance.[53]

American scholars were soon tracking down this music, in all sections of the country, and capturing it in musical notation and on phonograph discs.[54] Thus there is the same sort of material to work from, in studying this music and its "Americanization," as with ballads and songs.

But there is more to the story.

In the mid-seventeenth century, the cultured classes in England developed a taste for a style of dancing patterned after that done by the peasants. These "country dances" were accompanied by one or two fiddles, playing music also adapted from the country folk. This practice soon spread to the English colonies of the New World. William Byrd, an American-born member of the King's Council in Virginia in the first half of the eighteenth-century, and a man referred to as "the quintessence of Virginia Aristocracy," made frequent reference in his diaries to this sort of dancing:

---

[53] Cecil J. Sharp, *The Country Dance Book*, Part 5 (London: Novello & Company, 1909–1922), pp. 7 and 15.

[54] Among the most useful collections of fiddle music are *American Fiddle Tunes from the Archive of Folk Song* (Library of Congress AFS L62) and *The Old-Time Fiddler's Repertory* (University of Missouri).

Feb. 10, 1709. About 12 o'clock we went to the christening of Mr. Anderson's son, where we met abundance of company. There was a plentiful dinner but I ate nothing but bacon and fowl. Nothing happened particularly but there was dancing and mirth.[55]

Feb. 6, 1711. About 7 o'clock the company went in coaches from the Governor's house to the capitol where the Governor opened the ball with a French dance with my wife. Then I danced with Mrs. Russell and then several others and among the rest Colonel Smith's son, who made a sad freak. Then we danced country dances for an hour and the company was carried into another room where there was a very fine collation of sweetmeats.[56]

Nov. 2, 1711. In the meantime the Doctor secured two fiddlers and candles were sent to the capitol and then the company followed and we had a ball and danced till about 12 o'clock at night.[57]

Philip Vickers Fithian gave a glimpse of a similar event in Virginia a half-century later:

About Seven the Ladies & Gentlemen begun to dance in the Ball-Room first Minuets one Round; Second Giggs; third Reels; And last of All Country-Dances; tho' they struck several Marches occasionally—The music was a French-Horn and two Violins—The Ladies were Dressed Gay, and splendid, & when dancing, their Silks and Brocades rustled and trailed behind them!—But all did not join in the Dance for there were parties in Rooms made up, some at Cards; some drinking for Pleasure; some toasting the Sons of America.[58]

And the following brief account of a social evening in Albany, New York in 1782—which began with a sleighride—reminds us that the same sort of dancing was common in other parts of America as well:

The ball opened with a minuet, and a country dance was immediately called. They succeeded each other till supper, which was a good one, but plain. A few cotillions were then danced, with one or two reels, and the whole closed with a set of country dances. Broke up about three, and each retired with his partner.[59]

[55] Louis B. Wright and Marion Tinling, *The Secret Diary of William Byrd of Westover, 1709–1712* (Richmond: The Dietz Press, 1941), p. 2.

[56] Wright, p. 297.

[57] Wright, p. 431.

[58] Hunter Dickinson Farish, ed., *Journal and Letters of Philip Vickers Fithian, 1773–1774: A Plantation Tutor of the Old Dominion* (Williamsburg: Colonial Williamsburg, 1943), p. 76.

[59] Quoted in S. Foster Damon, "The History of Square-Dancing," *Proceedings of The American Antiquarian Society*, LXII (April–October 1952), p. 73.

In almost every mention of country dancing, there is a link to some sort of impropriety: drinking, gambling, intimacy between the sexes. Faulkland, a character in Richard Sheridan's *The Rivals* (produced in Londin in 1775), returns from a journey to discover that his lover Julia has been attending balls in his absence and says:

> A minuet I could have forgiven—I should not have minded that—I say I should not have regarded a minuet—but *country-dances!* Z—ds! had she made on in a *cotillion* I believe I could have forgiven even that—but to be monkey-led for a night!—to show paces like a managed filly!—O Jack, there never can be but *one* man in the world whom a truly modest and delicate woman ought to pair with in a *country-dance;* and even then, the rest of the couples should be her great uncles and aunts![60]

The dancers faced each other in two rows, men in one rank and women in another. This formation, dubbed "longways for as many as will," contrasted with round dances and with more disciplined ones done by several couples only. One attraction of country dancing was that any number of couples could take part; and since the dance figures were executed first by one or more couples at the head of the line, who then moved to the end with others moving up, even a beginner could participate by starting at the foot of the line and observing the more experienced couples. The country dance was thus a social, participatory affair, not a display of skill.

John Playford's *The English Dancing Master; or Plaine and easie Rules for the Dancing of Country Dances,*[61] was the first published source to record figures for country dances; it also contained the music for 105 of these, notated on a single line, without accompaniment, for the "treble violin." This collection went through eighteen editions, each with somewhat different contents, the last appearing about 1728. A handful of tunes surviving into the twentieth century in oral tradition can be traced back to Playford: a tune labeled "Sedanny, or Dargason" in his first edition is known today, in a somewhat altered but still recognizable form, as "The Irish Washerwoman":

"Sedanny, or Dargason," from Playford's *The English Dancing Master* (1651)

---

[60] Quoted in Damon, p. 71.

[61] Available in a modern edition: Margaret Dean-Smith, *Playford's English Dancing Master, 1651* (London: Schott & Company, 1957).

"Irish Washerwoman," from Howe's *The Musician's Omnibus* (1861)

and "Green Sleeves," mentioned as early as 1580 in England and referred to in Shakespeare's *The Merry Wives of Windsor,* made its first appearance in Playford's fourth edition of 1670; it is encountered in oral-tradition fiddle repertory as a jig:

"Green Sleeves," from Howe's *The Musician's Omnibus* (1861)

The popularity of country dances among America's literate classes led, soon after the Revolution, to the publication of collections of dance figures. The first, brought out by John Griffith—who identified himself on the title page as a dancing master in Providence—was entitled *A Collection of the newest and most fashionable Country Dances and Cotillions* (1788). A sample entry:

> No. 20. Fisher's *Hornpipe.*
> Cast off back—up again—lead down the Middle—up again, and cast off one Co.—Hands cross as Bottom—halfway—back again—right and left at Top

Some thirty collections of this sort were published in America by 1800; in addition a number of manuscript dance-books preserve some of the tunes to which they were danced.[62] A number of published collections of the nineteenth century contain both tunes and dance figures; *Howe's Complete Ball-Room Hand-Book* (Boston: Elias Howe, 1858), for instance, has scores of country-dance melodies popular throughout the first half of the nineteenth century, including the above-mentioned "Irish Washerwoman" and "Green

---

[62] Several of the most extensive of these are preserved in The American Antiquarian Society, Worcester, Massachusetts.

Sleeves," and also "Money Musk," "Fisher's Hornpipe,"[63] "Speed the Plough," "Durang's Hornpipe," "Soldier's Joy," "College Hornpipe,"[64] "Ally Croker," "Nelson's Victory," "Hunt the Squirrel,"[65] and "Opera Reel." Most of these are in the repertory of present-day fiddlers.

These tunes are reels (in 2 / 4 or ¢ time), jigs (in 6 / 8 or sometimes 9 / 8 meter), or hornpipes (2 / 4 or ¢). They are in two sections, each usually of 8 measures: the first, sometimes called the "coarse" or "thick" part, ends with an intermediary cadence known as the "tune"; the second, the "fine" or "high" section, usually lies at a higher pitch level than the first.

"Soldier's Joy," from Howe's *The Musician's Omnibus* (1861)

In performance, the two strains are played over and over until the dance figure has ended, or the fiddler feels he has done himself justice, if he is playing for an audience. Until the twentieth century, fiddlers played without accompaniment, normally seated in a chair, with the end of the instrument held against the chest rather than under the chin. Some traditional fiddlers hold the bow some distance up from the frog.

With a few exceptions, these tunes seem to date from no earlier than the eighteenth century. Most of them clearly outline chord progressions of common-practice harmonic style, and in contemporary performance are often backed by chord-playing instruments—piano, guitar, accordion.[66]

This music has been poised somewhere between oral and written tradition for two centuries. Many fiddlers were (and are) musically nonliterate, learning tunes by ear and teaching them to

[63] NW 294, s1 / 4.

[64] NW 294, s1 / 4.

[65] NW 294, s1 / 4.

[66] Several examples of accompanied fiddle tunes may be heard on NW 239: "A Medley of Scottish Fiddle Tunes," accompanied by piano, on s1 / 10; "Knit Stockings," also accompanied by piano, on s2 / 7; and "Cherish the Ladies," with the fiddle backed by accordian and guitar, on s2 / 11.

others in the same way; others learn at least part of their repertory from printed collections, though they always play from memory. Some tunes seem to have remained surprisingly intact, over a lifetime of two centuries or more. For instance, the reel entitled "Flowers of Edinburg," printed in a number of nineteenth-century American collections in the following form:[67]

"Flowers of Edinburgh," from Howe, *The Musician's Omnibus* (1861)

is essentially the same piece, differing only in some ornamental passages, as "The Flowers of Edinburgh" transcribed in 1943 from the playing of a fiddler near Davistown, Pennsylvania:[68]

"The Flowers of Edinburgh," from Bayard, *Hill Country Tunes*, No. 54

And the same tune is very much alive in oral tradition today.[69]

The repertory of fiddle tunes, like that of oral-tradition ballads and songs, is a constantly growing one. Individual fiddlers constantly add new tunes to their store; some may be older tunes which a given performer happens not to have known before, but others

[67] Elias Howe, *The Musician's Omnibus* (Boston: Elias Howe, 1861), p. 44.
[68] Samuel Preston Bayard, *Hill Country Tunes: Instrumental Folk Music of Southwestern Pennsylvania*. Memoirs of The American Folklore Society, 39 (Philadelphia: The American Folklore Society, 1944), No. 54.
[69] Cf. a recently recorded version, played on hammered dulcimers, on NW 239, s2 / 2.

may be new tunes, learned from another player or composed by the fiddler himself. The identity of the composer is soon lost in the process of transmission to other performers, and it is rare for a tune to be associated with the name of the person who created it. There is an interesting exception; the eighteenth-century American dancer, John Durang, wrote in his memoirs:

> While I was in New York I took lessons on the violin of Mr. Phile, and of Mr. Hoffmaster, a dwarf, a man about 3 foot, large head, hands and feet; his wife of the same stature. A good musician, he composed the following hornpipe expressly for me, which is become well known in America, for I have since heard it play'd the other side of the Blue Mountains as well as in the cities.[70]

Durang then gives the music to this piece, "as Composed by Mr. Hoffmaster, a German Dwarf, in New York, 1785"; essentially the same piece is found in many early collections of country dances and preserved today in oral tradition:

"Durang's Hornpipe," from Durang's *Memoir*, p. 22

"Durang's Hornpipe," from Howe's *The Musician's Omnibus* (1861)

These were the fiddle tunes, then, to which country dancing was done. A number of basic steps and movements could be pieced together in various sequences to form the "figure" for a given dance; since each tune is associated with a particular figure, announcement of the name of a tune to be played (or recognition of it by the dancers) was enough to identify the figure to be danced. At some point in the early nineteenth century, however, the practice began

[70] John Durang, *The Memoir of John Durang, American Actor, 1785–1816* (Pittsburgh: The University of Pittsburgh Press, 1966), p. 22.

Fiddling and dancing at a wayside inn, ca. 1811. From *A Portfolio of Water Color Sketches of the U.S.*, by Paul Petrovidi Svinin.

of having a "caller" shout out the sequence of movements for each dance. The following is a description of a dance in the mountains of Kentucky in the early twentieth century:

> The various movements, or "calls," are called in stentorian tones by someone present, who may or may not participate in the dancing. Sometimes the fiddler or banjo picker himself calls them, which is quite an accomplishment. At all times the tapping of the foot by the fiddler keeps time with the music. For the sake of those interested, a typical "set" is here reproduced:
>
> Eight hands up, circle to the left! Half way back on a single line! Lady before and gent behind! First gent lead out and swing his partner! First to the right and then to the left! Don't forget the two-hand swing! Break to the left on the Wild Goose Chase, and around that lady! Back to the right, and around that gent! Take on four and circle to the left! Half way and back on a single line! Lady before and gent behind! Swing your opposite partner, and promenade your own![71]

[71] Josiah H. Combs, *Folk-Songs of the Southern United States (Folk-Songs du midi des Etats-Unis)* (Austin and London: Published for The American Folklore Society by The University of Texas Press, 1967), p. 47.

"Calling" was an American innovation.[72] Mrs. Trollope, in her *Domestic Manners of the Americans* (1832), commented after observing it for the first time, "the figures are called from the orchestra in English, which has a very ludicrous effect on European ears."[73] But whatever the impression on visitors, Americans liked the practice, and it has flourished to the present day.

Fiddle tunes of the Appalachian region and other parts of the South are quite different from those of most of the rest of America, though their roots lie in the same soil, the country dance music of the British Isles. The repertory of the Southern fiddler contains, usually, only a scattering of reels, jigs, and hornpipes. He plays, rather, pieces associated with texts, unknown in the rest of the country:

> The Jigs were sung often as ditties on their own account, but their primary purpose was apparently to serve as an accompaniment to step-dances, or "hoe-downs," as they were called. The words appeared to be chosen from a large stock of phrases and fitted at random to the tune.[74]

Cecil Sharp offered the following as a sample of such Appalachian jigs:

"Eliza Jane," from Sharp, *English Folk Songs from the Southern Appalachians*, II, p. 356

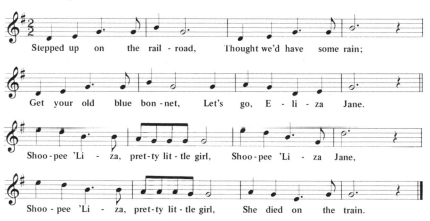

Most jig tunes are pentatonic. The upper strings of the fiddle are used for the melody and the lower as a drone. The resulting sound

[72] An example of twentieth-century calling may be heard on NW 223, s1 / 3.

[73] Frances Trollope, *Domestic Manners of the Americans* (New York: Dodd, Mead & Company, 1927), p. 127.

[74] Maud Karpeles, in the Introduction to Sharp's *English Folk Songs from the Southern Appalachians*, I, p. xviii.

is similar to that of a bagpipe, with the pentatonic melody sounding against the drone, and with the fiddle played in such a way to produce a type of tone that sounds harsh or nasal to an ear accustomed to the sound of a classical violin.[75] This is nonharmonic music; the tunes suggest no sequence of chords—and in fact it is difficult or impossible to fit a chordal accompaniment against such tunes—and the persistent drone also negates any harmonic feeling. This music must be descended from a nonharmonic (or preharmonic) tradition in the British Isles, and not only such fiddle tunes but other music of this region continued to exist as nonharmonic music into the twentieth century.

Among the most widely dispersed pieces of this sort are "Old Joe Clark," "Sourwood Mountain," "Cripple Creek," "Cumberland Gap," "The Hog-Eyed Man," "Bonaparte's Retreat," "Buffalo Girls," "Cluck Old Hen," "Arkansas Traveller," "Give the Fiddler a Dram," and "Run, Nigger, Run."

The banjo was also in common use in the southern Appalachian region in the nineteenth century. Introduced into America by black slaves, modeled after an instrument they had known in Africa, the banjo was played only by Afro-Americans until the nineteenth century. But gradually it became familiar and acceptable to whites, though at first only among the lower classes and usually in association with some "low-life" environment shunned by persons of culture and taste. An English traveler in America wrote of visiting an inn across the Ohio River from Cincinnati, in 1806:

> I entered the ball-room, which was filled with persons at cards, drinking, smoking, dancing &c. The *music* consisted of two bangies, played by negroes nearly in a state of nudity, and a lute [probably some sort of mouth-bow], through which a Chicksaw breathed with much occasional exertion and violent gesticulation. The dancing accorded with the harmony of these instruments. The clamour of the card tables was so great, that it almost drowned every other, and the music of Ethiope was with difficulty heard.[76]

And when the banjo first came to the attention of a much wider range of Americans in the 1830s and '40s, it was in the context of the minstrel show, widely accepted by most people—at least in the East and North—as an accurate depiction of the American black and his music. The instrument was used to play melodic elabora-

---

[75] Samples of this repertory and performance style may be heard on NW 226: "The Last of Sizemore," s2 / 1 and "Hunky Dory," s2 / 2.

[76] Thomas Ashe, *Travels in America Performed in the Year 1806* (London: n.p., 1809), pp. 90–91.

tions on the tunes sung by the performers, sometimes supporting these with bits of ostinato figures (reiterated melodie and rhythmic patterns).

The oldest style of banjo playing among Southern mountain people, known as "frailing" or "clawhammer" style, involves the same techniques and achieves the same sounds as early minstrel banjo playing. The performer strikes the proper string with a downward motion of the right hand, using only the thumb and the nail of the index finger. Complementary techniques involve two methods of producing a tone with the left hand: "hammering," in which a finger of the left hand is brought down on the fingerboard with enough force to produce a tone; and "pulling," in which a finger of the left hand plucks one of the strings. There are no chords; the style consists of melodic elaboration of a tune, or patterns of running notes acting as an accompaniment to a melody played by a fiddle, sung by the banjo player, or played on the banjo itself.[77]

The similarity between the music of the early minstrel show and the oral-tradition music of the Southern highlands extends beyond a common style of banjo playing. The songs sung on stage by the first generation of blackface and minstrel performers—George Washington Dixon ("Coal Black Rose," "Long Tail Blue"), Thomas Dartmouth Rice ("Jim Crow"), Bob Farrell ("Zip Coon"), Edward Harper ("Jim Along Josey"), Dan Emmett ("Old Dan Tucker," "Jordan Am a Hard Road to Travel"), Joel Sweeney ("Old Tare River")—have pentatonic tunes and texts consisting of a string of disconnected verses with puns, nonsense lines, commentary on events and persons known to the audience, and disparaging comments on blacks and their supposed dialect and habits. Typical is "Jim Along Josey," with such verses as:

> Oh! when I get dat new coat which I expects to hab soon,
> Likewise a new pair tight-knee'd trousaloons,
> Den I walks up and down Broadway wid my Suzanna,
> And de white folks will take me to be Santa Anna.
>
> Now way down South not very far off,
> A bullfrog died wid de hooping cough,
> And de odder side of Mississippi as you must know,
> Dar's whar I was christened Jim along Joe.
>
> De New York niggers tink dey're fine,
> Because dey drink de genuine,

---

[77] For an approximation of this style, Cf. "Granny Went to Meeting with her Old Shoes On," recorded on NW 226, s1 / 4. "Run, Banjo," on NW 226, s1 / 6, is played in a somewhat more modern style, with a different finger technique and suggestions of harmonic changes in the banjo accompaniment.

> De Southern niggers dey lib on mush,
> And when dey laugh dey say Oh Hush.

Each verse ends with the chorus:

"Jim Along Josey," from *Minstrel Songs Old and New*, p. 119

Hey get a-long, get a-long Jo-sey, Hey get a-long, Jim a-long Joe!
Hey get a-long, get a-long Jo-sey, Hey get a-long, Jim a-long Joe!

Cecil Sharp recorded the following jig in the Southern Appalachian region:[78]

> Works my horses in my team,
> And I work all grey before.
> Pretty near broke my true love's heart
> To hear the banjo roar.
>
> Beefsteak when I'm hungery,
> And whisky when I'm dry;
> Greenback for to carry me through
> And heaven when I die.
>
> Rabbit in the 'simmon tree,
> Possum's on the ground.
> Possum says: You big-eyed brute,
> Shake that 'simmon down.
>
> Called my wife a nigger,
> But she's neither black nor brown;
> She's just the color of a thunder-cloud
> 'Fore the rain pours down.

These verses were sung to a tune that would have been perfectly at home on the minstrel stage:

"Liza Anne," from Sharp, *English Folk Songs from the Southern Appalachians*, II, p. 355

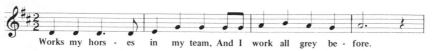

Works my hors - es in my team, And I work all grey be - fore.

[78] Sharp, *English Folk Songs from the Southern Appalachians*, II, p. 355.

Pret-ty near broke my true love's heart To hear the ban - jo roar.

And certainly such a song as "Old Joe Clark," which has survived into the present century, belongs to the same genre, both in
text,

> I went to see my honey babe,
> She's standing in the door,
> Shoes and stockin's in her hand,
> And her feet all over the floor.
>
> Old Joe Clark's a might rover,
> Tell you the reason why,
> Dashed through my field the other day,
> And threw down all my rye.

and in music:

Chorus of "Old Joe Clark"

Fare thee well, Old Joe Clark, good - bye Bet - sy Brown.

Fare thee well, Old Joe Clark, I'm bound to leave this town.

As recorded in 1927,[79] even the performance conforms to everything we know about the sound of early minstrel songs: the fiddle
and the banjo play the tune together, more or less in unison but
with each instrument engaging in some melodic elaboration; the
fiddler adds drone notes on his lower strings, the banjo adds fragments of ostinato figures; the voice sings the same melody as that
played by the two instruments; there is no sense of chord changes
or harmonic progression.

The similarities between the early minstrel song and some of the
oral-tradition music of the southern Appalachians are so numerous and striking as to be unquestionable.[80] Less clear is the sequence

[79] NW 236, s1 / 2.

[80] Other samples illustrating this style are the fiddle-banjo duo "Bigfooted Nigger," recorded on NW 226, s2 / 3, with the two instruments playing the tune together
in a nonharmonic, heterophonic fashion, and the banjo song "Oh My Little Darling," found on NW 245, s2 / 1. From what we know of the early minstrel style,
either would have been perfectly at home on the minstrel stage of the 1840s and
1850s.

Mr. Booth Campbell of Cane Hill, Arkansas performing a traditional banjo song in the early 1940's.

of events: whether the minstrel song was the progenitor of this sort of "mountain music," or vice versa; and just when the banjo passed from black American to white.

It seems unlikely that the Southern highlander adopted the instrument directly from the black man; blacks were virtually unknown in this region, remote from those areas where plantations, with their black slaves, were clustered. Much more plausible is the notion that the banjo and the style of music associated with it passed from the minstrel show to the musicians of this region.[81]

It is also possible that the banjo became part of the musical culture of the Appalachian region before the birth of the minstrel show, reaching this region by way of white musicians from other parts of the South who had learned to play it from plantation blacks before

[81] Evidence for this is summarized in Robert B. Winans, "The Folk, the Stage, and the Five-String Banjo in the Nineteenth Century," *Journal of American Folklore*, LXXXIX (1976), pp. 420–24. See also Arthur Woodward, "Joel Sweeny and the First Banjo," *Los Angeles Quarterly*, VII (1949), p. 7.

coming to the mountains.[82] If this were the case, the musical style of the first minstrel songs had been forged among white musicians quite early in the nineteenth century. It should be pointed out that not only songs in the style of early minstrel music have been recovered from oral tradition in the South, but a number of actual minstrel songs as well.[83]

In either event, it is clear that one of the most distinctive American musical dialects, the banjo and fiddle style of the Appalachian region, was forged from the traditional music of two quite different (and sometimes antagonistic) groups who found themselves in the New World: Afro-Americans and Anglo-Americans.

A postscript: the banjo dropped out of general use among Afro-Americans in the second half of the nineteenth century. Joel Chandler Harris, best remembered for his Uncle Remus stories, wrote in 1883, "I have never seen a banjo . . . in the hands of a plantation Negro."[84] Accounts of music among black Americans in the late nineteenth and early twentieth centuries rarely mention the banjo; there are only a few instances of banjo playing in the earliest recordings of Afro-American music; survivals of black banjo playing to the present day are rare, except in early jazz. Perhaps black Americans shunned the instrument after its association with the minstrel stage; perhaps there was a spontaneous evolution to other instruments and other kinds of music among them.

The only other instrument known to have been in use among the people of the Southern mountains in the nineteenth century was the dulcimer:

This strange instrument . . . has a slight resemblance to the violin, with a narrow and elongated body and a very short neck. It is usually made of walnut or maple wood, and is strung with three strings plucked by a crow-quill held in the right hand. One of the three strings, the one nearest the body as the instrument lies in the lap, is tuned an octave higher than the third one, and in unison with the second. The melody is produced on the first string by moving a bit of smooth reed back and forth over it, pressing it down between the fret and strumming all three strings with the quill; the second and third strings are used as tonic-drones. . . . The "dulcimore" is adapted to simple, one-part tunes rather than fast ones. Because of its simplicity many folk-airs even cannot be played upon it.[85]

---

[82] Winans, pp. 436–37.

[83] Numerous examples are given in Davis, *Folk-Songs of Virginia*.

[84] Joel Chandler Harris, "Plantation Music," *The Critic*, III (n.d.), p. 505.

[85] Combs, pp. 94–95. "My Little Pink," recorded on NW 226, s1 / 3, offers an example of dulcimer used as accompaniment to a song.

From this description by a man who knew the instrument as it was used in the nineteenth century, and from a handful of early twentieth-century recordings, it is evident that the dulcimer was used for playing simple melodies supported by a drone, or accompanying ballads or songs with a drone or fragments of a simple ostinato. Its original nature and function have often been obscured in the present century by "revivalist" performers who fit it with more strings and use it to play strummed or arpeggiated harmonic chords—all quite alien to the basic nonharmonic nature of the instrument and the music played on it until well into the twentieth century.

The music with which this chapter has been concerned was virtually invisible to literate Americans when the Civil War broke out in 1861. With the defeat of the South and the subsequent greater isolation of this region, it became even more remote from the mainstream of American culture. For more than a half-century it would develop in its own way, not to surface until the third and fourth decades of the twentieth century—when it would become the foundation for several types of the most distinctive and vital music ever to emerge from the complex currents of American life.

# 4

# Concert and Operatic Music
# in Colonial
# and Federal America

Boston newspapers record that on December 30, 1731, there was held a *"Concert of Music* on Sundry Instruments," for which tickets were sold. The event, which lasted from 6 to 9 P.M., was organized by a certain Peter Pelham, an engraver, dancing master, keeper of a boarding school, and tobacco retailer. In Charleston, South Carolina, a *"Consort* of Musick at the Council Chamber" was organized on April 8, 1732, by a Mr. Salter. The first mention of a similar event in New York dates from 1733, and in all likelihood Philadelphia too had concerts before mid-century.[1]

In succeeding decades, concerts of two types, benefit and subscription, became more frequent. The former were single events, with receipts going directly to some specified person or cause. The first such concert in Charleston was advertised "for the Benefit of Mr. Salter," the organizer, who paid performers' fees and all other expenses out of the proceeds and kept any balance for himself; a concert given in Fanueil Hall in Boston on December 6, 1744 was "for the benefit of the Poor of the Town," who benefitted to the sum of 205 pounds 5 shillings, according to reports published afterwards. Subscription concerts were a series of events, for which audiences paid in advance.

Eighteenth-century concerts were mixtures of instrumental and vocal music, combining solo and chamber pieces with works for

---

[1] For comprehensive information on such events, cf. O. G. Sonneck, *Early Concert-Life in America (1731–1800)* (Leipzig: Breitkopf & Härtel, 1907), pp. 1–4.

combined instrumental forces; they were organized into two or three sections, usually called "Acts," and lasted three hours or even longer. The concert was generally followed by a ball, with the performers furnishing minuets and other fashionable dances.

Several typical programs will serve to bring the shape and content of these events into sharper focus. Mr. Thomas Pike, a local dancing, fencing, and music master, organized an event in Charleston on October 16, 1765, announced in local newspapers:

> The Orange Garden, in Trade Street, will be opened for the Night only, when a *Concert of Vocal and Instrumental Musick* will be performed by Gentlemen of the place, for the entertainment of all lovers of harmony. . . . The subscription is two dollars for three tickets, to admit two ladies and a gentleman. . . . It is hoped no persons will be so indiscreet as to attempt climbing over the fences to the annoyance of the subscribers, as I give this public notice that I will prosecute any person so offending.

The announced program was:

Act I

French Horn Concerto
2d Concerto of Stanley
Solo on the Violincello
Bassoon Concerto
Song
Ouverture in Scipio

Act II

French Horn Concerto
Concerto on the Harpsichord
Trio
Bassoon Concerto
Song
French Horn Concerto of Hasse

Josiah Flagg offered a concert of "vocal and instrumental musick accompanied by French horns, hautboys, etc." in Boston on May 17, 1771:

| | | |
|---|---|---|
| Act I. | Overture Ptolomy | Handel |
| | Song "from the East breaks the morn" | |
| | Concerto 1st | Stanley |
| | Symphony 3d | Bach |
| Act II. | Overture 1st | Schwindl |
| | Duet to "Turn fair Clora" | (Harington) |

|  | Organ Concerto | |
|  | Periodical Symphony | Stamitz |
| Act III. | Overture 1st | Abel |
|  | Duetto "When Phoebus the tops of the hills" | |
|  | Solo Violin | |
|  | A new Hunting Song, set to music by | Mr. Morgan |
|  | Periodical Symphony | Pasquale Ricci |

The repertory is similar to that of contemporaneous concerts in the British Isles: a mixture of pieces by English composers, Handel, and European composers popular in England. The "Bach" is not Johann Sebastian, but one of his sons, John Christopher, who with Abel had organized a series of concerts in London.

Classical music was class entertainment, in America as in England; it was patronized by literate, educated persons. It would have been unthinkable for a peddler, a tradesman, or a farmer come to town to sell his produce, to attend. The price of admission would have been prohibitive for him to begin with. Quite beyond that, such a person would have known, by the dress and attitudes of those attending, that it was not a place where he was welcome. Furthermore, he would have had no opportunity to become acquainted with this kind of music.

Classical music was cultivated in the homes of cultured Americans, as part of their heritage and as something that was expected of persons of their class. This was true particularly in the larger cities and in the South, where planters and landowners were conscious of their heritage and their obligations to it:

> [They] were determined they should not revert to barbarism in the wilderness. At no time did they allow themselves to forget that they were inheritors of British civilization. Taking the English gentry as their model, they tried, insofar as colonial conditions would allow, to follow the ways of the country gentlemen of the homeland. On that pattern they fashioned their manners, their homes, their diversions; and with a similar aim they sought to acquire, and instruct their sons in, every branch of knowledge useful to a gentlemen.[2]

Philip Vickers Fithian, a young man from New Jersey hired in 1771 to tutor the children of Robert Carter at his Virginia plantation "Nomini Hall," summed up his impression of the expectations placed on young men raised in such an environment:

[2] Hunter Dickinson Farish, ed., *Journal and Letters of Philip Vickers Fithian, 1773–1774: A Plantation Tutor of the Old Dominion* (Williamsburg: Colonial Williamsburg, 1943), p. xxi.

Any young Gentleman travelling through the Colony . . . is presum'd to be acquainted with Dancing, Boxing, playing the Fiddle, & Small-Sword, & Cards.[3]

And his portrait of a young woman who often visited the Carters, Miss Jenny Washington, catches the essence of what was admired in a female member of this society:

[She] has but lately had opportunity of Instruction in Dancing, yet She moves with propriety when she dances a Minuet & without any *Flirts* or vulgar *Capers*. . . . She plays well on the Harpsichord, & Spinet; understands the principles of Musick, & therefore performs her Tunes in perfect time, a Neglect of which always makes music intolerable, . . . She sings likewise to her instrument, has a strong, full voice, & a well-judging Ear. . . . Her dress is rich & well-chosen, but not tawdry, nor yet too plain.[4]

Mr. Carter owned "a *Harpsichord, Forte-Piano, Harmonica, Guittar, Violin & German Flute*, & at Williamsburg, has a good *Organ*," performed chamber music with members of his family and neighbors, and had in his large library the score of Handel's oratorio *Alexander's Feast*, a volume of Italian music, two volumes of Handel's sonatas for flute and continuo, and "17 Volumes of Music, by various Authors," according to a catalogue of the library made by Fithian in 1774.[5]

Thomas Jefferson, who played the violin and sang, often had evenings of chamber music in his home, and was an inveterate concertgoer when in Philadelphia or Paris. His involvement in music was perhaps best summed up by one of his slaves, Isaac Jefferson:

He kept three fiddles: played in the afternoons & sometimes after supper. This was in his early time: When he begin to git so old he didn't play: kept a spinnet made mostly in the shape of a harpsichord: his daughter played on it. Mr Fauble a Frenchman that lived at Mr Walker's—a music-man used to come to Monticello & tune it. There was a forte piano & a guitar there: never seed anybody play on them but the French people. Isaac never could git acquainted with them: could hardly larn their names. Mr. Jefferson always singing when ridin or walkin: hardly see him anywhar out doors but what he was a-singin: had a fine clear voice, sung minnuits & sich: fiddled in the parlor. Old master very kind to servants.[6]

[3] Fithian, p. 212.
[4] Fithian, p. 163.
[5] Fithian, pp. 285ff.
[6] Isaac Jefferson, "Memoirs of a Monticello Slave," *William and Mary Quarterly* VIII (1951), p. 574.

George Washington playing the flute for his step-daughter Nettie Curtis.

Like other cultured colonials, Jefferson felt that involvement with the arts was a privilege and responsibility of persons of his class:

The ornaments too, and the amusements of life, are entitled to their portion of attention. These, for a female, are dancing, drawing, and music. The first is a healthy exercise, elegant and very attractive for young people. Every affectionate parent would be pleased to see his daughter qualified to participate with her companions, and without awkwardness. . . . Drawing is thought less of in this country than in Europe. . . . Music is invaluable where a person has an ear. It furnishes a delightful recreation for the hours of respite from the cares of the day, and lasts us through life. The taste of this country, too, calls for this accomplishment more strongly than for either of the others.[7]

Accordingly, he saw that his children were well instructed in music.

Though Jefferson lived in a region rich in oral-tradition music, he seems to have had no interest in it—he mentioned the music of blacks only once in his voluminous writings—nor in the native New England school of William Billings and his contemporaries. Nor did his feelings of pride and faith in the new nation he helped to establish encompass the music of the young country; writing to a certain John Fabroni, an Italian, on June 8, 1778, he said:

> If there is a gratification, which I envy any people in this world, it is to your country its music. This is the favorite passion of my soul, and fortune has cast my lot in a country where it is in a state of deplorable barbarism.[8]

Jefferson was by no means the only prominent figure of the late colonial period to have a passion for classical music. Patrick Henry often played violin duets with Jefferson; Governor John Penn of Philadelphia was also a violinist, and hosted evenings of chamber music for many years; Benjamin Franklin played the guitar and harp, invented an instrument called the glass harmonica (or glassychord),[9] often wrote about music, and may have composed a string quartet while in Paris;[10] and Francis Hopkinson of Philadelphia, signer of the Declaration of Independence and the first Secretary of the Navy of the United States, was an organist and harpsichordist, organized musical events from the time he was a student at the College of Philadelphia in the 1750s, and composed a number of songs and several larger dramatic-vocal works.[11]

Of all the forms of classical music, though, opera was far and away the most popular in the English colonies in the half century before the Revolution.

Eighteenth-century opera was part of the theatrical life of the time. Just as concerts were mixtures of vocal and instrumental

[7] Adrienne Koch and William Peden, eds., *The Life and Selected Writings of Thomas Jefferson* (New York: The Modern Library, 1944), p. 689.

[8] Koch, p. 363.

[9] A set of glasses, filled with varying amounts of water to give the different notes of the scale, rotated by a mechanical device and played by touching the spinning rims with a finger dampened with water.

[10] M. E. Grenander, "Reflections on the String Quartet(s) Attributed to Franklin," *American Quarterly* XXVII (March, 1975), pp. 73–87.

[11] O. G. Sonneck, *Francis Hopkinson, The First American Poet-Composer (1737–1791); and James Lyon, Patriot, Preacher, Psalmodist* (Washington: H. L. McQueen, 1905).

pieces, theatrical evenings combined spoken dramas, operas, and sometimes other forms of entertainment—pantomime, dance, even acrobatic acts and the like. Distinctions between several of these forms were often blurred; it is not always possible to distinguish between a spoken drama with interpolated songs, and a comic opera in which dialogue between musical numbers is spoken rather than sung. Thus it is difficult to pinpoint the precise date on which opera was first performed in America. The first theater in the English colonies was built in Williamsburg in 1716, by William Livingston; Tony Aston, son of a lawyer in Staffordshire, England, is known to have offered theatrical productions in Charleston and New York even earlier; a "New Theatre" was opened in New York in December of 1732. It is quite possible that operas, or at least operatic excerpts, were offered in these towns in the first third of the eighteenth century.

The first unequivocal evidence of opera in America comes from Charleston, where on February 18, 1735, a production of *Flora; or, Hob in the Well* (a condensation of the ballad opera *Country Wake; or Hob in the Well*) was mounted at the Courtroom, as part of the first theatrical season in that city.

A "Company of Comedians," organized in 1749 by Thomas Kean and Walter Murray, performed in New York, Maryland, and Virginia for several years; their repertory included such ballad operas as *The Beggar's Opera, The Mock Doctor,* and *The Devil to Play.* The most important theatrical group of the century arrived from England in 1752, calling itself the "London Company of Comedians." Financed and backed by William Hallan, the company landed at Yorktown in the summer of 1752, then moved on to Williamsburg. Under the management of Lewis Hallam, it offered an eleven-month season of plays and operas before relocating in New York, where some thirty-five different works were staged in the course of a six-month season. After similar seasons in Philadelphia and Charleston, the company disbanded, but was revived in 1758 by David Douglass. Renamed the American Company, it performed in cities and towns along the Atlantic seaboard for almost twenty years, until its activities were halted by political developments; the Continental Congress announced on October 4, 1774:

> We will discourage every species of extravagance and dissipation, especially horse-racing, and all kinds of gaming, cock-fighting, exhibition of shows, plays and other expensive diversions and entertainments.[12]

and the American Company went into exile in Jamaica.

The theatrical repertory was almost exclusively English. Thus

[12] O. G. Sonneck, *Early Opera in America* (New York: G. Schirmer, 1915), p. 52.

the ballad and comic operas dominating the musical stage in London and elsewhere in the British Isles were the core of the operatic repertory in the colonies from the first performance of *The Beggar's Opera* in 1728 to the end of the century.

Though music historians have judged that the quality of English music was at a low point throughout the eighteenth century, inferior to the creations of Italian, German, or even French composers, this period in fact represented the peak of popular musical theater in England, with the best composers of the century producing scores of works received with great acclaim at home and exported to other English-speaking countries with similar success. For almost a century, the English stage saw an unprecedented string of successful operas, including Thomas Arne's *Thomas and Sally* and *Love in a Village*, Stephen Storace's *No Song, No Supper* and *The Haunted Tower*, Thomas Linley's *The Duenna*, William Shield's *The Poor Soldier*, *The Woodman*, and *Rosina*, Charles Dibdin's *The Padlock* and *The Quaker*, and similar works by William Reeve, Samuel Arnold, James Hook, John Braham, and a host of others. These were the pieces performed on the American stage.[13]

Audiences for opera in eighteenth-century America were not only larger than those for concerts of classical music, they were also drawn from a much wider segment of the population. The theater was patronized by some of the same people who went to concerts; they sat in the boxes, above the level of the stage and the rest of the audience, conscious that their attendance at the theater linked them with certain stylish elements of English society:

> To judge from the dress and appearance of the company around me, and the actors and scenery, I should have thought I had still been in England. The ladies wore the small bonnets of the same fashion as those I saw when I left England; some of chequered straw, etc., some with their hair full dressed, without caps, as with us, and very few in the French style. . . . The gentlemen with rounded hats, their coats with high collars, and cut quite in the English fashion and many in silk striped coats.[14]

But the crowd in the lower level, the pit or gallery (or what would be called today the orchestra), was quite a different matter. Theatrical companies in eighteenth-century America played in an atmosphere not too far removed from that of Elizabethan England. There was often rowdiness, drunkenness, gambling, prostitution,

---

[13] Sonneck's *Early Opera in America* contains, in its various appendices, lists of operas performed in America in the eighteenth century by various theatrical troupes, verifying and detailing this repertory.

[14] Henry Wansley, as quoted in Sonneck, *Early Opera in America*, pp. 119–20.

A scene from a popular 18th century ballad opera at the John Street Theater, New York.

and a pervading atmosphere that made many Americans avoid the theater and prompted sermons, lectures, and essays against it. The manager of the American Company, Douglass, placed a notice in the New York newspapers in May of 1762 offering a reward to

> Whoever can discover the person who was so very rude as to throw Eggs from the Gallery upon the Stage, last Monday, by which the Cloaths of some Ladies and Gentlemen were spoiled and the performance in some measure interrupted.[15]

Members of the audience were sometimes seated on the stage, where they chatted with members of the cast not involved in the action of the moment. It was common for singers to interpolate favorite songs from other operas, or from the popular song repertory, into whatever piece was being offered. Audiences sometimes took it upon themselves to call out the names of songs they wished to hear, in the middle of dialogue or music from the stage. The members of the orchestra in Boston in 1794 were so annoyed by such interruption that they placed a notice in the local newspaper:

[15] Sonneck, *Early Opera in America*, p. 27.

The musicians that perform in the orchestra of the Boston Theatre, assure the public that it is not more their duty than it is their wish to oblige in playing such tunes as are called for. . . . They entreat a generous people so far to compassionate their feelings as to prevent the thoughtless, or ill-disposed, from throwing apples, stones, etc. into the orchestra, that while they eat the bread of industry in a free country, it may not be tinctured with the poison of humiliation.[16]

And a French visitor to America at the turn of the century wrote, after an evening at the theater in Philadelphia:

Neither order nor decency reigned in the theater. The noise of coming and going continually interefered with the attention of members of the audience who—despite posted warnings—often suffered from the odor of cigars, which were being smoked continually. The men kept their hats on their heads, and sat directly in front of women; one rarely saw a man chivalrous enough to offer his seat to a lady. Everywhere there was evidence that civilized behavior and liberty coexist with great difficulty.[17]

Many felt that the theater was an affront to decent citizens. Some righteous soul in Philadelphia inserted a notice in the *Pennsylvania Gazette* for November 10, 1773, protesting the presence of the American Company in the city:

It is a matter of real sorrow and distress to many sober inhabitants of different denominations to hear of the return of those strolling Comedians, who are travelling thro' America, propagating vice and immorality. . . . From what has been said, I think it appears: 1st, That common Players, etc., are vagrants and sturdy beggars. 2d, That the Playhouse in this city is a common nuisance.[18]

But the theater—incorporating opera—was far and away the most successful and popular form of entertainment of the day, and despite such reactions it flourished and expanded until the war broke out.

Concert and theater activity during the war was spotty. When the British were occupying such cities as Philadelphia and New York, there was music and theater for the entertainment of English officers and sympathetic colonists; when the Americans were in control, the seriousness and severity of the struggle for liberty produced a climate in which entertainment seemed inappropriate.

[16] Sonneck, *Early Opera in America*, p. 138.
[17] Perrin DuLac, "Voyage dans les deux Louisianes . . . en 1801, 1802, et 1803," quoted in Sonneck, *Early Opera in America*, p. 120.
[18] Quoted in Sonneck, *Early Opera in America*, p. 49.

There was widespread opposition to the theater, based on a conviction that the theater "threatens morals, diverts apprentices, subverts religion, and spawns brothels."[19] Rather than repealing the antitheater act of 1774, the Continental Congress, meeting in Philadelphia in 1778, reaffirmed official disapproval of such activities, in a proclamation issued on October 16:

> Whereas frequently Play Houses and theatrical entertainments, has a fatal tendency to divert the minds of the people from a due attention to the means necessary for the defence of their country and preservation of their liberties: *Resolved*, that any person holding an office under the United States who shall act, promote, encourage or attend such plays, shall be deemed unworthy to hold such office, and shall be accordingly dismissed.[20]

Despite this climate, several troupes attempted to revive theatrical life in America as soon as the fighting had ended. The Maryland Company of Comedians under the direction of Dennis Ryan took to the stage in Baltimore on January 15, 1782, and in the course of several seasons offered plays and operas such as Dibdin's *The Padlock* and the venerable *Beggar's Opera* to audiences in Maryland, Virginia, and South Carolina. The American Company returned from exile in Jamaica, picking up where they had left off almost ten years before with seasons in Philadelphia and New York. Though their personnel was much the same, there were some important differences—the presence of the eighteen-year-old John Durang, considered by historians to be the first professional American dancer, and a whole new repertory of English comic operas. On December 2, 1785, they introduced *The Poor Soldier* to America; written by John O'Keeffe and William Shield and first performed at Covent Garden in London on November 4, 1784, it had an unprecedented run of eighteen performances following its American premier at New York's John Street Theatre, and became the most popular opera in America of the entire century. The work serves to underline the difficulty in distinguishing between ballad and comic opera: though the music is credited to Shield, many of the songs were adaptations of oral-tradition tunes of the day. One of these, "A Rose Tree," became one of the most popular tunes of late eighteenth-century America, appearing in many other stage works and in instrumental arrangements and adaptations.

---

[19] Kenneth Silverman, *A Cultural History of the American Revolution* (New York: Thomas Y. Crowell Company, 1976), p. 546.

[20] Irving Lowens, *Music and Musicians in Early America* (New York: W. W. Norton & Company, 1964), p. 93.

"A Rose Tree," from *The Poor Soldier*

1. *(Patrick)* A rose tree in full bear - ing Had sweet flow-ers fair to see; One__
2. *(Norah)* How fine this morn-ing ear - ly, All sun - shin-y, clear, and bright; So__

[p]

rose, be - yond com - par - ing, For beau - ty__ at - trac-ted me.
late I loved you dear - ly, Though lost now each fond de - light.

The mood of the country remained grim, however, and city after city passed such laws as Philadelphia's "Act for the Prevention of Vice and Immorality" of 1785, which made it illegal—punishable by a fine of two hundred pounds—to

> erect, build or cause to be erected or built, any play house, theatre, stage or scaffold for acting, showing or exhibiting any tragedy, comedy, tragi-comedy, farce, interlude, pantomime, or other play, or any scene or part of any play whatsoever, or . . . act, show or exhibit any such play or any part of a play or . . . in anyway [be] concerned or employed therein, or [sell] any ticket or tickets for that purpose in any place within this commonwealth.[21]

Soon theater was legal only in Maryland and New York.

But the final ratification of the Constitution in the summer of 1788 brought a new mood to America, and on March 2, 1789 the Pennsylvania Assembly repealed the antitheater act. Hallam's troupe, now calling itself the Old American Company, established a regular circuit: Philadelphia–New York–Baltimore–Annapolis. It offered some fifty different operas, plays, and pantomimes in the first six years of its postwar activity; its operatic repertory was based on new works of the 1770s and '80s, by Dibdin, Shield, Arnold, and Linley.

[21] Quoted in Silverman, p. 556.

The success of the Old Americans led inevitably to the formation of rival companies. Thomas Wignell (for years one of the leading actors of the Old America Company) and Alexander Reinagle (an accomplished and versatile musician who had come to America in 1786) found financial backing for the construction of a new theater in Philadelphia. Modeled on the famous Theatre Royal in Bath, England, it opened on February 17, 1794 with a production of Samuel Arnold's *The Castle of Andalusia*. Wignell had recruited a splendid company, mostly from England; he had persuaded such established stars of the British stage as the singers Miss George and Miss Broadhurst (from Covent Garden) and the dancer-panto-mimists Mr. and Mrs. Francis to come to Philadelphia, and Rein-agle had assembled the best theater orchestra yet heard in America:

> The orchestra department was under the direction of manager Reinagle and the musicians were deemed equal in general ability with the stage artists—the celebrated violinist from London, George Gillingham the leader. In truth, the orchestra contained about twenty accomplished musicians, many of them of great notoriety as concert players on their respective instruments.[22]

With the Old Americans based in New York, both this city and Philadelphia now had resident theatrical companies. Boston had antitheater legislation until 1793; despite this, various operas were performed at the New Exhibition Rooms. Charles Stuart Foster traveled to England to recruit actors and musicians in 1793 and again the following year, and Boston's first legal theatrical season was launched at the Federal Street Theatre in February of 1794 with *The Farmer*. A second theater, the Haymarket, was opened on December 26, 1796; the repertory of both was drawn almost exclusively from the London stage.

Local theatrical companies offered seasons in Charleston, Richmond, Baltimore, Providence, Newport (Rhode Island), Worcester, New London (Connecticut), Hartford, Norfolk, Fredericksburg, and many other cities and towns, some with populations of no more than several thousand people. Some of these companies were quite small, and mounted only a few productions each year. But each managed to offer operas, even if their resources were limited to a handful of singer-actors and an "orchestra" of a single pianoforte. Opera, in America as in England, was part of a "people's theater" in the eighteenth and early nineteenth centuries—a character it was to lose in the years that followed.

[22] John Durang, as quoted in Sonneck, *Early Opera in America*, p. 117.

OLD AMERICAN COMPANY.
*Theatre—Cedar Street.*
Will open MONDAY, September 22.
(*For a few weeks only,*) *with an occasional*
Prelude, *called,* The
OLD & NEW HOUSES.
*The characters by* Meffrs. Hodgkinfon, King,
Ryan, Martin, Mrs. Miller &c.
*After which will be prefented, the Tragedy of the*
GRECIAN DAUGHTER.
Previous to the Tragedy the band will play
a New Federal Overture, in which is in-
troduced feveral popular airs ; Marfeilles
hymn, Ca ira, O dear what can the matter
be, Rofe Tree, Carmagnole, Prefident's
March, Yankee doodle &c. Compofed by
Mr. CARR.
To which will be added the mufical Farce of
Q              The
R  O  M  P.
The doors will be opened at half after fix,
and the curtain drawn up precifely at half
paft feven o'clock.
   *⁎* Meffrs HALLAM & HODGKIN-
SON, refpe&fully acquaint the Citizens in
general, that every expence has been chearful-
ly fuftained, that might tend to make the
*Old American Company,* worthy a fhare of
their patronage, during the fhort ftay the
nature of their engagements will permit them
to make here.
   ☞ PLACES in the Boxes may be had at
the Box Office, from ten to one every day
(Sundays excepted) and on days of perform-
ance from three to five P. M. where alfo
Tickets may be had, and at Mr. Bradford's
Book Store, No. 8, South Front ftreet, and
Mr. Carr's Mufic Store.
BOX, one Dollar—PITT three quarters—
GALLERY, half a dollar.

A newspaper advertisement dated September 20, 1794, for the Old American Company's Philadelphia Season.

Concert activity was in eclipse during the war years also. Since performances were usually given in theaters, and were followed by balls, they were subject to the prohibitions of the antitheater acts of the 1770s. When concerts were resumed in the mid-1780s, they followed the same format that had prevailed before the War. A notice in the *Pennsylvania Packet* for September 7, 1784 announced a season of subscription concerts:

Proposals

1st. That there shall be a Concert once in two weeks commencing in October: each concert to conclude at half past nine in the evening, after which rooms will be opened to Dancing and Cards.

2nd. That every subscriber shall be entitled to tickets for two ladies, besides his own admittance.

3rd. That each Subscriber pay two guineas and a half.

4th. That officers of the army and strangers (only) shall be admitted on paying 10 s. each.

The room, last season, having been found cold, proper care will be taken to prevent it this season, by placing stoves in different parts, in which the fire will be placed in the early part of the day.[23]

And various benefit concerts soon followed. In shape and content, such events were similar to those of the 1760s and '70s, as can be seen from the program of a "Grand Concert" offered in New York's Assembly Room on July 20, 1786:

### ACT FIRST

| | |
|---|---|
| Overture | Haydn |
| Song (Miss Storer) | Handel, from *The Messiah* |
| Sonata, Piano Forte | Mr. Reinagle |
| Song (Reinagle) | Handel, from *Samson* |
| Concerto Violin (Mr. Phile) | ——— |
| Song (Miss Storer) | Handel, from The Messiah |

### ACT SECOND

| | |
|---|---|
| Overture | Haydn |
| Song (Miss Storer) | Piccini, from *La Bona Figliuola* |
| Duetto, Violin & Violoncello | (Messrs. Phile and Reinagle) |
| Duetto (Miss Storer and Mr. Reinagle) | Handel, *Judas Maccabeus* |
| Miscellaneous Quartet | |
| Laughing Song (Mr. Reinagle) | Hook (?) |
| Overture | Haydn |

Concert life in the 1790s benefitted from the healthy state of the theater: subscription concerts were often organized by musicians who had come to America as members of theatrical troupes, and benefit concerts drew heavily on the talents of singers and instrumentalists who otherwise performed in operas. The postwar repertory underwent changes, again reflecting English tastes: Baroque instrumental music by Handel, Corelli, and Vivaldi, and the com-

[23] Quoted in Sonneck, *Early Concert-Life in America*, pp. 79–80.

positions of such Englishmen as Stanley and Arne, were gradually replaced by the newer music of Haydn and Pleyel, of foreign composers active in London (J. C. Bach and Abel), of "modern" Italians such as Martini and Sammartini, and by pieces from the Mannheim School.

Musical societies played a prominent role in the cultural life of postwar America. The prototype of one variety was the St. Caecilia Society of Charleston (South Carolina), founded in 1782 by persons in the town who enjoyed performing and listening to classical music with their peers. It was a private society, with membership by invitation; meetings consisted of programs of music played by members, joined by professional musicians, followed by a ball. Members were allowed to invite family and other guests; otherwise it was a closed affair.

Similar groups proliferated after the war. New York had a Musical Society, established in 1791 "with a view to cultivate the science of music, and a good taste in its execution." Meetings were held weekly, on Saturday evenings; "the principal professors of music" of the city were among the members and performers.[24] The Philharmonic Society of Boston was formed in 1809, meeting on Saturday evenings to perform the latest instrumental music for the enjoyment of members and an invited audience of family and friends; as the quality of performance improved, demand for attendance from nonmembers led to semipublic performances, in the format of open rehearsals.

The Philharmonic Society of New York, founded in 1799 as a merger of the St. Cecilia Society and the Harmonical Society, offered its first concert on December 23, 1800. The city also boasted a Euterpean Society, established about 1800 to afford musically inclined citizens the opportunity to play large-scale instrumental works together with professional musicians, for audiences made up chiefly of family and friends. The Musical Fund Society of Philadelphia was established in 1820, and in 1824 it moved into a new hall built especially for the group. Nor were such societies confined to the largest cities of America: Newport (Rhode Island) had an active St. Cecilia Society in the 1790s, and Fredericksburg had a Harmonic Society as early as 1784.

Though opera flourished during this period as a self-supporting form of entertainment, instrumental music was performed for a much smaller segment of the population, not large enough to support it as a public, commercial venture. It was from private societies, gradually gaining strength as the century unfolded, that the

---

[24] Cf. Sonneck, *Early Concert-Life in America*, p. 203.

permanent, public orchestras of America were eventually formed—not from the theater, which had housed many of the earliest concerts.

The Urania Society (or Academy) was a somewhat different sort of musical society. Founded in Philadelphia in 1784 by Andrew Adgate, it had the dual purpose of offering instruction in vocal music, and assembling enough singers and instrumentalists to perform oratorios and other pieces of sacred music requiring a trained chorus, orchestra, and soloists. No church in America had the musical resources to perform such compositions, as yet. Membership was drawn from the ranks of professional musicians in the city and private citizens willing to spend time in vocal training and chorus rehearsal. One of their first public offerings was a "Grand Concert of Sacred Music for the benefit of the Pennsylvania Hospital, Philadelphia Dispensary, and the Poor," given on May 4, 1786 at the German Reformed Church. The program opened with an overture by Martini, then alternated choral music with several concertos, and concluded with "that most sublime of all musical compositions, the grand chorus in the Messiah, by the celebrated Handel, to those words "Hallelujah! for the Lord God omnipotent reigneth," etc."[25] There were 230 members of the chorus and an orchestra of fifty—the most impressive array of musicians collected to this point for a musical performance in America. Adgate's inspiration was surely the Handel Commemoration in Westminster Abbey, London, held on May 26–29 and June 3–5, 1784, featuring a chorus of 275 and an orchestra of 250.

The Musical Society of Boston, founded by William Selby, offered such programs as one given on December 20, 1785 for the benefit of "the poor prisoners confined in the jails of this town." Between the opening overture (by Handel) and the closing overture (by J. C. Bach) were selections from Handel's *Messiah* and *Samson*, Selby's setting of the Doxology, several concertos, and a variety of anthems. Another concert, this one for the benefit of "those who have known better days," was given on January 16, 1787, and on the occasion of George Washington's visit to Boston during his triumphant inaugural tour of 1789, the Society performed an entire oratorio, *Jonah* (by the English composer Samuel Felsted).

Similar societies for the training of singers and the performance of sacred music were scattered throughout America. Stoughton (Massachusetts) boasts the oldest groups with uninterrupted histories reaching to the present: Ye Olde Musical Society, founded by residents of the town in 1762, has maintained its identity by annual

[25]*Pennsylvania Packet*, May 30, 1786.

meetings and occasional concerts, and the Old Stoughton Musical Society, founded in 1786 to join the best singers and instrumentalists from surrounding towns with those of Stoughton itself, also has annual meetings, as well as at least one concert each year. The Concord (New Hampshire) Musical Society, which was chartered on June 15, 1799 to "encourage the Knowledge and Practice of Sacred Music," had been active even before that date. The Psallonian Society of Providence, founded in 1815 by Oliver Shaw, grew to a size of 150 members and offered programs of pieces by the "best and most approved European masters" for sixteen years.

The largest and most influential group was the Boston Handel and Haydn Society, which has performed large-scale sacred works for chorus and orchestra from its founding in 1815 to the present day. An impetus for its formation was a grand "Peace Jubilee" given in Boston on February 22, 1815, celebrating the Treaty of Ghent (signed on December 25, 1814) and George Washington's birthday, simultaneously. Organized by the immigrant English organist and composer George K. Jackson, this program featured the largest assemblage of singers and instrumentalists yet heard in the city, and made such an impact that a number of Bostonians met to discuss the possibility of forming a permanent organization. A constitution was drawn up and adopted on April 26, 1815; the preamble laid out the aspirations of the founders:

> While in our country almost every institution, political, civil, and moral, has advanced with rapid steps, while every other science and art is cultivated with a success flattering to its advocates, the admirers of music find their beloved science far from exciting the feelings or exercising the powers to which it is accustomed in the Old World. Too long have those to whom heaven has given a voice to perform and an ear that can enjoy music neglected a science which has done much towards subduing the ferocious passions of men and giving innocent pleasure to society; and so absolute has been their neglect, that most of the works of the greatest composers of sacred music have never found those in our land who have even attempted their performance. Impressed with these sentiments, the undersigned do hereby agree to form themselves into a society, by the name of the Handel and Haydn Society, for the purpose of improving the style of performing sacred music, and introducing into more general use the works of Handel and Haydn and other eminent composers . . .[26]

The first concert, held on Christmas evening of 1815 in "the Stone Chapel in School Street," began with choruses and airs from

[26] Charles C. Perkins and John S. Dwight, *History of the Handel and Haydn Society of Boston, Massachusetts* (Boston: Alfred Mudge & Son, 1883–93), I, p. 39.

Haydn's *The Creation*, continued with airs, duets, and choruses from several of Handel's oratorios, and concluded with the "Hallelujah Chorus," already the traditional finale for such a program. The chorus of one hundred voices (males singing the alto, tenor, and bass parts, ten women on the soprano part supported by a few male falsetto voices) was accompanied by an organ and a dozen instruments; the audience numbered some one thousand.

In 1817, the society gave its first "complete" performances of Handel's *Messiah* and Haydn's *The Creation*, in a series of three concerts. These first efforts were widely praised, and attracted listeners from a wide area. The governor and members of the city council attended, and urged all members of the legislature to "avail themselves of the opportunity of hearing the performance, which, for excellence of style, it is confidently believed has not been equalled in this county."[27] This may well have been true, yet a review appearing in the *Centinel* for April 16, 1817 touches on some of the cold realities at this point in our musical history:

> Compare the effect of Hamlet's soliloquy when uttered by a Cooper and when uttered by a school-boy. The parallel will hold in music. The violins apparently played with no confidence in time or tune, the chorus was more than once completely thrown out by them, and the efforts of the vocal performers completely paralyzed by their want of spirit. . . .[28]

But the society persevered and continued to break new ground. It joined forces with the Philharmonic Society to offer a "Select Oratorio" on July 5, 1817 in honor of President James Monroe, who had chosen to celebrate the Fourth of July in Boston. The fourth season brought the first complete performance on a single program of *Messiah*, on Christmas Day of 1818, and of Haydn's *The Creation* on February 16, 1819. The program of April 1, 1819 was given over to large portions of Handel's *Dettingen Te Deum*, Haydn's *Mass in B-flat* was done on January 25, 1829, and Mozart's *Mass in C* was performed later that season.

Meanwhile, the society published several collections of choruses from the works of Handel, Mozart, Boyce, and other European composers in 1818, in conjunction with the Old Colony Musical Society of Plymouth. With the publication of the enormously successful *Boston Handel & Haydn Society Collection of Sacred Music* (1822) compiled by Lowell Mason (see Chapter V), the society entered a stage of financial stability. It offered a commission to Beethoven (whose *Mount of Olives* had been recently performed)

---

[27] Perkins, I, p. 46.
[28] Perkins, I, pp. 51–52.

for a new oratorio. Though he did not accept, he often mentioned the proposal as evidence of his growing worldwide fame.

Such activity and success sparked emulation. A Choral Society was formed in New York in 1823, offering programs of sacred music by Handel, Mozart, Haydn, and Beethoven; it was succeeded in the mid-1820s by the New York Sacred Music Society, which offered the city its first complete *Messiah* on November 18, 1831, with a chorus of seventy-four and an orchestra of thirty-eight.

This was the musical setting, then—subscription and benefit concerts, a lively operatic life, thriving musical societies of several sorts—for the first original instrumental and operatic composition written on American soil. With few exceptions, these pieces were the work of immigrant musicians, in musical styles similar to those favored in London.

The American Company was responsible for the creation of the only American ballad opera known to have been written before the Revolution. According to newspaper accounts, the troupe began rehearsal for *The Disappointment; or, the Force of Credulity*, written by American-born Andrew Barton, with tunes arranged from popular airs of the day. A first performance was announced for April 20, 1767, in Philadelphia; but at the last moment the work was withdrawn for fear that its political satire (of both British officials and certain native Philadelphians) would further complicate matters for the company, constantly under attack as part of the "immorality and depravity" of theatrical life.[29]

Of the many postwar composers who wrote music while in America, perhaps the most talented was Alexander Reinagle (1756–1809), born in Portsmouth, England and trained there and in Edinburgh. Coming to America in 1786, he soon settled in Philadelphia, where for many years he was the most important force behind the City Concerts, organizing them and participating as a pianist, singer, string player, and composer. In 1794 he assumed musical direction of the theatrical company formed by Thomas Wignell to perform at the New Theatre on Chestnut Street; among his duties were arranging and adapting English ballad and comic operas, often writing new overtures and new airs to be inserted in the scores.

Most of his compositions published in America were adaptations of songs by other composers, or of such traditional airs as "Auld Robin Gray." But he had composed instrumental pieces before

[29] The work was never performed until 1976, when it was reconstructed for performance at the Library of Congress in Washington. It was recorded on Vox/Turnabout TV-S 34650, as *The Disappointment: America's First Ballad Opera.*

*Sonata* (in C major) by Alexander Reinagle: beginning of first movement

leaving England—several sets of piano works, and six sonatas for the pianoforte, with the accompaniment of a violin—and he continued to write such pieces in the New World. The City Concerts for 1786–94 included sonatas for the pianoforte, attributed to Reinagle. They show his familiarity with the keyboard works of C. P. E. Bach (whom he visited in Hamburg before coming to America, and who praised his compositional talent), and recent performances and recordings reveal them to be compositions of considerable quality, idiomatic for the keyboard and quite expressive in content.[30] He also composed one or more concertos for pianoforte, various overtures, some chamber music, several marches, and was at work on a setting of Milton's *Paradise Lost* when he died in 1809.

[30]*Sonata in D Major* is available on MIA 126 (1966), and *Sonata in E* on MIA 101 (recorded in 1958).

John Christopher Moller, born about 1750, came to America from London in 1790, settling also in Philadelphia where he was organist at Zion Church, a codirector of the City Concerts with Reinagle, a frequent performer on the pianoforte and the glass harmonica, and one of the city's first music publishers. He moved to New York in 1795, assuming management of the Old City Concerts until 1803, the year of his death. Several of his compositions were listed on concerts in Philadelphia and New York, but his only published works were a *Sinfonia* (for pianoforte, though it may be a transcription of an orchestral piece) and his *Sonata VIII* for pianoforte. His set of six string quartets published in London[31] are in what might be called the London style of the late eighteenth century, combining the grace and transparency of Italian music with the more symmetrical structures of the German and English schools. They are more charming than profound—chamber music for casual listeners, easily playable by accomplished amateurs.

Jean Gehot, born in Brussels on April 8, 1756 but active as a professional musician in London from 1777, was one of the "professors of music from the opera house, Hanover-square, and Professional concerts under the direction of Haydn, Pleyel, etc. in London" recruited in 1792 for the Old American Company after it settled in New York. Recognized in London and elsewhere as a virtuoso on the violin, composer of numerous pieces of chamber music, author of several published treatises on the theory of music, he epitomized the much higher caliber of musician who came to America in the 1790s. A concert in New York on September 21, 1792 introduced him to the musical life of the city, as composer of a descriptive overture detailing his trip to America.

A fellow recruit in 1792 was James Hewitt, an excellent violinist and composer born in Dartmoor, England, in 1770, leader of the orchestra at the court of King George III at the age of twenty. The first performance in America of one of his compositions came on the same program in September of 1792 on which Gehot's work was played; Hewitt was represented by an *Overture in 9 Movements, Expressive of a Battle, etc.*[32] Hewitt's overture has been lost, but his *Battle of Trenton*,[33] a descriptive sonata for pianoforte dedicated to George Washington and introducing such familiar tunes

---

[31] Recorded on MIA 101, Quartet No. 6, and MIA 107 (1959), Quartets No. 1–5.

[32] This piece was in the mold of the most widely performed instrumental piece of the time, Franz Kotzwara's *The Battle of Prague*, a descriptive work in several sections, written c. 1788, commemorating the victory of the Prussians over the Austrians at Prague in 1757. A portion of this immensely popular piece, "Turkish Quickstep," is recorded on NW 299, s2/2.

[33] Available on a number of recordings, including Nonesuch H-71200 and Columbia ML-5496.

as "Yankee Doodle" and "Washington's March," was published in 1797, as was also his *New Federal Overture*, making similar use of well-known patriotic tunes.

Hewitt composed much more than program music, though. In addition to such instrumental works as *Three Sonatas for the Piano Forte*, Opus 5 (printed in New York in 1795–96) and *Six Easy Duetts* (Philadelphia, c. 1798), he wrote (or arranged) the music for *Tammany; or, the Indian Chief*, an opera with a book by Mrs. Anne Julia Hatton first performed by the Old American Company in New York on March 3, 1794, and the overture and some interpolated songs for the three-act play *The Patriot; or, Liberty Asserted*, done by the Old Americans on June 4 of the same year.

Victor Pelissier's name first appeared on concerts in America in 1792. A virtuosos on the French horn, he was a member of the Old American Company. He arranged and composed music for operas by other composers, and for several original stage works, the most ambitious being *Edwin and Angelina; or, the Banditti*, an opera to a libretto by Elihu Hubbard Smith, performed in New York on December 19, 1796. The music to this opera was never published, and only two songs from it survive—in Pelissier's *Columbian Melodies*, published in Philadelphia in 1811. Some music also survives from his *The Voice of Nature* of 1803, modeled on the blend of rococo–early Classical Italian and German music that soothed the ears of Londoners for many decades in the late eighteenth century.[34]

Benjamin Carr (1768–1831) was the third of the triumvirate of immigrant composers who wrote new operas in America in the 1790s. Coming to the New World in 1793, he made his stage debut as a singer with the Old American Company in New York. *The Patriot; or, Liberty Obtained*, a new work for which he wrote the music, was done in Philadelphia on May 16, 1796, and repeated in Baltimore. *The Archers; or, Mountaineers of Switzerland* was performed in New York by the Old Americans on April 16 of the same year.

His most widely played "American" work was the *Federal Overture*, premiered on September 20, 1794, during the last Philadelphia appearance of the Old American Company before it moved to New York. The piece is a potpourri of familiar tunes calculated to appeal to theater audiences with little or no acquaintance with classical instrumental music.[35] An unusually versatile man even for this period, Carr was a music publisher, concert organizer,

---

[34] A march-chorus-air from this work is recorded on NW 299, s2/4.

[35] Lowens discusses this piece, and Carr's reasons for selecting these tunes, on pp. 89–114.

organist (at St. Joseph's Church in Philadelphia), and teacher. In 1801 he accepted a post as organist and director of music at the Catholic Church of St. Augustine in Philadelphia, remaining in this position until his death in 1831. Much of his music written after 1800 was sacred, and two of his most important publications of these years were *Masses, Vespers, Litanies* and *Sacred Airs in Six Numbers*.

Many of his sixty-odd published songs were settings of substantial poetry, rather than the sentimental and often frivolous texts of pleasure-garden and comic-opera songs. Shakespeare's "Tell me where is fancy bred," "When Icicles hang by the wall" and "Take, oh! take those lips away" are found in his *Four Ballads* of 1794, and his *Six Ballads* (Opus 7) of 1810 set texts from Sir Walter Scott's *The Lady of the Lake*, published only months before Carr wrote these songs. They are filled with florid writing for the voice, difficult leaps and sustained high notes, text repetition, some difficult passages for the keyboard; their thoughtful and sensitive setting of the text and the balance between voice and accompaniment anticipate the lied style of Schubert and Schumann.[36] Written to be performed by professional singers, they move in the direction of art song, one of the characteristic genres of the nineteenth century.

Another English-born composer of unusually attractive music was Raynor Taylor (1747–1825). A member of the Chapel Royal as a child, then organist in Chelmsford, he moved on to London as violinist and composer at Marylebone Gardens and musical director at Sadler's Wells Theatre. He came to America in 1792, where his first programs were "musical evenings," comprising a string of songs and duets held together by the semblance of a plot and introduced by an overture. Settling in Philadelphia, he took a post as organist at St. Peter's and turned out a succession of songs, instrumental pieces, and an occasional work for the stage, all written in any easy, polished, thoroughly professional style.

His surviving instrumental pieces are attractive examples of the "London style," echoing the sounds and structures of early works by Haydn and Mozart but differing from them in their more pervasive lyrical character, the brevity or even absence of developmental sections, and their persistent refusal to exploit the dramatic potential of sonata-allegro form. His six sonatas for cello and continuo[37] may have been written for the son of Reinagle's brother-in-law, George Schetky, another immigrant to America; his *Sonata for the Piano Forte with an Accompaniment for a Violin*[38] was published in Philadelphia in 1797. His glee for three female voices,

---

[36] *Six Ballads* is recorded on NW 231, s1/1–4 and s2/1–2.
[37] Recorded on MIA 108 (1961).
[38] NW 299, s1/6.

"The Silver Rain"[39] and his *Rondo for the Piano Forte*[40] also tend to the lyrical and charming rather than the dramatic.

One of Taylor's later stage works, *The Ethiop; or, the Child of the Desert*, premiered in Philadelphia on January 1, 1814, serves as a reminder that English opera was beginning to move in new directions in the first decades of the nineteenth century. The libretto, by William Dimond, Jr., had first been set to music by Henry Bishop in London and presented as a "New Grand Romantick Drama" at Covent Garden in 1812. Bishop and Dimond were obviously familiar with such operas as Mozart's *Die Entführung aus dem Serail* (1782) and *Die Zauberflöte* (1790), and possibly von Weber's *Abu Hassan* (1811)—works set in exotic locales, combining spoken dialogue and simple strophic airs with more complex vocal ensembles, choruses, descriptive orchestral music, and finales involving soloists, chorus, and orchestra. *The Ethiop* is set in Baghdad; there is a dramatic overture, and the orchestra is sometimes used to accompany pantomime and spoken dialogue on stage. It was one of the first operas produced on the American stage to move so far from the style of the ballad/comic operas that had dominated the American musical stage from the first days of its history.[41]

Yet another talented English immigrant musician who wrote music after his arrival in America was George K. Jackson (1745–1822), who was in his fifty-first year when he arrived in Norfolk, Virginia in 1796. Holding a degree in music from St. Andrew's College, he had published a considerable amount of music in England, some of which had preceded him to these shores. A formidable organist and choir director, he worked his way north to New York, settling there in 1801 (at St. George's Chapel) and organizing the most ambitious programs of sacred music yet heard in that city before moving on to Boston in 1813.

Many of his "American" works were sacred; he brought out a collection of psalms for solo voice and organ in New York in 1804, and later published a *Choice Collection of Chants . . . as used in Cathedrals, Churches, and Chapels* (1816), and several anthems in the first publication of the Boston Handel and Haydn Society. He also composed music for the Masonic order, as well as various glees, songs, and patriotic works, such as his "Dirge for General Washington." His setting of Alexander Pope's "The Dying Christian to His Soul" for three voices, violin and pianoforte[42] is a curious but highly effective blend of elements of the early Classical style with

[39] Published in *The Ladies Collection of Glees, Rounds & Choruses* (Philadelphia, 1804–05) and recorded on NW 299, s1/2.
[40] Recorded on MIA 126 (1966).
[41] *The Ethiop* is recorded on NW 232, s2 (whole side).
[42] NW 231, s2/4.

those of older English music; expressive dissonances, chromaticism, word painting, echo effects, and text repetition suggest that Jackson knew and admired the music of Henry Purcell and contemporaries.

None of this music written in America made the slightest impact on musical life in England and the continent, and it would be foolish to suggest that these pieces were of the same quality as those written by the greatest European composers of the day. But many pieces by Reinagle, Taylor, and Jackson are skillful, expressive works, and in an age when new pieces were accepted and even expected by performers and audiences, these men played a vital role in the early musical life of America by supplying such music.

Concert music was still very much an imported product through the first decades of the nineteenth century, performed almost exclusively by musicians only recently arrived from England. Though some choral works by Handel, Mozart, Haydn, and Beethoven were becoming known to a wider audience through the activities of the numerous choral and sacred music societies springing up in so many American cities and towns, there was no comparable "grass roots" movement in instrumental music. The Boston Handel and Haydn Society was possible only because New England had a heritage of several generations nourished on the singing school. But except for persons living in cities and larger towns boasting one or more "professors of music," and wealthy planters, merchants, and professional men with the means to hire tutors for their children, there was virtually no opportunity for Americans to learn to play a musical instrument. Even when music was introduced into the public schools of America, beginning in Boston in the 1830s, instruction was in vocal music only.

Late in the eighteenth century, however, a handful of musicians—mostly in New England—began offering instruction in instrumental music in America's towns and villages. Perhaps the most important pioneer was Samuel Holyoke (1762–1820). A graduate of Harvard in 1789, he taught at singing schools in Massachusetts and southern New Hampshire for most of his life, was a prolific composer of hymns, psalms, and sacred songs, and brought out several of the largest collections of vocal music published in America. Late in the eighteenth century he began offering instruction in various instruments in such towns as Salem, Essex, and Exeter (New Hampshire), and organizing groups of instrumentalists for church and community performances. In 1800 he published *The Instrumental Assistant* (published in Exeter by Henry Ranlet), a "Selection of favorite Airs, Marches, &c. Progressively Arranged, and adapted for the use of Learners." The first pages are devoted to rudimentary instructions for the "Violin, German-Flute, Clarionett, Bass-Viol, and Hautboy"—fingering charts, scales, simple exercises, examples of ornamentation. The bulk of the book consists of three-part arrangements of pieces excerpted from the works of European composers, arrangements of such familiar tunes as "Yankee Doodle," "God Save the Queen" (appearing here as "God Save America"), "O Dear, What Can the Matter Be?", and unidentified marches and dances, some of which may be by Holyoke himself.

Volume 2 appeared in 1807; an introductory note explains that it was "prompted by the approbation with which the First Volume . . . has been received," and that it is intended to be "convenient for Instrumental Clubs," in contrast with the first, which had been intended for "learners." Instructions for the French horn and bassoon are contained in the first section, Holyoke explaining that the two volumes taken together give a "complete set of Scales for the Instruments, which are at present used in this Country." The new collection contains arrangements of "Minuets, Airs, Duettos, Rondos and Marches," for up to seven instruments. Typical are the *First Grand March* and the *First Grand Minuet*, a pair of pieces in simple binary form scored for two violins, two oboes, two clarinets, and bassoon. They may have been written by Holyoke, in which case they are among the earliest instrumental compositions by an American-born composer.[43]

The anonymous *Quintetto*, a three-movement work—Allegro, Affetuoso, Tempo Gavotta—is scored for two clarinets, two French horns, and bassoon. Idiomatically written for the instruments and moving smoothly and convincingly through formal structures of the early Classical period, it has the sound and shape of serenades and divertimentos for wind instruments by Mozart and his contemporaries. Its presence in this collection suggests that some American wind players had developed surprisingly advanced techniques. If it was written by Holyoke himself, as has been suggested, it is an important landmark in the history of instrumental composition by native-born American musicians.[44]

Similar collections were brought out by Oliver Shaw, Joseph Herrick, Ezekial Goodale, Amos Albee, Daniel Belknap, Uri K. Hill, and others. Most of these contain new pieces, such as Herrick's *Jolley's March*,[45] Shaw's *Governor Arnold's March* and *Air*,[46] and

[43] NW 299, s2/7.
[44] NW 299, s1/1.
[45] NW 299, s2/8.
[46] NW 299, s2/5–6.

Goodale's *Kennebec March.*[47] These collections, and the pieces contained in them, chronicle the birth and proliferation of the village band, an institution that was to be a central part of the musical education and experience of so many Americans in the nineteenth and early twentieth centuries. The simple marches and dances, sometimes written by local musicians and played by village bands, mark the true beginning of indigenous instrumental music in America.

[47] NW 299, s2/3.

# 5

## The African Slave and
## His Music in America

Slavery has existed for much of the known history of civilized man, but there has been nothing to equal the wholesale importation of Africans into the Americas in the sixteenth, seventeenth, and eighteenth centuries. The story of the Atlantic slave trade is one of the most shocking chapters in the entire history of Western man, and aftereffects of the human misery caused by this mass imprisonment linger to the present day. But, ironically, much of the cultural uniqueness of the New World, in both the Northern and Southern hemispheres, resulted from the introduction of Africans into the Western hemisphere.

African slaves in significant numbers were first introduced into modern Europe by the fifteenth-century Portuguese, who took slaves on the West Coast of Africa and sold them to the Spanish. Africans were first brought to the New World when it became evident that the native Indians of Haiti and other islands of the West Indies preferred death or imprisonment to a life of slavery.

Bishop Bartolomé de las Casas unwittingly provoked an acceleration in the African slave trade when, after witnessing the cruel treatment of the native Americans of Haiti by the Spanish settlers under Nicolas de Ovanda, he suggested to King Charles of Spain that each Spanish resident of the island be allowed a dozen black slaves—under the assumption that they would be better and more willing laborers than the Indians. Charles accordingly granted a patent for the importation of four thousand black slaves a year into

Haiti, Jamaica, Cuba, and Puerto Rico. The first of these did not arrive directly from Africa, but from Spain—first- and second-generation descendants of Africans brought to that country, many of them Christianized and Spanish-speaking. But there were not enough blacks in Spain to meet the continuing demand, and direct slave trade between Africa and the New World began.

Though the Atlantic slave trade was carried on by ships and crews of many nationalities—Portuguese, Dutch, French, Danish, Swedish—the English eventually dominated the industry. Sir John Hawkins, in 1562–63, was the first Englishman to bring African slaves to America, obtaining his cargo by robbing Portuguese slave ships off the coast of Africa. Slaves were first brought to an English colony in late August 1619, when a Dutch sea captain sold twenty Africans to settlers at Jamestown. Eleven Africans were brought to New Amsterdam (now New York) when it was founded in 1626; America entered the slave trade in 1638, when the slave ship *Desire* set sail for Africa from the Massachusetts Colony.

The English colonies had little need for slaves at first, because semiskilled labor was done mostly by white indentured servants, and there was little demand for large numbers of unskilled workers. But the growth of a plantation culture in Virginia and other Southern and middle colonies changed that situation radically, and by the mid-eighteenth century there were some 300,000 black slaves on the mainland of North America. In the meantime, more Africans were being brought to the West Indies and to South America; between 1700 and 1786, more than 600,000 of them were brought to Jamaica alone. The first census undertaken in the United States, in 1790, reported a black population of some 800,000; the census of 1860 made that figure 4,441,830. It has been estimated that as many as 15,000,000 Africans were brought to the Americas before the slave trade came to an end in the second half of the nineteenth century.

The process began with their capture or purchase by Arabs or other Africans, mostly along the central Atlantic coast—the so-called Gold Coast, or Slave Coast. Various tribes, among them the Ibo, Ashanti, Mandingo, Yoruba, and Fanti, were victimized for centuries. The captives would be taken to one of a series of "factories" (fortlike prisons, built and maintained by Europeans) strung along the coast and kept there until they were transferred to one of the flotilla of slave ships anchored just offshore to take on their human cargo. When the ship was filled, it would set off on the "Middle Passage," the Atlantic crossing to the West Indies or the mainland; upon arrival, the cargo would be sold directly to planters, or consigned to auction at a slave market.

Early European travelers in Africa were struck by the omnipresence of music; Richard Jobson, an Englishman who visited Gambia in 1620–21, wrote upon his return:

> There is without doubt, no people on the earth more naturally affected to the sound of musicke than these people; which the principall persons do hold as an ornament of their state, so as wee come to see them, their musicke will seldome be wanting.[1]

And one of the first Africans to write a book in the English language characterized his people as:

> . . . almost a nation of dancers, musicians, and poets. Thus every great event, such as a triumphant return from battle, or other cause of public rejoicing is celebrated in public dances which are accompanied with songs and music suited to the occasion.[2]

An African musician-scholar of the present century suggests that in his country, "music and life are inseparable, for there is music for many of the activities of everyday life as well as music whose verbal texts express the African's attitude to life, his hopes and fears, his thoughts and beliefs."[3]

Music was so ingrained in the nature of the slaves brought to the New World that they continued to perform it under every circumstance. They sang on board slave ships, with conditions so crowded and unhygienic that many of them failed to survive the crossing:

> They (sang) songs of sad lamentation. The words of the songs used by them were, Madda! Madda! Yiera! Bemini! Madda! Aufera! that is to say, they were all sick, and by and by they should be no more; they also sung songs expressive of their fears of being beat, of their want of victuals, particularly the want of their native food, and of their never returning to their own country.[4]

After their arrival and assignment, they sang while they worked, while they nursed their children and buried their dead, while

---

[1] *The Golden Trade or a Discovery of the River Gambra and the Golden Trade of the Aethiopians* (London: 1623), quoted in Eileen Southern, *The Music of Black Americans: A History* (New York: W. W. Norton & Company, 1971), p. 4.

[2] Olaudah Equiano, *The Interesting Narrative of the Life of Olaudah Equiano, or Gustavus Vassa the African, Written by Himself* (New York: printed by W. Durrell, 1791), I, p. 8.

[3] J. H. Kwabena Nketia, *African Music in Ghana* (Evanston: Northwestern University Press, 1963), p. 4.

[4] Ecroyde Claxton, *Minutes of the Evidence . . . Respecting the African Slave Trade,* XXXIV, 14–36, (Great Britain, Parliament, House of Commons), quoted in Dena J. Epstein, *Sinful Tunes and Spirituals: Black Folk Music to the Civil War* (Urbana: University of Illinois Press, 1977), p. 9.

entertaining themselves in the evenings, while playing games, while telling stories and legends to one another, while performing religious ceremonies or initiating new members into cults. And perhaps no aspect of their culture was more persistently misunderstood by the European-American world into which they were thrown, even by sympathetic observers:

> The system by which men are degraded to the level of brutes, or the arguments which justify such bondage, every unprejudiced mind must turn from with horror. . . . But when this is admitted, if it becomes a question whether the slave can be happy in his bonds—if not exposed to actual bodily suffering—the seven years I had an opportunity of witnessing his constitutional vivacity make me reply in the affirmative. . . . Toil, in ordinary cases, is but a dam to his animal spirits, which overflow with greater violence at the hour of relaxation. A dance, a song, and a laugh are his sole desiderata. All this is, no doubt, merely sensual, and far inferior to the pleasures which an elevation to his just dignity would afford him; but still, nothing can be more erroneous than the impression that the negro is not to the full extent as happy as any of the other unenlightened laborers with whom Europe abounds.[5]

And apologists for slavery would base much of their case on the argument that since the African slave sang and danced, he was obviously not unhappy.

The music brought to the New World by these black slaves was, of course, African. The problems in dealing with this music historically are similar to those encountered with the music of the American Indian, or any other nonliterate culture: since African music developed no system of notation, there is no direct way to deal with it before Europeans began recording it in their own system of notation and capturing it on discs, cylinders, and tapes. But such evidence as does exist before the present century—accounts of indigenous music by early European travelers in Africa, including descriptions and drawings of musical instruments; old instruments preserved in museums and private collections; the study of the music of isolated tribes, in the present century; early attempts by Europeans to transcribe African music into their own notational system; the myths and oral histories of Africans themselves; the musical practice of African Americans in remote areas of the American South—all supports the notion of a continuous musical tradition of many centuries, surviving into the twentieth century.

[5] John Bernard, *Retrospections of America, 1797–1811* (New York: Harper & Brothers, 1887), p. 126.

Such evidence enables us to make general comments about the state of music in Africa in the days of the slave trade, the music that was brought to America by many generations of black slaves:

—African music is nonnotated, played and sung—and passed on to succeeding generations of musicians—in oral tradition.

—Vocal music is sung by a single voice, by a group of singers, or—most typically—by a combination of both, in some variation of the call-and-response pattern: one or two solo voices give out a phrase, answered by the other voices. The chorus may echo the musical phrase sung by the leader(s), or it may respond with a different melodic phrase. There may be some overlapping of the solo lines with the choral response. Though there is no concept of European functional harmony, singing in two or three parts is common, particularly in the chorus of a call-and-response pattern.

—Drums, of many varieties, are the most common instruments. There are also instruments of the xylophone family, constructed of bars of woods of different sizes (and therefore different pitches) struck with some sort of mallet. There are plucked string instruments of the lute and harp variety, and blown reed instruments—flutes and whistles. Bowed string instruments are less common, and trumpets are occasionally encountered.

—Instruments may be used to accompany singing, or they may play alone, singly or in ensemble. The concept of ostinato—the reiteration of a single rhythmic / melodic pattern—is basic to African instrumental music. In ensemble playing, one instrument repeats the "time line" (a brief rhythmic pattern) for the duration of the performance. Other players take this as a point of rhythmic reference, coordinating their playing to it. The result is a complex web of simultaneous rhythms, or polyrhythms, each coordinated to the time line.

—Vocal music is usually accompanied by one or more drums, but the singers may supply percussive sounds made by the human body—hand clapping, foot stomping, and the like.

—As is true of most oral-tradition music, African music—both instrumental and vocal—is built on reiteration of brief rhythmic and melodic patterns, rather than on contrasts of tunes and rhythms, extended melodies, or developmental techniques. The effect is often cumulative, with the addition of more and more sound resources and a gradual increase in tempo as the piece progresses.

The extent of the role that music plays in the social and communal life of an African tribe is rarely encountered in Europe:

Organized games and sports, beer parties and feasts, festivals, and social and religious ceremonies or rites that bring the members of a community together provide an important means of encouraging involvement in collective behavior, a means of strengthening the social bonds that bind them and the values that inspire their corporate life. The performance of music in such contexts, therefore, assumes a multiple role in relation to the community; it provides at once an opportunity for sharing in creative experience, for participating in music as a form of community experience, and for using music as an avenue for the expression of group sentiments.[6]

Within such a communal or religious context, music serves to draw the participant into the ritual. The African believes in the reality of the spirit world, believes that his own life is transitory and less real than the world from which he came and where he will go when his present life ends. His rituals and ceremonies are designed to put him in touch with his deities and the spirits of his ancestors, invoked on such occasions.

In addition, since he lacks written histories, the African depends for knowledge of his cultural and historical heritage on tales, myths, and legends—and these are almost always associated with music. Thus an African deprived of his music is cut off from his past. And this is precisely what happened to some Africans in the New World. Family and tribal groups, even when captured together and brought on the same ship, were often broken up when sold or auctioned. Upon arrival at their new homes, they lived and worked with other slaves from different tribal groups in Africa, who spoke a different language. It was necessary for slaves to have enough command of the language of their owners and overseers to understand commands and orders; and since many of the slaves had no common African language anyway, they had no choice but to adopt Spanish or English. This was particularly true in the English colonies, where blacks tended to be in much closer contact with whites, where they were more closely supervised, and where their white masters often actively suppressed any evidence of the retention of their African heritage.

Nevertheless, many slaves retained elements of their ethnic and cultural heritage—in language, music, dance, and behavior. Account after account written during the era of slavery in America give witness to the survival of African elements, including ceremony and music, among black slaves:

[6] J. H. Kwabena Nketia, *The Music of Africa* (New York: W. W. Norton & Company, 1974), p. 22.

Nothing is more barbarous, and contrary to Christianity, than their . . . *Idolatrous Dances*, and *Revels* . . . That I may not be thought too rashly to impute Idolatry to their *Dances*, my conjecture is raised upon their ground . . . for that they use the Dances as a *means to procure Rain* . . .[7]

We young people had always been fond of occasionally going to the negro prayer meetings, but I remember a slight thrill of alarm one night (when I) saw a scene of barbaric frenzy that I have since thought the howling Dervishes reminded me of. The men sat around clapping and singing deep monotonous notes, but the women were shuffling and leaping in a circle, clapping with their hands high in the air, their heads thrown back so that some of their turbans had fallen off, and singing in high, shrill tones.[8]

In the city of New Orleans, the Place Congo was set aside on Sundays for slaves from the city and neighboring plantations to assemble for singing and dancing. It became a great attraction for visitors and tourists, and consequently we have many accounts of the activities there, particularly from the first half of the nineteenth century:

Twenty different dancing groups of the wretched Africans, collected together to perform their worship after the manner of their country. They

Slaves gathered at the Place Congo in New Orleans.

[7] Margan Godwyn, *The Negro and Indians Advocate* . . . (London: F. D., 1680), p. 33, quoted in Epstein, p. 28.

[8] Elizabeth Allen Coxe, *Memories of a South Carolina Plantation* . . . (n.p., privately printed, 1912), pp. 54–55, quoted in Epstein, p. 130.

have their own national music, consisting for the most part of a long kind of narrow drum of various sizes, from two to eight feet in length, three or four of which makes a band. The principal dancers or leaders are dressed in a variety of wild and savage fashions, always ornamented with a number of tails of the smaller wild beasts.[9]

Some observers provide specific details of musical instruments:

Approaching the common I heard a most extraordinary noise, which I supposed to proceed from some horse mill, the horses trampling on a wooden floor. . . . The music consisted of two drums and a stringed instrument. An old man sat astride of a cylindrical drum about a foot in diameter, & beat it with incredible quickness with the edge of his hand & fingers. The other drum was an open staved thing held between the knees & beaten in the same manner. They made an incredible noise. The most curious instrument, however, was a stringed instrument which no doubt was imported from Africa. On the top of the finger board was the rude figure of a man in a sitting position, & two pegs behind him to which the strings were fashioned. The body was a calabash. It was played upon by a very little old man, apparently 80 or 90 years old. . . .[10]

Sketches accompanying this narrative verify that the drums were of types still known in Africa, and that the string instrument was some variety of the instrument now known as the banjo.

Other instruments originating in Africa were in use among black slaves of the New World. These include the musical bow, an instrument common in parts of Africa and unknown elsewhere:

[The] "song-bow" [was] a simple contrivance, consisting of a string stretched tight from one end to the other of a long, flexible, narrow board or bow, and which the performer breathed upon in such a way as to cause a musical vibration, while at the same time he sang.[11]

Such instruments are occasionally encountered in the rural South even today, among both black and white musicians.[12]

Quills (or panpipes) and flutes are also mentioned as being played by black slaves. An observer visiting the South just after the Revolution wrote of hearing slaves play on flutes:

[9] Christian Schultz, Jr., *Travels on an Inland Voyage through the States* . . . (New York: Isaac Riley, 1810), II, p. 197, quoted in Epstein, p. 93.

[10] Benjamin Henry Boneval Latrobe, *Impressions Respecting New Orleans: Diary and Sketches, 1818–1820* (New York: Columbia University Press, 1951), pp. 49–50.

[11] W. H. Venable, "Down South before the War . . . ," *Ohio Archeological and Historical Society Publications*, II (March 1889), pp. 488–513.

[12] Cf. NW 223, s1 / 3, "Turkey in the Straw," for an example of an instrument of this type, played for country dancing.

I think the sounds they produce are the most affecting, as they are the most melancholy, that I ever remember to have heard. The high notes are uncommonly wild, but yet are sweet; and the lower tones are deep, majestic, and impressive.[13]

Quills—sets of five or more reeds of different sizes, played by blowing across the open tops—are common in various African cultures, and are still encountered in the South today. As the following transcription of a piece played on quills reveals,[14] the ties to African music go beyond the mere use of a musical instrument originating in that culture; the insistent but constantly varied reiteration of a brief melodic idea and the singer's vocal hoots are paralleled in African music.

"Emmaline," from the panpipes playing of Alec Askew

The presence of the balafo—an African-derived instrument of the xylophone family—in the New World is particularly interesting. It is mentioned in unambiguous terms in the eighteenth century:

Musicians arrived with an African Balafo, an instrument composed of pieces of hard wood of different diameters, laid in a row over a sort of box; they beat on one or the other so as to strike out a musical tune. They played two or three African tunes; and about a dozen girls, hearing it sound, came from the huts to a great court, and began a most curious and lascivious dance.[15]

While drums and an occasional small instrument could have traveled to the Americas on slave ships (and there is evidence that this sometimes happened), it is unlikely that such a large instrument as the balafo could have made its way with captured slaves to the factories on the African coast, and then been allowed aboard a slave ship, with its limited space. Its presence in the Americas can be explained only by the assumption that there were musicians among the slaves transported to the New World who knew how to build instruments of indigenous materials after their arrival in America.

[13] William Beckford, *A Descriptive Account of the Island of Jamaica* . . . (London: T. and J. Egerton, 1790), quoted in Epstein, p. 50.
[14] "Emmaline, Take Your Time," NW 252, s1 / 7.
[15] Sir William Young, "A Tour through the Several Islands . . . in the Years 1791 and 1792," in Bryan Edwards, *The History, Civil and Commercial, of the British West Indies* (London: J. Stockdale, 1793–1801), III, p. 276.

There is a great deal of evidence, then, both historical and empirical, that the introduction of black slaves into America resulted in the introduction of a number of African instruments to the New World. Nor was it merely instruments that came; other information makes it clear that the actual music played and sung by slaves was African in substance and function.

There are descriptions of slaves singing while performing such labors as hoeing, chopping, planting, harvesting, rowing or paddling boats, husking corn:

> The Negroes, when at work in howing Canes, or digging round Holes to plant them in, (perhaps forty Persons in a row) sing very merrily, *i.e.*, two or three Men with large Voices, and a sort of Base Tone, sing three or four short lines, and then all the rest join at once, in a sort of Chorus.[16]

Music of this sort can be found in Africa to the present day, and rural American blacks can still be heard singing such work songs.[17]

Other accounts of music among slaves describe the shape and content of song texts. A common pattern has a leader giving out a succession of verses, improvised and often referring to persons and events known to the group. Textual lines of quite different lengths could be fitted to the melodic fragment with which the leader framed his verses. The other singer-workers responded with an insistent refrain.

> The negroes at the corn huskings or picking matches, when they are singing one of their wild songs, often made as they go along. The leader sings his part, and all hands join in the chorus:

> *Leader:*   I loves old Virginny.
>    *Chorus:*   *So ho! boys! so ho!*
>         I love to shuck corn.
>         *So ho! boys! so ho!*
>         An old ox broke his neck.
>         *So ho! boys! so ho!*
>         He belong to old Joe R.
>         *So ho! boys! so ho!*
>         He cut him up for negro meat.
>         *So ho! boys! so ho!*
>         My master say he be a rascal.
>         *So ho! boys! so ho!*

[16] William Smith, *A Natural History of Nevis* . . . (Cambridge: J. Bentham, 1745), pp. 230–31.

[17] Recorded Examples include "Carrie Belle" on NW 278, s2 / 8, and "No More, My Lord" on NW 252, s2 / 1.

His negroes shall not shuck his corn.
*So ho! boys! so ho!*
No negro will pick his cotton.
*So ho! boys! so ho!*
Old Joe hire Indian.
*So ho! boys! so ho!*
I gwine home to Africa.
*So ho! boys! so ho!*
My overseer says so.
*So ho! boys! so ho!*[18]

African poetry abounds with examples of improvised texts, weaving events of the moment into a flexible structure; and many black American work-songs are obviously descended from such songs as the one mentioned above:

*Leader:* Massa kill the big old bull.
Give us people the lead to pull
Ain't I right?
*Chorus:* *You be right.*

Massa kill the big old duck,
Give us nigger the bone to suck.
Ain't I right?
*You damn right.*

Massa kill the big ol' duck,
Give us chillun the bone to suck.
Ain't I right?
*You damn right.* etc.

Farmer kill the big old bull,
Give us meat all to pull.
Ain't I right?
*John Henry right.* etc.

Well, all the Massa done for me,
Gimme a little piece of meat.
Ain't I right?
*You damn right.* etc.[19]

Examples persist to the present day in America. No mere music historian can settle the decades-long debate as to whether such things come about as direct cultural survivals from an African past or from inherent racial characteristics—or some combination of

---

[18] Thomas C. Thornton, *An Inquiry into the History of Slavery* . . . (Washington, D.C.: W. M. Morrison, 1841), pp. 120–21, quoted in Epstein, pp. 173–74.
[19] NW 278, s2 / 3.

both. But certainly, schoolgirls in Washington, D.C. in 1976 singing playground songs like the one below were following a centu-
ries-long African and Afro-American tradition:

> *Leader:*  Ronald McDonald loves a french-fry.
> Ronald McDonald loves a french-fry.
> Oooh, sissy wah-wah.
> *Chorus:*  (*A french-fry*)
>
> I found my lover.
> (*A french-fry*)
>
> He so sweet.
> (*A french-fry*)
>
> Jes' like a cherry treat.
> (*A french-fry*)
>
> Ronald McDonald loves a hamburger.
> Ronald McDonald loves a hamburger.
> Oooh, sissy wah-wah.
> (*A hamburger*)
>
> I found my lover.
> (*A hamburger*)
>
> He so sweet.
> (A hamburger)
>
> Jes' like a cherry treat.
> (*A hamburger*)[20]

These last two examples blend traditional African elements with
the language and culture of modern-day America; even the music
is somewhat modified by European-American elements. They are
examples of acculturation, the process whereby one cultural group
absorbs elements of another. And much of the story of Afro-American music has to do with the assimilation of European elements
into African music, almost from the time of the first arrival of black
slaves in America.

European-American dance music, for instance, quickly became
part of the slave experience in America. Some Africans were exposed
to it even before they landed in the New World. English and American sailors often danced aboard ship, to improve their health and
disposition, and a sailor who could play dance tunes was a valuable member of the ship's crew. It was a common practice for the
captain of a slave ship to force his captives to dance, to keep up
their health and insure that as many as possible would survive the
crossing:

[20] NW 291, s2 / 2.

[The slaves] were kept in irons, and in the afternoon, after being fed, the boatswain and the mate . . . make them dance; and if they do not, they had each of them a cat to flog them and make them do it which I have seen exercised repeatedly.[21]

They seemed more willing to dance if there was music. Sometimes they made their own, with improvised drums; sometimes they danced to the music of their captors:

We often at sea in the evening would let the slaves come up into the sun to air themselves, and make them jump and dance for an hour or two to our bagpipes, harp and fiddle, by which exercise to preserve them in health.[22]

By the second half of the seventeenth century, African slaves were being trained to play the fiddle, to accompany the dancing of their masters. Good fiddlers were in such demand that planters would resort to kidnapping to procure the best possible musicians for their entertainment.[23] Certain slave fiddlers became famous: Simeon Gilliat, of Richmond, was reputed to be the best fiddler in the state and played at the Governor's Palace in Williamsburg by demand. Numerous accounts specify that these men played minuets and cotillions for formal dancing, and jigs, hornpipes, and reels for country dancing; but there are occasional hints that they brought their own style of playing to European dances:

Unacquainted with the science of music, though gifted with decided musical powers, they played antics with the "high heaven of sound," while sawing violins.[24]

Slave fiddlers took music learned from white masters back to their own people and taught them the rudiments of European dancing.

At Christmas the slaves are allowed three days holiday. . . . One of them attends with a fiddle, and the men dress in the English mode, with cocked

[21] James Towne, *Minutes of the Evidence . . . Respecting the African Slave Trade,* XXXIV, 14–36 (Great Britain, Parliament, House of Commons), quoted in Epstein, p. 8.

[22] Thomas Phillips, "Voyage Made in the *Hannibal*," from Churchill, *Collection of Voyages and Travels* (London, 1732), quoted in Epstein, p. 8; concerns 1693 voyage of the British slaver *Hannibal.*

[23] Solomon Northup, a freeman living in New York, was kidnapped in 1841 and spent the next twelve years in the South as a slave-fiddler; he told his own story in *Twelve Years a Slave* (New York and Auburn: Derby and Miller, 1853).

[24] *Recollections of a Southern Matron* (New York: Harper & Brothers, 1838), quoted in Epstein, p. 150.

hats, cloth coats, Holland shoes, and pumps. They dance minuets with the mulattos and other brown women, imitating the motion and steps of the English, but with a degree of affectation.[25]

There are also hints that whites and blacks sometimes danced together. Isaac Jefferson, a slave at Thomas Jefferson's home of Monticello, reported that Thomas's brother Randolph was "a mighty simple man: used to come out among black people, play the fiddle and dance half the night."[26] Philip Fithian noted in his journal that on a certain evening in early 1774:

> . . . the Negroes collected themselves into the School-Room, & began to play the *Fiddle*, & dance. . . . I went among them, *Ben & Harry* (two white youths) were of the company—Harry was dancing with his Coat off—I dispersed them however immediately.[27]

When blacks danced among themselves to the fiddle, it was to music of a somewhat different character than that played by slave fiddlers for white dancing. The fiddle was often accompanied by

Fiddle, banjo, and bones accompany the dancers in this 1853 sketch by Lewis Miller.

[25] Peter Marsden, *An Account of the Island of Jamaica* . . . (Newcastle: S. Hodgson, 1788), quoted in Epstein, p. 83.

[26] Isaac Jefferson, "Memoirs of a Monticello Slave," *William and Mary Quarterly* VIII (1951), p. 22.

[27] Hunter Dickinson Farrish, ed., *Journal and Letters of Philip Vickers Fithian, 1773–1774: A Plantation Tutor of the Old Dominion* (Williamsburg: Colonial Williamsburg, 1943), pp. 61–62.

drums, handclapping, sticks pounded on the floor, and sometimes the banjo—none of which happened in European-style dance music. One observer reported that on these occasions "the fiddle would assume a low monotonous tone, the whole tune running on three or four notes only."[28] Southern whites themselves sometimes danced an "African jig" in the course of an evening's dancing. A guest at a ball in Virginia in 1775 observed that:

> Betwixt the Country dances . . . a couple gets up and begins to dance a jig (to some Negro tune), others comes and cuts them out, and these dances always last as long as the Fiddler can play. This is sociable, but I think it looks more like a Bacchanalian dance than one in a polite assembly.[29]

Other descriptions of the "African jig" confirm that it was something quite different from the European-American country dance, with music usually described as "African" and a unique dancing style: it was danced by a single couple at a time, as happens in certain African dances, with movements consisting of:

> a shuffling [of] arms and legs in artistic style, and [the] whole soul and body thrown into the Dance. The feet moved about in the most grotesque manner stamping, slamming, and banging the floor, not unlike the pattering of hail on the housetop.[30]

The dance became popular enough for several samples of its accompanying music to be published. The following, taken from *A Selection of Scotch, English, Irish and Foreign Airs* (printed in Glasgow in 1782 by J. Aird), conceivably could have originated as an African tune and been forced into European symmetries and cadential patterns by the person who wrote it down. Certainly its insistent repetition of a small number of melodic fragments makes it atypical for the time.

An "African Jig" printed in Glasgow in 1782

[28] Henry William Ravenal, "Recollections of Southern Plantation Life," *Yale Review* XXV (June, 1936), p. 768, quoted in Epstein, p. 123.

[29] Nicholas Creswell, *Journal of Nicholas Creswell, 1774–1777* (New York: L. MacVeagh [Dial Press], 1924), pp. 52–53.

[30] Ravenal, p. 769.

Despite the differences between African and European music, there are important common elements. West African music is based on pentatonic and heptatonic scales often similar in structure and tuning to those of European music. The use of harmony—or at least simultaneously sounding notes—in African music is another point of similarity. Call-and-response patterns resemble several wide-spread practices found in European religious music: the responsorial manner of singing some chants in the Catholic church and the lining out in Protestant psalm singing. The rhythmic, propulsive nature of African singing, dancing, and drumming could be related by the European to his own dance music, with its steady rhythmic movement keeping measure for the dancers.

Though the European often complained about the "wild" and "barbaric" music of the African and the Afro-American, it was not nearly so alien to his ears as was the music of the American Indian.

In spite of the strongly evangelical nature of Christianity, large-scale conversion of African slaves came about slowly. There was a fear among whites, stated succinctly by Governor Spotswood of Virginia in 1710, of any circumstance that would bring together large numbers of slaves, or improve communication among them:

> We are not to depend on either their stupidity, or that babel of languages among them; freedom wears a cap, which can without a tongue call together all those who long to shake off the fetters of slavery.[31]

But in 1701 the Church of England established a Society for the Propagation of the Gospel in Foreign Parts, and the Reverend Samuel Thomas was sent to the Carolinas the following year to begin the work of bringing Christianity to the black slaves of America. Progress was slow, at first; a report sent to London in 1724 painted a gloomy picture:

> Our Negroe Slaves imported daily, are altogether ignorant of God and Religion, and in truth have so little Docility in them that they scarce ever become capable of Instruction. . . . The Negroes cannot be said to be of any Religion for as there is no law of the Colony obliging their Masters or Owners to instruct them in the principles of Christianity . . . the poor Creatures generally live and die without it.[32]

The religious climate in America underwent radical changes with the advent of the Great Awakening. Such populist denomi-

[31] Quoted in Southern, p. 60.
[32] Quoted in Epstein, p. 102.

nations as Presbyterian, Methodist, and Baptist introduced mass public religious rallies conducted by evangelists who, through impassioned oratory, roused people to emotional heights causing them to embrace or reembrace Christianity, spontaneously and publicly. Jonathan Edwards (1703–58) began what were later to be called "revival meetings" in Northampton (Massachusetts) in 1734, marked by fiery sermons and large, emotional congregations; five blacks were among the "repentant sinners" baptized on one occasion in 1735. His follower, George Whitefield, carried the movement to other parts of Massachusetts and to Connecticut. By the 1750s, such men as Samuel Davies of Hanover, Virginia were "carrying the word" to the South. Davies reported in 1751:

> There is a great number of Negroes in these parts: and sometimes I see a 100 & more among my Hearers. I have baptized about 40 Adults of them within these three years.[33]

Bishop Francis Asbury, who enlisted the aid of a black man, Harry Hosier, to help attract members of his race to revival services, wrote from Virginia:

> The house was greatly crowded, and four or five hundred stood at the doors and windows, and listened with unabated attention. . . . I was obliged to stop again and again, and beg of the people to compose themselves. But they could not; some on their knees, and some on their faces, were crying mightily to God all the time I was preaching. Hundreds of Negroes were among them, with the tears streaming down their faces.[34]

Evangelical preachers understood very well the role that congregational singing could play in bringing people together. The most popular sacred poems of the time were the psalms, hymns, and spiritual songs of Isaac Watts (see pp. 43–45), and these—in musical settings by various British and American composers—made up the backbone of the singing during the first decades of the Great Awakening. Though Watts's religious poetry was written at an earlier time, his words and sentiments magically caught the mood of passion, yearning, ecstacy, and fervor that swept over so much of America in the middle and late eighteenth century:

> When I can read my title clear
> To mansions in the skies,

[33] Samuel Davies, *The State of Religion Among the Protestant Dissenters in Virginia* (Boston: S. Kneeland, 1751), p. 23.
[34] Francis Asbury, *The Journals and Letters of Francis Asbury*, Elmer T. Clarke, ed. (London: Epworth Press, 1958), I, p. 222.

I bid farewell to ev'ry fear,
    And wipe my weeping eyes.

Raise thee, my soul, fly up and run
    Through ev'ry heavenly street;
And say, there's nought below the sun,
    That's worthy of thy feet.

Thus will we mount on sacred wings,
    And tread the courts above;
Nor earth, nor all her mightiest things,
    Shall tempt our meanest love.

There is a land of pure delight,
    Where saints immortal reign;
Infinite days exclude the night,
    And pleasures banish pain.

Converted black Americans came to know this religious poetry. Along with the Bible, it was by far the most important Western literary influence on the culture of the African in America. Account after account stresses the role of these two:

> The Books I principally want for them are, *Watt's Psalms and Hymns,* and *Bibles.* . . . I cannot but observe, that the *Negroes,* above all the Human Species that I ever knew, have an Ear for Musick, and a kind of extatic Delight in *Psalmody;* and there are no books they learn so soon, or take so much Pleasure in.[35]
>
> I can hardly express the pleasure it affords me to turn to that part of the gallery where they (the Negroes) sit, and see so many of them with their Psalm or Hymn Books, assisting their fellows, who are beginners, to find the place; and then all breaking out in a torrent of sacred harmony, enough to bear away the whole congregation of heaven.[36]

White opposition to the conversion of slaves mounted. A Methodist minister in Virginia, a "circuit rider" who traveled to small rural churches, wrote in 1789:

> The dear black people was filled with the power & spirit of God, and began with a great Shout to give Glory to God—this vexed the Devil. He entered into the cruel whitemen with violence eagerly ran into the

---

[35] Benjamin A. Fawcett, *A Compassionate Address to the Christian Negroes in Virginia* . . . (London: Salop, 1755), p. 37 (appendix).

[36] Samuel Davies, *Letters from the Rev. Samuel Davies, and Others, Shewing the State of Religion in Virginia, South Carolina, and Particularly Among the Negroes* (London: J. & W. Oliver, 1759), p. 14.

Church with sticks clubs and caines—abeating and abusing the poor Slaves the outcast of Men for praising of God. O America how she groans under the burden of Slavery.[37]

But the tide of Christianity rolled on, picking up even more momentum at the turn of the nineteenth century with the second stage of the Great Awakening, sometimes called the Great Western Revival and sometimes the Camp-meeting Movement. The Reverend James McGready and Lorenzo Dow were among the leaders of this movement, which began in the West and the South; according to Dow:

> Camp meetings *began* in Kentucky—next N. Carolina—attended them in Georgia—introduced them in the centre of Virginia, N. York, Connecticut, Massachusetts and Mississippi Territory: 1803–4–5.[38]

Even more of a populist movement than the first wave of revivalism, this stage flourished mostly in rural and frontier areas. It featured outdoor meetings, often lasting several days; its message, delivered in an atmosphere supercharged with emotionalism, was that Christian salvation was a personal matter, available immediately to anyone who would repent of his sinful ways and accept Jesus as his saviour. The revival meeting became a combined religious, social, and recreational event, with a special flavor all its own:

> About an acre and a half was surrounded on the four sides by cabins built up of rough boards; the whole area in the centre was fitted up with planks, laid about a foot from the ground, as seats. At one end, but not close to the cabins, was a raised stand, which served as a pulpit for the preachers, one of them praying, while five or six others sat down behind him on benches. Outside the area . . . were hundreds of tents pitched in every quarter, their snowy whiteness contrasting beautifully with the deep verdure and gloom of the forest. . . . One of the preachers rose and gave out a hymn, which was sung by the congregation, amounting to about seven or eight hundred. . . . An elderly man gave out a hymn . . . then another knelt down in the centre and commenced a prayer . . . then another voice burst out into a prayer, and another followed him; then their voices became all confused together; and then were heard the more silvery tones of woman's supplications. As the din increased so did their

[37] James Meacham, "A Journal and Travels of James Meacham, Part I, 19 May–31 August, 1789," Trinity College *Historical Papers*, Series 9 (1912), p. 94.
[38] Quoted in Gilbert Chase, *America's Music* (New York: McGraw-Hill Book Company, 1966), pp. 209–10.

enthusiasm; handkerchiefs were raised to bright eyes, and sobs were intermingled with prayers and ejaculations. It became a scene of Babel; more than twenty men and women were crying out at the highest pitch of their voices, and trying apparently to be heard above the others. Every minute the excitement increased; some wrung their hands and called for mercy; some tore their hair; boys laid down crying bitterly, with their heads buried in the straw; there was sobbing almost to suffocation, and hysterics and deep agony. When it was at its height, one of the preachers came in, and raising his voice high above the tumult, intreated the Lord to receive into his fold those who now repented and would fain return. Another of the ministers knelt down by some young men, whose faces were covered up, and who appeared to be almost in a state of phrensy; and putting his hands upon them, poured forth an energetic prayer, well calculated to work upon their over excited feelings. Groans, ejaculations, broken sobs, frantic motions, and convulsions succeeded; some fell on their backs with their eyes closed, waving their hands with a slow motion, and crying out—"Glory, glory, glory!"[39]

The outdoor setting made it easier for black slaves to attend and participate. They flocked there in large numbers, attracted by the unrestrained mood, the use of music to punctuate the gathering with lively spiritual songs, and above all the message that anyone—even a slave—could be accepted into a large brotherhood, and in the process be assured of a better life after the present one had ended.

As the nineteenth century unfolded, then, the slave population of America was drawn more and more to Christianity. The opposition of most whites to the conversion of slaves crumbled, partly from inability to stem the tide and partly because it became evident that far from inciting slaves to rebellion, Christianity tended to make them more willing to accept lives of deprivation and labor, with its promised rewards in the next world if they conducted themselves "properly" in their present life. Christianity became a sort of tranquilizer for black Americans.

The earliest accounts of black participation in the Great Awakening describe them taking part in white-organized events, singing religious songs along with everyone else, with no hint that their singing was different from that of other participants. The first independent black church in America was the African Methodist Episcopal Church, established by Richard Allen in Philadelphia in 1794; the second, founded two years later, was the African Methodist Episcopal Zion Church in New York. Though it would be some time before organized Christianity flourished among blacks in the

---

[39]Captain C. B. Marryat, *A Diary in America, With Remarks on its Institutions* (New York: D. Appleton & Company, 1839), pp. 136–38.

South, converted slaves carried their new religion—and its music—to their fellow slaves and conducted spontaneous, nonstructured religious instruction and services, complete with spiritual songs.

Early in the nineteenth century blacks began adapting Christian songs to their own musical and cultural ways. A report written in 1819 records that:

> In the *blacks'* quarter, the coloured people get together, and sing for hours together, short scraps of disjointed affirmations, pledges, or prayers, lengthened out with long repetition *choruses*. These are all sung in the merry chorus-manner of the southern harvest field, or husking-frolic method, of the slave blacks; and also very greatly like the Indian dances. With every word so sung, they have a sinking of one or other leg of the body alternately; producing an audible sound of the feet at every step, and as manifest as the steps of actual negro dancing in Virginia, &c. If some, in the meantime sit, they strike the sounds alternately on each thigh. . . . I have know in some camp meetings, from 50 to 60 people crowd into one tent, after the public devotions had closed, and there continue the whole night, singing tune after tune, (though with occasional episodes of prayer) scarce one of which were in our hymn books. Some of these from their nature, (having very long repetition choruses and short scraps of matter) are actually composed as sung, and are indeed almost endless.[40]

Countless other accounts of black religious music, as sung in both North and South, verify and augment this picture of a distinctive black Christian music. A former slave wrote of religious services held near Heathsville, Virginia:

> The way in which we worshipped is almost indescribable. The singing was accompanied by a certain ecstacy of motion, clapping of hands, tossing of heads, which would continue without cessation about half an hour; one would lead off in a kind of recitative style, others joining in the chorus.[41]

And an English minister described a "religious meeting of Negroes" in Charleston, South Carolina in 1851:

> The minister walked among them and gave out a line, such as—"I go before you to Galilee"; then the rest sung "Hallelujah!" with great zeal. The burden of another song was to this effect—"We shall have nothing

---

[40] John Fanning Watson, *Methodist Error; or, Friendly Christian Advice, to Those Methodists, Who Indulge in Extravagant Religious Emotions and Bodily Exercises* (Trenton: D. & E. Felton, 1819), pp. 29–31.

[41] James L. Smith, *Autobiography . . . including, also, Reminiscences of Slave Life . . .* (Norwich: Press of the Bulletin, 1881), p. 163.

at all to do but ring Jerusalem"; and they did "ring Jerusalem" with amazing animation, the old men gesticulating, and the others waving to and fro and singing with the greatest earnestness.[42]

From such accounts, it is possible to piece together a description of religious song originating among black Americans in the half-century or so preceding the Civil War:

—Texts were taken from the Bible and the religious poetry of such eighteenth-century writers as Isaac Watts and Charles Wesley. These were fragmented and often pieced together from several different sources; grammatical structures were altered to fit the dialect of English spoken among blacks; many of the most popular texts dealt with people in captivity or slavery—the Israelites in Egypt, for instance.

—Solos lines were given out by a leader, often a minister, with the other singers responding. Though this pattern has similarities to the lining-out practice of rural Anglo-American psalmody and hymnody, there are critical differences: in lining out, the response echoes the melodic phrase sung by the leader; in spirituals, the response is a refrain, usually with its own melodic shape. It may consist of a short phrase, or even a single word, and it is usually sung in two- or three-part harmony.

—The singing is accompanied by percussive sounds made by hand clapping, foot stomping, and sometimes improvised percussion instruments.

This was oral-tradition music, but various bits of evidence enable us to reconstruct it with some assurance of accuracy and to identify certain ways of singing persisting to the present as closely approximating the sound and spirit of the pre–Civil War "shout" or "spiritual."

A certain Laurence Oliphant, traveling through the slave states in 1861, wrote of hearing religious music sung by blacks:

On some plantations in South Carolina they . . . never sang anything but their own sacred compositions. These chants break with their pleasant melodies the calm stillness of evening, as we glide down the broad bosom of the Wacamaw, and our crew with measured strokes keep time to the music of their own choruses. . . . Generally, indeed, the airs were appropriate to the spirit of the composition; some of them were sung with great vehemence and unction, and from the excitement of tone and manner, the susceptibility of the Negro to appeals of this nature to his

---

[42] Russell Lant Carpenter, *Observations on American Slavery After a Year's Tour in the United States* (London: E. T. Whitfield, 1852), p. 37.

devotional instrincts was evident. The sacred names were generally screamed rather than sung, with an almost ecstatic fervour. . . . [There are] a number of variations, often extempore, but with the same refrain ever recurring, and joined in by all

> I want to sing as the angels sing,      (solo)
> *Daniel!*                                (chorus)
> I want to pray as the angels pray,
> *Daniel!*
> I want to shout as the angels shout,
> *Daniel!*
> O Lord, give me the eagle's wing,
> *Daniel!*
> What time of the day?
> *Daniel!*
> In the lion's den?
> *Daniel!*
> I want to pray,
> *Daniel!*
> O Lord, give me the eagle's wing.
> *Daniel!* [43]

Similar pieces have persisted into the twentieth century, sung by ex-slaves and their descendents in isolated areas of the South. The following was recorded in 1960, by Alan Lomax, on St. Simons Island, one of the Georgia Sea Islands:[44]

The spiritual "Daniel," as sung in the Georgia Sea Islands

[43] Laurence Oliphant, *Patriots and Filibusters; or, Incidents of Political and Exploratory Travel* (Edinburgh: W. Blackwood & Sons, 1861), pp. 140–43.
[44] NW 278, s1 / 5.

(additional verses)

Shout the other way,      (four times)
  O Daniel!
Gimme the kneebone bend,  (four times)
  O Daniel!
On the eagle wing,       (four times)
  O Daniel!
Fly, I tell you, fly,       (two times)
  O Daniel!
Fly the other way,       (two times)
  O Daniel!

Pieces of just this sort—brief, improvisatory solo phrases answered by a two-part chorus exclaiming a single syllable or word—are common in African music. The following, for example, comes from the Akan region of Ghana:

A song from Ghana, from Nketia, *African Music in Ghana*, p. 121

The persistence of such pieces in Afro-American culture is astonishing; the following, recorded in Drew, Mississippi from the singing of a group of black schoolgirls in 1940, belongs to the same family as the pieces just mentioned:[45]

"Chariot," as sung by black schoolchildren in Drew, Mississippi

[45] NW 291, s2 / 4.

'round moun-tain,    side— by side,    You— and I    gon' take a ride.

Ju-bi-lee!    Ju-bi-lee!    Ju-bi-lee!    Ju-bi-lee!

Other shouts or spirituals from the nineteenth century have more extended solo sections and sometimes longer choral responses. The white Northern commander of the South Carolina Volunteers—the first slave regiment mustered during the Civil War—wrote of how his troops would improvise their "own wild hymns" as they marched:

> They constantly improvised simple verses, with the same odd min-gling,—the little facts of to-day's march being interwoven with the depths of theological gloom, and the same jubilant chorus annexed to all; thus,—

> We're gwine to de Ferry,
> *De bell done ringing;*
> Gwine to de landing,
> *De bell done ringing;*
> Trust, believer,
> *O, de bell done ringing;*
> Satan's behind me,
> *De bell done ringing;*
> 'T is a misty morning,
> *De bell done ringing;*
> O de road am sandy,
> *De bell done ringing;*[46]

"Live Humble," a spiritual recorded on St. Simons Island in 1940, alternates solo phrases, improvised on texts from various parts of the Bible, with the chorus responding:

> Live humble, humble,
> Humble yourself, the bell done rung.[47]

The events of the Civil War and its aftermaths brought about a sudden increase of interest in Negro spirituals, mostly among Northerners who came into contact with this music for the first

---

[46]Thomas W. Higginson, *Army Life in a Black Regiment* (Boston: n.p., 1870), pp. 24–25.
[47]NW 278, s1 / 4.

time. Thomas Higginson wrote at some length about these "quaint, monotonous, endless, negro-Methodist chants, with obscure syllables recurring constantly, and slight variations interwoven, all accompanied with a regular drumming of the feet and clapping of the hands."[48] He takes care to separate the spiritual from "Ethiopian Minstrel ditties" written and performed in the North, and also from the "long and short meters of the hymn-books," which the Southern blacks "sang reluctantly, even on Sunday . . . always gladly yielding to the more potent excitement of their own 'spirituals.' "[49] He was not a musician and was incapable of writing down the music of these spirituals; but he jotted down and later published the texts of some forty of them.[50]

The first large published collection of the music of these spirituals appeared in 1867: *Slave Songs of the United States* (New York: A. Simpson & Co.), the work of three collaborators—William Francis Allen (1830–99), Lucy McKim Garrison (1842–77) and Charles Pickard Ware (1840–1921). Allen says in his preface that though the ex-slaves still sang regular, white hymns—"at regular intervals one hears the elder 'deaconing' [i.e., lining out] a hymn-book hymn, which is sung two lines at a time"[51]—the pieces in this collection are something different, sung after the formal worship service has ended:

Old and young, men and women, sprucely-dressed young men, grotesquely half-clad fieldhands—the women generally with gay handkerchiefs twisted about their heads and with short skirts—boys with tattered shirts and men's trousers, young girls barefooted, all stand up in the middle of the floor, and when the "sperichil" is struck up, begin first walking and by-and-by shuffling round, one after the other, in a ring. The foot is hardly taken from the floor, and the progression is mainly due to a jerking, hitching motion, which agitates the entire shouter, and soon brings out streams of perspiration. Sometimes they dance silently, sometimes as they shuffle they sing the chorus of the spirituals, and sometimes the song itself is also sung by the dancers. But more frequently a band, at the side of the room to "base" the others, singing the body of the song and clapping their hands together or on the knees. Song and dance are alike extremely energetic, and often, when the shout lasts into the middle of the night, the monotonous thud, thud of the feet prevents sleep within a half a mile of the praise-house.[52]

[48] Higginson, pp. 16–17.
[49] Higginson, p. 222.
[50] Available in a modern printing in Eileen Southern, *Readings in Black American Music* (New York: W. W. Norton & Company, 1971), pp. 167–91.
[51] William Francis Allen, Charles Pickard Ware and Lucy McKim Garrison, *Slave Songs of the United States* (New York: A. Simpson & Company, 1867), p. xiii.
[52] Allen, pp. xiii–xiv.

The editors had difficulty in reducing these oral-tradition pieces to a notational system devised in Western Europe for a quite different sort of music. Some of the melodies they managed to transcribe have simple, repetitious phrases and brief exclamatory choral responses, suggesting African roots:

"Jine 'Em" (spiritual), from Allen, *Slave Songs*

or,

"Religion So Sweet" (spiritual), from Allen, *Slave Songs*

Others, however, show melodic resemblances to European music. The tunes imply an underpinning of functional harmonic chords; melodic phrases are shaped to accommodate common-practice harmonic cadences; and melodic sequence, virtually unknown in African music, is sometimes encountered. A tune such as the following must surely have been appropriated from a hymn or a secular tune sung by whites:

"John, John, of the Holy Order" (spiritual), from Allen, *Slave Songs*

Still others can be traced to specific American hymns. "Just Now (Sanctify Me)," for instance, is virtually a note-for-note adaptation of the hymn "Come to Jesus":

"Just Now" (spiritual), from Allen, *Slave Songs*

"Come to Jesus"

The model for spirituals was not always a religious song. "Lord, Remember Me" appears to draw phrases from two different songs by Stephen Foster—"Oh, Susannah" for its verse, and "Camptown Races" for its chorus:

"Lord, Remember Me" (spiritual), from Allen, *Slave Songs*

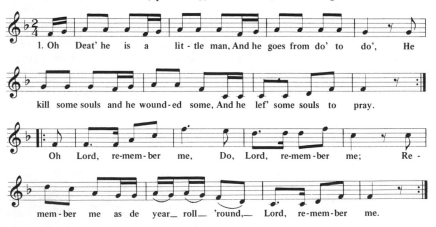

Though this may sound surprising, there is considerable evidence that minstrel songs were indeed known among slaves:

Although first published in the North, you there know nothing of the power and pathos given them here. The whites first learn them—the negroes catch the air and the words from once hearing, after which woods and fields resound with their strains—the whites catch the expression from these sable minstrels—thus Negro Melodies have an effect here not dreamed of at the North.[53]

There is a critical point to be made here. In the nineteenth century, the overwhelming majority of blacks were concentrated in the South. (It was not until well into the twentieth century that there was any wholesale migration of blacks to the North.) There were many terrible and tragic aspects of the Afro-American experience in the South, before and after emancipation. But it was only in this section of the country that prolonged and significant contact between the races took place—whatever the nature and quality of this contact. The story of Afro-American music, in all stages except the most recent, has been a Southern story.

[53] John S. Dwight, ed., *Dwight's Journal of Music: A Paper of Art and Literature* (Boston: Oliver Ditson & Company, 1852–81), February 26, 1853.

# 6

# William Billings
# and Lowell Mason:
# Birth and Reform

Late in 1770, Benjamin Edes and John Gill published, in Boston, a small book entitled, *The New-England Psalm-Singer: or, American Chorister,* the work of William Billings. A simple statistic will serve to place this book in historical perspective: no more than a dozen musical compositions known or suspected to have been written by native-born Americans had appeared in print to this point; Billings's collection contains 126 pieces, all by him. As the biographers of Billings have put it: "It would be difficult to find another single publication in the history of American music—in the history of western music, for that matter—whose priority in its tradition is more conspicuous."[1] The composition of psalms, hymns, and anthems had suddenly taken root in America, and in the coming decades dozens of Americans were to write thousands of such pieces, establishing the first native school of musical composition.

Billings, born October 7, 1746 in Boston, learned the rudiments of music at a singing school, perhaps at the New South Church where he was baptized. By 1769 he was conducting such schools himself; Boston newspapers carried an announcement of one led by Billings and John Barry at the Old South Meeting House. He was already composing; the preface to the *New-England Psalm-Singer* explains that the pieces contained therein had been completed some eighteen months earlier, with publication delayed by the difficulty of obtaining a quantity of suitable paper.

---

[1] David P. McKay and Richard Crawford, *William Billings of Boston* (Princeton: Princeton University Press, 1975), p. 41.

The frontispiece of *The New England Psalm-Singer* (1770) features a canon by William Billings engraved by Paul Revere.

The collection is similar to English tunebooks published in the colonies, particularly William Tans'ur's *Royal Melody Complete* (Boston: M'Alpine, 1767 and thereafter). But Billings had a sense of the historical position of this first American tunebook: his quotation on the title page of a passage from James 5:13—"Is any merry? Let him sing Psalms"—links his book with the first American book of psalmody, the *Bay Psalm Book* of 1640, on whose title page are the words, "If any be afflicted, let him pray, and if any be merry let him sing psalmes."

His second collection, the *Singing Master's Assistant* (Boston: Draper & Folsom), did not appear until 1778. A smaller and less elaborately printed volume, it was his most successful work: four editions came out, and fifty-one of its seventy-one pieces were reprinted in at least one later collection. He was typically candid and humorous in assessing his first effort:

Oh! how did my foolish heart throb and beat with tumultuous joy! With what impatience did I wait on the Book-Binder, while stitching the sheets

and putting on the covers, with what extacy, did I snatch the yet unfinished Book out of his hands, and pressing it to my bosom, with raptur-
ous delight; how lavish was I in encomiums on this infant production of
my own numb skull? . . . But since I have begun to play the critic, [and]
after impartial examination, I have discovered that many of the pieces
in that Book were never worth my printing, or your inspection.

This was the first collection of music to appear in the colonies
after the outbreak of hostilities, and Billings's political sympathies
were clear. The *New-England Psalm-Singer* had included a piece,
"Chester," with a text by Billings himself, that was to become one
of the most popular patriotic songs of the 1770s:

> Let tyrants shake their iron rod,
> And Slavr'y clank her galling chains,
> We fear them not, we trust in God,
> New England's God for ever reigns.

This was reprinted in Billings's new collection, with four added
stanzas referring to specific military events, and there were other
songs with patriotic texts. "Lamentation over Boston" begins with
a paraphrase of a famous passage in Psalm 137: "By the Rivers of
Watertown we sat down and wept, we wept when we remember'd
thee, O Boston." In "Retrospect," no fewer than nine biblical passages are pieced together and paraphrased into a narration
describing the British plan to cut the colonies in half and Burgoyne's failure to do so at Saratoga:

> Was not the Day dark and gloomy?
> The Enemy said, let us draw a line even from York to Canada.
> But praised be the Lord,
> the Snare is broken and we are escaped.

Such pieces gave the collection a character "nationalistic to a
degree unique among American tunebooks."[2]

His third book, *Music in Miniature* (1779, published by Billings
himself, Boston) was an even more modest effort. A tune supplement, it was intended for congregational singing. No texts were
given; psalm and hymn texts were to be fitted to tunes by matching meters. It was his only collection to contain music by other
composers: of seventy-four pieces, thirty-one were new tunes of his
own, thirty-two were reprinted from his two earlier collections,
and eleven were taken from other composers (ten of them European).

---

[2] McKay and Crawford, p. 80.

The *Psalm-Singer's Amusement* (Boston: Billings, 1781) was designed for experienced choirs or singing societies, rather than congregational singing or singing-school instruction. The collection contained some "Anthems, Fuges and Chorus's" promised by the composer since his first publication; most of the twenty-four pieces are lengthy, complex compositions. The *Suffolk Harmony* (Boston, 1786) marks a return to a simpler style of composition; the thirty-two pieces are predominantly homorhythmic settings of psalm and hymn texts. Though it had only one printing, it contained the most anthologized piece Billings ever wrote, "Jordan," a setting of a popular hymn by Isaac Watts. Billings's "Anthem for Easter," "far and away the most popular anthem by any American composer of the time,"[3] printed separately in 1787, is bound in the back of most extant copies.

Billings's music was now widely known. His compositions were sung on public concert programs in Boston, Philadelphia, and elsewhere; two of his pieces, "Marchfield" and "New England," were published in England, in Thomas Williams's *Psalmodia Evangelica* (London, 1789)—surely the first compositions by an American-born composer to be published abroad. But the absence of effective copyright legislation—the first comprehensive federal copyright bill did not come until 1790—prevented him from realizing any money from publication of his pieces in collections compiled by others. In 1786, he was appointed a street cleaner in the 11th Ward; the following year, he was given the position of "hogreeve," with the responsibility of seeing that pigs were properly penned and kept off the streets; a position with a more impressive title, Sealer of Leather, which he held from 1787 to 1796, was only part-time. By 1790 his plight was such that friends organized a "Concert of Sacred Musick, for the benefit of Mr. WILLIAM BILLINGS of this town—whose distress is real, and whose merit in that science, is generally acknowledged."[4] He was thus the first—but far from the last—American to discover that he could not support himself by musical composition alone.

His last publication, the *Continental Harmony* (Boston: Andrews and Thomas, 1794) was made possible through financial support from anonymous friends and admirers. Made up mostly of extended and difficult pieces intended for trained choirs and singing societies, this "large collection of new and elaborate music by America's foremost composer"[5] with its "store of vintage compositions" may "fairly be called an artistic success."[6] But its impact was slight:

[3] McKay and Crawford, p. 150.
[4] Notice in the *Columbian Centinel*, December 8, 1790.
[5] McKay and Crawford, p. 170.
[6] McKay and Crawford, p. 180.

no later editions followed the first, and only four of its fifty-one pieces were reprinted in other collections. Billings's wife died in 1795, leaving him with the care of six children, and "the father of our new England music"[7] died on September 27, 1800.

Several statistics will serve to underline his uniqueness: at the beginning of 1782, some 264 musical compositions by American-born writers had been published, 226 of them by Billings[8]; and of the some two hundred anthems published in America by 1810, more than a quarter were his.[9]

Like every other composer, Billings absorbed the music he knew during his formative years. Each of the several types of pieces contained in Billings's collections has obvious antecedents in the music of English composers of the eighteenth century.

Most of the compositions in the *New-England Psalm-Singer*, the *Singing Master's Assistant*, and *Music in Miniature* can be classified as "plain tunes"—simple homophonic, homorhythmic settings of the strophic and metrical texts of Tate & Brady and of Watts. At least half of these are simple, note-against-note, four-part harmonizations of diatonic tunes, similar in style to the sort of music sung in Britian and New England since the reform movement of the 1720s brought Regular Singing to the large city and town churches.[10] The style may be illustrated by the beginning of "Brookfield" (from the *Singing Master's Assistant*), one of the most popular pieces he ever wrote:

"Brookfield," by William Billings

---

[7] William Bentley, as quoted in McKay and Crawford, p. 186.
[8] McKay and Crawford, p. 139.
[9] McKay and Crawford, p. 96.
[10] For examples of pieces of this sort, cf. "Chesterfield" and "Richmond," on NW 255, s1 / 2 and s2 / 4.

Certain pieces in his first two collections are "fuging tunes"; these usually begin with a first section in the style of a "plain tune," and then, after a cadence and a pause, launch into a second section characterized by staggered entrances of the four voices, building up to block chords again at the close. Billings defines "fuge," in the Musical Dictionary included in the prefatory material to *Singing Master's Assistant,* as:

Notes flying after each other, altho' not always the same sound. N.B. Music is said to be Fuging, when one part comes in after another; its beauties cannot be numbered. It is sufficient to say, that it is universally pleasing.

"Washington,"[11] from the *Singing Master's Assistant,* is a good example of this style. The successive entrances have a similar rhythmic shape, but only a suggestion of melodic relationship:

"Washington," by William Billings

11 NW 255, s2 / 1.

For Billings, "fuging" sections were desirable in order to bring increased excitement, tension and variety to a composition. He wrote in the introduction to the *Continental Harmony:*

> It is an old maxim, and I think a very just one, viz. *that variety is always pleasing,* and it is well known that there is more variety in one piece of fuging music, than in twenty pieces of plain song, for while the tones do most sweetly coincide and agree, the words are seemingly engaged in a musical warfare; and excuse the paradox if I further add, that each part seems determined by dint of harmony and strength of accent, to drown his competitor in an ocean of harmony, and while each part is thus mutually striving for mastery, and sweetly contending for victory, the audience are most luxuriously entertained, and exceedingly delighted; in the mean time, their minds are surprizingly agitated, and extremely fluctuated; sometimes declaring in favour of one part, and sometimes another.—Now the solemn bass demands their attention, now the manly tenor, now the loftly counter, now the volatile treble, now here, now there, now here again.—O inchanting! O ecstatic! Push on, push on ye sons of harmony . . .

Forty-seven of Billings's compositions, even more complex and elaborate, are designated "anthems." Billings was neither the inventor of this form nor the first American composer to use it, but he wrote more of them than any other American composer of the day, and several achieved unmatched popularity.

The anthem had been popular in England throughout the eighteenth century, composed by such famous writers as Handel on the one hand and by obscure musicians at parish churches, on the other. It was, typically, a relatively brief work written for four-part unaccompanied chorus, though sometimes there was an organ accompaniment or instrumental doubling of one or more of the voice parts. The basic four-part homophonic texture (with melody in the tenor part) was varied by contrasting phrases for three, two, or even a solo voice, or by brief contrapuntal sections. The text—one or more portions of a Psalm or other biblical passage—was usually in prose; the music of each textual phrase or section usually contrasted in meter, texture, or key (flat or sharp). William Tans'ur was the most popular anthem composer in the colonies; fifteen of his anthems were printed here. William Knapp (11), Aaron Williams (7), and Joseph Stephenson (6) were other English writers of church music whose anthems were printed in America.[12]

The first anthems written by American composers were apparently an unpublished one written by Francis Hopkinson about 1760 and James Lyon's "Let the Shrill Trumpet's Warlike Voice," printed in his *Urania* in 1762.

The anthems in Billings's first two collections adhere to the description of the English anthem above, and to the extent that his later pieces depart from English style, they do so only in details. "Independence," from the *Singing Master's Assistant,* is typical with its contrasting tempos and rhythms in each section, its solo lines breaking up the prevailing four-part homophonic texture, and its bits of imitative counterpoint.[13]

Four canons in his first collection, including the widely popular "When Jesus Wept," were Billings's only attempts at pieces of this sort. If his music is "American," and in any way different from that written by his English predecessors and contemporaries, these differences were either in musical details or in more subtle areas involving their nature, spirit, character, or meaning.

---

[12] Cf. Ralph T. Daniel, *The Anthem in New England before 1800* (Evanston: Northwestern University Press, 1966). For a recent study of this music in its country of origin, cf. Nicholas Temperley, *The Music of the English Parish Church* (Cambridge: Cambridge University Press, 1979).

[13] Available on NW 276, s1 / 5.

Billings was a striking and unique character, even in physical appearance. The oft-quoted obituary written by the Rev. William Bentley describes him as:

> . . . a singular man, of moderate size, short of one leg, with one eye, without any address, & with an uncommon negligence of person. Still he spake & sung & thought as a man above the common abilities. He died poor & neglected & perhaps did too much neglect himself.[14]

A later writer, drawing on the testimony of people who had known him, filled in more details:

> Billings was somewhat deformed in person . . . with a mind as eccentric as his person was deformed. To say nothing of the deformity of his habits, suffice it to say, he had a propensity for taking snuff that may seem almost incredible, when in these days those that use it are not very much disposed to expose the article. He used to carry it in his coat-pocket, which was made of leather; and every few minutes, instead of taking it in the usual manner, with thumb and finger, would take out a handful and snuff it from between his thumb and clenched fist.[15]

As for the "eccentricity" of his mind, we can turn to his own words in the prefaces and introductions to his various tunebooks. He wrote openly and repeatedly about himself and his thoughts and actions in a style that was quite personal in mode of expression, syntax, even orthography. For instance, in pointing out that a given voice part reentering the musical fabric after several "empty bars" should sing its first notes with more accent and volume than otherwise, he inserts the observation:

> In fuging Music you must be very distinct and emphatic, not only in the Tune, but in the pronunciation; for if there happens to be a Number of greater Voices in the Concert than your own, they will swallow you up; therefore in such a case, I would recommend to you the resolution (tho' not the impudence) of a discarded Actor, who after he had been twice hissed off the Stage, mounted again, and with great Assurance he thundered out these words "I will be heard."[16]

His attitude toward composition was similarly idiosyncratic. Though he insisted that a writer must have a command of the

---

[14] William Bentley, *The Diary of William Bentley, D.D., Pastor of East Church, Salem, Massachusetts* (Salem: Essex Institute, 1905–14), II, pp. 350–51.

[15] Nathaniel D. Gould, *Church Music in America* (Boston: A. N. Johnson, 1853), p. 46.

[16] William Billings, *Singing Master's Assistant* (Boston: Draper and Folsom, 1778), Lesson XI.

materials and techniques necessary for putting together a piece of music, he emphasized that composition was a personal matter. Billings ended the introductory material to his first collection with a note "To all Musical Practitioners":

> *Nature is the best Dictator,* for all the hard dry studied Rules that ever was prescribed, will not enable any Person to form an Air any more than the bare Knowledge of the four and twenty Letters, and strict Grammatical Rules will qualify a Scholar for composing a Piece of Poetry, or properly adjusting a Tragedy, without a Genius. . . . For my own Part, as I don't think myself confin'd to any Rules for Composition laid down by any that went before me, neither should I think (were I to pretend to lay down Rules) that any who came after me were any ways obligated to adhere to them, any further than they should think proper: So in fact, I think it is best for every *Composer* to be his own *Carver.*

And some twenty-four years later, with almost all of his composition already written, he returned to the same theme:

> . . . although I am not confined to rules prescribed by others, yet I come as near as I possibly can to a set of rules which I have carved out for myself; but when fancy gets upon the wing, she seems to despise all form, and scorns to be confused or limited by any formal prescriptions whatsoever.[17]

The musical reformers of the 1710s and '20s had no particular desire to change the repertory of psalm singing, but merely to have singing done more "properly." But as the recent biographers of Billings pointed out, "New England religious leaders advocated the skill of note-reading as a guarantee of musical uniformity," but "that skill [became] just the opposite: an agent of musical diversity."[18] Billings could not have written his music had he not been musically literate, nor would it have been sung had there not been singing schools and congregations capable of "singing by note."

Billings wrote music passionately, as a form of self-expression—expression of his own religious, patriotic, and at times personal beliefs and feelings. Though his texts often glorify God, this praise is filtered through his personality and personal convictions, shaped by the idiosyncracies of his own character. Biblical texts are altered, if Billings believed they would be more effective in a different form.

Time and again Billings reveals, in his writings about music, an ecstatic, visceral, almost transcendental sense of his art. His excitement and passion break through the restraints of the written

[17] Billings, *Continental Harmony,* p. 31.
[18] McKay and Crawford, p. 24.

word in such passages as the following, taken from the *Continental Harmony*, in which the master is responding to a question put to him by a pupil—whether he prefers the flat (minor) or sharp (major) key:

> . . . let us suppose ourselves to be auditors to a company of musicians; how enraptured should we be to hear the sharp key, express itself in such lofty and majestic strains as these: *O come let us sing unto the Lord, let us make a joyful noise. . . . Sing unto the Lord all the earth, make a loud noise, rejoice and sing praise!* Do I hear the voice of men, or angels! surely such angelic sounds cannot yet proceed from the mouths of sinful mortals: but while we are yet warm with the thought, and ravished with the sound, the musicians change their tone, and the flat key utters itself in strains so moving, and pathetic, that it seems at least to command our attention to such mournful sounds as these: *Hear my prayer O Lord, give ear to my supplication . . . Have pity upon me, O ye my friends, for the hand of God hath touched me.* O how these sounds thrill through my soul! how agreeably they affect my nerves! how soft, how sweet, how soothing! methinks these sounds are more expressive than the other, for they affect us both with pleasure and pain, but the *pleasure* is so great it makes even *pain* to be pleasant, so that for the sake of the pleasure, I could forever bear the pain. But hark! what shout is that? It seems the sharp key is again upon the wing towards heaven; jealous, perhaps, that we pay too much deference to his rival: he not only desires, but *commands* us to join in such exalted strains as these. *Rejoice in the Lord, and again I say, rejoice, O clap your hands all ye people, shout unto God with the voice of triumph. . . .* What an ecstacy of joy may we suppose the Royal Author to be in when he composed this Psalm of praise! . . . The sharp and the flat key are so excellent each in its own way, that considering them in this light, though so different, they may (without impropriety) be said to excel each other.[19]

Billings's wild, manic flights of fancy sometimes took him even further afield. The introductory material to the *Singing Master's Assistant* contains a letter "To the Goddess of Discord." There had been criticism of Billings's lack of dissonances, so he informs "your uglyship" that he has composed a piece for the present volume "out of such materials as your kingdom is made up of" which will "fully compensate for my former delinquency." Instructions for performance follow:

> Let an Ass bray the bass, let the fileing of a saw carry the Tenor, let a hog who is extream hungry squeel the counter, and let a cart-wheel, which is heavy loaded, and that had been long without grease, squeek

---

[19] Billings, *Continental Harmony*, pp. 21–23.

the treble; and if the concert should appear to be too feeble you may add the cracking of a crow, the howling of a dog, the squalling of a cat; and what would grace the concert yet more, would be the rubbing of a wet finger upon a window glass.

The piece in question, "Jargon," is built of seconds, fourths, and sevenths, alone and in combination with consonant intervals.

Though the *music* of Billings appears similar to that of contemporary English composers, his written words suggest something quite different. We can resolve this apparent paradox by starting with the person and applying what we learn to the music, rather than the other way around. Knowing that Billings was passionately enthusiastic about music, manic, with an unbridled imagination, and that these traits carried over into his own singing ("[The Reverend Dr. Pierce of Brookline] said Billings had a stentorian voice, and when he stood by him to sing, he could not hear his own voice; and every one that ever heard Dr. Pierce sing . . . knows that his voice was not wanting in power."),[20] we can allow fervor and passion to dictate the interpretation of his music today, rather than restraint. Once this is done, the music begins to take on a different character; many of its musical details emerge in ways that remain hidden as long as the music remains on the printed page, or is sung in a "proper" manner.

The uniqueness of Billings's music is not to be found on the printed page, but in its sound. We have no direct way of knowing exactly how it sounded in eighteenth-century New England, but as is so often the case in America, oral tradition has preserved music and styles once thought to be lost. The singing school and much of its repertoire spread to the South and West in the early nineteenth century, and remnants of this tradition persevere to the present in remote areas of the rural South. To ears attuned to twentieth-century practices, a sound such as the Alabama Sacred Harp Convention singing Billings's "David's Lamentation"[21] will at first seem crude, harsh, insensitive, even unmusical. But if we compare such a performance, point by point—tempo, the timbres of the several voices, pronunciation, voice doubling—with Billings's instructions laid out in the prefaces to his tunebooks, we find close agreement on almost every point. And with closer familiarity with the style, a modern listener can begin to respond to the fervor and conviction that sets such a performance apart from most modern concert versions of Billings's music.

[20] Gould, p. 46.
[21] NW 205, s1 / 2.

The early 1770s were not productive years for psalmody and hymnody in America. The only significant new collection to appear between Billings's *New-England Psalm-Singer* of 1770 and the outbreak of the war was a tunebook printed in Newburyport in 1774, *Gentleman and Lady's Musical Companion*, compiled by John Stickney (1744–1827), a native of Stoughton. Stickney, a farmer and later a soldier in the Colonial Army, may have first learned music at a singing school taught by Billings, and for many years before and after the war conducted singing schools himself in the Connecticut River Valley in both Massachusetts and Connecticut. His tunebook was the largest collection of its kind published in America in the eighteenth century, with 140-odd psalm and hymn tunes and some thirty anthems; but aside from the inclusion of a dozen pieces by American writers, including four by Billings, it was an eclectic work, differing little from the earlier English collections of Tans'ur and Williams.

*Select Harmony* (Cheshire, Connecticut, 1779), the first tunebook brought out by Andrew Law (1748–1821), was a similar but smaller collection, with thirteen anthems by English composers included among its sixty-five works; compositions by Americans make up approximately a third of its contents, including thirteen pieces "purchased of the original compilers" and printed here for the first time.[22]

In the 1780s, the trickle of tunebooks compiled and published by Americans became a flood. In the words of a later, somewhat cynical observer of this phenomenon, "innumerable composuists, scarcely versed in the first principles of psalmody, sprung up on every side. The press groaned under the burden of their ponderous productions."[23] Hundreds of tunebooks were brought out in the last two decades of the eighteenth century and the first of the nineteenth. At first they appeared in Boston and its environs (some fifty tunebooks were printed in this area alone) and in towns scattered along the Connecticut River in Massachusetts and Connecticut; later they began to come out in other New England states.

Some were anthologies in the tradition of the prewar tunebooks of Tans'ur and Williams. *Laus Deo, or the Worcester Collection of Sacred Harmony*, published by Isaiah Thomas in Worcester in 1786—the first collection of this sort printed in America from movable type, rather than engraved plates—was an eclectic collection

[22] Descriptions and lists of contents of Laws's publications may be found in Richard A. Crawford, *Andrew Law, American Psalmodist* (Evanston: Northwestern University Press, 1968).

[23] Timothy Flint, *Columbian Harmonist* (Cincinnati: Coleman and Phillips, 1816), preface.

of English psalm and hymn tunes and anthems and also many American works, nineteen by Billings, for example. The preface includes the first historical assessment of Billings and his peers:

> Mr. WILLIAM BILLINGS, of Boston . . . was the first person we know of that attempted to compose Church Musick, in the New-England States; his musick has met with great approbation. . . . Several adepts in musick followed Mr. *Billing's* example, and the New-England States can now boast of many authors of Church Musick, whose compositions do them honour.[24]

A similar book was the *Chorister's Companion*, printed in New Haven by Simeon Jocelyn and Amos Doolittle in 1782; its mix of English and American works included twenty-four by Billings and several by the Massachusetts-born Lewis Edson—his popular fuging tunes "Lenox," "Bridgewater," and "Greenfield." Oliver Brownson's *Select Harmony*, published in New Haven in 1783 by Timothy and Samuel Green, was in the same mold, as was also *The Federal Harmony* (Boston, c. 1784).

Other tunebooks were made up in part or whole of pieces written by the compiler. The first American to follow Billings's lead in bringing out a collection entirely of his own compositions was Daniel Read (1757–1836), with his *American Singing Book* (New Haven, 1785), a "New and Easy Guide to the Art of Psalmody, Designed for the Use of Singing Schools in AMERICA," containing psalm and hymn tunes and two anthems. The following list is only a sample of the tunebooks published around the turn of the century that contain a substantial number of compositions by the compiler:

*The New American Melody* (Boston, 1789)—Jacob French
*American Harmony* (Boston: Isaiah Thomas & Ebenezer T. Andrews, 1792)  Oliver Holden
*Rural Harmony* (Boston: Isaiah Thomas & Ebenezer T. Andrews, 1793)—Jacob Kimball
*The Psalmodist's Companion* (Worcester, 1793)—Jacob French
*The Harmony of Maine* (Boston, 1794)—Supply Belcher
*The Responsary* (Worcester, 1795)—Amos Bull
*New England Harmonist* (Danbury, 1800)—Stephen Jenks
*New England Harmony* (Northampton, 1801)—Timothy Swan
*The Christian Harmony* (Exeter, New Hampshire, 1805)—Jeremiah Ingalls
These collections pale—quantitatively—before the work of Sam-

---

[24] Isaiah Thomas, *Laus Deo; or the Worcester Collection of Sacred Harmony* (Worcester: Isaiah Thomas, 1786), p. 1.

uel Holyoke (1762–1820), whose first collection, *Harmonia Americana* (Boston: Isaiah Thomas & Ebenezer T. Andrews, 1791), was a mere prelude to his mammoth *Columbian Repository of Sacred Harmony* (Exeter, New Hampshire: Henry Ranlet, 1803), which is nothing less than his setting to music of "the whole of Dr. Watts' Psalms and Hymns ... and some additional tunes suited to the particular meters in Tate and Brady's and Dr. Belknap's Collection of Psalms and Hymns"—732 compositions, in all!

These men were all native New Englanders. Some were college-educated: Andrew Law earned degrees from Rhode Island College (later Brown) and Yale; Jacob Kimball and Samuel Holyoke graduated from Harvard; Chauncey Langdon (the compiler of *Beauties of Harmony*) was a member of the Class of 1787 at Yale. Belknap, Belcher, Swan, Asahel Benham, Amos Bull had only a "common-school education." Some had served in the army during the Revolution: Daniel Read, Swan (a fifer), Kimball (a drummer boy). Their occupations were various: Law was an ordained minister, Belcher and Ingalls tavern keepers, Holden a carpenter, Swan a hatter, Belknap a farmer and mechanic, Read a librarian. Langdon studied law, became a judge, and was elected to the Connecticut State Legislature and to Congress; Holden served for many years in the Massachusetts House of Representatives; Belcher was also a member of the Massachusetts State Legislature. Justin Morgan taught reading and writing in district schools in Vermont, was a tavern-keeper, and bred horses—he developed the strain of Morgan horse, still popular. Benham, in the words of a biographer, "having no craft, devoted himself to teaching."[25]

Despite such diversity of education and vocation, these men all had certain important things in common. A recent writer has sketched a composite of the New England composer and tunebook compiler:

> He was Anglo-Celtic by lineage and Protestant (most likely Congregational) by religion. He was no professional musician but a tradesman who practiced music in his spare time. He was untutored in the ways of orthodox musical grammar, his only training probably having been picked up in singing schools like the ones he taught himself. He also studied music by other composers like himself, and he probably looked at some British treatises. ... He probably played no keyboard instrument. ... He embodied the qualities of independence and democracy, central elements of the image that Americans most like to associate with the Spirit of '76.[26]

[25] Frank J. Metcalf, *American Writers and Compilers of Sacred Music* (New York and Cincinnati: The Abington Press, 1925), p. 91.
[26] Richard Crawford, liner notes to NW 255, p. 1.

A somewhat more detailed portrait of one of these men, Timothy Swan, will serve to bring more clearly into focus just what sort of man turned to the composition of music in the decades immediately following the Revolution and what role music played in his life.

Swan, of second-generation Scottish stock, was born in Worcester, Massachusetts on July 23, 1758. After a few years of elementary school and a job as clerk in a country store, he moved with his family to Northfield. Upon the death of his father in 1774, he was placed in the care of an uncle in Groton, where he attended singing school for three weeks—his only "formal" musical training. After service in the Continental Army as a fifer, he became an apprentice hatter to his brother-in-law, Caleb Lyman, in Northfield, and it was here that he first wrote music:

> His first tune consisting of two parts, was composed at this time—and soon after others, with four parts followed. . . . They were made while engaged in his daily employment, by arranging in his mind a few notes, and setting them down from time to time, until the tune was completed. None of his music at this time was published but handed about in manuscript, and sung in private circles, , , , It was at this time he first heard of Billings as a composer, and felt such a desire to see him, that he was strongly tempted to run away from his brother in law.[27]

Moving to Connecticut, he settled in Suffield about 1780, remaining there some twenty-eight years. He continued to compose and to circulate his pieces in hand-written copies. Oliver Brownson visited him, writing to him afterwards, "I will tell you what I thought of you. I supposed you to be a man pretty well advanced with a wig on and a cocked hat"—Swan was in his late twenties! At any rate, Brownson's visit was fruitful· seven of Swan's pieces appeared in his *Select Harmony* (1783).

Two collections devoted to his own music eventually came out. *The Songster's Assistant* (Suffield: Swan and Ely, c. 1800) was a collection of twenty-two secular songs, and the *New England Harmony* (Northampton: Andrew Wright, 1801) contained all his known sacred pieces, those that had appeared in print elsewhere and a number of previously unpublished ones: forty psalm and hymn tunes, sixteen fuging tunes, and seven anthems and set pieces. Swan acted as agent himself; he was sent a total of 763

---

[27] Quoted in Guy Bedford Webb, *Timothy Swan: Yankee Tunesmith* (D.M.A. thesis, University of Illinois and Urbana-Champaign, 1972), p. 7. Most of my information comes from this source.

copies by the printer, of which 450 went out to various locations to be sold—but most of these seemed to have been returned. There was no second edition.

Dissolving the last of his several business ventures, a store selling "English and West India goods," Swan returned to Northfield. Again in business as a hatter, he may have taught singing schools, but there is no evidence of further musical composition. In retirement he became a well-known village character, an insatiable reader (particularly of Burns and other Scotch authors) who stayed up late and slept until noon, sometimes active in Masonic and political affairs, an infrequent church attender because of a feud with the pastor, a doughty old gentleman who always wore a hat, inside or out. He died on his eighty-fourth birthday, in 1842.

Swan and his fellow composers were content to write in the forms that had served Billings and his English predecessors and contemporaries so well. Most of the New England repertory consists of plain tunes—homophonic harmonizations of simple, straightforward tunes composed to fit metrical psalm texts and the hymns of Watts and others. These were intended for congregational singing and for singing-school pupils. A few have persisted in Protestant hymnody to the present.[28]

Of more interest to writers on American music and to choral groups that have revived the music of early New England composers are the fuging tunes. Something about these pieces—perhaps their energy, vigor, and propulsion—caused them to be viewed at the time, by both their supporters and detractors, as typically American products, despite their English origins. Many are available in recordings today, sung both by Southern shape-note singers who have kept this music in living tradition, and by modern concert groups who approach it with ears and voices attuned to European and American choral music styles of the two centuries between Billings's time and ours.[29]

Anthems and set pieces, longer and more complex settings of prose or metrical texts, make up a very small percentage of the repertory. These, too, are different only in details from anthems by

[28] Pieces of this type available on NW 255 are "Macedonia" by Oliver Holden (s2 / 5), "Summons" by Truman S. Wetmore (s2 / 7), and "Middletown" by Amos Bull (s2 / 8).

[29] On NW 205, as sung by the Alabama Sacred Harp singers are "Sherburne" by Read (s1 / 1), "Greenwich by Read (s2 / 1), and "Northfield" by Ingalls (s2 / 13); in "modern" performance on NW 255 are "Invitation" by Kimball (s1 / 5), "Montague" by Swan (s1 / 6), "Providence" by Read (s1 / 7), "New Jordan" by Shumway (s1 / 8), "Sunderland" by Strong (s2 / 3), and "Heroism" by Belcher (s2 / 2).

Billings and his English predecessors.[30] Much of this music has an oddly archaic sound. Two persistent characteristics contribute to this: the frequent use of the natural minor ("flat") key, and a fondness for chords built only of perfect consonances—octaves and fifths.

Since the flat key is different from either of the two scales perceived as "normal" by the nineteenth and twentieth centuries (the major and minor), and is encountered most often in either older music or in "folk" music not bound by the restraints of those two scales, a tune such as the following sounds ancient or folklike:

"Vermont" (anonymous)

Sharps were sometimes used by Billings and his contemporaries to bring a tune into the harmonic minor. But accidental sharps and flats proved to be confusing for some musicians in the early days of the new republic; some compilers simply refused to print them, and even when they did appear, they were often disregarded by pupil and master alike. Timothy Swan, for one, saw them as a needless complication: not a single accidental sharp or flat appears in his *New England Harmony*.

Beyond this, many tunes of this repertory have other characteristics generally attributed to folk music. The tune of Swan's "Montague"—one of his most popular pieces, printed in fifteen different tunebooks before it came out in his own collection—is based on a pentatonic scale on D, missing the fourth and sixth degrees (G and B flat):

[30] Several pieces of this type are available on NW 276: "Warren" by Wood (s2 / 3) and "A Hymn on Peace" by Wood (s2 / 5); and on NW 255: "An Anthem of Praise" by Belcher (s1 / 1), "Crucifixion" by Kyes (s1 / 4), and "Ode on Martyrdom" by King (s2 / 6).

"Montague," by Timothy Swan

This scale permeates not only the melody, but the other voices as well; the harmonization avoids these fourth and sixth degrees, touching on them only in passing.

"Montague," by Timothy Swan

And other tunes—"Love Divine" by Jeremiah Ingalls, for instance—are not only based on pentatonic scales, but proceed in rhythms reminiscent of dances of the day:

"Love Divine," by Jeremiah Ingalls

The fondness for perfect intervals in building chords may be traced directly to theoretical writings of earlier centuries, by way of Tans'ur and Morley. Billings writes:

> There are but four Concords, in Musick, viz. the Unison, Third, Fifth and Sixth, their Eighths or Octaves are also meant. The Unison is call'd a perfect Chord, the Fifth is also call'd a Perfect Chord, the Third and Sixth are call'd Imperfect, their Sounds being not so full and Sweet as the Perfect.[31]

It is astonishing enough to read, in the lifetime of Mozart and Haydn, that thirds and sixths are not as "full and Sweet" as octaves, unisons, and fifths. It is even more astonishing to observe that this concept is not merely a theoretical one, but a matter of musical practice and preference. Piece after piece proceeds, harmonically, in this style:

"Northfield," by Daniel Read

Such pieces—based on or suggesting folk tunes in their melodic lines and rhythms, harmonized with frequent imperfect triads, sung with vigor and fervor—were built on elements brought over from the British Isles, but they are somehow different, in sound and spirit.

No sooner was this lively and native school of composition launched by Billings and his peers than the same forces that had attacked Usual Singing some seventy years earlier—religious and educational leaders of Boston and its environs—launched a similar attack on the only indigenous American music to have emerged in the young country.

Andrew Law was the first to register dismay. His first tunebook (*Select Harmony*, 1779) had contained a goodly selection of pieces by Americans, Billings among them. But the number of American

---

[31] William Billings, *New-England Psalm-Singer* (Boston: Edes and Gill, 1770), p. 17.

pieces in his subsequent publications dropped off dramatically, and his *Musical Primer* (1793) contained an out-and-out attack on native composition and singing:

> European compositions aim at variety and energy by guarding against the reiterated use of the perfect cords. Great numbers of the American composers, on the contrary, and as it were, on purpose to accommodate their music for harsh singing, have introduced the smooth and perfect cords, till their tunes are all sweet, languid and lifeless; and yet, these very tunes, because they will better bear the discord of grating voices, are actually prefered, and have taken a general run, to the great prejudice of much better music, produced even in this country, and almost to the utter exclusion of genuine European compositions. . . . Sing the sweet-corded tunes of this country in sweet toned voices, and they will immediately cloy, sicken and disgust.[32]

Law attempted to alter the style of American singing by publishing instructions in "proper" vocal techniques and by stressing these in his own singing schools.

> The harshness of our singing must be corrected. Our voices must be filed. Every tone must be rendered smooth, persuasive and melting: and when a number of voices are joined together, they must all have the same pitch, or in other words, must be in the most perfect tune. Then, nor till then, shall we sing well, and be able to distinguish between compositions of genuine merit, and those that are merely indifferent.[33]

William Bentley, writing in his diary on May 23, 1796 after a public demonstration of "proper" singing by one of Law's classes in Salem, was struck by the enormous difference between their sound and what one was accustomed to hearing in other singing schools:

> He aims to have his music very soft, & the Treble is the leading part, not one note of tenour was heard through the Evening. The greatest good order prevailed, & the visiting Company was respectable. In their attempts to sing soft, many of the voices do not accent the notes so as to enable the ear to distinguish the strains from soft murmurs. He must have had above one hundred scholars.[34]

By now others had joined in the cry. William Cooper wrote in the preface to his *Beauties of Church Music* (Boston: Manning & Loring, 1804), "It has become a general opinion among good singers,

---

[32] Andrew Law, *Musical Primer* (Philadelphia: Robert and William Carr, 1793), p. 8.

[33] Law, p. 8.

[34] Bentley, *Diary*, II, pp. 184–85.

that the music in use before the revolution in 1775, is much better than that which has succeeded." The *Salem Collection* (Salem: Joshua Cushing, 1805) contained eighty-four pieces of church music, all by Europeans, and a preface attacking the "general and most deplorable corruption of taste in our church music." John Hubbard, a professor at Dartmouth College, helped found a Handel Society at that school in 1807, with the stated purpose of performing the best European music. Oliver Shaw took out a charter in 1815 for the Psallonian Society, which for sixteen years rehearsed and performed the music of the "best and most approved European masters"—Handel, Haydn, Mozart, and Beethoven. One of his pupils, Thomas Webb, removed to Boston, becoming the first president of the Boston Handel & Haydn Society, which offered its first public program in 1815. The attitude of this group toward Billings may be sampled in the official history of the organization:

> When Billings got the upper hand with his so-called fugue-ing tunes, hearts did indeed go "diddle-diddle," and wild were their dances. The paramount influence obtained by William Billings . . . is partly to be ascribed to the political enmities of the time, to his own zealous patriotism, and to the friendship and support of Samuel Adams. . . . His tunes and fugue-lings are what might be expected as the work of an uneducated man who knew but little of the laws of harmony, modulation, or the preparation and resolution of discords, and who had had no opportunities of purifying his taste or correcting the false theories.[35]

And it is made clear that such defects were a characteristic of American music in general; the state of music in New England during the first two decades of the nineteenth century was:

> a scandalous mockery of psalmody, led by a barrel organ or an incompetent professor . . . singing flat with a nasal twang, straining the voice to an unnatural pitch, introducing continual drawls and tasteless ornaments, trilling on each syllable, running a third above the written note; and thus, by a sort of triplet, assimilating the time to a Scotch reel, etc., etc.[36]

Thomas Hastings (1784–1872) was a central figure in this new reform movement. Born in Connecticut, he grew up in the village of Clinton, New York, where he led the village choir and a local musical society from the time he was eighteen. He put together a small collection of his own compositions, the *Utica Collection*, which

[35] Charles C. Perkins and John S. Dwight, *History of the Handel and Haydn Society of Boston, Massachusetts* (Boston: Alfred Mudge & Son, 1883–93), I, pp. 21–22.
[36] Perkins and Dwight, p. 26.

was later combined with *The Springfield Collection* (1813), a selection of sacred works by British composers compiled by Solomon Warriner of Springfield, Massachusetts. The result, *Musica Sacra; or, Springfield and Utica Collections United*, was published in Utica in 1819. An immediate success, it went into a new edition almost every year for some two decades.

At first glance, this book seems to be very much in the style of tunebooks from Billings's era: there are psalm and hymn tunes, and some anthems and set pieces, prefaced by brief instruction in the rudiments of music. But the New England repertory has disappeared—there are no pieces by Billings or Read or Swan. Identified composers are Purcell, Shrubsole, Handel, D. Clark, Tallis, Dr. Arnold, Madan, Arne, Dr. Callcott, Pleyel, Giardini, Haydn; the unattributed tunes prove to be by these same men or by American writers such as Hastings himself. There are no fuging tunes.

Hastings was a gentle reformer. An articulate man, despite his limited formal education, and deeply devout, he couched his attacks on American composers and his pleas for a new style of church music in temperate language, always affirming the religious and intellectual basis for his views:

> The distinguished composer does not usually set himself at work without a definite object and a corresponding design; and, like the skilful writer or eloquent speaker, he endeavors to accommodate himself as far as may be, to the science, taste, and susceptibility of those for whom his piece is chiefly intended.... The man of inferior talent pursues a different course. Imagining himself to excell in genius or practical skill, his object is similar to that of a superficial writer or conceited orator, who is more anxious to display himself than to elucidate his subject. ... Unhappily, however, musical science and taste are yet in a state of infancy among us: hence, men of inferior talent often succeed in practising upon the public credulity.
>
> Music is a language of feeling. When cultivated *merely* for the purpose of personal gratification, emolution, distinction or display, it is of course liable, in many instances, to awaken among its patrons and devotees some of the baser passions of the human heart; but when it is cultivated strictly for social and beneficial purposes, and especially for the promotion of the praise and glory of God, and the edification of his people, its tendencies are necessarily and decidedly of the opposite nature. It strengthens the social principle. It awakens sympathy, cherishes affection, and contributes to mutual gratification and refined enjoyment.[37]

[37] Thomas Hastings, *Dissertation on Musical Taste* (New York: Mason Brothers, 1853), pp. 13, 290.

As Hastings's fame grew, he moved to the larger city of Utica and then to New York (1832), where he advised the choirs of twelve churches. He directed the choir of the Bleeker Street Presbyterian Church for many years, published other collections almost until his death, and was awarded an honorary Doctorate of Music by the University of the City of New York in 1858. Several of his hymns have remained in common use to the present, including "Toplady," the tune most often used for the hymn "Rock of Ages."

The moving force of the reform movement, however, was Lowell Mason—a man who had as much impact on the musical life of nineteenth-century America as any other person.

Born in Medfield, Massachusetts on January 8, 1792, into a musical family—his father was a church-choir singer, his grandfather had taught singing schools—Lowell attended singing school himself. Mason's own copy of the *Norfolk Collection of Sacred Harmony* (Dedham, Massachusetts, 1805) is preserved, with his inscription: "This is the book used in first singing school I ever attended, which was taught by Amos Albee, the compiler. I must have been thirteen years old then . . ."[38]

Moving to Savannah, Georgia in 1812, he became a bank clerk, studied music with the German immigrant F. L. Abel, and became organist and choirmaster at the Independent Presbyterian Church. In his spare time he compiled a collection of church music; some pieces were taken from English collections, some were adapted from instrumental and vocal works by classical composers, some were new compositions. Mr. W. M. Goodrich, a Boston organ builder who had come to Savannah to install a new instrument, urged him to show his collection to members of the Boston Handel and Haydn Society. Dr. George K. Jackson, the organist for that organization, gave it his stamp of approval:

> The selection of tunes is judicious; it contains all the old approved English melodies that have long been in use in the church, together with many compositions from modern English authors. The whole are harmonized with great accuracy, truth, and judgement, according to the acknowledged principles of musical science. . . . It is much the best book I have seen published in this country.[39]

Five days later, on October 10, 1821, the Society signed an agreement with Mason to publish the book, under the title of *Boston Handel and Haydn Society Collection of Church Music*. Mason was

[38] Quoted in Metcalf, p. 154.
[39] Perkins and Dwight, pp. 81–82.

not to be identified as the compiler, since "I was then a bank officer in Savannah, and did not wish to be known as a musical man."[40] But within five years the collection had earned more than $4,000; eventually it went through twenty-two editions, selling more than fifty thousand copies and bringing some $30,000 to Mason and the Society, both consequently enjoying financial stability beyond their wildest dreams.

The preface, explaining that the Handel and Haydn Society had been "instituted for the purpose of improving the style of Church Music," suggests that while many valuable tunebooks have appeared, and "while much attention has been bestowed upon the selection of appropriate Melodies, it is evident that a corresponding attention has not been paid to correct Harmony."

> Of late years however, a great change has taken place in the public sentiment with regard to the importance of psalmody, and this has of course called the attention of the most eminent masters in England to the subject. Several of them have been recently employed in harmonizing anew, many of the old standard airs, and also in selecting and adapting movements from the works of Handel, Haydn, Mozart, Beethoven, and other great masters, whose mighty talents have been displayed and acknowledged throughout Europe.[41]

There are pieces attributed to Tallis and Thorley; to Corelli and Dr. Croft; to Haydn, Handel, and Harwood; to Mozart and Milgrove; to Giordini and Dr. Green; to Pleyel, Pergolesi, and W. Paxton; to Boyce and Dr. Blow and Beethoven; to Purcell and Jeremiah Clark, Viotti and Dr. Heighington. The first two-thirds of the pieces are homophonic, four-voice settings of psalm and hymn tunes, the remainder are anthems. All chords comprise complete triads, sometimes even seventh chords; the bass line is figured, to facilitate organ accompaniment. There is absolutely no trace of the repertory or style of the New England school of Billings and his contemporaries; the only American composer identified is Mason himself.

Many pieces attributed to "classical" composers were fashioned from fragments of melodies from instrumental or vocal works, wrenched out of context, whittled into simple sectional form to fit one of the metrical schemes into which sacred texts were cast, and reharmonized in the style of nineteenth-century English hymnody. "Bradford," for example, was carved from "I Know That My

[40] Perkins and Dwight, p. 82.

[41] Lowell Mason, *The Boston Handel and Haydn Society Collection of Church Music* (Boston: Richardson and Lord, 1822), p. iv.

Redeemer Liveth" from Handel's *Messiah,* forced into a four-phrase pattern to accommodate a CM (Common Meter, or 8.6.8.6.) text; the text was subjected to the same treatment, using only the first line from the oratorio.

"Bradford," adapted from Handel

In an address delivered in Boston in 1825, Mason confronted the issue of whether "the whole congregation be encouraged to join promiscuously, in this exercise?—or shall it be committed to a select choir?" Since congregational singing, as usually done, is "a jargon of sound . . . produced by a large assembly of all ages and descriptions, engaged each one in singing as seems good in his own eyes," it follows that "it is necessary, then, that in every church there should be a choir of cultivated singers." But this is not enough; it is also desirable that "others, sitting below, should join, provided they are qualified to do this with propriety and effect." As a matter of fact, all persons "should be invited and urged to sing: it is their duty to sing, to pray, to repent, to believe." *"Children must be taught music, as they are taught to read"* (italics mine). And congregational participation will be facilitated if there is "a small number of simple, easy, and solemn, tunes selected for the use of the choir in public worship. New tunes may be occasionally introduced . . . A change should be constantly going on, but it should be so gradual as to be almost imperceptible." If these steps are taken, "the songs of Zion will lie no longer neglected."[42]

The "simple, easy, and solemn" pieces found in the collections of Hastings and Mason—harmonized in four parts with completely triadic chords, and purged of any trace of "fuging" techniques—established a style of Protestant hymnody that has remained virtually unchanged for a century and a half. Such hymns by Mason as "Bethany" ("Nearer My God to Thee"),[43] "Missionary Hymn" ("From Greenland's Icy Mountains"), and "Olivet" ("My Faith Looks Up to Thee") are still sung today, in their original harmonization, without arousing the slightest feeling that they are in any way different from other pieces in modern hymnals.

No hymn writer of the entire nineteenth century was more successful than Mason. The *Hymnal of the Methodist Episcopal Church* of 1878 contains 68 of his original hymns and 22 of his arrangements of tunes by other writers; these represent three times the total of the next three most popular hymn composers combined. Even so late a collection as the *Methodist Hymnal* of 1935 contains 32 of his hymns.[44]

In 1827 three Boston churches—the Essex Street, the Hanover Street and the Park Street churches—invited him to come to Boston to be in charge of their music. He accepted, though he also took a position as a bank teller, in case his new career as a church musician did not prove to be sufficiently lucrative.

He moved quickly to the center of Boston's musical life and soon built his choirs to such a level that:

> Pilgrimages were made from all parts of the land to hear the wonderful singing. Clergymen who attended ministerial gatherings in Boston carried home with them oftentimes quite as much musical as spiritual inspiration.[45]

He was elected president of the Handel and Haydn Society in 1827, holding the post until 1832. One of his first actions was to:

[42] Lowell Mason, *Address on Church Music* (Boston: Hilliard, Gray, Little, and Wilkins, 1827), *passim*.

[43] NW 224, s2 / 7.

[44] Robert Stevenson, *Protestant Church Music in America* (New York: W. W. Norton & Company, 1966), pp. 80–81.

[45] Theodore F. Seward, *The Educational Work of Dr. Lowell Mason* (n.p., n.d.), p. 9.

... hire a room furnished with a pianoforte, where he could meet and instruct such members as in his judgement were likely to become proficient in the art of singing. ... First and foremost, he was not so very much superior to the members as to be unreasonably impatient at their shortcomings. Second, he was a born teacher, who by hard work had fitted himself to give instruction in singing. Third, he was one of themselves, a plain, self-taught man, who could understand them and be understood of them.[46]

Mason was determined to bring about universal musical literacy through the education of children. His first singing schools for children were organized among church congregations in Boston; within a few years, the number of children in these rose from fewer than a dozen to five or six hundred. His first book designed for children was written for these classes: *Juvenile Psalmist; or, the Child's Introduction to Sacred Music* (1829).

With George J. Webb and other local musicians, Mason organized the Boston Academy of Music in 1832. Some fifteen hundred children took advantage of the free musical instruction offered by the Academy in its first year, and the organization pushed for "the introduction of vocal music, as an ordinary branch of study, into common schools—not only those under private patronage, but public schools generally."[47] Five years later, Mason taught without charge at the Hawes School as a test of his theories and methods. At the end of the year, the principal reported to the mayor:

Many who at the onset of the experiment believed they had neither ear nor voice, now sing with confidence and considerable accuracy; and others who could hardly tell one sound from another, now sing the scale with ease. ... The alacrity with which the lesson is entered upon, and the universal attention with which it is received, are among its great recommendations.[48]

As a result, Mason was appointed Superintendent of Music in the Boston public schools in September of 1838. Boston was thus the first American town in which training in music became part of the normal instruction of children.

He held this post until 1845, sharing instruction with other members of the Boston Academy. His own assessment of the effect of this most massive attack yet on musical illiteracy, made some

[46] Perkins and Dwight, pp. 95–96.
[47] Boston Academy of Music, *Annual Reports* (Boston: various publishers), II (1834), p. 18.
[48] Boston Academy of Music, *Annual Reports*, VI, pp. 8–9.

Lowell Mason.

thirteen years after the inauguration of music teaching in the public schools, seems fair:

> The result already is, that a multitude of young persons have been raised up who . . . are much better able to appreciate and to perform music than were their fathers; and experience proves that large classes of young persons, capable of reading music with much accuracy may be easily gathered in almost any part of New-England.[49]

Mason's public school teaching methods were the same as those he had used so successfully in earlier situations, modified by his interest in the pedagogical methods of the Swiss music educator Pestalozzi: drill in the fundamentals of musical notation; simple scales and other patterns as a first step toward sight reading; simple unison and two-part pieces introduced as soon as possible, to help maintain the pupils' interest; and the use of a repertory made

[49] Mason, *Address on Church Music*, p. 16.

up of adaptations of pieces by European composers and new compositions in the same style by Mason and some of his contemporaries. Typical is the following, taken from his *Juvenile Singing School* (Boston: J. H. Wilkins & R. B. Carter, 1837):

"Shall We Oppressed with Sadness," adapted from Mozart

Mason's song literature for children was moralistic in character. Though he observed the distinction between school and church, and sacred songs are almost never found in his earliest juvenile collections, these latter are shot through with such texts as:

> Before all lands in east or west,
> I love my native land the best,
> With God's best gifts 'tis teeming;
> No gold nor jewels here are found,
> Yet men of noble soul abound,
> And eyes of joy are gleaming. (pp. 72 3)

> If I've fulfilled my daily task aright,
> And every duty done;
> Then joy to me when darkest shades of night
> Shall cloud the sinking sun!
> How cheering, then, how calming
> The golden lingering ray;
> The eventide is charming
> That ends a well spent day.

Designed specifically for use in the Boston public schools were *Musical Exercises for Singing Schools* (1838), and *The Boston School*

*Song Book* (1840), the latter designed to "introduce the singing of suitable songs as a relief from the severer study of the elements and as a exercise for the voice; also, as a means of improving the general taste and style of performance."

Mason's later publications included *The Boston Academy's Collection of Church Music* (twelve editions between 1835 and 1863), yet another anthology of psalm and hymn tunes and anthems; *The Boston Academy's Collection of Choruses* (1836), devoted to difficult pieces for experienced choirs; *The Boston Glee Book* (1838), glees, madrigals and rounds for social singing; and *The Song-Garden* (1864), probably the first graded (progressively arranged) series of school music books. The general musical literacy he was helping to foster resulted in a steadily expanding market for such books; *Carmina Sacra* alone sold more than 500,000 copies of its thirteen editions, between 1841 and 1860. Mason found himself a wealthy man by mid-century—the first American to amass a fortune from music.

Other men emulated his methods. William B. Bradbury (1816–68), for instance—born in York, Maine—took instruction in music through the Boston Academy of Music and eventually found his way to New York, where he undertook the musical education of young children on a large scale. His books—some sixty were published between 1841 and 1867—were aimed at the same markets that Mason tapped with such profit. There were books for children (*The Young Choir*, the *Sunday School Choir*); eclectic collections, for church choirs and musical societies (the *Shawn*, *The Jubilee*); collections of simple psalm and hymn settings, for congregational use (*The Devotional Hymn and Tune Book*). Like Mason, he mixed adaptations of European pieces and his own compositions.[50] His success approached that of Mason: it has been estimated that more than two million copies of his various publications were sold, including 250,000 of a single collection, *The Jubilee;* his own hymn tunes were second only to Mason's in dissemination during the nineteenth century.

Almost exactly a century after Regular Singing was introduced into New England churches Law, Hastings, Mason, and Bradbury sought to accomplish a second reform. Much has been made of the fact that they favored European music over American, that their efforts helped turn American musical taste back to European products. But Mason was, in his own eyes, first and foremost a com-

[50] Cf. his "Woodworth" on NW 224, s2 / 9.

poser. His activities as educator, organist, lecturer, compiler, and essayist revolved around his continuing productivity as a writer of hymns. History has justified him: of the thousands of pieces printed in his various collections, his own hymns sank deepest into American culture.

No matter what sources he turned to for his own musical vocabulary, Mason was doing nothing more and nothing less than every American composer of the past two centuries has done—drawing on other music for guidance and inspiration. He must be taken seriously as one of the most successful American composers of the entire century.

In the end, the chief issue with Mason and his fellow reformers was not their suppression of the psalms, hymns, and anthems of Billings and his fellow New England composers. Their criticisms of the "old ways" were more often of the *manner* of singing—vocal production, ornamentation, pitch, the changing of written notes by individual singers—than of the repertory, which was dying anyway. Their teaching methods, publications, and public pronouncements were based wholly on the premise that music should be a literate art, that nonliterate music was inferior to literate music, that universal musical literacy was the only way to improve the art in America.

The drive for universal musical literacy helped change and shape the character of music in America for the next century; it led to many positive accomplishments. At the same time, it was a powerful force in strengthening a dichotomy that was to mark Ameri-

Choir of the old First Congregational Church of Aurora, Illinois singing from a reform collection. ca. 1854.

can musical life well into the twentieth century, a dichotomy between the literate and the nonliterate, between music in written tradition and that in oral tradition.

# 7

# *The Origins and Beginnings of American Popular Song*

The first music to take on a typically American character was popular song. By the middle of the nineteenth century American singers were traveling to England to perform programs of their own works, and European songwriters were incorporating stylistic elements of this new music into their own compositions.

The story of indigenous popular song in the New World has the same shape as that of virtually every other sort of music with which this book is concerned: the importation of European music to America; the composition of pieces in a similar style here; and the shaping of a native style from elements of several different national or ethnic styles.

The first songs performed and published in America were brought from England—the pleasure garden songs of Thomas Arne and James Hook; airs from ballad and comic operas by Samuel Arnold, William Reeve, William Shield, and Charles Dibdin; concert songs by Dibdin, Hook, and Reginald Spofford. They were sung in the same settings as in Great Britain: in pleasure gardens, on the stage, on concert programs of mixed instrumental and vocal music. Beginning in the 1780s, they were printed and sold here in the form of sheet music, arranged for voice and keyboard accompaniment, sung by musical amateurs in their parlors for the amusement of themselves and their friends. The style had developed mostly in London, forged out of eighteenth-century musical elements: Italian opera and song, the vocal lines of Handel, and English songs by Purcell and his successors.

James Hook, "Listen, Listen to the Voice of Love"

Irish and Scottish song became increasingly popular at the turn of the century. The *Irish Melodies* of Thomas Moore (1779–1852) were published in Dublin and London in a series of volumes brought out between 1807 and 1834; they were traditional Irish tunes fitted to new texts by Moore, with keyboard accompaniments by Sir John Stevenson and Sir Henry Bishop. With their haunting and often familiar tunes and their delicate texts dealing mostly with nostalgia for lost youth and faded hopes, they were among the best-loved songs in the English language of the entire century, in the United States as well as in Great Britain. "The Last Rose of Summer," "Believe Me If All Those Endearing Young Charms," and "The Minstrel Boy" are merely three of several dozen to penetrate deeply into English-speaking culture around the globe.

A handful of the songs of Robert Burns (1759–96) also became popular at this time. Like Moore, Burns fitted his own poems to folk tunes, the results first appearing in various issues of the *Scots Musical Museum* between 1787 and 1803; among them were "Auld Lang Syne," "Coming thru the Rye," "John Anderson, My Jo," and "Scots What Hae wi' Wallace Bled." Other Scottish songs, most of them anonymous arrangements of traditional airs such as "The Blue Bell of Scotland," appeared also in the last decades of the eighteenth century and the first of the nineteenth.

Compared to the elegant, formalized music and texts of English song, these Irish and Scottish airs were earthy, direct in expression, and closer to the oral-tradition songs and ballads known to many Americans. James Hewitt, in the preface to *The Music of Erin*, warned his public that they might find the tunes he had arranged "wildly inelegant, or barbarously simple," but he found in them a "singular and plaintive beauty, a characteristic wildness and melting pathos," and he concluded:

> If the excellence of musical composition is to be estimated by the effect it produces on the human mind, by its power over the passions, or its influence over the heart, the Irish melodies, it must be allowed, graduate to a very high degree on the scale of musical excellence.[1]

Another national music flowered in Great Britain and the United States in the second, third, and fourth decades of the nineteenth century. The popular song repertory had already included an occasional piece fashioned from opera; "Away with Melancholy," an air from Mozart's *The Magic Flute* fitted with an English text, had been a popular item of sheet music since its first publication in America in the late 1790s, for instance. But the great operas of Rossini, Bellini, and Donizetti inspired an absolute craze for Italian melody. Manuel Garcia brought the New World its first taste of "modern" Italian opera when his troupe performed works by Rossini in New York and elsewhere, in 1825; Lorenzo Da Ponte, librettist of several of Mozart's late operas, had settled in New York and was responsible for the establishment of the first resident Italian operatic troupe in the city, in 1832; and a succession of other companies offered a steady stream of Italian operas to cities on the East Coast until the establishment of permanent companies in the 1850s.

At the same time, theaters all over America were offering English versions of favorite Italian operas, fashioned by Henry Bishop, Rophino Lacy, and others. In addition, several operas in the Italian style by British composers enjoyed tremendous popularity— Michael Balfe's *The Bohemian Girl* (1843) and William Vincent Wallace's *Maritana* (1845). Music publishers found a wide market for songs based on Italian operatic airs, from the first publication of a song from a Rossini opera in 1818 ("Here We Meet Too Soon to Part," from *Tancredi*) through almost a dozen songs from Bellini's *Norma* and almost as many from Donizetti's *Daughter of the Regiment*, right up to mid-century with songs based on early Verdi operatic arias.

---

[1] James Hewitt, *The Music of Erin* (New York, 1807), p. 2.

German *lied* also became popular in America. Songs by Franz Schubert ("Last Greeting," "Ave Maria," "Serenade"), Franz Abt ("When the Swallows Homeward Fly," "O! Ye Tears") and Friedrich Wilhelm Kücken ("Good Night, Farewell") were particular favorites as items of sheet music, with texts translated into English.

A second generation of British song writers flooded the American market with their products. Chief among these was Sir Henry Bishop (1786–1855), whose "Home, Sweet Home" was the single most popular song of the English-speaking world of the entire nineteenth century, allegedly selling more than 100,000 copies in America in the year following its publication in 1823 and a total of several million before the century had closed. Nor was this his only success; dozens of other songs sold well for a number of decades, among them "Love Has Eyes," "The Bloom Is on the Rye" and "My Pretty Jane." An older contemporary, John Braham (1774–1856), one of the most highly praised tenors of the day, wrote the most popular duet of the first part of the century—"All's Well," from his opera *The English Fleet in 1342*—and many other servicable songs. Samuel Lover (1797–1868) was the most successful Irish songwriter after Thomas Moore, contributing such perennial favorites as "Rory O'More" and "The Low-back'd Car." Like Moore, he wrote his own lyrics and performed his own songs on the stage as part of his "Irish Evening" in Great Britain and America. Charles Edward Horn (1786–1849), son of a German musician who had emigrated to England, wrote hundreds of songs of every sort, including "Cherry Ripe" and "I've Been Roaming." And there was Claribel—Charlotte Alington Barnard (1830–69)—the best female songwriter of the century whose output included such popular items as "I Cannot Sing the Old Songs," "Take Back the Heart" and "Come Back to Erin."

As living standards and musical literacy increased among the middle classes, more homes boasted family members who could sing and play the piano and who could afford to buy sheet music. Increasingly, songs were written with home performance in mind. Given the technical limitations of most amateurs, works designed for this market were often simpler, both in vocal line and accompaniment, than had been the case earlier in the century. Publishers also began to bring out simple arrangements of vocal pieces written for stage performance by professional singers. Though the distinction between classical and popular music was not as great as it would be in the twentieth century, one begins to see in the songs of a composer like Henry Bishop a clear distinction between vocal pieces written for professional performance and those headed for the living room, and most of Samuel Lover's and Claribel's songs were of limited range and low tessitura with relatively simple piano accompaniments.

The history of songwriting in America is best seen against this background of the continuing importation of songs of various national schools of melody.

Francis Hopkinson (1737–91), the first person known to have written songs for voice and keyboard in America, was a signer of the Declaration of Independence and the first Secretary of the Navy. While a student at the College of Philadelphia, he copied out some 100 pieces for voice and keyboard by Handel, Thomas Arne, Henry Purcell, William Boyce, and other composers popular in London in the middle of the eighteenth century. This manuscript also contains six works otherwise unknown, marked with the initials "F.H.", assumed to have been written by Hopkinson himself. Dating from about 1760, they are similar in style to the other songs in the manuscript, and were never published or circulated in any other way. Thus, though they are historical curiosities, they played no role in the history of song in America.[2]

Hopkinson's *Seven Songs for Harpsichord*, published in Philadelphia in 1788, bear a dedication to George Washington, and a remark in the preface:

If this Attempt should not be too severely treated, others may be encouraged to venture on a Path, yet untrodden in America, and the Arts in Succession will take root and flourish amongst us.

Though still reminiscent of the pastoral, amorous, and hunting songs of James Hook and his English contemporaries, they are substantial compositions and enjoyed some popularity at least within Hopkinson's circle. Like other songwriters, he hoped his creations would touch the passions; in a letter to Thomas Jefferson he described himself as "an Author who composes from his Heart, rather than his Head."[3]

There is no evidence that Hopkinson's songs were performed publicly, in concert or on the stage. But there were songs written in America in the first two or three decades of the new republic that were performed professionally and enjoyed some financial success from sales of sheet music. These were the work of immi-

[2] The first of these, "My Days Have Been So Wondrous Free," is available in Oliver Daniel (editor), *Songs by Francis Hopkinson* (New York: Carl Fischer, 1951).

[3] Three of these ("Beneath a Weeping Willow's Shade," "My Love Is Gone to Sea" and "O'er the Hills Far Away") are available in Daniel, *Songs by Francis Hopkinson*. The entire set of eight has been recorded on Cambridge Records (CAM. 711 / CRS 1711).

grant musicians, mostly from England, attracted to the New World by the blossoming of theatrical life after a wartime ban on theatrical activities was lifted in the late 1780s. These men were involved in both stage and concert activity, as performers, conductors, impresarios, and producers; they were versatile musicians who wrote and published songs not as a single preoccupation, but as one facet of their wide-ranging musical activity.

Benjamin Carr (1768–1831) had written operas and songs in London before coming to America in 1793, and he continued to do so in his new home, eventually publishing some sixty songs in this country. The first were "Four Ballads" to texts by Shakespeare, published the year after his arrival. Others were arrangements of traditional songs such as "Auld Lang Syne," intended for interpolation into stage works. His greatest success came with "The Little Sailor Boy" (1798), which seems to have had the widest distribution and longest life of any song written in America before 1800 and which, in its deliberate simplicity of style, seems to reflect an attitude "in which social position was determined economically, and which therefore treated music as a commodity whose value was best determined in the marketplace."[4]

One of his most ambitious vocal works was a set of *Six Ballads* (Opus 7) to texts from Sir Walter Scott's *The Lady of the Lake*, published in 1810; Carr appears to have been the first of many composers who found inspiration in the lyric and dramatic verses of this lengthy narrative poem based on the legend of James V, a sixteenth-century Scottish king. The various songs in Carr's set reflect the state of secular vocal music in America in the first quarter of the nineteenth century. All are strophic, with the several stanzas of text set to the same music. The first of the set, "Mary,"[5] reminds us that German music—specifically the vocal music of Beethoven—was known in America and also anticipates the lieder style of Schubert and Schumann. "Hymn to the Virgin," with its sustained tones, extended tessitura, and vocal flourishes, is much more indebted to Italian opera than Schubert's famous later setting of the same text, his "Ave Maria." "Coronach" makes repeated reference to Scottish-Irish song with its disjunct melodic line, its "Scottish snaps," and some strong hints of pentatonicism in the melodic line. The most "American" song of the set is "Soldier, Rest!"; like so many songs written and performed here in the decades following the Revolution, its text is a reminder that America had recently experienced a war on its own territory.

[4] Bill Brooks, liner notes to NW 231, p. 1.
[5] The entire set is available on NW 231, s1 / 1–4 and s2 / 1–2.

Other immigrant songwriters were James Hewitt, Alexander Reinagle, George K. Jackson, and Raynor Taylor.[6] Hewitt's "The Wounded Hussar" (1800) was one of the most popular items of sheet music in the first decade of the century; its text is concerned with the tragic effects of war. Reinagle adapted and arranged songs by other composers for stage performance in America; Jackson's most popular song was the romantic "One Kind Kiss" (1796);[7] Taylor's forty-odd songs published in America were mostly written for performance in the one-man musical evenings (or "olios") with which he made his reputation, though he also wrote music for such stage works as *The Ethiop; or, The Child of the Desert*, to a text by William Dimond, first performed in Philadelphia on New Year's Day of 1814.[8] Yet another immigrant composer for the musical stage was Charles Gilfert (1787–1829), who arranged and wrote many songs for interpolation into comic operas by other composers, and eventually managed the Charleston (South Caroline) Theatre and the Bowery Theatre in New York. Married to the singer Agnes Holman, he wrote such songs as "The Cypress Wreath"[9] for her to sing; this song was interpolated into the opera *Rokeby Castle*.

New England became the center of the first important songwriting movement in the United States. William Selby (1738–98), an English immigrant, and a number of other musicians living in and near Massachusetts wrote secular songs for voice and keyboard in the two decades following the Revolution. Some forty of these were published in the *Massachusetts Magazine*, others appeared in periodicals, a few were printed as separate items of sheet music, many were included in *The American Musical Miscellany* (Northampton, 1798) and subsequent anthologies. These songs were clearly derivative of English pleasure garden and comic opera pieces; none achieved wide or lasting circulation.

Oliver Shaw (1779–1848) enjoys the distinction of being the first American-born songwriter whose works were known and sung throughout the new nation. Blinded early in life, he nevertheless became a successful organist, teacher, singer, choirmaster, and composer, spending most of his life in Providence, Rhode Island. "By his sweet singing, which was simple and natural, without any pretension to style or ornament, Mr. Shaw often so touched the hearts of his audience that there would be hardly a dry eye in the house" wrote a contemporary,[10] and his songs themselves had a

[6] These composers are discussed in Chapter IV of the present book.
[7] Jackson's "The Dying Christian to his Soul" is available on NW 231, s2 / 4.
[8] The entire work is available on NW 232, s2.
[9] NW 299, s1 / 5.
[10] Charles C. Perkins and John S. Dwight, *History of the Handel and Haydn Society of Boston, Massachusetts* (Boston: Alfred Mudge & Son, 1883), I, p. 53.

similar effect on listeners. The most successful of these were written in the second decade of the century: "Mary's Tears" (1812) and
"All Things Bright and Fair Are Thine" (1817), both settings of
sacred texts by Thomas Moore, were printed and sold in various
parts of the United States, and were included on a "Select Oratorio" in Boston on July 4, 1817, celebrating the presence of President James Monroe in the city; and "There's Nothing True But
Heav'n" (1816),[11] also to a text from Moore's *Sacred Melodies*, had
gone through six editions within a decade and was alleged to have
earned its composer some $1,500 in royalties. An early biographer
summed up his accomplishments:

> His songs were sung and his other musical compositions performed in
> every state and in every large town and city in the Union. Ladies and
> Gentlemen, who never heard the name of their author, believed that
> they had the honor and happiness to learn and perform the most excel-
> lent and finished music of the first masters and doctors of Europe.[12]

Shaw performed, taught, and conducted the music of Handel,
Haydn, Mozart, and Beethoven all his life; his compositions are
rooted in the diatonic, balanced, symmetrical melodies and harmonies of the simpler works by the great masters of the eighteenth
century.

Oliver Shaw, "There's Nothing True But Heav'n"

[11] NW 231, s2 / 3.
[12] Thomas Williams, *A Discourse on the Life and Death of Oliver Shaw* (Boston:
Charles C. P. Moody, 1851), p. 24.

With the composition and publication in 1825 of "The Minstrel's Return'd from the War" by John Hill Hewitt (1801–90), American song reached a new peak of commercial success. The song itself is squarely in the mold of the day, laid out in strophic form with each stanza of text sung to a simple diatonic tune, supported by a keyboard accompaniment restricted to the three basic triads of the major key:

John Hill Hewitt, "The Minstrel's Return'd from the War"

It is dramatically and musically reminiscent of "The Wounded Hussar" (1810), one of the more successful songs written by the composer's father, James Hewitt. But somehow "The Ministrel's Return'd" struck the fancy of Americans; it sold all over the country in a number of editions and remained in print for more than half a century. Its success surprised and dismayed Hewitt and his brother James, who published the first edition; they had neglected to obtain a copyright, and thus any publisher could print it without payment of fee or royalties. The Hewitts estimated that their oversight cost them at least $10,000.

Hewitt continued to write songs for most of the remainder of his

long life. Some enjoyed modest commercial success; all were skillfully written. Many are clearly indebted to one or another of the
several schools of national song imported to American shores. His
first and greatest "hit," and a number of subsequent songs
("Farewell, Since We Must Part" of 1829, for instance), reflect the
English style of John Braham and James Hook; "Girls Beware"
(1832) reveals his mastery of the comic opera style of Henry Bishop;
"Ah! Fondly I Remember" (1837) is one of many songs that prove
Hewitt listened with care to the operas of Rossini and Bellini. The
brief popularity of several Swiss and Austrian singing families
prompted him to write his own "mountain songs" ("The Alpine
Horn" of 1843, for instance); the rise of black minstrelsy brought a
flood of songs for the minstrel stage from Hewitt's pen, including
the popular "Eulalie."

But he was no mere emulator. Though he was responsive to the
music around him, he was an assimilator rather than an imitator,
and his best songs incorporate elements of other song styles so
smoothly and convincingly that they sound like the products of no
other national school. "Mary, Now the Seas Divide Us" (1840) is
an American song not only because its composer was native born,
but because it could never be mistaken for a piece by a songwriter
of any other nationality:

John Hill Hewitt, "Mary, Now the Seas Divide Us"

Ma - ry, now the seas di-vide us, Dost thou think of me?—
Who that e'er a - dor'd could chide us Or my love for thee?

Income from sales of his songs was much too small to support
him and his family, and he earned his living as a journalist and

teacher. He cast his lot with the Confederacy in 1861 and spent the war years writing politically orientated plays and operas in Richmond and Atlanta. Perhaps the best song of his entire career was the powerful, dramatic, antiwar "All Quiet Along the Potomac" (1862), written to a poem by Mrs. Ethel Lynn Beers published in *Harper's Weekly* for November 30, 1861.[13] Like so many of the best songs of the war, it had equal appeal in South and North; like so many of Hewitt's mature songs, its style is unmistakably American.

It was the minstrel song that emerged as the first distinctly American genre, however. The minstrel show was created by white Americans, mostly in the North and Midwest, for the amusement of other white Americans. Though characters portrayed on the stage were black, the songs they sang and danced to had little to do with the music of black Americans of the day.

The stage portrayal of blacks was rooted in English comic opera of the late eighteenth and early nineteenth centuries. A number of works for the musical stage popular on both sides of the Atlantic included black characters. These roles were usually comic, spoken and sung in broken English, with tunes of deliberate simplicity intended to reflect supposedly primitive music. The English actor Charles Matthews, who came to America in the early 1820s in search of new material for his already popular one-man evenings, carefully recorded speech patterns of black Americans in phonetic form, then incorporated his "research" in his portrayal of a slave named Agamemnon for a new show titled "All Well at Natchitoches," which he tried out in Philadelphia and then offered to his home audiences back in Great Britain.

George Washington Dixon (1808–61) was probably the first American to specialize in stage portrayals of blacks; as early as 1827 he introduced comic black characters into his stage acts in Albany. George Nichols, J. W. Sweeney, and Bob Farrell were doing the same thing slightly later. Comic dialogue and pantomime, both supposedly based on characteristics of the black man, would lead into a song. The success of such acts prompted music publishers to bring out a number of these "nigger songs" in sheet music form— "Coal Black Rose," "Zip Coon," "Jim Along Josey," and "Long Tail Blue." All these were cut out of the same cloth: texts were in dialect, usually portraying the black person as a comical, illiterate, almost subhuman being; verses were strung together in rambling fashion, offering a series of disjointed episodes rather than an ordered sequence of events:

[13] NW 202, s1 / 2.

I went down to sandy hook todder afternoon,
And de fust man I met dare was ole Zip Coon,
Old Zip Coon is a very learned scholar,
And he plays upon de banjo, Cooney in de holler.

Ole Sukey Blue fell in lub wid me,
She vite me to her house to take a cup of tea;
What do you tink old Sukey had for de supper?
Chicken-foot, sparrow-grass, and apple-sauce butter.

Tunes were simple, diatonic, often pentatonic, sung in a lively, dancelike tempo. Recent research has identified most of these tunes as coming from oral-tradition Anglo-American music; "Zip Coon," for instance, was sung by both Farrell and Dixon in 1834 to one of the most venerable of all Anglo-American melodies, best known in the present century as "Turkey in the Straw."[14]

The most famous early blackface entertainer was Thomas Dartmouth ("Daddy") Rice (1808–60), born in New York City, an aspiring if not particularly successful actor on the legitimate stage before a sequence of improbable events brought him international fame. Finding himself stranded in the Midwest between engagements in the early 1830s, Rice observed an elderly black dancing for coins on the streets of Cincinnati, doing a somewhat awkward but distinctive shuffle while singing fragments of a curious song:

Turn about an' wheel about an' do jis so,
An' ebery time I turn about I jump Jim Crow.

Rice interpolated his own version of this song and dance as a skit in blackface, between acts of a local drama, to wildly enthusiastic response. Working his way eastward, through Cincinnati, Louisville, Philadelphia, Washington, and Baltimore, he found that word of his new act proceeded him and brought capacity crowds. "Jim Crow" was done in New York for the first time on November 12, 1832, at the Bowery Theatre. Rice was suddenly one of the best-known stage performers in all the United States, and his hit song was rushed into print in sheet music form by publishers in New York, Boston, and Baltimore. In 1836 he made a successful tour of England, where "Jim Crow" and other songs in a similar style were perceived by audiences and critics as being distinctly American. Thus the first American who carried to Europe a type of music accepted there as fundamentally different from their own was not

[14] Some sense of the persistence of this tune is suggested by the fact that it was recorded in 1970 in El Rancho, New Mexico, as played by fiddler Meliton Roybar; cf. NW 292, s2 / 6.

a composer of symphonies, operas, or choral pieces, but a song-writer and stage performer specializing in blackface comedy.

Musically, "Jim Crow" consisted of a simple, diatonic, strophic tune resembling a patchwork of several oral-tradition Anglo-American melodies, fitted—in its sheet music transcription—to a rudimentary keyboard accompaniment based on the simplest of chords. Its text was another string of disconnected verses, many with topical references; new ones could be inserted at the whim of the performer.

The next step was from individual blackface performers to a small group, or troupe. The first verified performance by a minstrel troupe took place on February 6, 1843 at New York's Bowery Amphitheatre:

> First Night of the novel, grotesque, original and surpassingly melodious ethiopian band, entitled the VIRGINIA MINSTRELS. Being an exclusively musical entertainment, combining the banjo, violin, bone castanetts, and tambourine; and entirely exempt from the vulgarities and other exceptional features, which have hitherto characterized negro extravaganzas.[15]

There were four of the Virginia Minstrels, none from Virginia or even the South: Billy Whitlock, born in New York City; Frank Brower, from Baltimore; Dick Pelham, another New Yorker; and Dan Emmett from Mount Vernon, Ohio. Their first programs were made up of "nigger" songs and dances, comic sketches and mock sermons in dialect, and instrumental pieces. Emmett played the fiddle, Whitlock the banjo, Brower the bones, and Pelham the tambourine, though they were all versatile enough to play other instruments as well. They performed songs already popularized by individual blackface entertainers—"Old Dan Tucker," "Lucy Long," "Boatman Dance." Tunes were borrowed or adapted from traditional Anglo-American pieces; the accompanying instruments were played in a traditional, nonharmonic style. A recent scholar suggests the following:

> The volume of the minstrel band was quite lean, yet anything but delicate. The tones of the banjo died away quickly and therefore could not serve as a solid foundation in the ensemble. On top was the squeaky, carelessly tuned fiddle. Add the dry "ra, raka, taka, tak" of the bones and the tambourine's dull thumps and ceaseless jingling to the twang of the banjo and the flat tone of the fiddle, and the sound of the band is

[15]*New York Herald* for February 6, 1843.

The sheet music cover for "Old Dan Tucker."

approximated: it was scratchy, tinkling, cackling, and humorously incongruous.[16]

---

[16] Hans Nathan, *Dan Emmett and the Rise of Early Negro Minstrelsy* (Norman: University of Oklahoma Press, 1962), p. 128.

This style was captured on some of the early recordings of music from the rural South, giving us as close an approximation of the sounds coming from the early minstrel stage as we will ever be able to obtain. "Old Joe Clark" may well have been a minstrel song, and a recording made in 1927[17] is in an archaic style surely tracing back to the mid-nineteenth century: the voice and fiddle are in unison, with an occasional drone note on a lower string; the banjo plays a supporting but nonharmonic ostinato pattern. "Bigfooted Nigger," as played in unison on the fiddle and banjo by the Helton Brothers of Ashville, North Carolina,[18] must be close in style to the music played to accompany the earliest minstrel dancing. And "Dr. Ginger Blue," available in a performance by Arthur Tanner and His Blue Ridge Corn Shuckers from 1929, is a piece of minstrel music from later in the nineteenth century, played in a somewhat later style with guitars supplying a rudimentary harmonic accompaniment.[19]

After a string of successful engagements in the winter of 1843–44, during which time their show expanded from a skit between acts of other entertainments to a featured presentation itself, the Virginia Minstrels followed in "Daddy" Rice's footsteps by going to England, in April of 1844. Their success in the British Isles led to the establishment of English minstrel troupes, and to the writing of minstrel songs by British composers.

The most famous and successful successor to the original Virginia Minstrels was Christy's Minstrels, which gave its first performances in Albany in the 1840s and came to New York in 1846. Their success opened a floodgate; dozens and then hundreds of minstrel groups were formed in the following two decades. Virtually every city and town in America was treated to performances by touring and resident groups with such names as the New Orleans Serenaders, the Sable Minstrels, the Virginia Harmonists, the Virginia Serenaders, the Nightingale Opera Troupe, the Ethiopian Operatic Brothers and Sable Sisters. The most famous troupes performed in the large cities of the East and toured to other parts of the country; small, regional groups operated within a more limited geographical area; there were even amateur groups, performing for neighborhood and family audiences. But all had in common that performers were white males, mostly from the North, performing in blackface; and their music was adapted from traditional Anglo-American pieces, from popular songs, even from Italian opera—or was newly composed in styles derived from such

[17] NW 236, s1 / 2.
[18] NW 226, s2 / 3.
[19] NW 245, s2 / 3.

The Virginia Serenaders, a typical minstrel group of the mid-19th century.

music. None of the music performed on the minstrel stage before the Civil War had any connection with the music of black slaves or freedmen.[20]

Meanwhile, several songwriters were moving in the direction of characteristically American products. Chief among these was Henry Russell (1812–1901), the most important and successful songwriter in America before Stephen Foster.

Russell, born in Sheerness, England, began his musical career as a boy soprano in a children's opera troupe specializing in adaptions of Italian operas, which once sang for King George IV. He went off to Italy when his voice changed, for further vocal study and with the hope of making a career in the land where his favorite music had been spawned. He claimed in his autobiography[21] that he studied with Rossini in Bologna and also knew Bellini and Donizetti, but he found both Italy and England swarming with gifted singers who afforded too much competition for a person of his somewhat limited talents, and he sailed for the New World. Settling first in Toronto, he soon accepted an offer in Rochester, New York, as organist at the First Presbyterian Church and "professor of music" at the Rochester Academy of Sacred Music.

The turning point in his career came there, in 1835, when he heard Henry Clay deliver one of his eloquent, fiery orations. Rus-

[20] Though this generalization seems valid for the melodies of minstrel songs, the banjo traces its ancestry to Africa, and the playing style of minstrel banjoists has points of similarity with the ostinato playing of certain African string instruments; cf. Chapter III, p. 76, of the present book.

[21] Henry Russell, *Cheer! Boys, Cheer!* (London: J. Macqueen, 1895).

sell was electrified, and decided on the spot to attempt to do in song what Clay had just done with speech; returning to his room, he immediately set to work on the composition of a song, choosing as a text the dramatic poem "Wind of the Winter's Night, Whence Comest Thou?" by Charles Mackay.

> All through the night I paced up and down my room arranging the music for the poem, and I remember that the notion uppermost in my mind was to infuse into my music the subtle charm, as it were, of the voice of Henry Clay.[22]

The song, which in concept and musical language resembles a *scena* from an Italian opera, was published in 1836. By this time Russell had launched a career as a ballad singer, armed with a number of additional songs of his own composition. He sang in New York for the first time in 1836, and within a year a contemporary writer could say:

> His fame was now fully established, and, devoting his whole attention to composition and singing, he traversed the States of America from extremity to extremity with a rapidity without parallel, singing at all places and at all times to multitudes that all but idolized him.[23]

His vocal programs were extraordinary events. He sang his own songs, to the virtual exclusion of those by other composers; he accompanied himself at the piano; he handled his own advance arrangements and publicity. His seventy-five-odd songs written in the United States fall into three general groups: extended, melodramatic pieces such as "The Maniac" and "Ship on Fire," drawing heavily on the style of Italian opera; more English-sounding strophic ballads, including "The Ivy Green" and "Cheer! Boys, Cheer!"; and simpler, sentimental songs such as "The Old Arm Chair," "My Mother's Bible," and "Woodman, Spare That Tree."[24] The latter group included his most popular and influential songs; they also draw on the musical conventions of Italian opera, with their diatonic but expressive melodic lines, their expressive use of appoggiatura and octave leaps, and their arpeggiated accompaniments. The style seems familiar and "American" to us because it suggests the sound of so many of Stephen Foster's songs, but its

---

[22] Russell, pp. 61–62.

[23] Quoted in John Anthony Stephens, *Henry Russell in America: Chutzpah and Huzzah* (Urbana: University of Illinois, 1975, unpublished doctoral thesis), p. 14. This is the most complete study of Russell and his music.

[24] Samples of each of these types of songs may be found on *An Evening with Henry Russell* (Nonesuch H-71338).

roots lie in Italian opera and it was Foster who knew Russell's songs, not vice versa.

Henry Russell, "Woodman, Spare That Tree"

It was not merely Russell's musical style that helped shape indigenous American song, but also his philosophy of what a popular song could and should be. His songs and his delivery of them were intended to be appealing to persons of varying and even non-existent musical backgrounds. Like Henry Clay, he strove for an emotional response from a mass audience. This somewhat revolutionary attitude was apparent from the beginning of his career; a reviewer in New York's *Commercial Advertiser* for October 15, 1838 commented:

> His vocal exertions to please are always regarded with a full attendance; and it is not surprising, for his voice and style are eminently qualified for general popularity.

Russell was fond of telling an anecdote that illustrates this point: in Boston one day, a street urchin pointed out the singer to one of his young friends, with the remark "That's Henry Russell, the song man"; with little encouragement he sang one of Russell's latest songs, "in excellent tune and voice"; the singer-songwriter later confided to a friend, "All of the applause of the entertainment I gave that evening did not gratify me more than the evident admiration of that little street-corner connoisseur." Equally telling was the adverse and often vitriolic criticism of his singing and his compositions from writers devoted to the notion that "good" music was and should be accessible only to an intellectual and musical elite: John S. Dwight of Boston called him a "great charlatan," and another critic insisted that his music "misleads to a false taste" and that his songs "were not genuine effects of art" but rather "bribe the untutored ear."

But tens of thousands of Americans flocked to his concerts and bought copies of his songs, and virtually every American songwriter of the next generation was touched in some way by both his music and his attitude. Though he was born in England of Jewish parents, studied and worshipped Italian music, and came first to Canada, Russell thought of himself as "half-American" and insisted that his songs reflected life in the United States. More than any other individual he contributed to the decisive split in style and function between popular and art song which came about in the first half of the nineteenth century.[25]

Shortly before Russell returned to his native England, four members of the Hutchinson family of Milford, New Hampshire formed a quartet, inspired by the success of the Rainer Family, a quartet of Swiss singers then touring America with programs of both traditional and original songs. After establishing a local reputation, the Hutchinsons set off in 1842 on a lengthy tour, taking them through New Hampshire and Vermont into New York State, as far west as Albany, then back eastward to Boston by way of Springfield, Pittsfield, Worcester, and many smaller towns and villages. The Hutchinson Family, as they eventually billed themselves, consisted of three brothers (Judson, John, and Asa) and their younger sister Abby. Their programs were made up of a mixture of solos by each of the four and quartet arrangements sung to their own accompaniment of two violins and a bass viol. They performed works by Henry Russell, Lyman Heath, and Bernard Covert, as well as a selection of songs, glees, and choruses from *The Social Choir*, a popular anthology brought out by George Kingsley in Boston in 1835. There were also a few songs written by the Hutchinsons themselves. The tour brought them a modest profit, favorable and even enthusiastic reviews, and the publication of four of their own songs by Oliver Ditson, the most important music publisher in Boston.

The next year they made a more ambitious and successful circuit through most of New England, down the East coast to New York, Philadelphia, and Baltimore, and eventually to Washington, where

---

[25]"A Life in the West" on NW 251, s1 / 3 is a fair sample of his style: the first phrases of both the piano introduction and the song itself anticipate the melodic writing of Stephen Foster, the following section shows clear traces of the style of Donizetti.

they were invited to dine with President Tyler at the White House. Suddenly they were the most famous singers in all of America; they cleared thousands of dollars, above expenses; a dozen of their songs were brought out by Firth-Hall & Pond in New York; they came to know such people as Henry Wadsworth Longfellow and Daniel Webster.

Their repertory now consisted mostly of their own songs: sentimental ballads ("My Mother's Bible" and "The Good Old Days of Yore"), narrative melodramatic pieces patterned after Henry Russell's most operatic pieces ("The Vulture of the Alps"), and moralistic songs ("King Alcohol," their first temperance piece). Some were new, some were adaptations: "The Old Granite State," an autobiographical song with which they opened or closed each program, was a reworking of the rousing gospel hymn "The Old Church Yard"; "Axes to Grind" seems to be based on a fiddle tune; their fiery abolition song, "Get Off the Track," borrows the tune of the minstrel favorite "Old Dan Tucker."

Having conquered their own country, the Hutchinsons set sail for Great Britain in the summer of 1845, following "Daddy" Rice and the Virginia Minstrels in bringing the newly emerging styles of American popular song to European audiences. London was unresponsive, but they enjoyed great success in smaller towns and with working-class audiences in Liverpool and other industrial cities. Some English critics saw the directness and simplicity of their music as American: "It is pleasant to hear music made subservient to the holy use of promoting good-will between man and man, and clothing the deep sympathy of the poet in the appropriate and winning garb of simple and unadorned harmony," wrote an observer in the *Birmingham Journal* in January of 1846.

They found great changes in America when they returned after an absence of less than a year; disagreements and tensions that were to lead ultimately to the Civil War had intensified. The Hutchinsons had pursued a dual career: they had become popular entertainers with their sentimental, humorous, and patriotic songs; they had also sung at temperance and abolitionist rallies. Now they decided to sing their political songs on public programs and associate themselves more openly with radical causes.

Some of their abolitionist songs were vignettes of individual slaves, underlining the inhuman conditions arising from the conditions of slavery:

> Oh! deep was the anguish of the slave mother's heart,
> When called from her darling for ever to part;
> So grieved that lone mother, that heart-broken mother,
>   In sorrow and woe.

The lash of the master her deep sorrows mock,
While the child of her bosom is sold on the block;
Yet loud shrieked that mother, poor broken-hearted mother,
   In sorrow and woe.

Oh! list ye kind mothers to the cries of the slave;
The parents and children implore you to save;
Go rescue the mothers, the sisters and brothers,
   From sorrow and woe.[26]

Others were impassioned calls for action; "Get Off the Track"
offered the image of abolition as a railroad train steaming through
the land, collecting passengers as it went:

See the people run to meet us!
At the stations thousands greet us;
All take seats with exaltation,
In the car, Emancipation.
   Huzza! Huzza! Emancipation,
   Soon will bless our happy nation.

Such songs had aroused unrestrained enthusiasm at rallies of
the already-converted. A writer for the *Herald of Freedom* described
the effect of "Get Off the Track" on a mass meeting in Boston's
Faneuil Hall:

The vast multitude sprang to their feet, as one man, and at the close of
the first strain gave vent to their enthusiasm in a thunder of unrestrained cheering. Three cheers, and three times three, and ever so many
more—for they could not count—they sent out, full-hearted and full-
toned, till the old roof rang again. Oh, it was glorious! I wish the whole
city, and the entire country could have been there—even all the people.
Slavery would have died of that music![27]

Elsewhere, though, the reception of their political songs was quite
different. They were hissed and objects were thrown at them when
they sang "Get Off the Track" on a public concert at Palmo's Opera
House in New York in 1845. More hissing greeted them at Yale
College. A critic who had praised them several years before wrote
in the *Philadelphia Courier* in 1846:

It is really time that someone should tell these people, in a spirit of
friendly candor, that they are not apostles and martyrs, entrusted with
a "mission" to reform the world, but only a company of common song-

---

[26] "The Bereaved Slave Mother," words by Judson Hutchinson.
[27] Quoted in John Wallace Hutchinson, *Story of the Hutchinsons (Tribe of Jesse)*
(Boston: Lee and Shepard, 1896), II, pp. 76–77.

singers, whose performances sound very pleasantly to the great mass of the people ignorant of real music.

But they persevered, even when the mood of the country became so ugly as to lead to rioting at rallies at which they were singing, the cancellation of some of their public concerts, and eventually violence at Faneuil Hall itself. Abby's marriage broke up the original quartet around 1850, and soon each of the brothers formed his own group. They supported Lincoln in his several campaigns, performed at war rallies when fighting broke out in 1861, sang arrangements of slave songs after the war to call attention to the continuing plight of Southern blacks after slavery had been abolished, and lent their support to the struggle for universal suffrage and women's rights.

None of the Hutchinsons was a songwriter of exceptional talent, and none of their songs took deep root in American musical culture.[28] But they were in the forefront of a movement bringing a new dimension to American popular song—involvement in social and political issues of the day.

By the middle of the nineteenth century, then, a clear profile of indigenous American song had emerged. All that was lacking was a songwriter of genius to weave various stylistic and expressive threads into great and enduring compositions.

[28] A selection of their songs is available on *There's a Good Time Coming: and Other Songs of the Hutchinson Family* (Smithsonian N-020).

# 8

## The Dawning of
## Classical Music in America
## (1825—65)

The first half of the nineteenth century saw America move slowly but inexorably away from its reliance on the musical habits and tastes of the English.

Opera was the first genre to embrace a non-British repertory, though the initial step in this direction reflected what was happening in England itself—the gradual adoption of Italian opera, beginning with certain works by Mozart and Rossini. These pieces were mounted not in their original form, but in adaptations for the English stage by Henry R. Bishop and other British musicians, who understood that the English public was not yet ready to accept foreign opera unreservedly. Bishop's *The Libertine* (fashioned from *Don Giovanni* in 1817) and *The Barber of Seville* (1818) did not offer merely an English translation of the Italian libretto; recitative was largely replaced by spoken dialogue, complex ensemble scenes and finales were transformed into strophic airs and simpler, homophonic choruses.

It was in this form that Italian opera first came to America. *The Libertine* was the first opera with Mozart's music to be performed in America, opening at the Park Theatre in New York on November 7, 1817 and in Philadelphia the following season. Bishop's version of *The Barber of Seville* brought Rossini's music to the American stage in 1818. These and other "Englished" Italian operas became the most popular musical fare on the American stage in the 1820s, '30s, and into the '40s. The most successful was *Cinderella; or, the Fairy-Queen and the Glass Slipper*, adapted from Rossini's *La*

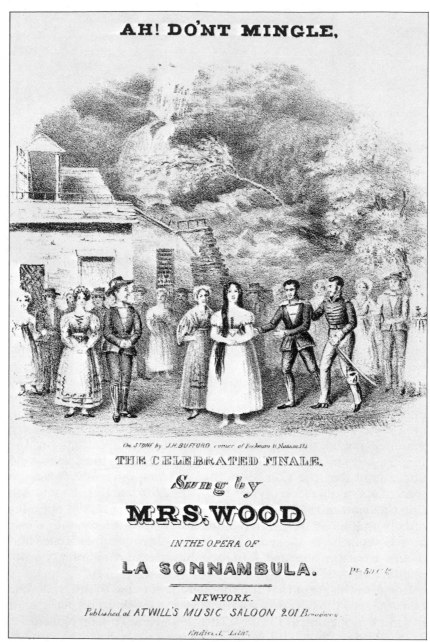

Sheet music cover for "Ah Don't Mingle."

*Cenerentola* by the Irishman Rophino Lacy, premiered at Covent Garden in 1830 and offered in America for the first time at the Park Theatre one year later.[1] It ran for some fifty performances in its first New York season, was chosen as the vehicle for the American debut of a number of visiting singers—such as Mrs. Wood, the prima donna of London's Covent Garden, who came here in 1833—and was given countless performances in this country for some three decades, not only in the large Eastern cities but wherever works for the musical stage could be mounted.

Bellini's operas were likewise first offered in English versions. *La sonnambula*, premiered (in English) at the Park Theatre in 1835, was sung for the rest of the season to the virtual exclusion of other works. *Norma* was introduced to Philadelphia in 1840, and for the next decade was America's most popular opera.

The popularity of this operatic music was not confined to the stage. Songs fashioned from airs by Rossini, Bellini, Donizetti, and other Italians became best-selling items of sheet music for several decades beginning about 1825. Texts were sometimes English translations of the Italian words, sometimes completely new lyrics. There was, for instance, "Little Nell," which grafts a melodramatic text based on the pathetic story of the young match-girl of Charles Dickens' *The Old Curiosity Shop* onto the melody of "Qual cor tradisti," the last-act finale of *Norma*:

"Little Nell," adapted from Bellini's *Norma*

---

[1] For a more detailed discussion of the dissemination of the music of Italian opera in America at this time, cf. Charles Hamm, *Yesterdays: Popular Song in America* (New York: W. W. Norton & Company, 1979), pp. 62–88.

Favorite tunes from Italian opera were also arranged for piano, instrumental ensemble, band, and even chorus. They were made into hymns and into vocal pieces sprinkled through collections published for use in public schools, singing schools, and social singing groups. Italian airs were made into cotillions, quadrilles, and other popular social dances. Italian melody became the most pervasive musical influence in America since Thomas Moore's *Irish Melodies*.

Italian opera in the original language made its way here much more slowly. Until the 1820s, opera had been offered only in English. The sole exception was in New Orleans, where French opera may have been performed as early as 1792, and a theatrical company directed by Jean Fornier had staged at least twenty-three French works in 1805–6, at the St. Peter Street Theatre. From 1806 to 1810, another troupe under the direction of Louis Tabary gave some 350 performances of 76 different operas by such French writers as Dalayrac, Grétry, and Méhul.[2]

On November 29, 1825, a visiting operatic troupe led by the great Spanish singer and vocal pedagogue Manuel Garcia performed Rossini's *Il barbiere di Siviglia* in Italian at New York's Park Theatre, and in the course of the next half-year they offered some eighty performances of nine different Italian works, all in the original tongue. Italian opera came again to New York in 1832, when a company headed by the tenor Montresor and the poet Lorenzo Da Ponte (librettist of Mozart's *Don Giovanni* and *Così fan tutte* and former court poet in Vienna, who had come to America in 1805) gave fifty-odd performances of works by Rossini, Mercadante, and Bellini. In 1833, a new theater built specifically for Italian opera—at a cost of some $150,000—was opened with Rossini's *La gazza ladra*, performed by a resident troupe assembled and directed by Da Ponte and Rivafinoli. Some eighty performances of Italian operas, most of them by Rossini, were given the first season.

Meanwhile a traveling company from New Orleans, directed by John Davis, had brought summer seasons of opera in French to New York and Philadelphia beginning in 1827, offering such works as Boieldieu's *La Dame blanche* and *Jean de Paris*, Méhul's *Joseph*, Hérold's *Zampa*, Auber's *La muette de portici*, and French versions of Weber's *Der Freischütz*, and Spontini's *La vestale*. Enough Italian singers could now be assembled in New York for productions at Niblo's Garden, which opened in 1835, and in 1844 another new

[2] For the early history of French opera in New Orleans, cf. Henry A. Kmen, *Music in New Orleans: The Formative Years, 1791–1841* (Baton Rouge: Louisiana State University Press, 1966), pp. 56–92.

The Astor Place Opera House, New York's most elaborate lyric theatre of the time and predecessor of the Academy of Music.

opera house (built by Signor Palmo) opened with Bellini's *I puritani.* The Astor Place Opera House, built in 1847, was the largest theater yet opened in America, with 1,500 seats; its construction was made possible when 150 persons pledged to support 75 nights of Italian opera each year for five years, and the opening production was Verdi's *Ernani.* The Park Theatre, a stronghold for English opera for a half-century, engaged the Havana Italian Opera Company for the season of 1847, in direct competition with the new opera house. The New York Academy of Music, built in 1853–54 at a cost of $350,000 "for the purpose of cultivating a taste for music by concerts, operas, and other entertainments," was still larger.

Thus, the quarter-century leading up to the outbreak of the Civil War saw a steady increase in the popularity of Italian opera in the original language, to the point where it could be enjoyed on something approaching a regular basis.

But this gradual Italianization of the operatic life of New York did not take place without opposition. Many Americans were disturbed by the experience of sitting through a theatrical evening featuring a language they could not understand:

> We want to understand the language; we cannot endure to sit by and see the performers splitting their sides with laughter, and we not to take the joke; dissolved in "briny tears," and we not permitted to sympathize

with them; or running each other through the body, and we devoid of the means of condemning or justifying the act.[3]

There was a persistent feeling that opera, and the circumstances surrounding its performance, were not in step with the mood and character of the United States of America. Box seats for the evenings of Italian opera put on by the Garcia troupe in 1825–26 were priced at $2.00, a large sum for the time; the audience that turned out for the opening night was described by a writer for the New York *American* as comprised chiefly of "elegant and well-dressed females. There were no unsightly bonnets detract(ing) from the array of beauteous and smiling faces, decked in native curls, or embellished with wreaths of flowers, or tasteful turbans."[4] One of the attractions of opera in a foreign tongue was precisely the style with which it was presented and the absence of the lower classes and their behavior, which had marred so many theatrical experiences in the eighteenth and early nineteenth centuries. The young Walt Whitman described a visit to the Academy of Music in the 1850s:

[It] is of elegant architectural appearance outside, especially at night— adorned with its plentiful, round, moon-like lights. Here we are at the front! What a gay show! The visitors are now in full tide. The lookers on—the crowds of pedestrians—the numerous private carriages dashing up to the great porch—the splendid and shiny horses—the footmen jumping down and opening the carriage doors—the beautiful and richly dresst women alighting, and passing up the steps under the full blaze of the lights.

But now from our seat let us take a good look around. Hundreds upon hundreds of gas-lights, softened with globes of ground glass, shed their brilliancy upon the scene. —Seated in the red velvet arm-chairs of the parquette, and on the sofas of the dress-circle, are groups of gentlemen, and of the most superbly dressed women, some of them with that high bred air, and self-possession, obtained by mixing much with the "best society." Just before the curtain rises, for fifteen or twenty minutes, line after line, party after party, come streaming down the passages, seeking seats previously engaged—most of them under the convoy of the ushers. —From every direction opera-glasses are level'd by white-gloved hands. —Those who have been in the habit of going only to the theatres or places of amusement, will be struck by the quietness and blandness that pervades the whole place, like an atmosphere—no hubbub—no "hi-hi's."[5]

[3] Philip Hone, Mayor of New York, as quoted in Julius Mattfeld, *A Hundred Years of Grand Opera in New York, 1825–1925* (New York: The New York Public Library, 1927), p. 34.

[4] Quoted in Mattfeld, p. 13.

[5] Emory Holloway, *The Uncollected Poetry and Prose of Walt Whitman* (New York: Peter Smith, 1932), p. 132.

For Philip Hone, a former mayor of New York and originally a supporter of Italian opera, the class distinction was symbolized by

> ... the private boxes, so elegantly fitted up, which occupy the whole of the second tier. They cost six thousand dollars each, to be sure, and the use of them is all that the proprietors get for their money; but it forms a sort of aristocratical distinction.[6]

Unlike the popular musical theater of ballad and comic opera that had prevailed in America for some seventy-five years, "grand" opera was unable to support itself ("There never was a peculiarly successful season of Italian opera in this city," wrote a critic for the *New York Courier and Enquirer* in the 1850s, "and, more, there never was a successful season of Italian opera anywhere. And we add, that the season at the Academy last year was eminently unsuccessful, in spite of crowded houses."[7]). According to a financial breakdown of the first (1833–34) season at the Italian Opera Theatre, fees and salaries paid to singers totalled some $56,000, out of a total budget of $81,000; receipts for the eight-month season were less than $52,000. Almost all singers for Italian opera were brought from Europe, and paid the fees they commanded there; various critics, including Walt Whitman (then writing for the Brooklyn *Eagle*), felt that the construction and operation of opera houses, the costs of which were met partly at public expense, should coincide with the employment of a substantial number of American singers and instrumentalists. As William Henry Fry, critic for the *New York Tribune*, put it:

> The expense of sustaining an opera-house so nurtured at home will be at the most not more than one-fourth what it would be if the artists were brought from Europe. In that way alone can the exorbitant demands of foreign artists be diminished; and the folly and extravagance of paying them from one to ten thousand dollars a night, as has been done in this city, will be forever avoided. In connection with this it may be mentioned that there are some Americans now studying for the operatic stage in Italy, and one lady of Boston has appeared in Naples with success.[8]

Though New York boasted the largest number of resident and visiting Italian troupes in the decades leading up to the Civil War, other cities were equally charmed with this exotic music, and it

[6] Philip Hone, as quoted in Mattfeld, p. 34.

[7] Quoted in Frédéric Louis Ritter, *Music in America* (New York: Charles Scribner's Sons, 1883), p. 295.

[8] Written in August of 1837, and quoted in William Treat Upton, *William Henry Fry, American Journalist and Composer-Critic* (New York: Thomas Crowell, 1954; Da Capo Press reprint, 1974), p. 37.

was in Philadelphia that the next step was taken in the absorption of Italian operatic music into American musical life—the composition of music in this style by an American-born composer.

Among the more ardent admirers of Italian opera were two sons of William Fry (1777–1855), a distinguished publisher who established the *Philadelphia National Gazette* in 1820—Joseph Reese Fry (1811–81) and William Henry Fry (1813–64). The latter studied theory and composition with Leopold Meignen, the most distinguished musician in the city. During a visit to Philadelphia in 1833 by the Montresor company from New York, the instrumentalists who had come with the troupe offered a benefit concert of overtures from favorite operas, other popular works, and an overture by "an Amateur of this city, pupil of Mr. Meignen," the twenty-year-old Fry. The following season, an operatic troupe directed by Rivafinoli gave a similar season in Philadelphia, again closing the visit with an instrumental program by members of the accompanying orchestra and again including an overture by "an American Amateur," otherwise unidentified but certainly Fry. Concerts in 1836 and 1838 included performances of a *Pastoral Overture*, again the work of the young Philadelphian.

William Henry Fry became a music critic in 1836 for his father's paper; from the beginning, he took a stand squarely on the side of Italian opera:

> It may not be unworthy of remark that the vulgar prejudices which exist in our country against Italian music are based upon erroneous impressions. It is sufficient that our public are beginning to think for themselves. They have discovered in Bellini's *Sonnambula*, even through a miserable translation and a very indifferent production in our theatre, that Italian music can be simple, passionate, and effective, and that its melodies are unequalled in commanding popular applause and affection.[9]

Fry and his brother Joseph did a translation of Bellini's *Norma* for a production premiered at the Chestnut Street Theatre on January 11, 1841. Every word of the original libretto was translated into English and fitted to the music as Bellini had written it. There was no replacement of recitative by spoken dialogue, no interpolation of music from other operas, no simplification of complex musical numbers; it was *Norma* as heard in Italy, only with an English text.

Fry tried his hand at composing an opera during this period. Only the overture and a duet remain from a projected work called

[9] Written in August of 1837, and quoted in Upton, *William Henry Fry*, p. 37.

*Cristiani e pagani,* abandoned in 1838. *Aurelia the Vestal,* to a libretto by his brother Joseph, was completed in 1841. The plot is strongly reminiscent of both Spontini's *La vestale* and Bellini's *Norma;* the music is what one would expect from a talented young composer under the spell of Italian melody. Fry sent his score to London with an Italian singer of his acquaintance, Signor Giubilei, hoping for a performance in a more musically sophisticated land. But this first full-length "grand" opera by an American-born composer remains unperformed to the present day.

Undiscouraged, Fry set to work on an even more ambitious piece, to a libretto once again fashioned by his brother, this one based on Bulwer Lytton's *The Lady of Lyons,* which had been premiered at Covent Garden in 1838. In the "Prefatory Remarks" to the published score (Philadelphia, 1846), Fry wrote:

> This Lyrical Drama was produced on the stage with a view of presenting to the American Public, a *grand opera,* originally adapted to English words. The class of opera technically so designated, is, on the continent of Europe, employed for works of a serious or tragic character. Its peculiarity lies in the absence of all spoken monologue or dialogue; every word being sung throughout, and accompanied by the orchestra. This is essentially the high, complete, and classic form to give to the opera; it imparts proper uniformity of style to the entire declamation; does not confound the strictly musical with the acting drama; and with an artistic performance confirms the interest of the representation. There is . . . no reason why in English serious opera, both *simple recitative* and dialogue may not be equally avoided; and all language which has sufficient dignity to merit a place in such an opera, may be sung in *recitative accompanied by the orchestra.*

There is no detail of the music of *Leonora* (as the opera was called) that does not derive directly from Rossini, Bellini, and Donizetti. A sample will suffice to illustrate this point:

"Every Doubt and Danger Over," from Fry's *Leonora*

light - ed, Comes my he-ro and my lov-er____ To my con-stant____ arms a-gain!

Premiered on June 4, 1845 by the Seguin Opera Troupe, at the Chestnut Street Theatre in Philadelphia, the work ran for a dozen performances. Several concert presentations were offered by the Musical Fund Society later that month, the Seguin company revived it at the Walnut Street Theatre in December of 1846, and it was given in New York in 1858 at the Academy of Music—in an Italian translation entitled *Giulio e Leonora*. The critic of the *New York Express* saw it for exactly what it was:

> The opera seems to us a study in the school of Bellini. It is full of delicious, sweet music, but constantly recalls the Sonnambula and Norma. The peculiarities which most strongly distinguish [it] are sweetness of melody and lack of dramatic characterization.[10]

But there is no denying *Leonora* its place in history as the first "grand" opera by an American composer to reach the stage, and the first to be published.

Fry spent the years between 1846 and 1852 in Europe, mostly in Paris as musical correspondent for the *Ledger* and the *New York Tribune*. Repeated attempts to have *Leonora* mounted in Paris failed, and he returned to America. His only other opera, *Notre Dame of Paris*, also with a libretto by his brother Joseph (based on Victor Hugo's "Notre Dame de Paris" of 1831), was composed at the end of his life. A note on Fry's autograph score reads:

> First performed by 350 executants at the Grand Musical Festival inaugurating the National Fair for the benefit of wounded and ill Soldiers and Sailors of the United States Army and Navy, held in Philadelphia at the great Academy of Music, May 4, 1864.

The half-dozen performances were conducted by Theodore Thomas; it was never performed again. The Philadelphia *Evening Bulletin*

---

[10] Quoted in Gilbert Chase, *America's Music: From the Pilgrims to the Present*, 2nd rev. ed. (New York: McGraw-Hill Book Company, 1966), p. 331.

for May 7 claimed that it was "better than some of Verdi's, Donizetti's and Bellini's, and far before those of Pacini, Petrella and
others that have won popularity," and the critic for the *New York
Times* found it

> . . . written in a fluent Italian style—the only style recognized by Fry as
> appropriate for the delineation of musical subjects. Opinions are divided
> on this question, but the gentleman is certainly true to his own theory.
> The repertoire of the Academy does not contain a work more thoroughly
> imbued with the spirit and fire of Italy.[11]

The Italian style permeates his other compositions as well. Even
his brief *Adieu* (*Song for the Piano*),[12] written in 1855, mirrors the
supple melodies and arpeggiated accompaniments of the Bellini-
Donizetti style.

Only one other opera by an American reached the stage before
the Civil War, *Rip Van Winkle* by George Frederick Bristow (1825–
98). Based on the famous story by Washington Irving, it was premiered at Niblo's Theatre in New York on September 27, 1855.

Bristow, son of an English immigrant, shared some of Fry's
admiration for Italian opera. But he was a violinist, who wrote
mostly chamber music and orchestral pieces; and his opera, like
his symphonies and other instrumental works, had more to do with
German music than Italian.

The increasing dominance of the Germanic repertory in America
may be traced through a brief history of the performance of works
from the "modern" school of German composition—Beethoven,
Schubert, Schumann, Mendelssohn, Abt, Kücken, Spohr, and lesser
contemporaries.

The Boston Handel and Haydn Society had performed music by
Handel, Haydn, Mozart, and early Beethoven, almost exclusively
until its fifteenth season, 1829–30, when portions of a Mass by a
now-forgotten German musician named Bühler were presented. The
following season the incumbent organist, Mrs. Ostinelli, was
replaced by the German-born Charles Zeuner.

An organ concerto of his was performed on November 20, 1830.
Selections from Neukomm's oratorio *David* were done in 1835, and
the entire work was done in 1836. The same composer's *Hymn of
the Night* was done in 1837, and his new oratorio *Mt. Sinai* was not
only performed in 1840, it was published at the society's expense.
The twenty-seventh season (1841–42) opened with the first perfor-

[11] Quoted in Upton, *William Henry Fry*, p. 228.
[12] NW 257, S2 / 4.

mances in Boston of Ludwig Spohr's cantata *God, Thou Art Great* and Sigismund Romberg's *Transient and Eternal;* later there was another work by Spohr, *The Last Judgement (Die letzten Dinge)*, with the composer's daughter as featured soloist. The first Boston performance of Felix Mendelssohn's *St. Paul* took place in 1843.

By this point, more than half the repertory of the society was German. Attendance and receipts fell, "partly owing to the want of special vocal attraction, and partly to the inability of the public to appreciate music so lofty in its strain of inspiration and so scientific in its character."[13] But Mendelssohn's *Elijah* was first performed by the society on February 13, 1848; by 1890 it had been done 47 times, trailing only *The Messiah* (82 performances) and *The Creation* (63). 1853 saw the society's first performance of Beethoven's *Ninth Symphony* by the Germania Society. The number of German-born members increased steadily through the middle decades of the century, and in 1854 a German, Carl Zerrahn, was appointed to the conductorship, holding the post until his retirement in 1895.

The same trend was evident elsewhere. The Musical Fund Society of Philadelphia, founded in 1820 to "first, cultivate and diffuse a musical taste; and secondly, to afford relief to its necessitous professional members and their families," included a number of German-born musicians among its charter members, including its first conductor, Charles Frederick Hupfeld. Its first program, given on May 8, 1821, included a *Grand Sinfonia in E* by Romberg and Beethoven's *Symphony No. 1.* The following decade brought the second and third symphonies of Beethoven, the overtures to Weber's *Oberon* and Mendelssohn's *Midsummer Night's Dream*, Neukomm's *David*, Romberg's *Son of the Bell*, and Karl Loewe's oratorio *The Seven Sleepers.*

In New York the same pattern prevailed. The Sacred Music Society, organized in 1823, progressed from programs of choruses and solo airs by Handel, Haydn, and Mozart to the first American performance of Mendelssohn's *St. Paul* on October 29, 1838, only two years after its composition. Such music did not fall easily on the ears of New York audiences, at first; Walt Whitman wrote of the performance of *Elijah* by the Sacred Music Society in 1847:

> Although the music, judged by the rules of the art, is of the highest order, it is too elaborately scientific for the popular ear. It is, besides, too heavy in its general character, and wants the relief of a proper proportion of

[13] Charles C. Perkins and John S. Dwight, *History of the Handel and Haydn Society of Boston, Massachusetts*, I (Boston: Alfred Mudge & Son, 1883–93), p. 132.

lightness and melody. There is scarcely a striking or pleasing air in it. To a mere musician, however, it would afford study and delight for a year. Although the audience, which was large, sat out the performance, it was evident that no great degree of pleasure was derived from it.[14]

But the flood of German music and musicians was not to be stemmed. By the early 1840s, German bands were performing at such places of entertainment as Niblo's Garden in New York, replacing the ensembles of English and French musicians who had formerly played such engagements. A German Music Society, formed in the late 1830s by immigrant musicians, advertised in New York newspapers the availability of a "full and effective band of Instrumental performers of twenty in number if required (with all the fashionable new music of Strauss, Lanner and Labitzky. [They] hold themselves in readiness to attend private parties, soirées, etc."[15] At another artistic level, the Mendelssohn Quintette Club of Boston, composed of German musicians, gave America its first public concerts of chamber music, featuring works by Beethoven, Mendelssohn, Haydn, Schubert, Gade, Weber, Hummel, and other composers of the "modern" German school.

In 1842 the Philharmonic Society of New York was founded, the oldest American orchestra with a history of continuous performance. The third (and last) organization to bear this name, its aim was simply "the advancement of instrumental music." Membership was limited to seventy "professors of music," and it offered its first public program in the Apollo Rooms on December 7, with Madame Otto and Charles E. Horn as vocal soloists:

*PART ONE*

1. Grand Symphony in C Minor (the 5th)    Beethoven
2. Scena, from *Oberon*                    Weber
3. Quintette in d Minor                    Hummel

*PART TWO*

4. Overture to *Oberon*                    Weber
5. Duett, from *Armida*                    Rossini
6. Scena, from *Fidelio*                   Beethoven
7. Aria, from *Belmont and Constantia*     Mozart
8. New Overture in D                       Kalliwoda

[14]Cleveland Rodgers and John Black, eds., *The Gathering of the Forces, by Walt Whitman*, II (New York and London: G. F. Putnam's Sons/The Knickerbocker Press, 1920), pp. 353–54.

[15]Quoted in George Clinton Densmore Odell, *Annals of the New York Stage*, IV (New York: Columbia University Press, 1927–49), p. 517.

This concert was seen as a historic event in the musical life of New York by an anonymous writer for *The Albion:*

> We must undoubtedly reckon Wednesday evening last, as the commencement of a New Musical Era, in this western world. The concert which was then given, at the Apollo Rooms, was the first of an attempt to form an approved school of instrumental music in this country.[16]

And *The Pathfinder* for May 6, 1843, in a retrospective review of the three programs making up the first season, asserted:

> We do not think any thing has ever been attempted in this city, that will more conduce to the advancement of musical taste, than the formation of the above society, whose first season arrived at so successful a termination on Saturday week last. Already has its influence been felt, not only in the quality of the music performed at the concerts of Madam Otto, Messrs. Scharfenberg and Timm, but what is of more importance, its influence has been felt upon the public. We, ourselves, in many houses have seen Beethoven's Symphonies arranged as duetts on the Piano Fortes of young ladies, where we used to see Quicksteps and Gallops. The music performed at the three Concerts given by the Society, has been of a character to elevate and improve the public taste.[17]

The repertory of the society was overwhelmingly Germanic. Only Rossini represented the non-Teutonic world on the opening program, and the second and third concerts offered Beethoven, Weber, and Hummel again, plus Romberg, Haydn, Mendelssohn, and Spohr. Twenty-two German-born musicians played in the first concerts, compared to 13 Americans, 4 Frenchmen, and 2 Italians. By 1855, 53 of the 67 members of the orchestra were German; by 1892, only 3 of the hundred-odd instrumentalists were of non-Germanic birth or heritage. Of the early conductors, Henry C. Timm, W. Alpers, and Louis Wiegers were German-born, and Ureli Corelli Hill—the spiritual leader of the young organization and its first president—had spent some years in Europe in the mid-1830s, studying with Moritz Hauptmann and Ludwig Spohr. Theodore Eisfeld, an immigrant from Germany, assumed the bulk of the conducting in the season of 1848–49 and was named sole conductor in 1852, holding the post until the season of 1865–66, when he was succeeded by another German, Carl Bergmann.

Praise for the society and its repertory was not universal. Max Maretzek, who arrived in New York in 1848 to manage the opera

[16] Quoted in Howard Shanet, *Philharmonic: A History of New York's Orchestra* (Garden City: Doubleday & Company, 1975), pp. 88–89.

[17] Quoted in Shanet, pp. 493–94.

company of the Astor Place Theatre, wrote to his friend Hector Berlioz:

> Their *répertoire* consisted always of the same few Symphonies, works of the old composers in our Divine Science, which everybody has heard, although few have comprehended, since childhood. The compositions of modern *maestri* had never even been put in rehearsal.[18]

And criticism of another sort was soon leveled against the Philharmonic. William Henry Fry, in a letter to the *Musical World* published on January 21, 1854, claimed that "the Philharmonic Society of this city is an incubus on Art, never having asked for or performed a single American instrumental composition during the eleven years of its existence." Though the officers of the Philharmonic disputed the accuracy of Fry's accusation, their own list of "all the grand instrumental pieces" in their repertory, totalling seventy-four works, listed only one composition by an American, a *Concert Overture* by George Bristow. Bristow himself angrily joined the debate:

> From the commencement there has been on the part of the performing members and the direction of the Philharmonic Society little short of a conspiracy against the art of a country to which they have come for a living; and it is in very bad taste for men to bite the hand that feeds them. If all their artistic affections are unalterably German, let them pack up and go back to Germany, and enjoy the police and the bayonets. What is the Philharmonic Society in this country? Is it to play exclusively the works of German masters, especially if they be dead?[19]

The Philharmonic, in defending itself, claimed there was no American classical repertory on which they could have drawn.

This was not strictly true. To begin with, there were overtures to Fry's several operas; there was his *Santa Claus: Christmas Symphony*, a lengthy programmatic orchestral work depicting the preparations for the Christmas season in an American household, performed in New York on Christmas Eve of 1853 by Jullien's orchestra; and his *Niagara*, a brief one-movement descriptive work, which was performed at a Grand Musical Congress held at the Crystal Palace in the summer of 1854. Excerpts from two other symphonic pieces, *A Day in the Country* and *The Breaking Heart*, were performed during the 1852–53 season. Jullien's orchestra played another large orchestral work by Fry, the *Symphony—Childe*

[18] Max Maretzek, *Crochets and Quavers: or, Revelations of an Opera Manager in America* (New York: S. French, 1855), p. 13.
[19] Quoted in Upton, *William Henry Fry*, p. 93.

*Harold,* on its Grand Farewell Benefit Concert of May 31, 1854; his *Sacred Symphony No. III, Hagar in the Wilderness,* dates from the same year.[20]

In addition, there were orchestral pieces, in great profusion, by Anthony Philip Heinrich (1781–1861), one of the extraordinary figures in the history of music in America. His output included some 36 orchestral compositions, 150 songs, a hundred or more piano pieces, and various choral and chamber works. *The Ornithological Combat of Kings: or, The Condor of the Andes,*[21] a descriptive "Grand Symphony" in four movements composed in the mid-1830s, was performed by the Musik Verein of Gratz, Germany, on May 25, 1836—but never played in America. His "Fantasia agitata dolorosa for a Full Orchestra" entitled *Complaint of Logan the Mingo Chief, Last of His Race,* was also composed in the 1830s. *The Mastodon, A Grand Symphony in Three Parts for Full Orchestra,* had movements portraying "Black Thunder, the Patriarch of the Fox Tribe," "The Elkhorn Pyramid, or, the Indians' Offering to the Spirit of the Prairies," and "Shenandoah, a Celebrated Oneida Chief." There was also an "American National Dramatic Divertissement, for a Full Orchestra" entitled *The Treaty of William Penn with the Indians: Concerto Grosso,* begun in the 1830s and completed in New York in 1847, and a "Capriccio Grande for a Full Orchestra" called *The War of the Elements and the Thundering of Niagara.*

The composer of these remarkably titled works, born into a well-to-do family in Schönbüchel in Bohemia, came to America in 1805, as a merchant dealing in linen, thread, wines, and other goods. Stranded here by the collapse of the Austrian economy in 1811, he turned to music for a livelihood. After holding a position as musical director of the Southwark Theatre in Philadelphia, circumstances too bizarre and complicated to be detailed here found him in Kentucky in 1817, where he conducted the earliest recorded performance of a complete symphony by Beethoven in America. Falling ill during the winter of 1818, he lived alone in a log cabin, practicing the violin and composing:

> In the Spring of 1818 J. R. Black, a young student of Bardstown, Kentucky, attracted by my well known seclusions in a retired loghouse interrupted my studious application on the violin, by desiring me to adjust the following ode from Collins [*How Sleep the Brave*] to music. I took pencil and instantaneously reciprocated with the present melody which in fact became the basis of all my after efforts.[22]

[20] The only orchestral piece by Fry available in recorded performance is his *Overture to Macbeth,* apparently written in 1862, on *MIA* 132.

[21] NW 208, S1 / 1.

[22] From a note accompanying the song as printed in *Journal of the Fine Arts,* III / 7 (December 1, 1851).

Within two years he had published a large collection of songs, piano pieces, and chamber works under the title *The Dawning of Music in Kentucky, or the Pleasures of Harmony in the Solitudes of Nature* (1820).[23] A writer for the *Euterpeiad, or Musical Intelligencer* (Boston), in the issue of April 13, 1822, found the compositions in this collection filled with "vigor of thought, variety of ideas, originality of conception, classical correctness, boldness and luxuriance of imagination," and concluded:

> There is versatility for the capricious, pomp for the pedant, playfulness for the amateur, learning for the scholar, business for the performer, pleasure for the vocalist, ingenuity for the curious, and puzzle for the academician. He seems at once to have possessed himself of the key which unlocks to him the temple of science and enables him to explore with fearless security the mysterious labyrinth of harmony. He may, therefore, justly be styled *the Beethoven of America.*

A stay in Philadelphia brought a performance of his melodrama *Child of the Mountain, or the Deserted Mother* at the Walnut Street Theatre in 1821, on a program featuring thirteen of his own compositions. Moving to Boston in 1823, he organized a program by members of the two leading musical organizations of the city, the Handel and Haydn Society and the Philharmonic Society; a critic hailed him as

> the first regular or general *American* composer—the first who, notwithstanding his great practical skill on various instruments, has almost exclusively devoted himself to the sublime study of harmony. His fame is rising fast, and America will have good reason to be proud of him.[24]

And when he left in 1826, for London, the best professional musicians of the city joined him in a Farewell Concert featuring three of his own compositions.

In London, he made his living as a violinist in the orchestras at Drury Lane and Vauxhall Gardens, while devoting most of his time to composition. A number of his songs and piano works were published and attracted favorable critical notice, and he completed his first orchestral piece, *Pushmataha: A Venerable Chief of the Western Tribe of Indians*, in 1831. A trip to the Continent, culminating in his first visit to his homeland since 1811, resulted in a concert in Graz by members of the Styrian Musik-Verein, featuring four of his compositions.

[23] Available in a facsimile edition, *The Dawning of Music in Kentucky and the Western Minstrel* (New York: Da Capo Press, 1972).

[24] Quoted in William Treat Upton, *Anthony Philip Heinrich: A Nineteenth-Century Composer in America* (New York: Columbia University Press, 1939), p. 70.

Heinrich returned to America in 1837, to New York, where he spent the next twenty years composing, teaching, participating in a variety of musical events. His first large program in New York took place at the Broadway Tabernacle on June 16, 1842, a "Grand Musical Festival" made up almost entirely of his own compositions. It opened with:

The Grand Overture to the Pilgrim Fathers.
  *Adagio Ottetto.* The Genius of Freedom slumbering in the Forest shades of America.

  *Adagio Secondo.* FULL ORCHESTRA—She is awakened into life and action by those moving melodies with which Nature regales her solitudes.

  *Marcia.* The efforts of Power to clip the wing of the young Eagle of Liberty.

  *Finale Allegrissimo.* The joyous reign of universal Intelligence and universal Freedom.

The Broadway Tabernacle was the scene of another benefit concert organized by Heinrich, this one devoted exclusively to his own compositions, ranging from songs and choruses to *A Monumental Symphony—To the Spirit of Beethoven* for "grand orchestra." A similar program was given in Boston, at the Tremont Temple, on June 13 of the same year and yet another at Metropolitan Hall in New York on April 21, 1853. A last trip to Europe was climaxed by an all-Heinrich program in Prague on May 3, 1857; he died in New York in 1861.

Despite the public and critical success of such concerts, his compositions were never performed by the large and influential musical organizations of America—the Philharmonic Society of New York, the Musical Fund Society of Philadelphia, the Boston Handel and Haydn Society, the Sacred Music Society of New York. Not one of his large instrumental compositions was accepted by a publisher. He lived a life of near poverty, and he died in circumstances as pathetic as had William Billings; a note in Dwight's *Journal of Music* less than two months before his death paints a pathetic portrait:

There is among us an aged artist numbering eighty years. Every reader of this paper knows him as a highly gifted musician. His many valuable manuscripts fill large trunks, and in the face of these riches this old man lies sick and without money in the second story of the house, No. 33 Bayard St. Anthony Philip Heinrich is too illustrious a person to be suffered to make his debut before the world in the character of a beggar. He has worked much and the world owes him.[25]

As he described his own life, in his last years:

> I am trotting about from morning till night, teaching little misses on the piano forte, for small quarter money, often unpaid. Sometimes I have had good cause to sink under my exertions, but still my spirits remain buoyant on the heated and dusty surface of the summer-earth. At night, I close my toilsome labors and lonely incubations, on a broken, crazy, worn-out, feeble, and very limited octaved piano forte. I believe my music runs full of strange ideal somersets and capriccios. Still I hope there may be some method discoverable, some beauty, whether of regular or irregular features. Possibly the public may acknowledge this, when I am dead and gone. I must keep at the work with my best powers, under all discouraging, nay suffering circumstances. The pitcher goes to the well till it breaks, and that I apprehend, will soon be the case with my old shell.[26]

Heinrich's compositional style grew out of the Germanic repertory. Heinrich Marschner wrote of his "joy on finding that the German school of music is so worthily represented by you in America; for in all your compositions honored sir, I remark that you exhibit the true German style most effectively."[27] But some aspects of his style are atypical of German music of the day. From his earliest pieces, he was fond of extraordinary chromatic passages, unexpected modulations, unexplained dissonances.

*A Chromatic Ramble*, by Heinrich

---

[25] *Dwight's Journal* for March 23, 1861, p. 415.

[26] From a letter written by Heinrich to *The Tribune* for May 5, 1846, quoted in David Barron, *The Ornithological Combat of Kings*, liner notes to NW 208, p. 3.

[27] From a letter of May 10, 1849 from Marschner to Heinrich, quoted in Upton, *Anthony Philip Heinrich*, p. 215.

His forms tend to be episodic and fragmentary, rather than unfolding according to the symmetries and architectural balances of Haydn, Mozart, Beethoven, and Mendelssohn.[28]

A contemporary remarked that "in the midst of this sublimity and grandeur, we are sometimes startled by the quaintest and oddest passages we ever heard. There is certainly a wonderful deal of originality in all of Mr. H.'s compositions."[29] He was fond of introducing such familiar tunes as "Yankee Doodle" at unexpected moments, and almost all of his compositions are programmatic:

> Mr. Heinrich belongs to the romantic class, who wish to attach a story to every thing they do. Mere outward scenes and histories seem to have occupied the mind of the composer too much, and to have disturbed the pure spontaneous inspiration of his melodies. In efforts to describe things, to paint pictures to the hearer's imagination, music leaves its natural channels, and forfeits that true identity which would come from the simple development of itself from within *as music*. Beethoven had no *programme* to his symphonies, intended no description, with the single exception of the *Pastorale;* yet, how full of meaning are they![30]

In retrospect, it appears that the music of Heinrich (and Fry) was excluded from programs of the Philharmonic Society of New York and similar musical organizations on grounds of musical style. The musical preference of the German musicians who dominated these groups was strongly on the side of abstract music rather than "modern" programmatic composition.

The Philharmonic was perfectly willing to play music by American composers—if it conformed to the style favored by its conductors, members and critics. George Bristow, whose brief flurry against the orchestra's supposed anti-American policies was mentioned above, remained a member of the violin section for some years, and was represented frequently on the Society's programs.

His *First Symphony* was played twice in public rehearsals in the Philharmonic's first years; his *Concert Overture* (Opus 3) appears

---

[28] His *Ornithological Combat of Kings*, recorded on NW 208, s1, is a good example of this style of putting a piece together.

[29] Quoted in Barron, p. 1.

[30] John S. Dwight in *The Harbinger* for July 4, 1846.

on concerts for the season of 1846–47; his *Second Symphony* was premiered on March 1, 1856 and his *Third Symphony* on March 26, 1859; his *Columbus Overture* was given its first performance by the Philharmonic on March 26, 1850; and his *Fourth Symphony*, the "Arcadian," was featured on the program of February 14, 1874. These were works based solidly on the Haydn-Beethoven-Mendelssohn symphonic tradition, as is evident both from contemporary criticisms:

> Its [the Symphony No. 2] chief fault is a pretty serious one: a decided want of originality. It is full of reminiscences of other composers, Weber, Mendelssohn, Spohr, Haydn, Mozart, and I know not what others, seems to be playing ball with snatches of their melodies, and tossing them to and fro in a merry confusion. In listening to it, I found myself constantly thinking: "What is that? where have I heard this? I surely know this melody," etc.; and the same experience has been related to me by many friends.[31]

and from examining his scores and listening to performances today.[32] Significantly, Bristow's orchestral works *not* played by the Philharmonic are precisely those which acknowledged the "modern" programmatic school, his *Niagara Symphony* and his symphonic ode entitled *The Great Republic*.

The musical life of nineteenth-century America depended as much on visiting artists as on resident performers. Until the 1840s, these were almost all singers, usually from the British Isles. They offered benefit concerts, took the leading roles in operas, and sang solo parts in large sacred choral works by Handel and Haydn.

This pattern was altered by a trio of celebrated violinists who made their American debuts in New York in late 1843: Alexandre Artôt was first, with his performance at the Washington Hotel on October 19; the great Norwegian violinist Ole Bull followed, at the Park Theatre, on November 25; and the Belgian virtuoso Henri Vieuxtemps first played for an American audience on December 11.

Pianists soon followed. Leopold de Meyer, "Imperial and Royal Pianist to the Emperors of Austria and Russia," made his New York debut on October 20, 1845; Henri Herz, "Pianist to the King of France," came to America in 1846; and Richard Hoffman, an

---

[31] *Dwight's Journal* for March 8, 1856, p. 180.
[32] Two of his symphonies are available in recorded form: *Symphony No. 2* in D minor (Opus 24), often referred to as the "Jullien" Symphony (MIA 143); and *Symphony No. 4* (Opus 49), the "Arcadian" Symphony (MIA 135).

English pupil of de Meyer's, came the following year. Before the decade was over, America had heard Charles Grobe and Maurice Strakosch ("Pianist to the Emperor of Russia"), Italian violinist Camillo Sivori, Hungarian violinist Edouardo Rementi, and Miska Hauser.

At first their programs were given mostly in theaters, and they played chiefly their own compositions or arrangements. Artôt shared his programs with the French soprano Cinti Damoreau; on a typical evening at the Park Theatre, they were on a bill with two farces: *The Married Rake* and *The Boarding School*. Ole Bull made his American debut at the Park, spotted between *A Thumping Legacy* and *The Lancers;* with the pit orchestra accompanying, he played two of his own compositions, a concerto and a *Grand Polacca Guerriera*. Soon he introduced pieces composed since his arrival in America, such as *Grand March to the Memory of Washington*, with "Yankee Doodle" and "God Save the King" played "amid discordant tremolos and battle storms of the whole orchestra."

Vieuxtemps played his own *Fantasia* "pour le violin sur la quatrième corde" with the Philharmonic Society in March of 1844. Leopold de Meyer's first program included his own "brilliant variations" on a melody from Donizetti's *Lucrezia Borgia* and *Grande Marche Marocaine*. Later programs included his sets of variations on themes from *Lucia di Lammermoor* and *L'elisir d'amore*, his arrangements of *The Carnival of Venice* and the overture to *William Tell*, and his *Fantasia on Russian Airs*. Sivori debuted with his own arrangement of the "Preghiera di Moise" by Rossini, played on one string of his violin. Hoffman's New York debut included de Meyer's *Introduction and Variations on Semiramis* and his own arrangement of the *William Tell Overture*, for three pianos.

Thus visiting European virtuosi offered American audiences fare that differed substantially from the programs of the Philharmonic Society of New York or the Boston Handel and Haydn Society: more programmatic; often based on familiar melodies; designed to show off the virtuosity of the artist.

Virtuosi of the time performed for a theatrical rather than a concert audience. Managers, then as now, were not adverse to gimmicks for drawing audiences into theaters; when Leopold de Meyer first played in New York, at the Broadway Tabernacle:

... it was difficult to fill the hall, even with the help of deadheads. De Meyer's agent, acting on the principle that "a crowd draws a crowd," hired a lot of carriages to make their appearance a little before the concert-hour, and to stand in front of the doors and then advance in turn, so that passers-by might receive the impression of activity on the part of the concert-goers.[33]

And the career of the most successful European virtuoso of the period, the "Swedish Nightingale" Jenny Lind, was orchestrated by no other than the greatest impresario and "master of humbug" of the day, P. T. Barnum.

Convinced that he could "sell" her to American audiences, Barnum guaranteed her $1000 for each of 150 concerts, depositing the sum of $187,500 in a bank in London as security. In the weeks preceding her arrival in American, he master-minded the most successful publicity campaign in the history of American entertainment. By the time of her arrival in New York on September 1, 1850, the city was in a frenzy:

> At length the vessel reached Canal Street; and here the crowd, who had been patiently waiting the arrival of the Northern Nightingale, was

Jenny Lind.

[33] William Mason, *Memories of a Musical Life* (New York: The Century Company, 1901), pp. 21–22.

immense. Some thirty or forty thousand people must have been collected together on the adjacent piers and shipping, as well as on all the roofs and in all the windows fronting the water. As the steamer slowly glided into her place, it became very obvious to Mr. Barnum that he would have considerable difficulty in getting Mademoiselle Lind to the Irving House, which has been selected as her hotel. Scarcely had she entered the carriage . . . than the multitude began to press against them. Some were thrown to the ground, while the tide of struggling and tossing humanity swept over them. Here lay persons protesting and screaming under the heels of the inexorable throng. At length the police succeeded in allaying the tumult and drove back the crowd, although, it must be confessed, with great difficulty, and the carriage containing the Singing Bird slowly started. As the people gradually fell back from it, they literally deluged its occupants with flowers.[34]

Jenny Lind was, by all accounts, a superb interpretor of the operatic and oratorio repertory, and her first American concert on September 11 was built partly on classical repertory:

### PART ONE

| | |
|---|---|
| 1. Overture to *Oberon* | Weber |
| 2. Aria, "Sorgete," from *Maometto Secondo* <br> Signor Belletti | Rossini |
| 3. Scena and Cavatina, "Casta Diva," from *Norma* <br> Mademoiselle Jenny Lind | Bellini |
| 4. Duet on two Piano Fortes <br> Messieurs Benedict and Hoffman | Benedict |
| 5. Duetto, "Per piacer," from *Il Turco in Italia* <br> Lind and Belletti | Rossini |

### PART TWO

| | |
|---|---|
| 1. Overture to *The Crusaders* | Benedict |
| 2. Trio for Voice and two Flutes, composed expressly for <br> Mademoiselle Lind, from *Camp of Silesia* <br> Lind, and Messrs. Kyle and Siede | Meyerbeer |
| 3. Cavatina, "Largo al Factotum," from *Il Barbiere* <br> Belletti | Rossini |
| 4. The Herdsman's Song, more generally known as "The <br> Echo Song"   Lind | traditional |
| 5. The Welcome to America, written expressly for this <br> occasion, by Bayard Taylor, Esq.   Lind | Benedict |

On closer inspection it proves to be the same sort of program offered by other visiting European artists. The Italian repertory of Rossini,

[34]C. G. Rosenberg, *Jenny Lind in America* (New York: Stringer & Townsend, 1851), pp. 9–11.

Bellini, and their peers had been widely known in America for a quarter-century. The newer works were written by a member of the company, Benedict, rather than more famous composers of the day. "The Echo Song," with which Lind closed almost every program in America, depended on a vocal trick, a type of ventriloquism, making it appear that echoing phrases came from offstage. And her encores were such familiar songs as "Home! Sweet Home!," "Coming through the Rye," and several of Stephen Foster's songs.

After five more concerts in New York, Lind and her assisting artists went to Boston, then Philadelphia, Baltimore, Washington, Richmond, Charleston, and Havana. Sailing back to New Orleans from Cuba, the company continued to Natchez, Memphis, St. Louis, Nashville, Louisville, Cincinnati, Wheeling, Pittsburgh, then back to Baltimore, Philadelphia, and New York.

On June 9, 1851, Lind exercised an option to break her contract with Barnum, hoping to realize more profit without a manager. To this point, after 93 concerts, the gross take had been some $712,000, of which she had received $177,000. She continued singing here for another year; her final American performance took place in New York on May 24, 1852, at Castle Gardens, where it had all begun.

More Americans heard her sing than any other performer in the history of the country; the intense excitement generated by her presence brought many people otherwise not involved in music to her concerts, and thus into contact with music. An American writer attempted to sum up her impact on the country:

> She brought the musical temperament of America to consciousness of itself. Her tour was the supreme moment in our national history when young America, ardent, enthusiastic, irrepressible, heard and knew its own capacity for musical feeling forever.[35]

There were visiting orchestras as well. The most successful and influential was the Germania Orchestra (or Musical Society), consisting of twenty-four young musicians from Berlin who left their native land in search of a more congenial artistic and political climate. They made their American debut in 1848 at Niblo's Garden in New York. It was well received by critics and a small band of musical enthusiasts, but their first popular successes came in Washington, where they had been invited to play for the inauguration of Zachary Taylor as twelfth president of the United States, and in Baltimore, with its large German population. The enthusiastic reception they received in Boston for the twenty-two con-

---

[35] Fanny Morris Smith, "What Jenny Lind Did for America," *The Country Magazine*, LIV (August 1897), pp. 558–59.

certs they gave there in the spring of 1849 led to a summer engagement at Newport, where they divided their time between playing "serious" programs for the summer inhabitants and more popular selections for dinner parties and dancing. They toured with Ole Bull for four months, shared programs with Strakosch and Adelina Patti, and accompanied Jenny Lind on thirty of her American concerts. They were also received with enthusiasm in the West—Cincinnati, St. Louis, Milwaukee, Louisville—with its large concentration of German immigrants. When they disbanded in the fall of 1854, they had given American audiences some 800 concerts and public rehearsals, and had appeared as the accompanying band on another 200; it has been estimated that more than a million Americans heard them at one time or another.[36]

Like other visiting performers, they mixed "selections of a popular nature" with pieces from classical repertory. They played all nine of Beethoven's symphonies at one time or another, and symphonies and overtures by Mozart, Haydn, Weber, Mendelssohn, Spohr, Gluck, Cherubini, Gade, Auber, Lindpainter, Marschner, and Schumann; they occasionally offered a "modern" work, such as Wagner's overture to *Tannhäuser*.

> These young artists have diffused among our people something nearer than we have had before, to a true idea of German music, both in its popular and in its classical forms. They have been to us in fact a live and genuine specimen of musical Germany, travelling about in the midst of us, and at each point again and again renewing the vibration from that vital heart and centre of the tone-sphere.[37]

Another visitor was Louis Antoine Jullien (1812–60), a French-born conductor who came to America in 1853 after a brilliant career in London. One of the supreme showmen of the century, Jullien understood as well as Barnum how to use the press to his advantage. His orchestras in England and America were advertised as the largest the world had ever seen; he had the largest instruments ever constructed—a huge ophicleide and his famous Monster Drum. He claimed that his repertory consisted of 1,200 different compositions. He conducted with white kid gloves to spotlight and dramatize his expressive hands; his jeweled baton was brought in on a silken pillow after he was on the podium; at the end of a piece he

---

[36] H. Earle Johnson, "The Germania Musical Society," *The Music Quarterly*, XXXIX (1953), p. 92. This is the best modern account of the Germanians. Valuable also is the more contemporary J. Bunting, "The Old Germania Orchestra," *Scribner's Monthly-Century Illustrated Monthly*, XI (November 1875), pp. 98–107.

[37] *Dwight's Journal* for April 10, 1852, p. 6.

would sink, melodramatically exhausted, into a red upholstered chair placed on the stage for that purpose.

Much of his repertory consisted of quadrilles, waltzes, mazurkas, polkas, schottisches, tarantellas, and galops. Each of his programs featured one of his "celebrated NATIONAL QUADRILLES, as the English, Irish, Scotch, French, Russian, Chinese, Indian, Hungarian, Polish, &c." with music of his own composition.

But there was more to Jullien than showmanship. By all accounts, his orchestra was the best yet heard in America:

> The orchestra he brought over with him, between forty and fifty in number, comprised some of the finest solo performers of Europe, —such as Koenig, the unrivalled cornettist; the great contra-bassist Bottesini; Lavigne, then considered the first living oboist. In New York the number of the orchestra was increased to ninety-seven,—then the largest orchestra that had ever appeared before an American audience. It was composed of three flutes, one flageolet, two oboes, two clarinets, two bassoons, three trumpets, three cornets, four trombones, four horns, three snare-drums, one bass-drum, one pair of cymbals, two pairs of kettledrums, seventeen first and sixteen second violins, ten violas, ten violoncellos, and eleven double-basses. The splendor and beautiful quality of this orchestra were a revelation to American musical amateurs.[38]

Each program included several overtures and movements of symphonies by famous European composers. In Boston and New York, he presented concerts devoted to the orchestral works of a single composer—Beethoven, Mozart, or Mendelssohn. And unlike America's resident orchestras, Jullien played works by American composers such as William Henry Fry's *A Day in the Country*, *The Breaking Heart*, and *Santa Claus: Christmas Symphony*, and the *Second Symphony* by George Bristow. As one writer summed it up,

> Although some critics of that day looked upon the lively Jullien as a humbug (others dubbed him the Napoleon among conductors), his humbug was really but the excessive theatrical expressions of a peculiar character and orchestral genius; and in his line he exerted a very excellent influence on orchestral performances. [His] enterprises, on a great scale, stirred up musical taste and emulation among rising American musicians.[39]

Among the most successful virtuosi of the period was Louis Moreau Gottschalk (1829–69). A native of New Orleans, he received most of his musical training in Paris and made his reputation

[38] Ritter, pp. 326–27.
[39] Ritter, pp. 327–28.

Louis Gottschalk.

abroad. He absorbed French ways so thoroughly that a critic said of him, "Il est Français d'espirit, de coeur, de goût et d'habitudes."[40] He spoke English with an accent, yet he considered himself an American and was taken as such by audiences in Europe and at home.

Gottschalk was hailed by Europeans not only for his playing, but also as a composer of talent and originality. His first pieces were written for the piano. Some were brilliant, virtuostic dance-based works, such as his Opus 1, *Polka de salon*, and a number of concert waltzes. Some were in the style of Chopin: Opus 6, *Colliers d'or*, various polkas and *Ossian, or deux ballades* (Opus 4). He attracted most attention, though, with a series of pieces evoking the music he had heard as a child in New Orleans. There was *Bamboula* (Opus 2), subtitled "Danse des nègres," based on a Creole tune called "Quand patate la cuite na va mangé li!" and taking its title from a type of Caribbean drum. *Le Bananier* (Opus 5) was a "Chanson

[40]Quoted in Louis Moreau Gottschalk, *Notes of a Pianist* (New York: Alfred A. Knopf, 1964), p. xvi.

nègre" drawing its chief melodic material from the Creole song "En avan' Grenadie"; *La Savane* (Opus 3) was a "Ballade créole" based on the song "Pov' piti Lolotte." All three were heard by European audiences as distinctively American.

In the century and a half since Gottschalk wrote *Bamboula*, so many pieces have made use of syncopated, Afro-Latin rhythms against reiterated melodic fragments that his piece, using these devices for probably the first time, has not received its proper due:

*Bamboula*, by Gottschalk

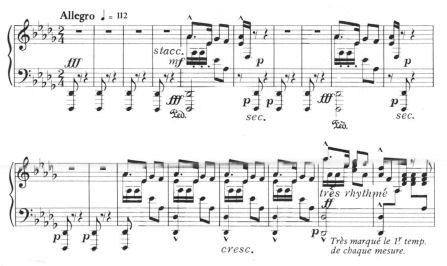

And his indebtedness to Chopin's style is more obvious now than when the piece was new, making it even more difficult for us to hear the "Americanness" that struck contemporary audiences:

*Bamboula*, by Gottschalk

Likewise, the opening of *Le Bananier*, with its insistent drumming of octaves and open fifths, and the structure of *La Savane*—a simple diatonic melody repeated for the duration of the composition against changing harmonizations and textures—remind us of many later pieces.[41] But contemporary audiences found these things new and exciting.

Gottschalk's American debut came on February 11, 1853 at Niblo's Salon in New York. He played mostly arrangements and transcriptions of pieces by other composers (the overture to Méhul's *La Chasse de jeune Henri*, a "Grand Triumphal Fantasia" for two pianos on themes from Verdi's *I Lombardi*, Liszt's paraphrase of the famous septet from Donizetti's *Lucia di Lammermoor*, his version of *La Carnaval de Venise*); and several of his own works, including a ballade from Opus 4; *La Bananier; La Moissonneuse* (Opus 8); and *Valse di bravura, pour deux pianos*.

Refusing an offer from P. T. Barnum for $20,000 a year, Gottschalk set out to tour America on his own. After four years of travel to almost every part of the country, he left for Havana in 1857, for a concert tour of Central America and the West Indies with the fourteen-year-old Adelina Patti. Resuming his American career with a program in New York on February 11, 1862, he continued the life of a traveling virtuoso:

> I have given eighty-five concerts in four months and a half. I have travelled fifteen thousand miles by train. At St. Louis I gave seven concerts in six days; at Chicago, five in four days. A few weeks more in this way and I would have become an idiot! Eighteen hours a day on the railroad! Arrive at seven o'clock in the evening, eat with all speed, appear at eight o'clock before the public. The last note finished, rush quickly for my luggage, and en route until next day, always to the same thing! . . . The railroad conductors salute me familiarly as one of the employees. The young girls at the refreshment room of the station, where five minutes are given, select for me the best cut of ham, and sugar my tea with the obliging smile that all well-taught tradespeople owe to their customers. In my black suit at 8 o'clock I salute my audience, and give them *Il Trovatore*. At a quarter to nine they encore the *Murmures éoliens*. At half-past nine they call again for the *Berceuse*, in the midst of the enthusiasm of some young romantic virgins and some papas slightly inclined in a semiconscious state to sleep, who find the piece full of agreeable affects. At ten o'clock I carry off my patriotic audience to the belligerent accents of *The Union* fantasia; and at half-past ten I throw myself, exhausted and depoetized, into the prosaic arms of the blessed Morpheus.[42]

[41] These early pieces, as well as a good selection of his later compositions for piano, are available in a modern printing in Louis Moreau Gottschalk, *Piano Music* (New York: Dover Publications, 1973). *Forty Works for the Piano*, performed by Alan Mandel (Desto DC 6470-73 Stereo), is the most comprehensive recording of Gottschalk's piano music, containing these early works and a large selection of later ones.

[42] Gottschalk, *Notes of a Pianist*, pp. 102 and 116.

Like most of the successful virtuosi of the time, he was a good showman. Handsome and elegant, he cut an effective and provocative figure on stage:

> It was the fashion at that time always to wear white gloves with evening dress, and his manner of taking them off after seating himself at the piano was often a very amusing episode. His deliberation, his perfect indifference to the waiting audience was thoroughly manifest, as he slowly drew them off one finger at a time, bowing and smiling meanwhile to the familiar faces in the front rows. Finally disposing of them, he would manipulate his hands until they were quite limber, then preludize until his mood prompted him to begin his first selection on the programme.[43]

He was a keen, bemused, and sometime vitriolic observer of the musical scene in America:

> Lately a gentleman among the audience did not cease repeating during the whole concert, "When are they going to play a tune?" And after three pieces sung by Madame S(trakosch), after those of Carlo Patti, after my five or six solos, he repeated, "I have not yet heard one tune," and he went away perfectly disgusted. . . . One of my friends lately told me that at one of my concerts he was seated in front of two ladies who consoled themselves for the total absence of "tunes" by seeing that in the third part I must play "Home, Sweet Home" with variations. They waited patiently. The concert went on, "Home, Sweet Home" was encored, which did not prevent the good women from saying, "But when is he going to play "Home, Sweet Home"?"[44]

He continued to write piano pieces incorporating the rhythms, melodies, and moods of the folk and popular music of the various lands he visited. His travels in Spain in the early 1840s yielded *Canto del gitano* and *La Jota aragonesa;* his several trips to Cuba resulted in *El Cocoyé; Grand Caprice cubain de bravura, Ojos criollos, La Gallina* (Opus 53), and others. Later "American" pieces were *The Banjo* (Opus 15) and the lost *Tennessee.* One of his most popular pieces on his last American tour was *The Union* (Opus 48), a "Paraphrase de concert sur les airs nationaux" dedicated to General McClellan, incorporating "The Star-Spangled Banner," "Yankee Doodle," and "Hail Columbia"—the latter two in counterpoint at the climax. His Opus 55, entitled *Le cri de délivrance* or *Caprice héroïque: Battle Cry of Freedom,* is a brilliant paraphrase of George F. Root's famous war song of 1863, described by Gottschalk as an

---

[43] Richard Hoffman, *Some Musical Recollections of Fifty Years* (New York: Charles Scribner's Sons, 1910), pp. 133–34.

[44] Gottschalk, *Notes of a Pianist*, pp. 210–11.

"obscure flower I have discovered on the heap of dirt that the poetasters and the *musicasters* have raised at the foot of their country's altar since the war began,"[45] and which he thought should become the national anthem.

Most successful of all was *The Last Hope* (Opus 16), a "Religious Meditation" for piano written as a parody of a popular parlor piece by a Miss Bardazewska entitled *The Maiden's Prayer*. Though Gottschalk often spoke cynically of it, he included it on almost every program and milked it for every last drop of sentiment. A woman wrote, after hearing him play it:

> His head was slightly bowed, and I'm sure his eyes were closed. He was praying a prayer of gratitude, giving back to God a measure of the music with which God had endowed him in such great abundance. I was crying so when he came to the end that I felt ashamed of myself. Then after I looked about and saw that nearly everybody else was crying also, I felt better.[46]

In his last years, Gottschalk organized concerts and festivals for gigantic groups of instrumentalists and singers. A "grand festival" in Cuba in 1860 brought together

> [An] orchestra of six hundred and fifty performers, eighty-seven choristers, fifteen solo singers, fifty drums, and eighty trumpets—that is to say, nearly nine hundred persons bellowing and blowing to see who could scream the loudest. The violins alone were seventy in number, contrabasses eleven, violoncellos eleven![47]

A second festival on March 21, 1861 assembled forty pianists, all the musicians of the military garrison of Havana, and "all the amateur vocalists of the city," for a program lasting five and a half hours. In San Francisco in 1865, he featured ten pianos (and pianists); the audience showed its approval by shouting and throwing gold dollars on the stage. Gottschalk promptly announced a "Farewell Concert" with thirty pianists performing his *The Battle of Bunker Hill*, but a scandal involving a young woman was blown out of proportion by several of his rivals, and he was forced to flee by ship to Mexico.

He spent the last four years of his life in Central and South America. Concerts in Peru, Chile, Argentina, and Uruguay brought him

[45] Gottschalk, *Notes of a Pianist*, p. 181.
[46] Quoted in Vernon Loggins, *Where the World Ends: The Life of Louis Moreau Gottschalk* (Baton Rouge: Louisiana State University Press, 1958), p. 147.
[47] Gottschalk, *Notes of a Pianist*, pp. 26–27.

to Rio de Janeiro, where he mounted a performance of Mendelssohn's *Grand Marche de Athalia* for 13 pianos (25 pianists) and orchestra. The emperor of Brazil placed all military bands of the city at Gottschalk's disposal for a program given on November 24, 1869. The performing forces totalled "800 performers and 80 drums," with the instrumentalists grouped into 15 different wind bands, an orchestra of "seventy professors of music," and two additional "German orchestras"; the program included Gottschalk's arrangement of the march from Meyerbeer's *Le Prophète*, the first movement of his *Night in the Tropics* symphony, and a piece written for the occasion, the *Marche solemne brasileira*, which included cannon among its percussion.

This concert was both the climax and the finale of Gottschalk's career; in poor health for some time, he died several weeks later, on December 18.

Three different strains of classical music coexisted in America during the quarter-century leading up to the Civil War. There was the Germanic repertory—the symphonies, chamber music and large choral works of Haydn, Mozart, Beethoven, Schubert, Mendelssohn, Gade, Lindpainter—which formed the core repertory of the German-dominated permanent musical organizations. The "modern" school of Berlioz, Liszt, Chopin, and the young Wagner was more discursive in form and increasingly complex in harmony and instrumentation; not much of this music was played here. And there was the music offered by virtuoso solo performers—concert dances, variations on familiar operatic airs and popular songs, programmatic pieces featuring technically dazzling passages.

The third repertory was heard by far the largest number of Americans, and has been dubbed "Music of Democratic Sociability" by a recent writer:

[It] was frankly directed to American popular taste as it then existed by composers who were in some degree public favorites. It includes striking and in some cases bizarrely autistic essays in the larger forms, particularly symphonies and operas, as well as countless waltzes, polkas, schottisches, galops, and marches for piano solo. It ranges from a vigorous frontier primitivism to brownstone-ballroom elegance to extraordinary examples of urban sophistication that prefigure jazz on the one hand and evoke a Rossinian or Offenbachian wit on the other. At its best it is so good that the musicological snobbery that suppressed it for a century seems nothing less than criminal. But even at its routine average it can surprise us with its capacity for rendering American subject matter in a deliciously fresh vernacular. Its tone is generally optimistic and it can be genial to a point of gregariousness—and that (plus its occasional roughneck associations) is probably what invited both its popular success and a considerable measure of critical disrepute.

By far the most interesting fact about it is that good, bad, or indifferent, it promptly found a place in the daily life of the nation wherever it managed to get heard. Those who first encountered it seemed to sense with delight that it was somehow about *them*, and today we see that it is actually a marvelously characteristic portrait of the society for which it was composed.[48]

The course of classical music in the United States might have been quite different in the second half of the nineteenth century had the major musical organizations of the country supported the efforts of American composers and regularly offered programs on the order of the following imaginary event:

PHILHARMONIC SOCIETY OF NEW YORK
Grand Concert of American Music
31 December 1857

*PART ONE*

| | |
|---|---|
| 1. Overture to *Aurelia the Vestal* | William Henry Fry |
| 2. "Pocahontas—the Royal Indian Maid and Heroine of Virginia, the Pride of the Wilderness." *Fantasia romanza (Cornette concertante)* | Anthony Philip Heinrich |
| 3. "Ossian" *Deux ballades, Opus 4* "Chant du Soldat" *Grand caprize de concert, Opus 23* "Bamboula," "Le Bananier," "La Savane," "The Banjo" | Louis Moreau Gottschalk |
| 4. "Hagar in the Wilderness" *Sacred Symphony No. 3* | Fry |
| 5. "War of the Elements and the Thundering of Niagara" *Capriccio grande for a full orchestra* | Heinrich |

*PART TWO*

| | |
|---|---|
| 1. *Concert Overture*, Opus 3 | George Bristow |
| 2. "The Harp's Last Echoes" | Heinrich |

[48] Robert Offergeld, "Gottschalk and Company. The Music of Democratic Sociability," liner notes to NW 257 (New York: New World Records, 1976), p. 1. Typical pieces of this genre are Gottschalk's *Pasquinade* (NW 282, s1 / 5) and *Romance* (NW 257, s2 / 3); Heinrich's *The Elssler Dances* (NW 257, s2 / 2) and *The Laurel Waltz* (NW 257, s2 / 2); Richard Hoffman's *Dixiana, Caprice* (NW 257, s1 / 6); George Bristow's *Dream Land* (NW 257, s1 / 2); and several pieces by Charles Grobe: *Natalie Polka-Mazurka* (NW 293, s1 / 5), *United States Grand Waltz* (NW 257, s1 / 3), and *The Flirt Polka* (NW 293, s1 / 8).

    a. 'Tis Echo's Voice
    b. The Soul Released
    c. Heaven and My Harp Are All That's
    Left
3. "Chant des Oiseaux" (voice, flute, piano)    Gottschalk
4. "The Hunters of Kentucky" *Sinfonia di*    Heinrich
    *caccia*
5. "Santa Claus: Christmas Symphony"    Fry

            soloists:  Louis Moreau Gottschalk, piano
                      Adelina Patti, soprano

# 9

## Stephen Foster and Indigenous American Song

*The air is full of his melodies. They are whistled, and sung, and played on all instruments every where. Their simple pathos touches every heart. They are our national music.*

—*Harper's New Monthly Magazine*, XXVIII (March 1864), p. 567

The above judgment of the songs of Stephen Foster (1826–64) has never been challenged. The rapidity with which they became known was astonishing; a contributor to the *Albany State Register*, addressing himself to the popularity of Foster's "Old Folks at Home" in 1852, the year following its publication, wrote:

Pianos and guitars groan with it, night and day; sentimental young ladies sing it; sentimental young gentlemen warble it in midnight serenades; volatile young "bucks" hum it in the midst of their business and their pleasures; boatmen roar it out stentorially at all times; all the bands play it; amateur flute players agonize over it at every spare moment; the street organs grind it out at every hour; the "singing stars" carol it on the theatrical boards, and at concerts; the chamber maid sweeps and dusts to its measured cadence; the butcher's boy treats you to a strain or two of it as he hands in the steaks for dinner; the milk-man mixes it up strangely with the harsh ding-dong accompaniment of his tireless bell; there is not a "live darkey," young or old, but can whistle, sing, dance, and play it. . . . Indeed at every hour, at every turn, we are forcibly impressed with the interesting fact, that—

> 'Way down upon de Swanee Ribber,
>   Far, far away,
> Dere's whar my heart is turnin' ebber,
> Dere's whar de old folks stay.'

Thomas Hastings told of encountering the tune in 1853, fitted with sacred words and intended as a Sunday-school song:

> A superintendent gave the music into the hands of a lady who had charge of about a hundred infant scholars. She saw the trick and remonstrated. "But," says the superintendent, "the children will never know it!" "Come and see," was her reply. She sang a line or two, and then said, "Children, have you ever heard anything like that before?" "Old folks at home! Old folks at home!" shouted the little urchins.[1]

William Vincent Wallace, the Irish composer of *Maritana* and other successful operas, played a set of "grand variations" for piano on "Oh! Susanna" on programs in America in 1852. Jenny Lind included "My Old Kentucky Home" and "Old Black Joe" on her programs. The American pianist and composer Louis Moreau Gottschalk performed *Variations on Old Folks at Home* while touring the United States in 1862–65. At the other end of the musical spectrum, a Scandinavian visitor to the South in 1850 heard so many of Foster's songs sung by black slaves that she assumed they were their own creations:

> Another young negro . . . sang with his banjo several of the negro songs universally known and sung in the South by the negro people, whose product they are, and in the Northern States by persons of all classes, because they are extremely popular. . . . Many of the songs remind me of Haydn's and Mozart's simple, artless melodies; for example, . . . "Oh, Susannah," "Uncle Ned," . . . These songs have been made on the road; during the journeyings of the slaves; upon the rivers, as they paddled their canoes along or steered the raft down the stream; and, in particular, at the corn-huskings.[2]

Never before, and rarely since, did any music come so close to being a shared experience for so many Americans.

Yet Foster's role as a songwriter has been consistently misunderstood and misrepresented. Since the songs that brought him such

---

[1] Quoted in William W. Austin, *Susanna, Jeanie, and The old folks at home; The Songs of Stephen C. Foster from His Time to Ours* (New York: Macmillan Publishing Company Inc., 1975), p. 265.

[2] Frederika Bremer, as quoted in Dena J. Epstein, *Sinful Tunes and Spirituals: Black Folk Music to the Civil War* (Urbana: University of Illinois Press, 1977), p. 241.

fame are brief pieces of apparent simplicity, most historians and critics have assumed that he had nothing more than a natural gift for memorable tunes and enough knowledge of practical harmony to fit three or four basic chords to these.

> Stephen has never mastered sufficiently the technic of composition to be able to produce interesting music on demand, and his vocabulary was so small that of necessity he repeated himself over and over again. He could usually find a melody of some sort without much trouble, but after a bar or two they are all apt to follow the same pattern. Many of his melodic ideas are worthy of better treatment, had he been able to handle them with greater skill.[3]

And even his most sympathetic biographer wrote:

> He had a natural gift of melody that shone because of its simplicity. . . . His limitations were his power; the few chords he used made his songs direct and simple, and always natural. Had he been a trained musician, his charm might have vanished.[4]

Actually, Foster had sound musical training, and was thoroughly familiar with the song literature of the day and the compositional techniques of the several schools of national song most popular in America when he began writing. His style was a matter of deliberate choice. In the words of George Frederick Root (1820–95), an American composer who progressed from emulation of the "proper" and "scientific" music of European composers to the writing of songs openly modeled on those of Stephen Foster:

> I saw that mine must be the "people's song," still, I am ashamed to say, I shared the feeling that was around me in regard to that grade of music. When Stephen C. Foster's wonderful melodies (as I now see them) began to appear . . . I "took a hand in" and wrote a few. . . . It is easy to write *correctly* a simple song, but so to use the material of which such a song must be made that it will be received and live in the hearts of the people is quite another matter. . . . It was much easier to write when the resources were greater.[5]

The issue is simply this: if a composer makes a conscious decision to write a people's music, music that will reach the broadest

[3] Harold V. Milligan, *Stephen Collins Foster* (New York: Schirmer, 1920), pp. 96–97 and 112–13.

[4] John Tasker Howard, *Stephen Foster, America's Troubador* (New York: Thomas Y. Crowell Company, 1934), pp. 188–89.

[5] George F. Root, *The Story of a Musical Life* (Cincinnati: John Church Company, 1891), pp. 83 and 96–97.

public, he must use a musical vocabulary understood by everyone. And Foster did make such a decision—he wanted to speak to the American people.

Born on July 4, 1826—the fiftieth anniversary of the signing of the Declaration of Independence, and the day on which John Adams and Thomas Jefferson died—into an educated and relatively well-to-do family, Foster attended a succession of public and private schools in and around Pittsburgh. In 1846 he went off to Cincinnati to take a position with his brother Dunning, a commission merchant. When the latter went off to the Mexican War, Stephen handled the business himself. With his native intelligence, his education, and his background, he could have pursued a successful business career. But he chose another path.

Music had been important to him since early childhood. His older sister Henrietta taught him simple melodies and chords on the guitar, and he was soon playing the flute and piano, studying with Henry Kleber, a German-born musician with the reputation of being the best "professor of music" in Pittsburgh. His father wrote in 1841 that Stephen's "leisure hours are all devoted to musick, for which he possesses a strange talent,"[6] and his brother Morrison recalled—perhaps not with perfect accuracy—that he "studied deeply, and burned much midnight oil over the works of the masters, especially Mozart, Beethoven, and Weber."[7] His first composition, the *Tioga Waltz*, was written in 1841, and his first published song, "Open Thy Lattice, Love," was brought out in 1844 in Philadelphia by George Willig. The first really successful songs he wrote, including "Old Uncle Ned" and "Oh! Susanna"—came out in 1847–48. By 1849, his reputation as a songwriter was such that two publishers (Firth, Pond & Company of New York, and F. D. Benteen of Baltimore) signed him to contracts guaranteeing a royalty of 2¢ a copy on all new songs. This was an unusual arrangement in a day when most songs were sold outright, for as little as $5, with the composer relinquishing all further claim to profits. For the last fourteen years of his life he made his living solely from writing songs—the first American to do so. Some 200 of these were published during his lifetime, in addition to a handful of piano pieces, hymns, and instrumental arrangements of popular melodies.

Foster was familiar with—and emulated—the various song styles of the day. His earliest attempts were solidly in the tradition of the English songs of Henry Bishop and Charles E. Horn: "Open Thy Lattice, Love," "There's a Good Time Coming," "Annie My Own

[6] Quoted in Howard, p. 81.
[7] Quoted in Howard, p. 108.

Stephen Foster.

Love" (1853), and "Come with Thy Sweet Voice Again" (1854). These are solo strophic songs, usually with a refrain line at the end of each verse, sentimental in content, and frequently dedicated to young women of his acquaintance.[8]

Others reveal Foster's familiarity with the Irish and Scottish songs so popular in America in the first quarter of the nineteenth

[8] Several of these, and many other songs by Foster, are available on *Songs by Stephen Foster* (Nonesuch Records H-71268) and *Songs by Stephen Foster, Vol. II* (Nonesuch Records H-71333).

century. He was of Irish ancestry, and Thomas Moore's *Irish Melodies* were part of his heritage, sung in his home by his older sisters. "Sweetly She Sleeps, My Alice Fair" (1851), "Jeannie with the Light Brown Hair" (1854), and "Gentle Annie" (1856) are direct descendants of the *Irish Melodies*—solo strophic songs, with texts dealing mostly with nostalgia for lost youth and happiness:

> Thou wilt come no more, gentle Annie,
>  Like a flow'r thy spirit did depart;
> Thou art gone, alas! like the many
>  That have bloomed in the summer of my heart.

And tunes suggesting the pentatonic scales of so much Irish music:

"Gentle Annie," by Stephen Foster

Foster was likewise familiar with the music of such Italian composers as Rossini, Bellini, and Donizetti. He is known to have attended concerts and recitals of this music, sometimes with Madame Eliza Ostinelli Biscaccianti, an operatic singer. His *Social Orchestra* (1854) contains a number of arrangements of Italian airs; the duet "Wilt Thou Be Gone Love" (1851) reveals his considerable skill at composing in the Italian style; and other songs written at various periods of his life—"The Voice of Days Gone By" (1850), "Come Where My Love Lies Dreaming" (1855), and "Beautiful Dreamer" (1864)—reveal their ancestry in Italian melody, with graceful melodic lines, expressive appoggiaturas, and arpeggiated and strummed accompaniments.

"Beautiful Dreamer," by Stephen Foster

Beau-ti-ful dream-er, wake un-to me, Star-light and dew-drops are wait-ing for thee;

But the genre in which he achieved his first and greatest success was the minstrel song. As a child of nine, in Pittsburgh, he organized neighborhood children into a minstrel troupe performing such songs as "Zip Coon" and "Jim Crow." Later, as a teenager, he belonged to a group of young men calling themselves the "Knights of the Square Table," who met regularly at his home to perform "songs in harmony" under his direction. Again the repertory was drawn largely from minstrel songs, and it was for this group that Stephen wrote "Lou'siana Belle" and "Old Uncle Ned."

The tremendous proliferation of the minstrel show, following the success of the Virginia Minstrels in 1843 and Christy's Minstrels the following year, created a great demand for new songs. Thus three of Foster's first minstrel songs—"Away Down South," "Old Uncle Ned," and "Oh! Susanna"—were published by the William C. Peters Company as part of a series of "Songs of the Sable Harmonists," and another edition of "Oh! Susanna" appearing the same year (1848) identifies the song as from the repertory of the "Original Christy Minstrels; The Oldest Established Band in the United States"; Foster's name is not mentioned.

Seven of Foster's minstrel songs came out in 1848–49, another seven followed in 1850. At least half of these fourteen quickly became staple items in the repertories of various minstrel troupes, including the most famous ones of the day. They included, in addition to the songs mentioned above, "Gwine to Run All Night" (or "Camptown Races"), "Nelly Bly," and "Nelly Was a Lady." It was the success of these songs that persuaded Foster to give up a career in business and devote himself to full-time songwriting.

These early minstrel songs were faithful to the genre, with simple diatonic melodies (often suggesting pentatonic scales), three-chord harmonic accompaniments, and texts depicting blacks as simple, irresponsible, good-natured creatures. "Dolly Day" (1850), for instance, is a virtual catalogue of the stock attributes of the minstrel-stage black:

> I've told you 'bout de banjo,
>   De fiddle and de bow,
> Likewise about de cotton-field,
>   De shubble and de hoe;
> I've sung about de bulgine,
>   Dat blew de folks away . . .

And others engage in crude caricature:

> I jumped aboard de telegraph
>   And trabbeled down de ribber,
> De 'lectric fluid magnified,
>   And killed five hundred nigger.
>             ("Oh! Susanna," 1848)

> My lub she hab a very large mouf,
>   One corner in de norf, tudder corner in de souf,
> It am so long, it reach so far,
>   Trabble all around it on a railroad car.
>             ("Away Down Souf," 1848)

But critical events in Foster's life and in the life of the country would change the nature of his songs.

He married Jane McDowell in the summer of 1850; within a year a daughter—Marion—was born. The couple separated after several years, and when Stephen decided to go to New York, Jane stayed behind in Pennsylvania. Once the young songwriter had taken up permanent residence in the East, his wife and daughter joined him, but they eventually returned to Pittsburgh and Stephen was alone when he died in 1864. He was constantly in debt in his last years, borrowing money from friends and relatives, drawing advances from his publishers, accepting gifts of clothing from his brother Morrison, turning out new songs for a few dollars.

The content of his songs changed radically during these years. "Jeanie with the Light Brown Hair" (1854), for instance, is a lament for the lost happiness of the early days of his marriage:

I long for Jeanie with the day-dawn smile,
   Radiant in gladness, warm with winning guile;
I hear her melodies, like joys gone by,
   Sighing round my heart o'er the fond hopes that die:
Sighing like the night wind and sobbing like the rain,
   Wailing for the lost one that comes not again:
Oh! I long for Jeanie, and my heart bows low,
   Never more to find her where the bright waters flow.

"Little Ella" (1853) is addressed to his daughter, then two years old:

Her brief absence frets and pains me,
   Her bright presence solace brings,
Her spontaneous love restrains me
   From a thousand selfish things.

And "Comrades, Fill No Glass for Me" (1855) is a melancholy hymn to "blighted fortune, health and fame":

When I was young I felt the tide
   Of aspirations undefiled,
But Manhood's years have wronged the pride
   My parents centered in their child.
Then, by a mother's sacred tear,
By all that memory should revere,
Though boon companions ye may be,
Oh! comrades, fill no glass for me.

Foster's mother had died a few months before this song was written; the year marked the nadir of his creative life, with only four other new songs copyrighted.[9]

His personal problems and anguish mirrored troubling and traumatic events in the life of the nation. Though he took no public stand on the issue of abolition and other political problems, and though none of his songs appears to address such matters, Foster was as deeply troubled by events in America as by the circumstances of his own life.

A new spirit begins to invade his minstrel songs in 1849–50. "Nelly Was a Lady" (1849) is a simple, eloquent lament of a slave for his loved one:

When I saw Nelly in de morning,
   Smile till she open'd up her eyes,

[9] For a more detailed discussion of the relationships of many of Foster's songs to persons and events in his life, see Austin pp. 89–122.

> Seem'd like de light ob day a dawning,
> Just 'fore de sun begin to rise.
>
> Now I'm unhappy and I'm weeping,
> Can't tote de cotton-wood no more;
> Last night, while Nelly was a sleeping,
> Death came a knockin' at de door.

"Angelina Baker" (1850) is a lament by a slave for a lover who has been sent away by "old Massa" with no concern for the resulting human misery. "Oh! Boys, Carry Me 'Long" (1851) begins with a theme common in the authentic Negro spiritual—death as a deliverance from a life of toil and pain:

> Oh! carry me 'long;
> Der's no more trouble for me:
> I's guine to roam
> In a happy home,
> Where all de niggas am free.

And "Old Folks at Home" (1851)—which was to become the most popular of all Foster's songs—transfers the pervasive sentiment of Thomas Moore's *Irish Melodies,* nostalgia for lost youth and happiness, to the minstrel stage:

> All up and down de whole creation
> Sadly I roam,
> Still longing for de old plantation,
> And for de old folks at home.

In much of the North, and in Europe, the minstrel show was accepted as an accurate portrayal of the black slave and his life. Advertisements claimed that the shows offered "songs, refrains, and ditties as sung by the Southern slaves at all their merry meetings such as the gathering in of the cotton and sugar crops, corn huskings, slave weddings, and junketings."[10] The image of a "cheerful, whistling, song-singing, loud-laughing, tobacco-chewing variety of the human family,"[11] was convincing to audiences with no direct contact with the black. But Foster began offering a different image, of the black as a human being experiencing pain, sorrow, love, joy, even nostalgia (the most fashionable of all emotions).

Foster had been ambivalent about the "Ethiopian" songs he

[10]Edward Le Roy Rice, *Monarchs of Minstrelsy, from "Daddy" Rice to Date* (New York: Kenny Publishing Company, 1911), p. 24.
[11]*The Musical World and New York Musical Times,* October 20, 1853.

wrote early in his career. But his attitude changed in the early 1850s. In a letter of February 23, 1850, written to Edwin P. Christy of Christy's Minstrels, he said, "I wish to unite with you in every effort to encourage a taste for this style of music so cried down by opera mongers." A letter to Christy the following year concerning "Oh! Boys, Carry Me 'Long," insists that it be performed "in a pathetic, not a comic style." Yet another letter to Christy, this one written on May 25, 1852, says:

> I find that by my efforts I have done a great deal to build up a taste for the Ethiopian song among refined people by making the words suitable to their taste, instead of the trashy and really offensive words which belong to some songs of that order. Therefore I have concluded to . . . pursue the Ethiopian business without fear or shame.[12]

When *Uncle Tom's Cabin* was performed on the stage, in New York and elsewhere (beginning in 1853), Foster's songs were felt to be sufficiently sympathetic to the spirit of this abolitionist drama for several of them, including "Old Folks at Home," to be interpolated into the show.

Increasingly after 1850, Foster used the term "plantation song" for his new compositions, thus differentiating them by title as well as content from his earlier minstrel songs. These pieces are gentle and nostalgic in text and music; though their melodic lines often hint at Irish or Italian ancestry, all were structured with solo verses followed by a chorus in three- or four-part harmony. These are the songs that established Foster as the most important and successful successor to Thomas Moore and served as a model for other American songwriters for almost half a century. Among Foster's most popular songs of this type are:

"Old Folks at Home" (1851)
"Farewell, My Lilly Dear" (1851)
"Massa's in de Cold Ground" (1852)
"My Old Kentucky Home, Good Night" (1853)
"Ellen Bayne" (1854)
"Hard Times Come Again No More" (1855)
"Old Black Joe" (1860)
"Cora Dean" (1860)
"Under the Willow She's Sleeping" (1860)
"Little Belle Blair" (1861)
"Why Have My Loved Ones Gone?" (1861)
"Little Jenny Dow" (1862)

Dialect virtually disappears from their texts; some refer to the

12 Quoted in Howard, p. 196.

A sympathetic depiction of a slave on the sheet music cover for one of Foster's most popular songs, "Old Black Joe."

South and slavery, some do not. Their verse-chorus structure makes them suitable for both the minstrel stage and for the parlor, where verses were taken by the more accomplished singers and choruses could be sung by everyone.

Similar pieces by other songwriters may be found in profusion in the American song repertory of the 1850s and '60s. Many are laments over the deaths of young women; some have black protagonists; others make no use of dialect and no reference to slavery. "Willie's Grave" (1857, by Joseph P. Webster)[13] is of the same genre, except that death has come to a young boy rather than a girl:

> The grass is growing on the turf
>   Where Willie sleeps,
> Among the flow'rs we've planted there,
>   The soft wind creeps. . . .
>
> (*chorus*)
> Sleep on, sleep on, sleep on dear Willie sleep;
> Sleep on, sleep on, sleep on dear Willie sleep.

"We Are Happy Now, Dear Mother" (1853, by Isaac B. Woodbury) is similar, except that the protagonists are a group of dead children singing to their mothers, left behind.[14]

American song had found a mold, different from that of any other national school of song. But the course of events created a climate requiring different sorts of songs, at least for a while.

> The making of the song of the people is a happy accident, not to be accomplished by taking thought. It must be the result of fiery feeling long confined, and suddenly finding vent in burning words or moving strains. . . . Almost always the maker of the song does not suspect the abiding value of his work; he has wrought unconsciously, moved by a power within; he has written for immediate relief to himself, and with no thought of fame or the future. . . . But when a song has once taken root in the hearts of a people, time itself is powerless against it.[15]

The Civil War was a people's war, more so than any other in the history of the United States. Almost everyone was passionately involved with the issues leading to the struggle, and a large percentage of the population actually participated, as members of the rival armies, or their immediate families. The war was fought on American soil, by citizen armies, with an intensity unmatched in any other war. As a historian put it recently:

[13] NW 220, s1 / 2.
[14] NW 220, s1 / 3.
[15] Brander Matthews, *Pen and Ink* (New York and London: Longmans, Green & Company, 1888), pp. 140–41.

No event in American history had more devastating results than the Civil War. . . . In the course of the struggle, a war of limited objectives had been translated into total war. The enemy was no longer armies but entire civilian populations. . . . When final defeat engulfed the South, its economy was in shambles; vast stretches of its territory were ruined; and its social institutions rooted in slavery had been smashed. . . . As one contemporary notes, the boundary between the two sections was drawn in blood.[16]

Political differences between North and South had existed almost from the first days of the formation of the new nation. The doctrine of States' Rights was first enunciated by John Calhoun (1792–1850), Senator from South Carolina, Secretary of State under President Tyler, and twice Vice President of the country. He opposed various tariffs imposed by the Congress in the 1820s and '30s on the ground that they were discriminatory to the agricultural South; the state legislature of South Carolina, rallying behind his leadership, voted to nullify the Federal Tariff Acts of 1828 and 1832, taking the position that an individual state was not necessarily bound by federal action. Even before mid-century, there was a widespread and deep feeling that the two sections of the country had drifted far apart:

We are essentially two people—we are not only not homogeneous but we have become radically heterogenous. . . . Our passions, our tastes, our character, our vices even, are different and dissimilar. Our interests conflict. We are no longer one family.[17]

Most scholars take the position that the first step toward armed conflict came with the establishment of the abolitionist movement by William Lloyd Garrison (1805–79). Though there had been agitation against slavery before, the publication of the first issue of Garrison's *The Liberator* in 1831 marked the beginning of organized antislavery activity. Garrison was a militant in his opposition to slavery, as well as alcoholic beverages, tobacco, freemasonry, and capital punishment. "I am in earnest—I will not equivocate— I will not excuse—I will not retreat a single inch—and I will be heard," he wrote in the first issue of *The Liberator*.

Garrison and his cause were considered wildly radical at first, even in the North. He was mobbed in Boston in 1835, dragged through the streets with a rope around his neck, and finally put in the city jail for his own safety. The English abolitionist George Thompson was stoned by a crowd of 300 men in Lynn, Massachu-

---

[16] James P. Shenton, foreword to *Flawed Victory; A New Perspective on the Civil War* by William L. Barney (New York and Washington: Praeger, 1975), p. vii.

[17] Dr. J. G. M. Ramsey, as quoted in William B. Hesseltine, ed., *The Tragic Conflict: The Civil War and Reconstruction* (New York: George Braziller, 1962), pp. 94–95.

setts the same year, and Elijah Lovejoy was killed in Alton, Illinois in 1837 while protecting his press, with which he printed a religious, abolitionist paper (*The Observer*), from a mob intent on destroying it. But gradually the cause of abolition gained wider acceptance in the North, and antagonisms were more focused between North and South. A motion offered by Garrison at a meeting of the Anti-Slavery Society held in Fanueil Hall in Boston, in January of 1843, was enthusiastically adopted by the gathering:

> RESOLVED, That the compact which exists between the North and the South is a covenant with death and an agreement with hell—involving both parties in atrocious criminality, and should be immediately annulled.[18]

And the South soon saw the abolitionist movement as a threat to its very existence:

> From this movement [abolition] dates the unremittingly hostile attitude of the two sections towards each other. Before there had been antagonism; now there was open hostility. Before there had been conflicting rights, but they had been compromised and adjusted; from this time there was no compromise.[19]

Events in Kansas in the mid-1850s helped convince the South that it faced a fight for its very life. South Carolina withdrew from the Union in December of 1860, confiscating federal property within its boundaries; other Southern states followed course during the winter; open hostilities began with the bombardment of Fort Sumter, in Charleston Harbor, by Southern batteries in mid-April of 1861. The *Charleston Courier* said, in its issue of April 13, 1861 (while the bombardment was in progress):

> The sword must cut asunder the last tie that bound us to a people, whom, in spite of wrongs and injustices wantonly inflicted through a long series of years, we had not yet utterly hated and despised. The last expiring spark of affection must be quenched in blood. Some of the most splendid pages in our glorious history must be blurred. A blow must be struck that would make the ears of every Republican fanatic tingle, and whose dreadful effects will be felt by generations yet to come. We must transmit a heritage of rankling and undying hate to our children.

---

[18] As quoted in John Wallace Hutchinson, *Story of the Hutchinsons (Tribe of Jesse)* (Boston: Lee & Shepard, 1896), I, p. 74.
[19] Thomas Nelson Page, *The Old South* (Chautauqua: The Chautauqua Press, 1919), pp. 38–39.

After the fall of Fort Sumter, President Lincoln issued a call for 75,000 troops and appealed to all citizens for aid "to maintain the honor, integrity and the existence of our National Union."

Both North and South still faced the problem of bringing their citizenry to the emotional state necessary to face—and kill—one another on the battlefield. The North had only a tiny standing army in early 1861, the South no organized military forces. After the first skirmishes and small battles, each side accused the other of barbaric conduct, in an attempt to fan hatred.

Important in polarizing sentiments and reducing political events to a personal, emotional level were some of the first songs of the war, the great patriotic, rallying songs that touched and excited both North and South. An eyewitness to the first singing of "Maryland! My Maryland!" before Southern troops, camped near Manassas, Virginia on the eve of the first great battle of the war, reported the scene; the singer was Miss Hetty Cary, a pro-Southern native of Baltimore who had fitted a poem written by James Rider Randall to the tune of the well-known German song "O Tannenbaum":

> Standing in the tent-door, under cover of darkness, my sister sang "My Maryland!" The refrain was speedily caught up and tossed back to us from hundreds of rebel throats. As the last notes died away there surged forth from the gathering throng a wild shout—"We will break her chains! She *shall* be free! She *shall* be free! Three cheers and a tiger for Maryland!" And they were given with a will. There was not a dry eye in the tent, and, we were told the next day, not a cap with a rim on it in camp. Nothing could have kept Mr. Randall's verses from living and growing into a power.[20]

Some of the first rallying songs were newly composed; "The First Gun Is Fired! May God Protect the Right!" by George F. Root, which came off the presses three days after the fall of Fort Sumter, was one of these. Others were fashioned by adding topical texts to familiar tunes. "John Brown's Body" is typical; early in the first year of the war, an anonymous text was fitting to the camp-meeting hymn, "Say, Brothers, Will You Meet Us on Canaan's Happy Shore?"

> John Brown's body lies a-mouldering in the grave,
> John Brown's body lies a-mouldering in the grave,
> John Brown's body lies a-mouldering in the grave,
>    His soul is marching on.

[20] Quoted in Matthews, p. 149.

Winslow Homer "Songs of the War." Wood engraving from *Harper's Weekly*, Nov. 23, 1861.

> Glory, glory hallelujah! (3 times)
> His soul is marching on!

The Twelfth Massachusetts Regiment adopted it as a marching song, and it spread like wildfire through the Union army. Julia Ward Howe, after hearing it sung by troops in Washington, wrote a new set of words; as "The Battle Hymn of the Republic," it became the single most popular and moving Northern song of the war:

> Mine eyes have seen the glory of the coming of the Lord;
> He is trampling out the vintage where the grapes of wrath are stored,
> He hath loosed the fateful lightning of His terrible swift sword;
>     His truth is marching on.
>
> Glory! Glory! Hallelujah! (3 times)
> His truth is marching on.

  The two great rallying songs of the Confederacy were likewise based on familiar tunes. "Dixie," the "wild refrain that brings the faint heart back to life again" (in the words of John Hill Hewitt), began life as a minstrel walk-around written by Dan Emmett for

Bryant's Minstrels in 1859.[21] The official anthem, "The Bonnie Blue Flag," has a text by the English-born Harry B. McCarthy fitted to the traditional Irish tune "The Irish Jaunting Car."

"The Battle Cry of Freedom; or, Rally 'Round the Flag" had such a stirring effect in the North that some commanders ordered their troops to sing it while marching into battle. Written by George F. Root in 1862, on the occasion of President Lincoln's second call for troops, the song sold some 350,000 copies of sheet music during the war, and its electrifying impact on civilians and soldiers alike prompted a veteran of the Union army to suggest that "the true and correct history of the war for the maintenance of the Union will place George F. Root's name alongside of our great generals," and Root himself remarked that he was "thankful that if I could not shoulder a musket in defense of my country, I could serve her in this way."[22]

Almost every battle, and the emergence of every new hero, produced a rash of topical songs, from Thomas D. Sullivan's "The Flag of Fort Sumter" through John W. Palmer's "Stonewall Jackson's Way" to Henry Clay Work's "Marching through Georgia." And even in the midst of fearful destruction and suffering, a steady stream of humorous and comic songs emerged. There was an endless stream of parody songs, with new words fitted to familiar sentimental and even religious songs. "The Army Bean," for example, replaces the words of the hymn "The Sweet Bye and Bye" with:

> There's a spot that the soldiers all love,
>   The mess tent's the place that we mean,
> And the dish that we best like to see there
>   Is the old-fashioned white Army Bean.
>
> (*chorus*) 'Tis the bean that we mean,
>   And we'll eat as we ne'er ate before:
> The Army Bean, nice and clean,
>   We'll stick to our bean evermore.

There were dialect songs, based on stereotyped ethnic traits and the accented English of several of America's minorities:

> Dem Deutschen mens mit Sigel's band
>   At fighting have no rival;
> Und ven Cheff Davis mens we meet,
>   We schlauch 'em like de tuyvil . . .
>     (from "I Goes to Fight mit Sigel," by Fitch Poole)

[21] NW 202, s1 / 1.
[22] Root, p. 133.

There were grotesque caricatures of the political and military leaders of the opposing sides[23] and a steady stream of newly composed humorous songs, such as "Goober Peas," with a tune attributed to "P. Nutt" and lyrics to "A. Pender":

> Just before the battle the Gen'ral hears a row,
> He says, "The Yanks are coming, I hear their rifles now."
> He turns around in wonder, and what d'you think he sees?
> The Georgia militia, eating goober peas!

> (*chorus*)  Peas! Peas! Peas! Peas! eating goober peas!
> Goodness, how delicious, eating goober peas!

But as the war wore on, with no end in sight to its ever-mounting casualties, its songs became reflections of the pain and heartbreak of the troops and their families and friends. There was, for instance, "Tenting on the Old Camp Ground," written late in 1862 by Walter Kittredge of New Hampshire. A self-styled "ballad singer" who was rejected for service in the Union army because of "feebleness of constitution," he soon thereafter wrote a song that transfers the sentiment of the prewar plantation song from the minstrel stage to the campfire of bivouacing troops:

> We've been tenting tonight on the old Camp ground,
> Thinking of days gone by,
> Of the lov'd ones at home that gave us the hand,
> And the tear that said, "Good bye!"

And the chorus is a lament for the return of peace and happiness:

> Many are the hearts that are weary tonight,
> Wishing for the war to cease,
> Many are the hearts looking for the right
> To see the dawn of peace.[24]

Similar in sentiment is Henry Tucker's "Weeping, Sad and Lonely; or, When This Cruel War Is Over," which was alleged to have sold over a million copies of sheet music following its publication in Brooklyn in 1863. This song, "Inscribed to Sorrowing Hearts at Home" by its composer on the title page, has been singled out in a study of songs of the Civil War: "If any single song

---

[23] For instance, "Jeff in Petticoats," NW 202, s2 / 2.
[24] NW 202, s1 / 5.

may be said to have expressed the emotions of millions in the 1860s, it was (this one)."[25]

Other songs dealt directly with the deaths of soldiers. John Hill Hewitt cast his lot with the South; his "All Quiet Along the Potomac" (1862), a setting of a poem by Mrs. Ethel Lynn Beers of Goshen, New York, paints in graphic detail the death of a picket killed by a sharpshooter. He falls, his "life-blood ebbing and plashing . . . moaning out all alone the death rattle," the lone casualty of a day described in the official dispatches as "All quiet long the Potomac," with "not an officer lost, only one of the men." One of the great antiwar songs of all time, it is a chilling anticipation of Erich Remarque's *All Quiet on the Western Front* of almost a century later.[26]

The statistics of casualties are staggering:

> During its four years—in a total population of less than 35,000,000 and a military population of 5,665,000—over 3,000,000 men were under arms. Of the 35,000,000 total, 26 were in the North, and 9—including 4,000,000 slaves—were in the South. The military populations were, respectively, 4,600,000 and 1,0675,000. More impressive still was the casualty list. Out of the 2,750,000 soldiers in the North, 360,000 were killed or died of wounds and disease, while the Southerners lost 385,000. Adding the estimated total wounded, and dying of disease in the South, the figure for the United States as a whole was over 1,000,000—1,000,000 out of a total army of little more than 3,000,000.[27]

There was no attempt to shield noncombatants from the magnitude and horror of the slaughter. Photography was unflinching in capturing images of the dead and maimed. Tens of thousands of volunteer nurses and hospital attendants, on both sides, witnessed the aftermaths of battles, in hospitals and even on the battlefield; a Northern nurse, one of the first to reach the field after the battle of Shiloh, wrote, "The foul air from this mass of human beings at first made me giddy and sick. When we give the men anything, we kneel in blood and water."[28] Journalists were unsparing with the details of what they witnessed. The point of all this is that such songs as "All Quiet Along the Potomac" or Hewitt's "Somebody's Darling" (1864) were understood as a direct reflection of reality:

[25] Willard A. and Porter W. Heaps, *The Singing Sixties: The Spirit of Civil War Days Drawn from the Music of the Times* (Norman: University of Oklahoma Press, 1960), p. 224, and NW 202, s2 / 3.

[26] NW 202, s1 / 2.

[27] Hesseltine, p. 11.

[28] Quoted in Charles Hamm, liner notes for NW 202.

Give him a kiss, but for Somebody's sake,
Murmur a prayer for him, soft and low;
One little curl from its golden mates take,
Somebody's pride they were once, you know;

Somebody's warm hand has oft rested there,
Was it a mother's so soft and white?
Or have the lips of a sister so fair,
Ever been bathed in their waves of light?

(*chorus*) Somebody's darling,
Somebody's pride,
Who'll tell his mother
where her boy died?

Popular song had never before been so intimately tuned to the pulse of the people; it would be almost a century before this was to happen again.

No great works of painting or sculpture—in the sense of classical European art—were created as a direct result of the Civil War; there was, rather, a mass of photography giving one of the first demonstrations of the power and poetry possible in that new medium. The war spawned a mere trickle of poetry and fiction of lasting worth (Walt Whitman's best poetry was written before and after the war, Stephen Crane's *The Red Badge of Courage* was written some thirty years after the war had ended); the most effective and enduring literary accomplishments of the era were in journalism. No great American symphonies, quartets, or operas were written while the country was in the grips of the terrible and dramatic events of the war; the early 1860s were, rather, one of the great eras of popular song.

The Civil War, a people's war, saw the first great flowering of what would later be called mass culture, or popular art.

The South was devastated by the war and faced with the problem of dealing with millions of former slaves who were mostly uneducated and unequipped at first for anything other than manual labor. The South existed in virtual isolation from the rest of America in the second half of the nineteenth century and into the twentieth. Few white Southerners chose to move to the North, only a trickle of ex-slaves made their way north of the Mason-Dixon line at first, not many Northerners settled in the South. As a result, life and culture in the South became even more idiosyncratic than in antebellum days.

Musically, no Southern city developed a major symphony orchestra or an important opera company in the half-century following the war, and it was exceptional to find a Southern-born instrumentalist in one of the major orchestras of the North or East. The popular music industry in the late nineteenth century was centered in the North; no Southern publishers competed significantly with the large firms located in New York, Chicago, Boston, and Cincinnati, few songwriters from the South were part of the postwar developments of the genre.

This is not to say that the South was devoid of music. On the contrary, the decades after the war brought developments in oral-tradition music that were to have the most profound effect on American music in the twentieth century. Despite problems and tensions between blacks and whites in the postwar era, the South was the only section of the country where significant contact between black and white Americans was possible. It is ironic that some of the most distinctive traits of American culture emerged from acculturation of European and African heritages, in a place and at a time when these two cultures were thrust into an almost totally antagonistic relationship.

The North, meanwhile, was turning its eyes to the West, and to an exciting new age of industrialization. As one historian has put it:

> In all respects save the abolition of slavery, the Civil War was not an end but a beginning. With it, industry and capital forever gained the upper hand over agrarian gentility. American society entered its rowdy adolescence, brash, confident, rebelliously amoral, reveling in its new eastern wealth and toughened northern muscle. In the quarter-century after Appomattox, steel took King Cotton's crown; the tracks of the Iron Horse bound the states into a new, unshakable union; factory workers replaced field hands as America's proletariat; millions of immigrants were lured, bought, or abducted by American wealth; and a splendid lot of rascals, heroes, thieves, and reformers staggered, marched, or slunk across the public stage.[29]

Curiously, American popular song, which had been so tuned to the life and mood of the country before and during the Civil War, quickly found itself out of step. In style and substance, it continued for another twenty-five years along paths laid out in the 1840s. The verse (solo voice)—chorus (four-part harmony) structure of the plantation songs remained the characteristic shape of the postwar song, and lyrics repeated the themes that had dominated popular song for some decades—social reform and nostalgia for lost youth, love, and happiness.

[29] William Brooks, "Progress and Protest in the Gilded Age," liner notes for NW 267.

The great social cause of postwar popular song became temperance. This was hardly a new topic for song in America: Henry Russell had written such songs as "The Dream of the Reveller" (1843) and "The Gin Fiend" (1860), and the Hutchinson Family had embraced temperance at the very beginning of its career, sprinkling their programs with "Cold Water" and "King Alcohol."

Henry Clay Work's "Come Home, Father" was the great classic of the temperance movement. Though written in 1864, its greatest popularity came after the war, when it was interpolated into William W. Pratt's *Ten Nights in a Barroom* and adopted as the official song of the National Prohibition Party. Cast in the verse-chorus form of the plantation song, it captures the intensity and passion of some of the best songs of the war years. Its three verses recount the melancholy tale of a young girl sent three times—at one, two, and three o'clock in the morning—to the bar where her father is drinking, to urge him to come home to comfort his son Benny, who is dying. The third verse brings the tragedy to its climax:

> Father, dear father, come home with me now!
>   The clock in the steeple strikes three;
> The house is so lonely—the hours are so long
>   For poor weeping mother and me.
> Yes, we are alone—poor Benny is dead,
>   And gone with the angels of light;
> And these were the very last words that he said—
>   "I want to kiss Papa good-night."

And the chorus comments softly, as it has after each verse:

> Hear the sweet voice of the child,
>   Which the nightwinds repeat as they roam!
> Oh, who could resist this most pleading of prayers?
>   "Please, father, dear father, come home!"

Similar songs often sought to achieve even more immediacy through the use of pathetic scenes on their lithographed covers, and by introductory vignettes linking their texts to actual incidents. A typically lacrymose song written in 1866 by a certain Mrs. E. A. Parkhurst prefaces the music with the following:

One dismal, stormy night in winter, a little girl—barefooted and miserably clad—leaned shivering against a large tree near the President's House. "Sissie" said a passing stranger, "why don't you go home?" She raised her pale face, and with tears dimming her sweet blue eyes, answered mournfully: "I have no home. Father's a Drunkard, and Mother is dead."

And the song takes this last line as its title.[30]

Such songs may strike us today as excessively melodramatic, but they were one of the factors that kept the Prohibition movement alive and healthy until the United States adopted the Eighteenth Amendment in 1919, prohibiting the sale of alcoholic beverages.

Another temperance song achieving the status of a best-selling item of sheet music in postwar days was Joseph Eastburn Winner's "Little Brown Jug" (1869), which has retained a measure of familiarity to the present, ironically enough as a party song. Its later verses, detailing the evil effects of alcohol, have been largely forgotten:

> 'Tis you that makes me wear old clothes,
> 'Tis you that makes my friends my foes,
> Here you are so near my nose,
> So tip her up and down she goes.[31]

An occasional song of the 1860s and '70s deals with other social problems. "Out of Work," written by Septimus Winner in 1877—during one of the several recessions that plagued the country after the war—is a portrait of an unemployed man who asks, "Must I starve in this great city, where there's food enough for all?"[32] Henry Clay Work's "The Song of the Red Man"[33] pleads for more humane treatment of the American Indian, in a day when the Native American was still considered a nuisance and a threat to the country's westward expansion. But the most characteristic songs of the era were concerned with purely personal matters.

Two songs written in 1866 by William Shakespeare Hays were the first great popular hits in the style that was to dominate American song until the birth of Tin Pan Alley. "Write Me a Letter from Home" and "We Parted by the River Side" each sold some 300,000 copies of sheet music, according to their publisher. The lyrics of the latter give a sense of their flavor:

> We parted by the river side,
> A tear-drop trembled on your cheek,
> In vain to tell my love I tried,
> My heart was sad—I could not speak;

[30] NW 267, s2 / 3.
[31] NW 267, s2 / 3.
[32] NW 267, s1 / 2.
[33] NW 267, s1 / 1.

> I promised that I would be true,
>> So long as I would live;
> The parting kiss I gave to you,
>> Was all I had to give.

Henry Tucker's "Sweet Genevieve" (1869) followed, then a succession of songs by H. P. Danks (including "Silver Threads among the Gold," which was alleged to have sold two million copies between its publication in 1872 and the turn of the century), "Put Me in My Little Bed Again" (1870) by Charles A. White of Boston, Thomas Westendorf's "I'll Take You Home Again, Kathleen" (1875), and Henry Clay Work's "Grand-Father's Clock" (1875).

These, and the thousands of other songs like them that poured from American presses in the second half of the nineteenth century, are direct descendants of Thomas Moore's *Irish Melodies* and Stephen Foster's plantation songs. Their sentiment is personal, their musical means are simple enough to allow amateur singers and pianists to give a decent account of them, they are verse-chorus songs with a prevailing mood of gentle nostalgia. Their texts are concerned with parted lovers, with the calming of passions by age:

> O Genevieve, I'd give the world
>> To live again the lovely past!
> The rose of youth was dew-impearled;
>> But now it withers in the blast.

and with death as a sentimental, lingering event:

> Mother dear come bathe my forehead,
> For I'm growing very weak,
> Mother let one drop of water
> Fall upon my burning cheek.

> Tell my loving little schoolmates,
> That I never more will play,
> Give them all my toys, but Mother
> Put my little shoes away.
>> ("Put My Little Shoes Away" (1870), by Charles E. Pratt)[34]

American songs of the mid-nineteenth century were widely sung, reprinted, and imitated in England and elsewhere in Europe. They were one of this country's contributions to the style and spirit of what came to be known as the Victorian era.

The verse-chorus song proved to be adaptable to a great variety

[34] NW 220, s2 / 3.

of texts. It turns up in instructional and moralizing pieces contained in song collections for Sunday schools and academies; typical is Rowland Howard's "You Never Miss the Water till the Well Runs Dry."[35] It was also taken over for religious songs, some of which had the shape of popular songs and were sold as individual items of sheet music for home performance. William G. Fischer's "I love to Tell the Story"[36] (1869), for instance, resembles the contemporary popular song in everything but text.

The form had originated on the minstrel stage, and it continued to flourish in this environment. The minstrel show remained America's favorite and most characteristic stage entertainment until almost the end of the nineteenth century. Companies grew larger, productions more lavish, performers more accomplished. American minstrel troupes crisscrossed this country and traveled to every continent in the world.

The abolition of slavery brought no change in the stage portrayal of the American black or to the type of song performed on the minstrel stage. Southern blacks were still projected as happy, innocent, childlike creatures, singing and playing the banjo all day and night—or as aging persons, remembering the happiness of their youth. Typical is "The Little Old Cabin in the Lane" (1871) by Will S. Hays, introduced by Manning's Minstrels:

> Dar was a happy time to me, 'twas many years ago,
> When de darkies used to gather round de door,
> When dey used to dance an' sing at night,
> I played de ole banjo;
>
> But alas, I cannot play it any more.
> De hinges dey got rusted an' de door has tumbled down,
> And de roof lets in de sunshine an' de rain,
> An' de only friend I've got now is dis good ole dog ob mine,
> In de little old log cabin in de lane.

This song and others like it can only be interpreted as a lament for the "good old days"—of slavery!

After the war, blacks took to the minstrel stage for the first time. The Georgia Minstrels, organized in 1865, was the first black troupe. Famous impresarios Callender and Haverley soon had black companies under their management, and such performers as Charles Hicks, Billy Kersands, Sam Lucas, and James Bland eventually rivaled the popularity of the most famous white minstrels. But there was no change in the style and content of the minstrel show, and

[35] NW 251, s1 / 7.
[36] NW 220, s2 / 4.

when Bland—the first successful black songwriter in the history of American song—published songs in the 1870s and '80s, they were in the same molds as those of his white predecessors and contemporaries. "Carry Me Back to Old Virginny" (1875) was a post-Foster plantation song, including such lines as "All dem happy times we used to hab will ne'er return again," and his "De Golden Wedding" offers a stereotyped view of the life of black Americans:

> All the darkies will be there,
> Don't forget to curl your hair;
> Bring along your damsels fair,
> For soon we will be treading.
>
> Won't we have a jolly time,
> Eating cake and drinking wine?
> All the high-toned darkies
> Will be at the Golden Wedding.[37]

The situation confronting black minstrels has been summed up thus:

> In antebellum times the minstrel show had been a white man's medium, with whites in blackface caricaturing what they and their audiences saw as the characteristics of the black man: oversize red lips, bulging eyes, exaggerated motion and gait, gaudy costuming. After the war black minstrels found they had to imitate the white man's burlesque of them in order to succeed. "Nothing seemed more absurd," said George Walker, Bert Williams' stage partner, "than to see a colored man making himself ridiculous in order to portray himself.[38]

But the minstrel show gave the black American his first opportunity to perform on the stage before white audiences, and was a first step leading to his eventual acceptance on the legitimate stage.

In the mid-1870s, the Fisk University Jubilee Singers introduced white audiences in the North, and in Europe, to black spirituals. This music was hailed by some writers as the first authentic American "folk music":

> There exists in the Southern States of the United States, a people's-song in a most original form,—the songs of the colored race. . . . These characteristic spiritual songs, with their often-repeated refrain or burden, possess a vehemence and intensity which are the passionate expression of this longing for that promised land of salvation and deliverance. . . .

[37] NW 265, s1 / 7.
[38] Richard M. Sudhalter, "Types and Stereotypes in American Musical Theater," liner notes for NW 265.

Poster advertising the Original Georgia Minstrels, the first all-black performing company after the Civil War.

> In this case the poor, ignorant, debased, ostracized colored slave finds strains, original, sweet, and touching, such as nature has refused to his white masters.[39]

Minstrel troupes began featuring newly composed pieces imitating these arranged spirituals, pieces that might be called minstrel-spirituals, with religious texts and call-and-response patterns. One of the first of these was Will S. Hays's "Angels, Meet Me at the Cross Roads" (1875):

> Come down, Gabriel, blow your horn,
> Call me home in de early morn;
> Send de chariot down dis way,
> Come and haul me home to stay.
> (*chorus*) O! Angels meet me at de Cross roads,

[39] Frédéric Louis Ritter, *Music in America* (New York: Charles Scribner's Sons, 1883), pp. 385 and 392.

*Meet me!*
Angels, meet me at de Cross roads,
*Meet me!*
Angels, meet me at de Cross roads,
*Meet me!*
Don't charge a sinner any toll.

James Bland's "Oh! dem Golden Slippers!" (1879), written for the minstrel stage, is in just this style, and his "Tell 'Em I'll Be There"[40] is a later example of this genre. Ironically, this first popular black songwriter learned about the spiritual from hearing such groups as the Jubilee Singers, and from the minstrel-spiritual as performed on the stage; he had grown up in a middle-class Northern home, in an educated family oriented to the white world.

The postwar years saw the establishment of a genre that would eventually replace the minstrel show as the most popular and characteristic form of American stage entertainment—vaudeville, or the variety show. Though similar in many ways to the minstrel show, with its string of songs, dances, comedy skits and the like, it developed important differences. Vaudeville introduced its various acts one after another, each as a separate entity, whereas a minstrel show was given unity by the presence on stage of the entire troupe. There was also more variety in an evening of vaudeville, with jugglers, child performers, acrobats, and even trained animals providing contrast to singers, dancers, and comedians.

Tony Pastor's Opera House, opened in 1865, was its first permanent house, and New York remained the nerve-center of vaudeville; the best performers were based there, and the important managers and agents had their offices in the city.

Songs were always an essential element in vaudeville. There were ballad singers, offering the sentimental popular songs of the day. There were blackface singers doing minstrel songs; dialect songs of all sorts—German, Jewish, Irish, Scandanavian—by singers skilled in the portrayal of racial and ethnic groups;[41] juvenile singers; character singers portraying old men, drunkards, and other types.

The most talented writer of songs for the variety stage in its first decades was the English-born David Braham (1838–1905), who learned his trade in the English music hall. After a decade of writing stage songs for a variety of performers—"Adolphus Morning Glory" (1867) was for the famous minstrel star J. B. Murphy, "Over the Hills to the Poor House" (1874) was a vehicle for the "Charac-

[40] NW 265, s2 / 3.
[41] NW 265 contains a number of songs of this sort.

ter and Comic Vocalist" James W. McKee, several other songs were written for Major Tom Thumb—Braham joined forces with Edward "Ned" Harrigan and Tony Hart (Anthony J. Cannon) to produce a string of dramatic sketches, beginning with "The Mulligan Guard" in 1873, that eventually evolved into stage comedies with interpolated music. Most of these shows revolved around the continuing adventures of the fictitious Dan Mulligan, with a cast of characters drawn from Harrigan's recollections of his boyhood in New York's sixth ward.

The sketches peopled the stage with "the newsboys and flower girls, the barbers and butchers, the Bowery toughs and South Street tailors, and the disreputable folk who hung out in the dives known as dance houses." The central characters were all "first- or second-generation Irish and German and Italian immigrants who came to New York during the nineteenth century and of whom Harrigan was in the habit of deploring, half-jestingly, that they wouldn't come to his theater because the incidents he showed on stage were indistinguishable from what they experienced at home."[42] But he wrote of these people with understanding and affection, and Braham—a city person himself—set his lyrics to appropriate and memorable tunes:

> If you want for information, or in need of merriment,
> Come over with me socially to Murphy's tenement.
> He owns a row of houses in the first ward, near the dock,
> Where Ireland's represented by the babies on our block.
>
> There's the Phalens and the Whalens
>     from the sweet Dunochadee,
> They are sitting on the railings
>     With their children on their knee.
>
> There's the Clearys and the Learys
>     From the sweet Blackwater side,
> They are laying on the Batt'ry
>     And they're gazing at the tide.
>
> There's the Brannons and the Gannons,
>     Far down and Connaught men,
> Quite easy with the shovel
>     And so easy with the pen.[43]

This was a new direction for popular song in America. The Harrigan-Braham songs deal with contemporary city life; Harrigan was

[42] E. J. Kahn, Jr., *The Merry Partners: The Age and Stage of Harrigan and Hart* (New York: Random House, 1955), p. 13.
[43] NW 265, s1 / 1.

the first person to articulate the role of popular song in an urban
environment:

> The short-lived bits of music, coming and going with the freedom and
> irresponsibility of wild flowers, helped to lighten the toil of the working
> people and were, and are now, potent peace-makers at many a gathering
> where they calm the angry passions of the poor, admitting sunshine into
> many a darkened life. Virtue, disguised as music, enters the home of
> poverty, and holds temptation at bay with the gentle weapon called the
> popular song. Make songs for the poor, and you plant roses among the
> weeds.[44]

But they had little currency outside of New York, never attaining
the general popularity of the other types of songs discussed in this
chapter. They were urban songs in an age when the majority of
Americans still lived in towns and rural areas, an anticipation of
what was to come next.

[44] As quoted in Kahn, pp. 152–53.

# 10

## Shape-Note, Camp-Meeting, and Gospel Hymnody

Nonliterate British immigrants to America and their descendants were drawn to the various populist religions and sects that sprang up in America in the eighteenth and nineteenth centuries. The Baptist church and its offshoots proved to be particularly attractive:

> Baptists share with Protestantism the exaltation of the Bible, an insistence upon the idea of the universal priesthood of believers and multiplicity of sects. They believe in absolute soul freedom with its corollary of the separation of church and state. Everyone has the inalienable right and duty to experience God in his own way. There can be no interference by creed, sacrament or priesthood between the soul and its Creator. The laity is not inferior to the ministry. The local church is sovereign.[1]

Such a credo was appealing to persons who had been excluded from participation in the most powerful and official institutions of their country. In New England, the Free Will Baptists, led by Benjamin Randall, became a force among the lower classes. In the South, the Separate Baptists, growing from a small colony settled at Sandy Creek, North Carolina, eventually spread into Virginia, South Carolina, and Georgia, then westward to Kentucky and Tennessee.

The predominant religion of the southern Appalachian region in the nineteenth and twentieth centuries was Primitive Baptist, an

[1] *Encyclopaedia Britannica*, 1956 ed., III, p. 87.

offshoot of the Separate Baptist movement carried into the mountainous areas by settlers from Virginia and North Carolina. The public worship services of this sect included sacred songs passed on by ear from generation to generation. In general style, these are similar to the Old Style of psalmody and hymnody practiced in the colonies in the late seventeenth and early eighteenth centuries. A leader sings the first line of a psalm or hymn, which is echoed by the congregation, the second line is done in the same fashion, and so on until the piece has been completed in this lining-out fashion. In actual practice, the congregation does more than simply repeat each phrase; they follow the basic contour of the tune, but each singer is free to elaborate it—anticipating or lingering on a given note, introducing vocal embellishment. The resulting sound must be close to what was heard in New England in the late seventeenth century, when the Usual Way of psalmody was in vogue:

> One Man is upon this Note, while another is a Note before him. . . . Much time is taken up in shaking out these Turns and Quavers; and besides, no two Men in the Congregation quaver alike, or together.[2]

As with the other music of the more remote sections of the Southern mountains, a style from earlier centuries has survived to the present, and the sound of a leader and congregation lining out a hymn is as close as we will ever be able to get to the sound of congregational psalmody in early colonial times.[3]

In other regions of the South, and in what was then the West, a different type of religious song based on oral-tradition music developed in the early nineteenth century.

Late in the eighteenth century the institution of the singing school, which had developed and flourished in New England, spread south and west. Typical of the Yankee singing-school master responsible for this expansion was Lucius Chapin (1760–1842), born in Springfield, Massachusetts, into a family dominated by the musical enthusiasms of the mother, the former Eunice Colton:

> Knowing nothing of notes or rules on paper, she was, by rote and mere memory, an admirable, perhaps it may be said a perfect singer of "psalms & hymns & spiritual songs." Her house was, for an extensive region around about, the center of vocal musick, her children, all of them, from their infancy, being furnished with that talent. Both she and they enjoyed

---

[2] Thomas Walter, *The Grounds and Rules of Musick Explained: Or, An Introduction to the Art of Singing by Note* (Boston: Printed by J. Franklin for Samuel Gerrish, 1721), pp. 4–5.

[3] Examples of this sort of lining out may be heard on NW 294, s1.

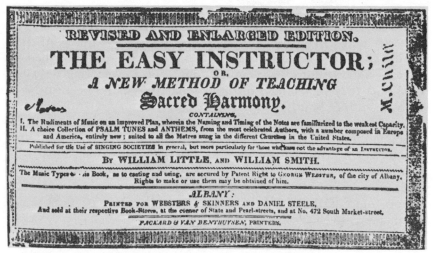

Title page of *The Easy Instructor*, an early shape-note book.

it—in practice, almost ceasing; for, with few exceptions, it was their everyday amusement.[4]

Enlisting in the Continental Army as a fifer in 1775, Lucius fought in the battles of Ticonderoga, Stillwater, Monmouth, and others; he passed the winter of 1777–78 with Washington at Valley Forge, suffering a "severe frosting of the legs" that troubled him for the remainder of his life. After the war he organized singing schools in Vermont, New Hampshire, Massachusetts, and Connecticut, and in 1787 he went to the South; he was the first to hold singing schools in the Shenandoah Valley of Virginia. He crossed the mountains into Kentucky in 1794, settling for a while in Vernon, Fleming County; from here he ranged throughout Kentucky and into Ohio and Indiana, for some forty years. His brother Amzi (1768–1835) followed him to Virginia, then ventured into North Carolina; later he was one of the first singing-school masters in western Pennsylvania and Ohio.

Other men carried the singing school into western New York, central and western Pennsylvania, and eventually into Illinois, Missouri, Arkansas, and other states in what is now the Midwest.

The earliest singing-school masters in these regions used New England books for instruction and repertory, and thus the compositions of Billings, Read, Swan, and their peers were disseminated to other parts of America. The first collection designed specifically

[4] From the Blinn Family Papers, housed in the Historical and Philosophical Society of Ohio, in Cincinnati, as quoted in Charles Hamm, "The Chapins and Sacred Music in the South and West," *Journal of Research in Music Education*, VIII / 2 (Fall 1960), p. 92.

for use outside of New England appears to have been *The Easy Instructor;* edited by William Little and William Smith, it was entered for copyright in Philadelphia in 1798 but not published until 1801.[5] Its greatest success came after it was published in Albany; new editions were brought out almost every year between 1805 and 1831, and much of its popularity was in western New York, the upper South, and the Midwest.

*The Easy Instructor* utilized a new system of musical notation, which came to be called "shape" or "patent" notes. In the four-syllable solmization system used at the time to instruct scholars in the rudiments of music, the octave was divided into two groups of three notes each, with the seventh note of the scale standing alone. Shape-note notation fixed this system visually, by assigning a different shape to each of the four syllables:

| (fa) | (sol) | (la) | (fa) | (sol) | (la) | (mi) | (fa) | (sol) | ... |
|------|-------|------|------|-------|------|------|------|-------|-----|
| C | D | E | F | G | A | B | c | d | |
| △ | ○ | □ | △ | ○ | □ | ◇ | △ | ○ | |

Shape-notes proved to be an effective pedagogical tool, particularly with the nonliterate, semiliterate, and newly literate people who made up a good percentage of the population of the South and West.

*The Easy Instructor* and several other early shape-note books contained a New England repertory, but in the second decade of the nineteenth century a number of collections printed on the fringes of the expanding country—John Wyeth's *Repository of Sacred Music, Part Second* (Harrisburg, Pennsylvania, 1813),[6] Robert Patterson's *Patterson's Church Music* (Cincinnati, 1813), Ananias Davisson's *Kentucky Harmony* (Harrisonburg, Virginia, 1815), the *Kentucky Harmony* (1817), compiled by Samuel L. Metcalf of Lexington, Allen D. Carden's *Missouri Harmony* (1820)[7]—began offering pieces of a somewhat different sort.

Dubbed "folk hymns" or "white spirituals" by twentieth-century writers, these pieces at first glance seem identical in style with the compositions of William Billings and his New England contemporaries. Settings of religious poetry by Isaac Watts, the Wesleys, and other popular writers of hymns and psalms, they proceed

[5] Cf. Irving Lowens, *Music and Musicians in Early America* (New York: W. W. Norton and Company, 1964), pp. 115–37.

[6] Cf. Lowens, pp. 138–58. The collection is available in a facsimilie edition, edited by Irving Lowens (New York: Da Capo Press, 1964).

[7] George Pullen Jackson, *White Spirituals in the Southern Uplands* (Chapel Hill: University of North Carolina Press, 1933; reprint, New York: Dover Publications, 1965) gives an extended if incomplete list of such books on p. 25. For a more complete list, cf. Richard J. Stanislaw, *A Checklist of Four-Shape Tunebooks* (Brooklyn: Institute for Studies in American Music, c. 1978).

in mostly homorhythmic fashion; the second section often introduces the several voices in staggered entrances, in the style of the fuging tune. But on closer inspection, important differences become evident.

The tunes are often pentatonic. More than that, these melodies take on the ubiquitous melodic shapes of the ballads, songs, and fiddle and banjo pieces of the oral-tradition music of this region. Such tunes as the following resemble those used for ballad and song texts:

"Idumea," from *The Southern Harmony*

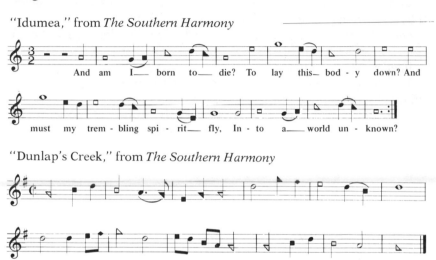

"Dunlap's Creek," from *The Southern Harmony*

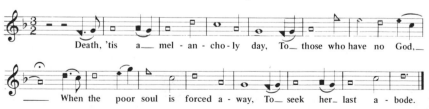

And the resemblance is often much closer than general melodic shape. "Tribulation," first published in the *Kentucky Harmony*, is surely the same tune as that collected by Cecil Sharp in Virginia for the ballad "Little Musgrave and Lady Barnard" (Child 81):

"Tribulation," from *The Southern Harmony*

"Little Musgrave," from Sharp, *English Folk Songs from the Southern Appalachians*, I, p. 182

how do you like your da - la - lay That lies in your arms a - sleep?

Though many of these pieces are attributed to the early teachers of singing schools in the South and West, they appear to be arrangements rather than new works. Apparently the composers drew on the indigenous melodic tradition of the people among whom they lived and worked, for pedagogical reasons. In doing so, they recorded—in musical notation—hundreds of oral-tradition tunes, and their collections are repositories of these melodies a century before Cecil Sharp and other scholars began their task of collecting "folk" music in these regions.

The pieces are written or arranged for three or four voices, in a unique "harmonic" style.

"Consolation," found in most of the early shape-note collections, has a gapped-scale tune, missing the seventh degree and touching on the fourth only in passing:

"Consolation," from *The Southern Harmony*

Once more, my soul, the— ris - ing— day Sa - lutes thy wak - ing eyes;

Once— more, my voice, thy trib - ute— pay To him that rules— the skies.

As fitted to a text by Isaac Watts, for three voices (with the melody in the middle, as usual in this style),

"Consolation," from *The Southern Harmony*

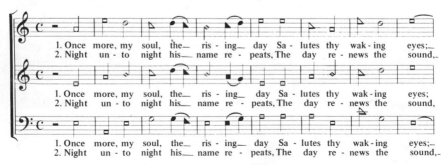

1. Once more, my soul, the— ris - ing— day Sa - lutes thy wak - ing eyes;—
2. Night un - to night his— name re - peats, The day re - news the sound,—

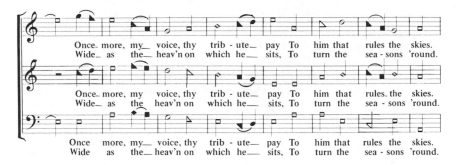

Once more, my voice, thy trib - ute pay To him that rules the skies.
Wide as the heav'n on which he sits, To turn the sea - sons 'round.

Once more, my voice, thy trib - ute pay To him that rules the skies.
Wide as the heav'n on which he sits, To turn the sea - sons 'round.

Once more, my voice, thy trib - ute pay To him that rules the skies.
Wide as the heav'n on which he sits, To turn the sea - sons 'round.

it becomes a composition quite different from any other Protestant hymnody of the day. Simultaneous combinations of notes are most often perfect consonances (fifths and octaves), sometimes fourths, often intervals regarded as dissonances in common harmonic practice (seconds and sevenths). There is only a single instance of a triad, the basic combination of notes in other eighteenth and nineteenth century hymnody. In addition, there are many parallel fifths, unisons, and octaves.

The logic in this "harmonization" lies in the melodic progression of the several voices rather than in their simultaneity. The upper voice has been shaped into a melody quite as attractive and logical as the tune itself, and the bass line likewise progresses mostly in a melodic fashion except at cadence points.

The origins of this style are not clear. Possibly oral-tradition polyphony among nonliterate Americans of Anglo-Celtic origin is reflected in these early shape-note collections. More likely, it was the creation of singing-school masters and the compilers of these books, who were faced with the problem of converting nonharmonic tunes into compositions for several voices, and who found a "harmonic" style appropriate to the nature of such melodies.

The singing-school movement and its characteristic music moved into the Deep South, which soon produced its own shape-note collections. The first of these was the work of William Walker, born in Union County in South Carolina in 1809 and a resident of Spartanburg, South Carolina from the time he was 18. According to a local historian:

> He joined the Baptist church at a very early age, and amid the ebullitions of his early Christian piety and religious fervor he conceived the idea that to praise the Lord on string instruments, the psaltery and harp, as well as with the human voice, was not only a requisite, but a grand concomitant of religious worship.
>
> To perfect the vocal modes of praise became the leading ambition of his long, laborious and useful life. Determined, *at once* he resorted to

pen and paper. From the deep minstrels of his own bosom he gathered and arranged into meter and melody a wonderful book suitably adapted to the praise and glory of God.[8]

This "wonderful book" was *The Southern Harmony*, first published in 1835. Walker claimed that some 600,000 copies of the various editions had been sold by the time of the Civil War, and his biographer wrote:

> Scarcely a hamlet, scarcely a church in the wooded coverts of those several sections [the South and Southwest], have not been made to reverberate the praises of God in accordance with the metrical spirit of [his book]. The Southern Harmony and his name, the name of the distinguished author, are as familiar as household duties in the habitations of the South.[9]

*The Southern Harmony* was used in singing schools, in church congregations, and in semisocial gatherings and conventions. As it passed out of everyday use in the late nineteenth century, a tradition sprang up of periodic "sings" from the book. One continues to the present, in Benton, Kentucky, where all-day sings from *The Southern Harmony* have been held on the fourth Sunday in May every year since 1884.[10]

*The Southern Harmony* contains hymns, spiritual songs and anthems by New England composers of the late eighteenth and early nineteenth centuries, many "folk hymns" found in early shape-note collections, and a number of new pieces—many of them written or arranged by Walker himself—based on the melodic tradition of Anglo-Celtic oral-tradition music. Typical of the latter is "New Britain," better known by the first two words of its text, "Amazing Grace" (see facing page). A pentatonic melody, lacking the fourth and seventh degrees of the diatonic scale, it is "harmonized" for three voices, each pentatonic itself; the bass is also lacking the fourth and seventh notes, the upper voice touches on the fourth degree only once, in passing. Thus the character of the melody permeates the entire composition.

The success of *The Southern Harmony* prompted the publication of other shape-note books in the Deep South. The most successful of these, and eventually the most widely dispersed shape-note book of the entire nineteenth century, was *The Sacred Harp*, the work of

---

[8] J. B. O. Landrum, *History of Spartanburg County* (Atlanta: Franklin Printing and Publishing Company, 1900), pp. 492–93.

[9] Landrum, p. 494.

[10] Cf. the description of this sing in Jackson, pp. 64–67.

"New Britain," from *The Southern Harmony*

Benjamin Franklin White (1800–79), a brother-in-law of William Walker. He moved to Georgia when he was about forty and continued to hold singing schools in this region, as he had in South Carolina:

> He never used his talent as a musician to make money. He had a higher, greater, and more glorious intention in view, and was untiring in his energy and efforts to bring simplicity to the singing of music and to furnish to beginners and to the poor a form of music that would find lodgement in the hearts and quicken the inner recesses of the soul; to look farther than to the mere rendering of the song, and to bring them to a higher and intimate relation to the Author of all music and in harmony with the fountain from whence blends all the charms and concords in music, and to teach them to sing such songs as would bring them in sacred nearness to their Maker.[11]

*The Sacred Harp* came out in 1844, with revised and enlarged editions following in 1850, 1859, and 1869. White organized the Southern Musical Convention in 1845; singing-school teachers and their pupils attended its annual meetings, centered around all-day

[11] Jackson, pp. 84–85.

sings from White's book; there were also discussions of how this music could best be taught, and the proper organization and conduct of singing schools. A committee formed within this organization, headed by White, planned and executed the later editions of *The Sacred Harp*. A similar group serving a different region of Georgia, the Chattahoochee Musical Convention, was formed in 1852, and others soon sprang up elsewhere, spreading to other states—Alabama, Arkansas, and Texas (where the East Texas Musical Convention was formed as early as 1855). These regional conventions granted licenses to teachers of singing schools within their jurisdiction and supervised the conduct of such schools. Needless to say, all used *The Sacred Harp*, and annual sings gave a focus to their organization.

Sacred Harp singing continued into the twentieth century. The largest organization in the history of the movement, the United Sacred Harp Musical Association, was established in Atlanta in 1904, and two separate new editions of the book came out in 1911. One of these, the *Original Sacred Harp*, restored many pieces from the first editions and contains no fewer than 609 pieces in all; more than two-thirds of the texts and tunes are attributed to Southern authors, most of them from Georgia and Alabama.

A visitor to a Sacred Harp sing in Mineral Wells, Texas in 1930 described the day's activities:

> The Friday morning session was just starting with a song as I entered. After the song the chaplain read from the scriptures, offered a prayer, and then singing, nothing but singing, filled the forenoon from nine to twelve excepting for a short recess in the middle.
> 
> I observed the singers. There were about two hundred of them, men, women, and children. They were all country folk, of course. [They] sat in folding chairs on four sides of a rectangular open space where the leader stood. The men and women "tenors" (sopranos) were in front of the leader, the men and women "trebles" (tenors) at his left, the women altos behind him, and the basses at his right. [Each leader's] time on the floor was three songs long. He called the page of his first song and then "keyed" the tune by singing its tonic and other opening tones without the help of even a tuning fork. "Faw, law, sol!" The singers of all four parts got their pitch instantly and, after the one deliberate chord with which all the *Sacred Harp* songs begin, the whole chorus was on its way singing the song through by "notes" (solmization syllables) only. Then came the words, one to three stanzas. This singing went on busily for over two hours. And one session was like all the others, but for the choice of leaders and songs.[12]

[12] Jackson, pp. 114–17, *passim*. An account of a similar sing in Alabama is given in the liner notes to NW 205, p. 1.

*The Sacred Harp* contains pieces from the New England school ("David's Lamentation" by William Billings,[13] "Sherburne" and "Greenwich" by Daniel Read,[14] "Northfield" by Jeremiah Ingalls[15]), even older pieces by English writers of the eighteenth century ("Amsterdam"),[16] pieces from the first shape-note books, and a number of compositions taken over from William Walker's *The Southern Harmony* (the anonymous "Wondrous Love,"[17] Walker's own "Hallelujah"[18]). But the repertory is not completely retrospective; each new edition contains a number of pieces appearing for the first time. "New Harmony,"[19] for instance, first appears in the 1869 edition, attributed to Miss M. L. A. Lancaster; but in style it differs little from earlier shape-note composition. The melody is pentatonic, as are the other voices, and parallel unisons, octaves, and fifths abound to such an extent that the sound of the piece approaches heterophony:

"New Harmony," from *The Sacred Harp*

*The Hesperian Harp* (1848), the work of William Hauser, a minister and medical doctor whose later life was spent in Georgia, was even larger than any of its predecessors; many of the thirty-six pieces attributed to Hauser himself were fashioned by "catching up melodies from the singing of individuals" and fitting them with two or three other voice parts. John G. McCurry of Hart County, Georgia, brought out *The Social Harp* in 1855, containing forty-nine of his own compositions or arrangements of traditional tunes in addition to the usual shape-note repertory.

[13] NW 205, s1 / 2.
[14] NW 205, s1 / 1 and s2 / 1.
[15] NW 205, s2 / 13.
[16] NW 205, s2 / 4.
[17] NW 205, s1 / 6.
[18] NW 205, s1 / 9.
[19] NW 205, s1 / 8.

These Southern and Western collections, then, not only preserved an older New England singing-school repertory, but also
gave birth to and nourished a new and distinctive tradition of
sacred part-songs. But the reform movement that had swept
through the Northeast a half-century before inevitably spread elsewhere. Jesse B. Aikin of Philadelphia brought out *The Christian
Minstrel* in 1846; widely sold and used in the South and West as
well as the East, it had gone through 171 editions by 1873. It was
a shape-note book; Aikin retained the four note-shapes and the syllables associated with them, but added three more to create a seven-
syllable solmization system:

| (do) | (re) | (mi) | (fa) | (sol) | (la) | (ti) |
|------|------|------|------|-------|------|------|
| C | D | E | F | G | A | B |
| △ | ○ | ◇ | ◣ | ○ | □ | ▽ |

*The Christian Minstrel* abounds with the rhetoric and music of
reform hymnody: the introduction expresses the hope that this book
will replace the "trashy publications which supplied the churches,
especially of the South and West"; the contents are drawn mostly
from the "approved and scientific" works of various English, German, and American writers; there are more pieces by Lowell Mason
than any other composer.

Meanwhile several of the largest Protestant denominations in the
South were bringing out official hymnals drawing on reform hymnody. *The Baptist Hymn and Tune Book* of 1857 and the first official
hymnal of the Southern Methodist Church, edited by L. C. Everett
of Virginia in 1859, were both printed in standard (nonshape) notation, and contained only a scattering of "Western Melodies," as the
indigenous pieces of the shape-note collections were called. These
and similar hymnals came to be used in cities and towns throughout the South and West, while shape-note books persisted in rural
areas. *The Harp of Columbia*, published in Knoxville in 1849 by W.
H. and M. L. Swan, adopted seven-shape notation, but clung to the
older shape-note repertory and style. A revised version, *The New
Harp of Columbia* (1867), was in print until the mid-twentieth century and was used for annual "Old Harp" conventions and sings in
the South and lower Midwest.

The perseverance of the traditional shape-note repertory into the
twentieth century is reflected by the success of a collection entitled
*The Good Old Songs*, first published in Thornton, Arkansas in 1913
by C. H. Cayce. The editor's preface could have been written in the
mid-nineteenth century:

For some years we have noticed a tendency among many people to drift
away from the good old songs that were loved and cherished by our

fathers and mothers, and to adopt the modern "jig" and operatic tunes. As a result of this there has been a great decline, and in our humble judgement, the *progress* has been downward, or backward. The singing is not as sweet and soul-cheering as it was in our younger days. We have lately observed that in many places there is a desire to return to the old tunes, but a suitable book for all occasions, containing the old music only, could not be had. We believe that in the following pages you will find the cream of the old music. The book contains none of the "modern sort."

Printed in the seven-shape system, the contents range from pieces by English and American singing-school teachers of the eighteenth century through the folk hymns and fuging tunes of such Southern shape-note collections as *The Southern Harmony* and *The Sacred Harp*. The twenty-second edition of 1960, containing 763 pieces, went through a printing of a million and a half copies, and 54¼ million of all editions had been printed by this time.

Shape-note music has been poised between oral and written tradition for more than a century and a half. The melodic style and many of the tunes came from oral-tradition music but became fixed in musical notation. Singing schools, the chief medium of dissemination of this music, were conducted with the use of the printed collections, but many people in attendance were nonliterate, learning by rote.

The melodic style was of Anglo-Celtic origin, and the texts of most of the pieces in early shape-note collections were written by such Englishmen as Isaac Watts and the Wesleys. But the harmonic style was an American innovation; it was, in fact, the first system of planned vertical combinations of notes to emerge from oral-tradition Anglo-American music. And in time, new texts were created by the Americans who shaped the musical style of shape-note hymnody. It is difficult to imagine a piece of music from the nineteenth century more American—in the sense of being unique to this country, unlike any other music in the world—than a composition like the following by William Walker:

"Complainer" (William Walker), from *The Southern Harmony*

mourn-ers, and lis-ten to my cries: I've man-y sore temp-ta-tions, and

mourn-ers, and lis-ten to my cries: I've man-y sore temp-ta-tions, and

mourn-ers, and lis-ten to my cries: I've man-y sore temp-ta-tions, and

sor-rows to my soul; I feel my faith de-clin-ing, and my af-fec-tions cold.

sor-rows to my soul; I feel my faith de-clin-ing, and my af-fec-tions cold.

sor-rows to my soul; I feel my faith de-clin-ing, and my af-fec-tions cold.

Music in America rarely remains stylistically pure, and shape-note music gradually absorbed compositions in other styles. From early in the nineteenth century, hymns and spiritual songs from the urban, reform school of Thomas Hastings, Lowell Mason, and William Bradbury were accepted into the shape-note repertory. Lowell Mason's "Missionary Hymn" became a particular favorite, sometimes sung with its original text ("From Greenland's icy mountains, from India's coral strand"), sometimes fitted with words more in the style of rural Christianity:

> O sir, we would see Jesus, the blessed Prince of Love,
> He only can relieve us, and all our griefs remove.
> O tell us, as a preacher, where Jesus Christ doth dwell,
> Describe His charming features, His glowing beauties tell.[20]

Bradbury's "Woodworth" also became a favorite in both the rural and urban South,[21] as did Lowell Mason's "Bethany" ("Nearer, My God, to Thee"), Simeon B. Marsh's "Maryn" ("Jesus, Lover of My Soul"), and Thomas Hastings's "Toplady," usually sung to a text beginning "Rock of Ages, cleft for me." And in the second half of the nineteenth century a scattering of hymns by the next genera-

---

[20] C. H. Elder Cayce, *The Good Old Songs*, 22nd ed. (Thornton, Arkansas: Cayce Publishing Company, 1960), p. 228.
[21] NW 224, s2 / 9, in a modern, urban performance.

tion of urban writers began creeping into the shape-note repertory; typical is J. P. Webster's "Sweet By and By."[22]

The presence of such urban products in the shape-note repertory suggests that the rural South was less isolated from big-city life by the late nineteenth century than it had been earlier, and anticipates the pattern we shall see with the beginnings of hillbilly and country-western music in this same region in the 1920s—an essentially conservative musical tradition overlaid with products of more modern times. Interestingly, urban hymns taken into the shape-note tradition retain their harmonic, triadic character. Stylistic dualism seemed to pose no problems; shape-note singers quite happily sang one piece in a pentatonic, nonharmonic style and the next with full triads on every beat.

Shape-note collections also preserve many of the pieces sung in the camp meetings of the various populist, ecstatic religious movements that swept over America in the late eighteenth and early nineteenth centuries. Such pieces as "The Morning Trumpet" preserve the actual music and suggest the mood of these meetings:

> O when shall I see Jesus,
> > And reign with Him above,
> And shall hear the trumpet sound in that morning?
>
> And from the flowing fountain,
> > Drink everlasting love,
> And shall hear the trumpet sound in the morning?
>
> Shout, O glory!
> > For I shall mount above the skies,
> When I hear the trumpet sound in that morning.[23]

The refrains of camp-meeting songs often featured some sort of echoing, or call and response, between the song leader and the congregation. This pattern became a feature of evangelical urban hymnody, in the late nineteenth century. Typical is "The Precious Name" by W. H. Doane and Mrs. Lydia Baxter, which appeared in *Gospel Hymns and Sacred Hymns*, brought out in 1875 by P. P. Bliss and Ira D. Sankey. After a first verse,

> Take the name of Jesus with you,
> Child of sorrow and of woe—
> It will joy and comfort give you,
> Take it then where e'er you go.

---

[22] NW 220, s1 / 1, in a modern performance.
[23] NW 205, s2 / 10.

the chorus sets up an echoing pattern between female and male voices:

"The Precious Name," by W. H. Doane

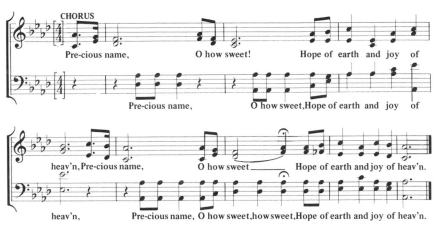

Dwight L. Moody (1837–99), born in Massachusetts, was a salesman in a shoe store in Boston when converted to evangelical Christianity. Moving to Chicago, he established his own church and began to devote himself fully to the business of "saving people for Christ." In 1870 he joined forces with Ira David Sankey (1840–1908), a musician and singer. They worked as a team, with Moody preaching and praying and Sankey singing what came to be called Gospel Songs, accompanying himself on a small reed organ. Their revival meetings in America and England "reduced the population of hell by a million souls," in the words of one of their converts. The songs associated with their efforts first appeared in print in 1875, as the above-mentioned *Gospel Hymns and Sacred Songs;* six volumes had been published by 1891, then all six were brought out together in 1894 as *Gospel Hymns Nos. 1–6 Complete.*[24] Moody eventually organized seminaries for both young men and women, offering a liberal education based on biblical studies, and a Bible Institute in Chicago concerned with both religious education and social reform.

Like all successful evangelists of the past two centuries, he reduced his religious messages to the personal level, and held out the prospect that everyone could be "saved," whatever their background or their history of sinful living. Likewise the music accom-

[24] Facsimilie edition, ed. by H. Wiley Hitchcock as *Earlier American Music,* 5 (New York: Da Capo Press, 1972).

panying his revival meetings was accessible to all who might attend, written in the most familiar style of the day and repetitious in nature so as to become quickly familiar. The harmonic style is fully triadic, usually drawing on only three or four chords; texts are concerned with sin and salvation; structures resemble those of popular songs of the day, with several verses each followed by a chorus or refrain line. Typical was Bliss's "Let the Lower Lights Be Burning":

"Let the Lower Lights Be Burning," by P. P. Bliss

Others were intended for dramatic, solo performance by Sankey; one of his most effective songs of this sort was "The Ninety and Nine."[25]

The late nineteenth and early twentieth centuries brought a flood of evangelists, many of them following Moody's example of teaming up with a singer–song leader. William A. ("Billy") Sunday enlisted the aid of Homer Alvan Rodeheaver (1880–1955) in 1909, and the two made an effective pair for many years. One of the latter's most successful songs was "Brighten the Corner Where You Are," written by Charles H. Gabriel and Ina Duley Ogdon; phonograph recordings of Rodeheaver singing this and other songs still exist.[26] Rodeheaver explained that the purpose of such songs was to

bridge the gap between the popular song of the day and the great hymns and gospel songs, and to give men a simple, easy lilting melody which

[25] NW 224, s2 / 3.
[26] NW 224, s2 / 5.

"Billy Sunday," a lithograph by George Bellows. (Courtesy National Portrait Gallery, Smithsonian Institution, Washington, D.C.)

they could learn the first time they hear it, and which they could whistle and sing wherever they might be.[27]

Revival meetings by Moody, Sunday, and hundreds of other evangelists were held in the South as well as the North, in both urban centers and rural locations. The songs which were such an important part of these occasions were likewise heard and sung in virtually every part of America, penetrating to even the most remote regions of the land. Thus any distinction between urban and rural hymnody disappeared; only the better educated middle and upper classes tended to shy away from populist, emotional religions. Gospel Songs became identified with the religious and musical experience of the working and lower classes.

The South was now the most conservative section of the United States. While accepting Gospel Songs, many people in the region also clung to older repertories, including shape-note and camp-meeting songs. The simultaneous presence of all these styles, and their occasional mixture, eventually brought about a new distinctive Southern idiom, in both sacred and secular music.

[27] Harry Eskew, liner notes to NW 224, p. 5.

# 11

## Marching and Dancing through Nineteenth-Century America

Military bands and their music were brought to America by the British Army in the eighteenth century. Foot troops marched to fife and drum, the cavalry had mounted trumpets and kettledrums. When British regiments came to the New World during the French and Indian War, some were accompanied by "bands of music" of eight to ten musicians—oboes, bassoons, clarinets, and French horns, in pairs. Sometimes called *Harmoniemusik*, these units were attached to the officer corps, and in addition to furnishing military music they would also play concerts (of overtures, concertos and symphonies) and dance music for balls.

Typical of the military music played by these bands in America before the Revolution are the marches written by General John Reid (1721–1807), a Scotsman who served under Lord Jeffrey Amherst in the 1760s. *March for the 3rd Regiment of Foot, Lord Amhersts,*[1] scored for winds in pairs, has a simple binary form (*AABB*), as did almost all marches of the time. *March for the 76th Regiment, Lord Macdonald's Highlanders*[2] is similar in instrumentation and form, with a flavor suggestive of Scottish traditional music.

The colonial militia also employed musicians. The Regiment and Artillery Company of Philadephia paraded in 1756 under the command of Benjamin Franklin, with "Hautboys and Fifes in Ranks."[3]

[1] NW 276, s1 / 1.
[2] NW 276, s2 / 2.
[3] Raoul F. Camus, *Military Music of the American Revolution* (Chapel Hill: The University of North Carolina Press, 1976), p. 43.

With the onset of war, a Continental Army was organized on the British model. Comprised of twenty-seven infantry regiments and one of artillery, with each regiment made up of eight companies, it included two fifers and two drummers in each company. Their music has been preserved in a number of manuscripts—the most important one written in 1777 by Giles Gibbs, Jr.—and in printed instruction books for fife, such as the *Compleat Tutor for the Fife*, published by George Willig in Philadelphia around 1805. Tunes were borrowed from the British; "British Grenadiers"[4] and "Yankee Doodle" were among the most popular. Many have the flavor of Irish or Scottish song.[5] Usually made up of two strains, they resemble fiddle tunes of the day, and, in fact, many melodies are common to both repertories.

The first evidence of "bands of music" in the Continental Army comes in 1777: there is mention of musicians in the Third Regiment of Artillery (from Massachusetts, commanded by Colonel John Crane), the Fourth Regiment of Artillery (from Pennsylvania, under Captain Thomas Proctor), and Webb's Regiment of Infantry from Connecticut. A letter from Colonel Christian Febiger, a Danish immigrant who had been given command of the Second Virginia Continental Infantry, addresses the problems of forming bands of this sort:

> Being perfectly sensible of the use and Necessity of good Music in an Army, I have allways been very desirous to have a good Band in my Regiment and have twice tried it and been as often disappointed, as no Musicians were to be had in this Country except prisoners or Deserters from the British Army. When the Time of Service of three of my best Fifers expird, I proposed to them to reinlist and I would make a Band of them, but to try them first and engagd a Mr. Schuetz a German Musician to teach them. In the course of January I was so much encouragd by their rapid progress, that I determined to compleat the Band on the following principles that they should reinlist and serve as long as I livd or Servd in the Army whether in War or peace as Musicians and Fifers, and as a Bounty for so doing, I would have them taught Instrumental Music Viz, 4 to learn Clarinetts and Violins, two Bassoons and Bass Viol, two French horns. I soon engagd the Number of men I wanted purchasd the Instruments provided a Master to teach the horns.[6]

Among marches known to have been popular with American bands are *Washington's March*,[7] first published in America in 1794, and

---

[4] NW 276, s1 / 2.
[5] Cf. NW 276, s1 / 3, *Lovely Nancy* by the Scotsman James Oswald.
[6] As quoted in Camus, p. 146.
[7] NW 276, s2 / 4.

*The March of the 35th Regiment*,[8] brought out both as a piece for band and as a fife melody. These are in the usual binary form of the day.

Though some bands organized during the Revolution continued their existence after the war, and new military bands were created—the United States Marine Band was formed in 1798 with an instrumentation of 2 oboes, 2 clarinets, 2 French horns, bassoon, and drums—the chief growth of the American band during the postwar decades took place in towns and villages. Samuel Holyoke offered instrumental instruction in several towns in New England and published the two volumes of his *The Instrumental Instructor*, in 1800 and 1807. *Jolley's March*,[9] brought out in a similar publication by Joseph Herrick (1772–1807) in Exeter, New Hampshire (*The Instrumental Preceptor*), is clearly designed for players just learning the rudiments of their instruments. Holyoke's second volume contains pieces for larger bands: *First Grand March*, which may have been written by Holyoke himself,[10] is scored for seven instruments—violins, oboes, and French horns in pairs, with a bass line for bassoon. The piece is in binary form, with a return to the A material at the end of the second strain giving a sense of recapitulation.

A reminiscence of such small, local wind bands appeared in the *Boston Musical Gazette* for July 25, 1838:

Full well do I remember when I first heard the sound of a *Clarinet, French Horn* and *Bassoon;* it was at regimental muster, where I went with my father, as a spectator. It was reported all over the country for weeks beforehand, that the *Boston Band* was to be at the muster, being hired at great expense by *Capt. Taylor*, the liberal and noble-spirited commander of the new troop of Cavalry. This band was all the topic of conversation among the boys, and many a luckless urchin had to do penance for listening to the wonderful stories of its performance, instead of attending to his task. Their number was only *four. Belsted* upon the Hautboy, *Granger* upon the Clarinet; the famous *Peter Schminch*, the French Horn; and old *Dr. Faegnol*, the Bassoon. The first and last belonged to Burgoyne's band, and were taken with him at Saratoga. I believe these musicians found constant employ in their vocation.[11]

As instruction in instrumental performance became more common, the size of instrumental forces in such bands increased. A

[8] NW 276, s2 / 1.
[9] NW 299, s2 / 8.
[10] NW 299, s2 / 7.
[11] As quoted by Jon Newsom in the liner notes to *Our Musical Past. A Concert for Brass Band, Voice, and Piano* (Library of Congress, OMP 101–102, 1976).

typical piece of about 1820, the *Kennebec March* by Ezekial Goodale,[12] (published in his *The Instrumental Director*, 1819, Hallowell,
Maine) is scored for eleven instruments—pairs of flutes, clarinets,
bassoons, and French horns, augmented by trumpet, serpent, and
drum. Pieces also became longer and more complex in structure.
Oliver Shaw's *Gov. Arnold's March*,[13] one of a series of marches
written by this Providence-based composer for the governors of
Rhode Island, is in the usual binary form with the addition of a third
strain, a trio: *AABB / CC / AB*.

Many bands of this era were not attached to military units. Boston had a civic group from about 1810, first called the Green Dragon
Band and later the Boston Brigade Band; the Independent Band of
New York was founded about 1825; the Allentown (Pennsylvania)
Band was formed by 1828; Jacob S. Paine organized the Portland
(Maine) Band in 1827; the Repasz Band of Williamsport (Pennsylvania) was founded in 1831; Milford (New Hampshire) had a band
in the 1830s, with a membership including several of the Hutchinson brothers. And Frank Johnson (1792–1844), a black resident
of Philadelphia, formed a "band of music" of flutes, clarinets, oboes,
bassoons, and French horns in the 1820s that not only played in
and around Philadelphia but went to England, where in 1838 it
gave a command performance for Queen Victoria at Buckingham
Palace.

A dramatic change in the makeup of American bands took place
in the mid-1830s, with the wholesale introduction of keyed brass
instruments. With the invention of the keyed bugle and an ophicleide,[14] a full range of brass instruments was now capable of playing complete diatonic—and even chromatic—scales. These new
horns could not only play melodic lines in any part of their range,
they could also supply full harmonic support, even in chromatic
and modulatory passages. Existing bands changed to an all-brass
instrumentation—New York's Independent Band became a brass
band in 1834, under the leadership of Thomas Dodworth—and new
brass bands were formed (Edward Kendall's Boston Brass Band
gave its first concert in March of 1835).

By combining these new instruments with trombones and French
horns, a group of eight or more brass instruments could cover a
range from soprano to bass and achieve a more homogeneous sound
than had been possible with mixed woodwinds and brass. A typi-

---

[12] NW 299, s2 / 3.

[13] NW 299 s2 / 5.

[14] Patented by Jean Hilaire Asté in 1821, the ophicleide was a keyed brass instrument with a baritone-bass range; the term was soon used generically, for an entire
family of keyed brass instruments.

cal instrumentation, as specified in one of the early printed collections of music for brass band,[15] consisted of:

1 E-flat bugle, 2 B-flat bugles, 2 E-flat trumpets, 1 cornopean
2 French horns, 2 alto ophicleides
3 trombones, 2 bass ophicleides
drums

Between 1842 and 1845, the Frenchman Adolphe Sax (1841–94) perfected an entire family of keyed brass instruments, making possible an even more homogeneous sound. They had the added advantage of standarized notation of fingering; they were all transposing instruments, and a player could switch from one to another without learning a new system of fingering. These saxhorns, as they were called, were accepted almost immediately in America; by 1849, Allen Dodworth (an important American bandleader) could write:

> What, in our opinion, would make the best arrangement for a Band of ten, would be as follows: Two E-flat Trebles, Two B-flat Altos, Two E-flat Tenores, One B-flat Baritone, One A-flat or B-flat Bass, Two E-flat Contra Bass. Many different kinds of instruments are used to take the parts here mentioned; but most of the Bands of the present day give

The Diston family with their saxhorns in 1848.

[15] E. K. Eaton, *Twelve Pieces of Harmony for Military Brass Bands* (New York: Firth & Hall, 1846).

preference to what is called the Saxhorn, which is made in all the different keys mentioned above.[16]

A manuscript collection of forty compositions copied for the Manchester (New Hampshire) Band in 1849 reveals an instrumentation of keyed bugles, valved trumpets and several sizes of ophicleides. A *Second Sett* copied in 1854 reflects the change of instrumentation in the American brass band mentioned above: most of the instruments are saxhorns, augmented by cornets and trumpets:[17]

3 E-flat cornets, 2 B-flat cornets, 1 E-flat trumpet
3 E-flat alto horns
2 B-flat tenor horns, 2 B-flat basso horns, 1 B-flat subbass horn
side drum, base drum, cymbals

Bands now played on military, patriotic, and political occasions, and also at concerts. The Portland Band was giving open-air concerts twice a week in the summer months as early as 1842, and the following year brought their first indoor concert; J. B. Smith's Independent Band gave its first outdoor concert, in Richmond's Capitol Square, in June of 1850; The Bangor (Maine) Band, formed in 1859, played more than sixty engagements in its first year of existence—military and fireman's parades and musters, concerts, serenades, excursions, private parties.

The military march remained the mainstay of the repertory, both in parade and concert. Some marches of mid-century represented little advance beyond the binary-form pieces of earlier days; one of these is *Lily Bell Quickstep* by G. W. E. Friedrich, published in the *Brass Band Journal* (New York: Firth, Pond & Co., 1854). Only the instrumentation, making greater technical demands on all of the players, marks it as a later piece.[18]

The very popular *Wood Up Quickstep* by John Holloway points in newer directions.[19] The first section is made up of the usual four eight-measure phrases; the second section introduces two new melodic phrases, featuring a florid, technically demanding virtuoso solo line played by an E-flat keyed bugle; and there is a third strain, a "trio," contrasting in instrumentation and melody. The shape of the piece:

A (aabb)—B (ccdd)—C (trio) (ee)—A (aabb)—B (ccdd)

[16]*The Message Bird* for August 1, 1849.

[17]Cf. the liner notes by Donald Hunsberger and Robert DeCormier, *Homespun America. Marches, Waltzes, Polkas and Serenades of the Manchester Cornet Band*, Vox SVBX 5309 (3 records), 1976.

[18]Cf. *Our Musical Past*, s1 / 4.

[19]*19th-Century American Ballroom Music, Smithsonian Social Orchestra & Quadrille Band*, Nonesuch H-71313 (1975), s1 / 10.

The band repertory of this era can best be judged from their concert programs, which included the compositions they played at all their functions. The Manchester Cornet Band offered the following program on July 1, 1858:[20]

*Eaton's Grand March*
*Giorno-d'Orrore* (from *Semiramide,* by Rossini)
*Free and Easy*—Quickstep
*Les Rendezvous*—Waltzes
*Neptune Galop*
*Departed Days*—Serenade
*Blues Quickstep*
*Knaebel's Waltz*
*Congo's Quickstep*

Most of the pieces are of greater length and complexity than those of early in the century, and the level of playing ability has risen dramatically, judging from the style of writing for all instruments and particularly the virtuoso writing in solo passages.

By the time of the Civil War, then, America's bands had become much more advanced in instrumentation, repertory, and playing techniques than in the decades following the Revolution.

A Yankee band during the Civil War.

[20] The entire program is available, played on instruments of the day, on *Homespun America. Marches, Waltzes, Polkas and Serenades of the Manchester Cornet Band.*

In 1861, America's brass bands went off to war. Virtually all military units had a regional identity: units of militia already in existence were brought into national service; officers recruited their own platoons or companies, locally; enlistment officers worked within a given city, town, or region, sending troops off as groups to national service; the military draft in the North also worked locally and regionally.

Town and regional bands often enlisted as a group, going off to war accompanying the soldiers from their area. The Portland (Maine) Band, at that time directed by Daniel H. Chandler, enlisted almost to a man and became the First Regiment Band of Maine serving throughout the war; the Manchester Cornet Band served the Fourth New Hampshire Regiment; the Armory Band of Richmond (Virginia) was attached to the Richmond Light Infantry Blues before and during the war.

Not all units could boast such large and well-organized bands. Those from rural areas often had only fifers and drummers; others, perhaps a handful of brass instruments. But whatever the size and composition of the band, it was an indispensable part of the unit to which it was attached. Their most important job was to furnish music for parading and marching; it was rare to see any military unit parade without some sort of accompanying music, and in a time when much transportation was by foot, even over considerable distances, band music—or at least drumming—helped make long marches less tedious. In camp, band concerts in the evenings were often the only form of entertainment available to the troops, and programs of dance music and arrangements of popular songs served both to entertain the men and to remind them of their homes and loved ones. As one Union soldier wrote in a letter home:

> I don't know what we would have done without our band. It is acknowledged by everyone to be the best in the division. Every night about sundown Gilmore gives us a splendid concert, playing selections from the operas and some very pretty marches, quick-steps, waltzes and the like. Thus you see we get a great deal of *new* music, notwithstanding we are off here in the woods.[21]

Bands played the same repertory as in civilian days. Walter Dignam, a member of the Fourth New Hampshire Regimental Band, copied a number of pieces in 1863–64, when the unit was stationed outside Charleston—dances, arrangements of songs, and operatic excerpts:

[21] Bell Irvin Wiley, *The Life of Billy Yank* (Indianapolis: Bobbs-Merrill Company, 1952), p. 158.

*Prayer* from *Der Freischütz* (Weber)
*General Stevenson's Quickstep* (Krebs)
*Hope Told a Flattering Tale* (Paisiello)
*Helene Schottische* (adapted from Chopin)
*Redoway* from *Le Prophète* (Meyerbeer)
*Waltz* (unidentified)
*Quickstep Medley* (Simon Knaebel)
*Wedding March* (Mendelssohn)
*Quickstep Medley* (unidentified)
*Black Brigade* (unidentified)
*No One to Love* (Stephen Foster)
*The Queen of Roses Waltz* (D'Albert)
*Come Where My Love Lies Dreaming* (Stephen Foster)
*Camp Polka* (D'Albert)
*Crystal Palace Waltz* (D'Albert)
*Ricordanza* from *Ione*

A typical Southern band was the one attached to the Twenty-sixth North Carolina Regiment. In prewar days, it had been a civilian group in Salem, North Carolina, dominated by the Moravians who had settled the community in 1766. The first formally organized band dated from 1831 and was a typical woodwind-dominated "band of music" of clarinets, a flute, French horns, bassoons, trombones, a bugle, a trumpet, and a bass drum.[22] By mid-century it had gone along with fashion and been transformed into the "Salem Brass Band."

In early 1862, they volunteered for military service. A member of the band recounted the circumstances:

> I was sitting in the lobby of the Gaston House, New Bern, when a man wearing a Colonel's uniform came in with a loaf of bread under each arm. This was Zeb Vance (of the Twenty-sixth Regiment). I spoke to him and told him my errand. Colonel Vance replied: "You are the very man I am looking for. You represent the Salem Band. Come to my regiment at Wood's brick yard, four miles below New Bern." Next morning, I went down to the camp, was met by Captain Horton, of Company C, and as the result of my visit, the band was engaged and at first it was paid by the officers.[23]

Eight members enlisted, all playing keyed brass instruments: E-flat cornet, 2 B-flat cornets, 2 E-flat altos, 2 B-flat tenors, 1 E-flat bass. Their duties included playing every morning at 8 o'clock for guard mount, every evening at dress parade, giving a concert every

---

[22] Harry H. Hall, *A Johnny Reb Band from Salem: The Pride of Tarheelia* (Raleigh: The North Carolina Confederate Commission, 1963), pp. 4–5.
[23] As quoted in Hall, p. 10.

evening for the troops, and playing at regimental inspection on Sunday morning. They also played appropriate music for religious services.

When the regiment saw action, the members of the band were pressed into service as hospital attendants. After a winter spent in camp in southeastern Virginia, the regiment was reassigned to Lee's Army of Northern Virginia, taking part in the campaign of Gettysburg.

This battle proved a disaster for the Twenty-sixth, as it was for the fortunes of the Confederacy: the regiment lost most of its officers, and casualties approached 90 percent. The band worked ceaselessly in field hospitals, though in one curious episode it played "polkas and waltzes" in the midst of the fighting, the music heard by members of both armies. In the relatively quiet months that followed, Lee reshaped his army. The band had the opportunity to hear—and exchange music with—many other Confederate bands in the same camp, including the Sixteenth Mississippi Regiment. which allowed them to copy a number of arrangements made by their leader, William H. Hartwell.

Subsequent engagements included the campaign of the Wilderness and the Battle of Cold Harbor; several times the band was ordered to play in the midst of battle, in the hope that music would improve morale. In the final month of the war the band was cut off from its command, and on April 5, 1865, surrendered to the Yankees:

> Our instruments were taken from us and that seemed to be the bitterest experience of all. I had learned to love my B-flat cornet more than all the rest of my few possessions and to see it go into the hands of another and know that I would never see it again, was a very hard thing to endure.[24]

After three months in a federal prison at Point Lookout, Maryland, the members of the band were released. Reunited in Salem, they offered a concert on December 29, 1865; the flyer for this concert states that "having lost nearly all their instruments about the time of the close of the last Virginia campaign, and being desirous of replacing them with a new and good set," they "propose raising funds for this purpose by giving one or more Concerts."

In the Northern army, the best band in the first two years of the war was that of the Twenty-fourth Massachusetts Regiment, directed by Patrick Gilmore (1829–92). Born in Ballygar, County Galway, Ireland, Gilmore came to Canada in 1848 as a cornettist

[24] Hall, p. 104.

with the band attached to an army regiment from Athlone. He moved to Boston, opened a music store, played in the Boston Brigade Band, became director of the Boston Brass Band (1852), and assumed the leadership of the Boston Brigade Band in 1859.

The first appearance of Mr. Gilmore's new band last Saturday evening gave assurance of much success in its future operations. The audience was immense, and the applause abundant, compelling many encores not anticipated. The formation of a thorough and complete military band has been the object of Mr. Gilmore's efforts, and he has done better and gone farther in this direction than any of his predecessors. Hitherto we have had only brass bands regularly organized, all attempts to combine a well balanced body of brass and reed instruments having failed. Mr. Gilmore seems to have affected this arrangement, and declares himself determined to perpetuate it. His military band consists of some thirty-five members, among whom are the proper proportions of players upon reed instruments—flutes, clarinett, hautboys, bassoons. In the disposition of the brass department, some thought has been given to more harmonious, and less noisy, combinations than are common among us.[25]

The use of woodwind instruments was continued in his wartime group; an observer in 1862 commented that the twenty-fourth Massachusetts Regimental Band included "five reed instruments, of which no other band can boast."[26] The excellence and growing fame of this organization led to his appointment as director of all bands in occupied Louisiana in 1863.

In 1872, Gilmore brought a number of famous European military bands to America, including England's Grenadier Guards, Germany's Kaiser Franz Grenadier Regiment, and the National Band of Dublin. Their repertory consisted of marches, transcriptions from opera, and fantasies on familiar airs. Excited by the size and professionalism of these European bands, Gilmore set out to emulate them. Leaving Boston for New York in 1873, he accepted the leadership of the band of the Twenty-second Regiment of the New York Militia, with the provision that the band bear his name. By 1878 the band numbered 66 players, with a full range of wind instruments:

2 piccolos, 2 flutes, 2 oboes, 2 bassoons, 1 contra bassoon
clarinets: 1 A-flat sopranino, 3 E-flat soprano, 16 B-flat, 1 alto, 1 bass (22)

[25] John S. Dwight, ed., *Dwight's Journal of Music: A Paper of Art and Literature* (Boston: Oliver Ditson and Company, 1852–81; reprint edition, Johnson Reprint Corp., 1967), April 16, 1859.
[26] As quoted in Wiley, p. 158.

saxophones: 1 soprano, 1 alto, 1 tenor, 1 baritone (4)
1 E-flat soprano cornet, 4 B-flat cornets, 2 trumpets, 2 fluegel-horns
4 French horns, 2 E-flat alto horns, 2 B-flat tenor horns, 2 euphoniums
3 trombones, 5 bombardons
4 percussionists

With this group trained to a degree of professionalism unprecedented in the history of the American band, Gilmore set out on tour, first of the United States and Canada, then Europe.

Though Gilmore composed many of the pieces played by his band—*Astor House Polka* (1859), *On the Road to Salem Quickstep* (1853), *The 22nd Regiment March* (1874)—none of them achieved much success beyond his own group. Several typical and popular marches of the last quarter of the nineteenth century will serve better to give an idea of the prevalent style.

The *Second Connecticut Regiment March*, written in 1880 by D. W. Reeves (1838–1900), leader of the American Band, was as widely played as any American march of the time. It is in double binary form—*AABB / CCDD*—with fanfarelike introductions leading into each of the two large sections. Clarinets dominate in much the same way as violins in a symphony orchestra; lower winds and brass furnish a harmonic and rhythmic accompaniment; snare drum and bass drum are heard throughout. The second section, the trio, contrasts in instrumentation and dynamic level. Trombones are given the melody in Section *C*, with clarinets playing an obligato countermelody; part *D* is quite soft, though scored for full band; and a brief coda returning to a fanfare motif brings the piece to a crashing conclusion. The melodic material frequently suggests marches and marchlike passages in the operas of Donizetti, Bellini, and Verdi.

A. F. Weldon's *Gate City* (1890) is a paraphrase march, drawing its melodic material from familiar tunes.[27] A brief introduction ushers in the first eight-measure phrase, the first section of Stephen Foster's "Old Folks at Home" scored for full band; another fanfare leads to a repeat, this time with the first phrase of "Dixie" fitted against it in counterpoint. A third eight-measure section brings the second half of "Dixie," the second half of "Old Folks at Home" follows, and the first section concludes with the two tunes played in counterpoint. The trio consists of a harmonization of "Maryland, My Maryland."

*Boston Commandery* was written in 1892 by Thomas M. Carter

[27] NW 266, s1 / 4.

(1841–1934), whose band (established in 1871) was popular throughout New England.[28] After a brief introduction, the symmetrical first strain, *AABB*, has the melody carried as usual by clarinets (sometimes doubled with cornets), with prominent trombone running passages at ends of phrases; another fanfare leads to the trio, with the brass playing the hymn "Onward, Christian Soldiers" and the clarinet section furnishing a virtuoso obbligato part above it.

Gilmore led the band until his death, which occurred unexpectedly in 1892 in St. Louis, where they had gone to participate in the Great Exposition of that year. Curiously, that very year saw the formation of the band which soon became the most famous of its kind—Sousa's Band.

John Philip Sousa (1854–1932) was born in Washington, D.C., the son of a Portuguese father and German mother. His father was a member of the United States Marine Band, and Sousa served a period of apprenticeship with that organization. His principal instrument was the violin, and his early musical experiences ranged from accompanying a dancing class, or playing in "social orchestras," to playing under Offenbach when this famous composer came to America for the Centennial celebration of 1876. He also conducted theater bands, variety shows, and eventually a touring production of *H. M. S. Pinafore*.

The United States Marine Band with leader John Philip Sousa on tour, September 1891. (National Archives)

[28] NW 266, s1 / 2.

In 1880 he was named the fourteenth conductor of the United States Marine Band, and in 1892 he resigned from this prestigious post to organize a professional civilian band. Their first concert took place on September 26, 1892 at Stillman Music Hall in Plainfield, New Jersey; the program began with Sousa's arrangement of Patrick Gilmore's song "The Voice of a Departing Soul," honoring the recently deceased bandmaster. The band remained in existence until 1931. Each year it toured the United States for at least six months; there were four European tours (1900, 1901, 1902, 1905), and a world tour in 1910–11.

Sousa's band numbered some 50 players in 1892:

2 flutes, 2 oboes, 2 bassoons
16 clarinets: 2 E-flat, 12 B-flat 1 alto, 1 bass
3 saxophones
4 cornets, 2 trumpets
4 French horns, 3 trombones, 2 euphoniums, 3 basses (tubas)
3 percussionists

The instrumental makeup was still quite similar to Gilmore's later groups. By 1924, the distribution of players had changed somewhat:

6 piccolos and flutes, 2 oboes, 1 English horn, 2 bassoons
29 clarinets: 26 B-flat, 1 alto, 2 bass
8 saxophones: 4 alto, 2 tenor, 1 baritone, 1 bass
6 cornets, 2 trumpets
4 French horns, 4 trombones, 2 euphoniums, 6 sousaphones
3 percussion

Clarinets ae even more dominant; oboes, bassoons, and flutes are represented in an even smaller ration than in Gilmore's band; cornets are more numerous than any other brass instrument; and the lower brasses are more prominent, buttressed by the sousaphone, a flexible and powerful bass tuba built to Sousa's specifications in the late 1890s.

The repertory placed greater emphasis on transcriptions of classical compositions, and Sousa often employed instrumental and vocal soloists, including the famous American violinist Maud Powell and singers Marjorie Moody, Virginia Root, and Estelle Liebling. Most of the arrangements were by Sousa himself. Also, Sousa composed original pieces for bands in the nineteenth century, and encouraged and commissioned other composers to do the same. In the mixture of large instrumental pieces, dances and marches, and pieces featuring solo performers, his programs resemble concerts from the first decades of the nineteenth century. One of his typical programs from the early 1920s:

| | |
|---|---|
| 1. Overture. "The Red Sarafan" | Erichs |
| 2. Cornet Solo. "Centennial Polka" | Bellstedt |
| 3. Suite. "Leaves from my Note-book" | Sousa |
| 4. Vocal Solo. "Ah Fors e Lui" (from *La Traviata*) | Verdi |
| 5. Intermezzo. "Golden Light" | Bizet |

Interval

| | |
|---|---|
| 6. Fantasia. "A Bouquet of Beloved Inspirations" | Sousa |
| 7. Xylophone Solo. "Witches' Dance" | MacDowell |
| 8. March. "The Gallant Seventh" | Sousa |
| 9. Violin Solo. "Romance and Finale from Second Concerto" | Wieniawski |
| 10. Cowboy Breakdown. "Turkey in the Straw" | Guion |

The audience also demanded and was given encores, mostly Sousa's familiar and famous marches, arguably the most universally known music in the United States in the first quarter of the twentieth century. Sousa composed 136 of those, from the *Review March* and *Salutation March* of 1873 to a cluster of marches written in 1931, the year before his death. Among these are several dozen classics which have continued to be the core of the march repertory to the present day: *The Thunderer* (1889), *The Washington Post* (1889), *El Capitan* (1896), *The Stars and Stripes Forever* (1896), and *Hands Across the Sea* (1899).

*Revival March* (1876), an early work,[29] has a formal design no different from what one would expect for the time:

*AABBA'A' / CD/ABA'*

and many of the musical details are equally expected: the use of clarinets and sometimes cornets to carry the chief melodic material and to play obbligato countermelodies when the tune is given to other instruments; a trio contrasting in melody, instrumentation, and dynamic level; a familiar tune ("In the Sweet Bye and Bye") in the trio; the use of trombones to play introductory and concluding running passages for several sections. *Bonnie Annie Laurie March* (1883)[30] looks back to an even older pattern, with a three-strain trio, the second and third sections based on the familiar tune.

The *Washington Post March* (1889) has a different shape and character. The trio has become as long and as important as the

[29] NW 266, s2 / 3.
[30] NW 266, s1 / 7.

first strain, and there is no *da capo*. The tempo broadens with the last two repetitions of *C* and a sturdy countermelody in the trombones supports and strengthens the winds and upper brass; the piece comes to a resounding climax with this intensified *C* strain:

$$AABB \mid C(x) \, C'(x) \, C'$$

*The Stars and Stripes Forever* (1896), surely the most famous march ever written, carries these techniques even further. A brief introduction and the first two strains start things off. The trio is soft, with both the tune and the accompaniment played by woodwinds. A "break strain" featuring brilliant and loud brass and percussion serves as a powerful interlude; the trio is repeated, still soft but intensified by a brilliant piccolo obbligato against the clarinet melody; the "break strain" returns, more powerful than before; and in a final play-through of the trio the tempo broadens a bit, the melody is now supported by brass and full percussion, the trombones fill pauses in the melody with rapid running passages, and the piccolo countermelody sounds out over everything.

Most of Sousa's later marches are written in this same form; *Federal March* (1910) is typical.[31] But none of his marches written in the twentieth century captures quite the spirit and energy of his early pieces, and none has approached the popularity of the best of his marches of the 1880s and '90s.

Contemporary audiences and critics, both in America and abroad, took Sousa's marches to be uniquely American. "In Germany they hold his music so typically representative of America that they play his marches on international occasions," wrote an American historian in 1904.[32] It is no easy matter to identify specific elements that are uniquely American, however. The military band and the march originated in Europe and continued to flourish there into and beyond Sousa's lifetime; the instrumentation of Sousa's band and the formal designs of his marches differ only in details from European bands and marches written by European composers.

The answer would appear to be both simple and complex. By the end of the nineteenth century, bands and their music had become deeply ingrained in American life. Virtually every city, town, and village had its own bands, with membership drawn from the community. Band music was omnipresent, heard in evening concerts, parades, political rallies, social events, picnics, civic ceremonies, educational functions. Few Americans traveled abroad in those days. Music was part of their life—their American life. The fact

---

[31] NW 282, s1 / 1, in a performance by the Sousa Band.
[32] Louis C. Elson, *The History of American Music* (New York: The Macmillan Company, 1904), p. 226.

that similar music existed in Europe had no effect on their perception of the band and its music as distinctly American, because it was an important part of their own life and culture.

Sousa was receptive to new musical currents flowing in America at the turn of the century, and his band played a role in popularizing these. He may have heard ragtime music for the first time in 1893 at the Columbian Exposition in Chicago. By 1900, Sousa was playing his own arrangements of early ragtime pieces like Kerry Mills's *Whistling Rufus, At a Gerogia Camp Meeting*,[33] *Southern Hospitality*, and *An Arkansas Huskin' Bee* by Arthur Pryor, a member of his band. It was at just this time that the group made its first European tour—the first American band to play abroad since Gilmore in 1878. Their programs at the Paris Exposition of 1900 and throughout France and Germany included ragtime pieces; it was the first time European audiences had heard American syncopated dance music. Sousa's recordings of these pieces were among the most popular and widely disseminated early phonograph discs, and though a military band could not impart the same flavor as a black ragtime pianist, Sousa's championing of this music played some role in its acceptance and popularity.

Somewhat later, when jazz was emerging, Sousa wrote a humoresque entitled *Showing Off Before Company* (1919), which not only featured syncopated rhythms, but also had various members of the band improvising jazzlike solo passages.

Musical currents flowed the other way, also. Some of the earliest jazz was played by bands in New Orleans and elsewhere in the South, using the instruments of the military / concert band—trumpets, clarinets, trombones, saxophones, drums. The trombone "smear" originated in Sousa's band,[34] and surely some jazz of the 1920s, in which the melody was played by a cornet, with obbligato passages in the clarinet and trombone, was rooted in the trios of some of Sousa's famous marches.

Though Sousa's other compositions for band have not had the enduring success of his marches, they are important as early attempts to create a serious repertory for the wind band. They include suites, descriptive pieces, overtures, fantasias, pieces featuring one or more solo performers, and humoresques. Though Sousa was familiar with classical literature and forms and was capable of writing music of this sort, he was deeply committed to a populist view of music.

[33] NW 282, s1 / 3.
[34] Cf. Arthur Pryor's *Trombone Sneeze*, recorded by the Sousa Band in 1901, NW 282, s1 / 7.

My theory was, by insensible degrees, first to reach every heart by simple, stirring music; secondly, to lift the unmusical mind to a still higher form of musical art. This was my mission. The point was to move all America, while busied in its varied pursuits, by the power of direct and simple music. I wanted to make a music for the people, a music to be grasped at once.[35]

His more serious compositions gave the untrained listener something easy to grasp—a familiar tune, a descriptive program, the stirring playing of a virtuoso instrumentalist.

The first of his eleven suites for band, *The Last Days of Pompeii* (1893), takes us into a quite different musical world than that of his marches. The three sections ("In the House of Burbo and Stratonice," "Nydia the Blind Girl," and "The Destruction of Pompeii and Nydia's Death") are each prefaced with quotations from Bulwer Lytton's novel; the musical style is derived from the tone poems of Liszt and his successors. The sound is fully orchestral, with woodwinds replacing the strings of the conventional orchestra; there are passages of a brilliance and color not available with a string-dominated orchestra. It is a well-constructed composition, accessible to Sousa's audiences because of its programmatic content and the compelling brilliance of its sound.

At the other end of the spectrum is Sousa's *Fantasia for Band* entitled *Rose, Thistle and Shamrock* (1901), featured on his second European tour; it is a marchlike potpourri of traditional tunes of the British Isles—"The Minstrel Boy," "The Campbells are Coming," and the like.

The greatest era of the American concert / military band lasted from the 1890s to the onset of the Depression. The bands of the military forces increased in size and professionalism; other professional bands were formed to compete with Sousa's Band, including that of Arthur Pryor, a great trombone virtuoso with Sousa until he formed his own group in 1903;[36] municipal bands became larger, the caliber of performance improved, and they tackled more difficult literature. "Serious" composers began writing for concert bands[37] but few of these works achieved permanent status in the band repertory, which is still based on marches, concert dances, suites, and transcriptions of operatic and orchestral works of the nineteenth century.

[35] "Bandmaster Sousa Explains his Mission in Music," *Musical America* (April 16, 1910).
[36] A selection of recordings by the Pryor Band is on NW 282, s2.
[37] Five "serious" American compositions for band are available on NW 211.

Social dancing had been popular in eighteenth-century America, mostly among upper-class colonials and British civil servants and army officers. The decades following the Revolution saw a decline in such activity, because of the political climate and a resurgence of opposition from the church. Sermons and published tracts hammered away at this evil:

> The Primitive Fathers spoke of dancing as a most atrocious and scandalous evil; so saith St. Ambrose: "None may dance but the daughter of an adultress; but she who is chaste, let her teach her daughter prayer, not dances." . . . St. Chrysostom saith, "Where wanton dancing is, there certainly the devil is present; for God hath not given us legs to dance but that we should walk modestly, not skip like camels; but if the body be polluted by dancing impudently, how much more may the soul be thought to be defiled? The devil danceth in these dances." . . .[38]

But despite this, dancing masters set up shop in many of America's cities and towns, and the aristocracy of the new republic continued to enjoy this diversion.

The most popular social dance of the late eighteenth and early nineteenth centuries was the cotillion, defined by Noah Webster in his *An American Dictionary of the English Language*[39] as "a brisk dance, performed by eight persons together; also, a tune which regulates the dance." Danced by four couples—or a larger group divided into four-couple units—it was a pattern or figure dance, with steps and movements learned in advance by participants. The accompanying music, usually in 2/4 or 6/8 meter, consisted of two or three phrases or strains. Typical patterns were *ABA, ABCA, ABBA, AABBA, AABBCCA*. The second phrase was sometimes in the dominant; the third phrase was often in a minor key. The following, the seventh cotillion in a set of thirty-two dances selected, arranged, and figured by Alexander Dupouy "for the use of his Cotillion parties" and published by George Willig in Philadelphia, is typical:

A dance tune from *Cotillions and Country Dances* by Alexander Dupouy

<hr />

[38] John Phillips, *Familar Dialogues on Dancing* (New York: Kirk, 1798), pp. 17, 19.
[39] Springfield, Massachusetts, 1861.

The figures printed just under the music give the movements associated with this dance:

$A$ { 2 & 2 lead to the sides (4)
round 4 & 4 (4)

$B$ { chassez cross all (8)

$C$ { forward & back (4)
back & back (4)

$A$ { Promenade (4)
right & left (4)

Thus proficiency in social dancing consisted of learning "figures" for a number of dances and executing these with ease and grace.

For contrast during an evening of cotillions, contra dances (or country dances) would be performed. All dancers would form two facing lines; in the words of a dance scholar:

> The fundamental nature of this dance is that the couples facing each other at the head of the line dance with or around dancers from other positions and then by various means move into a new position in the line, either second or at the bottom. The other couples move progressively up to the point where they too will dance the figures.[40]

Everyone danced, and it was not necessary to know the figures in advance; by observing the lead couple, the uninitiated could learn a given dance on the spot.

The music was drawn from older and often traditional music—jigs, hornpipes, reels, familiar Irish and Scottish tunes.[41] It was

[40] Thornton Hagert, liner notes to NW 293.
[41] Six pieces known to have been used for country dancing in this period are available on NW 293, s1 / 4, played by a single fiddle.

simpler in structure, consisting of only two strains or phrases, repeated as many times as necessary to give everyone a chance to dance. A typical country dance tune:

A dance tune from *A Collection of Country Dances* by G. Graupner (c. 1808)

has the usual two strains, and much simpler instructions than most cotillions:

> Hands four round and back again,
> Down the middle, up again,
> Pausette and lead outsides.

Two other dances were encountered in America during this time. The minuet was archaic by the first decades of the nineteenth century, associated with the European aristocracy of the previous century, stiff and static in execution, with slow-paced formal music; its occasional inclusion during an evening of cotillions was a concession to older members of the party. The waltz, on the other hand, was brand new. Of German origin, first widely popular in Vienna in the closing years of the eighteenth century, it was a couples dance which aroused great opposition because of the proximity and intimacy of the executants. Cotillions could be danced to music of a variety of meters and tempos, and waltzes were apparently first danced in cotillion formation rather than in couples. Jullien's *Prima Donna Waltz*,[42] with its simple two-strain shape, each of eight measures and each repeated as necessary, is typical of the early waltz in America.

By the 1820s and '30s, a cotillion consisted of five or six separate dances, done in sequence. These were learned, danced, and published as sets, with identifying names: "Fanny Jones' Sett," "Opera Sett," "St. Lawrence Sett," "Niagara Sett," "Battle of New Orleans Sett." The "Columbian Sett," Cotillion No. 14 in a collection published in the 1830s, consists of six separate but continuous dances:

1. 6 / 8 (*ABACA*)
   Right and left 4, balance, swing round, chassa, &c.
2. 2 / 4 (*ABA*)
   First gentleman forward twice, cross over and forward 3, opposite lady balance &c.
3. 6 / 8 (*ABACA*)
   All gentlemen balance to the right, turn partners, chassa. Ladies the same.
4. 2 / 4 (*ABACA*)
   First 2 balance to the right, chassa and balance to the next, &c.
5. 6 / 8 (*ABACA*)
   All forward and back, swing partners, balance to corners, &c.
6. 2 / 4 (*ABA*)
   First lady balance to the gentleman on her right, swing round, and so on through the sett. Others the same.

The American cotillion was an adaptation of the French quadrille, popular in Paris during the First Empire and introduced into Germany and England in the second decade of the nineteenth century. The quadrille was highly formalized, a set of five figures always bearing the names *Le pantalon, L'été, La poule, La pastourelle*, and *Finale*. Such rigid structures were sometimes found in America, with the French names of the five sections retained, but more commonly the American cotillion was a more informal collection of dances strung together.[43]

It was no simple matter to remember the figures for an entire

---

[42] NW 293, s1 / 1.

[43] A truncated performance of an American cotillion from this period, *La Sonnambula Quadrille, Number Two*, by the black bandleader and composer Francis (or Frank) Johnson, is available on NW 293, s1 / 9. Only four of the five sections are performed, and most repeats are omitted, but it gives an idea of the sytle and sequence of several dances comprising a cotillion.

evening of dances. Booklets were sometimes printed with summaries of cotillion figures; these could be slipped in a pocket and consulted as necessary:

LA FAYETTE FOREVER

All round, chasse four open, back again, balance in the middle, then
half right and left, the gentlemen balance and turn the ladies to their
left hand only half way, set, chasse la Marquis all eight, that you may
be in your former places; the third and fourth couples do the same.[44]

But a better method was devised in America sometime before 1820:
a "caller" (one of the musicians) would shout out the figures over
the music.

Social dancing was held in a variety of environments in the first
half of the nineteenth century. Well-to-do families had private balls
in their own homes; others were held in public buildings. Robert
Waln describes a cotillion party held in the Masonic Hall in Philadelphia around 1818 ("The room was about half-filled with a most
splendid collection of belles and beaux, the greater part engaged
in dancing cotillions, after the fashion of my country").[45] Frances
Trollope described a ball in Cincinnati:

In noting the various brilliant events which diversified our residence in
the western metropolis, I have omitted to mention the Birthday Ball, as
it is called, a festivity which, I believe, has place on the 22nd of February, in every town and city throughout the Union. It is the anniversary
of the birth of General Washington, and well deserves to be marked by
the Americans as a day of jubilee. I was really astonished at the *coup
d'oeil* on entering, for I saw a large room filled with extremely well-dressed company, among whom were many very beautiful girls. The
gentlemen also were exceedingly smart; but I had not yet been long
enough in Western America not to feel startled at recognising in almost
every full-dressed *beau* that passed me, the master or shopman that I
had been used to see behind the counter, or lolling at the door of every
shop in the city. . . . The dancing was not quite like, yet not very unlike,
what we see at an assiz or race ball in a country town. They call their
dances cotillions instead of quadrilles, and the figures are called from
the orchestra in English, which has a very ludicrous effect on European
ears.[46]

[44] From *A Collection of the Newest Cotillions and Country Dances*, Worcester, Massachusetts, early nineteenth century.

[45] Quoted in Eileen Southern, *Readings in Black American Music* (New York: W. W. Norton & Company, 1971).

[46] Frances Trollope, *Domestic Manners of the Americans* (New York: Dodd Mead & Company, 1927), pp. 126–27.

Considerable credit for making social dancing respectable, fashionable, and highly popular in America must go to Allen Dodworth, a member of an important musical family in New York. Allen was a member of the Independent Band, the National Brass Band, and eventually the Philharmonic Society of New York, as a violinist. But his chief love was dancing. After a number of years as a private dancing instructor, he opened an Academy of Dance in a fashionable part of the city about 1842, and for half a century this academy, in a series of locations, was considered the most fashionable institution at which to learn dancing and associated social graces. His book, *Dancing and Its Relation to Education and Social Life, with a New Method of Instruction* (New York: Harper, 1885), went through a series of editions both here and in Britain.[47]

Dancing in the early nineteenth century was most often accompanied by one or two violins. As the piano became more popular, cotillions, country dances, and waltzes were published as piano pieces, and this instrument—alone or with a violin—was often used to accompany dancing. But as the century wore on, a larger (and louder) ensemble was needed for larger halls. In his *Complete Ball-Room Hand Book,*[48] Elias Howe recommends a "social" or "quadrille" orchestra of two violins, flute, clarinet, cornet, and a bass instrument (usually a cello), with optional piano or harp. But there was great flexibility; another collection of dance music suggests:

> When you have not four instruments besides the pianoforte, omit the third violin or the cornet part. When you have not three instruments, omit the second violin or clarinet part. When you have not two instruments, omit the bass. Any of the pieces can be performed with or without the pianoforte. The upper two parts will generally be found the best as duets. Add the bass when you can do so.[49]

Many bands functioned either as military / concert groups or—with a change in instrumentation or personnel—as "social orchestras." By adding strings, Frank Johnson transformed his "band of music" into a "social orchestra" that was in demand for balls as far south as Virginia.

As the nineteenth century unfolded and music in the United States became more complex and varied, the stylistic range of the music to which cotillions were danced grew. There were sets based

---

[47] For a fuller account of his life and activity, cf. "The Dodworth Family and Ballroom Dancing in New York" by Rosetta O'Neill, the fifth chapter in Paul Magriel, ed., *Chronicles of the American Dance* (New York: Henry Holt & Company, 1948).

[48] Boston: Oliver Ditson, 1858.

[49] Quoted in the liner notes to *Homespun America*, from John W. Moore, *The American Collection of Instrumental Music* (Boston: Henry Tolman & Company, 1856).

on minstrel tunes ("Jim Crow"), classical pieces ("Beethoven") and operatic melodies ("Norma," "Martha," "Trovatore"). By the 1830s there were entire cotillions made up of strings of waltzes—*Opera Waltz, Tiger Waltz*. And the 1840s brought new European dances to the United States, with new rhythms and new steps.

The first was the polka, a round or couples dance originating in Bohemia in the early nineteenth century. It was introduced into Prague as a social dance in 1837, reached Vienna and St. Petersburg in 1839, became the rage of Parisian society in 1843–44, was first performed in London in 1844, and probably reached America the same year. Its appeal lay in the much greater freedom and spontaneity allowed dancers and its lively, hopping character. The music was in 2 / 4, moving along in segments of two measures (since a two-measure phrase formed the basis for the steps of this dance), with a rhythmic stress or some sort of brief pause on the second beat of the second measure:

*Ocean Wave Polka*, from Elias Howe's *Musician's Omnibus* (Boston, 1861)

A typical and popular polka of the 1840s was the *Jenny Lind Polka*.[50] Like all social dances, it is in a simple, sectional form (*ABACA*), each phrase 8 measures in length. There is no development, transition, or any other sophisticated compositional device; the purpose of the music is to give the dancers the simplest possible structure for their steps and figures.

Similar but more extended is *The Flirt Polka*[51] by Charles Grobe (1817–80), a prolific German-born composer (whose last published work bore the opus number 1994). The first section is a full binary form (*AABABA*); the trio has two strains (*CDCD*); the *da capo* repeats both original strains (*BABA*).

The schottische also came from Central Europe. Its rhythmic character was somewhat like that of the polka, though it was performed at a slower tempo; its gliding, turning steps had something to do with the waltz, hence its name (the "Scottish waltz").[52] The polka redowa was in triple time, "composed of the same step as the Polka, with the exception that you slide the first step instead of springing, and omit the pause, as in this dance you count three,

[50] NW 293, s1 / 2.
[51] NW 293, s1 / 8.
[52] Cf. *Flying Cloud Schottische* on NW 293, s1 / 6.

both for the music and dance"[53]—in other words, it was a polka danced to triple rather than duple music. The mazurka was also in triple time, and—at least in America—was danced with polka steps, so that it was often indistinguishable from the polka redowa.

All of these "fancy dances" were done by couples. Resistance to the "intimacies" of this kind of dancing lingered in America into the 1830s and even 1840s, and the polka and other new dances of the era were apparently first introduced into this country as cotillions, or quadrilles (as they were increasingly called as mid-century approached)—that is, as figured dances done by four couples. But round dancing was increasingly tolerated, and in the decade before the Civil War a large public ball would consist of both round and figured dances. A Grand Holiday Ball, given on January 4, 1859 in Worcester, Massachusetts, featuring "dancing throughout the evening without intermission" to the music of two bands, with coffee rooms and whist tables, offered 14 Quadrilles, 1 Polka Quadrille, 1 Waltz Quadrille, 2 Lancers Quadrilles, 1 Waltz and Schottische, 1 Waltz and Polka Redowa, 1 Polka and Mazurka, 1 Polka Redowa and Varsoviana, 1 Polka and Polka Redowa, 1 Highland Schottische and Mazurka, and 2 Contra Dances. (All quadrilles were figured dances; all others were round dances for couples).

The galop, a fast, lively dance in 2 / 4 meter was also popular. It was first done as a section of a cotillion or quadrille, then later as a couples dance. Like all dances discussed to this point, it was in simple sectional forms, usually with two or three eight-measure strains, repeated several times.[54]

A distinction must be made between the utilitarian dance repertory and concert dances for piano intended to be performed in the parlor or on the stage. Charles Grobe's *Natalie Polka-Mazurka*[55] has the formal shape and rhythmic patterns of a polka; but an introduction and an interlude after the trio that break the formal pattern would have confused dancers and the mood (and some of the melodic shape) of the piece has more to do with the concert mazurkas and polkas of Chopin than with music for dancing. *The Laurel Waltz*[56] by A. P. Heinrich has even less of a dancelike nature, with its extended two-part introduction, its extensions of phrases beyond the normal eight-measure length, its developmental sections and variations on the main theme where a dancer would expect a new strain, its irregularities of tempo, and its emphasis

[53] Howe, *Musician's Omnibus*, p. 55.
[54] Cf. *Victoria Galop* by Francis Johnson on NW 293, s1 / 7. Other recorded examples of mid-nineteenth century dances may be heard on *19th-Century Ballroom Music, Homespun America*, and *Stephen Foster's Social Orchestra*.
[55] NW 293, s1 / 5.
[56] NW 257, s2 / 2.

on piano virtuosity. Homer N. Bartlett's *Grande Polka de Concert*[57] was typical of the compositions for virtuoso pianists that poured from American and European presses in the second half of the nineteenth century. Except for the title and suggestions of rhythms and melodies characteristic of the polka, it has absolutely nothing to do with social dancing.

Social dancing during the Civil War served as a diversion for officers between campaigns and battles and as entertainment for those at home. In the decades following the war, round dancing gradually replaced cotillions and quadrilles, at least in cities and towns, until virtually all social dancing was done by couples. New dances were introduced and enjoyed fleeting popularity. The tempo at which the waltz was danced was increased, new steps were devised for it, and many waltzes took on the character of the waltz-song of early Tin Pan Alley.[58]

The galop evolved into the two-step, a fast dance done to music in 2 / 4 or 6 / 8 meter. Much of its music had a martial sound; indeed, Abe Holzmann's *Blaze-Away!*[59] has all the characteristics of a Sousa march: the fanfarelike introduction, the trio with piccolo obbligato, the "break strain," and a final trio strain featuring Sousa's characteristic three-part instrumentation—melody played by clar-

A waltz scene depicted on the sheet music cover of Charles K. Harris's popular song "After the Ball" (1892).

[57] NW 257, s2 / 5.
[58] Cf. *Eliza Jane McCue* on NW 293, s2 / 1.
[59] NW 293, s2 / 1.

inets and cornets, piccolo obbligato, and running trombone passages. In fact, many of Sousa's marches served to accompany the two-step, both in America and Europe. Thus marching and dancing, two activities closely related throughout the nineteenth century, came together with identical music serving both.[60]

It would be difficult to claim anything distinctively American about the dance music discussed to this point. These dances, without exception, originated in Europe, and their characteristic rhythms and melodies remained essentially unchanged when they were transported to the United States. Though many waltzes, polkas, and mazurkas were written in America, nothing in their music reflects the unique features of American culture and its indigenous music. Nineteenth-century social dancing and its music were American in the same sense as marches: they were assimilated into our culture, and became part of the experience of millions of Americans.

But all this began to change in the last years of the nineteenth century. Just as the Sousa Band began to perform pieces which incorporated the syncopated patterns of ragtime, two-steps were danced to music with the same flavor. Fred S. Stone's *Ma Ragtime Baby*[61] looks like a march, with its introduction, *AABB* first section, a contrasting trio, a "break strain," and a concluding play-through of the trio with full band and obliggato parts. But the sound is dominated by syncopated rhythms.

These rhythms were taken by both Americans and Europeans to be characteristically American, and they soon generated a new style of dance, this time spawned in the New World, not the Old.

[60] *Hiawatha* by Neil Moret on NW 293, s2/2, is another example of a two-step from the turn of the century with all the characteristics of a military march.
[61] NW 293, s2/2.

# 12

# *The Rise of Classical Composition in America: The Years after the Civil War*

The mid-nineteenth century saw the first of America's large music festivals, in emulation of such affairs in London's Crystal Palace and elsewhere in England, Germany, and France.

This story has its beginning in Boston, where the Handel and Haydn Society organized the first such event in late May of 1856. The festival began with Haydn's *The Seasons*, continued with Mendelssohn's *Elijah*, and concluded with Handel's *Messiah* on the third evening; three "miscellaneous concerts" of instrumental and vocal music occupied the afternoons. The chorus of the venerable society was expanded to 600, and the orchestra, augmented by a number of New York professionals, numbered 78—the largest group heard in the city to that date. Officers of the society took pains to point out that there was no pandering to the "popular taste," and the official historian proudly observed:

> For the first time almost in our country has an artistic demonstration here been made, and carried through, upon a grand scale, without false pretence, vain show, or *humbug*. The best thing, the most hopeful thing about it is, that it has all been *honest*. Nothing of artistic integrity and value has been sacrificed to mere money-making views.[1]

A second festival in May of 1865 was even grander. Coming just after the end of the Civil War and the assassination of President

---

[1] Charles C. Perkins and John S. Dwight, *History of the Handel and Haydn Society of Boston, Massachusetts* (Boston: Alfred Mudge & Son, 1883), I, p. 179.

**307**

Lincoln, the emphasis was on peace, unity, and healing. The opening concert, on May 23, had a dramatic and emotional beginning: the audience was confronted with a chrous of some 700 singers and an orchestra of 100:

> Up went the conductor's baton, up rose all the ranks of chorus singers on their feet, and the flood-gates of harmony broke loose. The first burst was overwhelming, chorus, orchestra, and organ uniting their full volume in one massive rendering of Luther's chorale, *Ein' feste Burg*.[2]

Then followed Nicolai's *Religious Festival Overture,* based on the chorale melody just heard, and the featured piece for the evening, Mendelssohn's *The Hymn of Praise.* The following four days brought four additional instrumental / vocal concerts, an organ recital, two more oratorios, and Handel's *Messiah*—the fiftieth performance of the piece in the fifty-year history of the society.

In May of 1868, what was advertised as the first Triennial Festival took place. Again, "miscellaneous" instrumental / vocal programs in the afternoons were followed by performances of oratorios in the evenings. High points included the first American performance of Mendelssohn's *Reformation Symphony* (No. 5) and the "first really satisfactory performance in this country" of Beethoven's *Ninth Symphony.*

Before a second Triennial Festival could be mounted, Boston was the scene of a musical extravaganza dwarfing anything ever done anywhere in the country—the "Grand National Celebration of Peace and Musical Festival," the brainchild of Patrick Scarsfield Gilmore.

His flair for organizing events for huge musical forces first showed itself in New Orleans, where he put together a spectacular concert for the inauguration of Governor Hahn in Lafayette Square on March 4, 1864:

> In the centre of the park a monster ampitheatre had been erected. From the circular stand on which the solemnities of the day were held, the immense structure radiated in the form of a semicircle, seat after seat rising up step after step, until more than fifteen thousand seats were formed. At the base of this was the orchestra of five hundred performers, with the fifty blacksmiths that kept time on their anvils like so many real Vulcans. In front and on each side of the stand was another great platform, on which were seated invited guests, distingui hed strangers, civil and military dignitaries.[3]

[2] Perkins and Dwight, p. 222.
[3] *The True Delta,* March 4, 1864.

The 15,000 seats were for a chorus of more than 10,000 children, an orchestra of 500, and dozens of bands from New Orleans and other cities in Louisiana.

After the War, Gilmore—back in Boston—nursed the idea of organizing the "Grandest Musical Demonstration that the world has ever witnessed," as an appropriate celebration of "The Restoration of Peace throughout the Land, the most important event in American History."

He enlisted the support of Boston's political leaders, press, business men, and musicians. A new auditorium, the Coliseum, was constructed. The performance forces included almost 10,000 voices, from Massachusetts (8,500 singers from 65 different communities), New Hampshire (810 from 15 cities and towns), Maine (279), Vermont (94), Connecticut (199), Rhode Island (136), New York (111), and even Illinois (95 members of the Chicago Mendelssohn Society) and Ohio (60 singers); a "Select Orchestra" of 484 instrumentalists (410 strings, 74 woodwinds and brass), mostly from Massachusetts and New York, though a few players came from as far away as St. Louis and Washington; and a "Grand Orchestra," which joined in the more popular and less demanding selections and accompanied the chorus, of 590 players drawn from brass, military, and cornet bands. A journalist recorded his impressions of the opening program, held on June 15, 1869:

> The scene on entering the huge Coliseum was indeed most imposing. The sight of all those faces turned toward you from the vast ampitheatre filled by ten thousand singers and a thousand instrumentalists, all full of glowing expectation, and of the audience of more than twelve thousand, covering floor and balcony, was inspiring. We can only say that the success of Tuesday was in the main glorious and inspiring. The vast audience were greatly stirred, delighted. The best effects were those achieved by the great Chorus. The unity of impression was much better than we had dared to expect; for it had seemed a very doubtful problem whether the sound of the nearest and farthest voices, hundreds of feet apart, could reach the ear at the same instant. But in all, the wonder was that so vast a chorus sang so well together.[4]

The "Grand Classical Programme" of the second day was attended by President Grant and an audience of more than 20,000. The featured work was Schubert's *Symphony in C*, but the President requested "The Star Spangled Banner" and the "Anvil Chrous," so only the second and fourth movements of the Schubert were played. By the time the festival ended on Saturday the 19th

[4]*Dwight's Journal* for June 19, 1869, p. 55.

with a program sung by 7,000 school children, more than 200,000 people had attended the various events and some 20,000 musicians had participated.

*Dwight's Journal of Music* characterized the event as "a plan so vain-glorious in the conception, so unscrupulously advertised and glorified before it had begun, and having so much of claptrap mixed up with what there was good in its program."[5] But in the end all participants and observers were caught up in the excitement. Dwight observed that "the wide, stupendous advertising filled thousands of minds with an enthusiasm which, if ignorant, was entirely honest; the mustering of all the clans of song, in such vast numbers, all within one city and one building, fired the imagination of the singers far and wide";[6] and a New York correspondent found the Festival "freighted with great consequence to American art," explaining:

Heretofore America has had no standing in the musical art-world. England has looked down on us. Germany has supposed that no festival could be given here except by her Sängerbunds. Italy and France have recognized for us no higher possibilities than the production of their operas. At one step, without any preliminaries, without more special preparation than could be crowded into a few weeks, we have lifted ourselves, so far as great musical gatherings are concerned, to an artistic level with these nations. The journals of Europe, heretofore silent on all questions concerning our musical art, are now called upon to tell their surprised leaders that the largest gathering of singers and players ever brought together has just been held in the United States. The enterprise has been conceived and executed on a scale in keeping with the vastness of the country, with the breadth and largeness of the American methods, and with the expedition and fearlessness that characterize all our attempts in untried fields of effort. But it has done more. It has shown that our people can think of something beyond mechanical inventions and the almighty dollar, and it has given earnest promise of a noble musical future for America.[7]

The Festival was the most widely and favorably publicized musical event in the history of the United States to that point, and plans for a sequel were underway almost with the last concert. This one was billed as the "World's Peace Jubilee and the International Music Festival," celebrating the end of the Franco-Prussian War. It opened on June 17, 1872 and spanned more than two weeks, with a grand conclusion on the 4th of July. A chorus of some

[5]*Dwight's Journal* for June 19, 1869, p. 55.
[6]*Dwight's Journal* for June 19, 1869, p. 55.
[7]*New York Sun* for June 23, 1869.

17,000 voices was mustered this time, and an orchestra of 1,500; 40 vocal soloists from Europe and America sang arias from opera and oratorio, in unison; military bands were brought in from various European countries. Johann Strauss (The Younger) came from Vienna to conduct his *Blue Danube Waltz*, Franz Abt came from Germany to conduct some of his choral pieces, so popular in America. There was an English Day, a German Day, and a French Day, each with appropriate music and performers.

Despite great press coverage, the presence of international musical celebrities, and some good performances, the second Jubilee was less successful than the first. It was, evidently, simply too large: the performance forces were too massive for most of the music to be heard to the best advantage, and logistical problems stemming from the presence of such hordes of people in the city interfered with enjoyment of the event.

Nevertheless, Chicago mounted an enormous Jubilee in 1873, with Gilmore as impresario. Cincinnati organized a four-day festival in May of 1873, built around a large chorus drawn from the numerous singing societies of the city and nearby communities. Featured works were Beethoven's *Ninth Symphony*, Handel's *Dettingen Te Deum*, Mendelssohn's *Walpurgis Night*, and selections from Haydn's *The Creation* and Handel's *Messiah*. The chorus numbered almost 700 voices and was supported by an orchestra of 108 professional players. The event was such a success that a second festival was organized two years later; as the Cincinnati May Festival, it has continued to take place every other year.

The Philadelphia Centennial Exposition opened with a monster concert on May 10, 1876, attended by President Grant and his cabinet and held in an open-air setting with some 100,000 persons attempting to listen. Both this concert and a similar one closing the celebration on November 10 featured the *Centennial Inauguration March* by Richard Wagner, commissioned for $5,000; both included performances of Handel's "Hallelujah Chorus" by massed choirs, a huge orchestra, a number of military bands, and organ, with chimes ringing throughout the city and a 100-gun salute serving as a coda. New York staged a gigantic festival on May 2–6, 1882, held in the Seventh Regiment Armory and featuring a chorus of 3,000 and an orchestra of 300. Pittsburg mounted a three-day festival in 1883, San Francisco followed with a similar event on June 7–13, of the same year, St. Louis and other cities followed suit.

It was during this era of gigantic celebrations that something more important for the future of classical music in America took place: the establishment of a number of resident, permanent

An orchestra concert in New York City in the 1870's with Hans von Buelow as piano soloist.

orchestras and musical societies. The Brooklyn Philharmonic Society was founded in 1857, with Theodore Eisfeld as its first conductor. Philadelphia had its own Germania Orchestra from 1860 to 1895. The Harvard Musical Association, founded in 1866 under the baton of Carl Zerrahn, supplied the Boston area with orchestral programs until 1882, when it yielded to the competition of the Boston Symphony Orchestra, founded in 1880 and offering its first program on October 22, 1881 under Georg Henschel.

No one person had a more profound impact on the development of classical music in America than Theodore Thomas (1835–1905). Born in the German town of Esens, the son of a local musician, Thomas came with his family to America in 1845. As he remembered it, "the metropolitan city was then a provincial town of two-story houses, and the pigs ran through Broadway and ate the refuse. For the benefit of any European who may read this, I will say that there were plenty of negroes to be seen, but no Indians."[8] A violinist, Thomas was playing in theater and opera orchestras soon after his arrival in the New World, and in 1854 he became a member of the Philharmonic Society.

In 1855 the American pianist William Mason formed a chamber music ensemble consisting of himself, Theodore Thomas and Joseph

[8] Theodore Thomas, *A Musical Autobiography* (Chicago: A. C. McClurg & Co., 1905, edited by George P. Upton), I, p. 20.

The chamber music ensemble formed by William Mason, photographed in 1856: left to right G. Matzka, T. Mosenthal, F. Bergner, Theodore Thomas, and Mason.

Mosenthal (violinists), George Matza (viola), and Carl Bergmann (cello). The seventy-odd programs given by this group over a period of thirteen years brought New York its first series of public, professional performances of the trios, quartets, and quintets of Beethoven, Schubert, Schumann, Haydn, Mozart, Mendelssohn, Brahms, and occasionally Bach.

Thomas's ambition, however, was to conduct, and after honing his skills with various theater and opera orchestras and bands, he resolved in 1862 "to devote my energies to the cultivation of the public taste for instrumental music."[9] Convinced that "what this country needed most of all to make it musical was a good orchestra, and plenty of concerts within reach of the people,"[10] he called a meeting of the best instrumentalists in New York and "told them of my plans to popularize instrumental music, and asked their cooperation."[11] A first concert on May 13, 1862, in Irving Hall, was followed by a series of ten matinee concerts between October 24 and December 26 of 1863.

Thomas's strategy was to attract the largest possible audience by featuring popular performers and compositions, then to offer a

[9] Thomas, I p. 50.
[10] Thomas, I, p. 50.
[11] Thomas, I, p. 51.

scattering of more "serious" pieces. Typical is the program of October 31, with Louis Moreau Gottschalk as soloist:

*PART ONE*

| | |
|---|---|
| 1. Symphony in E Flat | Haydn |
| 2. "The Union," Paraphrase on National Airs | Gottschalk |
|     Gottschalk, piano | |
| 3. "Aurora Ball," Polka | Strauss |
| 4. Cavatine from *La Sonnambula* | Bellini |
|     Miss Fannie Riddell, soprano | |
| 5. "Ojos Creollos" | Gottschalk |
|     Gottschalk and Harry Sanderson, pianos | |
| 6. *Il Ballo in Maschera* (selections) | Verdi |

*PART TWO*

| | |
|---|---|
| 1. *Merry Wives of Windsor,* Overture | Nicolai |
| 2. Romanza from *Robert le Diable* | Meyerbeer |
|     Miss Riddell | |
| 3. "Hydropathen," Waltz | Gung'l |
| 4. "Minuit à Séville" | Gottschalk |
|     Gottschalk | |
| 5. *Tannhäuser,* March | Wagner |

Thomas next inaugurated a series of evening concerts in direct competition with the Philharmonic Society, calling these his *soirée* concerts and later the New York Symphony Concerts. Critics agreed that Thomas offered better and more varied programs; his programming philosophy produced effective results:

In earlier years (my programmes) always included a Beethoven number; first, because Beethoven is the nearest to us in spirit; second, because he expresses more than any other composer; and third; because he has reached the highest pinnacle in instrumental music, which became through him a language. Thus Beethoven answers a double purpose; he gives delight to the educated, and teaches the uneducated. His place was always in the first part of the program.

I have always believed in climaxes, also in giving people the most recent musical productions, and Wagner is the composer who satisfies both these essentials. Like Beethoven, he also answers a double purpose. He represents the modern spirit, and his effective scoring makes the desired climax. Wagner excites his hearers, especially the younger generation, and interests the less musical.

In this way Beethoven and Wagner became the pillars, so to speak, of my programmes. The effect of these composers on the public was plainly apparent. So I placed them where they belonged, and then filled out the rest of the programme so as to keep within a certain limit of time, have each piece prepare for the one to follow, observe a steady *crescendo,* and "keep a trump" for last.[12]

A concert offered by the New York Symphony Orchestra on November 9, 1872 illustrates Thomas's thesis:

| | |
|---|---|
| 1. *Iphigenia in Aulis,* Overture | Gluck |
| 2. Aria from "Belmont and Constance" | Mozart |
|     Mr. George L. Osgood, tenor | |
| 3. Symphony No. 7, in A, opus 92 | Beethoven |
| 4. "Five Poems by Lenau." opus 90 | Schumann |
| 5. "Wotan's Farewell," from *Die Walküre* | Wagner |
| 6. "Mephisto Waltz" | Liszt |

Fewer compositions were offered than earlier in the century, and each was brought to a higher level of performance; chamber music no longer appeared on orchestral programs; a vocal or instrumental soloist was usually featured, for contrast, accompanied by the orchestra; entire symphonies and concertos are played, rather than isolated movements. The shape and general content of today's orchestral program was forged by Thomas in these concerts.

His repertory was international, and he offered a steady stream of new pieces to balance the standard literature. In his first season alone, 1864–65, he introduced American audiences to works by Lachner, Berlioz, and Raff, he gave the American premiere of Beethoven's *Triple Concerto* (for piano, violin, and cello, Opus 56), Mozart's *Symphony Concertante* for viola and violin, and Bach's great *Passacaglia in C minor,* in an arrangement by Esser. In succeeding seasons American audiences heard their first performances of Berlioz's Overture to *Benvenuto Cellini,* Brahms's second and third symphonies, Bruckner's fourth and seventh symphonies, a host of pieces by Dvořák (including his first two symphonies), Grieg's *Peer Gynt Suite,* Handel's *Royal Fireworks Music,* Liszt's *Piano Concerto* and five of his symphonic poems, many pieces by Anton Rubinstein and Saint-Saëns, Schubert's *Unfinished Symphony,* most of the tone poems by Richard Strauss, and a raft of pieces by Richard Wagner including the preludes to *Die Meistersinger* and *Parsifal.*

Thomas also gave "Garden Concerts" in the summer months, from 1865 until 1891. Reminiscent of the pleasure garden concerts of the late eighteenth and early nineteenth centuries, while also anticipating "pops" concerts of the twentieth century, these were

[12] Thomas, I, p. 73.

Cartoon of a Central Park Garden Concert, Theodore Thomas (center) conducting. (From a contemporary print)

open-air affairs with tables and refreshments available for the audience.

Beginning with the season of 1869–70, Thomas took his orchestra on an extended tour at least once a year, bringing professional performances of both the standard and the "modern" orchestral literature to dozens of American cities and towns. The "Thomas Highway" included the following stops:

New York—New Haven—Hartford—Providence—Boston—Worcester—Springfield—Albany—Schenectady—Utica—Syracuse—Rochester—Buffalo—Cleveland—Toledo—Detroit—Chicago—St. Louis—Indianapolis—Louisville—Cincinnati—Dayton—Springfield (Ohio)—Columbus—Pittsburg—Washington—Baltimore—Philadelphia—New York

He also conducted the Brooklyn Philharmonic Society orchestra from 1862 until 1891 and organized the first May Festivals in Cincinnati. In 1877 he became conductor of the Philharmonic Society of New York, holding that position until 1891. In 1891 he accepted an invitation to establish a permanent orchestra in Chicago. In order to give the new orchestra financial stability in its early stages fifty local businessmen pledged $1000 each for three years. Thomas took sixty musicians with him from New York, added thirty local players, and inaugurated the Chicago Symphony Orchestra on October 17, 1891 with the usual pieces by Beethoven (*Symphony No. 5*) and Wagner (*A Faust Overture*) balanced by several more modern compositions—Tchaikovsky's *Piano Concerto No. 1*, with Rafael Joseffy as soloist, and Dvořák's *Husitzka* overture. In addition to twenty concerts each year in Chicago, the orchestra traveled to Milwaukee, St. Paul, Minneapolis, Duluth, Omaha, Kansas City, Nashville, Indianapolis, Detroit, Grand Rapids, and South Bend. More than $700,000 was donated by the citizens of Chicago for a new auditorium, and on December 14, 1904 Thomas lead the orchestra in the Dedicatory Concert for Orchestra Hall, the most modern concert hall in the country at the time. The next year he died.

When Thomas organized his New York Symphony Orchestra in 1864, New York was the only American city that already had a permanent orchestra offering regularly scheduled public concerts—the Philharmonic Society. By his death, the situation had changed dramatically: New York had another orchestra, the New York Symphony Society, established by Leopold Damrosch in 1878; the St. Louis Symphony had been established in 1879; the Boston Symphony Orchestra had been giving regular concerts since October 22, 1881; there were orchestras in Chicago (1891), Cincinnati (1895), Pittsburg (1895), and Philadelphia (1900); and smaller towns like New Haven and Bangor (Maine) enjoyed regular if abbreviated concert seasons.

The period of Thomas's activity in the United States was thus a critical time in the evolution of the symphony orchestra into a permanent institution in a number of American cities and towns. Though the increased popularity of symphonic music would have undoubtedly come about even if Thomas had not come to the New World, there can be no denying him the role of being the single most influential individual in this chapter of American musical life.

William Mason (1829–1908), the youngest son of Lowell Mason, wrote in 1901:

Enormous progress in the art and science of music has been made in America since I began my studies in Germany in the year 1849. There are now teachers of the piano of the first rank in all of our principal cities, who secure better results with American pupils than foreign teachers do, because they have a better understanding of our national character and temperament. Our country has also produced composers of the first rank, and the names MacDowell, Parker, Kelley, Whiting, Paine, Buck, Shelley, Chadwick, Brockway, and Foote occur at once to the mind.[13]

He might have added that he himself established a pattern of travel and study subsequently followed by almost all successful American performers, teachers, and composers of the second half of the nineteenth century.

After early lessons in Boston, he was sent off to Germany at the age of twenty. His piano study was with Alexander Dreyschock in Prague ("I remained with Dreyschock for over a year, taking three lessons a week and practicing about five hours a day. I played also in private musicales at the houses of the nobility and at the homes of some of the wealthy Jews, two classes of society which were entirely distinct from each other, never mingling in private life."[14]), with Liszt in Weimar, and with Moscheles in Leipzig. He met Meyerbeer, Wagner, Joachim, Brahms, Peter Cornelius, Raff, and other prominent composers and pianists; he gave several public performances while in Europe, and at least one of his compositions, "Amitié pour Amatié," was published abroad, by Hofmeister in Leipzig.

Returning to America in 1854, he settled in New York as a teacher and performer. His most important performances were the Mason-Thomas Chamber Concerts between 1855 and 1868, and he attracted many of the most talented American pianists as students. His treatise on piano method, *Touch and Technique for Artistic Piano Playing* (Opus 44, 1889), was accepted as an important contribution to piano pedagogy in both America and Europe. As a composer, he confined himself almost exclusively to writing for the piano; among his most successful pieces were *Silver Spring* (Opus 6),[15] *Ballade* (Opus 12), *Serenata* (Opus 39), and *Capriccio Fantastico* (Opus 50).

James Cutler Dunn Parker (1828–1916) followed the same path. Sent off to Leipzig in 1851 from his home town of Boston, he studied at the Conservatory there for four years under Moscheles, Plaidy,

---

[13] William Mason, *Memories of a Musical Life* (New York: Century Company, 1902), pp. 261–62.
[14] Mason, pp. 70–71.
[15] NW 257, s2 / 6.

Hauptmann, and Richter, then returned to Boston and a succession of posts as organist, choirmaster, and "professor" of theory and keyboard. An assiduous composer, he wrote sacred works—cantatas, anthems, and other choral pieces—in a style based solidly on Mendelssohn. The peak of his career came late in his life, in 1890, when the Boston Handel and Haydn Society performed his cantata *St. John.*

John Knowles Paine (1839–1906) was the first American composer to write major works in the Germanic style fully comparable in quality to the products of European writers. Born in Portland, Maine, he was the grandson of an organ builder; his father organized and directed the first concert band in Portland and owned a music store; his sister Helen was a contralto soloist of considerable regional fame and taught both voice and piano. John became a pupil of Hermann Kotschmar, a member of the Saxonia Band. Under his tutelage, the young man wrote a string quartet at the age of sixteen, made his public debut as an organist at eighteen, and in 1858 offered three subscription concerts to raise enough money to complete his musical education in Germany.

His teachers at the Hochschule für Musik in Berlin included Carl August Haupt in organ, Wieprecht and Teschner in theory and composition. Within a year he was appearing in public as an organist, specializing in the music of J. S. Bach, and it was as an organist that he enjoyed his first success upon his return to America in 1861, with a recital in his home town and a subsequent appointment as organist at Boston's West Church. As a result of his performances and teaching, "the taste for organ music according to the standards of the Germany School then began to form itself" in Boston.[16]

Typical of his early style is his *Fantasia über "Ein' feste Burg,"* Opus 13.[17] The venerable tune is stated first by the pedals, then the full organ, with rhapsodic passage work giving some sense of improvisation; a contrasting, slower section leads through fugatos and virtuoso pedal work to a final statement for full organ again. Though there are echoes of Bach's organ music, Paine has drawn on his revered master more for inspiration than for precise models of formal structures.

In 1859, while still in Germany, he had begun work on a *Mass in D* for chorus, soloists, and orchestra, and on February 16, 1867 he conducted the first performance at the Singakademie in Berlin.[18]

[16] George Thornton Edwards, *Music and Musicians of Maine* (Portland: Southworth Press, 1928), pp. 123–24.

[17] NW 280, s2 / 3.

[18] NW 262 / 263.

It was the first large-scale classical composition by an American-born composer to be performed in Europe, and the first such piece to be published. Even more important, it is a splendid composition, skillfully and convincingly written, highly effective and often quite moving. As the conductor who revived the piece in the present century wrote:

> How can one explain that an American composer in his early twenties and in a young, not even half-settled land, in a society with as yet only the merest cultural accoutrements (and those imported from Europe at that), could write a work so impressive, so precocious, so technically sophisticated, and so profoundly musical as this Mass? Of course he was musically gifted. Of course he must have heard Beethoven's *Missa Solemnis* or Mendelssohn's *St. Paul* and *Elijah* or some of the other popular large-scale choral works performed at the time. But all of this cannot explain a work of such grandeur and haunting beauty ... by a composer so young. The answer lies, as it must in all otherwise inexplicable manifestations of genius or great talent, in the creator himself and in the largely ineluctable mysteries of the creative process.[19]

Paine's model was Beethoven's *Missa solemnis,* as one can deduce from the key of the piece, certain formal similarities, and many of his techniques for chorus and orchestra. His own words give us a good notion of what he thought of this work:

> Beethoven's music, more than any other before his time, is characterized by vivid contrasts in the themes and passages, rhythmical effects, bold dissonances and modulations, dynamic expression, varied and massive instrumentation. He made sudden progressions into remote keys. His bold modulations were unprecedented. In the adagio, or other slow movement, the master gives utterance to his pathetic, solemn, and religious feelings. Here he speaks the language of his inmost soul. Beethoven considered the "Mass in D" as his greatest work. ... It is not church music so much as the direct, subjective expression of a religious heart, which cannot be restrained by the barriers of mere form and ritual.[20]

Friends arranged for a performance of Paine's Mass in Boston in the spring of 1868, at the Music Hall, but the event received almost no critical attention and there is no record of other performances for over a century: in May of 1972 it was programmed during a Festival of Americana at the New England Conservatory of Music in Boston and conducted by Gunther Schuller.

[19] Gunther Schuller, liner notes for NW 262 / 263, p. 3.
[20] John K. Paine, *The History of Music to the Death of Schubert* (Boston and London: Ginn and Company, 1907), pp. 274–80 *passim.*

*St. Peter* (1873) was an even more ambitious work, a full-length oratorio for soloists, chorus, and large orchestra. A first performance in Portland on June 3, 1873 was followed by another in Boston on May 9, 1874, during the Third Triennial Festival of the Boston Handel and Haydn Society. The venerable society had never before devoted an entire program to a composition by an American, and the event brought mixed reactions:

> Nearly as much time was given to the rehearsal of its choruses as to that of all the other choral pieces of the Festival together; and it was serious up-hill work,—more work than recreation. Indeed it was a common complaint among the singers that, in many of the choruses, the music did not help them, take them up and carry them along with it, by that sort of charm which made the difficulties of Bach, for instance, or of Mendelssohn, or Handel, or even the Ninth Symphony, melt away before them to their own surprise. It was a trying position for Mr. Paine's work to be placed thus immediately between the master works of Bach and Handel (*St. Matthew Passion* and *Messiah*). Without attempting to describe or criticise the work itself, the composition, which had many musician-like, impressive numbers in it, was wholly free from slavish imitation, thoroughly in earnest, sometimes quite dramatic, sometimes showing depth of feeling, and as a whole won respect if not admiration.[21]

Paine next turned to the composition of large-scale instrumental works, beginning with his *Symphony No. 1* (Opus 23).[22] The piece is clearly a homage to Beethoven, whom Paine considered to be "the greatest of all instrumental composers,"[23] who had furthermore "established the new form and spirit of modern music."[24] Even more specifically, Paine's piece reflects his admiration for that composer's *Symphony No. 5*. Both pieces are in C minor and each movement of Paine's symphony is in the same key and has the same general formal design as the corresponding movement of his model: the first movement is an *allegro con moto* sonata-allegro form, in C minor; the second is a scherzo; the third a slow movement in E flat; and the finale a vigorous and marchlike movement in C major. The orchestra is modeled precisely on Beethoven's, and many passages recall the motivic development and instrumentation of the *Fifth Symphony*. But Paine was too good a composer to be content with a single model. Other sections suggest the melodic and harmonic vocabulary of slightly younger German composers, Schub-

[21] Perkins and Dwight, I, pp. 347–48.
[22] Available on *MIA* 103.
[23] Paine, p. 266.
[24] Paine, p. 269.

ert and Mendelssohn for instance. In the end he integrates the styles of these several masters into a convincing and pleasing whole.

Theodore Thomas gave the work its first performance in Boston on January 26, 1876, with his touring orchestra. Audience and critics alike left Music Hall with the conviction that they had attended a historic event:

> Whatever anxiety or lack of entire faith any one may have felt beforehand must have been removed by the very first phrase, which with its rushing bass and powerful stroke of chords (as if with some resistless hammer of Thor) proclaims at once the technical skill and boldness of design that belong only to masters of symphonic writing. The pauses between the movements were made unduly long by the applause in which the excitement sought to vent itself; and at the end there burst forth such a storm of delighted approval as, during many years of concertgoing, we had never before witnessed. Seldom has a composer obtained a more splendid triumph; seldom, too, have original genius and untiring diligence more thoroughly deserved such success.[25]

Thomas went on to introduce New York audiences to Paine's music with a performance of *The Tempest*, a symphonic fantasia, in 1877; in 1880 he premiered the *Symphony No. 2* ("Spring Symphony"), Opus 34, with the orchestra of the Harvard Musical Association in Cambridge. A *Centennial Hymn* for chorus and orchestra was featured on the inaugural program of the Philadelphia Centennial celebration on May 10, 1876; six choruses for male voices accompanied by orchestra were interpolated into Harvard College's production of *Oedipus Tyrannus* in the spring of 1881; the Boston Handel and Haydn Society undertook the cantata *The Nativity* (Opus 38) during its sixth Triennial Festival in May of 1883; another cantata, *A Song of Promise* (Opus 43), was commissioned by Theodore Thomas for performance on the Eighth May Festival in Cincinnati in May of 1888; a *Columbus March and Hymn* was performed under Thomas's direction on the dedicatory program opening the Music Building at the Chicago World's Fair on October 22, 1892.

Appointed Musical Instructor at Harvard College in 1862, Paine had functioned as chapelmaster, organizing and directing choral music for chapel services, serving as college organist, and offering instruction in voice and organ. In 1873 he was made Assistant Professor of Music, Harvard's first academic post in the discipline; his courses in music theory now carried full credit. He became a Professor of Music in 1875, offering both undergraduate and graduate

[25]*Atlantic Monthly* for June 1876, pp. 763–64.

courses; such a position was unprecedented in the history of higher education in America. Under his leadership Harvard developed an entire department of music, eventually offering a variety of academic courses in theory, history, and composition.

Despite his earlier successes, Paine's later music did not appeal to performers or audiences of the late nineteenth and early twentieth centuries. Once Thomas had broken the resistance of an older generation of German musicians to the "modern" music of Liszt and Wagner, the compositions of these men and certain of their younger contemporaries (Dvořák and Tchaikovsky, for instance) quickly became the most popular items on orchestral programs. Paine had first been attracted to the music of Bach and Beethoven, then Mendelssohn and Schumann; he never came to terms with "modern" music. His musical credo was stated in an Inaugural Lecture given at Boston University in October of 1872:

> The techniques of music, like Wagner, Liszt, and their adherents, have become so extremely involved and complicated, both in composition and performance that there must soon be a healthy reaction. The only hope for the present and future is the adherence to the historical forms, as developed by Bach, Händel, Mozart, and Beethoven, in church music, the oratorio, opera, and instrumental music.[26]

Academic life came to be, for him, an escape from the contemporary world of music. He felt his isolation from the musical life of America acutely, nevertheless, and the following passage surely was written as much about his own later life as about the Cantor of Leipzig:

> Popularity and an easy comprehension of a master's works are not always the infallible criterion of merit. Full appreciation comes only after years, generations, and even centuries of neglect.
>
> [Bach] was one of the most intellectual musicians who ever lived, yet made his skill and learning subservient to his emotional nature, which his religious fervor ennobled and intensifed. Those who find his music cold and passionless are simply ignorant of his style, which must first become familiar, or else they are incapable by nature from being moved and elevated by his music. [He] could make new discoveries in the domain of musical sound without being arrested halfway by external affairs or practical considerations. He did not write for a public, but for himself and his ideal critic; his music, therefore, cannot grow antiquated. He appears modern now, and must remain so, because he stood above fashion.[27]

[26] As quoted in M. A. DeWolfe Howe, "John Knowles Paine," *The Musical Quarterly* XXV / 3 (July 1939), p. 265.

[27] Paine, pp. 227–29.

It was an ominous portent for America that its first greatly talented composer of classical music made so little impact on the musical life of his country and ended his days more embittered than praised.

Next to Paine, the most widely praised American composer of this era was Dudley Buck (1839–1909), a native of Hartford, Connecticut.

Early study with local musicians was followed by some years in Germany. After working at the Conservatory in Leipzig in theory, composition, and piano, he went to Dresden, where he concentrated on organ technique. Like Paine, he made his first impression on his countrymen, upon his return from abroad, as an organist. He was appointed organist at the Music Hall in Boston, went to New York as an assistant conductor of the Central Park Garden Concerts under Theodore Thomas, then settled in Brooklyn as an organist and choir director.

His music was as indebted to Germanic models and ideals as Paine's, but it took somewhat different directions. His *Grand Sonata in E Flat* (Opus 22, 1866),[28] one of many works for his favorite instrument, has many trappings of the Germanic style in its formal designs and reliance on contrapuntal techniques. But the third movement, a scherzo cast in a simple *ABA* shape, is almost totally homophonic, and has the character of some of the most direct and accessible piano works of Mendelssohn. And while the fourth movement is indeed a fugue, its theme is an elaborated version of "Hail, Columbia" and the climax drops contrapuntal writing altogether in favor of a loud, rhetorical, easily comprehended succession of chords.

His first public success as a composer came during the World's Peace Jubilee in Boston (1872), with a performance of his *Festival Hymn*, written to his own text:

> O Peace! on thine upsoaring pinion,
> Thro' the world thine onward flight taking,
> Teach the nations their turmoil forsaking,
> To seek thine eternal dominion.

Since the piece was to be sung by a chorus of some 20,000 voices, Buck confined himself to simple, diatonic melodies and harmonies, realizing that anything more complex would be drowned in a sea of sound; it struck critics as being "written with more view to popular effect."[29] The Third Triennial Festival of the Boston Handel and Haydn Society brought a first performance of his *Forty-sixth Psalm* for chorus, soloists, and orchestra, which proved to be

[28] NW 280, s1.
[29] *Dwight's Journal* for July 27, 1872, p. 279.

not quite what critics had come to expect on these solemn occasions. "Mr. Buck's work was somewhat light and popular in style, but nearly always pleasing, musical, felictious, if not very original in thoughts or very skillful in the treatment," wrote one journalist, adding that some of it was "a little operatic like the modern Italian sacred music."[30]

Mid-1874 brought *Don Munio*, a cantata to a text taken from Washington Irving, and in 1876 Buck was commissioned to write a cantata for the Centennial Celebration in Philadelphia. The piece, entitled *The Centennial Meditation of Columbia*, was to a text by Sidney Lanier of Georgia, a poet, critic and musician; the idea was to have a "Yankee" and a "Rebel" combine talents, as a symbol of reconciliation between North and South. But Lanier's poem was criticized for its obscurity, its unintelligibility, and its unsuitability for musical setting; Buck's music was damned with faint praise ("A very favorable example of the composer's style. Mr. Buck does not write with a very Titanic pen, but his style is so pure and unforced, his effects are so easily and naturally brought about, that we cannot but overlook an occasional tendency to the trivial and commonplace."[31]) The piece is vintage Buck, from its fugal writing in the final chorus demonstrating his command of the "learned style":

*Centennial Meditation,* by Dudley Buck

---

[30] Perkins and Dwight, pp. 339–40.
[31] *Atlantic Monthly* for July 1876, pp. 122–24.

to solo passages with echoes of the Italian style, to sections of extreme chromaticism, reminding us that he was the first American composer of the nineteenth century to appropriate some of the harmonic language of the "modern" German school:

*Centennial Meditation,* by Dudley Buck

His most frequently performed work was *The Golden Legend* (1880), based on scenes from Longfellow's "Christus." It was the winning composition in a competition held by the Cincinnati Festival Association for a new piece for chorus and orchestra and was premiered on May 20, 1880 in a concert that included Berlioz's *King Lear Overture* and selections from Wagner's *Siegfried* and *Die Götterdämmerung*—a thorougly modern program.

Immersed in music making all his life, as an organist and choir director, he wrote music that his performers could handle and that would be accessible to audiences and congregations. A recent writer summed up his style:

> Despite the old-world forms, the music is distinctly American. One looks in vain for Gallic passion, stifling Teutonic earnestness, or British reserve. Instead we find qualities that have always been associated with the American people, particularly in the nineteenth century. If we occasionally find maudlin sentimentality, we also find light-heartedness; if we find pomposity, it is balanced by fresh exuberance. Through it all runs a thread of naïvité and even wonder that was perhaps the one thing common to all American art during the nineteenth century.[32]

William W. Gilchrist (1846–1916), born in Jersey City but a long-time resident of Philadelphia, was an organist and choirmaster who wrote mostly vocal music. In 1877, he won several prizes offered by the Abt Society for new part-songs for male voices; his choral music won an award from the Mendelssohn Society of New York in 1880; and his *Forty-sixth Psalm* was the winning work in a competition held by the Cincinnati May Festival Committee in 1882. A contemporary comment:

> One constantly sees in Gilchrist's compositions a strong composer fettered by contrapuntal rules and by an evident desire not to stray from the highroad of art. There is never anything astonishing, but rather a constant display of skill and ease in the leading of voices. Whenever counterpoint can be used it is present, and always correct, ingenious, and commendable; but one sometimes longs for an outburst of ferocity.[33]

Silas Gamaliel Pratt (1846–1916) might have become better known had he lived and worked in Boston or New York. A native of Vermont, he took up residence in Chicago, which had no per-

[32] Barbara Owen, liner notes to NW 280, p. 4.
[33] Louis C. Elson, *The History of American Music* (New York: Macmillan, 1904) p. 240.

manent orchestra or major choral organization. He went twice to Berlin for study, in 1868 and again in 1875, and composed prolifically after his return to America, everything from small piano pieces to operas (*Zenobia*, 1882, and *Lucille*, 1887), symphonies (three of them), descriptive pieces for orchestra (*The Battle of Manila* and one depicting Paul Revere's ride), and orchestral marches. His enthusiasm for native subject matter and the blend of Germanic compositional devices with frequent quotation of familiar tunes remind one of Heinrich, and sometimes even Charles Ives. But Pratt was judged to be nothing more than an enthusiastic amateur by the foreign conductors who ruled the repertories of America's performing organizations, and his music remained little more than a rumor to most audiences, except for occasional performances in his adopted city of Chicago.

Frederic Grant Gleason (1848–1903) was another New Englander, born in Middletown, Connecticut; he settled in Chicago after study with Dudley Buck and the obligatory pilgrimage to Germany. Most of his performances took place in Chicago, though an occasional piece was played elsewhere in America. He was a "Modernist," employing Wagnerian leitmotifs in his cantatas and operas, writing descriptive and programatic orchestral pieces, and indulging in chromatic harmony and colorful orchestration.

Frank Van der Stucken (1858–1929) lived in Europe from 1866 to 1884; his father, a captain in the Confederate cavalry, left the country after the Southern defeat. Frank studied in Antwerp, became a Kapellmeister in Breslau, gave a concert of his own compositions in Weimar in 1883 under the sponsorship of Liszt, and was invited to give a similar program in Antwerp in 1891. Upon his return to America he took over the directorship of the Arion Male Chrous of New York in 1884; he conducted a program of orchestral pieces by American composers during the Paris Exposition of 1889; and in 1895 he assumed the direction of the Cincinnati Symphony Orchestra, holding this post until 1907. Various of his orchestral compositions, including the symphonic poems *William Ratcliff* and *Pax Triumphans*, were performed in Boston, New York, Cincinnati, Chicago, and also in Germany.

Louis Adolphe Coerne (1870–1922) also spent much of his life in Europe. Born in Newark, he was in France and Germany for most of his childhood; after study at Harvard under John Knowles Paine, he returned to Germany, where he studied composition and organ under Rheinberger and directed his symphonic poem *Hiawatha* upon his graduation in 1893. After a series of organ concerts in Germany, Italy, France, and England, he returned to America, holding a succession of positions in Boston, Buffalo, and Columbus. His opera *Zenobia*, staged in Bremen in 1905, was the first opera by an American to be produced in Germany.

Arthur Foote (1853–1937) was able to find excellent instruction in the Germanic style without leaving the country; such had been the progress of American musical life as the nineteenth century moved into its last decades. Born in Salem, Massachusetts, Foote studied at the New England Conservatory and at Harvard under Paine. He was in his mid-twenties before he "attempted to write real music."[34] As he described his progress:

> My influence from the beginning, as well as my predilection, were ultra-conservative: as a boy, General Oliver, later Emery and Paine, later still Dresel were my mentors; and I formed myself, so to speak, on Mendelssohn (having none the less a love for Schumann and Chopin). My harmony was correct but with little variety, the structure of my pieces conventional; and it was only much later that I absorbed harmonic finesse and became sensitive to it. Somehow, although deeply moved by Wagner, I did not have sense enough for a long time to learn from his music, and was late in appreciating the early Debussy. The idea that certain things simply must not be had become too thoroughly ingrained.[35]

One of his best compositions is a *Violin Sonata in G minor* (Opus 20),[36] written for and dedicated to Franz Kneisel, concertmaster of the Boston Symphony Orchestra with whom Foote often played chamber music. The spirit of Mendelssohn hovers over it, from the statement of the first theme of the opening movement through the graceful *alla siciliano* of the second movement and the lyric *adagio* (recalling several of Mendelssohn's *Songs without Words*) to the robust but controlled *allegro molto* of the last movement. There are gently chromatic passages recalling the best of early German Romanticism:

*Sonata for Piano and Violin* (Opus 20), by Arthur Foote

[34] Arthur Foote, *Arthur Foote (1853–1937). An Autobiography* (Norwood: Plimpton Press, 1946), p. 55.
[35] Foote, pp. 57–58.
[36] NW 268, s2.

The texture is sometimes varied with bits of contrapuntal writing:

*Sonata for Piano and Violin* (Opus 20), by Arthur Foote

And the writing for both instruments is sure and highly idiomatic; even those passages impressing the listener as brilliant and difficult lie well for the performer.

Later compositions included a *Quartet* (Opus 23) and a *Quintette* (Opus 38) for piano and strings, many songs; several suites for string orchestra; and many piano pieces, including *5 Poems after Omar Khayyam for the Pianoforte* (Opus 41), which he considered his best work. His only piece for full orchestra was *Francesca da Rimini* (Opus 24), a "symphonic prologue" premiered by the Boston Symphony in 1891.

After holding various church positions in Boston and teaching piano and organ privately, he joined the faculty of the New England Conservatory of Music in 1920. Though he struggled to keep in touch with new trends, he confessed that "a severe strain has been put

upon one's willingness to be hospitable to new ideas" as the twentieth century unfolded, and he was finally led to ask plaintively,
"Is it that hearing is not so sensitive as formerly? Is our feeling for
logic lost?"[37]

George Whitefield Chadwick (1854–1931) fit into the same mold.
Born in Lowell, Massachusetts, he was trained at the New England
Conservatory under Dudley Buck, George E. Whiting, and Eugene
Thayer; his German study was in Leipzig (Reinecke and Jadas-
sohn) and Dresden (Rheinberger and Abel). He once remarked to
an interviewer, "They kept me at harmonizing chorales for four
years, but I've always been grateful for that incomparable disci-
pline."[38] Several of his pieces were given public readings in
Leipzig—two string quartets and an overture entitled *Rip Van
Winkle*—and when he returned to Boston in 1880 he discovered
that the overture had already been played by the Harvard Musical
Association.

His five string quartets were written between 1878 and 1898. His
second and third symphonies were played by the Boston Symphony Orchestra, in 1886 and 1894, and his *Melpomene Overture*,
premiered by the same group in 1887, was perhaps the most widely
performed American orchestral piece of the decade; it was done
not only in other American cities (Chicago, Cincinnati, New York,
St. Louis, and Detroit), but in Paris and Copenhagen as well. He
also wrote piano pieces, songs, and choral works. His most extended
work was a "sacred opera," *Judith* (1901), performed in concert but
never on the stage.

Appointed to the faculty of the New England Conservatory
immediately upon his return from Germany, he became director
in 1897 and retained the post until his death in 1931. Not even his
most successful compositions, solid and serious though they may
have been, broke new ground; a contemporary offered the following evaluation:

> Chadwick has imbibed the traditions of Germany through direct con-
> tact with the teachers of Leipsig and Munich. His facility and strength
> in the handling of the factors of composition are most admirable. A crit-
> ical mind and sincere admiration for logic and symmetry save him from
> the excess radicalism into which young composers are so prone to fall.[39]

Amy Marcy Cheney, born in 1867 in Henniker, New Hampshire,
debuted in Boston at the age of sixteen as a pianist; within two

[37] Foote, pp. 105–7.
[38] Liner notes to *MIA* 104.
[39] H. E. Krehbiel, *Music in America*, Vol. 6 of *Famous Composers and Their Music*
(New York: Merrill & Baker, 1901), pp. 951–52.

years she was soloist with the Boston Symphony in Chopin's *F-minor Concerto* for piano and orchestra. Her first publicly acclaimed composition was *Festival Jubilate*, written for the dedication of the Woman's Building at Chicago's Columbian Exposition of 1892, and her first major instrumental piece was a *Gaelic Symphony*, played by the Boston Symphony in 1896.[40] Three years later, the same orchestra performed her *Piano Concerto in C-sharp minor*, with the composer (now calling herself Mrs. H. H. A. Beach) as soloist.

A *Sonata in A minor* for piano and violin (Opus 34, 1896) is a fair

Mrs. H. H. A. Beach.

[40] Available on *MIA* 139.

sample of her music.[41] Solidly constructed, lyrical, more varied in harmonic language than the works of most of her New England peers (perhaps because of her fondness for Chopin), it is an altogether successful piece, fully as effective in performance as the best compositions of Paine and Foote.

Just before the outbreak of World War I she performed her piano concerto with various German orchestras; her symphony was played in both Leipzig and Berlin during this time. The largest part of her output consists of piano music[42] and songs; several of the latter, including "The Year's at the Spring" (1900),[43] were among the most widely performed concert songs of the first half of the twentieth century.

Horatio Parker (1864–1919), born in Auburndale, Massachusetts, became a pupil of Chadwick in Boston in 1880, spent several years of study in Munich, settled in New York upon his return, and eventually became a professor of music at Yale University. His first major work was a *Scherzo for Orchestra*, conducted by Van der Stucken in New York in 1886; his most praised composition was a sacred cantata, *Hora novissima*, first performed by the Oratorio Society of New York in 1893. He was also an organist, choirmaster, and choral conductor; his *Fugue in C minor* for organ[44] demonstrates his skill in contrapuntal writing. But his limitations were the same as those of his New England peers:

> Philip Hale, in what was meant to be high praise, wrote that *Hora Novissima* was a work to which "an acknowledged master of composition in Europe would gladly sign his name." Perhaps this sort of accomplishment was important while America's music was coming of age. It meant that, judged by European standards, American music had no need to be ashamed of itself; the imitation was getting to be practically as good as the model. But what we really needed was some American music to which no European master of composition could sign his name and get away with it. This the Boston classicists were incapable of giving us.[45]

By the last decades of the nineteenth century, cultural life in the United States had made enormous strides since Theodore Thomas had arrived in New York to find pigs running in the streets. Some details of the New York musical season of 1885–86 will serve to

---

[41] NW 268, s1.

[42] A selection of her piano music is available on Genesis 1054, performed by Virginia Eskin.

[43] NW 247, s1 / 2.

[44] NW 280, s2 / 2.

[45] Gilbert Chase, *America's Music* (New York: McGraw Hill, 1966), pp. 377–78.

dramatize the new vitality and sophistication of America's musical life.

From October through April Theodore Thomas conducted forty-eight orchestral concerts at the Academy of Music, the New York Philharmonic Society gave six concerts, the Symphony Society under Walter Damrosch gave another six programs, Frank Van der Stucken conducted five concerts, and Anton Seidl offered an all-Wagner evening. All nine of Beethoven's symphonies were played by one group or another, and New York audiences also heard Schumann's first and second symphonies, two by Schubert, two by Mendelssohn, three by Haydn, and two by Raff. There were piano concertos by Beethoven, Chopin, Grieg, Liszt, Mozart, Mendelssohn, Schumann, Henselt, Hiller, Saint-Saëns, Rubinstein, and others. The "modern" school of composition was represented by Berlioz (*Symphonie fantastique*, selections from *Roméo et Juliette*, even the rarely performed *Grande symphonie funèbre et triomphale*), Liszt (*Les Préludes*, *Festklänge*, *Tasso*, *Orpheus*), and dozens of preludes and orchestral excerpts from Wagner's operas.

The Metropolitan Opera Company, in its third season, gave 52 performances of 9 different operas, the most popular being Goldmark's *Die Königin von Saba* (15 times) and Wagner's *Die Meistersinger* and *Rienzi*. Average attendance was 2,500; thus some 125,000 individual admissions were sold during the season. The American Opera Company gave another 66 performances of 9 operas, all in English, including Gluck's *Orpheus*, *Lakmé* by Delibes, and Wagner's *Lohengrin*. Gilbert and Sullivan's *The Mikado* was given its first American performances under the direction of Mr. R. D'Oyly Carte, and there were seasons of German opera and operetta at the Thalia Theatre, French light opera at Wallack's, and English light opera at a variety of halls.

The Oratorio Society of New York offered Berlioz's *Messe des morts*, Wagner's *Parsifal*, and of course the inevitable *Messiah*. Various churches offered oratorios and cantatas at festive seasons; chamber music programs, organ recitals, benefit concerts, concerts by various German singing societies, and miscellaneous musical events filled out the calendar.

The myth of America as a cultural wasteland crumbles before such data. Few European cities could boast of a concert and operatic season of comparable richness, variety, and comprehensiveness.[46]

---

[46] This information was condensed from H. E. Krehbiel, *Review of the New York Musical Season. 1885–1886* (New York & London: Novello, Ewer & Company, 1886).

Such a survey also enables one to place the performance of pieces by American composers in perspective. A summary of the careers and accomplishments of these men and women, with mention of performances of their works, may leave the impression that compositions written in this country were a frequent part of the repertory. But the New York season of 1885–86 will serve to remind us that this was not the case; in the course of more than seventy orchestral concerts and recitals, not a single extended American composition was performed by a major organization. Silas Pratt's brief *Court Minuet* was included on the twenty-first concert of the Thomas Popular Series at the Academy of Music; the only other orchestral pieces played the entire year—Horatio Parker's *Scherzo for Orchestra*, Frank Van der Stucken's incidental music to Shakespeare's *Tempest*, the prologue to Dudley Buck's *The Golden Legend*—were done on several "Novelty Concerts" organized and conducted by Van der Stucken at Steinway Hall. William Sherwood included William Mason's *Scherzo in B-flat minor* (Opus 41) on his piano recital given January 23, 1886, and a handful of other recitalists included songs and piano pieces by Americans, usually as novelty or encore numbers.

A similar ratio of European to American compositions made up the repertory of the ninth season (1899–1900) of the Chicago Symphony Orchestra, even though the conductor was Theodore Thomas, who was more sympathetic to American composers than most. Twenty-two concerts were given with 124 different pieces played. Two were by Americans—the symphonic poem *Lancelot and Elaine* by Edward MacDowell, and Horatio Parker's *Northern Ballad* (Opus 46). By contrast, the season brought 24 pieces by Wagner, 11 by Beethoven, and 9 by Tchaikovsky.

The Germanic music which dominated the musical life of America during the second half of the nineteenth century was never cut off from its origin. There was a continuing flow of musicians from the Germanic countries into America. Instrumentalists, conductors, singers, and teachers from Germany dominated the performing organizations and music schools of America. Aspiring American musicians accepted these immigrants as role models, representing the peak of musical culture. The German style and aesthetic were never questioned, only emulated.

Even Theodore Thomas, who came to America as a youth and liked to think of himself as an American, was described by a contemporary as "German born, associated with German musicians all his life, meeting them daily, and living as it were in a German atmosphere."[47] When news came of the defeat of the French at Sedan in September of 1870, Thomas conducted his orchestra in a celebratory playing of *Wacht am Rhein*—to the acute discomfort of the single non-German player, who happened to be French.[48]

Quite naturally, German music—old and new—was of more interest than anything written by an American. There was disdain for all elements of American culture. Theodore Thomas dismissed all "so-called popular music in America" as "representing nothing more than sweet sentimentality and rhythm, on the level of the dime novel."[49] And many American critics and journalists echoed this elitist attitude:

> Supposing that our aspiring composers should devote themselves to the composition of such music as can be well assimilated by the multitudes, instead of following their own highest ideal, and that both composers and music-lovers should for a period of ten or twenty years concentrate their aesthetic energies upon leading the masses step by step to an understanding of the higher music. The whole country would be steeped in the most disheartening mediocrity. We must never forget what an overwhelming influence the fit individual has upon the whole culture of his age. The higher above the common herd the individual stands, the greater and surer will his influence be in the end. Instead of wasting so much breath and ink upon a chimerical gradual cultivation of the masses, it would be much more to the purpose to do all in our power towards the still higher and higher cultivation of the already enlightened few.[50]

On the other hand, not one of the American-born composers of the era claimed that there was anything distinctly American about the style of his or her pieces, nor was such a claim made by critics or supporters of native compositions. The prevailing attitude was expressed by one of the foremost American writers on music of the day:

> German ideals have mastered the world of music, for which reason it was possible for Dr. von Bülow a few years ago to say that the best German music at the time was composed in Paris, Moscow and St. Petersburg. By that he meant no reflection on the French and Russian composers; on the contrary, he was praising them at the expense of his own countrymen. So far as the future is concerned, the American composer who is following the example of his brethren of Great Britain,

[47] Thomas, I, pp. 254–55.
[48] Charles Edward Russell, *The American Orchestra and Theodore Thomas* (Garden City: Doubleday, Page & Company, 1927), pp. 171–72.
[49] Thomas, I, p. 18.
[50] *Atlantic Monthly* for January 1875, pp. 122–23.

France, Italy, and Russian in studying German ideals will stand an equal chance with them in the struggle for recognition as soon as he is put upon their level in respect of appreciation and encouragement at home and abroad.[51]

Almost all music transplanted to the New World underwent change on American soil, absorbing and reflecting aspects of American life and culture. Classical music of the Germanic tradition resisted change, because of the attitudes of its practitioners and enthusiasts. Their view was that Americans themselves would have to change before they could come to terms with symphonies, quartets, concertos, and operas written in German classical style. Surely this is one of the reasons for the continuing difficulties many Americans had with this music, whether it was written by European or American composers.

[51] Krehbiel, *Music in America*, p. 960.

# 13

# *The Music*
# *of Tin Pan Alley*

For the entire lifespan of the era known as Tin Pan Alley, popular song in the United States was dominated by New York City and by the musical stage.

New York had become the largest and most vital city in America. Its population passed the quarter-million mark in the 1830s, and in the years following the Civil War it became the first American metropolis to have a million inhabitants. It became the country's largest port, the center of commerce and fashion, and the heart of theatrical life in the New World.

The rest of the country regarded it with ambivalence, however. An observer wrote in 1909:

New York is the metropolis of a jealous and disparaging country that seldom has anything good to say of it. Practically the entire country seems to take pleasure in it; reads about it continually—for it is the greatest contributor of news to the papers; visits it when it can and enjoys the visits; is amused with its shows and interested in its hotels, shops, parks, streets, tall buildings, rivers, bridges, slums, tunnels and people. It pays a constant tribute of attention and spends money in it according to its means, but it seldom shows pride in it, or speaks any better of it than it can help. Perhaps when Kansas goes to Europe (as it does abundantly) it brags a little about New York as an American product, and the greatest-city-to-be in all the world. But at home Kansas is apt to see in New York a greedy city, wrapped up in itself, incredulous of Western wisdom, inhospitable to "broad American ideas," perched on the shore of the Atlantic Ocean and careless of the great land behind it except as a vast productive area from which it draws endless wealth. New York is merely one of the fruits of that great tree whose roots go down in the Mississippi Valley, and whose branches spread from one ocean to the other, but the tree has no great degree of affection for its fruit. It inclines to think that the big apple gets a disproportionate share of the national sap.[1]

Immigrants from all over Europe came to the New World by way of New York, and many of them stayed there. The census of 1900 revealed that only 36 percent of the population of the city had been born in this country, and some 60 percent of these were the children of parents born in Europe. There were more than three times as many first-generation Americans whose parents had been born in Germany and Ireland alone as there were New Yorkers whose families had been in the country for more than two generations.[2] Edward "Ned" Harrigan, who rose to fame on the musical stage in the Harrigan and Hart shows of the 1870s and '80s, was born and raised in the city's sixth ward, where the census revealed 812 Irish, 218 Germans, 189 Poles, 186 Italians, 39 Blacks, various "unclassifiable persons"—and 10 native-born white Americans. As he once put it, "the U.S. language was a hard find" in his neighborhood.[3]

Changes in patterns of immigration in the last decade of the nineteenth century and the first years of the twentieth brought a massive influx from the Mediterranean countries and Central and Eastern Europe. By the 1920s, almost 50 percent of the population of New York was Catholic (chiefly Irish and Italian), a third was Jewish, and no more than 15 percent was Protestant—in a country traditionally dominated by Protestants.

The ambivalence of the rest of the country was simply a matter of regarding most New Yorkers as foreign, not part of the cultural mainstream of America.

But most foreign-born and first-generation New Yorkers wanted nothing so much as to become part of their new country—to learn its language, adopt its culture, leave their own heritage behind. The most remarkable part of the story of American popular music from the 1890s through the 1950s was the fact that it did indeed become a musical language accepted all over America, even though

[1] Edward Sandford Martin, *The Wayfarer in New York* (New York: The Macmillan Company, 1909), p. xv.
[2] These figures are taken from Ira Rosenwaike, *Population History of New York City* (Syracuse: Syracuse University Press, 1972), p. 79.
[3] E. J. Kahn, Jr., *The Merry Partners: The Age and Stage of Harrigan and Hart* (New York: Random House, 1955), p. 58.

it was shaped in a city where there was little contact with America's older cultural heritages.

The commercial center of popular song gradually shifted from Boston, Philadelphia, Chicago and even Cincinnati, to New York. Several new publishing houses, including those of Frank Harding, T. B. Harms, and the Witmark family, began amassing large sales of sheet music through a policy of concentrating on vocal music and marketing their products aggressively. Their offices were located in the heart of the entertainment district of the city: some were in the Union Square section, on East 14th Street, but the Witmarks moved uptown, to 28th Street, and by the late 1890s virtually every publisher had an office on that street. Monroe H. Rosenfeld gave it the nickname of "Tin Pan Alley," descriptive of the sounds heard on the street from the cheap upright pianos playing simultaneously in salesrooms of various publishers. In time this term was applied to the popular song industry itself, and then to the type of music written by songwriters of the era.

At first these songs were mostly sentimental verse-chorus tunes mining the rich stream of nostalgia for lost youth and love that had served so many generations of American songwriters: "White Wings" (1884) by Banks Winter; Paul Dresser's first hit, "The Letter That Never Came" (1886); "The Picture That Is Turned toward the Wall" (1891) by Charles Graham. And when America's best songwriters began making their way to New York, in response to its growing commercial importance, their songs did not change in style, as may be seen from Charles K. Harris's "Break the News to Mother" and " 'Mid the Green Hills of Virginia" and Dresser's "The Pardon Came Too Late" and "On the Banks of the Wabash."

But an increasing number of songs written in New York were designed for Irish singers and comedians, in a successful appeal to the large Irish population of the city: "Remember, Boy, You're Irish" by William Scanlan (1885); the anonymous "Drill, Ye Tarriers, Drill" of 1888;[4] Joseph Flynn's "Down Went McGinty" (1889). And the 1890s saw the emergence of the first distinctly New York product, the waltz-song. Though triple meter had been utilized in songs before, such songs as "The Bowery" (Percy Gaunt, 1892);[5] "Daisy Bell" (Harry Dacre, 1892), "The Sidewalks of New York" (Charles B. Lawlor and James W. Blaker, 1894), "She May Have Seen Better Days" (James Thornton, 1894), "The Band Played On" (Charles B. Ward, 1895), "Sweet Rosie O'Grady" (Maud Nugent, 1896), and "My Wild Irish Rose" (Chauncey Olcott, 1899) were per-

[4] NW 267, s1 / 2.
[5] NW 221, s2 / 7.

ceived as a new trend. Their lyrics often made reference to the Irish living in New York:

> Down in front of Casey's, old brown wooden stoop,
> On a summer's evening, we formed a merry group;
> Boys and girls together, we would sing and waltz,
> While the "Ginnie" played the organ, on the sidewalks of New York.
>
> That's where Johnny Casey, and little Jimmy Crowe,
> With Jakey Krause the baker, who always had the dough;
> Pretty Nellie Shannon, with a dude as light as cork,
> First picked up the waltz step, on the sidewalks of New York.

A series of factors brought a new ethnic flavor to America's popular songs at the turn of the century, however. The minstrel show had retained considerable popularity, and now a vigorous new musical dialect called ragtime swept in from the West and was enthusiastically embraced by the New York–based writers. The black population of the city had increased from some 10,000 persons during the Civil War era to more than 60,000 by 1900—a figure that would more than triple in the first two decades of the twentieth century. The international character of New York made it more receptive to black performers than was the case elsewhere, and large numbers of black musicians and stage performers made their way to the city. There were now black minstrel troupes, black dancers began appearing in shows with white casts, and soon after the turn of the century black performers (singers, comedians, dancers) were accepted in some vaudeville houses.

*A Trip to Coontown,* written by two blacks (Bob Cole and Billy Johnson) and performed by an all-black cast, had a brief run in April of 1898; later that year *The Origin of the Cake Walk or, Clorindy,* with book and lyrics by Paul Laurence Dunbar and music by Will Marion Cook, starring the great black minstrel performer Ernest Hogan, became the first all-black show to run for white audiences. A scattering of songs by black composers began appearing in the catalogues of Tin Pan Alley publishers; Gussie Davis's "In the Baggage Car Ahead," brought out by Howley, Haviland & Company in 1896, became the first piece by a black songwriter to sell a million copies of sheet music. *In Dahomey,* by Dunbar and Cook and featuring the vaudville team of George Walker and Bert Williams, was the first all-black musical show to be performed at a major theater on Broadway, opening on February 18, 1903. By this time the black presence was being felt so strongly in New York, and ragtime was so popular that in the curious words of a contemporary observer:

The 'possum replaced Widow Nolan's goat in the popular songwriter's lexicon. The razor replaced the shillelagh, Mandy became more commonplace than Kathleen, and gin supplanted the Cruikeen lawn.[6]

Another ethnic presence in New York, the Jews, had a no less profound but quite different impact on American popular song.

In the decades following 1880, more than a third of the Jews of Eastern Europe left their homelands; 90 percent of them came to the United States, and the overwhelming majority settled in New York, where the Jewish population rose from no more than 60,000 in 1880 to approximately a million by the turn of the century.

As was the case with so many immigrant groups of this period, the Jews of New York were torn between a desire to retain their identity and the necessity of adapting to their new home. Many found a satisfactory compromise: they retained their language, religion, and traditions in the privacy of their homes and ethnic communities, but assimilated American culture in public and professional life. "To be an American, dress like an American, look like an American, and even, if only in fantasy, talk like an American became a collective goal, at least for the younger immigrants."[7]

In the world of entertainment, this assimilation of indigenous culture was nothing short of astonishing. While retaining and developing Yiddish theater, literature, and music for their own people, these immigrants also absorbed popular forms of theater and music. Jewish singers and comedians became outstanding and popular performers on the minstrel and vaudeville stage; Jewish songwriters began turning out Irish waltz songs and ragtime tunes as though these had been part of their heritage for generations. As a historian of this era said of the similar involvement of foreign-born and first-generation Jews in American film in the early years of Hollywood, "they were brilliantly attuned to the needs of their business; they commanded and used to the full a profound instinct for the common denominator of taste; and they left a deep imprint on American popular culture."[8]

Popular song in the United States was shaped chiefly by Jewish songwriters and lyricists (most of them living in New York) for the entire first half of the twentieth century; they drew on elements of indigenous American music, including ragtime, other syncopated

---

[6] Edward B. Marks, *They All Sang; From Tony Pastor to Rudy Vallée* (New York: The Viking Press, 1934), pp. 91–92.
[7] Irving Howe, *The World of our Fathers* (New York and London: Harcourt Brace Jovanovich, 1976), p. 128.
[8] Howe, p. 165.

dance music, and then jazz—which they responded to and absorbed much more willingly and effectively than most native-born white Americans.

Curiously, another large ethnic component of New York, the Italians, contributed very little to American popular song during this era, despite their numbers and their reputation as a musical people. An occasional performer came out of the Italian sections of the city, but one would look in vain for any Italian influence on America's popular songs in the early twentieth century.

The minstrel show and vaudeville were both made up of individual acts or numbers with no semblance of dramatic unity. Though there were stage pieces in which drama, music, dancing, and spectacle were combined—the most notable being *The Black Crook*, which ran for 475 performances after its opening at Niblo's Garden on September 12, 1866—music was not part of the original concept of these shows:

> Music was used either as insertions and embellishments to otherwise complete and independent works for the stage. . . . The songs and dances rarely assisted the flow of the plot, and particularly when they were intended as lavish production numbers, comic relief, or sentimentality they brought the dramatic action to a standstill. Many such songs and dances were borrowed or adapted from traditional or currently popular material.[9]

Even when a songwriter furnished a number of pieces for a specific show, as Percy Gaunt did for *A Trip to Chinatown*—which broke the *The Black Crook* record by running for 657 performances in New York after its premier in 1891—these songs rarely figured in the dramatic action and could be eliminated or replaced at the whim of the director or even individual performers, with no damage to the dramatic shape of the show.[10]

It is in this context that the place of Geroge M. Cohan in the history of the American musical stage may best be understood.

Cohan (1878–1942) literally grew up on the stage. His father, an itinerant performer on the minstrel and vaudeville circuits, incorporated his wife into his act, then George, and finally daughter Josie; the family was billed as The Four Cohans. George, almost totally self-taught in music and knowing only the vocal repertory he had encountered on the stage, wrote songs from the time he was

[9] Deane L. Root, *American Popular Stage Music, 1860–1880* (Ann Arbor: UMI Research Press, 1981), p. 175. This book gives an excellent coverage of the American musical theater for the period in question.

[10] Songs from a number of these shows are available on NW 221.

Sheet music cover of George M. Cohan's great hit "Yankee Doodle Boy."

in his early teens, and by the late 1890s he was providing all the material for the family act—skits, dramatic routines, songs. Beginning with *The Governor's Son* in 1901, he wrote a string of "musical plays" that moved in the direction of a distinctive American musical comedy. Writing both book and songs, he created unified pieces for the stage in which songs were spotted at strategic moments and contributed to the flow of the drama. His best and most popular songs were written for the most important of these shows: *Little Johnny Jones* (1904) brought "Give My Regards to Broadway" and "The Yankee Doodle Boy"; *Forty-Five Minutes from Broadway* (1906) introduced "Mary's a Grand Old Name," "So Long Mary," and the title song; *George Washington, Jr.* (1906) featured "You're a Grand Old Flag."

The subject matter of Cohan's musical plays is American, usually with an aggressive patriotism running through them. His songs tend to be of two types: waltz-songs, often with texts reflecting Cohan's Irish heritage; or brash, breezy songs in march tempo, evoking the rhythms and spirit of American marches of the day and often quoting familiar patriotic airs. "The Yankee Doodle Boy," for instance, incorporates fragments of "Yankee Doodle," "Dixie," "The Girl I Left Behind Me," and "The Star Spangled Banner."[11] Their march rhythms sometimes evoke a sense of ragtime, underlining the close ties between ragtime and march music in the first decade of the twentieth century.

Jerome Kern (1885–1945), whose cultural and musical orientation was quite different from Cohan's, was similarly involved in writing for the musical stage from early in his career. Born in New York, he studied piano and musical theory at the New York College of Music, then went off to Europe for further training, with the intention of becoming a composer of classical music. Caught up instead in the popular musical stage, he set out to learn the trade of songwriting by working for several Tin Pan Alley publishers as a song plugger, while also holding jobs as rehearsal pianist for Broadway theaters. His first hit song, in 1905, "How'd You Like to Spoon with Me?", was inserted into the imported English musical comedy *The Earl and the Girl.*[12]

For almost a decade Kern wrote for interpolation into musicals; not until 1912 did he do a complete show, *The Red Petticoat.* His most important contributions to the American musical stage began on April 20, 1915, with the opening at the Princess Theatre of *Nobody Home*, with a book by Guy Bolton and most of the music by Kern. The two had worked together from the beginning on this rewriting of Paul Rubens's *Mr. Popple of Ippleton;* lyrics and music were written to be sung in specific dramatic situations. The small house (229 seats) proved ideal for the projection of the spirited, intimate show, which ran for 135 performances and was succeeded by the even more successful *Very Good, Eddie*, which ran for almost a year, before going on the road. As one theater historian put it:

[11] NW 221, s1 / 2.
[12] NW 221, s1 / 7.

More than any other piece it formed the mold out of which poured a half-century of American Musical Comedy. Its people were everyday people—neither cartooned clowns nor cardboard lovers. Its situations were plausible—however unlikely. Its easily singable songs helped the story flow but were lovely and natural away from the stage.[13]

*Oh, Boy!* followed at the Princess, opening on February 20, 1917— one of three musicals with songs by Kern that season. P. G. Wodehouse was now a collaborator with Kern and Bolton, as lyricist.

There were other talented songwriters and other forms of musical stage serving as an outlet for American songs. Irving Berlin, born in Temun, Russia in 1888, worked his way up in the world of Tin Pan Alley, beginning as a singing waiter, song plugger, and lyricist for the Ted Snyder publishing house. His first songs cover the range of vaudeville types: sentimental Irish ballads; ragtime songs; nostalgic songs of the old South, still performed in blackface; dialect songs of several types, including Yiddish ones. He first appeared on the stage himself in 1910, in a revue entitled *Up and Down Broadway*, touching two ethnic bases with "Sweet Italian Love" and "Oh, That Beautiful Rag."

At just this time Florenz Ziegfeld was inaugurating his annual *Follies*, which were to be a mainstay of the New York stage for two decades. They were little more than glorified vaudeville shows, a string of individual acts and production numbers, presented in Broadway theaters rather than vaudeville houses. The *Follies of 1910* introduced two performers to the series, the veteran black star Bert Williams and the nineteen-year-old singer-comic Fanny Brice, who had come to Ziegfeld's attention with her performance of Berlin's "Sadie Salome" on the burlesque circuit, and who introduced Berlin's "Goodbye Becky Cohen." *The Passing Show of 1912* was a competing extravaganza produced by the Schuberts; Berlin contributed a song to it also.

By this time, with the success of "Alexander's Ragtime Band" (1911), introduced in a vaudeville act in Chicago by Emma Carus and quickly picked up by Sophie Tucker, Berlin was in great demand. The year 1914 brought his first complete show, *Watch Your Step*, starring Vernon and Irene Castle, filled with ragtime and syncopated songs by Berlin including a sequence set at the Metropolitan Opera House featuring "ragged" versions of favorite operatic arias. The show confirmed that Berlin's strength was in individual songs, as did also the following year's *Stop! Look! Lis-*

---

[13] Gerald Bordman, *American Musical Theatre. A Chronicle* (New York: Oxford University Press, 1978), p. 312.

*ten!*, notable chiefly for "The Girl on the Magazine Cover," one of Berlin's most enduring songs.[14]

Berlin continued to write individual numbers, for vaudeville or revues and sometimes interpolated into other shows. *Yip Yip Yaphank* (1918), a wartime revue with a cast of servicemen from Camp Upton, featured Berlin himself singing "Oh, How I Hate to Get Up in the Morning."[15] Ziegfeld's *Follies of 1919* celebrated the return of peacetime with the most lavish production in the series, and the best array of songs by Berlin to appear in a single show, including "A Pretty Girl Is Like a Melody"; the neo-minstrel "Mandy," a comic-romantic duet for the vaudeville team of Van and Schneck;[16] new songs for Bert Williams and Eddie Cantor; and a duet for these two, "I Want to See a Minstrel Show."

With a series of *Music Box Revues* beginning in 1921, staged at a beautiful, new, rather small Broadway theater, Berlin for the first time was in a position to conceive and write shows from scratch, and the four revues done there represent a peak of his career as a writer for the musical stage. They contained some of Berlin's most memorable songs—"Say It with Music," "What'll I Do?," "All Alone," "Rock-a-Bye Baby"[17]—and cemented his reputation as the master of the revue, just at the time Jerome Kern was acquiring a similar stature in musical comedy.

The season of 1916 brought a new name to the Broadway musical stage: George Gershwin, only seventeen years old, contributed "The Making of a Girl" to the *Passing Show* revue of that season. Gershwin, classically trained as a pianist, was encouraged to write for the popular stage after hearing Kern's songs from *The Girl From Utah*, and spent several years as a pianist and song plugger for a Tin Pan Alley publisher before signing a contract as house song-writer with T. B. Harms.

Success came early, and almost overnight. "Swanee" was picked up by Al Jolson for a concert, then interpolated into the musical *Sinbad* while the show was on the road in 1919. Jolson recorded it, for Columbia, and sales of both sheet music and disc quickly reached the hundreds of thousands. *La, La, Lucille*, a musical with a complete score by Gershwin, opened on Broadway on May 26, 1919, and the following year he did most of the music for the *Scandals of 1920*, the second edition of this new, dance-oriented series conceived by George White. Gershwin was the major contributor to the *Scandals* through 1924, when he decided to concentrate on

[14] NW 233, s1 / 2.
[15] NW 238, s1 / 1.
[16] These two are on NW 238, s1 / 2–3.
[17] NW 238, s1 / 4.

book shows. Evidence of his maturity as a writer for the musical stage came on December 1, 1924 with the opening of *Lady, Be Good.* The score included some of Gershwin's finest songs (the title song, "Fascinating Rhythm," "The Man I Love," "So Am I"), all to lyrics by his brother Ira. Gershwin's jazz-flavored style, sound instinct for dramatic situations, and gift for memorable melody brought a new dimension to the American musical comedy.

*A Lonely Romeo,* an otherwise unmemorable light musical entertainment which enjoyed a brief run in the summer of 1919, was the vehicle for the first stage song by Richard Rodgers, a seventeen-year-old New Yorker about to enter Columbia University. Entitled "Any Old Place with You," it had a lyric by another unknown, Lorenz Hart. After writing the university's annual musical stage production for 1920, the two returned to the commercial stage with a number of songs for *Poor Little Ritz Girl* (1920), produced by Lew Fields. Rodgers teamed up with Hart again in 1925 to write seven songs for *The Garrick Gaieties,* a benefit revue for the Theatre Guild which ended up running for 211 performances, largely because of the effectiveness of the Rodgers-Hart songs. Soon, the two had another show, *Dearest Enemy,* running at the Knickerbocker Theatre with such success that some critics compared it to the best works of Gilbert and Sullivan.

All necessary ingredients were thus assembled for a productive era in the American musical theater: the involvement of many of the country's most talented songwriters; the emergence of equally talented lyricists with a strong interest in dramatic pieces; a healthy though brief tradition of indigenous stage works; a receptive mood on the part of audiences and critics toward American pieces. And the period from the early 1920s until the end of World War II did indeed prove to be the zenith of the American musical stage. The *Ziegfeld Follies,* George White's *Scandals,* the *Earl Carroll Vanities, Artists and Models,* the *Greenwich Village Follies,* and the *Grand Street Follies* appeared in annual installments throughout most of the 1920s, reaching new peaks of stage spectacle, dancing, and quality of music.[18] Even more important, the period brought an unprecedented number of dramatic works combining tight and effective books with well-integrated songs and musical numbers by the best songwriters and lyricists in the country. A highly selective list will suffice to underline the point that American musical comedy had become one of the stunning artistic products of the New World:

1925: *No! No! Nanette* (Vincent Youmans)
   *Sunny* (Jerome Kern)

---

[18] NW 215 contains a selection of songs from some of these shows.

1926: *The Girl Friend* (Richard Rodgers)
    *Oh Kay!* (George Gershwin)
1927: *Funny Face* (George Gershwin)
    *Showboat* (Jerome Kern)
    *Hit the Deck* (Vincent Youmans)
    *A Connecticut Yankee* (Richard Rodgers)
1930: *Girl Crazy* (George Gershwin)
    *Strike Up the Band* (George Gershwin)
1931: *Music in the Air* (Jerome Kern)
    *Of Thee I Sing* (George Gershwin)
    *The Cat and the Fiddle* (Jerome Kern)
1932: *Gay Divorce* (Cole Porter)
    *Face the Music* (Irving Berlin)
1933: *Roberta* (Jerome Kern)
1934: *Anything Goes* (Cole Porter)
1936: *On Your Toes* (Richard Rodgers)
1937: *Babes in Arms* (Richard Rodgers)
1938: *The Boys from Syracuse* (Richard Rodgers)
    *Knickerbocker Holiday* (Kurt Weill)
1940: *Louisiana Purchase* (Irving Berlin)
    *Pal Joey* (Richard Rodgers)
    *Panama Hattie* (Cole Porter)
1941: *Lady in the Dark* (Kurt Weill)
    *Let's Face It* (Cole Porter)
1943: *Oklahoma* (Richard Rodgers)
1944: *Mexican Hayride* (Cole Porter)
1945: *Carousel* (Richard Rodgers)
1946: *Annie Get Your Gun* (Irving Berlin)

All were the work of composers and lyricists working in New York City; many were in fact natives of the town.

The subject matter of most earlier works for the musical stage had been local, set in New York or its suburbs, concerned with topics of interest to metropolitan audiences. Most of the numbers in revues and other vaudeville-like shows had been likewise topical; caricatures (sympathetic or otherwise) of Irish, Jewish, German, black, and Italian types had formed the basis of most of the humor. In other words, the American musical stage in the first two decades of the twentieth century was dominated by works aimed at New York audiences.

But just as America's classical composers began using indigenous melodic material and making reference to America's history, literature, and legends, the creators of works for the musical stage also began reaching beyond the geographical and cultural boundaries of New York. An obvious unifying feature of the pieces in the

The immortal Helen Morgan singing "Bill" in the 1927 Ziegfeld production of *Showboat*. (Courtesy of The Institute of the American Musical, Inc.)

list above is that they are all set in various parts of America, and involve characters and situations to which a wide range of Americans could relate. Songwriters for these shows attempt to suggest dimensions of the American experience in their music. *Show Boat* does not draw on traditional tunes in its portrayal of life along the Mississippi River in the late nineteenth century; all of its songs, including the moving "Ol' Man River" sung by a black stevodore, were written by Kern in the mold of the Tin Pan Alley song. But subtle inflections in melody and harmonic structure made each seem appropriate for the character singing it, and even for the time and place in which the story was set. Nor is there any hint of the traditional music of New England in "If I Loved You" or the other songs written by Richard Rodgers for *Carousel*, but they seem appropriate in style. For that matter, none of the music in *Oklahoma* had anything to do with the culture of that part of America, but many of the songs have *now* become a part of American musical tradition.

Some music attempts to become part of the culture of a people by drawing on familiar material; other music creates its own traditions. Albert Von Tilzer's "Take Me Out to the Ball Game" (1908) did not draw on music already part of baseball in America; but it was such a good song and so appropriate for the setting, that in time it *became* part of the tradition of baseball. Likewise the songs from *Oklahoma*, written by two men with no contact with the culture of that part of the United States, were considered appropriate because they appeared in a drama set in that region, and because they were of such high quality. The latter point is most important. Surely Aaron Copland's *Appalachian Spring*—written in the same year as *Oklahoma*, incidentally—became one of the most widely performed pieces of orchestral music by an American composer because of its excellence and because it was offered in an American setting, not because of its use of an American traditional melody (which was unknown to most people, in any event).

American musical comedy in its Golden Age (the 1920s, '30s, and '40s) broke through regional cultural boundaries and reached the entire country because it deliberately set out to transcend the cultural isolationism of New York, and because its music was written by songwriters of great talent and even genius.

The first successful discs by singers were those of Enrico Caruso and other opera stars in the first decade of the twentieth century; their strongly projected, focused voices overcame much of the distortion inherent in recording techniques of the time, and their recordings were at least an approximation of their voices in live performance. But the scattering of discs by popular singers early in the century were much less satisfactory, and the phonograph was much more successful with the instrumental dance music of the period.

By the early 1920s, recording techniques could capture on wax the voices of many popular singers, Al Jolson for instance, in a relatively faithful way, and sales of phonograph discs of certain songs approached and even surpassed those of sheet music. This development had little or no impact on the popular music industry for many years, however; the major New York publishers effectively controlled the distribution of popular music and the phonograph disc became a highly profitable extension of the industry without changing it.

Commercial radio, which had its beginnings in the early 1920s, depended almost entirely on live programming for the first decade of its existence. Music was a major component: singers, accompanied by a studio band or orchestra, were featured on variety shows and soon had programs of their own; dance bands were broadcast from hotels and clubs. Certain performers built reputations from radio alone, without ever appearing on the vaudeville or musical comedy stage: Vaughn De Leath, Will Osborne, Lanny Ross, "Whispering" Jack Smith, Rudy Vallee, Kate Smith. But the new medium did not generate new music at first. Radio performers depended on what was available from music publishers, and Tin Pan Alley songs went over the airwaves for several decades. Even when a network show, "Your Hit Parade," began bringing popular songs to a wider audience than that reached by any other medium, the repertory, in 1935, was for the most part songs already popularized on the musical stage or movie screen and already disseminated via phonograph discs and sheet music. It would be several decades before radio would begin to play a critical role in the initial popularizing of songs.

The silent film developed its own musical traditions in the first three decades of the twentieth century. Almost from the beginning, films were accompanied by music, at first played on an upright piano and later on large, elaborate theater organs designed and constructed for this purpose. The keyboard player would piece together a potpourri of musical fragments appropriate to the action of the film, drawing on everything from popular songs to classical works.[19] Some films, *The Son of the Sheik* (1926), for instance, came to theaters accompanied by elaborate cue-sheets keyed to anthol-

[19] Cf. NW 227, s2 / 2, for a typical silent film accompaniment, used for the movie *For Heaven's Sake* of 1926.

ogies of musical selections widely used by theater organists, specifying just what music should accompany certain scenes and sequences.[20] Others came with actual scores for the theater organist, either stitched together from diverse compositions (D. W. Griffith's *Intolerance* of 1916)[21] or, in a few instances, newly composed: Griffith's *Orphans of the Storm* (1921) had a score by Louis Ferdinand Gottschalk.[22]

But with the introduction of the sound film, movie music became an extension of the New York musical stage.

The first film to make extensive use of dialogue and music, *The Jazz Singer* (1927), was based on a Broadway play of 1925, featured songs from a number of different productions for the musical theater, and starred Al Jolson, a veteran of vaudeville. *The Coconuts* (1929) was essentially a filming of a show which had opened on Broadway in 1925, with much of the same cast (including the Marx Brothers) and many of the songs Irving Berlin had written for the stage production. This pattern was to persist: dozens of musical comedies and revues were remade as movies, retaining the music written for them on Broadway. When songs began to be written for the screen, they were mostly the work of established songwriters for the New York musical stage. Jerome Kern spent much of his time in Hollywood in the 1930s and '40s working on film versions of his stage musicals and also writing new scores for such films as *I Dream Too Much* (1935), *High, Wide and Handsome* (1937) and *Cover Girl* (1944). George Gershwin was there even earlier, doing the music for *Delicious* in 1931 and following with *Shall We Dance* and *A Damsel in Distress* in 1936–37. Cole Porter's first contributions were songs for *Born to Dance* (1936) and *Rosalie* (1937). But it was Irving Berlin who made the most prolonged contributions to the new medium. From *Puttin' on the Ritz* (1929) through *Top Hat* (1935), *Follow the Fleet* (1936), *Second Fiddle* (1939), *Holiday Inn* (1942), *Blue Skies* (1946), and *Easter Parade* (1948), he contributed to the screen such masterpieces of Tin Pan Alley craft as "Cheek to Cheek," "Let Yourself Go," "White Christmas," "Be Careful! It's My Heart," and "I've Got My Love to Keep Me Warm."[23]

A few songs for films were written by composers who had not enjoyed success in New York, and even by musicians with no Broadway experience. *Sunny Side Up* (1929) brought several excellent songs by Bud DeSylva, Lew Brown, and Ray Henderson,

---

[20] Part of this score is available on NW 227, s1 / 3.
[21] NW 227, s2 / 6.
[22] NW 227, s1 / 5.
[23] "Puttin' On the Ritz" and "Cheek to Cheek" are on NW 238, s2 / 2 and 7.

including "If I Had a Talking Picture of You,"[24] and *Hollywood Revue of 1929* is best remembered for "Singin' in the Rain," with music by Nacio Herb Brown, a native of New Mexico who was virtually unknown before he began writing for film. Harry Warren had enjoyed only sporadic success in New York before writing songs for a series of spectacular Hollywood musicals during the early years of the Depression, beginning with *Forty Second Street* (1932) and *Gold Diggers of 1933.*[25]

The songs written by these and other men for Hollywood films in the 1930s and '40s were no different in form and expressive content from other songs of the Tin Pan Alley period. The sound film had brought a lively new medium to American life, but it was filled with the same sort of music that had been written in the several decades preceding its invention.

The Tin Pan Alley song was proving to be a remarkably durable and adaptable product.

Virtually all Tin Pan Alley songs are in verse-chorus form. For the first several decades of the new era, songs normally had three or more verses, which lay out a brief drama; the chorus follows each verse with a commentary on the emotional situation developing in the verses. The verse is usually twice as long as the chorus, but the chorus has the more memorable music, the "tune" which the songwriter hopes will appeal to his listeners and stick in their minds. Charles K. Harris's "After the Ball" (1892), the first great hit song of the era, is a classic example of this structure:

> A little maiden climbed an old man's knee,
> Begged for a story—"Do Uncle, please.
> Why are you single; why live alone?
> Have you no babies; have you no home?"
> "I had a sweetheart, years, years ago;
> Where she is now pet, you will soon know.
> List to the story, I'll tell it all;
> I believed her faithless after the ball.

> *Chorus:* After the ball is over, after the break of morn,
> After the dancers' leaving; after the stars are gone;
> Many a heart is aching, if you could read them all;
> Many the hopes that have vanished after the ball.

> Bright lights were flashing in the grand ball room,
> Softly the music, playing sweet tunes.
> There came my sweetheart, my love, my own—

---

[24] NW 233, s2 / 8.
[25] "We're in the Money" from this film is available on NW 270, s1 / 8.

"I wish some water; leave me alone."
When I returned dear there stood a man,
Kissing my sweetheart as lovers can.
Down fell the glass, pet, broken, that's all;
Just as my heart was after the ball.

*Chorus:*
Long years have passed child, I've never wed,
True to my lost love, though she is dead.
She tried to tell me, tried to explain;
I would not listen, pleadings were vain,
One day a letter came from that man,
He was her brother—the letter ran.
That's why I'm lonely, no home at all;
I broke her heart, pet, after the ball.

*Chorus:*

A song put together in this way was well-suited to the vaudeville
stage. Many singers delivered the verses in a semireciting voice, to
make sure the audience could follow the dramatic action. The chorus would then be sung in a more lyric and melodic style, and once
the song became popular, the audience might sing along with the
chorus.

It was a flexible form, allowing for a wide variety of dramatic
situations and musical styles. In "The Bowery" (1892) by Percy
Gaunt and Charles H. Hoyt, the biggest hit song in *A Trip to Chinatown,* a young man tells of a series of misadventures that overtook
him on his first night in New York; each of the six verses details an
incident, each is followed by the chorus in the usual waltz style of
the era.[26] In a quite different mood, Charles E. Trevathan's "Bully
Song" (1895),[27] introduced by May Irwin in *The Widow Jones,* lays
out the story of a black bully who terrorizes his neighborhood; this
is a "coon song," with text in dialect and syncopated rhythms.

Subtle changes mark the songs of the first two decades of the
twentieth century. Two verses became standard, rather than three
or more, and while these still delineate a dramatic situation, it is
usually much less complex than the stories told in the earliest Tin
Pan Alley songs and in fact tends to be more a vignette—a single
dramatic or emotional situation—than an unfolding drama moving from episode to episode and an eventual climax. George M.
Cohan was one of the first songwriters to standardize the two verse-
chorus, seminarrative song; virtually all of his successful compositions fit into this mold:

[26] NW 221, s2 / 7.
[27] NW 221, s1 / 8.

My mother's name was Mary, she was so good and true;
Because her name was Mary, she called me Mary too.
She wasn't gay or airy, but plain as she could be;
I hate to meet a fairy who calls herself Marie.

*Chorus:*   For it is Mary, Mary, plain as any name can be;
But with propriety, society will say Marie;
But it was Mary, Mary, long before the fashions came,
And there is something there that sound so square,
It's a grand old name.

Now, when her name is Mary, there is no falseness there;
When to Marie she'll vary, she'll surely bleach her hair.
Though Mary's ordinary, Marie is fair to see;
Don't ever fear sweet Mary, beware of sweet Marie.
*Chorus:*

Similar in shape and content is "Come, Josephine, in My Flying Machine" (1910) by Fred Fisher and Alfred Bryan,[28] in which the experience of flying is described in two verses but not made into a drama with developing dangers and a safe resolution. And the next generation of Tin Pan Alley songwriters, led by Irving Berlin, took the two-verse shape as the norm. Berlin's "The Girl on the Magazine Cover" (1915)[29] and "Mandy" (1919)[30] are among his most successful songs of this sort, in two quite different moods and rhythms. And songs of the World War I era, including the antiwar "I Didn't Raise My Boy to Be a Soldier" (1915, by Al Piantadosi and Alfred Bryant),[31] George M. Cohan's super-patriotic "Over There" (1917),[32] and the postwar favorite "My Buddy" (1922, Walter Donaldson and Gus Kahn) conform to the same format.

It is not altogether clear why the narrative-dramatic song with three or more verses gave way to the two-verse "situation" pattern, but surely technology played some role. Phonograph discs (or cylinders) could record only three or four minutes of music; early Tin Pan Alley songs with many verses took considerably longer to perform, and in recordings it was necessary for one or more verses to be omitted. A songwriter hoping to have his products recorded had good reason to create a piece that would last no more than three minutes.

The 1920s brought further deemphasis of the verse, which was now often only half the length of the chorus and was even more clearly of an introductory nature:

[28] NW 233, s1 / 6.
[29] NW 233, s1 / 2.
[30] NW 238, s1 / 2.
[31] NW 222, s1 / 2.
[32] NW 222, s1 / 4.

Wishing is good time wasted, still it's a habit they say;
Wishing for sweets I've tasted, that's all I do all day.
Maybe there's nothing in wishing, but, speaking of wishing I'll say:

*Chorus:*  Nothing could be finer than to be in Carolina in the morning,
No-one could be sweeter than my sweetie when I meet her in the morning.
Where the morning glories twine around the door,
Whispering pretty stories I long to hear once more.
Strolling with my girlie where the dew is pearly early in the morning.
Butterflies all flutter up and kiss each little buttercup at dawning.
If I had Aladdin's lamp for only a day,
I'd make a wish and here's what I'd say:

Nothing could be finer than to be in Carolina in the morning.

Dreaming was meant for nighttime, I live in dreams all the day;
I know it's not the right time, but still I dream away.
What could be sweeter than dreaming, just dreaming and drifting away.[33]

*Chorus:* Nothing could be finer, *etc.*

John Steele recorded Irving Berlin's "A Pretty Girl is Like a Melody" in 1919 with the first verse (of 16 measures), the chorus (32 measures, in *ABAC* form), then another run-through of the chorus. The second verse is simply omitted—given the limited time available on a disc, two chorus were deemed more important.[34] Al Jolson recorded "April Showers" (1921, Louis Silvers and Bud G. De Sylvia) in just the same way, with a first verse (of a mere 8 measures), a chorus (again 32 measures in *ABAC* shape), and then a second chorus in which Jolson, in venerable vaudeville style, delivers the text in a semisinging style. Again the second verse was considered expendable.[35]

Gene Austin's recording of "My Blue Heaven" (1927, Walter Donaldson and George Whiting) underlines the increasing dominance of the chorus as the Tin Pan Alley era reached its midpoint. The verse is only 8 measures, the chorus 32 (*AABA*); a second chorus gives the melody of the first two phrases to a cello, then Austin sings the last two phrases; a third chorus follows, this time with whistling dominating the first two phrases and the singer returning for the last two. The second verse is never heard, even though three choruses were fitted on the disc.[36]

[33] "Carolina in the Morning" (1922), by Walter Donalson and Gus Kahn.
[34] This performance is available on NW 238, s1 / 3.
[35] NW 279, s1 / 2.
[36] NW 279, s2 / 5.

By the end of the decade, the verse was disappearing altogether from many recorded performances. It was sometimes relegated to instruments: a version of "Deep Night" (1929, by Charlie Henderson and Rudy Vallee) by Rudy Vallee and His Connecticut Yankees begins with a 32-measure chorus (*AABA*) played by the band; the verse functions as an instrumental break: then another full chorus is sung by Vallee.[37] Performances of Tin Pan Alley songs by jazz bands usually ignored the verse in favor of a string of choruses, as can be heard in a performance of "Ain't Misbehavin' " (1929, by Thomas Waller, Harry Brooks and Andy Razaf) by Louis Armstrong and His Orchestra, with three choruses—the first by the band, the second with Armstrong singing, the third featuring Armstrong on trumpet.[38]

The verse had lost its dramatic function; the typical song had become a vignette, developing a single, simple emotional situation, usually summed up in the title:

[The title] encompasses the grand idea, the crux of the obsession, the thought; it all goes into that; that is, somehow, the bringing together of all of it; that's what hits first, that's what's way back in your mind brought together in sharp focus: the title hits like a bullet, and if it's right, there you have it, all of it, ready to go, in a succinct package—all the crazy, unconscious groping has merged into something real.[39]

Choruses were now almost always written in four eight-measure phrases, shaped into such patterns as *AABA, ABAB, AABC,* or *ABAC.* Even the dramatic shape of these four phrases became more or less stereotyped:

State your theme in the first eight bars—which should include the title. Then amplify in the next eight bars. Then build further in your next eight bars. And then come in strong with punch line and title again. These are the fundamental rules, as a study of the standards will disclose.[40]

Most of the songs of the 1930s and '40s adhere to these patterns. For example, the title "Blue Moon" (1934, by Richard Rodgers and Lorenz Hart) epitomizes the dramatic-emotional content; it is imbedded in the first, second, and fourth phrases of the song; a climax occurs in the third phrase:

[37] NW 279, s2 / 6.
[38] NW 279, s2 / 7.
[39] Johnny Mercer, as quoted in Henry Kane, *How to Write a Song* (New York: Avon Books, 1962), p. 85.
[40] Kane, p. 217.

1st phrase  Blue Moon, you saw me standing alone
           Without a dream in my heart,
           Without a love of my own.

2nd phrase  Blue Moon, you knew just what I was there for,
           You heard me saying a pray'r for
           Someone I really could care for.

3rd phrase  And then there suddenly appeared before me
           The only one my arms will ever hold;
           I heard somebody whisper "Please adore me,"
           And when I looked, the moon had turned to gold!

4th phrase  Blue Moon, now I'm no longer alone
           Without a dream in my heart,
           Without a love of my own.

In a typical performance from the time, by Connee Boswell,[41] there is no trace of a verse but merely two choruses. Hart did indeed write two verses, but the chorus is self-sufficient. Except in performances on stage, and sometimes in nightclubs by singers who liked to take advantage of whatever dramatic and vocal differences there still existed between verse and chrous, the verse effectively disappeared from Tin Pan Alley song in the 1930s.

The transformation of the Tin Pan Alley song from its original verse-chorus structure to chorus alone was completed in the early 1930s when songwriters themselves began turning out verseless pieces. Both "Smoke Gets in Your Eyes" and "Yesterdays" from *Roberta* of 1933 (Jerome Kern and Otto Harbach) were written without a single verse, and another "evergreen" from the same year, "Stormy Weather" (Harold Arlen and Ted Koehler), likewise consists of only a chorus:

Don't know why there's no sun up in the sky,
Stormy weather,
Since my gal and I ain't together, keeps rainin' all the time.

Life is bare, gloom and mis'ry ev'rywhere,
Stormy weather,
Just can't get my poor self together, I'm weary all the time.

When she went away the blues walked in and met me.
If she stays away old rockin' chair will get me.
All I do is pray the Lord above will let me walk in the sun once more.

Can't go on, ev'rything I had is gone,
Stormy weather,
Since my gal and I ain't together, keeps rainin' all the time.

[41] NW 248, s1 / 5.

The lyrics were written so that an introductory or explanatory verse is unnecessary. In a typical contemporary recording made by Leo Reisman and His Orchestra with the composer himself as vocalist,[42] the band takes a complete chorus and the singer follows with another; since there was a bit of time left to fill out the disc, the last eight-measure phrase is repeated.

A song written for stage or screen would be more likely to have a verse. Oscar Hammerstein, for instance, one of the most successful lyricists of the time who wrote mostly for the musical stage in collaboration with Jerome Kern or Richard Rodgers, clung to an introductory verse even into the 1950s. Typical is "It Might as Well Be Spring" for the movie *State Fair*, with music by Rodgers:

> The things I used to like I don't like any more,
> I want a lot of other things I've never had before.
> It's just like mother says, I "sit around and mope,"
> Pretending I am wonderful and knowing I'm a dope.

> *Chorus:*  I'm as restless as a willow in a windstorm,
> I'm as jumpy as a puppet on a string.
> I'd say that I had spring-fever,
> But I know it isn't spring.

> I am starry-eyed and vaguely discontented,
> Like a nightingale without a song to sing
> Oh, why should I have spring-fever
> When it isn't even spring?

> I keep wishing I were somewhere else,
> Walking down a strange new street,
> Hearing words I have never heard
> From a girl I've yet to meet.

> I'm as busy as a spider spinning day dreams,
> I'm as giddy as a baby on a swing.
> I haven't seen a crocus or a rosebud, or a robin on the wing,
> But I feel so gay in a melancholy way
> That it might as well be spring,
> It might as . . . well be . . . spring.

The emphasis on big-band performance that marked most of the 1930s was an ever further deterrent to the inclusion of a verse; and the singers who dominated the last decade of Tin Pan Alley—Frank Sinatra, Doris Day, Perry Como, Eddie Fisher—were interested chiefly in projecting lyric, melodic lines and thus had no interest in narrative-dramatic verses. This brought about the final demise of the verse in Tin Pan Alley song.

[42] NW 248, s1 / 1.

Through its half-century of existence, Tin Pan Alley song was flavored musically by changing patters of American dance.

Most successful songs written in the 1890s were in waltz rhythm. The reasons for the great popularity of the waltz-song at just this time are not altogether clear. The dance had first swept over Europe—and the rest of the Western world—in the late eighteenth century, and had retained some popularity for more than a century. Perhaps the increasing popularity of German dance music in the United States after the Civil War as part of the dominance of Germanic music during this period contributed to the new surge in popularity of the waltz at the end of the century; perhaps the popular success of the Strauss operettas was a factor. Whatever, the fortunes of the early Tin Pan Alley publishers were built on melodramatic or sentimental songs moving along in 3/4 time:

"The Band Played On," by Charles E. Ward

Harmonies were simple and mostly diatonic, in the style of the popular (as opposed to concert) waltz of the nineteenth century.

Songs of this sort continued to be written into the twentieth century. "A Bird in a Gilded Cage" (1900, Von Tilzer) sold more than 2,000,000 copies of sheet music in the year following its publication; "The Mansion of Aching Hearts" (1902, Von Tilzer), "Meet Me in St. Louis, Louis" (1904, Kerry Mills), and "My Gal Sal" (1905, the last hit song by Paul Dresser) were all waltz-songs.

By this time, however, a new rhythm was beginning to dominate Tin Pan Alley song. The minstrel show spawned a final product, the "coon song," with simple syncopated patterns believed to be characteristic of black music. Among the first of these were Jacob J. Sawyer's "The Coon Dinner" (1882) and J. S. Putnam's "New Coon in Town" (1883). The genre peaked in the 1890s with Ernest Hogan's "All Coons Look Alike to Me" (1896), Barney Fagan's "My Gal Is a High Born Lady" (1896),[43] and the "Bully Song" introduced by May Irving—the most famous "coon shouter" of the day—in a show called *The Widow Jones* which opened in New York at the Bijou Theatre in 1895. The composer, a sportswriter named Charles E. Trevathan, claimed to have heard it performed by a black singer named Mama Lou in St. Louis.

> I'm a Tennessee nigger, and I don't allow
> No red-eyed roustabout with me to raise a row.
> I'm looking for dat bully and I'll make him bow.
>
> I went to a wingin' down at Parson Jones',
> Took along my trusty blade to carve dat nigger's bones.
> Just a'lookin' for dat bully to hear his groans.[44]

Reaction to the crudity and racism of the "coon song" was a factor in the emergence of a related genre, the ragtime song, which retained the same sort of music but used less offensive texts. The first popular hit in this style was "Hello! Ma Baby" (1899) by Joe Howard and Ida Emerson. A vignette of a courtship carried out over the telephone, the use of dialect in the lyrics and the illustration on the sheet-music cover make it clear that the protagonists are black:

> I'se got a little baby, but she's out of sight,
> I talk to her across the telephone;
> I'se never seen my honey but she's mine all right;
> So take my tip, an' leave this gal alone.

[43] NW 265, s2/1.
[44] NW 221, s1/8.

Sheet music cover of "Hello Ma Baby."

But there is nothing particularly offensive or racist in the portrayal of the two characters, with the exception of a single use of the word "coon."[45] Musically, rhythmic patterns suggesting the

[45] NW 272, s1 / 2.

cakewalk or the just-emerging ragtime style make it indistinguishable from contemporary "coon songs."

"Hello! Ma Baby," by Joseph E. Howard

"Hel-lo! ma ba - by, Hel-lo! ma hon-ey, Hel-lo! ma rag-time gal,

"Hello! Ma Baby" generated a flood of songs sharing its general
characteristics. 1902 brought Hugh Cannon's "Bill Bailey, Won't
You Please Come Home?" and Bob Cole's "Under the Bamboo
Tree." Rhythmic syncopation quickly became so fashionable that
songs making no reference to blacks would use it—Joe Howard's
"Good Bye, My Lady Love" (1904) and "Waiting for the Robert E.
Lee" (1912, Lewis A. Muir) are examples. By the time Irving Berlin
wrote his first songs, ragtime was all the rage, not only in rhythmic
patterns but even in song titles: "Yiddle on Your Fiddle, Play Some
Ragtime" (1909), "Stop That Rag" (1910), "Oh, That Beautiful Rag"
(1910), and of course "Alexander's Ragtime Band" (1911) were
among his first successful songs.

Popular song became even more permeated with syncopated
dance rhythms in the second decade of the century, with the introduction of new dances—the foxtrot, turkey trot, tango, bunny hug—
all in duple or quadruple meter and all featuring syncopated
rhythm. Songwriters quickly adopted the new rhythmic patterns,
and the characteristic instrumentation—stressing saxophones,
clarinets, and trumpets rather than strings and the softer winds—
of the syncopated dance bands of Jim Europe, Ford Dabney, and
W. C. Handy began permeating the sound of orchestras accompanying singers. This seems to have happened first with novelty songs,
having texts related to "modern" events,[46] and with black performers. Bert Williams, the first black to appear in an otherwise
all-white Broadway show, recorded a number of songs backed by
a studio orchestra playing in syncopated style,[47] and the success of
the musical show *Shuffle Along*, written, produced, and performed

[46] Cf. "Take Your Girlie to the Movies" (1919), on NW 233, s1 / 8.
[47] Cf. his performance of "Everybody Wants a Key to My Cellar" (1919), on NW
233, s1 / 7.

by blacks, created even more of a taste for syncopation. A number of songs from *Shuffle Along* enjoyed brisk phonograph sales: "In Honeysuckle Time" and "Gee, I'm Glad That I'm from Dixie," as recorded by Noble Sissle and His Orchestra[48] illustrate the syncopated dance sound of the day.

The popular music industry was still centered in New York, and the fact that bands accompanying Tin Pan Alley songs in the 1920s were flavored by jazz had a great deal to do with the increased contact between black and white musicians. Even though New York was still a segregated society, like the rest of the United States, it became fashionable for whites to attend events in Harlem, and many white musicians, among them George Gershwin, Harold Arlen, and other Tin Pan Alley songwriters, heard jazz played by the best black Jazzmen of the day. Jazz flavored Tin Pan Alley songs of the 1920s at every level: syncopated rhythms became more and more common:

"Sweet Georgia Brown," by Ben Bernie, Maceo Pinkard, and Kenneth Casey

lyrics took on a new light-hearted, gently humorous quality;[49] and the sound of trumpets and other favorite jazz instruments became characteristic of the decade.[50] White singers imitated the style of

[48] NW 260, s1 / 2 and s2 / 3.
[49] Cf. "Yes Sir, That's My Baby" by Walter Donaldson and Gus Kahn (1925), on NW 279, s2 / 3.
[50] Cf. "Deed I do," as sung by Ruth Etting on NW 279, s1 / 7.

blacks, and recordings were made with the accompaniment of jazz piano alone; Irving Berlin's "It All Belongs to Me," as recorded in 1927 by Ruth Etting,[51] and W. Benton Overstreet's "There'll Be Some Changes Made," as recorded in 1927 by Sophie Tucker,[52] are examples of this new jazz-flavored style.

But the songs themselves didn't change. They still were written in verse-chorus form, still dealt with vignettes concerned with some aspect of romantic love, still were shaped in conventional Tin Pan Alley song forms. "Sunday," as recorded in 1926 by Cliff Edwards and His Hot Combination,[53] features some of the best white jazz-men of the era, including Red Nichols (cornet) and Jimmy Dorsey (saxophone and clarinet). The song, however, consists of a brief verse setting the situation, then a 32-measure chorus in *AABA* form; in this performance the chorus is done three times, first with voice, then instrumentally (allowing several of the players to take brief solos), then once again with voice.

Jazz-flavored songs persisted into the early 1930s; "On the Sunny Side of the Street" (1930) by Jimmy McHugh and Dorothy Fields in a classic of the genre.[54] But the emergence of the sound film contributed another change in the sound of the Tin Pan Alley song. Almost from the beginning, Hollywood opted for spectacle, opulence, and entertainment rather than dramatic intensity or social relevance; and with the onset of the Great Depression the film industry judged that Americans would respond to images on the "silver screen" of the very things they could not have. Films stressed wealth, travel, fashionable society, lavish sets and costumes, wildly extravagant production numbers. A large orchestra with massed strings, approaching the instrumentation of a symphony orchestra, seemed in keeping with the image Hollywood had chosen to project. Accordingly 1929 brought a new sound to the Tin Pan Alley song, a string-dominated accompaniment. One can hear this in "If I Had a Talking Picture of You" from the film *Sunny Side Up* (1929), starring Janet Gaynor (who sang this song) and Charles Farrell.[55] Al Jolson sang, in *Mammy* (1930), to the accompaniment of an orchestra containing more strings than he had ever encountered before.[56] And with new electrical microphones and pickups, a balance could be achieved in both recordings and live performances between such large orchestras and even small voices, such as that

[51] NW 238, s1 / 6.
[52] NW 279, s2 / 1.
[53] NW 279, s2 / 2.
[54] NW 215, s2 / 2.
[55] NW 233, s2 / 8.
[56] Cf. his singing of "Let Me Sing and I'm Happy" from this film, on NW 238, s2 / 1.

of Ginger Rogers,[57] and even the seven-year-old Shirley Temple singing "On the Good Ship Lollipop" in the film *Bright Eyes* (1934).[58]

Once again the Tin Pan Alley song proved durable and versatile enough to survive the switch to a new medium and a new style of accompaniment. The chief difference is one of mood: songs written for movies tend to be more lyric and sentimental than those of the "jazzy" decade of the 1920s. One can see this trend in the songs of individual songwriters; most of George Gershwin's rhythmic, jazz-influenced songs were written before he went to Hollywood ("Swanee" in 1919, "Fascinating Rhythm" in 1924, "I Got Rhythm" in 1930, "Clap Yo' Hands" in 1926, "Strike up the Band" in 1927); typical of his Hollywood songs are "A Foggy Day" from *Damsel in Distress* (1937), and "Love Walked In" from *The Goldwyn*

Ethel Merman and the chorus in the Gershwin's *Girl Crazy*, 1930. (Billy Rose Theatre Collection, the New York Public Library at Lincoln Center, Astor, Lenox and Tilden foundations)

[57] Cf. her singing of Irving Berlin's "Cheek to Cheek" from the movie *Top Hat* (1935), on NW 238, s2 / 7.
[58] NW 270, s1 / 6.

*Follies* (1938).[59] In fact, a more lyric mood seemed to radiate from Hollywood back to New York, and many songs of the 1930s are more mellow in style and in performance than had been the case in the previous decade.[60]

Fred Waring, Rudy Vallee, and particularly the Casa Loma Orchestra (formed in 1929) continued to perform and record with a sound dominated by brass, reed, and rhythm. They usually featured a mixture of vocal and instrumental music; often the band would take a first chorus, then accompany a singer on a second.[61] Sometimes the band would play a piece alone;[62] but even in the latter case the composition was usually a Tin Pan Alley song, or more precisely the 32-measure chorus of such a song, played several times to allow the several sections of the band and perhaps a soloist or two to be heard to best advantage. And in the mid-1930s a rash of new bands appeared, featuring arrangements similar to those of a cresting wave of black bands—Count Basie, Fletcher Henderson, Jimmie Lunceford, Benny Carter—playing in a style called "swing."

The bands were indeed big, with trumpet, trombone, reed, and rhythm sections of as many as five players each; some bands added string sections. It was instrumentally oriented music, no question about it.

But the Tin Pan Alley song survived even this. The big-band repertory consisted almost entirely of songs in the now-venerable verse-chorus format—though in performance the 32-measure chorus dominates. The big bands had one or more vocalists; most performances alternated between vocal and instrumental choruses. Arrangers showed considerable ingenuity in juggling vocal, sectional, and solo emphasis within the three-minute time frame imposed by the phonograph disc. One can hear all this in a recording made by Johnny Long and His Orchestra of Harry Warren's "No Love, No Nothin' " in 1943: a brief introduction features the sound of the entire band; the first 32-measure chorus is instrumental, with a trumpet solo dominating the first 8 measures, the brass and reed sections the second phrase, a saxophone solo the third, and the entire band joining in the final 8 measures; the vocalist, Patti Dugan, takes a 32-measure chorus, backed by the band; and

[59] NW 270, s1 / 5.

[60] Cf. "Once in a While" (1939), by Michael Edwards and Bud Breen, as performed by Martha Raye, on NW 248, s2 / 4.

[61] Cf. the performance of "Deep Night" by Rudy Vallée and his Connecticut Yankees, on NW 279, s2 / 6.

[62] Cf. "In the Still of the Night" in an instrumental performance by the Casa Loma Orchestra, on NW 270, s1 / 4.

a coda based on the final 8-measure phrase brings the singer and the entire band together in a rousing ending.[63] Similarly, a performance of "The White Cliffs of Dover" by Glenn Miller and His Orchestra[64]—the most popular big band of the war years—has an introduction for the entire band, an instrumental performance of the first two 8-measure phrases of the song featuring muted brass in the first and reeds in the second, a full 32-measure chorus by the vocalist, and an 8-measure instrumental ending with prominent saxophone and piano.

By now the Tin Pan Alley song was almost half a century old, yet it had enough vitality to withstand one final change in musical style. Inexplicably, swing decreased in popularity as World War II drew to a close. Increasingly a song recorded by one of the favorite singers of the day, Bing Crosby or Dick Haymes, for instance, would be released under the name of the singer and not the accompanying band. And late in 1943 a disc having nothing whatsoever to do with either swing style or big bands—the Mills Brothers' recording of Johnny S. Black's "Paper Doll"—not only became the best-selling song of the year, but the greatest commercial success of the entire decade. It remained on the *Billboard* charts for a total of 30 weeks, longer than any other disc of the 1940s or 1950s; it eventually sold more than 10,000,000 copies. A typical Tin Pan Alley product in structure and substance, it was almost totally voice-dominated, with the three singers backed by a jazz-flavored rhythm section of guitar, piano, and bass. Nothing could have been a more dramatic change from the sound of a big band.

Big bands lingered on for another five years, steadily losing ground to the emerging big singers—Bing Crosby, Perry Como, Eddie Fisher, Jo Stafford, Vaughn Monroe, Dinah Shore, Doris Day, Patti Page, the Andrews Sisters, Nat "King" Cole, Frank Sinatra. Tommy Dorsey had a hit record as late as 1949 ("The Huckle-buck"), Freddy Martin occasionally had a moderately successful disc into the early 1950s. But the decade beginning in 1945 was dominated by the voice, with bands once again relegated to an accompanying role, rarely taking more than an introduction or at best a half-chorus without the singer.

Instrumental accompaniments for singers varied widely. Some emulated the Mills Brothers, using little more than a rhythm section for support; some retained the characteristic brass-wind sound of the big bands. But many preferred the string-dominated sound of the Hollywood-Broadway tradition, and by the 1950s Frank Sin-

[63] NW 222, s2 / 7.
[64] NW 270, s2 / 8.

Frank Sinatra preparing for a recording session, 1947. (© William P. Gottlieb)

atra and others were accompanied by bands approaching small symphony orchestras in instrumentation and sound, with lush arrangements by Nelson Riddle and David Raskin that went beyond even the Hollywood style of the 1930s. None of these singers had voices, or singing styles, capable of being heard against such an array of instruments. But amplification and microphone placement, in both live performance and recording studios, enabled engineers to balance intimate singing styles with a full, rich instrumental sound produced by thirty or more players.

This technology had its roots in the mid-1920s, with the development of electrical pickups, microphones, and amplification. Early radio performers had discovered that by singing directly into a microphone, they could project even a small, intimate voice. "Gimme a Little Kiss, Will Ya, Huh?" (1926)[65] as sung by "Whispering" Jack Smith illustrates not only this new singing style, but also a new variety of Tin Pan Alley song springing up in response to new technology, more intimate and personal in its lyrics.

It was this intimacy of singing style, and of song style, that was picked up again in the postwar era. With the aid of increasingly sophisticated sound systems, the big singers projected songs of personal anguish, affection, love, and minor tragedy. No longer fettered by having to share the spotlight with a band and no longer restricted in their expressiveness by the necessity of maintaining the inflexible pulse of swing, they could now interpret in highly personal styles the pathos and sentimentality of the lyrics they were given to sing—slowing down the tempo if emotion seemed to demand it, "crooning" and even whispering the words if dramatic context justified it, pausing for melodramatic effect, lingering on climactic notes. Amplification captured every vocal nuance; the band was there to accompany them in whatever rhythmic eccentricities they elected.

But something was missing which had been part of earlier Tin Pan Alley song: there was no connection with dance music. Dancers did what they could, clinging to one another and shuffling slowly around the floor. But there was no vitality to the music, no spark, no rhythmic life.

Tin Pan Alley music was vulnerable, and was soon to succumb to a new music bursting with rhythm, movement, and life—and having nothing to do with the city of New York.

[65] NW 279, s1 / 6.

# 14

## *Soulful Singing and Syncopated Dance Music; or, The Roots of Jazz*

The Civil War brought legal freedom from slavery to black Americano, but little else at first. Cast adrift in a largely hostile society, without effective leadership, mostly nonliterate in an age moving rapidly toward high technology, skilled only in manual labor, they nevertheless made significant progress in the half-century between freedom and the outbreak of World War I.

This progress is epitomized in music. In this fifty-year span they forged several types of the most dynamic, expressive, and commercially successful music yet produced in the New World. In an age which saw white composers groping for means to make their music characteristically American, several generations of black musicians created a body of music accepted in virtually every part of the world as reflective of cultural elements distinctive to the United States.

In the first flush of enthusiasm, upon learning of their emancipation and identifying their liberators as the armies of the North, many freed slaves gravitated toward the Union armies.

They flocked in upon the line of march by bridle-paths and across the fields; old men on crutches, babies on their mothers' backs; women wearing the cast-off jackets of Yankee cavalry-men, boys in abbreviated trousers of rebel gray; sometimes lugging a bundle of household goods snatched from their cabins as they fled, sometimes riding an old mule "borrowed" from "mas'r," but oftener altogether empty-handed, with

**373**

nothing whatever to show for their life-time of unrewarded toil. But they were *free;* and with what swinging of ragged hats, and tumult of rejoicing hearts and fervent "God bless you's," they greeted their deliverers! "The year of jubilee," of which they had sung and for which they had prayed and waited so many years had come at last![1]

But neither this army nor its government was geared, politically or economically, to offer sustained assistance to the four million or so former slaves. Their chief advocates were private and religious organizations in the North, including the American Missionary Association, established in 1846 to sustain educational missions in Africa, the Caribbean, and the American South. Within several years there were seventeen schools for the general education of blacks throughout the South, and seven institutions were chartered for collegiate and theological education.

Fisk University—one of the seven—was opened in Nashville in January of 1866 with an enrollment of one thousand students. Its staff was white and Northern; typical was the treasurer, George L. White. In addition to his administrative tasks, he organized and directed a college chorus, which gave its first public concert in the spring of 1867. The repertory consisted of arrangements of popular and sacred songs, including many by Stephen Foster, and soon the singers were skillful enough to perform classical selections as well; their proudest achievement was Handel's *Esther.* White also allowed them to sing some of "their" music: arrangements (in four-part triadic and tonal harmonizations) of songs remembered from their childhood days in slavery. In time these "spirituals" formed the core of their repertory.

Within several years of its founding, Fisk faced an acute financial crisis. The chorus had attracted large and enthusiastic audiences to its public concerts, both in Nashville and away from home; now it set off on an extended tour, hoping to raise funds to sustain the school. In the words of W. E. B. Dubois, the black author, lecturer and political leader who began his education there:

So in 1871 the pilgrimage of the Fisk Jubilee Singers began. North to Cincinnati they rode—four half-clothed black boys and five girl-women—led by a man with a cause and a purpose. They stopped at Wilberforce, the oldest of Negro schools, where a black bishop blessed them. Then they went, fighting cold and starvation, shut out of hotels, and cheerfully sneered at, ever northward; and ever the magic of their song kept thrilling hearts, while a burst of applause in the Congregational Church at Oberlin revealed them to the world. They came to New York and Henry Ward Beecher dared to welcome them, even though the metro-

[1] J. B. T. Marsh, *The Story of the Jubilee Singers: with their Songs* (Boston: Houghton, Osgood and Company, 1880), p. 4.

The Fisk Jubilee Singers.

politan dailies sneered at his "Nigger Minstrels." So their songs conquered till they sang across the land and across the sea, before Queen
and Kaiser, in Scotland and Ireland, Holland and Switzerland. Seven
years they sang, and brought back a hundred and fifty thousand dollars
to Fisk University.[2]

Their success spurred emulation. In 1872 a student choir was
formed at Hampton Institute in Virginia, singing similar arrangements of spirituals and jubilee songs[3] under the direction of Thomas
P. Fenner. Other black schools followed suit, professional groups
began offering programs of spirituals (the McAdoo Jubilee Singers,
for instance), and professional minstrel shows added "minstrel-
spirituals" to their shows.[4] Collections of spirituals appeared in
print, arranged for chorus and sometimes for solo voice with piano
accompaniment;[5] the first of these were the work of the white lead-

[2] W. E. B. DuBois, *The Souls of Black Folk* (Chicago: McClurg, 1903), pp. 379–80.
[3] The term "jubilee song" was sometimes used to refer to songs of a joyful nature,
as opposed to the more solemn spirituals.
[4] Charles Hamm, *Yesterdays. Popular Song in America* (New York: W. W. Norton
& Company, 1979), pp. 272–73.
[5] Theodore F. Seward, *Jubilee Songs: As Sung by the Jubilee Singers of Fisk University* (New York: Biglow & Main c. 1872); Thomas P. Fenner, *Cabin and Plantation
Songs as Sung by the Hampton Students* (New York and London: G. P. Putnam's
Sons, 1874); Marsh, *The Story of the Jubilee Singers.* Cf. Fenner, p. iii: "There are
evidently, I think, two legitimate methods of treating this music: either to render
it in its rude simplicity, or to develop it without destroying its original characteristics; the only proper field for such development being in the harmony."

ers of the several black Jubilee college choruses, but in time, the first black instructor of music at Fisk—John Wesley Work, Sr.—and other black musicians (Harry Burleigh, R. Nathaniel Dett, James W. Johnson) arranged and published spirituals in essentially the same style.

Millions of Americans had their first sympathetic response to the new black citizens of their country through these songs. But it was black music filtered through white culture. Texts, melodic material and the expressive character of the spiritual grew out of the black religious experience. Texts were adapted from the Bible:

> Five of them were wise when the bridegroom came,
> Five of them were wise when the bridegroom came,
> O Zion, O Zion, O Zion, when the bridegroom came.
>
> Five of them were foolish when the bridegroom came,
> Five of them were foolish when the bridegroom came,
> O Zion, O Zion, O Zion, when the bridegroom came.
>
> ("The Ten Virgins")[6]

from spiritual songs by Isaac Watts and his peers:

> Oh, the land I am bound for,
> Sweet Canaan's happy land I am bound for,
> Sweet Canaan's happy land,
> Pray give me your right hand.
>
> '("Sweet Canaan")[7]

from popular abolitionist and temperance songs:

> The gospel train is coming,
> I hear it just at hand,
> I hear the car wheels moving,
> And rumbling thro' the land.
>
> Get on board, children,
> Get on board, children,
> Get on board, children,
> For there's room for many a more.
>
> ("The Gospel Train")[8]

and from a variety of other sources. These texts had as a common denominator the plight of oppressed people and their longing for

[6] Marsh p. 159.
[7] Marsh p. 243.
[8] Marsh p. 150. The text of this song is based on a famous abolitionist song of the Hutchinson Family, "Get Off the Track."

freedom, and they had been transformed into language reflecting the characteristic rhythms, turn of phrase, and inflections of English as spoken at the time by the American black.

But the harmonizations of these spirituals reflect white musical practice, and forcing them into musical notation robs them of one of their most distinctive features—a flexible, complex rhythmic character rooted in rhythmic tradition more sophisticated than that of European music. ("The first peculiarity that strikes the attention is in the rhythm. This is often complicated, and sometimes strikingly original. (But) its irregularities invariably conform to the 'higher law' of the perfect rhythmic flow."[9]) One can observe this process of simplification by comparing a recording of spirituals performed by rural blacks relatively untouched by white culture[10] with arranged spirituals by classically trained musicians. Nevertheless, even in the latter, reminiscences of African style still peek through, such as call-and-response patterns between a leader and the other singers:

"De Ole Sheep Done Know de Road," from Fenner, *Cabin and Plantation Songs*, p. 26

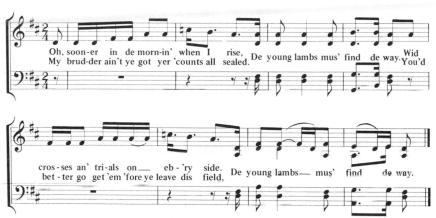

and syncopated rhythmic patterns:

"Nobody Knows the Trouble I See, Lord!" from Marsh, *The Story of the Jubilee Singers*, p. 125

[9] Theodore F. Seward, as quoted in Marsh p. 122.
[10] Cf. NW 278, *Georgia Sea Island Songs*.

No-bod-y knows the trou-ble I see, Lord, No-bod-y knows like Je - sus.

Literacy among blacks progressed slowly and selectively. The eleventh U.S. census, taken in 1890, revealed that only 30 percent of the black population of more than seven million possessed any degree of skill in reading and writing. There thus developed a dual tradition of black church music. Nonliterate blacks, living mostly in the rural South and in ghettos in Southern towns, continued the singing traditions of prewar days: a "shouting" style characterized by call-and-response patterns between a leader and the congregation, improvisatory in nature, accompanied by hand clapping and other percussive sounds, with the choral response often involving improvised polyphony. As W. C. Handy remembered from his childhood:

> The Baptists had no organ in their church and no choir. They didn't need any. The lusty singers sat in the amen corner and raised the songs, raised them as they were intended to be raised, if I'm any judge. None of the dressed-up arrangements one sometimes hears on the concert stage for them. They knew a better way. Theirs was pure rhythm. While critics like to describe their numbers as shouting songs, rhythm was their basic element. And rhythm was the thing that drew me and other members of our home town quartet to attend the Baptist services.[11]

Literate, urban blacks increasingly depended on rehearsed music sung by choirs or smaller vocal groups, indebted in style to arrangements of spirituals popularized by the various jubilee singing groups of the day. Congregational support came as hand clapping and supportive ejaculations, not as singing. Modern black gospel music derives from this stage, though its history is difficult to trace because of the virtual absence of written or recorded documentation.[12] A handful of phonograph discs made by the Dinwiddie Colored Quartet and other groups in the first years of the present century confirm that the harmonically based jubilee style had spread to other areas of black vocal music;[13] field recordings made in the rural South and in Southern prisons in the 1930s and '40s tell us that triadic, tonal vocalizing had extended to orally dissem-

[11] W. C. Handy, *Father of the Blues* (New York: Macmillan Company, 1941), p. 157.
[12] For a history of this era cf. George Robinson Ricks, *Some Aspects of the Religious Music of the United States Negro* (New York: Arno Press, 1977).
[13] Cf. their performance of "Down on the Old Camp Ground," recorded in 1902, on *Folk Music in America*, Vol. 1, s2/1.

inated music and that the male quartet (usually featuring one or two exceptionally high tenor voices) had become a popular medium;[14] commercial recordings made in the 1920s of both sacred and secular music document the vocal and rhythmic viruosity which had become part of these traditions.[15] A flood of recordings by black male gospel quartets in the 1930s and '40s, by the Golden Gate Jubilee Quartet,[16] the Famous Blue Jay Singers,[17] the Kings of Harmony,[18] the Soul Stirrers,[19] and many others, preserve some of the most complex music for small vocal ensemble ever performed, while underlining the successful integration of harmonic and formal aspects of white music into the expression of intensely black religious and musical expression. Other recordings from the same period inform us of the early utilization of instruments in black religious music.[20]

The modern era of gospel music, taken by most scholars to begin with the compositions of C. A. Tindley and Thomas A. Dorsey, falls outside the scope of the present chapter. However, its most important musical impulses were surely derived from spirituals and jubilee songs of the decades leading up to World War I.

It has been said that the blues "represent the full racial expression of the Negro, the expression of the emotional life of a race."[21] This solo secular vocal form took shape at just the time the spiritual was emerging in the postwar South, and like the latter it reflects aspects of African style and expression modified by circumstances of black life in America:

> (The) intensely personal nature of blues-singing is the result of what can be called the Negro's "American experience." African songs dealt, as did the songs of a great many of the preliterate or classical civilizations, with the exploits of the social unit, usually the tribe. There were songs about the gods, their works and lives, about nature and the elements, about the nature of man's life on the earth and what he could expect after he died, but the existence of blues verses on the life of the individ-

---

[14] Cf. "Do You Call that Religion" as recorded in 1934 by a quartet of prisoners at Reed Prison Farm, South Carolina, on *Folk Music in America*, Vol. 1, s2/2.

[15] Cf. "What's the Matter Now?" as recorded by the Monarch Jazz Quartet in 1929, on NW 290, s1/4.

[16] Cf. "What Are They Doing in Heaven Today?," recorded in 1938, on *Folk Music in America*, Vol. 15, s2/3.

[17] Cf. "Canaan Land" (1947) on NW 224, s1/2.

[18] Cf. "God Shall Wipe All Tears Away" (1946) on NW 224, s1/1.

[19] Cf. "Walk Around" (1944) on NW 224, s1/3.

[20] Cf. NW 224, s1/6–7, for several examples.

[21] Handy p. 119. For an excellent general history of the blues, cf. Paul Oliver, *The Story of the Blues* (London: Barrie & Rockliff, 1969).

ual and his individual trials and successes on the earth is a manifestation of the white Western concept of man's life, and it is a development that could only be found in an American black man's music. The whole concept of the *solo*, of a man singing or playing by himself, was relatively unknown in Western African music.[22]

The first stage in the development of the blues is thought to be the "field holler," a spontaneous solo utterance—usually of a plaintive nature—by a worker engaged in nonrhythmic labor (such as picking cotton) or taking a respite from his work. It is quite different from work-songs themselves, which are usually sung by a group of workers, in call-and-response patterns, and are strongly rhythmic, coordinated with the physical activity of hoeing, chopping, pounding, or rowing. Texts are often commentaries on the work being done or complaints on other aspects of the singer's existence:

> Oh, if I ever make it, baby, I be long gone.
>
> Wo, I'm goin' down in Lou'siana, oh, don't you wanna go.
> Wo, I'm goin' down in Lou'siana, don't you wanna go.
> Wo, you look for me in Lou'siana, oh, I be long gone.
> Wo, you look for me in Lou'siana, I be long gone.
>
> Wo, you can tell everybody that I'll be gone.
> Wo, I'll be by to see you 'fore the summer gone.
> Wo, I might be in a hurry, I can't stay very long.[23]

At some point, two developments transformed the field holler into the modern blues. Texts took on a structure of three lines to each stanza, with the second line a repetition or slight variation of the first:

Oh, black night fallin', my pains comin' down again.
Oh, oh, black night fallin', my pains comin' down again.
Oh, I feel so lonesome, oh, I ain't got no frien'.

Oh, oh, just another pain, oh Lord, it hurts so bad.
Mm, just another pain, oh Lord, oh, it hurts so bad.
Lord, I feel so lonesome, baby, lost the best frien' I've ever had.

Oh, sheets and pillow cases torn all to pieces, baby, blood stain all over the wall.
Mm, sheets and pillows torn all to pieces, baby, blood stain all on the wall.

[22] LeRoi Jones, *Blues People* (New York: William Morrow and Company, 1963), p. 66.
[23] NW 252, s1 / 1, as sung by Henry Ratcliff.

Oh, Lord, I wasn't aimin' when I left, baby, and the telephone, wasn't in the hall.[24]

The second factor was the addition of an instrumental accompaniment. It is impossible to reconstruct with certainty the sequence of events, since few recordings were made before the 1920s and the few literary references to the blues before 1900 offer only the most general information. But some commercial recordings made in the 1920s and '30s capture the singing and playing of musicians who apparently performed in a similar style during the first two decades of the century, and field recordings made more recently by blues performers whose style may trace back to the early days of the genre give us material on which to base a speculative chronology.

The guitar was probably the first instrument used to accompany blues singing. In some recordings of the earliest style of accompaniment, it furnishes little more than a rhythmic underpinning to the vocal line, strumming combinations of notes giving no sense of harmonic progression. In a field recording of "Old Original Blues" made by Alan Lomax, performed by Fred McDowell and Miles Pratcher:[25]

Lord, I'm goin' down in Lou'siana, I'm goin' buy me a mojo hand.
Lord, I'm goin' down in Lou'siana, I'm goin' buy me a mojo hand.
I'm goin' fix my baby, so she won't have no other man.

the two guitars play ostinato figures with no sense of changing chords.

A second function of the accompanying guitar was to echo or answer the voice at the ends of vocal phrases. In "Rolled and Tumbled," as performed by Rose Hemphill and Fred McDowell:[26]

Rolled an' I tumbled, cried whole night long.
Rolled an' I tumbled, cried whole night long.
Got up this mornin', didn't know right from wrong.

the guitar plays a dual role: it furnishes a rhythmic accompaniment to the voice, and it acts as a second melodic voice, "singing" along with the vocalist in heterophonic fashion and—when the singer reaches the end of a phrase—continuing and expanding the melodic line on its own.

[24] Harry Oster, *Living Country Blues* (Detroit: Folklore Associates, 1969), p. 184.
[25] NW 252, s1 / 5.
[26] NW 252, s2 / 6.

Gradually, the accompanying guitar assumed the harmonic patterns. In the earliest recordings by blues singers untouched by intervening commercial and urban developments (Blind Lemon Jefferson of Texas and Charley Patton of Mississippi, for instance),[27] we can hear the emergence of standardized progressions for each of the three lines making up a blues stanza:

the first line begins and ends on a tonic chord;
the second line moves to a subdominant chord, then returns to a tonic;
the third line has some sort of dominant harmony at the beginning, and ends on the tonic.

Thus in singing "Po Boy Blues," John Dudley ( a performer in the classic Mississippi blues tradition of Patton and Sun House) underlines his text with the following harmonic scheme:[28]

I'm a poor boy, and I'm great long way from home.
   I _____
I'm a poor boy, and I'm great long way from home.
   I ___ IV _____ I _____
I'm a poor boy, and I'm great long way from home.
   I ___ V _____ IV _____ I _____

And Richard "Rabbit" Brown recorded "James Alley Blues" in New Orleans in 1927 with almost exactly the same chord sequences:

Oh times ain't now nothing like they used to be.
   I _____
No times ain't now nothing like they used to be.
   I ___ IV _____   I
And I'm telling you all the truth, oh take it from me.
   I _____ V _____ IV _____ I

The earliest blues, whether unaccompanied or sung with the support of an instrument, seem to have been irregular in structure. Even after the three-line verse had become the norm, there might be considerable variation in the lengths of lines from verse to verse, the singer might draw out words or syllables with vocal embellishment, and the melodic response by the accompanying instrument was flexible in length. Guitar techniques dependent on strummed chords rather than ostinato figures or melodic lines began bringing

---

[27] Cf. Samuel Charters, *The Bluesmen* (New York: Oak Publications, 1967) and Samuel Charters, *Sweet as the Showers of Rain* (New York: Oak Publications, 1977) for biographical and musical information on the earliest known blues singers of the rural South.
[28] NW 252, s1 /2.

a sense of meter to this music, and the length of all lines began to be equivalent. In Pillie Bolling's performance of "Brownskin Woman" recorded in Atlanta in 1930,[29] the regular strumming of the guitar imparts an almost metronomic unfolding of musical time as the piece progresses; the Western mind, with its tendency to organize beats into simple duple or triple patterns, perceives the piece in 4/4—with some slightly irregular lines:

| | |
|---|---|
| I got a brownskin woman, she's allright with me. | (5-1/2 bars) |
| I got a brownskin woman, she's allright with me. | (4 bars) |
| Got the finest woman that a man most ever seen. | (5 bars) |
| | |
| Lord, I can't stay here, and my lover gone. | (4 bars) |
| Lord, I can't stay here, and my lover gone. | (4-1/2 bars) |
| Sometimes I wonder, my brownskin she won't come home. | (4-1/2 bars) |

The musician is keeping time to a different drumming, of course—one in which the patterns 11–8–10/8–9–9 are not exceptional.

Increasing contact between black and white musicians eventually brought much Afro-American music into the metrical patterns of western Europe, and at the same time the growing practice of singing the blues to the accompaniment of a small ensemble of instruments made it desirable to have a relatively simple rhythmic pattern underlying the form. The blues gradually adapted to a regular 4/4 meter and the length of each line was standardized at four measures. The resulting structure has been given the name of 12-bar blues. The following diagram—of the first verse of "Violin Blues," recorded by the Johnson Boys in 1928 with guitar, violin, and mandolin backing the singer[30]—lays out this form:

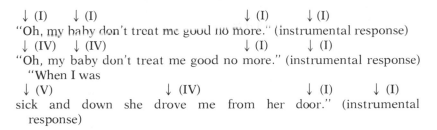

```
↓ (I)     ↓ (I)                    ↓ (I)      ↓ (I)
"Oh, my baby don't treat me good no more." (instrumental response)
↓ (IV)   ↓ (IV)                    ↓ (I)      ↓ (I)
"Oh, my baby don't treat me good no more." (instrumental response)
    "When I was
↓ (V)                  ↓ (IV)              ↓ (I)      ↓ (I)
sick  and  down  she  drove  me  from  her  door."  (instrumental
response)
```

This pattern was taken over into instrumental music as well. Some blues singers began to use the piano as an accompanying instrument, and some pianists began playing solo piano pieces built

[29] NW 290, s1/2.
[30] NW 290, s1/3.

on the 12-bar blues form, repeating the chorus as many times as their imagination and audience permitted, all over the same insistant harmonic pattern:[31]

phrase 1: I     –   –   I    (4 bars)⎫
phrase 2: IV  IV   I   I    (4 bars)⎬12 bars
phrase 3: V  (IV)   I   I    (4 bars)⎭

Virtually none of this music as performed by black musicians was recorded before the 1920s.[32] But we know that the 12-bar blues form had become standardized before this time from scattered discs made by white performers clearly imitating black musicians,[33] and from composed and published songs and pieces of dance music by both black and white musicians from the 1910s incorporating the 12-bar blues pattern into longer pieces.

The first published blues appeared in 1912, among them "Dallas Blues" by Hart Wand and Lloyd Garret and the first version of W. C. Handy's "The Memphis Blues"—written in 1909 as a campaign piece for Edward H. Crump, running for the mayorship of Memphis. Handy's "St. Louis Blues," published in 1914 and probably the most often recorded composition of the entire jazz era, will serve as a demonstration of the relationship between the published blues of this decade and its "folk" form, as described above. The first section is a complete 12-bar blues pattern, the three vocal phrases supported by the standardized harmonic scheme already described; the second section is shaped in the same way, and appears to be merely a second verse of a normal strophic blues. But the third section shifts to a minor key and is cast in a 16-bar (4x4) pattern, with a harmonic pattern having nothing to do with a 12-bar blues form; the fourth section then returns to a 12-bar blues pattern. Handy has thus employed the classic 12-bar blues structure as part of the usual *AABA* form of a Tin Pan Alley song:

*A*      *A*      *B*      *A*
*aab*    *aab*    *cd*    *aab*

and the result bears the same relationship to a "folk" blues as a composed and published ragtime piece by Scott Joplin does to the syncopated dance music played by nonliterate black pianists in

---

[31] For examples of piano pieces from the 1920s based on the 12-bar blues form, cf. NW 259, s1 / 1–5.

[32] Cf. John Godrich and Robert M. W. Dixon, *Blues and Gospel Records, 1902–1942* (London: Storyville, 1969), for a complete listing of early discs.

[33] For instance, cf. "Nigger Blues" as recorded in 1916 by white entertainer George O'Connor, in 12-bar blues form, on NW 290, s1 / 8.

bars and dancehalls in the decades before the first piano rags appeared in print.

Blues are characterized by much more than their formal design, of course. From the first, they seem to have made use of a scale unlike any found in Western music: the third and the seventh degrees may be either major or minor, and, in fact, these two pitches

The blues scale

are treated with subtle inflection often resulting in pitches somewhere between the raised and lowered forms of these notes in Western intonation. Thus, blues make use of a seven-note scale in which five of the notes (1, 2, 4, 5, 6) are similar in intonation to the tempered scale and the other two (3, 7) are unstable. One can hear this in the vocal line of virtually all of the earliest recorded blues:[34]

"Mistreatin' Mamma," as sung by Walter "Furry" Lewis in 1928; from Jeff Todd Titon, *Early Downhome Blues*, No. 43

and also in the guitar accompaniment, in which several methods of "bending" notes were developed: "pulling" the strings with the left hand to give fluctuations in pitch; or using some hard object—a metal bar or a bottleneck, usually—to stop the strings on the fretboard, making it possible to slide from one pitch or chord to another and to play any inflection of a given note.

Though the flatted seventh is found in music of West Africa, the blues scale as such does not exist in music from this part of the world, nor is expressive pitch fluctuation a common feature of West

[34]"Mistreatin' Mamma" as recorded in 1928 by Walter "Furry" Lewis. Transcription taken from Jeff Todd Titon, *Early Downhome Blues* (Urbana: University of Illinois Press, 1977), No. 43.

African music. A recent scholar has suggested that all notes of the blues scale may indeed be found in African music when one takes into consideration the fact that harmonization of a melody in parallel fourths and fifths is common, and the African thus deals with two scales, the one which forms the basis for melody and another used for harmonization.

> When the Negro made his first tentative attempts to combine his African melodic heritage with the European diatonic system, he found that he could readily do so by alternating, as equivalently as in his native land, the two seven-note scales he already knew. At first these attempts must have been somewhat cautious, but by the latter part of the nineteenth century definite patterns in which blues notes were used became established.[35]

Inflected notes were used by blues singers to underline the expressiveness of their texts, and in time this practice spread to instruments used to accompany blues singing, then to purely instrumental music, until it was one of the most distinctive features of the emerging jazz style in the first quarter of the twentieth century.

The most important aspect of the blues, its meaning to the black people of the United States during this excruciatingly difficult time in their history, cannot easily be put into words. All blues texts deal with personal misfortune, of one sort or another; "many maintain one cannot play the music unless one has 'a blue feeling' or 'feels blue,' (and) indeed the blues is considered a perpetual presence in the lives of black Americans and is personified in their music as 'Mister Blues'."[36] Singing or playing the blues was regarded by black Americans as a sort of catharsis: "it is generally understood that a blues performer sings or plays to rid himself of 'the blues.' "[37] On the personal level this music projected the larger problems and sufferings of the entire black race in America and afforded most black Americans "an effective discharge with symptomatic relief but not necessarily a cure of the underlying pathology."[38]

Until the 1920s, the blues remained a true folk music, disseminated orally and the property of a single race. White Americans

[35] Gunther Schuller, *Early Jazz* (New York: Oxford University Press, 1968), p. 46.
[36] Paul Oliver, "Blues," *The New Grove Dictionary of Music and Musicians*, Stanley Sadie, ed. (London: Macmillan Publishers, 1980), II, p. 813.
[37] Oliver, p. 813.
[38] From the definition of "catharsis" in *The American College Dictionary* (New York: Random House, 1947, edited by Clarence L. Barnhart), p. 190.

knew this music only in the last few years of this period, and then only in a somewhat distorted and "whitewashed" form.

It was obvious, early in the nineteenth century that the music sung and played by black slaves possessed a rhythmic character unlike that of any European music.

The first substantial body of printed music purporting to have something to do with the music of the black American was the minstrel song, which came into prominence in the 1920s and '30s. Performers and songwriters were white, for the first half-century of the existence of this curious genre, and though many claimed to have learned their songs and dances from blacks, most of these pieces are characteristic of traditional Anglo-American and Celtic-American music, including pentatonic melodies and the distinctive short-long "Scottish snap":

"De History Ob de World," from *The Ethiopian Glee Book* (1848), p. 126

In fact, many early minstrel songs have been traced to specific traditional tunes from the British Isles.[39]

But that is not all there is to it. The banjo became the most popular instrument of the minstrel stage, and it is certainly of African origin and was first constructed and played in the New World by

[39] Cf. Hans Nathan, *Dan Emmett and the Rise of Early Negro Minstrelsy* (Norman: University of Oklahoma Press, 1962), pp. 159–88.

Sheet music cover for "The Banjo" by Louis Gottschalk.

black slaves. More than that, the oldest style of banjo playing in the minstrel tradition, involving the use of rhythmic-melodic ostinatos, has much more to do with African music than European, and must have been learned from black Americans. Since this instrument and its playing style were taken over from Afro-American culture, it seems likely that melodic and rhythmic patterns from this same tradition found their way into minstrel songs. Once one takes a closer look, one finds features in some early minstrel songs not at all typical of Anglo-American culture. For example, it is not unusual to find a simple extension of the rhythmic peculiarity of the "Scottish snap." But there is a significant difference. The "Scottish snap" involves a single note, falling on a stressed beat, shortened to give a simple rhythmic inversion; its origin lies in language rather than music—it is first found in songs, where it captures the Scottish fondness for a short, clipped first syllable in certain words:

"Annie Laurie" (traditional)

The rhythmic pattern that begins to crop up in many minstrel songs is a purely musical phenomenon, not associated with specific language patterns. It represents a first attempt by the white to capture the rhythmic nature of black music, a simplification of something much more complex.

At just about the same time, Louis Moreau Gottschalk was using similar rhythmic patterns in some of his piano compositions.

*The Banjo*, by Gottschalk

Gilbert Chase, in the most pointed discussed of this matter,[40] reminds us that in his youth, Gottschalk was influenced by the culture and music of the Caribbean Islands, with its mixture of African, Spanish, and French elements.

Slightly later, other types of piano pieces featuring similar rhythmic patterns, and making reference to blacks in their titles or the illustrations on sheet music covers, began to appear. There

[40]Gilbert Chase, *America's Music* (New York: McGraw Hill, 1966), pp. 304–14.

was, for instance, the "patrol," a marchlike composition characterized by a soft beginning, a progressive buildup in dynamic level as the piece reaches its climax, and a final decrescendo. Pieces of this sort bore such titles as *The Hottentots: Patrol Characteristic* (Fred Neddermeyer, 1889). There were also character pieces for performance in the American parlor by amateur pianists, with titles making the same reference to blacks—G. L. Lansing's *The Darkie's Dream* (1891), for instance, in which the ♪♪♪ rhythmic pattern is featured prominently.[41] And beginning in the early 1880s, "coon songs" made use of the same rhythmic motif.

For almost half a century, then, music with either a real or pretended connection with the culture of the American black—minstrel songs and dances, arranged spirituals, "coon songs," a variety of piano pieces—shared a rhythmic figure almost certainly derived from Afro-American music. And at the end of the century this rhythmic impulse became a central feature of a genre that was taken both in this country and abroad as the most characteristic music to emerge from America—ragtime.

One of the dances done on the minstrel stage was the cakewalk, a couples dance featuring high-stepping, strutting antics. It may have originated on plantations in antebellum days, with slaves competing for prizes (perhaps including cakes); some dance historians see it as a descendant of the Ring Shout dance known to have been done by slaves, which in turn traces its ancestry to the African circle dance.[42] It was incorporated into the minstrel show before mid-century as part of the "Walk Around," which served as a finale to the evening's entertainment; by the 1880s it had appeared in several Harrigan and Hart shows; and in the 1890s a number of black dancers, including the team of Bert Williams and George Walker, were featuring it in vaudeville. *Clorindy, the Origin of the Cakewalk*, an all-black show with music by Will Marion Cook which had a successful run on Broadway in 1898, included a sensational production number built around this dance, and at just this time it became popular off stage as well, as a recreational and competitive dance. In well-publicized competitions held in Madison Square Garden and Coney Island, prizes were awarded to the most acrobatic and stylish couples; one held in Chicago in 1898 was described in the press:

[41] Cf. Edward A. Berlin, *Ragtime. A Musical and Cultural History* (Berkeley: University of California Press, 1980), pp. 106–11, for a discussion of this repertory.

[42] Marshall and Jean Stearns, *Jazz Dance. The Story of American Vernacular Dance* (New York: The Macmillan Company, 1968), pp. 122–24.

Mr. Dave White led off with Miss Patty Willow, a very stout colored woman in a ballet dancer's costume made from yellow calico, and behind them seventy-five more couples. From the judge's stand it was a whirl-ing ring of kaleidoscopic colors accompanied by shuffling feet in time to the music. The friends of the walkers stood around the outside and yelled encouragement to the candidates and as the music got into full swing and quickened its time a bit, they began to shuffle and to sway in rhythm. Every walker strained his or her muscles to put in extra steps.[43]

Piano pieces identified in their titles as cakewalks were pub-lished in the 1890s. In form, they were similar to marches and dances of the day: made up of from two to four repeated strains, with the third often contrasting in key and character, forming a "trio." Rhythmically, they resembled the syncopated marches and coon songs of that decade, with pervasive use of the ♫♩ rhythmic pattern. Some published cakewalks incorporated strains from familiar coon songs into their second sections or trios.

A new term for syncopated dance music first appeared in print in 1897, with the publication in Chicago (on January 25) of *Missis-sippi Rag* by the white bandmaster William Krell; the cover iden-tifies the piece further as "The First Rag-Time Two-Step Ever Written and First Played by Krell's Orchestra, Chicago." *Ragtime March* by Warren Beebe came out two days later, and before the year was out pieces identified as "rags" or "ragtime" had appeared in New Orleans, Cincinnati, New York, St. Louis, and elsewhere. In September, Ben Harney's *Rag Time Instructor* was published in New York. Scott Joplin's *Maple Leaf Rag* (1899) became the first great commercial success of the new genre, and the rage for rag-time—which was to last for almost two decades—had hit America.

Ragtime did not represent a new sort of music in its early stages, but was rather the application of a new label to music that had been around for awhile. The first piano pieces identified as rags were virtually identical in style and form with many cakewalks, patrols, syncopated two-steps, and character pieces of the previous decade; rhythmically, they involved nothing more intricate than the sim-ple syncopated figure mentioned repeatedly above. Their titles underline the close associations among the cakewalk, the march (or two-step), and early ragtime: *Carpet Rags—Characteristic March and Two-Step* (Raymond W. Connor, 1903); *Aunt Dinah's Cake Walk—Ragtime March* (William Weidenhammer, 1899); *Timbuctoo March—Ragtime Dream* (E. C. Ramsdell, 1899); *The Ragtime Patrol* (R. J. Hamilton, 1897); *Ragtime Belles—Rag Time March and Dance*

---

[43] From the *Chicago Inter-Ocean* for January 2, 1898, as quoted in Rudi Blesh and Harriet Janis, *They All Played Ragtime* (New York: Oak Publications, 1971), p. 99.

(Alfred Paulsen, 1898). Joplin's *The Entertainer* (1902) is one of many of his pieces identified as a "Rag Time Two Step."

The performance style of ragtime emerged before its literature, as would be the case several decades later with jazz. The World's Columbian Exposition held in Chicago in 1893 brought together many pianists already playing in the characteristic style of ragtime, though no pieces with such a label had yet been published:

> Pianists from all over the central United States converged on the amusement thoroughfare called the Midway, as well as the huge Chicago red-light district that extended from Eighteenth Street to Twenty-second and from Dearborn all the way to the Illinois Central tracks. Few were the players who went unemployed as the thousands of visitors poured into the Windy City, and all amusements, both licit and illicit, flourished.
>
> Joplin formed a small band and went to work straight off in the district. During the exposition year he met the pioneer ragmen in Chicago, among them "Plunk" Henry, named for the banjo he had played earlier and from which he had derived his piano ragtime rhythms.[44]

Ben Harney's *Ragtime Instructor* demonstrates how a pianist may apply ragtime rhythms to popular songs and even hymns, implying that he and other ragtime pianists had played in this way long before the publication of the book. Also,

> (Ben Harney's) performances included the "ragging" of such popular classics as Mendelssohn's *Spring Song*, Rubinstein's *Melody in F*, and *Intermezzo* from Mascagni's "Cavalleria Rusticana," which he would first play in their orthodox form. The effect was startling.[45]

When a body of instrumental ragtime music appeared, in the first decade of the twentieth century, formal patterns emerged, usually similar to those of march and dance music of the day. There was often an introduction, of 4 or 8 measures; the simplest design—found in such classics as *St. Louis Rag* (Thomas Turpin, 1903) and *Wall Street Rag* (Scott Joplin, 1909)—consisted of four strains, each repeated: *AABBCCDD*. A common variation entailed a return of the original strain in the middle of the piece (*AABBACCDD*), as in *Maple Leaf Rag* (Joplin, 1899) and *Pine Apple Rag* (Joplin, 1908). Some rags bring the material of the introduction back again: Joplin's *The Entertainer* (1902) is shaped *Intro AA BB A CC Intro DD*. The third and fourth strains are often in the subdominant,

---

[44] Blesh, p. 41.

[45] Isidore Witmark and Isaac Goldberg, *The Story of the House of Witmark: From Ragtime to Swingtime* (New York: L. Furman, 1939), p. 155.

raising the question of whether or not there should be a return to the first strain at the end, to bring the piece back into the tonic key.[46]

It was rhythm, of course, not formal design, that made ragtime distinctive. From Joplin's earliest published rags, the simple syncopated rhythmic germ alluded to above is expanded and made more complex. It is no longer merely a matter of accents being dislocated within the time span of a quarter note (or a single beat), but over a longer span as well:

*Original Rags*, by Scott Joplin

The Western mind tends to view these as syncopations or dislocations of beats in the upper voice, rhythmic stresses falling just ahead or just after one would expect them. But with what we know about African music, it is possible to see the process of additive rhythms at work, and to see (and hear) the passage as:

*Original Rags*, by Scott Joplin

From this perspective, a famous passage in the *Maple Leaf Rag* would become:

*Maple Leaf Rag*, by Scott Joplin

[46] Cf. Berlin, pp. 89–97, for a discussion of formal structure in piano rags.

There is a very real difference between these two ways of viewing such passages; the difference between smoothly unfolding rhythmic units of twos and threes in one voice, not grouped in regular metrical units, against a steady pulse in the other; and two voices bound by the same meter, with one constantly clashing with certain expected patterns of accent and stress.

Another common rhythmic feature of ragtime, the use of repeated patterns of groups of three eighth notes in the course of the relentlessly duple organization of the notated music, can also be understood as the use of additive rhythms shifting freely between groups of two and of three:

*Black and White Rag*, by George Botsford

The corpus of published ragtime compositions, then, reflects elements of both black and white music of the late nineteenth century. The most characteristic rhythmic impulses come from Afro-American music; the formal patterns and the instrument on which this music was played come from white culture.

The career of Scott Joplin reflects this same mingling of black and white culture. Born in Texas in 1868, the son of a violin-playing ex-slave, he began playing piano in bars and clubs in the Mississippi Valley as a teenager, had instruction in piano and rudimentary music theory from an immigrant German musician, and by 1885 was more or less settled in St. Louis, as one of the piano players at "Honest John" Turpin's Silver Dollar Saloon. After a visit to Chicago in 1893, on the occasion of the World's Columbian Exposition, he established himself in Sedalia, a new, lively, bustling town some seventy-eight miles southeast of Kansas City, finding employment at the Maple Leaf Club owned by the Williams brothers.

The town offered other important attractions for Joplin. He was able to attend the George R. Smith College, for further instruction in musical theory, and there were individuals who became aware of his unusual musical talent and helped him: Marie Walker, owner of a music store in Hannibal, and John Stark, who published his earliest rags.

He also joined the Queen City Concert Band, as a cornettist, and in 1895 he organized the Texas Medley Quartette, arranging popular songs and plantation medleys for them and eventually booking the group on the vaudeville circuit in Missouri, Kansas, Oklahoma, and Texas. In the meanwhile his first published compositions appeared—two sentimental songs ("A Picture of Her Face" and "Please Say You Will," both brought out in 1895), and several marches and waltzes for piano in 1896.

To this point, then, Joplin was operating in two musical worlds simultaneously: playing the piano in social establishments patronized chiefly by blacks, performing a largely improvised, syncopated repertory; and performing, arranging, composing, and publishing music in the style of white popular songs and piano pieces.

Stark published Joplin's *Maple Leaf Rag* on September 18, 1899 in Sedalia. It has come to occupy such a central position in the history of the genre not because it was the first piece of its kind in print, but because it is thought—by some—to represent an earlier type of ragtime than most published rags, and because of its sheer popularity: it influenced the compositions of many composers who turned to the new genre.

After the commercial success of *Maple Leaf Rag*, he moved (with Stark) to St. Louis, giving up playing in order to concentrate on composition, teaching, and collaboration with other musicians. He seems to have been involved with an opera company, as pianist, and he mounted productions of two extended compositions: *Rag Time Dances*, a twenty-minute piece conceived as a ballet, and *A Guest of Honor*, labeled by Joplin himself "A Rag Time Opera." Piano rags continued to appear; Stark insisted on publicizing these pieces as "classic" rags, implying a comparison with the classical piano repertory; Joplin himself said that there was nothing improvisational about his art any longer, and that his music should be played with absolute precision and at a moderate tempo. In his *The School of Ragtime—Six Exercises for a Piano*, published by Stark in 1908, he wrote:

> It is evident that, by giving each note its proper time and by scrupulously observing the ties, you will get the effect. So many are careless in these respects. Play slowly until you catch the swing, and never play ragtime fast at any time. We wish to say here, that the Joplin ragtime is destroyed by careless or imperfect rendering, and very often good players lose the effect entirely, by playing too fast.

After moving to New York in 1907, Joplin set to work on a more ambitious opera, *Treemonisha*, completed in 1911, revised a few years later, but never published or performed publicly in his lifetime.

Joplin's life thus offers a paradox. His most successful and influ-

Carmen Balthrop and Willard White in the Houston Grand Opera's 1975 production of Scott Joplin's *Treemonisha*.

ential compositions, his piano rags, drew their rhythmic character and "soul" from the music and culture of black Americans. His own ambition, however, was to integrate elements of this style with classical European forms; as his first important biographer put it, "until he died he persisted in believing that his syncopated music belonged with the European classics."[47]

Other ragtime composers emerged from the same environment. Thomas M. J. Turpin, whose father "Honest John" ran the Silver Dollar Saloon in St. Louis, was resident pianist at Babe Conner's Castle Club before opening his own establishment, the Rosebud, which became a popular center for syncopated piano playing. His *Harlem Rag* (1897) was the first published piece of ragtime by a black musician; despite its title, neither he nor the piece had any connection with New York. A handful of later rags by Turpin were published, including *A Ragtime Nightmare* (1900) and *St. Louis Rag* (1903). James Scott (1886–1938), Arthur Marshall (1881–1968), Scott Hayden (1882–1915), and Louis Chauvin (1881–1908) also learned their trade in and around St. Louis, built their reputations as pianists in the clubs and bars of this region, and had their first pieces brought out by regional publishers. White pianist-composers of ragtime whose music was shaped by the same environment

[47] Blesh, p. 145.

included Charles Hunter (1876–1906), Charles Johnson (1876–1950), and Calvin Woolsey (1884–1946).[48]

The interracial nature of ragtime is seen clearly in the career of Ben Harney (1871–1938). Born in Middleboro, Kentucky, he built a reputation as a singer and pianist on vaudeville stages along the Ohio River and in Chicago before coming to New York in 1896. The *New York Clipper* for February 17 of that year reported that he had "jumped into immediate favor through the medium of his genuinely clever plantation Negro imitations and excellent piano playing," and though Harney never published a piece of piano ragtime, the term itself was first widely used in connection with his performance style and with several songs published under his name, "You've Been a Good Old Wagon but You've Done Broke Down" (1895) and "Mister Johnson Turn Me Loose" (1896). This judgment of Harney as the first popularizer of the ragtime style was widely current in the last years of the century:

> Mr. Ben Harney is believed to have been the first Caucasian to translate ragtime to the piano. He learned it from a Negro whose songs he accompanied and made it the rage of Chicago and the West before it was heard in the East.[49]

As is evident in this quotation, Harney was taken at the time to be white, but some scholars now believe that he was a mulatto who succeeded in passing for white. His *Ragtime Instructor*, as mentioned above, demonstrates how the rhythmic patterns of ragtime playing can be applied to popular and religious music by white composers, and his song "You've Been a Good Old Wagon" (1896) employs the syncopated patterns of ragtime in the piano part against a pentatonic melody borrowed from traditional Anglo-American music.

"You've Been a Good Old Wagon," by Ben Harney

48 Cf. David A. Jasen and Trebor Jay Tichenor, *Rays and Ragtime* (New York: The Seabury Press, 1978) for biographical information on these men and lists of their ragtime compositions.
49 Rupert Hughes, "A Eulogy of Rag-Time," in *Musical Record* for April 1, 1899.

The first decades of the twentieth century brought the commercial peak of ragtime. Joplin wrote and published piano rags until 1914, and James Scott's ragtime pieces appeared into the early 1920s. Talented younger composers appeared, many of them inspired by Joplin's piano rags—Percy Wenrich, George Botsford, Joseph Lamb. Ragtime lost all sense of geographical identity, and was written and published in all parts of the United States.

Some scholars see Joplin's later ragtime compositions as moving away from the true nature of this music. They view ragtime as a form of black folk music, beginning as a playing style in the Mississippi Valley in the vicinity of St. Louis, spreading up and down the river and then overland to both west and east. After it reached Chicago, Cincinnati, and particularly New York, it became contaminated in the course of being taken over by commercial (mostly white) interests.

Whatever the truth of this matter, there is no question but that many Americans took ragtime to be a product of black America and an assault on the moral and musical standards of the country. Writer after writer in the national press hammered away at the theme that "its vicious influences are highly detrimental to the cause of good music,"[50] and that widespread acceptance of such an "artistically inferior" product would result in a lowering of moral standards:

> This cheap, trashy stuff could not elevate even the most degraded minds, nor could it possibly urge any one to greater effort in the acquisition of culture in any phase.[51]
>
> It is an evil music that has crept into the homes and hearts of our American people regardless of race, and must be wiped out as other bad and dangerous epidemics have been exterminated.[52]

Some openly equated the acceptance of "Negro music" with a decline in American life and cluture:

> (Ragtime) is symbolic of the primitive morality and perceptible moral limitations of the negro race. America is falling prey to the collective soul of the negro.[53]

---

[50]"The Ragtime Rage," in *Musical Courier* for May 23 1900, p. 20. This and the following five quotations came to my attention through Berlin, *Ragtime. A Musical and Cultural History*.

[51]Paul C. Carr, "Abuses of Music," *Musician* for October 6, 1900, p. 229.

[52]"Musical Impurity," *Etude* for January 1900, p. 16.

[53]Walter Winston Kenilworth, "Demoralizing Rag Time Music," *Music Courier* for May 28, 1913, pp. 22–23.

while others used insinuation and code words to get across the same message:

> There is no element of intellectuality in the enjoyment of ragtime. It savors too much of the primeval conceptions of music, whose basis was a rhythm that appealed to the physical rather than to the mental senses.[54]

The final step in this classic pattern of intolerance invoked Christianity against the evil influence of ragtime, and by implication against the race whose culture had brought it into being:

> Let us take a united stand against the *Ragtime Evil* as we would against bad literature, and horrors of war or intemperance and other socially destructive evils.
>
> In Christian homes, where purity of morals is stressed, ragtime should find no resting place.
>
> Avaunt with ragtime rot! Let us purge America and the Divine Art of Music from this polluting nuisance.[55]

But even though opposition to ragtime became so intense that members of the musician's union "swore to play no rag-time, and to do all in their power to counteract the pernicious influence exerted by 'Mr. Johnson,' 'My Rag-Time Lad' and others of the negro school,"[56] it became too popular to be resisted, there was too much commercial potential in it for the music industry to ignore, and the talents of Tin Pan Alley were put to work to exploit the rage for ragtime. Established songwriters, who had been turning out verse-chorus waltz songs, began producing ragtime. From Joe Howard's "Hello! Ma Baby" (1899)[57] and Hughie Cannon's "Bill Bailey, Won't You Please Come Home?" (1902) through Irving Berlin's "Alexander's Ragtime Band" (1911) and Lewis F. Muir's "Waiting for the Robert E. Lee" (1912), the most viable Tin Pan Alley products were songs echoing the simplest rhythmic patterns of piano rags and making reference in their lyrics either to ragtime music itself, or to the black American culture out of which this music had sprung. Some of the same men even tried their hand at writing piano rags: Jean Schwartz (*Whitewash*, 1908); Egbert Van Alstyne (*Honey Rag*, 1909); Muir (*Heavy on the Catsup*, 1913); even Goerge M. Cohan (*Popularity*, 1906).

[54] Carr, "Abuses of Music," p. 299.
[55] Leo Oehmler, "Ragtime: A Pernicious Evil and Enemy of True Art," *Musical Observer* for September 1914, p. 15.
[56] "War on Rag-Time," *American Musician* for July 1901, p. 4.
[57] NW 272, s1 / 2.

White America had successfully and profitably absorbed rag-time.

The new syncopated music slowly became part of social (or ball-room) dancing in America. It entered the mainstream of American life as instrumental music, for piano or band, or as a spectator dance:

> For most of the general public—at least outside the South—such black dances were seldom seen in a natural social setting. They were more apt to be seen—in much modified form—in low-life sporting resorts cater-ing to sensation seekers, or on the stage, generally done in blackface by Irish clog dancers. It was the "cakewalk contest" that caught the public fancy at the turn of the century, and only a few of the steps survived translation into popular social dancing.[58]

As syncopated rhythms spread to band music at the turn of the century, dancers—without changing the basic patterns and move-ments of the two-step—began modifying their steps and postures to reflect the new rhythmic impulses of ragtime. Two-steps, now mostly in 2 / 4 or ¢, were often so close in character to ragtime com-positions as to be virtually indistinguishable from them, and arrangements of ragtime pieces for concert band came to be used for two-step dancing.[59]

Around 1910, the two-step began giving way to a number of dif-ferent dances, many of them taken over from "low-life" establish-ments of the South and West—the turkey trot, the grizzly bear, the chicken glide, the bunny hug, the bull frog hop—and all requiring fast, syncopated music. Though these "belly-rubbing" dances, done with the two partners holding one another closely, were soon inter-polated into stage productions in New York and elsewhere, they were still associated in the public mind with their place of origin, and were resisted by many:

> A Paterson, New Jersey, court imposed a fifty-day prison sentence on a young woman for dancing the turkey trot. Fifteen young women were dismissed from a well-known magazine after the editor caught them enjoying the abandoned dance at lunchtime. Turkey trotters incurred the condemnation of churches and respectable people, and in 1914 an official disapproval was issued by the Vatican.[60]

[58] Thornton Hagert, liner notes for NW 293, p. 3.
[59] Examples are *Ma Ragtime Baby* (1898) by Fred S. Stone on NW 293, s2 / 2, and *At the Mississippi Cabaret* (1902) by Albert Gumble on NW 293, s2 / 4.
[60] Sylvia G. L. Dannett and Frank R. Rachel, *Down Memory Lane* (New York: Greenberg Publishers, 1954), p. 75.

It was Vernon and Irene Castle who brought respectability to these new forms of social dancing and ushered in a new era in American dance.

Vernon Castle had come to America from his native England in 1906, enjoyed some success as a dancer and actor in New York, and married an American woman (Irene Foote). The two went to Paris in 1911, where they built a reputation with their dancing at cafes and casinos. Back in New York they offered tea dances at Louis Martin's restaurant, then starred in the musical *The Sunshine Girl* (1913), creating a sensation with their energetic yet elegant dancing of the turkey trot and the tango. Sensing a ground swell of enthusiasm for a new sort of social dancing in America, they opened the Castle House, a dance studio where they offered instruction in the turkey trot and other new dances, retaining some of the earthiness but stripped of their overt sexuality. In other words, they did in dance what Tin Pan Alley composers were doing in music—taking a new, vital style with roots in the black subculture of America, retaining enough of its distinctiveness to preserve the energy that had attracted people in the first place, but modifying it enough to make it palatable to mainstream American culture.

Some considerable part of the Castles' success is traceable to their musical director, one of the most remarkable and influential American musicians of the first decades of the twentieth century, James Reese Europe.

Born in Mobile in 1881, Europe moved with his family to Washington, D.C. in early childhood, becoming a violin student of Enrico Hurlei, assistant director of the United States Marine Band. Removing to New York in 1904, Europe directed the music for several all-black shows, and in 1910 organized more than 100 black musicians into the Clef Club, which not only served as a clearing house for the employment of small ensembles to play syncopated dance music, but on occasion performed as a gigantic ensemble under Europe's direction.

The Castles understood very well the superiority of black musicians in playing the sort of music they were using, so they hired Europe to assemble and conduct a dance band for their stage performances and their studio, and to keep them supplied with the newest syncopated dance music. This association with the Castles was undoubtedly a factor in Victor's decision to record and release two discs by Europe's Society Orchestra in December of 1913 and four more in February, 1914. Victor's publicity stressed that the band, in addition to playing for the Castles, "has become very popular in society circles in New York and vicinity, and has played for social affairs in the homes of wealthy New Yorkers and at functions at the Tuxedo Club, Hotel Biltmore, Plaza, Sherry's, Delmonico's, the Astor and others," and that Europe had been hailed as "the Paderewski of syncopation" by the *Sunday Press.*

The pieces chosen for the first recording session include several one-steps or turkey trots (*Too Much Mustard* and *Down Home Rag*) and a tango (*Irresistible*).[61] The second session featured dances even more directly associated with the Castles. *Castle House Rag,*[62] gives a vivid picture of the state of syncopated dance music in the critical period bridging ragtime and jazz. In formal design, it is identical with many of Joplin's classic ragtime pieces for piano, including the *Maple Leaf Rag* itself—*AABBACCDD.* The first strain is dominated by several ragtime melodic and rhythmic patterns; the second is more reminiscent of a march by Sousa; the third strain, a trio, is softer and makes use of contrasting instrumentation, as was common in both marches and rags. The fourth strain begins with patterns suggesting the beginning of the piece, but the playing is less restrained and suggests a degree of improvisation; the drummer (Buddy Gilmore) dominates more and more, until the last measures become virtually a drum solo—surely the first time that music so dominated by percussion had been captured on a phonograph disc.

Perhaps the most important result of the collaboration between the Castles and Europe was the emergence of the most popular of all dances associated with the new syncopated music, the fox trot. Though its name suggests another of the "animal dances" originating in black dance halls and bordellos, it was in fact developed in New York by the Castles. As a dance historian describes the earliest stage of the fox trot,

> It had an emphatic 4/4 rhythm at about forty bars a minute, peculiar structures of twelve or twenty bars in place of the customary sixteen, and some really crazy breaks in the rhythm—right in the middle of the tune. The solution that evolved was to borrow some steps and breaks from the glide of several years back, some from the one-step and trot, and some from the tango, and to put them together in brief sequences of two or four bars so that no one would be caught off balance by the unaccustomed shapes of the music. The fundamental steps alternated in various patterns between "slow" (two to the bar) and "quick" (one to a beat).[63]

---

[61] Brian Rust, *Jazz Records, 1897–1942* (New Rochelle: Arlington House, 1978) has full discographical information.

[62] NW 269, s1/1.

[63] Thornton Hagert, liner notes for NW 293, p. 4.

Fox-trotting at a Y.W.C.A. Hostess Hut in 1917.

Europe offered the following account of the musical origins of the new dance:

> The fox trot was created by a young negro of Memphis, Tenn., Mr. W. C. Handy, who five years ago wrote "The Memphis Blues." This dance was often played by me last season during the tour of the Castles, but never in public. Mr. Castle became interested in it, but did not believe it suitable for dancing. He thought the time too slow, the world of today demanding staccato music. Yet after a while he began to dance it at private entertainments in New York, and, to his astonishment, discovered that it was immediately taken up. It was not until then that Mr. and Mrs. Castle began to dance it in public, with the result that it is now danced as much as all the other dances put together. Mr. Castle has generously given me credit for the fox trot, but the credit, as I have said, belongs to Mr. Handy.[64]

The critical point here is the equating of the fox trot with the blues.

An examination of Handy's *Memphis Blues*—referred to by Europe as a fox trot—in a performance by a band under Europe's direction[65] reveals that the piece takes the following shape,

$$x // A\ A // B\ B // x // A'\ A'\ A'\ A'\ A'\ A' /$$

[64] *New York Tribune* for November 22, 1914.
[65] NW 269, s1 / 3.

in which $x$ is a four-bar introductory phrase; $A$ is a 12-bar blues structure; $B$ is a 16-bar section with a phrase structure of $aa'ba''$, with rhythmic patterns reminiscent of piano rags; and $A'$ is another 12-bar blues section. Thus, a traditional 12-bar blues pattern is embedded in a longer and more complex dance piece. The $A'$ section is particularly interesting in this performance; it is played 6 times with various instrumentalists taking solos which were surely not written into the score Europe had prepared for his band.

Other composed dance pieces of the prewar era entitled "blues" are similar in that they incorporate 12-bar blues patterns into larger structures. *Kansas City Blues* by Euday L. Bowman, as recorded in 1916 by the Victor Military Band,[66] is a mixture of melodic and rhythmic elements drawn from ragtime, marches, and the blues. Each section is based on the harmonic formula associated with traditional blues, but lengths of the several sections are irregular; the first section is 16 bars long (*abbc*); the second has the three-phrase shape of the blues (*aab*), but the first phrase is 6 measures long, giving a total length of 14 bars; the third is again 16 bars (*abbc*); and so on.

As such pieces became more viable commercially, because of their association with the most popular dance of the day, relationships with the traditional 12-bar blues form became more tenuous. In fact, the large majority of "blues" published and recorded commercially in the decade after 1915 either have no relationship whatsoever to the formal and harmonic patterns of traditional blues—the popular *Wang Wang Blues*, written in 1921 by Gus Mueller, Buster Johnson and Henry Busse, is typical in being cast in the verse-chorus pattern of Tin Pan Alley songs, with a 32-bar chorus—or at the most have a 12-bar blues phrase or two embedded in a larger structure. Most of the pieces with the word "blues" in their title recorded before the 1920s are actually fox trots, intended for fashionable dancing rather than soulful singing.

Returning to James Reese Europe: when the United States entered the war in 1917 he enlisted in the Fifteenth New York Regiment, which became the 369th Infantry, eventually earning the nickname of "The Hell Fighters." The commanding officer, recognizing Europe's talent as well as the potential contribution of music to the morale of his troops, assigned Europe the task of organizing a band. With the aid of a $10,000 gift from Daniel Gray Reid, a director of the United States Steel Corporation, Europe recruited black musicians from various parts of the country, shaped them into a functioning band, wrote a series of arrangements for them, and they were off for Europe.

[66] NW 293, s2 / 5.

Jim Europe in uniform, 1917. (Noble Sissle Archives)

Like Civil War bands, they had multiple functions: playing for marching and drilling; giving evening concerts for soldiers and civilians; playing hymns for religious services; furnishing music for dances. The common factor in these several repertories was the playing style; even though Europe wrote out arrangements, the players introduced complex rhythmic passages and idiosyncratic articulation:

> I have to call a daily rehearsal of my band to prevent the musicians from adding to their music more than I wish them to. Whenever possible they all embroider their parts in order to produce new, peculiar sounds.[67]

[67] Quoted in Eileen Southern, *The Music of Black Americans. A History* (New York: W. W. Norton & Company, 1971), p. 365.

The music of Europe's band was received with enthusiasm not only by American armed forces, but by the French as well. A correspondent sent to cover the war in Europe by the St. Louis *Post-Dispatch* filed a story on June 10 1918 after an interview with Noble Sissle, the regimental drum major:

> Lieut. Europe, before raising his baton twitched his shoulders apparently to be sure that his tight-fitting military coat would stand the strain, a musician shifted his feet, the players of brass horns blew the saliva from their instruments, the drummers tightened their drumheads, everyone settled back in their seats, half closed their eyes, and when the baton came down with a swoop that brought forth a soul-rousing crash both director and musicians seemed to forget their surroundings; they were lost in scenes and memories. Cornet and clarinet players began to manipulate notes in that typical rhythm (that rhythm which no artist has ever been able to put down on paper); as the drummers struck their stride their shoulders began shaking in time to their syncopated raps.
>
> Then, it seemed, the whole audience began to sway, dignified French officers began to pat their feet, along with the American General, who, temporarily, had lost his style and grace. . . . (Europe's) body swayed in willowy motion, and his head was bobbing as it did in days when terpsichorean festivities reigned supreme.
>
> The audience could stand it no longer, the "jazz germ" hit them and it seemed to find the vital spot loosening all muscles and causing what is known in America as an "eagle rocking it."
>
> All through France the same thing happened. Troop trains carrying allied soldiers from everywhere passed us en route, and every head came out of the window when we struck up a good old Dixie tune.
>
> We were playing our Colonel's favorite ragtime, "The Army Blues," in a little village where we were the first American troops there, and among the crowd listening to that band was an old woman about 60 years of age. To everyone's surprise, all of a sudden she started doing a dance that resembled "Walking the Dog." Then I was cured, and satisfied that American music would some day be the world's music.

Sent to Paris in August to play a concert in the Théâtre des Champs-Elysées, the band created such a sensation that it remained in the city for eight weeks, a stay climaxed by a concert in the Tuileries Gardens for a crowd estimated at 50,000.

Now referred to as the 369th U.S. Infantry Jazz Band, they returned to America in triumph—"The Band that Played the Hell Fighters on to Victory at the Battles of Champaigne and Argonne Forest" and "The Band that Set all France JAZZ MAD" read posters announcing their parade down Fifth Avenue, which drew a million people. They gave a concert in the Manhattan Opera House, cut twenty four discs for Pathe in the early spring of 1919,[68] then set off to tour America. Jim Europe got only as far as Boston, where on May 9 he was stabbed to death by Herbert Wright, one of his drummers.

Europe's bands were not the only groups playing syncopated dance music. Will Marion Cook (1869–1944) organized and led a succession of black bands in New York from the turn of the century into the 1920s; a member of the Clef Club and a charter member of ASCAP, he formed the New York Syncopated Orchestra in 1918, took it on a four-month tour of the United States, then took the group—now called the American Syncopated Orchestra—to London and Paris. Will Vodery (1885–1951) led a syncopated dance band at the Coconut Grove Club for many years, was musical supervisor for productions by Florenz Ziegfeld, and organized a black band for the 807th Infantry during the war. Tim Brymn (1881–1946) led a black band during the war years (the 350th Infantry), played in a number of New York clubs for several decades, and cut a series of discs in 1921 with his Black Devil Orchestra. Other black dance bands in New York were led by Ford Dabney, William H. Tyers, and J. Leubrie Hill. Noble Sissle and Eubie Blake, who had been associated with Jim Europe and had formed a songwriting team, combined forces to write and produce *Shuffle Along*, a successful all-black musical which opened in New York on May 23, 1921. Each also led a succession of instrumental groups, which performed and recorded under such names as the Eubie Blake Trio, Blake's Jazztone Orchestra, Eubie Blake and his Shuffle Along Orchestra, and Noble Sissle and his Sizzling Syncopators.

W. C. Handy had formed his first band in Memphis in 1903. Chicago numbered among its black bands Wilbur Sweatman's Orchestra, Erskine Tate's Orchestra, and Dave Peyton's Symphonic Syncopators; Finney's Quadrille Orchestra was from Detroit. New Orleans had bands of this sort as early as the last decades of the nineteenth century; Buddy Bolden's band was only one of some twenty-five New Orleans groups with black or Creole personnel known to have been in existence around the turn of the century and into the early 1900s.

Except for a cylinder made by Sweatman's band in about 1904, the first phonographic evidence of this music dates from 1913 and 1914, the discs cut by Europe's Society Orchestra in New York. The popularity of black bands during the war and afterwards prompted several recording companies to issue discs of bands led

---

[68]*Mirandy* on NW 260, s2/4 and *On Patrol in No Man's Land* on NW 260, s2/6 came from these sessions.

by Handy, Dabney, Sweatman, Blake, Sissle, Brymn, and others. From this time on we have ample recorded evidence of the development of jazz, as syncopated dance music had come to be called; for its early history we must depend on the handful of recorded pieces, photographs, reminiscences by various musicians, accounts of the day, and less reliable sources.

Much of this music existed in oral tradition, at first; black musicians would memorize pieces, learn to play them together, and teach them to other blacks. But the black musicians who formed commercially successful urban bands, and who made the first recordings of syncopated dance music, had training in notated music. We know from Europe's own testimony, from photographs,[69] and from other evidence, that Jim Europe's several bands played from music—from published band pieces or from his own arrangements. The same appears to be true for the bands of Handy, Dabney, Sissle, and the others mentioned above.

The syncopated dance music of the last years of the nineteenth century and the first two decades of the twentieth, then, represents a blend of elements from both African and European cultures.

The several types of music with which this chapter has been concerned—spirituals, blues, ragtime, other syncopated dance music—share a similar history in the half-century between the freeing of the slaves during the Civil War and the end of World War I.

Each emerged among American blacks as an oral music, with a distinctive style of performance. Each remained in this form, in rural and isolated areas of the country until well into the twentieth century, relatively uncontaminated by the music of white Americans. For some historians of Afro-American music this is the most interesting and valuable period. Later developments—the arrangement and composition of similar pieces by white musicians, the gravitation of some blacks toward white musical styles, the skimming off of superficial elements of spirituals, ragtime, or blues by urban white musicians for commercial gain—are taken to represent the exploitation by the dominant white culture of America of a musical style originating among one of the country's oppressed minorities.

Each type can also be seen as interracial music, with rhythmic and expressive character coming from the music of black Americans, formal patterns and instruments from white. In the first two decades of the twentieth century, elements of American musical

[69] Cf. Robert Kimball and William Bolcom, *Reminiscing with Sissle and Blake* (New York: The Viking Press, 1973) for a photograph of Europe's Clef Club (p. 58) and his army band (p. 70).

life—the popular musical theater, the American military—concert band, popular piano music, popular song, social dancing—absorbed more and more of this style. The result was a dialect of music regarded both here and abroad as not only characteristically American, but as the *most* American style.

It seems unnecessary to choose between these two views. Both seem equally valid.

# 15

## *The Search for a National Identity*

My own duty as a teacher, I conceive, is not so much to interpret Bee-thoven, Wagner, or other masters of the past, but to give what encour-agement I can to the young musicians of America. I must give full expression to my firm conviction, and to the hope that just as this nation has already surpassed so many others in marvellous inventions and feats of engineering and commerce, and has made an honorable place for itself in literature in one short century, so it must assert itself in the other arts, and especially in the art of music.

—Antonín Dvořák, 1894

Mrs. Jeanette M. Thurber, wife of a successful wholesale grocer in New York, had a noble dream: to help establish a "national Amer-ican school of composition." As a step in this direction she founded a National Conservatory of Music. Classes began in 1885, but though some talented musicians were enrolled, the school attracted little attention and produced few notable results. Deciding that only a bold stroke could save the Conservatory, Mrs. Thurber offered the directorship to Antonín Dvořák, one of the leading European com-posers of the day, who accepted; Dvořák arrived in New York on September 27, 1892.

He was the most distinguished composer ever to come to Amer-ica. Born in the Czech village of Nelahozeves in 1841, the son of a butcher, he had become a violist in the Provisional Theatre Orchestra in Prague, worked steadily at acquiring compositional skills, and eventually established some local reputation for his operas, symphonies, and chamber music. Within a few years his works were becoming known all over Europe, and in America as well. Many of his compositions—several symphonies, his two sets of *Slavonic Dances* for orchestra, some of the chamber music— became standard fare throughout the Western world. With the death of Wagner in 1883, critical opinion placed him second only to Brahms as the most important living composer. Dvořák was indeed a prize for Mrs. Thurber and her National Conservatory.

Within a few months of his arrival he began work on his *Symphony No. 9* ("From the New World"); completed in May of 1893, it was premiered in New York on December 16, 1893, and became his most widely played orchestral work. The summer of 1893 was spent in a small Czech settlement in Iowa, Spillville, where he wrote a string quartet (No. 12, in F Major) and a string quintet in E-flat, both premiered in January of 1894. These three pieces were his major compositional efforts during his stay in America.

Dvořák became familiar with Negro spirituals through the singing of a black student at the conservatory, Harry T. Burleigh. He examined a handful of early transcriptions of Indian melodies, visited Buffalo Bill's Wild West Show when it came to New York, and may have heard singing by American Indians during his summer in Iowa. From this limited contact with these two bodies of music, Dvořák found similarities between them:

> The music of the two races bore a remarkable similarity to the national music of Scotland. In both there is a peculiar scale, caused by the absence of the fourth and seventh, or leading note. In both the minor scale has the seventh and invariably a minor seventh, the fourth is included and the sixth omitted.[1]

The principal themes of the *New World Symphony* and both chamber works written in the summer of 1893 are characterized by pervasive use of a pentatonic scale and struck the ears of many listeners as suggesting melodic contours of Negro spirituals and/or Indian songs.

In an essay, the composer expressed his views on the subject of nationalism in music:

> A while ago I suggested that inspiration for truly national music might be derived from the negro melodies or Indian chants. I was led to take this view by the fact that the so-called plantation songs are indeed the most striking and appealing melodies that have yet been found on this

[1] *New York Herald* for December 15, 1893.

side of the water, but largely by the observation that this seems to be recognized, though often unconsciously, by most Americans.

It is a proper question to ask, what songs, then, belong to the American and appeal more strongly to him than any others? What melody could stop him on the street if he were in a strange land and make the home feeling well up within him, no matter how hardened he might be or how wretchedly the tune were played? The most potent as well as the most beautiful among them, according to my estimation, are certain of the so-called plantation melodies and slave songs, all of which are distinguished by unusual and subtle harmonies, the like of which I have found in no other songs but those of old Scotland and Ireland.

The point has been urged that many of these touching songs, like those of Foster, have not been composed by the negroes themselves, but are the work of white men, while others did not originate on the plantation, but were imported from Africa. It seems to me that this matters but little. The important thing is that the inspiration for such music should come from the right source, and that the music itself should be a true expression of the people's real feelings. . . .

The music of the people is like a rare and lovely flower growing amidst encroaching weeds. Thousands pass it, while others trample it under foot, and thus the chances are that it will perish before it is seen by the one discriminating spirit who will prize it above all else. The fact that no one has as yet arisen to make the most of it does not prove that nothing is there.[2]

Dvořák did *not* urge American composers to base their composition on Indian and Negro melodies, as has often been alleged. Instead, he urged them to be receptive to whatever music was taken most to heart by their fellow citizens. This is precisely what he had done himself with the music of his own land: he knew the popular and folk songs and dances of Czechoslovakia from his youth and kept in touch with this music throughout his life. Melodic and rhythmic elements of his pieces grow out of this music; many of his own compositions capture the essence of Czech life and culture. As a result, his compositions were taken to heart by the Czech public and struck audiences in other countries as being significantly different from the products of German, Russian, Scandinavian, British, and Italian composers.

Dvořák's stay in the New World lasted less than three years; in 1895 he returned to Prague to reassume his chair as professor of composition.

Musical nationalism was one of the great issues of the nineteenth century. In country after country in Europe, critics debated whether

---

[2]Antonín Dvořák, "Music in America," *Harper's New Monthly Magazine*, XC (February 1894), pp. 432–33.

or not music could reflect the character of a national or ethnic group. Scales and melodies drawn from traditional music were taken as a basis for melodic material in classical compositions, the rhythms and forms of indigenous dances were appropriated and elaborated, national languages were used for the lyrics of songs and the librettos of operas, inflections and rhythms of national languages were incorporated into instrumental music, the sounds of distinctive regional instruments were imitated in the classical orchestra, national history and legend became the subject matter of symphonic poems and even chamber music.

Such matters were of little concern to American composers until the very end of the nineteenth century. True, Heinrich had attempted to write "American" music before the middle of the century, an occasional piece by another composer would bear a descriptive national title, and most of the virtuoso performer-composers incorporated familiar American tunes into their display pieces for their instruments. But those Americans who were seen as "serious" composers were convinced that the Germanic style was the only basis for successful composition.

The career and compositions of Edward MacDowell (1860–1908) dramatize the turn of the century shift away from the Germanic style toward a new path for American composition.

Born in New York, MacDowell was taken to Paris by his mother when he was fifteen in order to develop his obvious talent as a pianist. He was accepted at the Conservatory in 1877, but was soon persuaded that a more stimulating musical environment could be found in Germany. Several years in Stuttgart, Wiesbaden, and Frankfurt honed his piano technique, brought his first public performances, and led to study in theory and composition with Joachim Raff. Successful private piano teaching in Frankfurt and a growing reputation as a performer resulted in his appointment as instructor in piano at the Darmstadt Conservatory. He was drawn increasingly to composition, however, and the performance of his *First Modern Suite* (Opus 10) for piano before the Allgemeiner Deutscher Musikverein in Zurich in July of 1882 persuaded him to give up his teaching post in order to devote his energies to composition. By the end of 1884, a dozen or so of his pieces had been published by German companies, his compositions were receiving frequent performances in both Europe and America, and he was settled in Frankfurt, turning out a steady stream of piano pieces, songs, and an occasional work for orchestra.

His compositions were indistinguishable in general style from those of many German composers of his age. He published settings of German texts and his piano pieces were published with German titles. When he decided to return to the United States in 1888, he had spent a dozen years in Europe.

His Boston years, from 1888 to 1896, were the most successful and productive of his life. Solo and chamber recitals quickly established his reputation as a pianist. His *Piano Concerto No. 2*, completed just before he returned to America, was premiered in New York, then played in Boston and Paris. Several symphonic poems and suites for orchestra were played in Boston, New York, Louisville, Chicago, Worcester, Cincinnati, Philadelphia, and elsewhere.

In 1896 MacDowell accepted an appointment at Columbia University as the first professor of music at that institution, which thus joined Harvard (John Knowles Paine) and Yale (Horatio Parker) in focusing academic work in music around a distinguished American composer. Though his compositional output declined in his New York years, several major compositions for piano, including his last two sonatas, date from this period.

Much of MacDowell's rhetoric in his lectures and publications emphasizes his opposition to the trend toward musical nationalism:

> One point must be very distinctly understood, namely, that what we call harmonization of a melody cannot be admitted as forming any part of folk song. Folk melodies are, without exception, homophonous. This being the case, perhaps my statement that the vital principle of folk music in its best state has nothing in common with nationalism (considered in the usual sense of the word), will be better understood. And this will be the proof that nationalism, so-called, is merely an extraneous thing that has no part in pure art. . . . So-called Russian, Bohemian, or any other purely national music has no place in art, for its characteristics may be duplicated by anyone who takes the fancy to do so. On the other hand, the vital element of music—personality—stands alone.[3]

But his most ambitious orchestral work, the *Suite No. 2* (Opus 48), begun in 1891 and premiered by the Boston Symphony Orchestra in 1896, is subtitled *Indian Suite*. MacDowell had obtained a copy of Theodore Baker's *Über die Musik der nordamerikanischer Wilden*, with its transcriptions of Indian melodies, and had used some of these as the thematic basis for the five sections of his piece:

1. Legend
2. Love Song
3. In War-time
4. Dirge
5. Village Festival

[3] Edward MacDowell, *Critical and Historical Essays*, W. J. Baltzell, ed. (Boston: Arthur P. Schmidt, 1912), p. 146; Lawrence Gilman, *Edward MacDowell. A Study* (New York: John Lane Company, 1908), p. 83.

The "Dirge" draws its opening theme from a Kiowa chant of mourning, yet lush chromatic harmonies and rich scoring for strings and lower winds obscure the fact that the melodic material is drawn from another culture.[4]

*Woodland Sketches* (Opus 15, 1896), the most popular of all his piano compositions, includes "From an Indian Lodge" with the accompaniment of the entire lyric middle section by a drone bass surely intended to suggest the sound of Indian music. "From Uncle Remus" suggests a minstrel song, with its skipping melody and hints of pentatonic scales. His last two sets of piano pieces, *Fireside Tales* (Opus 61, 1901–2) and *New England Idyls* (Opus 62, 1901–2), contain pieces with similar titles and similar musical invocations of folk material.

A recent discussion of MacDowell concludes:

> It is ironic that in his day MacDowell should have been widely regarded as "the great American composer," since it is hard to find anything distinctively American about his music. Indeed he never aspired to write nationalistic music; his ambition was to be a fine composer who also happened to be American. He had an explicit aversion to concerts consisting only of American works, and finally he refused to allow his music to be performed at these increasingly popular events, insisting that music ought to be presented on its merits and not on account of its composer's nationality.[5]

When MacDowell left America, Germanic music was taken to be the ideal (and indeed only) model for an aspiring composer. Upon his return to America, after a successful career in Germany, he was hailed as a hero. His first years in Boston brought adulation, his compositions were performed repeatedly, orchestras and individual performers stood in line to play his newest compositions, the press treated him as one of the country's heroes.

But Dvořák's arrival in America changed this. Ironically, it was the foreigner who raised the consciousness of Americans, who suggested the desirability of a native style. Attention and praise shifted from MacDowell to the visiting Bohemian, and the American lashed out at his competitor:

> We have here in America been offered a pattern for an "American" national musical costume by the Bohemian Dvořák—though what Negro melodies have to do with Americanism in art still remains a mystery.

---

[4] MIA 137.

[5] Margery Morgan Lowens, "Edward MacDowell," in *The New Grove Dictionary of Music and Musicians*, Stanley Sadie, ed. (London: Macmillan Publishers, 1980), II, p. 420.

Music that can be made by "recipe" is not music, but "tailoring." To be sure, this tailoring may serve to cover a beautiful thought; but—why cover it? and, worst of all, why cover it (if covered it must be: if the trademark of nationality is indispensable, which I deny)—why cover it with the badge of whilom slavery rather than with the stern but at least manly and free rudeness of the North American Indian?[6]

Despite this statement, MacDowell was ambivalent in his own compositions until his death: some continued to be unyieldingly European in style,[7] others did just what he criticized Dvořák for doing.

MacDowell was a composer of great talent. Perhaps if he had taken a clear stand on one side or another of the issue of musical nationalism, his contributions to American music would have been even more substantial.

For many other American composers, there was no ambivalence: they accepted Dvořák's challenge and set out to create a national school of composition.

There were, first of all, Dvořák's own students. Rubin Goldmark (1872–1936) was one of the first talented young musicians to come to the American Conservatory to work with the famous Czech. Among his more successful compositions were the *Hiawatha Overture* (1899), a *Negro Rhapsody*, and a descriptive piece for orchestra entitled *Call of the Plains*. Harvey Worthington Loomis (1865–1930) had few public performances of his some 500 compositions, though a handful of them—including *Lyrics of the Red Men*, for piano— were published. William Arms Fisher (1861–1948) had more success as a music historian than as a composer, but some of his arrangements of Negro spirituals were widely performed. And Harry Thacker Burleigh (1866–1949), the black American whose singing of spirituals had brought this music to the attention of Dvořák, composed some 200 pieces, most of them songs and short works for chorus or piano. His most ambitious pieces were *Six Plantation Melodies for Violin and Piano* (1901) and *From the Southland* (1914) for piano, but his collection of *Jubilee Songs of the United States of America* (1916) had the greatest impact on the musical life of his country: many of these settings of spirituals for voice and piano became standard recital fare for the greatest singers of the day.[8]

[6] Gilman, p. 84.

[7] Cf. his *Twelve Virtuoso Studies* for piano (Opus 46, 1893–94) on NW 206, s2.

[8] Three of them—"Go Down, Moses," "Deep River," and "Heav'n, Heav'n," are available on NW 247, s1 / 8–10.

Other American composers with no direct contact with Dvořák began writing similar pieces. Arthur Farwell, born in St. Paul, Minnesota in 1872 earned a degree from the Massachusetts Institute for Technology in 1893. Residence in Boston also brought him into serious contact with music: he studied theory and composition, then went off to Germany and Paris for further training with Engelbert Humperdinck, Hans Pfitzner, and Alexandre Guilmant. He returned to America in 1899 with a quite respectable list of compositions—songs, piano pieces, several compositions for orchestra—and was promptly offered a teaching position at Cornell University. A safe academic career, combining teaching with composition in European style, seemed to stretch ahead of him.

But Farwell was troubled by the direction his composition had taken. He became convinced that:

> The promise of our national musical art lies in that work of our composers which is sufficiently un-german; that is, in which the German idiom is not the dominant factor. It will cost American culture many pangs to learn this simple fact. The German masterpieces are unapproachable, especially from another land and race. All that we do toward imitating them must necessarily be weak and apologetic, bringing honor neither to German tradition nor to American music. It is only by exalting the common inspirations of American life that we can become great musically.[9]

Accordingly, Farwell wrote a set of *American Indian Melodies* (Opus 11) in 1900, taking the tunes from a book published that year by Alice C. Fletcher.[10] The tunes had already been fitted with simple harmonizations by John C. Fillmore, "determined partly by the Indian's preference, but more particularly by the tonal structure of the melodies themselves"; but Farwell felt that much more could be done:

> It struck the writer, however, that a heightened art-value could be imparted to them, if the composer should consult, not merely this melodic structure, but the poetic nature of the particular legend or incident of which each song was the outcome. For it must be understood that these songs are entirely dependent upon mythical or legendary occurrences, which they qualify or interpret, or upon religious ceremonies of which they form a part. The writer realized that if the musical imagination could be fired by a consideration of the particular legend pertaining to a song, it would give rise to a combination of harmonies

[9] From the preface to the issue of the Wa-Wan Press for September 1903.
[10] Alice C. Fletcher, *Indian Story and Song From North America* (Boston: Small, Maynard & Company, 1900).

far more vitally connected with the song's essence, its spiritual significance, than any which should be the outcome of a mere consideration of the melodies' tonal structure.[11]

Farwell set off for New York to find a publisher; a number of his earlier pieces had been brought out by Oliver Ditson and H. B. Stevens, and he expected no difficulty. But no commercial firm would bring out music of this sort, and Farwell encountered other young American composers having the same problem. The solution was simple: the establishment of a press dedicated to American music.

The Wa-Wan Press, set up in Newton Center, Massachusetts, in December of 1901, took its name from a ceremony of the Omaha tribe, a celebration of "peace, fellowship and song." Run on a subscription basis by Farwell and his father, with the printing and engraving done in Boston, it published several hundred compositions by thirty-seven composers in the decade of its existence.[12]

Farwell was not concerned with the wide stylistic discrepancies between his borrowed melodies, which were often pentatonic, and the harmonic vocabulary of late nineteenth century European music, which he enthusiastically incorporated into his accompaniments. *Three Indian Songs* (Opus 32, 1908)[13] draw their melodies from Indian music captured on phonograph cylinders by Alice Fletcher. The text of the second of these, "Inketunga's Thunder Song":

> Wakonda Wakonda!
> Deep rolls thy thunder! Wakonda!
> They speak to me, my friend; the Weeping Ones,
> Hark! In deep rolling thunder calling.
> Wakonda! O friend, they speak to me,
> Far above, hark,
> Deep-voiced in thunder calling.

struck Farwell as intensely dramatic; the voice is given outbursts on the word "Wakonda" (the Omaha name for the Great Spirit), and subsides to melodramatic low-pitched musings on other lines; the piano accompaniment is highly chromatic, shifting in tonality, sometimes hinting at a whole-tone scales and chords. In the end,

[11] From the introduction to *American Indian Melodies* (Wa-Wan Press, 1900).

[12] For a history of the press, cf. Gilbert Chase's introduction to Vera Brodsky Lawrence, ed., *The Wa-Wan Press, 1901–1911* (New York: Arno Press, 1970), and Edward N. Waters, "The Wa-Wan Press: an Adventure in Musical Idealism," in *A Birthday Offering to Carl Engel*, Gustave Reese, ed. (New York: G. Schirmer, 1943).

[13] NW 213, s1 / 1.

Western elements overwhelm the Indian: one is scarcely aware of the pentatonic nature of the melody.

"Navajo War Dance" and "Pawnee Horses" for piano, two sections of *From Mesa and Plain*,[14] have less European flavor. With their pentatonic melodies moving along in 9/8 and 6/8 meter, supported by left-hand figurations sometimes based on open fourths and fifths, they suggest the character of an Irish jig. The most remarkable passage comes at the end of "Navajo War Dance," where virtuoso piano figuration momentarily loses contact with tonal harmony, anticipating some of the polytonal experimentation that lay ahead in the twentieth century.[15]

Farwell went to New York in 1909 to take a position as critic for *Musical America,* and the Wa-Wan Press soon foundered. He continued to compose, more prolifically than before. Virtually abandoning the notion of using Indian materials, he turned instead to other philosophies of creating indigenous American music. In 1925, he established a "Theater of the Stars" on Big Bear Lake in the San Bernardino Mountains of California in 1925, composing *The March of Man* for the opening of this idealistic venture in "a people's outdoor musical and dramatic ampitheater."

But performances of his music became increasingly rare. One of his last compositions, an "operatic fantasy of music in America" entitled *Cartoon* (1948), is concerned with the theme of "the American composer struggling against European domination." The synopsis of the first act reads, in part:

Act I. Temple of Europus, the Music God. Impecunious young composer, *Americus,* get a raw deal at hands of Robber-Priests (powers of the musical world). He loves *Columbia,* music-loving girl of social position, who believes in him. Love scene in Temple; *Columbia* will wed *Americus* when he triumphs in the Temple with his music. Beethoven (elevated status) comes to life, tells *Americus* to go forth and gain strength from the folksongs of his people.

Even though Farwell largely abandoned the notion of utilizing American folk material in his compositions, other composers pushed resolutely along this path. Henry F. Gilbert (1868–1928) was perhaps the first American to draw on Negro spirituals in an orchestral piece: his Opus 2, written in 1895, is entitled *Two Episodes*, the second section a "Negro Episode." His *Americanesque on Negro-Minstrel Tunes* (c. 1903) follows Dvořák in failing to dif-

[14] NW 213, s2/2.
[15] A later arrangement of "Navajo War Dance" for unaccompanied voices, his Opus 102, attempts to suggest the singing style of Navajo chant; cf. NW 213, s2/1.

ferentiate between black folk music and the minstrel songs of white composers. Subsequent pieces included a *Comedy Overture on Negro Themes* (1905) and *Negro Rhapsody* (*Shout*) of 1912; he also wrote *Six Indian Sketches* (1911) for orchestra, and *Indian Scenes* (1912) and *Negro Dances* (1914) for piano. He joined most of his peers in calling for an American school of composition; "as long as we run after foreign gods with too great an assiduity we shall never have a god of our own really worthy of our respect and worship."[16]

His most ambitious composition based on indigenous melodic material is *The Dance in the Place Congo*,[17] written in 1906–8 as a symphonic poem, then revised as a ballet in 1916. Inspired by George Washington Cable's article of the same title, which had appeared in *Century Magazine* for February of 1886, Gilbert's piece draws its chief melodic material from Creole melodies quoted by Cable. A slow, gloomy introduction, depicting the slaves gathering for a Sunday afternoon of dancing at New Orleans's Place Congo, insinuates syncopated rhythms and introduces a Creole song, "Eh! pou' la belle Lalotte," as a "poignant cry of rage and revolt" given out by the assembling slaves:

"Eh! pou' la belle Lalotte" (Creole)

The dancing begins, to the music of a bamboula, "Quand patate la cuite na va mangé li!"

"Quand patate la cuite" (Creole)

A lyric middle section, loosely based on the tune of the introduction, works to a broad climax; the dancing resumes, to the bamboula tune; six bells ring, announcing the end of the day's festivities, and the piece concludes with a somber coda as the slaves return to their life of bondage with a "cry of racial revolt against slavery."

The tunes are merely the foundation for a complex orchestral piece, developing along lines strongly reminiscent of the tone poems

---

[16] Henry Gilbert, "The American Composer," in *The Musical Quarterly*, I (1915), p. 184.
[17] NW 228, s1 / 2.

of Liszt. Ridding oneself of "foreign gods" was proving a difficult task for the American composer.

John Powell, born in Virginia in 1882 and trained in piano and composition in Vienna from 1902 to 1907, had a successful career as a pianist in both Europe and America and composed a series of pieces drawing upon or suggesting Negro melodies: *In the South* (1906) for piano; *Sonata Virginiesque* for violin and piano; and *Rhapsodie Nègre* for piano and orchestra, stimulated by Joseph Conrad's novella *Heart of Darkness* and first performed with the composer as soloist by the Russian Symphony in New York's Carnegie Hall on March 23, 1918.[18]

But Powell's search for national identity took on a darker note:

> The only possible root upon which we can engraft our culture is the Anglo-Saxon root, and that, not because the founders of our country were almost exclusively Anglo-Saxon, but because those ideals upon which our republic was based are characteristically and distinctively Anglo-Saxon. The Anglo-Saxon spirit of good sportsmanship and sense of fair play and justice have been, up to this time, the basis of everything that is fine, that is liberal, that is progressive in our past and in our present.[19]

After outlining ways in which this ideal could be implemented— restriction of immigration, removal from the country of individuals and groups "who have proved themselves unworthy of the benefits our country bestows," prohibition of the use of any language other than English in the United States, the establishment of closer cultural and political ties with England—Powell turns his argument to music by examining and rejecting the several schools of composition which had sprung up in the search for a "characteristic and distinctive American music."

> 1. *Red Indian School.* It is already apparent that the Red Indian School can never give us a national American music. In the first place, the Indian material is too scanty, monotonous, and inelastic to lend itself to musical development in the higher and more complicated forms. But the fundamental trouble lies deeper. We Americans are not Red Indians; we are not even Americans; we are Europeans in race and language. And it could never be possible to express our European culture and psychology in terms of the musical idiom of an alien and primitive race.
> 2. *Negro School.* When the negro music is analyzed, we see at once that that part of it which is purely African is almost as meagre and monotonous as the Indian music. In addition to all this, the same objec-

[18] Available on NW 228, s2 / 2.
[19] John Powell, "Lectures on Music," *The Rice Institute Pamphlet*, X / 3, (July 1923), p. 137.

tion that was made to the Indian School holds good here. We Americans, so-called, are no more black Africans than we are red Indians; and it is absurd to imagine that the negro idiom could ever give adequate expression to the soul of our race.[20]

After similarly disposing of the Stephen Foster School, the Popular Music School ("I put this question to you. Do the musical comedy and the vaudeville stage represent the real spirit of our land and people?"), and the Ultra-Modern School, Powell at last comes to his solution:

> 6. *Anglo-Saxon Folk Music School.* We have seen that our only hope for a nation in America lies in grafting the stock of our culture on the Anglo-Saxon root. Is it not equally evident that, if we desire a music characteristic of our racial psychology, it must be based upon Anglo-American folk-song? Here the whole gamut of life is aptly and beautifully expressed—crude brutality, as in the primitive ballads, gay abandonment, impish merriment, farcial horse-play, gentle humor, sturdy adventurousness, unwavering fidelity, tender lyricism, passionate romanticism, delicate sadness, touching pathos, witty comedy, poignant tragedy. I must urge all American composers to avail themselves of this unparalleled opportunity. In this way, not only will our racial heritage be used to give us a national music, but the resulting music will become one of the most important means towards the end of achieving a national consciousness.[21]

Powell devoted the remainder of his life to the encouragement of Anglo-American folk music (he was an organizer of the White Top festival) and the composition of classical pieces based on it—*In Old Virginia* for orchestra, *Natchez-on-the-Hill* (a set of "Virginian country dances"), arrangements of Anglo-American folk songs, and his crowning achievement, *Virginia Symphony*, premiered in Richmond in 1951.

It is not my purpose to castigate Powell, at this late date, for his blatant racism, but to underline two points relevant to the present discussion: his comments on "The Red Indian School" and "The Negro School" give at least a germ of explanation for the fact that little music of lasting value emerged from these movements; and history tells us repeatedly that racism can ride on the coattails of nationalism.

With the emergence of ragtime and then jazz, the American composer had another source of indigenous music to draw on in his search for a national style.

[20] Powell, pp. 146–48.
[21] Powell, pp. 152–62, *passim.*

This material was first utilized in Henry Gilbert's *Dances in Ragtime Rhythm* (1915) and a *Concertino for Piano and Orchestra* of the same year written by John Alden Carpenter (1876–1951), a native of suburban Chicago. Carpenter made a considerable stir in 1921 with *Krazy Kat*, a ballet score first performed as an orchestral piece by the Chicago Symphony Orchestra. Its subject matter is drawn from American popular culture, the famous comic strip by George Herriman that excited both the hoi polloi and the intelligentsia of the country for many years; the ballet[22] makes considerable use of popular dances of the early jazz era; the orchestration includes instruments associated with jazz—piano, saxophone, a full complement of wind and brass instruments; Carpenter called it a "jazz pantomime" and it was described at the time as "music replete with jazzy inflections."[23] But hearing it today,[24] it is difficult to understand what the excitement was all about. Its most important musical reference is to French and Russian ballet music of the late nineteenth and early twentieth centuries; its most prominent "exotic" rhythms are those of Spanish dance, emphasized by use of castenets; and it is only in Krazy Kat's final "Katnip Blues" that occasional suggestions of jazz instrumentation and rhythm come through, in trombone and clarinet glissandos, the brief use of a muted "wa-wa" trumpet, and some hints of syncopated rhythms.

The most successful piece of this era combining jazz and classical elements was not the work of a "serious" composer, but of a musician whose chief background and experience was in popular music. *Rhapsody in Blue* (1924) by George Gershwin (1898–1937), a work for large jazz band and piano, was hailed by some critics on the occasion of its first performance as one of the most important pieces of concert music by an American composer to date:

> The audience was stirred, and many a hardened concertgoer excited with the sensation of a new talent finding its voice, and likely to say something personally and racially important to the world. A talent and an idiom, also rich in possibilities for that generally exhausted and outworn form of the classic piano concerto.[25]

It has been a problematic piece for critics and historians, however. Though Gershwin had some familiarity with classical music— he had studied piano as a child, and had retained sufficient skill to accompany the soprano Eva Gauthier in a program of songs by

[22] It was first done as a ballet on January 20, 1922 in New York's Town Hall with choreography by Adolf Bolm, who also danced the title role.

[23] Nicolas Slonimsky, *Music Since 1900* (New York: Charles Scribner's Sons, 1971), p. 350.

[24] It is available on NW 228, s1 / 1.

[25] Olin Downes, *New York Times* for February 17, 1924.

Byrd, Purcell, Bellini, Hindemth, Schoenberg, Milhaud, Kern, and Gershwin himself in New York in 1923—he had no formal training in counterpoint, composition, or orchestration, and was in fact not able to complete the scoring of *Rhapsody in Blue,* turning that task over to Ferdie Grofé (the arranger of Paul Whiteman's orchestra, which gave the first performance). Critics from the day of the premier until the present have harped on the same perceived deficiencies of compositional skill:

> This music is only half alive. Its gorgeous vitality of rhythm and of instrumental color is impaired by melodic and harmonic anemia of the most pernicious kind. How trite and feeble and conventional the tunes are, how sentimental and vapid the harmonic treatment, under the disguise of fussy and futile counterpoint![26]
>
> Gershwin had only limited experience in developing musical material, and . . . his serious works are structurally defective. The orchestral and piano pieces are filled with repetitive rather than developed melodies, motifs, sequences, and ostinatos, and often sections are separated by abrupt pauses.[27]

Just what were American composers striving for in their search for a national identity? Was it music faithful to nineteenth-century European compositional style, made American by the insinuation of bits and pieces of rhythms, melodic patterns, scales, and instrumental usage drawn from indigenous folk or popular music? Or was it music in which basic structural procedures would also grow out of these styles? Gershwin's subsequent "serious" music gives *his* answer to this dilemma: even though he sought out composition teachers, his *Concerto in F* (1925) for piano and orchestra, *An American in Paris* (1928), *Second Rhapsody* (1931) for piano and orchestra, and *Cuban Overture* (1932) reveal no greater sophistication in formal, developmental, and contrapuntal techniques than did *Rhapsody in Blue.* His episodic, fragmented, mosaiclike formal designs, growing out of the Tin Pan Alley song style and the popular dance music of the day, helped give these pieces what no "serious" American composer of the 1920s was able to achieve—a sense of being truly American in character.

America did indeed produce a composer during this period who wrote music so deeply rooted in American life and music as to have an unmistakable nationalistic character—yet he and his music went

[26] Lawrence Gilman, *New York Tribune* for February 17, 1924.
[27] Charles Schwartz, *The New Grove Dictionary of Music and Musicians,* VII, p. 303.

(left) George E. Ives as a young man (courtesy of Bigelow Ives); (right) his son Charles E. Ives in his later years.

virtually unnoticed and had no impact on either the musical life of the country or on other composers.

Charles Edward Ives was born in Danbury, Connecticut in 1874. His father, George E. Ives (1845–94), had been a bandmaster in the Union Army; afterward he directed choirs, led community bands, and taught theory and various instruments. His son absorbed a wide range of music—playing in his father's bands from an early age, singing in the church choir and becoming a church organist at fourteen; playing and singing popular songs at home; learning the classical repertory from piano and organ study. With the older man's blessings and encouragement, after the "serious" part of a day's instruction in music had been completed satisfactorily, Ives was allowed to "roam a little for fun":

> Father was not against a reasonable amount of "boy's fooling" if it were done with some sense behind it—as playing left-hand accompaniment in one key and tune in right hand in another. He made us stick to the end, and not stop when it got hard. This led into trying to write duets and pieces in more than one, or two keys together, also a fugue going up in fourths in four keys, or up in fifths in four keys, etc. Also I remember there was a kind of game—a way of playing off-beats *pp* on the nearest

black notes (as the *Arkansas Traveller*), singing the air, right-hand chords in G, left-hand bass in G, and off-beats *pp* in G♭, etc.[28]

Ives's first compositions, dating from his early teens, reflect the various musical threads that made up his background. There were songs, marches for piano and band, and organ pieces played as preludes and postludes at local churches, in the nature of fantasias on familiar hymns. Most remarkable were the settings of psalm texts, written when Ives was seventeen or eighteen, making use of bitonality, densely dissonant triadic writing, pandiatonic fugatos, freely atonal mirror writing, and whole-tone structures.

At Yale, where he matriculated in 1894, Ives studied for four years with Horatio Parker.

(I showed him) a couple of fugues with the theme in four different keys, C–G–D–A—and in another, C–F–B♭–E♭. It resulted, when all got going, in the most dissonant sounding counterpoint. Parker took it as a joke (he was seldom mean), and I didn't bother him but occasionally after the first few months. He would just look at a measure or so, and hand it back with a smile, or joke about "hogging all the keys at one meal" and then talk about something else.[29]

On assignment from Parker, he wrote songs to German and French texts, and for his thesis he produced his *First Symphony*, completed in June of 1898. It is a remarkable work, a four-movement symphony in late-nineteenth century Germanic style exhibiting a solid command of thematic statement and development, orchestration and counterpoint; a personal style combining compelling lyricism with infectuous ebullience shines through the restrictions imposed by his teacher. Parker's reaction was typical:

[The symphony] was supposed to be in D minor, but the first subject went through six or eight different keys, so Parker made me write another first movement. But it seemed no good to me, and I told him that I would much prefer to use the first draft. He smiled and let me do it, saying "But you must promise to end in D minor."[30]

Ives's other major composition during his Yale years was his *First String Quartet*, subtitled "From the Salvation Army." Some or all of the four movements originated as organ pieces—preludes, offer-

[28] Charles E. Ives, *Memos*, John Kirkpatrick, ed. (New York: W. W. Norton & Company, 1972), pp. 46–47.
[29] Ives, p. 49.
[30] Ives, p. 51.

tories, postludes—improvised by Ives at Centre Church in New Haven, based on familiar hymns. According to a note on the autograph manuscript, the quartet version was written for a series of revival services held in the church in 1896–97. The first movement takes the tune of Mason's famous hymn "Missionary" as the subject for a fugue:

*String Quartet No. 1,* by Charles Ives

and later introduces "Coronation" by Oliver Holden in a way which underscores the melodic similarity of the two tunes:

*String Quartet No. 1,* by Charles Ives

Graduation from college in 1898 posed for Ives the problem of a career. Apparently he never considered music:

(1) As a boy I was partially ashamed of it [music]—an entirely wrong attitude, but it was strong—most boys in American country towns, I think, felt the same. When other boys, Monday A.M. on vacation, were out driving grocery carts, or doing chores, or playing ball, I felt all wrong to stay in and play piano.

(2) Father felt that a man could keep his music-interest stronger, cleaner, bigger, and freer, if he didn't try to make a living out of it. If he has a nice wife and some nice children, how can he let the children starve on his dissonances! So he has to weaken (and as a man he should weaken for his children), but his music (some of it) more than weakens— it goes "ta ta" for money—bad for him, bad for music, but good for his boys!![31]

He took a position in New York with the Mutual Insurance Company. Musical activity—composition, playing the organ, and directing the choir at several churches—was confined to evenings, weekends, and holidays. Despite this, his twelve years in New York (from 1898 to 1911) were immensely productive. He wrote songs, dozens of them; organ pieces, played for church services; sacred choral pieces, including a seven-section cantata entitled *The Celestial Country* performed in 1902 at the Central Presbyterian Church in New York.

The *Second Symphony,* completed in 1901 or 1902, was based on earlier compositions, some dating back to his days at Yale. A five-movement work for full orchestra, it is cast in the same traditional harmonic and formal vocabulary as his first symphony. But it is hardly a conventional piece in its melodic material, being shot through with quotations from hymns, patriotic songs, and classi-

[31] Ives, p. 131.

cal pieces. Ives gave a score of the symphony to Walter Damrosch in 1910, hoping to hear at least a reading of it, but this never came about and the score was apparently misplaced.

The *Third Symphony*, completed in 1904 (subtitled "The Camp Meeting"), draws virtually all of its melodic material from familiar hymns. Its sound is quite different from that of the *Second Symphony*—there are successions of triads tonally unrelated to one another, polytonal structures, intensely chromatic developmental sections, complex interrelationships of themes. Written at a time when Ives first sensed that his music was not destined for public performance, the composer found that "I worked with more natural freedom when I knew the music was not going to be inflicted on others."[32] Several sets of *Ragtime Pieces* written in 1902–4 demonstrated his receptivity to yet another kind of American music. A number of brief keyboard works show him moving further than before in the direction of polytonal and even atonal harmonic structures.

Most remarkable are his *Two Contemplations* for small orchestra, written in 1906. In both, the orchestra is divided into two parts, which are not metrically coordinated and thus require two conductors. The first, *The Unanswered Question*—originally entitled "A Contemplation of a Serious Matter or The Unanswered Perennial Question"—has prompted more rhetoric than any piece Ives wrote:

> Muted strings, distantly playing immensely slow diatonic concords with virtually no temporal pulse, represent eternity and the unknowable mysteries. A solo trumpet becomes Man asking the "Perennial Question" in an angular, jagged, upward thrusting phrase to which what Ives calls the "Fighting Answerers" (flutes and other people) heroically attempt to give answers. The string concords proceed implacably on their way, however; so the Fighting Answerers get increasingly distraught, bumping into one another in polytonal, polyrhythmic chaos until they end in despairful mockery of the trumpet's phrase.[33]

The second, *Central Park in the Dark*—originally "A Contemplation of Nothing Serious or Central Park in the Dark in 'The Good Old Summer Time' "—opposes a chromatic, spiraling, pulseless backdrop in the strings and a foreground of fragments of popular tunes and other sounds from the contemporary world played by winds, percussion, and piano ("sounds of the manmade world—car hooters, subway roars, yelling newsvendors, jazz bands and theatre

---

[32] Ives, p. 129.
[33] Wilfrid Mellers, *Music in a New Found Land* (London: Barrie & Rockliff, 1964, and New York: Alfred A. Knopf, 1965), p. 46.

hubbub"[34]). Surely the fragments from "Hello! Ma Baby!" and other ragtime tunes represent the first use of such material in a "serious" composition.

The *First Piano Sonata*, worked on from 1901 until 1909, most clearly anticipates the compositional techniques and expressive depth of the extended pieces of his mature years. A five-movement piece (about fifty minutes long) requiring heroic technique and dedication from its performer, the *First Sonata* was said by Ives to be "about the outdoor life in Connecticut villages in the '80s and '90s—impressions, remembrances, and reflections of country farmers in Connecticut farmland."[35] On another occasion he told a friend that the two outer movements represented a family together, the second and fourth movements—based on ragtime rhythms—portrayed the son "sowing his oats," and the middle (third) movement reflected parental anxiety. Unity comes from the use of the same hymns and songs in various movements, thematic similarities among the tunes chosen for quotation, and a consistent and highly personal harmonic, melodic, and pianistic idiom throughout the piece.

The third movement will serve to underline some of Ives's technical and expressive methods. The opening slow section is unbarred and progresses from chords built on open fifths to a complexly harmonized version of the opening bars of Charles C. Converse's hymn "What a Friend We Have in Jesus," followed by dissonant chromatic chords of seven or eight notes:

*Piano Sonata No. 1,* by Charles Ives

[34] Mellers, p. 46.
[35] Ives, p. 75.

The fast section begins as a mad fantasy on Converse's hymn, but almost immediately Ives suggests the melodic similarity between this tune and a fragment of Stephen Foster's "Massa's in the Cold Ground":

*Piano Sonata No. 1*, by Charles Ives

Depending on the listener's familiarity with the hymn and song literature of the nineteenth century, fragmentary references to as many as a dozen tunes may be heard through the fearsomely complex piano writing and the excruciating dissonances that follow. A return to the slow tempo of the beginning brings more extended and more easily recognizable references to "What a Friend," and the movement closes with an almost exact quotation of the last measures of the hymn and an unambiguous subdominant–tonic cadence in the key of E major. Simplicity and clarity have emerged out of chaos.

Ives heard ragtime pianists in Connecticut as early as 1892, and in New York he was fond of listening to piano rags in bars. The *First Sonata* makes it clear that he—alone of the white musicians of the day—understood that the rhythmic essence of ragtime depended on additive rhythms:

*Piano Sonata No. 1*, by Charles Ives

In harmonic language, structural concepts, and technical demands on the performer, Ives had pushed far beyond what any other composer of the day was attempting. And he had done it on his own.

> I found that I could work more naturally and with more concentration if I didn't hear much music, especially unfamiliar music. To make a long story short, I went to few concerts. I've never heard or seen the score of the *Sacre du Printemps*, yet I've been told that some of my music had been strongly influenced by [it]. Personally I don't believe they have anything in common. The pieces which some say come from Stravinsky were written before Stravinsky wrote the *Sacre* (or at least before it was first played).[36]

In 1911 Ives moved out of the city to Hartsdale; the following year he bought a farm in West Redding. Success in business and a more peaceful setting seemed to spur him to even greater heights in composition, and the early 1910s brought an outpouring of major pieces of unparalleled vigor, vision, and expressiveness.

Ives was at the peak of his creative life; the pieces of this period were written for himself, utterly uncompromising in their demands on performer and audience. Tunes from hymns, marches, patriotic songs, dance music, popular and college songs, and the classical repertory were woven into intricately interlocking thematic relationships, implying that all music is part of a single tonal universe.

This period produced the *First Orchestral Set* (1911–14), better known as *Three Places in New England*, cast in three movements:
1. "The Saint Gaudens in Boston Common," inspired by a statue commemorating the 54th Massachusetts Regiment of Black Contrabands, a black regiment commanded by Colonel Robert Shaw. Ives wrote at the end of the score of this slow march, which quotes several Civil War and Stephen Foster songs:

> Moving—Marching—Faces of Souls!
> Marked with a generation of pain,
> Part freers of a Destiny,
> Slowly, restlessly swaying us on with you
> Towards other Freedom! . . .

A marginal jotting by Ives reads "this can never be played or make sense to anyone."
2. "Putnam's Camp, Redding, Connecticut," a portrait in sound of a child attending a Fourth of July picnic on a site marking the

[36] Ives, pp. 137–38.

winter quarters of General Israel Putnam's soldiers during the Revolution, hearing military bands, falling asleep, and dreaming of Putnam's men marching to the fife and drum music of the 1770s. In a celebrated passage, two bands are heard playing in different tempos.

3. "The Housatonic at Stockbridge," invoking "the colors one sees, sounds one hears, feelings one has, of a summer day near a wide river—the leaves, waters, mists, etc. all interweaving in the picture and a hymn singing in church away across the river," according to a note in the score. The strings play swirling, shifting, chromatic masses of sound; the melody is a highly elaborated version of a familiar hymn.

Cut out of the same cloth are four orchestral pieces—*Washington's Birthday* (1909), *Decoration Day* (1912), *The Fourth of July* (1911–13), and *Thanksgiving* (first sketched in 1904)—which Ives conceived as separate compositions but which may be "lumped together as a symphony," entitled *New England Holidays.*

The crowning achievement of this period, and perhaps of Ives's entire career, is the *Fourth Symphony,* which occupied Ives off and on between 1910 and 1916. It epitomizes Ives's art on many levels: virtually every compositional device in his entire repertory is drawn upon; more than a dozen of his earlier pieces were worked into the fabric of the symphony; many of the tunes that he drew upon throughout his career are found here; the philosophical attitudes which become inseparable from his later compositions are very much in evidence. The piece is concerned with nothing less than "the searching questions of What? and Why? which the spirit of Man asks of life."[37]

The first movement poses the "Eternal Question." Fragments of a number of hymns are given out by the orchestra, divided into a large group in the foreground and a frequently inaudible chamber group in the distance; a chorus sings Lowell Mason's "Watchman, Tell Us of the Night"; the brief movement dissolves into mists of sound.

The first answer, given in the second movement, is that life is a "comedy, in the sense that Hawthorne's Celestial Railroad is a comedy."[38] The music is at times an utterly mad melange of sounds, a jumble of dozens of tunes, skipping from dense clusters of orchestral sound to patches of familiar songs and dances, then back to explosions of sound so complex that two conductors are necessary. The mood skips abruptly from ominous to trivial to sentimental to

[37] From notes prepared by Henry Bellman in 1927 for a performance of two movements of the symphony.

[38] From a note by Ives in the score.

martial; the ending is enigmatic, a single sustained note after torrents of sound.

The third movement gives a second answer—"the expression of life into formalism and ritualism." Ives dipped into his days at Yale with Horatio Parker for this answer; the movement is a reworking of the slow movement of his *First String Quartet*, with its subject drawn from Lowell Mason's "Missionary Hymn."

Ives's own answer seems to be given in the last movement, "an apotheosis of the preceding content, in terms that have something to do with the reality of existence and its religious experience."[39] It is perhaps Ives's most personal statement; a hushed rhythmic ostinato played by drums, cymbal, and gong continues throughout; the orchestra, consisting of several discrete units—the main body; a "distant choir" of chamber-music proportions; organ; solo piano—builds a complex fabric of fragmentary references to Mason's hymn and others; at the climax, an invisible choir hums "Nearer My God To Thee." The movement dissolves into silence, and only the soft ostinato of the percussion section is heard in the final measures.

The *Second String Quartet* was completed in 1913. Ives set out to write it, "half mad, half in fun," after hearing a concert by the Kneisel Quartet in Mendelssohn Hall in New York.

> It used to come over me that music had been, and still was, too much of an emasculated art. Too much of what was easy and usual to play and to hear was called beautiful, etc.—the same old even-vibration, Sybaritic apron-strings, keeping music too much tied to the old ladies. The string quartet music got more and more weak, trite, and effeminate.[40]

The three movements are entitled "Discussions," "Arguments," and "The Call of the Mountains"; Ives jotted on the score that the piece was a "string quartet for 4 men—who converse, discuss, argue, fight, shake hands, shut up—then walk up the mountain side to view the firmament!" Parts of it are the most unrelentingly dissonant music ever written for string quartet; fragments of patriotic tunes and hymns (and also symphonies by Brahms, Beethoven, and Tchaikowsky) emerge from a thicket of atonal, polytonal sounds made even more strident by the extreme difficulty of the instrumental writing; even in the most professional performance the four players appear to be scrambling to approximate the notes.

Ives himself is responsible for the subtitle "Concord, Massachusetts, 1840–1860" to his *Second Piano Sonata*, and later wrote that

[39] Ives, p. 66.
[40] Ives, p. 74.

the piece "is an attempt to present one person's impression of the spirit of the literature, the philosophy, and the men of Concord of over a half century ago." The four movements are entitled "Emerson," "Hawthorne," "The Alcotts," and "Thoreau"; characteristically, much of the music is drawn from earlier unfinished pieces. The sonata was essentially completed by 1912, when Ives played it for Max Smith in Hartsdale; his friend liked the Alcott movement, but the rest of it "made him half sore, half cuckoo, etc."[41] Ives later explained that the piece was "called a sonata for want of a more exact name." Many years later, reacting to a criticism that the piece was "formless," he wrote:

> A natural procedure in a piece of music, be it a song or a week's symphony, may have something in common with—I won't say analogous to—a walk up a mountain. There's the mountain, its foot, its summit—there's the valley—the climber looks, turns, and looks down or up. He sees the valley, but not exactly the same angle he saw it at the last look—and the summit is changing with every step—and the sky. Even if he stands on the same rock at the top and looks toward Heaven and Earth, he is now in just the same key he started in, or in the same moment of existence.[42]

Enough has been written about the *Concord Sonata* elsewhere[43] to make it unnecessary to continue here. Suffice it to say that it has long since been accepted as a crowning achievement of Ives's compositional career, and as one of the handful of works of pure genius written for the piano in the present century.

America's entry into World War I in 1917 brought a flurry of patriotic songs from Ives, who tried to enlist as an ambulance driver. A serious heart attack in September 1918 prompted him to revise and make clear copies of many of his larger compositions, and to publish some of his music at his own expense. The *Second Piano Sonata* was privately printed in 1920, together with a lengthy introductory *Essays Before a Sonata*. A collection of *114 Songs*, again accompanied by an essay, was printed in 1922. Several brief pieces were completed in the early 1920s, including several dozen songs.[44] But he was unable to mount sustained creative effort, and the last thirty years of his life were spent in almost complete retirement from both business and music.

[41] Ives, p. 186.
[42] Ives, p. 196.
[43] Cf. Henry and Sidney Cowell, *Charles Ives and His Music* (New York: Oxford University Press, 1955), pp. 190–201 and Gilbert Chase, *America's Music* (New York: McGraw-Hill, 1966), pp. 418–27, for instance.
[44] The last of these, "Sunrise," is available on NW 300, s1 / 5.

It was during this time, however, that his music began to be performed. His *Third Violin Sonata* was played at the Carnegie Chamber Music Hall in 1917; the *Second Violin Sonata* was performed at Aeolian Hall in New York on March 18, 1924; on January 29, 1927, the first two movements of the *Fourth Symphony* were played. Nicholas Slonimsky conducted the first performance of *Three Places in New England* in New York on February 16, 1930, on a program of the American section of the International Society for Contemporary Music, then repeated the piece in Town Hall with the Boston Chamber Orchestra in early 1931; on June 6 Slonimsky conducted the piece in Paris under the auspices of the Pan American Association—the first time a piece by Ives was heard in Europe.

The number of performances thereafter accelerated: *Washington's Birthday* was done in San Francisco in September of 1931; the Havana Philharmonic premiered *Decoration Day* in December; *The Fourth of July* was done in Paris and Berlin in 1932; seven songs by Ives were performed by Hubert Linscott, with Aaron Copland accompanying, at the Yaddo Music Festival in May of 1932. The first recording of a piece by Ives was made in 1934: "General William Booth Enters into Heaven," sung by Radiana Pazmor, accompanied by Genevieve Pitot; the following year brought the first commercial publication of one of his compositions, *Three Places in New England.*

But other major pieces waited much longer for their first performances. Though Henry Bellamann and other pianists had played sections of the *Second (Concord) Piano Sonata* within several years of Ives's publication of the score, the first public performance of the entire piece awaited the historic recital by John Kirkpatrick at Town Hall on January 20, 1939. The *First Piano Sonata* and the *Second String Quartet* were premiered in 1946. The *Fourth Symphony* did not receive its first complete performance until 1965.

Virtually no one had the chance to respond to Ives's music until the late 1920s because of his decision to make a career in another field and his refusal to seek performances for his compositions, to establish contact with other composers, to become a functioning part of the musical life of the country. His music was not so much ignored as it was totally unknown. Horatio Parker, when asked in 1910 for information about his erstwhile student, could only reply, "Your query baffles me. There was a Charles Ives in my class when I first came to Yale, but I cannot think he is the same."[45]

As a result, the music of Charles Ives played no role in the struggle

---

[45] David Woolridge, *From the Steeples and Mountains. A Study of Charles Ives* (New York: Alfred A. Knopf, 1974), p. 206.

for a national identity which occupied most American composers in the decades when his compositions were written.

Ives succeeded in writing truly American music where his peers had mostly failed, for three reasons:

—The indigenous musical material on which he drew—hymns, patriotic songs, band music, popular tunes, ragtime—was at the core of his own musical vocabulary. Using it was not a deliberate or patronizing act; it came naturally and often unconsciously to him.

—His attitudes toward aesthetic and cultural issues were based on American traditions and literature.

—He was the most talented composer of his generation.

Had he persevered, had his remarkable symphonies, songs, string quartets, and sonatas become known to American audiences and other American composers in the first two decades of the century, a viable school of American composition might have become a reality.

In the 1920s many talented American composers still found their way to Europe, but now they went to Paris rather than Berlin, Munich, or Frankfurt, and consequently turned out pieces characterized by Gallic attitudes and techniques.

Virgil Thomson, for instance, born in Kansas City in 1896, had a musical background much like that of Charles Ives: his family had its roots in Virginia, they were Southern Baptists, and he grew up amidst the hymns of Protestant America and the sentimental songs and piano variations of the nineteenth century; ragtime came into the house through his sister and her friends; Virgil himself became a church organist, and sometimes played the piano for silent movies; he made his own way through some of the standard classical literature for piano and piano-vocal scores of standard operas; there were nightly band concerts in the summer. He responded with enthusiasm to all of this music, and it became part of his musical vocabulary.

At Harvard and later in Paris he was attracted to the music of Eric Satie and Les Six, with its emphatic rejection of German Romanticism in favor of simplicity, lucidity, and emotional detachment. Like so many of his contemporaries he studied with Nadia Boulanger, whose teaching stressed a rational and intensely musical approach to composition. His own pieces, from the beginning, drew on the music he had known as a child: *Two Sentimental Tangos* for piano (1923); *Variations and Fugues on Sunday School Tunes* for organ (1926–27); *Symphony on a Hymn Tune* (1928). Though he used various "learned" devices in these pieces, they are characterized by a directness and economy of means and a transparency of orchestration.

A series of film scores written in the 1930s and '40s brought Thomson's "American" period to a climax. The first, written to a documentary film entitled *The Plow that Broke the Plains* made by Pare Lorentz in 1936, is a beautiful and highly effective demonstration of the composer's use of American material in a style shaped by French lucidity. Thomson wrote the score quickly and easily:

> I knew the Great Plains landscape in Kansas, Oklahoma, New Mexico, Texas; and during the War I had lived in a tent with ten-below-zero dust storms. I came to the theme nostalgic and ready to work; and the film itself, when I first encountered it, was highly photogenic—broad grasslands and cattle, mass harvesting, erosion by wind, deserted farms.[46]

A six-part orchestral suite made from the score became one of the most widely played American pieces of its decade.

Thomson used similar techniques in other film scores—*The River* (1937), another documentary by Lorenz; Robet Flaherty's *Louisiana Story* (1948)—and in the ballet *Filling Station*. But the end of the Depression, America's involvement in another great war and a flood of European musicians seeking refuge in the New World brought America out of its introspective mood of the 1930s and planted fresh musical ideas in the consciousness of most of our composers, Thomson among them.

Aaron Copland, born in Brooklyn in 1900, also went off to Paris to study with Nadia Boulanger in the early 1920s.

> Remember that I was an adolescent during the First World War, when Germany and German music were very unpopular. The new thing in music was Debussy and Ravel—also Scriabin. Germany seemed like that old-fashioned place where composers used to study music in Leipzig. All the new things seemed to be coming from Paris—even before I knew the name Stravinsky.[47]

For four years the young American absorbed the full range of European music. From his earliest compositions a characteristic style emerged, shaped partly by his musical instincts and partly by his exposure to the rational, concise, precise music favored by French composers of the day and by his teacher. The central elements of Copland's style, in the view of a fellow composer, are:

---

[46] Virgil Thomson, *Virgil Thomson* (New York: Alfred A. Knopf, 1966), p. 270.

[47] Edward T. Cone, "Conversation with Aaron Copland," in *Perspectives on American Composers*, Benjamin Boretz and Edward T. Cone, eds. (New York: W. W. Norton & Company, 1971), p. 173.

Economy of means, the transparency of his textures, the preciseness of his tonal vocabulary—all of them rare accomplishments at a time when approximate effects are often considered sufficient because they seem to serve a composer's immediate end in works heard from a distance in large concert halls.[48]

In addition, the age was still haunted by the concept of musical nationalism:

The period of the Twenties (was) colored by the notion that Americans needed a kind of music they could recognize as their own. It's a very unpopular idea now but seemed very much in the cards then. Don't forget that it was the Hungarianness of Bartók that seemed so fascinating; not only was he writing good modern music, but it was Hungarian in quality.[49]

From the perspective of Paris in the 1920s, jazz was the most characteristic and exciting form of American music. Copland set out to make use of it:

The identification of jazz with the *Zeitgeist* formed the text of many an article during the '20s. What interested composers, however, was not so much the spirit of jazz, whatever it symbolized, as the more technical side of jazz—the rhythm, melody, harmony, timbre through which that spirit was expressed.

From the composer's viewpoint, jazz had only two expressions: the well-known "blues" mood, and the wild, abandoned, almost hysterical and grotesque mood so dear to the youth of all ages. These two moods encompassed the whole gamut of jazz emotion.[50]

Copland absorbed elements from jazz into his own compositional style as a conscious, intellectual maneuver to enrich his vocabulary and to make reference to music of his own country. Audiences and critics indeed perceived jazz influences in his compositions of the 1920s—the *Symphony* for organ and orchestra (1924), commissioned and first performed by Boulanger as a gesture of confidence in the talent of her young student; *Music for the Theatre* (1925), a suite for small orchestra; pieces for piano.[51]

Obvious references to jazz became less fashionable in both Europe and America in the 1930s, but rhythmic impulses from this music had become so ingrained in Copland's vocabulary that traces

[48] Arthur Berger, *Aaron Copland* (New York: Oxford University Press, 1953), p. 39.
[49] Cone, p. 177.
[50] Aaron Copland, *The New Music. 1900–1960* (New York: W. W. Norton & Company, 1968), pp. 63–64.
[51] NW 277, s2 / 3.

may be spotted in later compositions. The second movement of his *Piano Sonata* (1939–41),[52] for instance, is shot through with "the wild, abandoned, almost hysterical and grotesque mood" that he had found in jazz and with the polymetrical (or additive) rhythmic patterns that help generate this mood.

The Great Depression of the 1930s brought a new and somewhat different impetus to the continuing search for a national music. As Copland saw it:

> In all the arts the Depression had aroused a wave of sympathy for and identification with the plight of the common man. In music this was combined with the heady wine of suddenly feeling ourselves—the composers, that is—needed as never before. Previously our works had been largely self-engendered: no one asked for them: we simply wrote them out of our own need. Now, suddenly, functional music was in demand as never before. Motion-picture and ballet companies, radio stations and schools, film and theater producers discovered us. The music appropriate for the different kinds of cooperative ventures undertaken by these people had to be simpler and more direct. There was a "market" especially for music evocative of the American scene—industrial backgrounds, landscapes of the Far West, and so forth.[53]

Recognizing that most of his compositions had been "difficult to perform and difficult for an audience to comprehend," Copland set out to "say what I had to say in the simplest possible terms."[54] Much as he had done with jazz, he turned to music that had been no part of his own cultural heritage—the traditional music of several ethnic groups—but would help stamp his compositions as distinctively American. The results were historic: no orchestral works by an American composer have received more performances, for more responsive listeners, than the following:

*El salón México* (1933–36), orchestral suite

*Billy the Kid* (1938), ballet; orchestral suite

*An Outdoor Overture* (1938)

*Quiet City* (1939), incidental music; arranged for small orchestra

*Our Town* (1940), film score; arranged for orchestral suite

*Rodeo* (1942), ballet; orchestral suite

*Lincoln Portrait* (1942), speaker and orchestra

*Fanfare for the Common Man* (1942)

*Appalachian Spring* (1943–44), ballet; orchestral suite

*Danzón cubano* (1944)

*The Red Pony* (1948), film score; arranged as an orchestral suite

Most of these pieces make prominent use of traditional tunes.

[52] The piece is available in a performance by Leonard Bernstein on NW 277, s1 / 2.
[53] Copland, pp. 161–62.
[54] Copland, p. 160.

*Billy the Kid,* by Aaron Copland

Copland's technique with this material is somewhere between Ives (who introduced fragments of borrowed melodies in ambiguous surroundings) and Thomson (who often merely harmonized and orchestrated folk melodies). *Billy the Kid, Rodeo,* and *Lincoln Por-*

*trait* present their traditional melodies in easily recognizable form, but Copland cannot resist tampering: "durations are stretched unexpectedly or notes omitted, motifs are detached, new phrases are formed, so that the flow of the music is by no means determined by the tunes."[55]

The most elaborate use of a borrowed melody comes in *Appalachian Spring*, where the Shaker tune "The Gift to be Simple" is taken as the subject of a prolonged and climactic set of variations.

Like virtually all American composers, Copland turned to European models after World War II. His *Piano Quartet* (1950) was a twelve-tone piece, and "the Schoenberg method (not the aesthetic) continued to intrigue me in subsequent works"[56]—such serially organized compositions as the *Piano Fantasy* (1957) and *Connotations for Orchestra* (1962).

Both his search for a national style and his romance with American audiences had ended.

A scene from a 1966 performance of Martha Graham's ballet *Appalachian Spring*. (Photograph by Martha Swope)

[55] William Austin, *The New Grove Dictionary of Music and Musicians*, Vol. 4, p. 723.
[56] Copland, p. 168.

The long wait for the Great American Composer seemingly ended in the early years of the Depression with the meteoric emergence of Roy Harris. His background was appropriate: birth (in 1898) in a log cabin on Lincoln's birthday, in Lincoln, Nebraska; childhood in the San Gabriel Valley of California; a proletariat adolescence and young adulthood, including several years spent driving a truck for a dairy company; early self-instruction in music. His talent as a composer was honed in Paris in the late 1920, under Nadia Boulanger. He had a strong sense of the cultural identity of America and an equally strong sense of how this identity could be expressed in music:

> Our rhythmic impulses are fundamentally different from (those) of Europeans; and from this unique rhythmic sense are generated different melodic and form values. Our sense of rhythm is less symmetrical than the European rhythmic sense. European musicians are trained to think of rhythm in its largest common denominator, while we are born with a feeling for its smallest units. Our struggle is not to invest new rhythms and melodies and forms; our problem is to put down into translatable symbols and rhythms and consequent melodies and form those that assert themselves within us.[57]

Performances of his *Concerto* (1927) for clarinet, piano, and strings, *Piano Sonata* (1928), and *String Quartet No. 1* (1930) inspired an article by Arthur Farwell hailing him as a genius.[58] Serge Koussevitzky, conductor of the Boston Symphony Orchestra, became his most important champion, performing his *First Symphony* in 1933 and proclaiming it the "first truly tragic symphony by an American." An overture, *When Johnny Comes Marching Home* (1935), was widely played, and his career peaked with the *Third Symphony*, written in 1937 and premiered in Boston on February 24, 1939. The piece was filled with Harris's now-characteristic devices: a broad opening motif, mostly in unison:

*Third Symphony*, by Roy Harris

[57] Roy Harris, "Problems of American Composers," in Henry Cowell, ed., *American Composers on American Music* (Palo Alto: Stanford University Press, 1933), pp. 149–66.

[58] Arthur Farwell, "Roy Harris," *The Musical Quarterly*, XVIII / 1 (January 1932), p. 18.

lyric, pastoral, and dramatic sections with asymmetric modal tunes harmonized with chords built on perfect intervals, simple triads, and more complex chords built of superimposed harmonic structures; a fugue, with a subject suggesting the American penchant for rhythmic patterns based on the smallest units of measurement (see facing page).

The piece quickly became the most often played symphony in the entire history of American music. Critics across the country found in this music precisely those qualities which Harris had earlier identified as characteristically American; their reviews were filled with such terms as "sinewy," "elemental," "stark," "rugged," and "gaunt"; the music evoked images of "wind-swept prairies" and "seas of wheat."

The outbreak of World War II seemed to stimulate him to even greater productivity. There were more symphonies (three during the war years) and other orchestral pieces, choral and chamber works,[59] and a spate of compositions for concert band. Critical

*Third Symphony*, by Roy Harris

commentary continued to range from favorable to ecstatic. Copland wrote of his music in 1940:

> The outstanding thing that sets Harris apart from other composers is the fact that he possesses one of the most pronounced musical personalities of anyone now writing. . . . What (he) writes is music of real sweep and breadth, with power and emotional depth such as only a generously built country could produce. It is American in rhythm, especially in the fast parts, with a jerky, nervous quality that is peculiarly our own. It is crude and unabashed at times, with occasional blobs and yawps of sound that Whitman would have approved of.
>
> American, too, is his melodic gift, perhaps his most striking characteristic. His music comes nearest to a distinctively native melos of anything yet done, at least in the ambitious forms. Celtic folksongs and Protestant hymns are its basis, but they have been completely reworked, lengthened, malleated.[60]

But the postwar years were not kind to him. Though he continued to compose almost until his death in 1979, performances of his music became rarer and critical attention turned to other sorts of music. Copland wrote in 1967:

[59] His *String Quartet No. 2* (*Three Variations on a Theme*) is available on NW 218, s1.

[60] Copland, pp. 119–20.

Harris the composer has remained very much what he was, but the musical scene around him (and us) has radically altered. . . . As it has turned out, the young men of [today] show no signs of wishing to build on the work of the older American-born composers, the generation of the '20s and '30s. Today's gods live elsewhere.[61]

Opera is potentially the most effective genre around which to build a national school of music. Plots may be constructed from legends, episodes in national history, incidents in the lives of patriots and other famous men and women, well-known works of national literature. Visual references to national culture are possible: stage sets depicting typical locations, costumes indigenous to certain regions. National dances may be introduced, distinctive singing styles or choral repertory may be utilized in choruses.

Within a decade of the first stirrings of musical nationalism in America, composers were indeed beginning to write operas intended to reflect the American experience. Henry Gilbert spent some years on an operatic version of *Uncle Remus*, but the project was abandoned around 1906. Charles Wakefield Cadman began an "Indian" opera, *The Land of the Misty Water*, in 1909; the piece occupied him for three years but never reached the stage. The first opera of this sort to be performed seems to have been Arthur Nevin's *Poia* (1909), produced by the Royal Opera in Berlin but never staged in the United States.

The first "Indian" opera seen on an American stage was *Natoma* by Victor Herbert (1859–1924), the Irish-born composer of such successful operettas as *Babes in Toyland* (1903), *The Red Mill* (1906), and *Naughty Marietta* (1910). Herbert wrote *Natoma* for the Manhattan Opera Company of Oscar Hammerstein, but the troupe disbanded before the piece was finished, and the first performance was given in Philadelphia on February 25, 1911 by the Philadelphia-Chicago Opera Company. A brilliant cast included Mary Garden in the title role and John McCormack as the romantic lead; the libretto, by Joseph Deighn Redding, concerns a noble Indian maiden who saves a white friend by killing a villainous tribesman and then becomes a nun; Herbert supposedly incorporated Indian melodies into his score. But the piece was poorly received—the press described it as "A dull text set to mediocre music, an antiquated 'book' written in stilted speech and silly verse that contains neither operatic drama nor operatic characters"[62]—and any refer-

[61] Copland, p. 125.
[62] Boston *Evening Transcript* for February 27, 1911.

ences to Indian musical materials were obscured by Herbert's usual operetta language.[63]

American opera found an important champion in an unlikely place. Giulio Gatti-Casazza (1869–1940) assumed the post of general manager of the Metropolitan Opera Company in 1910, after successful tenures at the Teatro Comunale in Ferrara and La Scala in Milan. Coming from a tradition in which contemporary opera was an important part of the repertory, Gatti-Casazza instituted a policy of seeking out and performing American works. Frederick Converse's one-act *The Pipe of Desire* was given the first season (it had been premiered in Boston in 1906); Gatti-Casazza then set up a competition—with a prize of $10,000—for a new, full-length American opera. The winning work was Horatio Parker's *Mona*, with a "gory libretto wherein an early British noblemaiden stabs her Roman lover to death in 99 A.D. when he meddles in her druidic rites"; this text, so reminiscent of the era of Spontini and Bellini, was wedded to a score in late-nineteenth-century Germanic idiom, and the costly production endured for only four performances. But the first decade of Gatti-Casazza's tenure was a period of unprecedented opportunity for American opera, and with the Chicago Opera and other companies adopting a similar attitude, few operas by major American composers went unperformed in the decade of the 1910s. The following works were performed in New York or Chicago:

1913—*Cyrano de Bergerac*, Walter Damrosch
1914—*Madeleine*, Victor Herbert
1917—*Azora*, Henry Hadley
1917—*The Canterbury Pilgrims*, Reginald de Koven
1918—*A Daughter of the Forest*, Ethelbert Nevin
1918—*Shanewis*, Charles Wakefield Cadman
1919—*The Legend*, Joseph Breil
1919—*The Temple Dancer*, John Adam Hugo
1920—*Rip Van Winkle*, Reginald de Koven
1920—*Cleopatra's Night*, Henry Hadley

And when this list is augmented by other American operas performed elsewhere in the United States during this decade—*The Sacrifice* by Converse (Boston, 1911), *Narcissa* by Mary Carr Moore (Seattle, 1912), *The Atonement of Pan* by Hadley (San Francisco, 1912), *The Dove of Peace* by Damrosch (Portsmouth, 1912), *Fairyland* by Parker (Los Angeles, 1915), *Hearts of Erin* by Herbert

[63] The arias "I List the Trill" and "No Country Can My Own Outvie" are available on NW 241, s1 / 1–2.

(Cleveland, 1917), *Bianca* by Hadley (New York, 1918), and *The Sunset Trail* by Cadman (San Diego, 1920—it appears that this was indeed a golden age for opera in this country. The problem is that none of these works enjoyed a lengthy run, none was performed by an operatic company other than the one responsible for the premiere, none was revived, almost none appeared in print.

A truly successful opera by an American composer did not appear until 1927, when *The King's Henchman*, by Deems Taylor (1885–1966), was premiered by the Metropolitan Opera on February 17. It held the stage for three seasons and was given a record (for an American opera) fourteen performances. Its strengths were a sound and poetical libretto by Edna St. Vincent Millay and a craftsmanlike score by a composer who had made it his business to master the various components of opera—recitative, aria, chorus, descriptive orchestral music, ensembles, finale. It is set in tenth-century England, and Taylor's music is eclectically European in style. But it works, dramatically and musically: the story is laid out in simple, elegant language; the leading characters are sketched with subtlety and depth; Taylor's music allows all critical parts of the text to come through to underline and heighten the drama.[64] It is more an opera by an American than an American opera, but it carried a critical message: no opera can succeed unless its composer masters the basic techniques of the genre.

It was not until 1933 that the Met finally presented an opera distinctively American in style and competently crafted for the stage. *The Emperor Jones* by Louis Gruenberg, based on a play by Eugene O'Neill, was given its first performance on January 7, 1933. The opening-night audience was ecstatic; the *New York Times* ran a headline the following morning announcing that "The Emperor Jones Triumphs as Opera," and went on to say that the "drama [was] swift, tense, emotional, with fantastical music and a spectacular finale."

O'Neill's plot revolves around Brutus Jones, a former slave who has become a pullman porter; after murdering a man in a dice game, he escapes to an island in the Caribbean, where he sets himself up as an emperor. His subjects eventually rebel and pursue him into the jungle where, in a final moment of hallucination, he kills himself with a silver bullet. The "spectacular finale" is an intensely dramatic monologue in which Jones rambles about his past, repents the murder, turns to the religion of his childhood (in Gruenberg's operatic version, he sings the spiritual "Standing in the Need of Prayer"), then shoots himself—all this against the

[64] Two excerpts are available on NW 241, s1 / 3–4.

counterpoint of offstage voodoo drums and the chanting voices of his pursuers.[65]

Despite the initial success of *The Emperor Jones*, it disappeared from the repertory of the Metropolitan Opera after two seasons, never to be revived. Subsequent criticism suggested that it was more a play with music than a true opera; after the first wave of enthusiasm, New York audiences found its persistent percussive nature wearying and the absence of traditional arias and ensembles regrettable.

If there were to be native American opera, the Met had become an unlikely place for it to flourish. George Gershwin's *Porgy and Bess* demonstrated this in spectacular fashion. After opening in Boston at the Colonial Theatre on September 30, 1935, it moved to New York for a sixteen-week run at the Alvin Theatre, then went on the road for three months. Successful revivals in 1938 and 1942 were also mounted in commercial theaters rather than opera houses. Its first European performance came in Copenhagen in 1943; an all-black cast took it to Europe in 1952, and essentially the same cast performed it both in New York and on the road in 1952–53; many of the same performers were part of the company that took it to Russia in 1955—the first theatrical company from the United States to be invited to the Soviet Union. But it has yet to be performed in a major American opera house.

The libretto is based on the novel *Porgy* by Du Bose Heyward, set in the black district of Charleston, South Carolina. Gershwin had an unusual affinity for black musicians and their music. His friends included Jim Europe, James P. Johnson, Luckey Roberts, and Will Vodery; he haunted musical events in Harlem in the 1920s; Vodery worked with him on a one-act opera entitled *Blue Monday Blues* (1922). Black singers and jazz musicians in turn were much more responsive to his music that to that of any other Tin Pan Alley composer. While working on the opera, Gershwin spent some time in and around Charleston, particularly Folly Island, ten miles out from the city and with a large population of Gullah blacks with only intermittent contact with white culture. Heyward observed:

> To George it was more like a homecoming than an exploration. The Gullah Negro prides himself on what he calls "shouting." This is a complicated pattern beaten out by feet and hands as an accompaniment to the spirituals and is indubitably an African survival. I shall never forget the night when, at a Negro meeting on a remote sea-island, George started "shouting" with them. And eventually to their huge delight stole

[65] Part of this monologue, without the offstage drums and chorus, is available on NW 241, s1/5.

the show from their champion "shouter." I think he is the only white man in America who could have done it.[66]

*Porgy and Bess* is a fully developed opera; it has recitatives and arias, choruses and ensemble scenes, descriptive orchestral music, duets, large-scale production numbers. Gershwin does not draw on "folk" material, except briefly in a street scene, but rather the popular musical idiom of his own time—which he himself had helped to shape, in his songs. Since this idiom is indebted in various ways to black Americans, and since it is a natural style for Gershwin himself, it is more effective in laying out the emotions of his simple, soulful characters than if he had tried to draw directly on their music.

Americans often observe that strains from Italian opera may be heard on the streets and in the shops of Italy. The songs from *Porgy and Bess*—"Summertime," "It Ain't Necessarily So," "I Got Plenty o' Nuthin' "—may not be heard in the streets, but they were heard for several decades on the radio, on television, on the phonograph. Gershwin came closer to bridging classical and popular musical culture than any other operatic composer of the twentieth century; his opera functions equally well as a formal stage entertainment and as people's song. It is the greatest nationalistic opera of the century, not only of America but of the world.

Virgil Thomson's *Four Saints in Three Acts*, premiered the year before Gershwin's opera, is vastly different in concept and musical style, yet its history is remarkably similar: it made its way to the stage and enjoyed considerable success outside the professional operatic life of America.

Thomson, while in Paris early in his career, met the American expatriate Gertrude Stein, whom he had admired since his days at Harvard. Stein had little interest in music, but she found Thomson and his compositions fascinating, and in early 1927 they began discussing the possibility of writing an opera together.

Stein's libretto for *Four Saints in Three Acts* has no roots in operatic history. "Instead of presenting a linear series of dramatic events that are progressive in their development of characters and plot, Stein unveils a taspestry of images. It is an abstract assemblage of words and images patterned after the techniques of Cubist painting."[67] Thomson saw the theme of the opera as "the religious life— peace between the sexes, community of faith, the production of miracles";[68] his music was intended to "evoke Christian liturgy,"

[66] As quoted in David Ewen, *A Journey to Greatness. The Life and Music of George Gershwin* (New York: Henry Holt, 1956), pp. 257–58.

[67] Robert Marx, liner notes for NW 288–89, pp. 8–9.

[68] Thomson, p. 105.

Leontyne Price and William Warfield sing the title roles in a memorable production of George Gershwin's *Porgy and Bess*.

but that of his own childhood in the Southern Baptist church, not of Europe. It is mostly tonal, triadic, monophonic, and static, with reference to hymns, nursery tunes, and the like.

The first performance was in Hartford, Connecticut, on February 8, 1934, for the opening of the Avery Memorial Theater. The production has become one of the legends of American theatrical history: an all-black cast, mostly from Harlem and Brooklyn, had been selected and coached by Thomson; John Houseman was stage director; Frederick Ashton did the choreography; the American painter Florine Stettheimer designed the sets and costumes; Alexander Smallens conducted. The mix of elements and styles was preposterous—a "Cubist" libretto set to Southern Baptist music, with an urban black cast (directed and choreographed by Englishmen) singing and dancing in front of a semiabstract American set—but somehow it all worked. The show moved from Hartford to Broadway, for a six-week run, then to Chicago. There were sixty performances the first year alone.

Stylistically, it is difficult to imagine three more different operas than *The Emperor Jones, Four Saints,* and *Porgy and Bess.* But the appearance of the three at virtually the same time suggested that indigenous American opera was at last becoming a reality, and 1937 brought two more successful—and very different—pieces for the musical stage, *The Cradle Will Rock* by Marc Blitzstein and Gian Carlo Menotti's *Amelia Goes to the Ball.*

A pattern had been set for American opera, not of musical style but of venue. The successful works of the next decade—Aaron Copland's *The Second Hurricane* (1937),[69] Douglas Moore's *The Devil and Daniel Webster* (1939), Menotti's *The Medium* (1945), *The Telephone* (1946), and *The Consul* (1949)[70]—were produced commercially, on Broadway or by well-subsidized theater departments at America's colleges. The handful of new works mounted by America's professional operatic companies were mostly failures—the Metropolitan Opera's productions of Howard Hanson's *Merry Mount* (1934)[71] and Menotti's *The Island God* (1942), for instance.

When Thomson and Stein collaborated on another opera just after the war, *The Mother of Us All,* the premiere took place at Columbia University (on May 7, 1947), and most subsequent productions were mounted at colleges and music schools. The central character was Susan B. Anthony (1820–1906), the famous fighter for women's suffrage. The style of both libretto and music is often whimsical—both Stein and Thomson appear as characters, and the composer set the complete text, including stage directions:

| | |
|---|---|
| Susan B. Anthony | Yes I was, |
| Gertrude S. | said Susan. |
| Anne | You mean you are, |
| Virgil T. | said Anne. |
| Susan B. | No, |
| Gertrude S. | said Susan, |

[69] Cf. NW 241, s2 / 1, for an excerpt.
[70] A highly effective dramatic sequence is available on NW 241, s2 / 2.
[71] Cf. NW 241, s1 / 6, for an excerpt.

Gertrude S. and Virgil T. in the Santa Fe production of *Mother of Us All*.
(Photograph by Ken Howard)

| | |
|---|---|
| Susan B. | no. When this you see remember me, |
| Gertrude S. | said Susan B. |
| Anne | I do, |
| Virgil T. | said Anne.[72] |

Much of the libretto is more narrative than that of their first opera,
and some sections in fact approach the recitative-area patterns of
traditional opera:

[72] From Act 1, scene 1. NW 288–89 is a complete recording of the opera.

| Anne | Oh it was wonderful, wonderful, they listen to nobody the way they listen to you. |
| Susan B. | Yes it is wonderful as the result of my work for the first time the word male has been written into the constitution of the United States concerning suffrage. Yes it is wonderful. |
| Anne | But. |
| Susan B. | Yes but, what is man, what are men, what are they . . .[73] |

Thomson sets the words in a mostly syllabic way, in a style that does not "attempt to do any of the things already done by the words. It merely explodes them into singing and gives them shape."[74]

The stylistic similarity among the successful American operas of the 1930s and '40s is that each composer—Gershwin, Menotti, Blitzstein, Thomson, Gruenberg, Moore—utilized a melodic and harmonic vocabulary that stays in touch with the musical experiences of performers and audiences of the time, and each set his text so that the voice dominates and the orchestra functions as an accompaniment. But the late 1940s and early '50s brought sweeping changes of technique and aesthetic to American music. Most composers were no longer concerned with finding a common ground with their audiences; the human voice became one thread in a web of dissonant, complex polyphony, and its text could rarely be heard.

It is a matter of historical record that no American opera of the past quarter-century has made a substantial impact on our audiences.

Ironically, the genre that most successfully developed a distinctively American character in the first quarter of the twentieth century—the art-song—did so without soul-searching on the part of its composers, without endless discussion and debate in the press.

American composers first turned to "serious" songs for voice and piano in the last quarter of the nineteenth century. John Knowles Paine, Dudley Buck, George Chadwick, Horatio Parker, Arthur Foote, and a host of less prominent musicians produced songs in profusion; Chadwick alone wrote 128. But there was nothing distinctive about these pieces, any more than there was in the symphonies and sonatas written at the same time.

If one song were to be singled out as an exception to this trend, it would surely be "the Rosary" by Ethelbert Nevin (1862–1901), published in 1898. Within a decade it had sold a quarter-million

[73] From Act II, scene 2. Cf. NW 288–89.
[74] Thomson, p. 105.

copies and become far and away the most often programmed song by an American. It is no easy matter to isolate stylistic details that make this song distinctive. Nevin's most important teacher had been Karl Klindworth in Berlin, and one would search in vain for hints of "American" traits:

"The Rosary," by Ethelbert Nevin

The hours I spent with thee, dear heart, Are as a string of pearls to me;

Yet something is there, perhaps more in the spirit of the piece than in technical details, not found in German and French songs of the time. Most critics and historians have been ambivalent and even patronizing in their discussions of his "distinctly not unimpressive" songs:

> Nevin possessed no profundity of musical thought, [though] he did have to a marked degree a feeling for fluent melody, a limited but expressive (though unfortunately often oversentimentalized) harmonic sense, and a certain buoyancy of style not at all to be despised.[75]

Edward MacDowell seems to have grasped the same thing in his later songs. Many of these take on some of the character of American parlor songs of the nineteenth century, dominated by the theme of nostalgia for lost youth and lost love:

> Long ago, sweetheart mine,
> Roses bloomed as n'er before,
> Long ago the world was young
> For us, sweetheart.

> Fields of velvet, azure skies,
> Whispering trees and murmuring streams,
> Long ago life spread his wings
> For us, sweetheart.[76]

[75] William Treat Upton, *Art-Song in America* (Boston and New York: Oliver Ditson Company, 1930), p. 125.
[76] NW 247, s1 / 1.

The piano accompaniment plays a subordinate role, supporting the voice without calling attention to itself, unlike most contemporary European art-songs.

The same traits dominate the products of two female song-writers of the turn of the century. Critics have had difficulty dealing with the songs of Carrie Jacobs-Bond (1862–1946), uncertain whether to classify "I Love You Truly" (1906) and "A Perfect Day" (1910) as popular or art songs. Singers of the day had no such problems; many, Mme. Schumann-Heink and David Bispham among them, included these songs on their vocal recitals, and audiences made no distinction between them and other pieces offered on such occasions. Mrs. H. H. A. Beach, on the other hand, was labeled a "classical" composer, but her setting of Browning's "The Year's at the Spring" (1899)[77] and her many other successful songs utilize the same techniques and invoke the same response as do the songs of Jacobs-Bond.

Perhaps this is the secret: American songwriters of the first decades of the twentieth century found a middle ground between art-song and popular song, in both the sentiment of their texts and in their musical means. Charles Wakefield Cadman, as noted above, was one of the most enthusiastic "Indianists" of this period, yet in "At Dawning" (1906)[78] he moved to the direct expression of simple, universal sentiments increasingly shared by American songwriters of varied stylistic and philosophical persuasions.

A. Walter Kramer (1890–1969) was imitating the style of French Impressionistic composers in his instrumental music, yet "Swans" has more of the sound and sentiment of the American style of song-writing than of the French;[79] John Alden Carpenter is best remembered for his attempts to forge an American symphonic style out of elements of ragtime and jazz, yet his two major song cycles— *Gitanjali* (1913) and *Water Colors* (1918)—fit comfortably into the profile of American song sketched here;[80] and even Charles Tomlinson Griffes (1884–1920), America's most successful Impressionist composer, sometimes wrote songs more reflective of the American art-song than of European models, even when his texts were translation from other languages.[81]

"Do Not Go, My Love" (1917), Richard Hageman's setting of a poem by Rabindranath Tagore, is solidly in this new mainstream of American song.[82] The piano accompaniment is richly sonorous,

[77] NW 247, s1 / 2.
[78] NW 247, s2 / 1.
[79] NW 247, s1 / 5.
[80] NW 247, s2 / 4–5, contains two songs from the first cycle.
[81] Cf. his "By a Lonely Forest Pathway" on NW 247, s2 / 2.
[82] NW 247, s2 / 3.

but subordinate to the voice. The text is set in an almost completely syllabic fashion, mostly in a medium range, and the singer has no difficulty in projecting the entire lyric to the audience. And "When I Have Sung My Songs" (1934)[83] by Ernest Charles could be described in precisely the same terms, though it was written almost twenty years later. It is instructive to compare these songs with Roger Sessions's "On the Beach at Fontana" (1929),[84] a piece of infinitely greater compositional sophistication and much more in touch with the language of contemporary instrumental composition. But the jagged vocal line and the prominence of the piano part—no longer an accompaniment—make the text virtually unintelligible after the first few words, and the listener is forced to hear it as a piece of abstract music, a brief duo for soprano and piano.

Of the next generation of American composers, Samuel Barber (1910–81) was the most talented and successful songwriter. Louise Homer, the famous American contralto, was his aunt; her husband, Sidney Homer, had been a talented and widely performed songwriter, best known for a number of settings of poems by Robert Louis Stevenson; these two encouraged and influenced the young man, before and during his formal training at the Curtis Institute in Philadelphia. His style was viewed by most of his peers as conservative:

> Romantic music, predominantly emotional, embodying sophisticated workmanship and complete care. Barber's aesthetic position may be reactionary, but his melodic line sings and the harmony supports it.[85]

"Dover Beach" (1931) for baritone and string quartet, written while Barber was still a student at Curtis, is fully representative of his songs, despite its early date. The voice dominates, laying out Matthew Arnold's pessimistic text in such a way as to underline its dramatic impact; the strings play a mostly accompanimental role, becoming involved in the melodic material only when the voice is not singing; the harmonic language is tonal and triadic, differing from late-nineteenth-century practice only in idiosyncratic chromaticism and gentle dissonance.[86]

Many of Barber's subsequent songs became staples of the vocal repertory: *Three Songs* (Opus 10, 1936), to texts by James Joyce; *Four Songs* (Opus 13, 1940), including two of the most frequently performed American songs of the entire twentieth century, "A Nun

[83] NW 247, s2 / 7.
[84] NW 243, s2 / 3.
[85] Virgil Thomson, *Twentieth-Century Composers. American Music Since 1910* (New York: Holt, Rinehart and Winston, 1970), p. 121.
[86] NW 229, s1 / 1, has a performance of "Dover Beach" sung by Barber.

Takes the Veil" and "Sure on This Shining Night";[87] *Mélodies passagères* (Opus 27, 1950), to French texts by Rilke but very much in Barber's "American" song style;[88] the cycle *Hermit Songs* (Opus 29, 1952–53). Though some of Barber's instrumental pieces also enjoyed wide popularity—*Adagio for Strings* (Opus 11, 1936), *The School for Scandal* overture (Opus 12, 1937), the *Piano Sonata* (Opus 26, 1949)—his songs will probably remain in the performing repertory long after his instrumental music has been forgotten.

A dichotomy between vocal and instrumental composition grew up in America after about 1925; the best song composers were either disinterested in writing abstract music or enjoyed little success when they did so, the most highly praised instrumental composers had little interest in songs. Ned Rorem (born in Richmond, Indiana in 1923) has written more than 400 songs, the majority of which have been published and many of which have found their way onto vocal recitals over the past thirty years.[89] Like Barber, he writes in a tonal and somewhat eclectic style, which has helped make his songs accessible and pleasing to performers and audiences.

Theodore Chanler (1902–61) first attracted attention with his setting of Archibald MacLeish's "These, My Ophelia" in 1925; two sets of *Epitaphs* (Walter de la Mare) and *The Children* (1945, to texts by Leonard Feeney) were among the most successful song cycles of the period.[90] Paul Bowles, born in New York in 1910, contributed graceful and often touching songs, in a harmonic style much closer to the popular song literature of the day than to the classical repertory;[91] he virtually gave up composing in 1949 in favor of the novel. Kurt Weill also tried his hand at art-song, with settings of Robert Frost ("Stopping by Woods on a Snowy Evening," 1939) and *Four Songs of Walt Whitman* (1942); he too relied on the melodic and harmonic idiom of the popular musical stage.

Changes in musical style sweeping across Europe and America in the 1940s and '50s were no more congenial to the art-song than they were to opera. No American composers of the generation after Barber, Rorem, and Bowles have revealed unusual talent for art-song; musicians with lyric gifts, such as Stephen Sondheim and Paul Simon, have gravitated toward the popular musical theater and rock music, where one must look for the distinctive American song of the last quarter century.

[87] NW 243, s2 / 5.
[88] NW 229, s1 / 2–6.
[89] A selection of his songs is available on NW 229, s2 / 1–11.
[90] NW 243, s2 / 4 and s1 / 1.
[91] Cf. his "Once a Lady Was Here" and "Song of an Old Woman," on NW 243, s1 / 3–4.

A succession of individual composers, beginning with Charles Ives, discovered ways of making their music reflect the musical and cultural life of America in the first half of the twentieth century. The 1930s in particular produced an extraordinary series of operas, symphonies, other orchestral works, songs, ballets, and film scores which drew composers, performers, audiences, and critics together in common cause, in a way never witnessed before in America—and unfortunately never recaptured.

It cannot be said that this period produced a national *school* of composition, however. Each composer found his own way.

Perhaps this is the way it should be in America.

# 16

## Diamonds in the Rough— Hillbilly and Country- Western Music

The American South played virtually no role in mainstream American culture in the half-century following the Civil War. Crushed economically and harboring feelings of extreme bitterness toward the North, it had withdrawn into a protective shell, nourishing its regional identity and history, resisting most of the political and cultural changes that swept over the rest of the country. Southern life and culture became so idiosyncratic that a recent scholar has suggested that Southerners might well be considered one of America's ethnic groups:

> Like other ethnic groups, Southerners have differed from the national norm: they have been poorer, less well-educated, more rural, occupationally more specialized. They also differ culturally in important respects; and their political behavior has been distinctive. Although Southerners are not usually identifiable by name or appearance, their accent usually serves as an ethnic marker. . . . They are seen, and see themselves, as less energetic, less materialistic, more traditional and conventional, more religious and patriotic, more mannerly and hospitable, than other Americans.[1]

Nevertheless, several types of highly distinctive music were developing in the South at just this time and became highly visible

---

[1] John Shelton Reed, in *Harvard Encyclopedia of American Ethnic Groups*, Stephen Thernstrom, ed. (Cambridge: Harvard University Press / Belknap Press, 1980), pp. 944–45.

for the first time in the early 1920s, when the phonograph industry stumbled on it. Victor recorded two southern fiddlers in 1922— Henry Gilliland and A. C. "Eck" Robertson—but was so unsure of the market that the first disc was released only the following year (a pairing of "Arkansas Traveller" and "Sally Gooden"). Meanwhile, Ralph Peer of Okeh Records recorded the harmonica playing of a southern millhand named Henry Whitter in March of 1923. Later that year, while in the South searching for black musicians, he recorded several pieces by Fiddlin' John Carson, an old-time musician who had attracted a considerable following on Atlanta's first commercial radio station, WSB. Two pieces recorded by Carson on June 14, 1923—"The Little Old Log Cabin in the Lane" and "Old Hen Cackled and the Rooster's Going to Crow"—were released on Okeh 4890, a disc marking the beginning of the commercial history of what was soon called hillbilly music.[2]

The term "hillbilly" had been in use from at least the end of the nineteenth century as a deprecatory label for rural whites of the South; the *New York Journal* for April 23 1900 commented that "a Hill-Billie is a free and untrammelled white citizen of Alabama, who lives in the hills, has no means to speak of, dresses as he can, talks as he pleases, drinks whisky when he gets it, and fires off his revolver as the fancy takes him."[3] It was appropriated for this music in 1925 when four musicians from the vicinity of Galax, Virginia (Al and Joe Hopkins, Tony Alderman, John Rector) traveled to New York to record with Okeh. Peer asked for the name of the group. "We're nothing but a bunch of hillbillies from North Carolina and Virginia. Call us anything,"[4] was the reply, and Peer, delighted with the sound of the word, promptly dubbed them the Hill Billies. With characteristic Southern humor, the band not only accepted the name but stressed their rural mountain heritage in publicity photographs and copy. Within a year, the term "hillbilly" was in wide use for all music of this sort.

The first commercial discs preserve the various sorts of vocal and instrumental music of the rural South in the nineteenth and early twentieth centuries.

Radio and the phonograph industry did not create country music; these commercial media merely exploited and popularized a preexistent tra-

---

[2] The best account of Carson—and of most of the musicians with which this chapter is concerned—is found in Bill C. Malone and Judith McCulloh, eds., *Stars of Country Music: Uncle Dave Macon to Johnny Rodriguez* (University of Illinois Press, 1975).

[3] Quoted in Archie Green, "Hillbilly Music: Source and Symbol," *Journal of American Folklore* LXXVIII (1965), p. 204.

[4] Quoted in Green, p. 213.

dition of singing and string-band playing. Although subjected to new commercial influences in the 1920s, the hillbilly performer remained a folk musician who was molded and shaped by the complex religious, social, cultural, and economic patterns of his traditional environment.[5]

A number of Child ballads were scattered through the early commercial repertory, though no one at the time was able to identify them as such. "Old Lady and the Devil," recorded by Bill and Belle Reed in 1928 for Columbia, proves to be a version of Child 278; "The House Carpenter" (Child 243) was recorded by Clarence Ashley for Columbia in 1930;[6] Charlie Poole and the North Carolina Ramblers recorded a version of Child 95, as "Hangman, Hangman Slack that Rope"; Vernon Dalhart was one of a number of singers to record a version of "Barbara Allen" (Child 84).[7]

Other ballads brought over from the British Isles are part of the early commercial repertory. "The Knoxville Girl" by Arthur Tanner and His Corn Shuckers (Columbia, 1927) and "Knoxville Girl" by Fiddlin' Jim Burke (Silvertone, 1928) are versions of "The Berkshire Tragedy; or, The Wittam Miller" (Laws P 35), which narrates the tale of a murder in Oxford. Fiddlin' John Carson, Vernon Dalhart, and Frank Hutchinson recorded versions of "Botany Bay" (Laws L 16), transposed to an American setting. And "Billy Grimes, the Rover,"[8] as recorded by the Shelor Family for Victor in 1927, is surely of British origin.

Even more common are native American ballads. "John Henry" (Laws I 1), the immortal story of a "steel driving man" who pits himself and his hammer against the new steam drill ("Before I let the steam drill beat me down, I'm gonna die with that hammer in my hand"), was recorded by virtually all of the early hillbilly performers. Almost as popular was "The Wreck of the Old 97," a recounting of the events of September 17, 1903 just outside of Danville, Virginia. In venerable ballad style, it lays out its tale in vivid but dispassionate language, shaped into four-line strophes.[9]

A similar native American ballad is "Been on the Job Too Long,"

---

[5] Bill C. Malone, *Country Music. U.S.A.* (Austin: The University of Texas Press, 1968), p. 45.

[6] Both available on Harry Smith, ed., *Anthology of American Folk Music* (New York: Folkways Records, 1952).

[7] Cf. Judith McCulloh, "Some Child Ballads on Hillbilly Records," in *Folklore and Society: Essays in Honor of Benjamin A. Botkin* (Hatsboro, Pa., Folklore Associates, 1966), for a more complete listing and discussion.

[8] NW 236, s1 / 3. Ballads will be identified by the numbering system of G. Malcolm Laws in his *Native American Balladry* (Philadelphia: The American Folklore Society, 1959).

[9] Cf. Richard K. Spottswood, ed., *Folk Music in America* (Washington: Library of Congress, 1977), Vol. 9, s2 / 5.

based on an incident in Lamar County, Mississippi, in which a deputy sheriff named Alfred Bounds killed a holdup man; it was recorded commercially by Wilmer Watts and the Lonely Eagles in 1929.[10] And ballads based on actual occurrences continued to be created and sung for several decades after the first commercial recordings; Wilf Carter's "The Rescue from Moose River Mine" was written and recorded in 1936.[11]

All these ballads, whether native to the British Isles or to America, are strophic, with a single four-phrase tune used for each verse. Many retain tunes dating back at least to the nineteenth century. Though unaccompanied ballad singing was still widespread in remote areas, virtually all commercially released ballads are accompanied. In some, the voice is supported by a fiddle playing in unison.[12] Others have banjo accompaniment in nonharmonic style, with the instrument "frailing"—playing ostinato patterns, often pentatonic in nature.[13]

But most recorded ballads utilized a guitar as accompaniment, alone or in combination with other instruments. It is not certain when and by whom the guitar was introduced into rural Southern music: perhaps it came in from the Southwest, an area in touch with Latin music, perhaps through mail-order catalogues which offered instruments cheaply. Once it was adopted widely, it sparked a major stylistic change, from a pentatonic, nonharmonic music to a diatonic, tonal, and harmonic idiom.

Not all hillbilly music has it roots in traditional Anglo-American music, however. "The Little Old Log Cabin in the Lane," found on one side of the historic 1923 disc by Fiddlin' John Carson, was written in 1871 by Will S. Hays and published that year by J. L. Peters in New York. Widely sung on the minstrel stage and in the American parlor, it is cast in the ubiquitous verse-chorus format of the period, with the several verses sketching a sentimental vignette of an old man yearning for his childhood home in the South. It is thus a composed song which passed into oral tradition, kept alive in the rural South by the same word-of-mouth process that preserved traditional ballads. Many other hillbilly singers brought out versions of it (Riley Puckett, Uncle Dave Macon, and Ernest V. Stoneman among them), and it was published in many regional folk-song collections—recovered from oral tradition by

[10] NW 245, s2 / 2.

[11] NW 287, s2 / 2.

[12] Cf. Fiddlin' John Carson's performance of "The Farmer Is the Man That Feeds Them All" on NW 245, s1 / 6.

[13] Cf. "The Wagoners Lad" as performed by Buell Kazee in 1928, on Smith, *Anthology of American Folk Music*, Vol. 1, No. 7.

scholars who were not aware of its origin as a composed and published song.[14]

In fact, the early hillbilly repertory is rife with popular songs of nineteenth-century America. Riley Puckett and Wilf Carter both recorded Charles E. Pratt's "Put My Little Shoes Away" (1870); Charlie Poole and the North Carolina Ramblers recorded a version of Paul Dresser's first hit, "The Letter That Never Came" (1886); Clayton McMichen paired "Silver Threads Among the Gold" (H. P. Danks, 1873) with "When You and I Were Young, Maggie" (J. A. Butterfield, 1866); Carson Robison recorded "Darling Nelly Gray" (B. R. Hanby, 1856); and there were at least a dozen different versions of Henry Clay Work's classic temperance song, "Come Home, Father" (1864).[15] The Blue Sky Boys recorded Charles K. Harris's "There'll Come a Time" (1895) for Bluebird in 1936,[16] and as late as 1951 Lester Flatt and Earl Scruggs recorded "Over the Hills to the Poorhouse," written in 1874 by David Braham.[17]

Though these songs came from a tradition quite different from that of the ballads discussed above and are in a somewhat different musical style, both types were sung by the same performers for the same audience and were taken to be part of the same repertory. Thus, the hillbilly tradition was a mixed one from the beginning of its recorded history.

Just as the creation of new ballads was accepted in this musical culture, so was the composition of new sentimental songs. "By the Cottage Door," recorded in 1930 by the Perry County Music Makers,[18] sounds for all the world like something from the 1870s or '80s, but was written in the 1920s by Nonnie Presson. And "The Village School," from a disc by Nelstone's Hawaiians (1929), has the style and substance of a popular song of the second half of the nineteenth century, but is the work of an anonymous song maker of the early hillbilly period:[19]

> Our village school was crowded on examination day,
> Some they came to see those children pass.
> They felt so glad, of all of them, except two they knew
> Who was always at the bottom of their class.

[14] Arthur Kyle Davis, Jr., *Folk-Songs of Virginia: A Descriptive Index and Classification* (Durham: Duke University Press, 1949), and Randolph Vance, *Ozark Folksongs* (Columbia: The State Historical Society of Missouri, 1946–50), for instance.

[15] Cf. "Poor Little Bennie," as recorded in 1927 by Bela Lam and His Greene County Singers, on Spottswood, ed., *Folk Music in America*, Vol. 13, s2 / 7.

[16] NW 287, s1 / 10.

[17] Spottswood, *Folk Music in America*, Vol. 7, s2 / 5.

[18] NW 236, s1 / 8.

[19] NW 245, s2 / 6. The chorus was surely intended to be sung after both verses, but was sung here only once because of limitations of time on the disc.

*Chorus:* We have no one to care for us now,
No one to put us to bed;
No one to kiss and caress us at night,
When our evening prayers have been said.

Since mother's been taken away,
We don't get along somehow;
That's why we don't pass with the rest of the class,
We have no one to care for us now.

This day they missed as usual, their little hearts were sad,
The rest of them they seemed to be so gay;
When told no one would love them if they did not learn at school,
With tearful eyes the teacher she heard them say:

*Chorus:* We have no one to care for us now, etc.

Dance music, descended from the fiddle tunes used for country dancing in the eighteenth and nineteenth century, was an important part of the early hillbilly repertory. Though this music was still played by only one or two fiddles in the rural South, most of the early commercial recordings feature a more elaborate instrumentation. "Old Joe Clark" was recorded in 1927 by DaCosta Woltz's Southern Broadcasters, consisting of fiddle, banjo, and voice. Like all fiddle tunes, it is made up of two alternating strains, played as many times as desired or necessary. In this performance, the voice sings intermittently, with verses fitted to one strain of the tune and a chorus to the other ("Fare you well, Old Joe Clark . . ."):[20]

*A A B A A B B A A B A A A B B A A B A A B A* . . .

The fiddle, banjo, and voice are all in unison, with an occasional double-stop on the fiddle and frailing patterns on the banjo giving rhythmic and pitch support to the tune.

The introduction of the guitar into dance music in the late nineteenth or early twentieth century brought a shift to a harmonically based style; commercial recordings of the 1920s capture this emerging style in its transitional and often awkward stages. Sometimes the guitar is used as a melodic instrument with only hints of chords;[21] sometimes the performers have difficulty with chord changes, with one player shifting to a new chord while another remains on the previous one.[22] Other performers developed a solid harmonic sense, and their performances are marked by fully real-

[20] NW 236, s1 / 2. Italicized sections have text.
[21] Cf. "Cotton-Eyed Joe" as recorded in 1928 by the Carter Brothers & Son, on NW 236, s1 / 6.
[22] Cf. "George Washington" as recorded by Pope's Arkansas Mountaineers in 1929, on NW 236, s1 / 4.

ized chordal progressions. Uncle Dave Macon and His Fruit Jar Drinkers, for instance, understood very well what they were doing harmonically,[23] and Gid Tanner and His Skillet Lickers had such strong harmonic instincts that instrumentalists often felt free to interpolate running passages and obbligato lines, with a resulting texture that approaches early jazz.[24]

Eventually, a bass instrument was introduced as a foundation for the harmony. The first stage in this evolution came with the use of the lower register of the guitar to play a bass line. But as early as 1930, the string bass was introduced into hillbilly music: "Bibb County Hoedown," recorded by Seven Foot Dilly and His Dill Pickles,[25] looks both to the past, with its two-strain form derived from the traditional fiddle tune, and to the future, with its solid harmonic style.

These groups are several of the string bands of the period, representing a separate though parallel development to the ballad and song repertory. String bands usually featured several fiddles, a banjo or two, and one or two guitars, sometimes augmented by mandolin or bass. Though their sound was dominated by instrumental playing, the musicians would sing an occasional verse or chorus. Dance music of the nineteenth-century rural South did not draw a sharp distinction between vocal and instrumental music. "Old Joe Clark," "Arkansas Traveller," "Cluck Old Hen," "Cotton-Eyed Joe," and similar pieces were dance songs, with texts associated with their melodies. This tradition is continued in the music of the string bands of the 1920s and 1930s.

Other popular string bands were the Virginia Reelers, the Dixie Mountaineers, Chenoweth's Cornfield Symphony Orchestra, Charlie Poole and his North Carolina Ramblers, and the Hill Billies themselves. A typical piece is "Georgia Wildcat Breakdown," recorded in 1932 by Clayton McMichen and his Georgie Wildcats.[26] The band consists of two fiddles, three guitars, and a banjo; the music is in the usual two strains; text consists of an occasional fragment of the traditional words associated with the tune, and interpolated verses directed at the dancers, almost in the nature of dance calls:

> Swing low, swing far,
> Swing that gal from Arkansas;
> Rope that cow and choke that calf,
> Swing your partner round and half.

[23] Cf. their recording of "Carve That Possum" on NW 236, s1 / 9.
[24] Cf. their recording of "Molly Put the Kettle On" on NW 236, s2 / 1.
[25] NW 226, s2 / 9.
[26] NW 287, s1 / 1.

An occasional disc uses a piano to accompany dance music; these are thoroughly harmonic in concept, since the piano was associated with a musical tradition which had been harmonically based for centuries. "Rymer's Favorite,"[27] recorded in Bridgeport (Connecticut) in 1925, is a version of a traditional fiddle tune (often known as "Billy in the Lowground") played by fiddle and piano. There is the usual alternation between a first and a second strain (*AABAABAABAAB* ...); the piano plays a sequence of simple diatonic chords, mostly tonic but with subdominant and dominant chords giving tonal cadences at phrase endings. Though the piece was recorded in the North, the fiddler (Allen Sisson) was born in Tennessee; he brings a typical Southern touch to the piece, assymetry—the *A* strain always has 8 beats, the *B* strain has 11.[28]

In summary, the hillbilly repertory in its first decade included traditional ballads and songs, both British and American; newly composed ballads; sentimental popular songs written in the second half of the nineteenth century; new songs in the same style; and two-strain fiddle tunes, for dancing, played on a variety of instruments. Some pieces retain the nonharmonic style of the nineteenth century, but the majority are based on the emerging harmonic style of rural Southern music.

Ralph Peer, now with Victor, went south again in July of 1927 in search of new talent for his new company. In a remarkable period of four days, he located and recorded in Bristol (Virginia) the musicians who were to shape and dominate the next several decades of this music, and become its brightest stars—the Carter Family, on August 1 and 2, then Jimmie Rodgers on August 4.

Alvin Pleasant Carter (1891–1960), his wife Sara Dougherty Carter (b. 1898), and his sister-in-law Maybelle Addington Carter (1909–78) came from nearby Maces Spring, Virginia, and had only a local reputation. By the time they had ended their recording career in 1941 and made their last radio appearance in 1943, they had cut more than 300 discs, had performed regularly on radio stations in the South and West, and had established a song style that was to change little for almost half a century.

They sang and recorded a number of strophic, narrative ballads, including Child ballads—"Sinking in the Lonesome Sea" is a version of "The Golden Vanity" (Child 286)—and other ballads brought over from the British Isles. Native American ballads make up a portion of their recorded repertory; "Engine One Forty Three" is a

---

[27] NW 226, s2 / 6.

[28] Similar but somewhat more elaborate is "That's My Rabbit, My Dog Caught It," recorded in 1933 by the Walter Family (NW 226, s2/4), in which a jug and washboard support the fiddle and piano in such a way as to suggest a bass line.

The Carter family in 1927 when they made their first recording.

railroad disaster song in the mold of "The Wreck of the Old 97." The ballad lays out the tragic tale of the engineer, George Alley, who ignores his mother's warning that "many a man has lost his life, in trying to make lost time," and comes to a sad ending:

> His face was covered up with blood,
> His eyes it could not see;
> And the very last words poor Georgie said
> Was "Nearer my God to Thee."

Other Carter Family ballads have not been traced to earlier performers and may have been the work of A. P. Carter himself. "Old Ladies' Home" paints a picture of the lonely and dreary lives of abandoned old women, not to record a specific event but to urge any listener with a mother to sit down and write her a letter, and "Broken Down Tramp" is not a saga of lurid crime or brave deeds, but rather a pathetic tale offered to dissuade young men from drifting into a life of dissolution:

> I'm a broken down tramp without money,
> My clothes are all tattered and torn;
> And I am so sad and so lonely,
> I wish I had never been born.
>
> Now drink was the cause of my downfall,
> And the money I had I've outrun;
> And the friends that were mine when I had it
> Now pass by and call me a bum.

Their repertory also included sentimental songs in verse-chorus form, some borrowed and some perhaps original. "Hello Central, Give Me Heaven" is an early Tin Pan Alley song, published by Charles K. Harris in 1901; "Wildwood Flower" traces back to a nineteenth-century song entitled "The Pale Amaranthus."

"Wildwood Flower," as sung by the Carter Family

Oh, I'll twine with my ming-les and wav-ing black hair, With the ros-es so red and the lil-ies so fair; And the myr-tle so bright with the em-er-ald dew, The pale and the lead-er and eyes— look like blue.

It is often not clear whether a given song was written by the Carters or if it was taken over from another source. There was no intent to defraud; it must be remembered that the Carters came out of an oral tradition in which songs were common property. As far as is known, A. P. Carter composed the following song; but it is so much in the style of popular songs of the last quarter of the nineteenth century that it would come as no surprise if it proved to be the work of some obscure songwriter of that era:

> Every night I'm dreaming of a little home
> Down among the hills of Tennessee;
> And I'm always lonely, longing to return
> To the place that means the world to me.

*Chorus:* Just a little shack, roof all turning black,
    Still it is a palace to me;
    Songbirds always singing 'round my kitchen door,
    In my little home in Tennessee

"Sweet Fern" is similar, with its three verses laying out a vignette—a lover has left, promising to return—and the chorus addressing the "sweet lonesome bird" whose name gives the piece its title.[29]

"I'm Thinking Tonight of My Blue Eyes," probably the most perennially popular of all their songs, also has three verses sketching a vignette of an absent lover, each followed by the chorus:

    Oh, I'm thinking tonight of my blue eyes,
    Who is sailing far over the sea;
    Oh, I'm thinking tonight of him only,
    And I wonder if he ever thinks of me.

And many of their other favorite songs—"When the Roses Come Again," "I Cannot Be Your Sweetheart" and "Shall the Circle Be Unbroken," for instance—are sentimental verse-chorus songs in a style shaped by nineteenth- and early-twentieth-century American songwriters.

Musically, Sara was the lead singer, accompanying herself with strummed chords on the guitar or autoharp. Maybelle played lead guitar in a characteristic style that was widely imitated—the melody on the lower three strings, with frequent "hammered" notes, the upper strings adding a rhythmic-chordal accompaniment. Ballads were usually sung by Sara alone, with Maybelle's guitar doubling the melody at the unison or octave. Verse-chorus songs were usually done with Sara singing the verses; Maybelle and A. P. join in the chorus, in three-part harmony.

No other instruments were used—no fiddles, no banjos—though Sara sometimes used a steel (Hawaiian) guitar. There is no true bass line; Maybelle's melody on the lower strings of her guitar is the lowest part. Harmonic language is limited on the earliest recordings to two chords (tonic and dominant) and later expanded to include the subdominant and even an occasional secondary dominant. Melodies are mostly diatonic, with an occasional hint of the pentatonic scale so characteristic of older rural Southern music. Sara's singing style is traditional, somewhat nasal and inexpressive by the standards of "cultured" European singing.

Every song was performed in the same way, whether it was an oral-tradition ballad or a recently composed sentimental parlor

[29] NW 287, s1 / 3.

song. This consistency of sound and expression created a sense that everything they sang was part of a single repertory.

Although Jimmie (James Charles) Rodgers (1897–1933) had his roots in the same rural Southern culture as the Carter Family, his career and music differed in significant ways from theirs.

Much of his childhood was spent in the town of Meridian, Mississippi. Traditional ballads and fiddle tunes were part of his earliest musical experiences, but he also attended minstrel shows, circuses, and medicine shows, and he heard urban church music and the popular songs of Tin Pan Alley on the phonograph and sung in the parlors of family friends. He learned to play the guitar and banjo, and in the early 1920s he spent endless hours with the phonograph, playing and singing along with his favorite discs. He was probably the first American musician whose most important formative musical experiences came via the phonograph.

Through the mid-1920s he performed with a succession of short-lived amateur and semiprofessional musical groups and acts. Between such engagements he wandered and drifted to New Orleans, Texas, Florida, and Arizona, supporting himself with temporary jobs on the railroad. But he always came back to Meridian, and to music.

The winter of 1927 found him in Asheville, North Carolina, where a powerful new radio station, WWNC, had just begun operation. Rodgers was asked to perform on the air, first with a musician named Otis Kuykendall and then with a small string band, the Tenneva Ramblers. Most of his material was drawn from popular songs of Tin Pan Alley composers, and Rodgers projected an urban image with his dress and manner. When Ralph Peer auditioned the Tenneva Ramblers in Bristol on August 3rd, he was taken with Rodgers's singing style and asked him to cut two discs alone the following day. Rodgers chose several songs that had been well-received at WWNC, a lullaby ("Sleep, Baby, Sleep") and a sentimental ballad ("The Soldier's Sweetheart," based on the tune "Where the River Shannon Flows"). Later that year he recorded four more of his songs: a railroad disaster song ("Ben Dewberry's Final Run); a hillbilly song written and recorded earlier by Kelly Harrell ("Away Out on the Mountain"); a Tin Pan Alley song written by Joseph Stern and Edward B. Marks ("Mother Was a Lady"); and, almost as an afterthought, a song by Rodgers himself (first called "T for Texas," it was released as "Blue Yodel"). The latter was the most successful, selling more than a million copies and establishing Rodgers as the brightest star of the hillbilly world.

From 1927 until his death in 1933, Rodgers recorded 111 songs, in studios in New York, Atlanta, Hollywood, Dallas, San Antonio, Louisville, and New Orleans. Always restless, he continued his wanderings, but now as the headlined performer in theater shows through the South and Southwest. He was given his own radio show on WTFF in Washington, and appeared on other stations across the South. A month after his death from tuberculosis in 1933, 30,000 people collected in Meridian for the unveiling of a statue and memorial, with an inscription by the Nashville journalist H. B. Teeter:

> His is the music of America;
> He sang the songs of the people he loved,
> Of a young nation growing strong,
> His was an America of glistening rails,
> Thundering boxcars and rainswept nights,
> Of lonesome prairies and rainswept nights.
>
> We listened. We understood.

And when the Country Music Hall of Fame was established in Nashville, he was the first person elected to membership.

Rodgers never recorded traditional ballads of either British or American origin, though some of his songs are narrative and strophic. "Moonlight and Skies" has lyrics telling of a man imprisoned for murder and a tune obviously derived from "On Top of Old Smoky," and "Mother, the Queen of My Heart" is close in style and mood to some of the narrative-moralistic songs of the Carter Family; the story is of a man who, despite warnings from his mother, turns to a life of drinking and gambling. Needing to draw the queen of hearts to make his hand in a poker game, he does indeed get his card, but as he looks at it, "I saw my mother's picture," and he repents:

> My winnings I gave to a newsboy,
> I knew I was wrong from the start;
> And I'll never forget the promise
> To mother the queen of my heart.

Mostly, though, he performed sentimental songs in a lyric rather than narrative style up to his last sessions in May of 1933, when he recorded "Dreaming with Tears in My Eyes":[30]

> Why should I always be lonely,
> When sunny and blue are the skies?

[30] NW 287, s1 / 4.

> While shadows of loneliness linger,
> I'm dreaming with tears in my eyes.

His thirteen songs labeled "blue yodels" reveal another dimension of hillbilly music. The first is typical of the set: phrase structure and harmonic design are based on the 12-bar blues form developed by black musicians, modified by Rodgers's erratic metrical sense; its lyrics consist of a string of episodic, improvisatory verses concerned with personal misfortune:[31]

> T for Texas, T for Tennessee;
> T for Texas, T for Tennessee;
> T for Thelma, that girl that made a wreck out of me,
>
> Rather drink muddy water, sleep in a hollow log;
> Rather drink muddy water, and sleep in a hollow log,
> Than to be in Atlanta, treated like a dirty dog.

At his first and last recording sessions, and many between, he sang to the accompaniment of his own guitar, with no other musicians involved. His guitar style consisted almost entirely of simple strummed chords. His technique was clumsy, and he often played a chord different from the one implied by the melodic line. He had little sense of meter, and often added or dropped beats. But many of his most effective and popular songs are among these self-accompanied ones; his chief appeal was in his voice, in its sweet and plaintive sound, and his minimal guitar playing focuses even more attention on the voice and text.

Almost all his songs feature yodeling, usually as a tag at the end of a phrase or verse, and though he was not the first or the only hillbilly singer to yodel, the technique became his trademark. No one knows for sure how and when yodeling penetrated into the rural South; it may trace back as far as the 1830s and '40s, when singing families from Switzerland and Austria enjoyed a vogue in America.

Rodgers recorded with other musicians on more than half his sessions. The range was from one other guitarist, to the more usual hillbilly complement of fiddle, banjo, and guitar, to backing by a Hawaiian band with its characteristic sliding sounds on the steel guitar, all the way to a studio or theater band. The character of his music varies somewhat with these changes in backing instruments. Fiddle and banjo give his music more the sound of the ear-

---

[31] Cf. "Blue Yodel No. 11," recorded in 1929, on NW 287, s1 / 2, for another of these with the same musical and textual characteristics.

liest hillbilly performers, while the use of an ensemble including cornet, clarinet, piano, and string bass brings some of his discs close to the sound of Dixieland jazz, as in his recording of "Waiting for the Train" (1928).

The rural South, where much of the audience for this music was still concentrated, was hard hit by the onset of the Great Depression. By the early 1930s, sales of phonograph records had plummetted to 20% of what they had been a few years earlier. Even star performers like Rodgers were affected by the economic disaster sweeping the country, and younger musicians found it virtually impossible to launch careers. Like their black contemporaries in jazz and the blues, country-western performers wrote an ever-increasing number of songs reflecting the human misery surrounding them; some of these made direct commentary on the situation, others were simply dark in mood. Southerners were still intensely patriotic, and many topical songs of the Depression years voiced support of the government and its efforts to deal with the disaster, particularly after Franklin Roosevelt took office in 1932. But there were more pessimistic and defiant songs as well, by Woody Guthrie and others, and the tradition of protest songs was to become an important thread in American life in coming decades.[32]

It quickly became evident that the audience for hillbilly music extended far beyond the South—through the Southwest (Texas, Oklahoma, Missouri, Arkansas, even California) and into much of the Midwest (Indiana, Illinois, Ohio). These areas, like the South, had large populations descended from nonliterate immigrants from the British Isles, with musical roots in the oral-tradition ballads, fiddle tunes, and sentimental songs out of which hillbilly music had been forged.

The Southwest had developed its own cultural identity, based largely on the image of the cowboy. Jimmie Rodgers identified himself with this area; he performed frequently in the Southwest, built a $50,000 mansion ("Blue Yodeler's Paradise") in Kerrville, Texas in 1929, made reference in many of his songs to Texas and its cowboys, and was made an honorary Texas Ranger in 1931.

Even before this, a handful of performers from the Southwest had begun recording songs based on an indigenous tradition with its roots in the same Anglo-American music that had developed

---

[32] For a more extended discussion of the impact of the Depression on American songs, see Charles Hamm, "Brother, Can You Spare a Dime," liner notes to NW 270.

into hillbilly music.[33] Carl Sprague was one of these; Victor recorded his performances of "When the Work's All Done This Fall" and other songs of Texas origin in 1925.

Gene Autry, born in Tioga, Texas in 1907, was the first great popularizer of western—as opposed to hillbilly—music. Autry learned much of Jimmie Rodgers' repertory, imitated his yodel, then traveled to New York in 1929 (after losing his job as a railroad telegrapher with the onset of the Great Depression) to make several recordings for Victor, billed as "Oklahoma's Singing Cowboy." Engagements with radio stations in Tulsa and Chicago followed. Meanwhile, he recorded a number of discs for the Sears-Roebuck label, widely publicized in the mail-order catalogues of the company. These reveal Autry's close ties with traditional Anglo-American music: "The Death of Mother Jones," from 1931, is strophic and narrative in the style of a traditional ballad, sung in the inexpressive and somewhat nasal voice of Southern mountain music, accompanied by simple strummed chords on the guitar.[34] His first hit recording, released in 1932, was "That Silver-Haired Daddy of Mine," written by Autry and his father-in-law (Jimmy Long) in the style of the popular song repertory of the late nineteenth century. It eventually sold more than a million copies.

His first film role came in 1934, when he played a small part in *In Old Santa Fe.* Hollywood was just discovering the potential of the cowboy movie, and Autry became the brightest star of the new genre, eventually playing in more than a hundred films for Republic and Monogram. His image was of a hard-riding, honest hero determined to uphold justice, who could also play the guitar and sing when the occasion arose. The songs were written mostly by urban commercial songwriters with little or no contact with the musical and cultural traditions that had produced hillbilly music. Typical is "The Last Roundup," featured in one of his early films and first recorded soon after the beginning of his Hollywood career.[35] It was written by Billy Hill, a native of Boston who had studied at the New England Conservatory and performed as a violinist with the Boston Symphony Orchestra before launching a successful commercial songwriting career. Autry sings it to the

---

[33] As early as 1910, John A. Lomax had brought out a collection of songs from the region, *Cowboy Songs and Other Frontier Ballads* (for a full citation, see bibliography). An early commerical recording of one of these, "Whoopee-Ti / Yi-Yo," as sung by John White to the accompaniment of guitar and harmonica in 1931, may be heard on NW 245, s1 / 9.

[34] NW 270, s2 / 6.

[35] Cf. NW 287, s1 / 7, for a somewhat later recording of this song by Autry.

accompaniment of a studio orchestra, complete with strings, muted trumpet, and wind instruments; his voice had become much more mellow, almost approaching the crooning style of Bing Crosby and other popular singers of the era.

The title song of the first film in which he was given a starring role, *Tumbling Tumbleweeds* (1935), was written by Bob Nolan and became one of Autry's greatest hits. His film career lasted into the early 1950s and produced such successful and popular songs as "Back in the Saddle Again," "Mexicali Rose," "South of the Border," "The Yellow Rose of Texas," and "Deep in the Heart of Texas."

Autry's life is a classic American success story, with his rise from childhood poverty to fame as a film and recording star, great wealth, ownership of a chain of radio stations, hotels, and, eventually, a major league baseball team. At the same time, his singing career underlines how western music moved away from its traditional roots in the 1930s and '40s and was colored to a great extent by the songwriting style of Tin Pan Alley. Cowboy movies were produced for urban audiences; Autry's recordings after the mid-1930s were aimed at these audiences in all parts of the country.

Roy Rogers, born in Cincinnati in 1912, starred in a hundred or more films, the first in 1938. Many of his songs were written by Bob Nolan, born in Canada but raised in Arizona and New Mexico, who in 1934 formed a group called the Sons of the Pioneers, with Rogers and Tim Spender. Though the musical roots of all three were to some extent in traditional Anglo-American music, and their early recordings were in the style of hillbilly and western string bands of the early 1930s, a move to Hollywood and success in films propelled them in the direction of increasingly larger instrumentation and songs in the Tin Pan Alley style. Nolan wrote such songs as "Tumbling Tumbleweeds" and "Cool Water," and the group itself gradually assumed Hollywood's image of western music. "Chant of the Wanderer," recorded in Hollywood in 1946,[36] reveals how far from their musical origins the Sons of the Pioneers had moved. Rogers, meanwhile, was performing and recording not only songs by Nolan but also those of a number of urban Eastern songwriters, including Cole Porter ("Don't Fence Me In") and Johnny Mercer ("I'm an Old Cowhand").

Woodward "Tex" Ritter came from a background including college, law school, classical vocal training, and dramatic roles in New York. One of the first performers of "cowboy" music in New York, on radio stations WOR and WHN, Ritter made the first of his 78 cowboy movies in 1936; most of his film songs were newly

---

[36] NW 287, s2 / 6.

composed pieces by commercial songwriters, suggesting authentic cowboy music but avoiding its musical and textual "crudities." His greatest success came near the end of his career with the song "High Noon," written for the film in 1952 by Ned Washington and Dimitri Tiomkin. Typical of cowboy film songs, it sold well with urban audiences but never appeared on *Billboard's* country-western charts.

The commercial success of these singing cowboys spurred other performers to assume a cowboy image. Many singers and groups in the South, Midwest, and Southwest—and even Hank Snow in Canada—donned cowboy hats, shirts and boots, and featured songs referring to the American cowboy and his life and legends. Patsy Montana and the Prairie Ramblers brought out "I Wanna Be a Cowboy's Sweetheart" in 1935, invoking a western image in its text, its yodeling (now associated in the popular mind with cowboy music, despite its origins in earlier hillbilly music), and in the dress of the performers.[37] Yet Patsy was born in Arkansas and spent much of her life in urban California, and the Prairie Ramblers had originated as a string band in Kentucky.

Soon the term "country-western" came into general use as a general label for both the older hillbilly style and the new western dialect.

A somewhat different western style, more instrumentally oriented, came to be called "western swing." Its first stages may be heard in recordings from the late 1920s and early 1930s by Prince Albert Hunt's Texas Ramblers, the East Texas Serenaders, and the Cowboy Ramblers. A decisive step came in 1931–32 with the formation of a group in Fort Worth, first known as the Aladdin Laddies, around the talents of fiddler Bob Wills and Singer Milton Brown. Employed by the Light Crust Flour Company to perform manual labor and also to advertise company products through their performances, they took the new name of the Fort Worth Doughboys, added two guitars (Durwood Brown and C. H. "Sleepy" Johnson), and cut several discs for Victor in early 1932.[38] Their style reflects the receptiveness of some white Southern performers to the developing urban jazz style dominated by blacks.

The original members of the Doughboys soon went their separate ways. Milton Brown and His Brownies, whose first appearances were on radio station KTAT in Fort Worth in 1933, was a somewhat larger group—several fiddles and a rhythm section of piano, guitar, and bass. Their guitarist, Bob Dunn, was probably

[37] NW 287, s2 / 1. This was the first million-selling disc by a female western performer.

[38] "Nancy Jane," on NW 236, s2 / 6, is from their first recording session.

the first commercial performer on the electric guitar;[39] his solo guitar breaks suggest the improvisational style of early jazz saxophonists. The group performed and recorded some traditional country-western pieces, given a new color by the jazz orientation of the band, but more typically they played popular song and jazz. One can hear all elements of their style in "Ida, Sweet As Apple Cider" (1936),[40] a venerable Tin Pan Alley song written in 1903 by Eddie Leonard; both the instrumental playing and the sound of Brown's voice approach the style of commercial, eastern, jazz-flavored bands of the 1930s.

Bob Wills and His Texas Playboys moved from Fort Worth to Tulsa, where they played for a decade over the powerful station KVOO. Beginning with fiddles, guitars, and bass, the group was soon augmented with electric guitar, piano, drums, brass, and winds. By 1938 the Playboys numbered fourteen, and their sound approached that of the big bands of the era, though modified by the sounds of fiddles and yodeling. But more than Milton Brown's band, Wills and his group maintained musical ties with their rural Southern background. They did versions of old-time fiddle tunes— "Goodbye Liza Jane" and "Cotton-Eyed Joe"—and other pieces maintained much of the flavor of traditional country dance music. Their style tended to vary according to the type of piece being played; "Cotton-Eyed Joe," though recorded late (in 1946), plays down swing elements in favor of more traditional fiddling and guitar-playing techniques.[41] Their most successful single piece was "San Antonio Rose" (1940), chosen by Wills as the title of his biography.

Other western swing groups proliferated in the middle and late 1930s. Bill Boyd made his reputation on the Dallas radio station WRR with a group called the Cowboy Ramblers, then signed a recording contract with RCA Victor. By the late 1930s he had moved much further than either Milton Brown or Bob Wills in the direction of mainstream jazz, with a driving rhythm section of piano, banjo, and bass, and virtuoso solo playing and improvising by members of his band.[42] On the other hand, Ted Daffan's Texans featured a more lyric, vocal-dominated style, given western swing color by the syncopated rhythms of piano, bass, and rhythm guitar, and by Daffan's own steel guitar breaks.

The Light Crust Doughboys remained active after the defection of Brown and Wills. Of the various personnel performing with this

[39] Cf. Malone, *Country Music U.S.A.*, p. 171, for details.
[40] NW 287, s1 / 9.
[41] NW 287, s2 / 8.
[42] For an example, cf. "Jig," recorded in 1938, on NW 226, s2 / 10.

band in the late 1930s, the most prominent was "Knocky" Parker, whose piano playing dominated the group for some years. And even though western swing did not survive the 1940s and the proliferation of new styles ushered in by that decade, individual performers have kept the style alive to the present,[43] and the 1970s brought a revival of interest in this particular offshoot of hillbilly music.[44]

Yet another dialect of hillbilly music developed in Louisiana, among the Cajun people inhabiting the southern part of that state. They had come there in the second half of the eighteenth century as refugees from Acadia, a region including Nova Scotia, New Brunswick, and Prince Edward Island, where they had settled in the seventeenth century. Under a provision of the Treaty of Utrecht they came under British rule in 1713; the British expelled them by force in 1755. Many found their way to Louisiana, then a French colony, where they established new homes in the bayou country and along the Mississippi River south of New Orleans. Living in virtual isolation from mainstream American life, they clung to their own language, customs, and culture well into the present century.

Little is known of their music before a scattering of commercial phonograph discs appeared in the mid-1920s. These reveal a dance music with the fiddle as chief instrument, though the fiddling style is different from that found elsewhere in the South. Typically two fiddles play together, one taking the melody and the other alternating between doubling the melody and supporting it with rhythmic-linear figures. The style[45] is related to Anglo-American fiddle tunes in that a piece is usually made up of two sections; there are resemblances to the fiddling styles of Nova Scotia and surrounding regions, which themselves grew out of the music brought to the region by Scottish settlers in the seventeenth century. All this suggests that the Cajuns brought Scottish-Acadian fiddling to Louisiana with them some two centuries ago, and that their music has roots in the British Isles.

Early recordings also preserve vocal music. "Mon Cherie Bebe Creole" (1928)[46] alternates vocal and instrumental verses based on the same melody, though with considerable variation. The two violins play mostly in unison, with one sometimes assuming a sup-

[43] Cf. Bob Wills's "Fat Boy Rag," as recorded in Nashville in 1975 by Johnny Gimble and others, on NW 287, s2 / 9.

[44] The most comprehensive recorded anthology is *Western Swing* (Old Timey LP 105, Arhoolie Records, 1966), edited by Chris Strachwitz.

[45] Cf. "Le Rille Cajun," recorded about 1930 by Dennis McGee and Ernest Fruge, on NW 226, s2 / 6.

[46] NW 245, s1 / 10.

porting—but nonharmonic—role; in vocal verses they play in unison with the singer.

Following an evolutionary pattern similar to that of hillbilly music, Cajun music assumed a harmonic nature with the introduction of a chord-playing instrument, in this case the concertina, a small accordion. No one has been able to pinpoint the date or the circumstances of the arrival of the concertina in Cajun territory, but it probably happened a bit earlier than the introduction of the guitar into other rural Southern music. The concertina may be heard in some recordings made in the late 1920s, for instance "Fe Fe Ponchaux" (1928) by Joseph Falcon.[47] A dance piece in two strains, the melody is accompanied by tonic and dominant chords, with the dominant harmony just before the final chord of each phrase accomplishing a clear tonal cadence. Armede Ardoin, the most widely recorded Cajun musician of this period (more than thirty discs, for various companies), accompanied his singing with a concertina, usually augmented by one or two fiddlers: as in some early hillbilly music, chord changes do not always correspond to harmonic progressions implied by the melody.[48]

Cajuns came more into contact with their neighbors, both white and black, as the twentieth century progressed. By the late 1930s their commercially recorded music was in danger of losing its distinctive character. The Hackberry Ramblers, the most successful Cajun band of the time, performed with a collection of instruments almost identical with that of country-western bands—fiddle, guitar, mandolin, bass. Their facile harmonic sense and playing styles suggest little of their Cajun heritage, as may be observed in such a piece as "Fais Pas Ça" (1937).[49] Only the continuing use of the French language distinguishes this music from mainstream country-western style.

But traditional Cajun styles were kept alive by noncommercial performers. The distinctive fiddling, the use of concertina, the fondness for waltz rhythms could be heard in music played at picnics, festivities, bars, and local dance halls; and the past several decades have brought increased interest and pride in ethnic heritage among Cajuns, as among so many groups in the United States, and a revival of more traditional Cajun music.

Despite the proliferation of dialects of hillbilly music in the 1930s and 1940s—western songs, cowboy film music, western swing,

[47] NW 226, s1 / 11.
[48] An example of his accordion playing, a recording of "Two Step de Eunice," made in 1929, may be heard on Spottswood, *Folk Music in America*, Vol. 12, s2 / 3.
[49] NW 287, s1 / 6.

Roy Acuff (right) and his publisher Fred Rose. (Courtesy of the Country Music Foundation and Media Center, Nashville, Tennessee)

Cajun music—the original style persisted. The most important successor to the Carter Family and Jimmie Rodgers was Roy Acuff, born in Maynardville, Tennessee in 1903.

Acuff's musical sense was shaped by his father's fiddle playing, by the church music he heard in Knoxville as a child, and by the classic hillbilly music he heard on the radio and phonograph. His career began with a touring medicine show and then local radio; his first recording was made in 1936, for Columbia. That disc, "The Great Speckle Bird," was one of the greatest hits of his entire career, and another early session for Columbia yielded "The Wabash Cannonball," one of the classics of the entire country-western repertory. Far and away the most commercially successful performer of his generation, Acuff performed into the 1960s; it has been estimated that total sales of his discs surpassed 30,000,000. His several profitable business ventures included partnership in the Acuff-Rose publishing house, the first company to be concerned with country-western music. His most important and prolonged exposure was on the weekly shows of the "Grand Ole Opry," originating from radio station WSM in Nashville. The show had been on the air since 1925, but it reached its greatest popularity only after 1940, when Acuff became a regular performer.

Acuff's music clung to the style of traditional ballads and songs. His songs—most of which he wrote, adapted, or coauthored—are mostly strophic and narrative, with texts and tunes drawn from or related to traditional sources. The text of "The Great Speckle Bird" is drawn from verse 9, chapter 12, of the Book of Jeremiah, and seems to have been circulated in oral tradition before Acuff recorded it; the tune is related to "I'm Thinking Tonight of My Blue Eyes," a song popularized by the Carter Family. "The Wabash Cannon Ball" also may have been known in oral tradition, possibly as a prison song, and yet another of his successful songs, "The Precious Jewel," has a tune resembling the traditional ballad "The Hills of Roane County." None of this brands Acuff a plagiarist; in the oral tradition from which he came, tunes and texts were considered common property, to be borrowed and changed as a given performer saw fit.

His performance style was also traditional. His singing voice was descended from the nasal, mournful "high country" sound of the Southern uplands, and his backing band, the Smoky Mountain Boys, consisted of fiddle, guitar, bass, and dobro (a steel guitar popular in early hillbilly music, capable of producing the sliding sound which is still one of the most distinctive features of country-western music). "Railroad Boomer," recorded in 1939,[50] will serve to illustrate all these features. Strophic and narrative, in the style of a traditional ballad, it has a last verse functioning as a moral, with a sentiment common to railroad songs of the hillbilly era:

> If you want to do me a favor,
> When they lay me down to die,
> Dig my grave beside the railroad
> So I can hear the train go by.

And the sound of Acuff's voice and the backing instruments is an extension of the mainstream hillbilly style of the 1920s and '30s.

The subject matter of Acuff's songs affirms the conservative religious and moral attitudes prevalent among white Southerners of the time. Many are openly religious ("The Great Judgement Morning" and "The Songbirds are Singing in Heaven"), many others pass moral judgment on the evil influences of modern life. "Wreck on the Highway" deals with a car crash; the narrator observes

[50] NW 287, s2 / 3.

"there was whiskey and blood all together, mixed with glass where they lay," then comments sadly and piously in the chorus,

> I didn't hear nobody pray,
> I didn't hear nobody pray;
> I heard the crash on the highway,
> But I didn't hear nobody pray.

Many other country-western performers of the 1930s and '40s built careers around similar songs.[51] Eddy Arnold, born near Henderson, Tennessee in 1918, began singing on local radio shows in 1936 as "The Tennessee Plowboy," made his first appearance on the Grand Ole Opry in 1942, and cut his first commercial disc in 1944. By 1947 one of his recordings ("I'll Hold You in My Heart") had sold a million copies, and four more became top-selling hits on the *Billboard* country-western charts in the next several years. "Bouquet of Roses" (1948) is typical of his early style.[52] A love ballad with a refrain, rather than a narrative ballad, it features an accompanying group of guitar, fiddle, dobro, and bass. Arnold's voice is more mellow and less nasal than Acuff's, closer to Jimmie Rodgers than the Carter Family.

Hank Snow, born in Nova Scotia in 1914, began his career on Canadian radio in 1934 as "Hank, the Singing Ranger," featuring songs by Jimmie Rodgers and imitating his yodel. His first American performance was in Dallas in 1944, his first American recording dates from 1949, and he joined the cast of the Grand Ole Opry in 1950. "I'm Movin' On" (1950) was a train song; "I Don't Hurt Anymore" (1954) was a sentimental ballad. His other successful songs cover the entire topical and expressive range of country-western music of the era.[53]

Ernest Tubb, born in 1914 in Crisp, Texas, also began as an emulator of Jimmie Rodgers, and was in fact encouraged and aided by Rodgers's widow. His own songs dealt mostly with personal and often painful emotions rather than the narration of historic or tragic events. Signed to a recording contract by Decca, his breakthrough came in 1941 with "Walking the Floor Over You," which not only sold more than a million copies in his own performance but was also recorded with great success by Bing Crosby. "Try Me One More Time" (1942) is in the same mold,[54] with its sentimental lyrics of

---

[51] Typical in textual and musical style is "The Forgotten Soldier Boy," recorded by the Monroe Brothers in 1936. Cf. NW 287, s1 / 8.

[52] NW 207, s1 / 1.

[53] "Squid Jiggin' Ground," (1957), for instance, is a strophic narrative ballad. Cf. NW 207, s1 / 4.

[54] NW 207, s1 / 6.

personal anguish, its strophic structure (with a refrain line), and its performance with traditional country-western instrumentation and singing style. Noteworthy is Tubb's use of the electric guitar—which was brought into the country-western mainstream by Tubb and other performers from the Southwest—and the characteristic interpolation of odd beats, yielding occasional triple measures in a piece in duple meter.

Kitty Wells (b. 1919 in Nashville) was the most successful female country-western singer of the decades surrounding World War II. Her career progressed through the same stages as did those of so many of her male peers—initially at family, religious, and social occasions; first professional exposure on local radio (WSIX in Nashville); a hit recording ("It Wasn't God Who Made Honky Tonk Angels" for Decca) leading to appearances on the Grand Ole Opry; a continuing string of successful recordings. "There's Poison in Your Heart" (1955)[55] perfectly defines her style and underlines its position in the mainstream country-western style, now centered in Nashville—a vocal sound shaped by rural Southern heritage, an instrumental backing of fiddle, dobro, and guitars, with a rhythm section of guitar and bass.

Through the 1930s, hillbilly music had remained on the fringe of American culture. Perhaps the first recognition in the national press was an article entitled "Thar's GOLD in them Hillbillies" in the April 30, 1938 issue of Collier's. The author, Kyle Crichton, takes a somewhat humorous approach to his subject, which cannot conceal his attitude of condescension and cultural superiority. A legend under the title informs the reader that "Songs are legal tender anywhere. Some of the worst circle the globe."

> The young man with the Adam's apple seemed out of place in a New York elevator. Very definitely he was not a New Yorker and in addition he was not welcome in the crowded car because he carried under his arm a case that looked like a rough box for a horse.
>
> "Will y'all pahdon me?" he said plaintively. "Ah'm havin' some trouble with this here git-tar."
>
> He carried the trouble with him when he got off at the eleventh floor and was presently in a room before a microphone having an audition for phonograph records. . . . This was the rare thing of a New York audition for hillbilly songs and race records. The general practice is to take a recording outfit into the territory where such songs grow. A hint from New York that David Kapp of Decca or Eli Oberstein of Victor is headed South will find the tidings flying over mountains and the result will be that when the city slickers arrive they will be unable to get into their

---

[55] NW 207, s1 / 5.

hotels for the presence of mouth-organ virtuosos, yodelers, blues singers and specialty bands equipped with instruments made up of tissue paper on combs, washboards, assorted saws and rutabaga gourds.

If there needs to be another picture at this point, the camera can leap agilely to such distant parts of South Africa and Australia where the native bushmen are busily humming a little number written by Jimmie Davis of Shreveport, Louisiana.

But the years following World War II brought a boom period to country-western music and extended its geographical and cultural boundaries. Military service and wartime employment had taken millions of Americans from rural areas into the cities of the North and East, where many of them remained, prompting some radio stations and retail phonograph outlets to concern themselves with country-western music for the first time. Talented new performers were emerging—Webb Pierce, Ray Price, George Jones, Carl Smith—and the phonograph industry began responding to the widening market for country-western music.

It was at this propitious time that the most talented and magnetic performer since Jimmie Rodgers embarked on his meteoric career.

Hank (King Hiram) Williams was born on a tenant farm in Mt. Olive, Alabama, in 1923, formed his first band when he was thirteen, and made his first radio appearance (station WSFA in Montgomery, Alabama) a year later. Many years of performing in clubs, bars, theaters, and medicine shows led to a recording contract in 1946, with a small company (Sterling); his first discs were country gospel songs. A contract with MGM finally brought stardom: between his first top-selling disc in 1949 ("Lovesick Blues") and his death on New Year's Day of 1953, Williams dominated country-western music, releasing eleven million-selling discs, many others which sold almost as well, and becoming the most sought-after radio performer of the day.

His voice retained the nasal "country twang," his instrumental backing—usually by the Drifting Cowboys—was dominated by guitars, fiddle, steel guitar or dobro, and bass. At the same time his music reflected the life and music of the rural South at midcentury. His songs were not traditional ballads, but rather lyrical reactions to brief and usually bitter relationships between the sexes, often set in the honky-tonk bars and dance halls of the modern South. Their mere titles suggest their concerns—"Why Don't You Love Me?," "Cold, Cold Heart," "I'll Never Get Out of This World Alive," "Your Cheatin' Heart." They are usually simple stanzaic pieces with four-line verses, often with the last line a refrain:

Hank Williams in performance. (Courtesy of the Country Music Foundation and Media Center, Nashville, Tennessee)

> I could say it's over now,
> That I was glad to see you go;
> I could hate you for the way I'm feeling,
> My lips could tell a lie, but my heart would know.

Like other white musicians growing up in the South, Williams had considerable contact with black performers and their music. His guitar teacher was said to have been a black street singer named Teetot, and his music is colored by the music of black Americans, from the rhythm section of his band (drums, rhythm guitar, and bass, more prominent than in earlier country-western music) to the fact that many of his songs reflect the sentiment and sometimes the structure of the blues.

His bitter but honest lyrics and the strong simplicity of his singing and instrumental backing were in sharp contrast to the maudlin sentiments and cloying musical style offered by New York and Hollywood musicians caught in the death throes of the venerable Tin Pan Alley style. America's urban whites were not quite ready for the vocal and instrumental sounds of country-western music, but they responded to the music of Hank Williams in "cleaned-up" interpretations; in the early 1950s, "cover" versions of his songs by Tony Bennett, Jo Stafford, and Rosemary Clooney sold well. They were straws in the wind, signaling that urban popular song in America had reached a dead end and audiences were casting around for something very different.

The 1960s brought a new generation of country-western musicians, who took Hank Williams as their most important model. Their songs were almost all performed in traditional singing styles and backed with small instrumental groups with more or less standard instrumentation. Most of these performers had been born in the rural South or Southwest and they continued to cultivate an image attractive to audiences in these areas. Their songs often voiced the socially and politically conservative attitudes still dominating the South and other parts of rural America; though the single most popular topic was disappointed or frustrated love and attendant unhappiness and loneliness, many songs continued to deal with the traditional topics of death, family ties, religion, problems with alcohol, and the preservation of the moral code of the region. It seems fair to say that such songs represent the continuation of a tradition dating back to the Carter Family and Jimmie Rodgers, whose songs in turn were based on much older traditions. Though country-western music contributed to the musical style of early rock 'n' roll, the latter had a much less lasting impact on mainstream country-western music than on urban popular music. Thus the period which brought the century's most dramatic stylistic revolution to urban popular music was marked by continuity and stability in country-western music.

The songs of Johnny Cash, born in Kingsland, Arkansas in 1932, will serve to suggest the lucrative aspects of country-western music in the post–Hank Williams decades and the types of songs making up the repertory.

Cash's first disc, "Cry, Cry, Cry," was cut in 1954 for Sun Records in Memphis, the same year that Sun released Elvis Presley's first recording. His first million-seller came in 1956, and by the end of the 1970s more than 100 of his recordings had appeared on *Billboard*'s country-western charts, at least half of them in the Top Ten.

Fans photographing Johnny Cash at the Grand Ole Opry. (Courtesy of the Country Music Foundation and Media Center, Nashville, Tennessee)

"I Walk the Line" (1956), his first top hit, shows his indebtedness to Hank Williams. A simple, strophic song with the title serving as a refrain line at the end of each verse, the text deals with romantic love. Cash's rich, deep, gravelly voice retains clear elements of traditional country singing; the instrumental backing is dominated by guitar and bass. Interestingly, in this year of Elvis Presley, Chuck Berry, Jerry Lee Lewis, and Little Richard, "I Walk the Line" enjoyed considerable success with urban white audiences and appeared on *Billboard*'s "pop" charts for twenty two weeks. Cash's song makes no overt bow to the new rock 'n' roll style, but urban audiences understood that the roots of rock 'n' roll lay partly in country-western music and could listen to this latter music with an appreciation not possible even a few years before, as a result of several years' exposure to rock 'n' roll. This was the first disc by a country-western performer making no concessions to urban popular song style to appear on the "pop" charts; even Hank Williams never managed that.

Cash's later songs never lose touch with stylistic elements

stamping them as country-western music. There are railroad songs ("Rock Island Line," 1970); narrative ballads of brave and tragic deeds and events ("The Ballad of Ira Hayes," 1964, and "Smiling Bill McCall," 1960); tales with moralistic overtones ("Don't Take Your Guns to Town," 1959); prison songs ("Folsom Prison Blues," 1956, and "In the Jailhouse Now," 1962); sad and lonesome love laments in the tradition of Hank Williams ("Oh Lonesome Me," 1961); comic tales ("A Boy Named Sue," 1969); songs with political undertones ("Singing in Vietnam Talking Blues," 1971); and an occasional song reminding one of the venerable link between country-western music and the popular song style of the nineteenth century ("Lorena," a Civil War ballad, released in 1959).[56]

Texas-born Buck Owens, who had more No. 1 songs on *Billboard*'s country-western charts in the 1960s and early '70s than any other performer, is cast in much the same mold,[57] as are also Conway Twitty (born in Mississippi) and Merle Haggard. Though Haggard's first successful song, "Sing a Sad Song" (1963),[58] was a love ballad, the range of his texts is greater than that of most of his contemporaries, and he has never hesitated to write and perform songs with political and social implications. "Hungry Eyes" (1969) is very much a protest song in the style of Woody Guthrie and some of the political urban folk songwriters of the 1960s, dramatizing the plight of one of America's least-publicized subcultures, poor rural whites. And his "Okie from Muskogee" of the same year was a humorous but sharp condemnation of the radical youth movement in America, voicing strong support for traditional American—or at least Southern—values. Charley Pride should also be mentioned, as the only successful black performer of country-western music.

There were female stars in the 1960s and '70s, as well. Loretta Lynn, the daughter of a coal miner in Butchers Hollow, Kentucky, followed the well-charted path to commercial success—a beginning in local clubs and bars, performances on local radio, bookings in larger establishments, growing local and regional reputation, a hit single with a small recording company ("I'm a Honky-Tonk Girl" [1960] with Zero),[59] a contract with a major company (Decca), appearances on the "Grand Ole Opry," a flood of top-selling discs, and bookings at top clubs and with major radio networks. Tammy Wynette and Dolly Parton also emerged in the 1960s; the latter, in addition to being an effective and popular per-

[56] NW 207, s2 / 4.
[57] For a sample of his style, cf. "Don't Let Her Know," (1964), on NW 207, s2 / 5.
[58] NW 207, s2 / 7.
[59] NW 207, s2 / 3.

former, has proved to be a songwriter of unusual gifts. Her "Coat of Many Colors (1971),[60] for instance, is a contemporary country-western song retaining the most important characteristics of the genre, with clear ancestry all the way back to the Carter Family and still aimed at an audience of rural and working-class Americans in the South and elsewhere.

On September 16, 1946, Bill Monroe and His Blue Grass Boys cut several discs for Columbia Records. The group, made up of Bill Monroe (mandolin and vocals), Lester Flatt (guitar and vocals), Earl Scruggs (banjo), Chubby Wise (fiddle), and Cedric Rainwater (bass), created the most distinctive new dialect of country-western music in the decades following World War II, and gave this new style its name—bluegrass.

All the characteristics of bluegrass are defined in the discs cut at this historic session. The style is in some respects conservative: there are no electric instruments; there is a mix of vocal and instrumental performance. The core of the band consists of five-string banjo (which had virtually disappeared from commercial country-western music), fiddle, and guitar. New features include the introduction of mandolin and bass, a lively and often break-neck tempo, and most of all, virtuoso playing on all instruments, particularly the banjo, with Scrugg's new right-hand technique of three-finger "picking" enabling him to play passages of much greater speed and complexity than had been possible with the older banjo techniques of frailing, strumming, or plectrum picking.

"Why Did You Wander," from this first session,[61] illustrates all these features, new and old. A first chorus is played by the entire band, the sound dominated by Scruggs's banjo racing along in a style never before heard in country-western music. A chorus with Flatt and Monroe harmonizing mostly in thirds and fourths, and an instrumental chorus featuring Wise's fiddle, complete the introductory section. The core of the piece consists of three verses sung by Scruggs, each followed by a vocal (two-part harmony) and then an instrumental chorus, the latter dominated by one of the instrumentalists; a final vocal chorus brings the piece to an end. Though more than half the verses and choruses are vocal, one is left with the impression of instrumentally dominated music. Though there are few suggestions of jazz in rhythmic patterns and instrumental style—less than one hears in western swing, or even the music of Ernest Tubb and his peers—the emphasis on instrumental virtu-

[60] NW 207, s2 / 8.
[61] NW 225, s1 / 1.

Lester Flatt and Earl Skruggs (the last two on right) after forming their Blue Grass group. (Courtesy of the Country Music Foundation and Media Center, Nashville, Tennessee)

osity and the way in which the various players are featured in successive choruses is very much in the tradition of small-group jazz.

Though the band had been in existence since 1938, when it was formed in Atlanta, and had performed on the "Grand Ole Opry" and cut earlier discs for Columbia, the distinctive style of bluegrass did not jell until Scruggs joined the band as a nineteen-year-old banjoist in December of 1945. The band stayed together for only three years after the recording session of 1946—time enough to stylize and popularize the new bluegrass techniques. Scruggs and Flatt left to form their own band, the Foggy Mountain Boys, which played in a style virtually indistinguishable from that of the original Blue Grass Boys.[62] By this time other groups were imitating the sounds of bluegrass, and the late 1940s and the 1950s saw a great proliferation of bluegrass bands.

Bluegrass is a style of playing, applicable to the several types of songs comprising the country-western repertory of the era. Many

[62] Cf. their performance of "Blue Ridge Cabin Home," (1955), on NW 225, s1 / 2.

of the earliest bluegrass hits were in verse-chorus form, a structure that allowed sequences of solo vocal verses, harmonized choruses, and instrumental choruses.[63] The new style could also be used for strophic, narrative ballads, with alternation between vocal and instrumental stanzas;[64] religious songs;[65] old-time, two-strain fiddle tunes, done without voices;[66] and even nineteenth-century popular songs,[67] older hillbilly pieces by Jimmie Rodgers and his peers, and newly composed songs.

Once fixed in the late 1940s, the bluegrass style remained virtually static for the next thirty years. Bill Monroe still performs, in the same style as that of his recordings of the 1940s; new groups, and new players, seek mostly to emulate the sound of the first bluegrass bands. The audience has been a curious mixture; many followers of country-western music responded to it, but almost from the beginning bluegrass had an appeal also for many middle- and upper-income Americans, many of them college-educated. Bill Clifton, leader of the Dixie Mountain Boys,[68] attended the University of Virginia, and Emerson and Waldon[69] are from urban backgrounds. Bluegrass performances are as likely to take place on college campuses as in country bars; bluegrass festivals, such as the one in Bean Blossom, Indiana, attract audiences mixed in age and background. The appeal of this kind of music has been persistent, but few discs have had commercial success comparable to those of the country-western singers discussed above. It is a commentary on the changing face of American culture that the only disc by Flatt and Scruggs ever to be listed as a top seller on *Billboard*'s country-western charts was "The Ballad of Jed Clampett" (1962)—the theme song of the television series "The Beverly Hillbillies."

In 1924, in an attempt to capitalize on the new hillbilly market, Victor asked a singer named Vernon Dalhart to record one of the

---

[63] Cf. "You'd Better Wake Up," by Mac Wiseman and The Country Boys (1953), on NW 225, s1 / 5; "Your Old Standby," by Jim Eanes and the Shenandoah Valley Boys (1956), on NW 225, s1 / 6; and "Raise a Ruckus Tonight," (c. 1961), by the Lonesome River Valley Boys on NW 225, s2 / 6, for samples of verse-chorus songs played in bluegrass style.

[64] Cf. "Twenty-One Years," (1952), by the Lonesome Pine Fiddlers, on on NW 225, s1 / 7.

[65] Cf. "Daniel Prayed," (1959), by the Stanley Brothers and the Clinch Mountain Boys, on NW 225, s1 / 3.

[66] Cf. "Blackberry Blossom," (1965), by Billy Baker and group, on NW 225, s2 / 1.

[67] Flatt and Scruggs recorded "Over the Hills to the Poorhouse," (1951), written in 1894 by David Braham. Cf. Spottswood, *Folk Music in America*, Vol. 7, s2 / 5.

[68] Cf. their version of "Springhill Disaster," (1958), on NW 225, s1 / 8.

[69] Cf. "Fox on the Run," (c. 1969), on NW 225, s2 / 7.

most popular ballads of the "old-time" repertory, "The Wreck of the Old 97." Another song was needed for the flip side of the disc, and Dalhart suggested "The Prisoner's Song," a simple strophic piece depicting a prisoner pining away in confinement:[70]

> Oh I wish I had someone to love me,
> Someone to call me their own;
> Oh I wish I had someone to live with,
> 'Cause I'm tired of living alone.
>
> Now if I had wings like an angel,
> Over these prison walls I would fly;
> And I fly to the arms of my poor darling,
> And there I'd be willing to die.

Born in Texas (in 1883, as Marion Try Slaughter), Dalhart had gone to New York for classical vocal training, had become a member of the Century Opera Company, and was a frequent performer in Gilbert and Sullivan operettas. His singing of "The Prisoner's Song" reveals his classical training, though he attempts to imitate some of the nasal style of hillbilly singers; the accompaniment consists of simple strummed chords on a single guitar, in carefully correct harmonies, and a viola (played in classical style, suggesting nothing of the sound of traditional fiddling).

"The Prisoner's Song" became the single most successful composition of the pre-electrical era of the phonograph. The original disc for Victor sold somewhere between 4,000,000 and 6,000,000 copies and Dalhart eventually recorded it on twenty eight different labels, with total sales in the neighborhood of 25,000,000. The disc sold well in the South and in rural areas of the Southwest and Midwest, as Victor had hoped; but it sold even better elsewhere. Millions of Americans who did not otherwise respond to hillbilly music found Dalhart's performance of this song appealing and irresistible. It was thus the first instance of a "crossover" record—one aimed at a certain audience which had appeal for other listeners as well.

Some western dialects of hillbilly music, particularly those of Hollywood cowboy movies, were also aimed at both rural and urban audiences in all parts of the country, and recordings by Gene Autry and Roy Rogers were later examples of crossover discs. But

[70] Dalhart claimed that the song had been written by his cousin, Guy Massey; but like so many hillbilly songs on the 1920s and '30s, it appears to have been known in oral tradition before it was recorded. Cf. Randolph, *Ozark Folksongs*, Vol. 4, p. 226, for information on this point, and a similar song entitled "Meet Me Tonight," which appears to predate "The Prisoner's Song."

it was not until the decade following the end of World War II that record companies launched a campaign calculated to attract a larger and more varied audience for country-western music.

Led by Decca in the early 1950s, several major recording companies set up studios in Nashville, in order to be close to the best singers and instrumentalists, many of whom performed regularly on the "Grand Ole Opry." This trend brought something new to country-western recordings—a producer involved in artistic decisions formerly left to performers.

Typical of the Nashville producers was Chet Atkins, who was put in charge of the country-western repertory of RCA Victor. Born in Luttrell, Tennessee in 1924, a country-western singer and guitarist of some success in his early professional days, Atkins expanded his musical horizons to include jazz, urban popular music, and even classical music, and became fluent in a multiplicity of styles.[71] In a series of discs brought out under his direction in the late 1950s and early 1960s, many of the characteristic features of country-western music gradually disappear—the use of fiddles, banjo, and guitar, and the traditional country vocal style—and are replaced by a sound moving closer to urban popular music of the day, the style of the declining years of Tin Pan Alley.

Jim Reeves's "Four Walls," released by RCA in 1957, uses a backing group of humming voices (a sound alien to earlier country-western music), piano, bass, and several sustaining instruments; Reeves's voice is closer to the crooning style of Tin Pan Alley singers than the vocal sound of traditional Anglo-American singing. Born in Texas, and coming from a legitimate country-western background, Reeves was accepted by country-western audiences, and "Four Walls" spent 25 weeks on the *Billboard* charts, rising as high as the No. 2 position. It also placed on the "Hot 100" pop charts for 22 weeks, and combined sales soon passed the million mark.[72] Within a few years, with such songs as "Welcome to My World" (1964), Reeves was singing to the accompaniment of a large, lush, string-dominated orchestra virtually indistinguishable in sound from that used to back Frank Sinatra at many of his recording sessions. But despite the ever-increasing distance between Reeves's music and the traditional Anglo-American style

[71] Cf. NW 207, s1 / 8, for Atkin's performance on the guitar of "Jean's Song," by Marguerite Monnot—also known as "The Poor People of Paris"—in a style which demonstrates both his own virtuosity as a performer and his grasp of sophisticated musical materials.

[72] "Little Ole You," recorded by Reeves in 1962, available on NW 207, s2 / 1, is a sample of his later pop style.

and its offshoots, he carried the country-western audience with him. Stylistic incongruities are often of more concern to the scholar and critic than to listeners. Another large chunk of his audience consisted of older urban people searching for alternatives to rock 'n' roll, who would not have listened to Reeves had he performed in a mainstream country-western style.

Eddy Arnold was singing in a similar way, at just the same time; RCA Victor was also his company. By the mid-1960s, Arnold was being accompanied by a large studio orchestra with a full complement of strings; the songs themselves are lyric, sentimental pieces almost indistinguishable from the products of the last generation of Tin Pan Alley songwriters.[73] In fact, Arnold often performed songs from the New York–Hollywood repertory, and was booked into clubs in Las Vegas and other spots catering to older, conservative, wealthy clientele, where earlier country-western singers had never set foot. Patsy Cline was the most successful female singer of this persuasion. One of her most successful songs was "Love Letters in the Sand,"[74] written in 1931 by the Tin Pan Alley songwriter J. Fred Coots and published by Irving Berlin.

Glenn Campbell was one of many singers emerging in the 1960s who was poised so convincingly between country-western and pop style and repertory as to enjoy equal success with both audiences. A number of his discs, including "By the Time I Get to Phoenix" (1967), "Wichita Lineman" (1968), "Galveston" (1969), and "It's Only Make Believe" (1970), placed in the Top Ten on both the country-western and the "Hot 100" charts in *Billboard*.

By the 1970s, much of the country-western audience was so attuned to country pop as to be willing to accept performers with no cultural ties to the rural Southern heritage which had spawned virtually all performers of hillbilly and country-western music, singing pieces with only the most superficial relationship to the musical traditions underlying this branch of American music. The British-born, Australian-trained Olivia Newton-John placed a number of songs in the Top Ten of the country-western charts in the mid-1970s—"Let Me Be There" (1973), "If You Love Me Let Me Know" (1974), and "Have You Never Been Mellow" (1975), among others—and was voted female vocalist of the year (1974) by the Country Music Association. Songwriters with no cultural ties to traditional Anglo-American music began writing country-western songs. Kris Kristofferson's background included a degree from

---

[73] Cf. "Bouquet of Roses," on NW 207, s1 / 1, for a sample of Arnold's earlier style.
[74] NW 207, s1 / 7.

Pomona College in California, a Rhodes scholarship to Oxford University in England, service in the U.S. Army, and a teaching assignment at the U.S. Military Academy at West Point. His "Me and Bobby McGee," popular with white rock audiences as performed by Janis Joplin, enjoyed some success on the country-western charts in versions by Jerry Lee Lewis and Roger Miller,[75] and other urban songwriters began furnishing material for Nashville-based singers.

The Country Music Association was founded in Nashville to "improve, market and publicize country music . . . to the end that it would become an even greater industry."[76] One tactic was to create a new image of the people who performed, wrote, promoted, and listened to country-western music, an image bringing them closer to the mainstream of American life and culture.

The "Grand Ole Opry" became the symbol of country-western music's growing affluence and its new image. Originally broadcast from the studios of WSM, it is subsequently housed in the large Ryman Auditorium. After a successful fund-raising campaign backed by both the city of Nashville and the phonograph industry, it moved in 1974 into a new, fifteen-million dollar building, "Opry Land, U.S.A.," designed and executed by the same firm that had created Disneyland. The inaugural program was carried by some 200 radio stations in all parts of America; President Nixon and his wife were in the audience. Several years later, ABC-TV carried a ninety-minute live telecast celebrating the fiftieth anniversary of the first radio broadcast of the "Grand Ole Opry," and Robert Altman's film *Nashville*, with many scenes shot in the new complex, was a top-grossing film in 1975.[77]

The urbanization of country-western music has intensified in the late 1970s and early '80s. President Carter's championing of Willie Nelson and other country singers brought them publicity and exposure in circles previously hostile to this sort of music; Kenny Rogers and Dolly Parton are only two of many country-western performers who have modified their style in the direction of country pop and even rock, and in doing so have attracted a more eclectic following; the film *Urban Cowboy* (1979), starring John Travolta, spurred a trend toward "country chic"—the affecting of western-styled clothing by city dwellers, the popularity of fashionable bars with western decor and country-western music in cities across

[75] A sample of Kristofferson's songwriting style is available on NW 207 s2 / 9, his own performance of "Help Me Make It through the Night," (1969), later recorded with great success by Sammi Smith (1971).

[76] Malone, *Country Music U.S.A.*, p. 264.

[77] Curiously, the music featured in the movie consisted not of older country-western classics, or even new songs by established songwriters, but rather undistinguished and atypical songs written by members of the cast.

America. New performers have emerged with styles poised somewhere between urban popular and country-western music.[78]

The present chapter differs from other writings on hillbilly and country-western music in its emphasis on the mixture of traditional and popular elements which shaped this music from its earliest days. It might appear that country pop is merely the latest chapter in a continuing story; there is a subtle but nevertheless critical difference, however. In earlier decades, even though country-western music brought together elements from both traditional and popular cultures, it retained a distinctive style; country pop has come to be so strongly flavored by musical and expressive elements of the late Tin Pan Alley period as to become urban popular music with mere traces of traditional musical styles.

Country pop is remarkably conservative, with its most important features derived from the era before 1955. But the rejection of this style by a portion of the country-western audience in recent years, in favor of older performers clinging to a more traditional style and new performers who pattern their music on older classics of country-western music, suggests that many people in those parts of America that gave birth to hillbilly music still prefer their own brand of tradition and conservatism and their own regional and cultural identity.

[78] Discs released in recent years by Crystal Gayle, Mickey Gilley, Barbara Mandrell, and Eddie Rabbitt give testimony of this trend.

# 17

# *The Golden Age of Jazz*

"Scoop" Gleason filed a story with the *San Francisco Bulletin* on the first day of spring training for the baseball season of 1913, reporting to his readers on the spirit of the Seals, the local professional team:

> Everyone has come back to the old town full of the old "jazz" and they promise to knock the fans off their feet with their playing. What is "jazz"? Why, it's a little of that "old life," the "gin-i-ker," the "pep," otherwise known as the enthusiasalum. A grain of "jazz" and you feel like going out and eating your way through Twin Peaks. It's that spirit which makes ordinary ball players step around like Lajoies and Cobbs. The team which speeded into town this morning (has) trained on ragtime and "jazz" and Manager Del Howard says there's no stopping them.[1]

Later Gleason was to explain that he got the term "jazz" from Art Hickman, a band leader and baseball fan who led a dance orchestra at Boyes Springs, near the training camp. Featuring the popular syncopated dance music of the day, the band built a reputation as "the jazziest tune tooters in all the Valley."[2]

It may or may not be a coincidence that a black band from New

---

[1] From the issue of March 6, 1913, as quoted in Nicolas Slonimsky, *Music Since 1900* (New York: Charles Scribner's Sons, 1971), p. 1405.

[2] "Scoop" Gleason in *The Call Bulletin* (San Francisco) for September 3, 1938, as quoted in Slonimsky p. 1406.

Orleans calling itself the Original Creole Orchestra, headed by cornettist Freddie Keppard, had come to California the year before.

Several years later in Chicago, a member of another dance band from New Orleans led by Nick LaRocca reported that during their engagement at the Booster Club:

> One frenzied couple kept yelling for more jazz. (The club manager), hearing them call out "play some more jazz" or "jazz it up!" had the idea to bill (us) as such a band. The word Jazz is of northern origin. We never heard this word Jazz down South. It was used in the theatrical profession, meaning various things, one meaning to pep or excite one.[3]

"Brown's Dixieland Jass Band, Direct from New Orleans, Best Dance Music in Chicago," may have arrived in the city before LaRocca's group, and it is also possible that the Original Creole Band had played there before either. In any event, by 1916 a number of clubs in Chicago were featuring "Jazz" bands, and Brown's group had taken this music on the road, playing an eleven-week engagement at the Century Theatre in New York. LaRocca's band opened at the Paradise Club in that city on January 15, 1917, as the "Dixie Jasz Band," and within a few weeks they had cut discs for both Columbia and Victor, now calling themselves the "Original Dixieland Jazz Band."

The new term was quickly appropriated for the syncopated dance music of the period. Jim Europe's army band, which had gone off to Europe in 1917 as the 369th Infantry Band, was hailed on its return in the fall of 1918 as the 369th U.S. Infantry Jazz Band.

America had a new term and, perhaps, a new type of music.

Though the long-cherished notion that jazz originated in New Orleans has been challenged by recent scholars, most of the musicians who played important roles in the development of the stream of music to which the term "jazz" is applied learned their musical trade in that city, and these men themselves believed that the style in which they played originated there.

Tracing its early history is difficult, since no recorded or notated evidence is available for the first quarter-century. We know the names of individual performers and the bands in which they played. Oral tradition identifies Charles "Buddy" Bolden (1868–1938), a cornet player whose career ended in 1907 with his committment to the East Louisiana State Hospital, as the first musician to play in this distinctive style. Joseph "King" Oliver (1885–1938) was his

---

[3] LaRocca, from a letter quoted in Slonimsky p. 272.

most important immediate successor, and Freddie Keppard (1889–1933) was another important early cornet player and bandleader, probably the first to take the New Orleans playing style out of the city. Other musicians who helped forge the tradition before 1920 were Sidney Bechet (clarinet), Johnny Dodds (clarinet) and his brother Warren "Baby" Dodds (drums), Willie "Bunk" Johnson (cornet), Johnny St. Cyr (banjo), Edward "Kid" Ory (trombone), Clarence Williams (piano), and of course Louis Armstrong (1900–71), who as a child heard Buddy Bolden and received instruction and his first cornet from King Oliver, and who came to be regarded as the greatest jazz player to come out of New Orleans.

Most of these men were members of marching bands, usually connected with black fraternal organizations, which accompanied funeral processions with hymns and other appropriate pieces, then played livelier music on the walk home. Some played in orchestras featuring the music of social dances of the day. Their most important employment, however, was in Storyville, an area in uptown New Orleans bounded by Canal and Basin Streets where legal prostitution flourished from 1897 to 1917 under legislation introduced by Alderman Sidney Story. Live music could be heard in bars, brothels, and dance halls; the emerging jazz style seemed quite appropriate for the environment. Surely the widespread employment of local musicians in a limited geographical area was a powerful stimulus to the growth of an indigenous and relatively homogeneous playing style.

The new style was employed for all the types of pieces played by these musicians—syncopated dance music, blues, marches, ragtime compositions, the hymns and other pieces played by marching bands. The most important factor was that it was an oral music. All evidence is emphatic on this point. For instance:

> King Buddy Bolden was the first man that began playing jazz in the city of New Orleans, and his band had the whole of New Orleans real crazy and running wild behind it. Now here is the thing that made King Bolden's Band the first band to play jazz. It was because they could not read at all.[4]
>
> Buddy Bolden was more of a ragtime cornet player at that time than Manuel Perez. He didn't use music.[5]

Louis Armstrong played for years before learning to read music. George Lewis, a clarinet player, said in 1955, "I never had a music

---

[4] Bunk Johnson, as quoted in Nat Shapiro and Nat Hentoff, eds., *Hear Me Talkin' to Ya* (New York: Rinehart & Company, 1955), p. 26.
[5] Alphonse Picou, as quoted in Shapiro and Hentoff, p. 28.

lesson in my life, and still can't read music."[6] Jack Weber, explaining how Leon Rappolo—the clarinet player of the New Orleans Rhythm Kings—learned the jazz style from black players who stopped at his father's saloon, said:

> Those clarinetists who gave Rappolo tips on clarinet playing were fakers, every one of them. Some of them thought that if they learned how to read, it would ruin their ability to improvise.
>
> Their tunes came from a million sources. Many of them were stolen from old marches (*High Society*, for instance) and were the leader's interpretation of the old marches. Because he couldn't read, the band played it differently from the original. Other band leaders stole it in turn, and, because he couldn't read either, the tune was played with many variations. After the leader had shown the trumpet man the melody (or what he *thought* was the melody), the trumpeter would play it for the band, and the men would come in, making a complete arrangement. It was "every man for himself," with the trumpeter taking the lead and everyone else filling in the best he could.[7]

By the 1910s, a characteristic ensemble had emerged: cornet, clarinet, trombone, and a rhythm section made up of some combination of banjo, piano, guitar, drums, and bass. Each instrument had a clearly defined role; and while it is true that the musicians improvised their parts, players in this tradition understood the nature of what their particular instrument was expected to play and had mastered typical phrases and motifs.

The first recordings of black musicians playing in this style date from the early 1920s. A band led by Kid Ory recorded two pieces in Los Angeles in 1922—"Ory's Creole Trombone" and "Society Blues."[8] King Oliver cut almost fifty discs in 1923 and 1924, mostly in Chicago; Clarence Williams' Blue Five cut a number of sides in New York these same years;[9] Louis Armstrong and His Hot Five began recording in Chicago in 1925; Freddie Keppard's Jazz Cardinals were first recorded in the same city in 1926.[10]

Two pieces by the Clarence Williams Blue Five will serve to define the basic stylistic elements of this music.

"Texas Moaner Blues" was recorded in New York on October 17, 1924, with Louis Armstrong (cornet), Charlie Irvis (trombone), Sidney Bechet (clarinet and soprano saxophone), Clarence Williams

---

[6] Shapiro and Hentoff, p. 28.
[7] Shapiro and Hentoff, p. 59.
[8] NW 269, s1 / 7–8.
[9] "Old Fashion Love" is available on NW 269, s2 / 7.
[10] "Stock Yard Strut" is on NW 269, s1 / 6.

(piano), and Buddy Christian (banjo).[11] The piece is made up of five 12-bar blues choruses:

1. The cornet takes the melody; the clarinet has an obbligato part above this, most prominent between phrases; the trombone functions as a tenor voice supporting the melody and a lower obbligato part at phrase endings; the piano and banjo give a simple, steady rhythmic-harmonic base.

2. The lead passes to the trombone, which elaborates the tune according to the character of the instrument; clarinet counter-melodies, again most prominent between phrases, become more elaborate and prominent; the cornet slips into a harmonic filler role.

3. The melody, back in the cornet, is now highly ornamented; an elaborate "break" at the end of the second phrase is left unsupported by the other two instruments, which otherwise continue their roles.

4. Bechet switches to the soprano saxophone for a highly elaborated version of the melody, reaching a climax with another florid "break" at the end of the second phrase. The cornet and trombone play even more subordinate roles than before.

5. This "stoptime" chorus—punctuated by carefully coordinated rests—has the melody once again in the cornet, with the other two melody instruments performing obbligato roles. A solo flourish by the clarinet, in the nature of a brief coda, finishes off the performance.

Thus each of the three melody instruments is given a chance to play an elaborated solo. The texture is contrapuntal; at times, each of the three instruments seems to be going its own way, held together only by the harmonic structure of the piece.

"Old Fashion Love," recorded in November of 1923 with a somewhat different personnel—Thomas Morris on cornet, John Masefield on trombone—is in essentially the same style.[12] The performance is based on a song written by James P. Johnson, in the verse-chorus style of Tin Pan Alley: a 4-bar introduction; a 16-bar verse; a 32-bar chorus in *ABAB* shape, based on the traditional song "Careless Love." The cornet has the lead for the entire verse, playing a rather straightforward version of the melodic line, while the clarinet and trombone fluctuate between harmonically supporting sustained notes and more active countermelodies, again mostly at cadences. Two choruses follow: the trombone takes the melody for the first half-chorus, the cornet the second; Bechet has the lead for the entire second chorus. When not soloing, each

[11]*Jazz Odyssey. Volume 1: The Sound of New Orleans* (Columbia Records C3L 30), s1 / 5.

[12]NW 269, s2 / 7.

instrument falls back into a supporting obbligato part. The most active three-part polyphony comes between phrases and sections; the rhythm section is unobtrusive, furnishing only the necessary foundation for the melody instruments.

Contemporary discs by Freddie Keppard and Kid Ory feature the same instrumentation, with each instrument performing the same roles. King Oliver had a second cornet (Louis Armstrong), playing a discreet harmonic-obbligato part, and a drummer. In solo choruses, the other melody instruments would often rest, play simple harmonic parts, or play their obbligato lines only in the final bars of a solo chorus. Thus the contrast in texture and contrapuntal activity between ensemble and solo choruses becomes much more pronounced, and in a piece like "Dippermouth Blues," recorded in June of 1923, the effect is almost that of a classical rondo:[13]

Chorus  1. ensemble (maximum texture and activity)
           2. ensemble (maximum texture and activity)
           3. clarinet solo (accompanied mostly by rhythm section)
           4. clarinet solo (accompanied mostly by rhythm section)
           5. ensemble (maximum texture and activity)
           6. cornet solo (subdued accompaniment by other instruments)
           7. cornet solo (subdued accompaniment by other instruments)
           8. ensemble (maximum texture and activity)
           9. ensemble (maximum texture and activity)

Some groups were even larger. Sam Morgan's Jazz Band recorded eight pieces for Columbia in 1927, in New Orleans itself—"the only recordings of a first-rate (local) band playing anywhere near its prime"[14]—with two cornets, trombone, two reed players, and a rhythm section of piano, banjo, drums, and bass. Yet all the characteristics of the style are there, despite the denser texture.[15]

The peak of this early, New Orleans–dominated jazz style came in the mid-1920s, with the playing of Louis Armstrong and the musicians associated with him. Louis Armstrong and His Hot Five cut their first discs in Chicago on November 12, 1925; the group consisted of Armstrong (cornet), Kid Ory (trombone), Johnny Dodds (clarinet), Lil Armstrong (piano), and Johnny St. Cyr (banjo). The Hot Seven was first recorded on May 7, 1927, adding Pete Briggs (brass bass) and Baby Dodds (drums) and with John Thomas

[13] Available on *The Smithsonian Collection of Classic Jazz* (Washington: Smithsonian Institution, 1973), selected and annotated by Martin Williams, s1/6.
[14] Samuel B. Charters, *Jazz: New Orleans (1885–1963). An Index to the Negro Musicians of New Orleans* (New York: Oak Publications, 1963), p. 134.
[15] NW 269, s2/1.

The Hot Five in 1925: (left to right) Johnny St. Cyr, banjo; Kid Ory, trombone; Louis Armstrong, cornet; John Dodds, clarinet; Lil Armstrong, piano.

replacing Ory on trombone. There was some slight change in personnel from session to session, and Armstrong switched from cornet to trumpet in 1928. The general style of ensemble playing changed very little from that of the early 1920s, but the solo playing of Armstrong, in technique, expressiveness, virtuosity, and imagination, became a model for jazz soloists for more than a decade. In the opinion of an eminent jazz historian, Armstrong's playing "stood out like a mountain peak over its neighboring foothills," for four reasons:

(1) His superior choice of notes and the resultant shape of his lines; (2) his incomparable basic quality of tone; (3) his equally incomparable sense of swing, that is, the sureness with which notes are placed in the time continuum and the remarkably varied attack and release proper-

ties of his phrasing; (4) and, perhaps his most individual contribution, the subtly varied repertory of vibratos and shakes with which Armstrong colors and embellishes individual notes.[16]

"Come Back, Sweet Papa," recorded by the Hot Five in February of 1926,[17] starts off with a brief introduction in which each of the first-line instruments (cornet, trombone, clarinet) takes its usual melodic role. But immediately Dodds takes a 32-bar solo chorus, accompanied only by the two rhythm instruments, and a second chorus is dominated by Armstrong, with the trombone and clarinet in subordinate roles. A second strain is split between ensemble playing and an unaccompanied piano solo, 16 bars each, and a 16-bar return to the first strain brings the performance to a close. More than half of the piece is given over to solo playing, and most of the ensemble passages are dominated more by Armstrong's lead than had been customary in such passages.

By June of 1928, when "West End Blues" was recorded,[18] the Hot Five had a somewhat different roster—Armstrong (now playing trumpet), Fred Robinson (trombone), Jimmy Strong (reeds), Earl Hines (piano), Mancy Cara (banjo), and Zutty Singleton (drums)—and a rather different musical character. Armstrong opens with an unaccompanied cadenzalike passage, then dominates the first 12-bar chorus with expressive and brilliant playing; though the other players support him, it is mostly with sustained chords rather than obbligato lines. The second chorus is given to the trombone, accompanied only by rhythm; Armstrong (with textless vocals) and Strong share the next chorus, echoing one another; Hines takes a chorus; and the final chorus brings the entire band together for the first time, though once again the trombone and clarinet play mostly sustaining notes against Armstrong's lead. The piece is most memorable for the musicianship and personality of the several soloists; there is virtually none of the contrapuntal ensemble playing so characteristic of the first years of this music.

Virtually every jazz historian has singled out the recordings made by the Hot Five and the Hot Seven as central to the evolution of jazz in the 1920s:

The Hot Five recordings constitute the most impressive, if not the most authentic, evidence of what the New Orleans style was like in its Golden Age. More than a quarter century later, these records, which are faded

[16] Gunther Schuller, *Early Jazz. Its Roots and Musical Development* (New York: Oxford University Press, 1968), p. 91.
[17] Available on *Jazz Odyssey*, s3/4.
[18] *The Smithsonian Collection*, s2/9.

in some spots but as fresh as ever in others, show clearly that Johnny Dodds and Kid Ory may have been precursors but Louis Armstrong was the first great classical figure of jazz.[19]

Armstrong was the greatest *solo* performer of the first several decades of jazz, and its most effective and appealing personality on stage. His acceptance by white audiences is a factor not to be underestimated in any assessment of the impact of jazz on commercial musical interests in America. But in some ways his talents, and his career as a "personality," went against what jazz had been from the beginning and was to continue to be at most of the peaks of its subsequent history—ensemble music.

By contrast, a series of recordings made at the same time by Jelly Roll Morton's Red Hot Peppers reaffirms and expands the ensemble nature of early jazz, and points more in the directions this music was to take in the following decade.

Ferdinand Joseph Morton (1885–1941) was one of the more fascinating characters in the drama of early jazz. Childhood in New Orleans brought him into contact with a wide range of music, both popular and classical. He became an itinerate ragtime and blues pianist and composer, leaving New Orleans in 1907 for a career in which fact is difficult to distinguish from fiction; he claimed, for instance, to have "invented jazz" in the first years of the century.[20] The discs made by his Red Hot Peppers—made in Chicago, beginning in 1926—are based on the improvised ensemble playing of New Orleans jazz, modified by his own talents and musical personality. Working with a larger number of instrumentalists than Armstrong, Morton functioned as a composer-arranger, shaping complex patterns of solo and ensemble playing. No matter how talented any of his performers (including himself) might have been, no one musical personality dominates the ensemble.

"Grandpa's Spell," recorded in Chicago in December of 1926 with a classic instrumentation of three front-line players (trumpet, trombone, and clarinet) and a rhythm section featuring Morton's piano, will serve to illustrate the control he exerted and the emphasis on subtly varied ensemble patterns. Based on one of his earlier piano pieces, it is a three-strain composition (each strain 16 bars in length):[21]

[19] Andre Hodeir, *Jazz. Its Evolution and Essence* (New York: Grove Press, 1956), p. 62.
[20] For an excellent summary and evaluation of the life and music of Morton, cf. Schuller, *Early Jazz*, pp. 134–74.
[21] *The Smithsonian Collection*, s1 / 7.

*Introduction: A A' B B' A'' C C C' C''*

The *A* strain is comprised of four 4-bar segments in an *abab* pattern, each *a* given to a solo instrument (guitar, trumpet, and trombone / bass) and each *b* to an answering ensemble. *B* is played by the ensemble, with a 2-bar piano break in the middle; *B'* is a 16-bar clarinet solo. C is a 16-bar trumpet solo; the three repetitions of the strain are given to a solo clarinet, piano, and then clarinet, and a concluding ensemble section. It is thus a mosaic of ensemble and solo sections, some only four bars long and some as many as sixteen; even this does not convey the complexity of the texture: some of the solos are accompanied only by the rhythm section; others are counterpointed by fragmentary breaks or bits of countermelodies from the other players.

While it is doubtful that Morton put any of this down in musical notation, and the character of the playing is still clearly improvisational, the complex sequence of events must have been carefully planned in advance.

All performers discussed to this point were black, and many histories of jazz have assumed the attitude most pointedly expressed in the opening statement of a book by Andre Hodeir: "Jazz is the Negro's art and almost all the great jazz musicians are Negroes."[22]

However, it is historical fact that the Original Dixieland Jazz Band, which brought jazz to New York and Europe and made the first recordings of it, was a white group. Clarinetist Nick LaRocca, the leader, had formed a band in New Orleans with the classic instrumentation of early jazz (cornet, trombone, clarinet, percussion) as early as 1908; a number of other white bands were playing music in what must have been a similar style in the 1910s; and a number of early jazz musicians, both black and white, have attested to the fact that there was frequent and fruitful musical interchange between instrumentalists of the two races. Before the first recordings of black jazz players were made, a number of other white bands—some from New Orleans, others formed in imitation of white New Orleans groups—had released discs: Earl Fuller's Famous Jazz Band (1917); the Original New Orleans Jazz Band, headed by Jimmy Durante (1918); the Louisiana Five (1918); the Original Memphis Five (1922); the New Orleans Rhythm Kings (1922).

Surely this situation only reflects the fact that the United States was a white-dominated society, and that it was easier for a white

[22] Hodeir, p. 7.

band to obtain recording contracts. Still, jazz by white musicians existed, and it must be examined.

The first disc cut by the Original Dixieland Jazz Band was made in New York on January 30, 1917, of Shelton Brooks's "The Darktown Strutter's Ball,"[23] a Tin Pan Alley song. After a brief introduction, the ODJB alternates verse and chorus:

*verse—chorus 1—chorus 2—verse—chorus 3—chorus 4—chorus 5*

Throughout, the cornet (LaRocca) plays a somewhat embellished version of the melody; the clarinet (Larry Shields) takes mostly an upper obbligato part; the trombone (Eddie Edwards) plays a harmony line in the tenor-bass range that takes on the nature of another obbligato part at the ends of some phrases. The only variation in this texture comes when the trombone or clarinet takes the melody for a few bars, with the cornet slipping into a supporting role. In general style, instrumentation, and the role each player takes in the three-part texture, the piece resembles the first music of this sort recorded by black musicians, five years later.

"She's Cryin' for Me," recorded by the New Orleans Rhythm Kings on March 26, 1925, near the end of their playing career, is much more oriented toward solo playing.[24] After a mostly homophonic introduction, the clarinet (Paul Mares) takes a solo for the first 8 bars of the first strain, answered by the ensemble with each instrument taking its traditional role in a three-part contrapuntal texture. A 16-bar solo for cornet follows; a brief transition leads to another strain, shaped as a 12-bar blues, with two choruses played by the clarinet (Charlie Cordilla). A return to the first strain finishes off the piece, with cornet and clarinet solos and a final half-chorus with the ensemble playing in traditional style and texture. Solos are accompanied by the rhythm players alone; ensemble playing takes up only two half-choruses.

The New Orleans jazz style of the 1910s and '20s encompassed both black and white performers, then. If there is a difference in the playing of the two races, it must be sought at a level other than general style.

For many jazz historians, it is a cultural and ethnic matter. An English critic, comparing the Original Dixieland Jazz Band with King Oliver's Jazz Band, finds that:

> The wildness of the blues, the tension of the heterophony, have vanished, leaving only a eupeptic jauntiness. Oliver makes something positive, even gay, out of a painful reality; the Dixieland Band, purging

[23] Available on *Jazz Odyssey*, s1 / 1.
[24] NW 269, s2 / 4.

away both the passion and the irony, leaves us with the inane grin of the black-faced minstrel.[25]

And comparing the playing of Bix Beiderbecke, the best white jazz cornetist of the 1920s, with that of black musicians:

> The basis of (his) playing was in the regular beat, the perky dotted-note fillip, the comparatively sweet sonority of the Original Dixieland Jazz Band.
>
> To us, at this date, Beiderbecke's playing survives as much for social-historical as for musical reasons. We see him as a symbol of the Jazz Age of Scott Fitzgerald . . . Always playing the old-world cornet rather than the more aggressive trumpet, Beiderbecke sought the presumed innocence of Negro music, but avoided, no less than did the white Dixieland Band, the hard realism of Armstrong or the ecstatic melancholy of Bechet. Instead he discovered, within the deliberate inanity of Dixieland style, a frail charm and plaintive melancholy.[26]

The debate over whether or not white musicians can play good jazz has persisted through the entire history of the genre, often exacerbated by intellectual and political climates. The first critical writing on jazz came at a time when even liberal whites could not shake the notion of black intellectual and cultural "inferiority." Gilbert Seldes wrote in 1923:

> I say the negro is not our salvation because with all my feeling for what he instinctively offers, for his desirable indifference to our set of conventions about emotional decency, I am on the side of civilization. To any one who inherits several thousand centuries of civilization, none of the things the negro offers can matter unless they are apprehended by the mind as well as by the body and the spirit. So far in their jazz the negroes have given their response to the world with an exceptional naivete, a directness of expression which has interested *our* minds as well as touched our emotions; they have shown comparatively little evidence of the functioning of *their* intelligence.[27]

In the 1960s and into the '70s, on the other hand, the climate of black consciousness and militancy made it impossible for most blacks (and many whites) to see jazz by white musicians as anything more than sterile imitation and exploitation.

These matters cannot be settled here. For the moment I will merely point out that the term "Dixieland," taken from the name

[25] Wilfrid Mellers, *Music in a New Found Land* (New York: Alfred A. Knopf, 1965), p. 289.

[26] Mellers, p. 308.

[27] Gilbert Seldes, "Toujours Jazz," in *The Dial* LXXV (1923), pp. 159–60.

of the first popular white jazz band, has come to be used in two different ways in recent years: as a generic name for the style of early New Orleans jazz; and as a label for music of this sort by white performers, continuing to the present in the playing of Pete Fountain, Al Hirt, and their peers.

The style of jazz discussed to this point might be thought of as a sort of chamber music, played by a small ensemble with each musician taking an individual line. In the 1920s a somewhat different sort of jazz emerged, played by larger groups and characterized by ensemble rather than solo playing. Its history is complex; it will be useful to begin with a consideration of the band that brought this style to its first peak, Fletcher Henderson and His Orchestra.

Born in Cuthbert, Georgia in 1898 into a well-educated, upper-middle-class family—Henderson's father was principal of the Randolph Training School in Macon, his mother taught piano—he studied chemistry and mathematics at Atlanta University and came to New York to pursue a degree at Columbia University. He took a job with the music publishing firm of Pace and Handy as a song plugger, then joined the staff of the Black Swan recording company as house pianist and music director. He accompanied several early blues singers, and, as accompanist to Ethel Waters, went on the road to New Orleans and Chicago, where he heard his first authentic jazz. Several discs by Henderson's Dance Orchestra, released as early as 1921, were undistinctive dance pieces in the commercial style of the day.

The critical point in his career came in early 1923 when he began collaborating with Don Redman (1900–64), a reed player with sound musical training at Storer College who had begun his professional career as an arranger with Billy Paige's Broadway Syncopators. The two became the nucleus of the house band at the Club Alabam and also began recording as Fletcher Henderson and His Orchestra. The personnnel usually consisted of two cornets, trombone, two reeds, and a rhythm section of piano, banjo and drums—a traditional Dixieland ensemble augmented by a second cornet and reed. But it was a reading band, with a style shaped by Redman's arrangements and careful rehearsing.

"Dicty Blues," recorded on August 9, 1923, reveals the disciplined character of Henderson's music at even this early stage.[28] Ensemble sections are tightly arranged: the introductory chime-

---

[28] Available on *A Study in Frustration. The Fletcher Henderson Story* (Columbia Records C4L 19), s1 / 1.

like passage is played by horns in parallel chords, and even though the following eight-bar phrase has some of the sound of New Orleans jazz with the several instruments suggesting their traditional roles, it is more homophonic than improvised jazz and less spontaneous in mood. Several of the interior solos are taken by saxophonist Coleman Hawkins, an eighteen-year-old recently arrived in New York from St. Joseph, Missouri, considered to be the first player to bring a distinctive jazz style to that instrument, which rarely featured in New Orleans jazz.

Henderson hired Louis Armstrong away from King Oliver's Chicago band in the fall of 1924. It was a challenge for Armstrong:

> Where I had come from I wasn't used to playing in bands where there were a lot of parts for everybody to read. Shucks, all one man in the band had to do was to go to some show and hear a good number. He keeps it in his head until he reaches us. He hums it a couple of times, and from then on we had a new number.[29]

But he adapted to life in a reading band, and the other players responded to his imaginative solo playing. By now the band had added a third trumpet and a bass. Redman, in his arrangements, began to play off the trumpet trio against the three-man reed section, and the members of the band were developing precision and flexibility in such a way that an entire section plays with something of the spirit of an improvised solo. "Copenhagen," recorded in late October of 1924,[30] underlines these new features. The piece itself is another multistrain dance composition in which the first strain features a four-bar trumpet trio echoed by a four-bar clarinet trio, each answered by four bars of ensemble playing. A contrasting strain is given to the clarinet trio; only after all this do we have the first solo, 12-bar blues strain given to Armstrong. The piece continues with alternation of 16- and 12-bar strains for the ensemble, with the only other solo taken by the trombone for the first four bars of a later chorus. Though one is aware of the brilliance of Armstrong's playing, and several ensemble sections suggest the collective improvisation of the New Orleans style, one is left with the overriding impression of arranged and disciplined sectional and ensemble playing.

"The Henderson Stomp,"[31] recorded in November of 1926 after Armstrong had gone back to Chicago, unveils an even more complex arrangement by Redman. The introduction features the clar-

---

[29] Shapiro and Hentoff, p. 204.
[30] *A Study in Frustration*, s1 / 5.
[31] *A Study in Frustration*, s2 / 6.

The Fletcher Henderson Band in 1926. (Courtesy Jazz Magazine)

inet trio. All sections are sixteen bars in length; some are dominated by the reeds, often playing passages requiring considerable virtuosity and coordination, some by the brass, some by the entire band. There are scattered solo breaks and a sixteen-bar piano solo by Fats Waller, who had joined the band that year. But again the dominant impression is of carefully rehearsed ensemble performance.

The climax of this era of the Henderson band came in 1927 with the release of such discs as "Rocky Mountain Blues" and "Tozo." New electrical recording techniques give us a much better idea of the sound of the band. Redman's arrangements alternate sectional trios, solos (sometimes accompanied by complex ensemble playing), controlled group improvisation, and passages for the entire band. Solos are no more than interludes.

Redman left the band later that year for the Detroit-based McKinney's Cotton Pickers, but Benny Carter emerged as an arranger with an equally strong talent and personality. His tenure with the band coincides with a shift of repertory, with more emphasis on popular songs by Tin Pan Alley composers, consisting of a 32-bar chorus made up of four 8-bar phrases, played several times with different instrumentation. Harmonically they were more complex, however, with seventh and ninth chords, chromatically altered harmony, and modulations even within the limited time span of a brief song.

Carter's arrangement of Harold Arlen's "Sweet and Hot" will serve to illustrate these changes.[32] After a four-bar introduction, the band plays four choruses of the song, which is structured in the usual *AABA* pattern. The full band takes the first chorus; the second is split into sixteen-bar trumpet and trombone solos, the third chorus is sung by Jimmy Harrison, one of the trombone players, with a brief "scat" break at the end; the last chorus combines several improvised solos with the entire band. In ensemble passages, a section or a single instrument plays a written-out version of the melody against the arranged accompaniment of the band; the brief improvised solos are also accompanied. There is no group improvisation.

When Carter himself left, Henderson and his brother Horace began doing the arrangements. The band was further enlarged; by the mid-1930s it had three trumpets, two trombones, four reeds, and a four-man rhythm section. The first and last choruses were usually given to the entire band, with antiphonal interplay between brass and reeds, and interior choruses were given to one or more soloists. The sound is rich and full, the rhythm is flexible and supple without ever being as flamboyant or boisterous as that of Dixieland jazz. Somewhere along the way the word "swing," used both as a noun and a verb, was coined for this new dialect of jazz.

Henderson's supremacy in this New York brand of jazz was challenged in 1925 by Charlie Johnson, who brought a band of comparable size and talent to Harlem's Cotton Club. "The Boy in the Boat," which they recorded in 1928,[33] reveals them playing in a style similar to that of Henderson's band. Duke Ellington, who came to New York from Washington in 1922, began recording in 1924 and took over at the Cotton Club in 1927; his career and music will be dealt with later in the present chapter. Chick Webb began an eleven-year tenure at the Savoy Ballroom in 1928, with an orchestra of the same size and personnel as Henderson's. And the 1930s were to bring a proliferation of such bands in the city.

Nor was New York the only place where jazz bands of ten or more pieces were playing in the 1920s. In Chicago, Erskine Tate's Vendome Orchestra, formed in 1918 to play syncopated dance music, made a transition to the jazz style—just as Jim Europe's band would surely have done, had he lived. They recorded only twice; "Static Strut," from their second session in May of 1926, reveals a band of two trumpets, trombone, three reeds, a rhythm section of four. They were a reading band, and though the arrange-

[32] *A Study in Frustration*, s6 / 1.
[33] NW 256, s1 / 3.

ment is much more stiff and unimaginative than those of Redman, it allows several soloists (including Louis Armstrong) to take solo choruses in up-to-date jazz style.[34]

Chicago had attracted many of the first generation New Orleans jazz players, but did not play an important role in the transition from Dixieland style to swing. The many discs made in the late 1920s by Louis Armstrong and His Orchestra, for instance, retain both the typical instrumentation and the solo-dominated style of New Orleans jazz. But other parts of the country, other "territories," were producing large bands playing from arrangements. The Southwest was particularly fertile, though the history of jazz in this region is difficult to reconstruct because of a paucity of recordings.

For instance, only eight sides were ever recorded by the most noted band of the territory, led by Alphonso Trent, and the earliest of these dates from 1928, more than five years after the group was formed. Trent, born in Arkansas in 1905, was college-educated, like so many of the pioneers of arranged jazz. His first band was organized in 1923, and in 1925 it began playing at the Adolphus Hotel in Dallas, the first black band to play in a white establishment in Texas. After two years there and a series of broadcasts over a Dallas radio station, they toured most of the United States, as far east as New York.

"After You've Gone" (1930)[35] dispels any notion that they were inferior to the New York–based bands. The piece is a Tin Pan Alley song, written by Henry Creamer and Turner Layton; the band comprises four trumpets, a trombone, four reed players, a violin, and a four-man rhythm section. The arrangement features ensemble playing, with only two brief solos (for trumpet and trombone). Complex, chromatic harmonies abound and the three choruses are taken in different keys. And their "Black and Blue Rhapsody" (1928)[36] is an even more forward-looking piece. An introduction and modulating transitional passages transform this three-strain dance piece into a fluid, continuous composition; the instrumentation is varied and flexible, sometimes changing in mid-phrase; repeated strains are played with different combinations of instruments. One is left with the impression not of a dance piece, but of a jazz composition, comparable to contemporary pieces by the Henderson band and even Duke Ellington. If it seems curious to find such progressive music being played by a band located far from the cities regarded as the centers of jazz in the 1920s, it must

[34] NW 256, s1 / 1.
[35] NW 256, s2 / 8.
[36] NW 256, s2 / 7.

be kept in mind that the phonograph recording was making a mockery of geographical boundaries by enabling musicians in any part of the country to become familiar with what their peers were doing elsewhere.

The most-recorded band of the Southwest was Bennie Moten's Kansas City Orchestra. Moten, born in Kansas City in 1894, organized a ragtime trio in 1918, and his first recordings were made in St. Louis in 1923. Beginning with a New Orleans–style ensemble of cornet, trombone, clarinet, and rhythm, Moten expanded his reed section to three players, added a second cornet and a bass, and by 1927 had the same personnel as Henderson's orchestra. At the same time the style of his band progressed from the improvised playing of early jazz to reliance on "head charts"—collectively worked out arrangements, often making use of reiterated short phrases or "riffs"—to the use of full arrangements or "charts," the work of trombonist Eddie Durham. The band by this time had been strengthened by a remarkable group of talented young musicians: Oran "Hot Lips" Page (trumpet); Durham (trombone and guitar); Eddie Barefield (clarinet); Jack Washington and Ben Webster (saxophones); Count Basie (piano).

"Toby,"[37] recorded in December of 1932 at their last session, shows off the band at its best. The tempo is so fast that eight full choruses were fitted on a single phonograph disc, yet the ensemble playing is so sure that entire sections handle passages of rhythmic complexity that only soloists would have attempted in the 1920s. There is alternation between ensemble playing and soloists; but the full band plays with such virtuosity and exuberance that there is no sense of stylistic difference between solo and ensemble playing.

So few recordings were made of "territory" bands that we have only a hint of what was happening in wide-flung parts of the country.[38] But these few discs, combined with whatever other evidence remains,[39] suggest that bands in these regions were also playing arranged jazz in the late 1920s and early '30s, incorporating the more sophisticated chord changes of Tin Pan Alley songs into their arrangements and emphasizing ensemble playing.

The popularity of social dancing to syncopated music in the late 1910s and early '20s spawned hundreds of white bands playing music for the fox trot, tango, and other fashionable steps. The first

[37] NW 217, s2 / 1.
[38] NW 217 and 256 offer a representative selection of territory band performances.
[39] For the most complete survey of these bands, cf. Albert McCarthy, *Big Band Jazz* (New York: G. P. Putnam's Sons, 1974), pp. 88–181.

wave of jazz, spurred by the popularity of the Original Dixieland Jazz Band in Chicago and New York, likewise encouraged the formation of new bands playing in a similar style and learning to cope with its improvisational nature:

> Each orchestra made its own arrangements, nor were these reduced to manuscript. The system was to obtain a piano, violin or song copy of the piece to be performed and to learn it at rehearsal. The pianist played it through till the others caught the rhythm and a general idea of the harmony, though the latter was not important except for the pianist. Those instruments that did not play the melody devoted themselves to free fantasias, either contrapuntal devices or *obbligati*. All this was arranged *impromptu* and *viva voce*, according to suggestions from the leader or to the player's own ideas.[40]

In time white bands began playing arranged jazz. The unchallenged leader of this genre, dubbed the "King of Jazz" by New York critics, was the classically trained Paul Whiteman (1890–1967), whose band featured arrangements by the equally well-trained Ferde Grofé. The attention given his band in the 1920s and the insistence by many writers that his orchestra represented the peak of jazz obscured for many Americans the true nature of jazz. The first book published on the subject, in 1926, devoted entire chapters to Whiteman, Grofé, George Gershwin, and Irving Berlin while covering the subject of black musicians in a single footnote:

> Nowhere have I gone into detail about negro jazz bands. There are so many good ones, it would be hard to pick out a few for special mention. None of them, however, are as good as the best white bands, and very rarely are their best players as good as the best white virtuosos. Their playing makes up for what it may lack in smoothness and finish by abandon, dash, spirit and warmth. There are fewer trained musicians, consequently more of the improvisations and variations which characterized early jazz.[41]

The chief problem in assessing Whiteman's place in the history of jazz is that his orchestra played and recorded in a variety of styles and with considerable fluctuation in personnel. For their first hit, "Whispering" (1920),[42] Grofé blended winds and strings to suggest the sound of a miniature symphony orchestra; the melody is given to the violin; there is not the slightest suggestion of the

---

[40] Henry O. Osgood, *So This Is Jazz* (Boston: Little Brown & Company, 1926), p. 106.
[41] Osgood, p. 103.
[42] NW 279, s1 / 1.

rhythmic vitality and spontaneity of black jazz. Only a year later, however, Whiteman's band recorded "Gypsy Blues"[43] in an altogether different style: there are suggestions of the three-part contrapuntal texture of Dixieland and its characteristic rhythms, particularly in the last chorus, with its faster tempo and florid upper obbligato part. But everything is carefully written out, and there is none of the exuberance and flexibility that gave New Orleans jazz its special flavor.

In the mid-1920s, Whiteman employed a number of the best white jazzmen, including Bix Beiderbecke, Frank Trumbauer, Tommy and Jimmy Dorsey, Eddie Lang, Bunny Berigan, Red Nichols, Jack Teagarden, and Red Norvo; on occasion he played arrangements by blacks ("Whiteman Stomp" of 1927 was the work of Don Redman).

Some jazz historians have ignored Whiteman, some have condemned him, others have been equivocal ("The influence of the Whiteman band, even over some quite irreproachable jazz groups, is something that most jazz followers are not anxious to admit.")[44] The most useful attitude would seem to be that of Duke Ellington:

> We've all worked and fought under the banner of jazz for many years, but the word really has no meaning. What is the relationship between Guy Lombardo, Stan Kenton, Count Basie, and Louis Armstrong—all of whom people regard as playing jazz? Music is limitless.[45]

Or, as Gunther Schuller put it, "There is in the best Whiteman performances a feeling and a personal sound as unique in its way as Ellington's or Basie's."[46]

The same comments could be applied to many of the white bands of the early and mid-1920s, led by Vincent Lopez, Roger Wolfe Kahn, Sam Lanin, Ted Weems, Ben Selvin, and others. Ben Pollack's band featured several outstanding white jazz players—Benny Goodman, Jack Teagarden, Jimmy McPartland. The French-born Jean Goldkette assembled a band in the fall of 1926 which played in the Roseland Ballroom in New York, sharing billing with Fletcher Henderson and His Orchestra; its personnel included Bix Beiderbecke, Frank Trumbauer, Bill Rank, and Eddie Lang, and its performances excited admiration from both white and black musicians. And the Casa Loma Orchestra, organized in 1929, is indistinguishable in instrumentation and general style from the

[43] NW 260, s1 / 7.
[44] McCarthy, p. 189.
[45] Edward Kennedy Ellington, *Music Is My Mistress* (Garden City: Doubleday, 1973), p. 465.
[46] Schuller, *Early Jazz*, p. 192.

contemporary black bands of Henderson, Ellington, and Moten. In their "Casa Loma Stomp," recorded in late 1930,[47] we hear an ensemble of three trumpets, two trombones, three reeds, and a rhythm section of four playing a tight arrangement (by Gene Gifford) in a precise and crisp style; ensemble choruses frame a series of brief solos in interior choruses; the brass and wind sections are set off antiphonally, sometimes in close riff patterns. This piece, and their "White Jazz" and "Black Jazz" of 1931, aroused admiration and emulation in the jazz world.

As the 1930s unfolded, jazz bands became even larger, ensemble playing became more polished, and solo improvisation became more firmly encased within the framework of arranged jazz.

Earl "Fatha" Hines, a jazz pianist and bandleader who spent most of his career in Chicago, played at the Grand Terrace for more than a decade. By 1933 his instrumentation had become the same 3–3–4–4 used by Henderson, and their playing was marked by smoothly coordinated ensemble work interspersed with brief solos. Their repertory at first was made up mostly of multistrain dance pieces, many of them written by Hines and his saxophonist-arranger James Munday;[48] later they depended more on arrangements of Tin Pan Alley standards, always structured in a 32-bar chorus— "On the Sunny Side of the Street," "My Melancholy Baby," "It Had To Be You"—and a fourth trumpet and reed player increased the size of the group to sixteen.

Don Redman established his own band in 1931, with the same 3–3–4–4 instrumentation. The repertory from the beginning was based on his arrangements of popular songs or of other pieces sharing their 32-bar chorus structure.[49] Jimmie Lunceford led a similar band through the 1930s;[50] Benny Carter formed his own band in 1932 and cut his first discs in June of that year with an instrumentation of 3–1–3–4, but within several years he had a three-man trombone section and had added a fourth reed. Chick Webb and His Orchestra recorded in the early 1930s with a 3–1–3–4 lineup, playing an older 1920s repertory with emphasis on solo choruses;[51] during their extended engagement at the Savoy Room in New York the orchestra was built up to the size of the other big bands of the era. Lionel Hampton began with a smaller ensemble (a single trumpet, no trombone), in order to spotlight his own vibraphone playing, but by 1940 his band was up to the size of the others.

---

[47] NW 217, s1 / 2.
[48] Cf. "Madhouse" on NW 217, s1 / 4.
[49] Cf. "Doin' the New Low-Down" on NW 215, s1 / 6.
[50] Cf. " 'Tain't What You Do" on NW 248, s2 / 7.
[51] Cf. "Heebie Jeebies" on NW 217, s1 / 5.

Louis Armstrong and His Orchestra first recorded in Chicago in December of 1928; the makeup of the band reflected the evolution of the big bands of the swing era, and by 1937 Armstrong was playing with 3–4 trumpets, 3 trombones, and 4 reeds. Though the band contained some excellent musicians, they are usually kept in the background, supporting Armstrong's playing and singing. "I Double Dare You" (1938) is taken at a fast enough tempo to allow for four choruses, and though Armstrong is again dominant with vocal and instrumental solos, the band is given the second half of the first chorus, and the third chorus consists of sixteen-bar solos by J. C. Higginbotham (trombone) and Bingie Madison (saxophone).[52]

Cab Calloway likewise built an orchestra to support his own talents, as a singer specializing in "scat" effects and outlandish stage deportment. Beginning in Chicago in 1928 and moving on to the Savoy Ballroom in New York in 1929 and then the Cotton Club in 1931, the band backed Calloway in such hits as "Minnie the Moocher" and "Keep That Hi-De-Ho in Your Soul." But he insisted on using the best players available—Eddie Barefield (saxophone), Ben Webster (saxophone), Chu Berry (reeds), Milt Hinton (bass), Cozy Cole (drums), Dizzy Gillespie (trumpet)—and the band eventually recorded some of the outstanding instrumental discs of the time, particularly between 1939 and 1941.[53]

The most distinctive band of the swing era was that of Count Basie, however.

Born in Red Bank, New Jersey in 1904, Basie began his career in New York as a member of the "stride" school of jazz piano. Finding his way to Kansas City, he played with Walter Page's Blue Devils and then Benny Moten's Kansas City Orchestra; after Moten's death, Basie brought some of the players together in a group of his own, with a first engagement at the Reno Club in Kansas City and a first disc cut in January of 1937. The strongest rhythm section of the decade—Walter Page (bass), Joe Jones (drums), Freddie Green (guitar), and Basie (piano)—laid down an absolutely firm and driving beat, marked by Jones's use of high-pitched percussion (particularly the high-hat) rather than the bass drum for the fundamental beat. Against this, the best array of soloists of any band of the time played with a rhythmic drive and spontaneity that often suggests the exuberance of the best New Orleans jazz. There was more emphasis on solo playing backed by riffs than was usual in big bands.

All of this can be heard in their most famous numbers: "One

[52] NW 274, s2 / 1.
[53] Cf. "Pickin' the Cabbage" and "Ebony Silhouette" on NW 217, s1 / 6–7.

O'clock Jump," "Doggin' Around," "Jumpin' at the Woodside." "Every Tub" (1938)[54] shows off the band at its absolute best. A multistrain dance piece rather than the more usual 32-bar song form, it has an introduction dominated by saxophonist Lester Young, the most talented and original jazz soloist of the decade. Young continues with a solo of three eight-bar phrases, against the riffs of the band; Basie, backed by drums and bass, answers with a solo of equal length. A brief transition leads to a new strain dominated by a trumpet solo, again accompanied by riffs. Three final choruses are taken by the entire band, with the third phrase of each given to a different soloist—piano, saxophone, and trumpet. A brief coda is played by the entire ensemble.

The big-band swing style was accepted by much of white America and became a viable commercial product, but in the process inevitably lost some of its close identification with black American culture.

For almost a decade, beginning in 1935, white popular music in America was dominated by the big bands of Benny Goodman, Tommy and Jimmy Dorsey, Glenn Miller, Artie Shaw, Charlie Barnet, Hal Kemp, Freddy Martin, Hal McIntyre, Vaughn Monroe, Harry James, Charlie Spivak, Gene Krupa. Instrumentation was identical to that of the black bands discussed above; arrangements were often the work of black musicians: Fletcher and Horace Henderson, Jimmy Mundy, Mary Lou Williams for Benny Goodman; Sy Oliver for Tommy Dorsey. But white big bands reached their peak of popularity only after they allied themselves with Tin Pan Alley and the dominant popular music industry, still centered in New York. There is a clear progression from the instrumentally oriented pieces that featured frequent solos in the early 1930s to the popular songs played in a relatively straightforward fashion as an accompaniment for vocalists, by the early 1940s—and a corresponding shift to a more mellow or "sweet" playing style. For instance, Tommy Dorsey and His Orchestra recorded "Weary Blues" at its first recording session in September of 1935 as a purely instrumental piece, with successive solos by Sid Stoneman (clarinet), Paul Mitchell (piano), Johnny van Eps (tenor saxophone), and Dorsey (trombone) played off against ensemble sections virtually indistinguishable in arrangement and playing style from what contemporary black bands were doing; but most Americans came to know the Dorsey orchestra from their recordings of such Tin Pan Alley favorites as "Once in a While" (1937), "Music, Maestro,

[54] NW 274, s1 / 1.

Please" (1938) and "I'll Be Seeing You" (1944), the latter with a vocal by Frank Sinatra. "The White Cliffs of Dover," as recorded by Glenn Miller and His Orchestra in 1941,[55] is built around a central vocal chorus, with no significant solo instrumental work and little hint of the imaginative sectional playing that characterized the best black bands.

Some bands stressed instrumental playing, to be sure, and excellent soloists in such bands as those of Charlie Barnet and Buddy Berigan were allowed improvised solos. In live performances, many bands played more instrumental music and would sometimes play an extended string of choruses to accomodate a string of solos. But these were deviations from what mainstream big band was understood to be by the publishing and recording industries: a medium for the promotion of popular songs.

White big-band music was essentially an episode in the continuing history of Tin Pan Alley song.

The music of Duke Ellington and his band occupies a special place in the history of jazz.

Edward Kennedy Ellington was born in Washington, D.C. on May 24, 1899. The family lived a comfortable, middle-class life, with music occupying an important role in the family: "My mother used to play the piano, pretty things like 'Meditation,' so pretty they'd make me cry. My father used to play too, but by ear, and all operatic stuff."[56] Duke played the piano from an early age, learning from both trained "reading" pianists and others who played by ear.

But opportunities for creative and professional development were limited in Washington, and in 1922 Ellington went to New York to take a job in Wilbur Sweatman's Orchestra with two musicians with whom he had played in local bands, Toby Hardwick (saxophone) and Sonny Greer (drums). The three were the core of a group that became the house band at the Hollywood Cafe, soon renamed the Kentucky Club; other members were Arthur Whetsol (trumpet) and Freddy Guy (banjo). Soon Charlie Irvis (trombone) was added, bringing the band up to the standard trumpet-trombone-clarinet-rhythm instrumentation of classic New Orleans jazz, and Bubber Miley replaced Whetsol on trumpet. This was the group that cut several discs in November of 1924, as The Washingtonians.

In 1926, the band was augmented by Joe Nanton (trombone), Harry Carney (saxophone), and Wellman Braud (bass), the reper-

---

[55] NW 270, s2 / 8.
[56] Ellington, *Music Is my Mistress*, p. 20.

tory came to be made up of pieces written or arranged by Ellington, often in collaboration with one or another of the band members; a distinctive style began to emerge, based largely on the talents and musical personalities of the various players. Three pieces from this time, "East St. Louis Toodle-Oo," "Black and Tan Fantasy," and "Creole Love Call," are the earliest distinctive products of the Ellington band.

The first of these[57] suggests the widening gap between Ellington's music and that of other bands of the day. A collaboration between Ellington and Miley, the piece begins with a passage remarkable for the time, an 8-bar sustained, moaning phrase in a minor key scored by Ellington for three saxophones (in their lowest register) and bass. Miley takes a 32-bar solo against a continuation of this strange music, with punctuations by the cymbals and other percussion not usually heard in jazz of the 1920s; his playing is marked by a distinctive use of a "dirty" tone and several mutes. A second strain, modulating to major, brings an 18-bar improvised solo by Carney on the baritone saxophone—again a most unusual sound for jazz—and a matching solo by Nanton on trombone, marked by idiosyncratic tone production and flexible intonation. The piece ends with a brief clarinet solo, a repeat of the second strain by the entire band, and a final 8-bar solo by Miley against the low, dark, minor chords that had opened the piece. It is a moody and quirky composition, dominated by dark instrumentation and strongly personal, mannered solo playing. It suggests none of the dances associated with jazz in the 1920s, has none of the infectious rhythmic propulsion of the Dixieland style, and yet is not a blues.

Ellington and his band played at the Cotton Club in Harlem for the first time on December 4, 1927, remaining there until 1932. Three more excellent players were added: Cootie Williams (trumpet), Johnny Hodges (saxophone), and Barney Bigard (clarinet). The instrumentation was now that of the other leading bands of the time, 3–2–3–4; though Ellington continued to be the pianist, taking occasional solos, his role became more and more that of composer and arranger, and it was at this time that he became convinced that "my instrument is the orchestra."

The cotton Club was patronized by whites, both New Yorkers and tourists, who wanted to observe the black culture of Harlem. The club was decorated with murals suggestive of Afro-American images, and was lavishly furnished; there were elaborate stage shows, with some of the best black dancers, singers, and enter-

[57] *The Smithsonian Collection*, s6 / 4.

tainers of the day; the band dressed in tuxedos. Much of the band's music from its Cotton Club days was devised for this environment. There were pieces in "jungle style," built around the growling, muted, tricky sounds of Miley on trumpet and Nanton on trombone, underscored with percussion and atmospheric backing from the other instruments—"Hottentot" (1929), "Jungle Jamboree" (1929), and "Jungle Night in Harlem" (1930). Other pieces were designed for the production numbers on stage, and the band also played for dancing by the patrons, who expected the latest in jazz dance music. But Ellington also found time for abstract compositions, including *Echoes of the Jungle* (1931), *Creole Rhapsody* (1931), a six-minute piece released on the two sides of a phonograph disc), *Reminiscing in Tempo* (1934–35, requiring four sides), and an even more ambitious piece begun in 1934 which would eventually become his *Black, Brown and Beige*.

Instrumental pieces were made into songs, and vice versa; "serious" pieces were made from the same harmonic, melodic, and rhythmic elements as all of his other music. This flexibility is apparent in his most famous composition of this time, recorded first as an instrumental piece with the title "Dreamy Blues" on October 17, 1930, recorded again as *Mood Indigo*, published and frequently performed as a piece for piano under the same title, and later fitted with a text by Irving Mills and published as a song. As first recorded by the band,[58] the opening 16-bar phrase (*aa'ba*), distinguished by a striking augmented chord in the second bar, is scored for muted trumpet and trombone and clarinet, in homophonic style; a second 16-bar section is given to a clarinet solo, supported by bass and drums, then repeated by the trumpet; a solo break for piano leads to a repetition of the first phrase, scored just as before. It is a mood piece, lyrical and dreamy, with unusual scoring; there is no trace of either the rhythmic propulsion or improvisation that had characterized jazz of the 1920s.

Ellington's band reflected certain aspects of the big-band era. By 1931 the instrumentation was 3–2–3–4, and in the mid-1930s the addition of a third trombone and a fourth reed player brought the personnel up to fourteen. They were capable of emulating the swing style of their contemporary bands, particularly after Billy Strayhorn joined the band as arranger and second pianist in 1939. "Take the 'A' Train" (1941) became their most popular swing arrangement and was used as their theme song; Ellington's "Harlem Air Shaft" (1940)[59] suggests the best Kansas City playing, with its pro-

[58] NW 272, s2 / 1.
[59] *The Smithsonian Collection*, s6 / 7.

Duke Ellington with Billy Strayhorn. (Photograph by Frederick Plaut)

pulsive energy and rifflike work in the brass and reed sections. But even at the peak of the swing era, Ellington continued to search for more distinctive voicings, tried out unusual chords, continued to play various small groups of instruments off against one another and the entire band, and created more examples of lyric mood pieces. "Passion Flower" (1941)[60] is as far from swing as one could imagine; in the tradition of "Mood Indigo," though more complex in its compositional devices, it featured the fluent and expressive playing of Johnny Hodges on alto saxophone.

A succession of pieces from the late 1930s and early '40s represent another creative peak for Ellington. "Ko-Ko" (1940) and "Blue Serge" (1941)[61] are both blues-based compositions, though their minor keys and the richness and complexity of their harmonic and instrumental language transforms them into almost purely abstract pieces. *Concerto for Cootie* (1940),[62] one of a series of pieces written

[60] NW 274, s2 / 2.
[61] *The Smithsonian Collection*, s7 / 2–3.
[62] *The Smithsonian Collection*, s6 / 8.

to spotlight the talent of individual members of his band, features the playing of Cootie Williams on trumpet. The piece is simple in design, built around a central chorus in *aaba* song form followed by a second 16-bar strain and a brief recapitulation, bracketed by an introduction and a coda. The central chorus was later reworked into one of Ellington's most successful songs, "Do Nothing Till You Hear from Me" (1943, with lyrics by Bob Russell). Williams's solo part is not what one might expect from the title, stressing lyric, expressive playing rather than the pyrotechnics one usually encounters in the solo parts of classical concertos.

By this time Ellington's band had toured Europe twice, to great popular and critical acclaim, adding fuel to the European intellectuals' contention that jazz was America's answer to their own classical music. Ellington's *Black, Brown and Beige*, a 57-minute "tone parallel to the history of the American Negro," was performed by the band as part of a concert at Carnegie Hall on January 23, 1943. Similar programs followed, at least one each year, each bringing one or more extended new compositions by Ellington: *New World a-Comin'* (1943) for piano and the band; *Perfume Suite* (1944), *The Deep South Suite*, *The Tonal Group*, and *The Beautiful Indians*, all from 1946; *The Liberian Suite* (1947); *The Tattooed Bride*, *Symphomaniac*, and *The Manhattan Murals* in 1948. The Ellington band made its first appearance with a symphony orchestra in 1949, playing with the Philharmonic Symphony at Robin Hood Dell that summer; similar performances with orchestras in America and in Europe were to follow. *Harlem*, a "concerto grosso for band and symphony orchestra," was written in 1950 on commission from Arturo Toscanini and the NBC Symphony; *Night Creature*, commissioned in 1955 by the Symphony of the Air, was subsequently played by orchestras in Detroit, Buffalo, New Haven, Washington, Paris, and Stockholm.

"*Jazz* is only a word and really has no meaning. We stopped using it in 1943," Ellington once said.[63] He then quoted the black American composer William Grant Still:

In actual fact, American Negro music (which is indeed a fusion of African and various European elements) encompasses a great deal more than jazz, and any teacher who claims to teach the subject should be aware of all its forms, from the Negro folk product to the advances now being made in serious music. The only reason there has been such great emphasis on jazz is that it has been pushed by commercial interests, and this doesn't mean that it is the *only*—or even the most important— form in existence.

[63] Ellington, *Music Is my Mistress*, p. 471.

The parallel between Ellington and Scott Joplin is haunting. Both absorbed the music of both black and white culture; each achieved his greatest popularity with composed popular dance music; both aspired to large-scale classical composition. Ellington was able to realize this latter goal better than Joplin because he lived much longer, perhaps because he was more talented, and because of changing attitudes toward black people in the United States in the decades following the Second World War.

Jazz and blues have a long and complex relationship.

Though they were both products of Afro-American culture, taking shape at just the same time, they had little in common at first: the blues was vocal music, originally sung by a solo voice only and later accompanied by a single chord-playing instrument; jazz was an instrumental performance style.

At some point in the early decades of the twentieth century the two came together on the black vaudeville circuit. Professional blues singers began to be accompanied by instrumentalists, performing in the style of early New Orleans jazz. The historic "Crazy Blues" was recorded by singer Mamie Smith on August 10, 1920, accompanied by Perry Bradford's Jazz Hounds, a group comprised of the classic cornet-trombone-clarinet-rhythm instrumentation of early jazz. Like so many blues of the time, it is a multistrain composition, some sections of 16 bars and some shaped into the 12-bar blues pattern. Each instrument takes the traditional role assigned it in Dixieland style, but since the voice has the melody, the cornet usually slips into an accompanying role. This disc is not only the earliest recorded evidence of the blues, it is also the first recording of jazz instrumentalists playing in New Orleans style, almost two years before the first discs of instrumental black jazz.

"Crazy Blues" demonstrated the commercial potential of recordings by black performers aimed at black audiences, by selling well enough to prompt a flood of similar discs. Among the many blues singers discovered and recorded in the early 1920s were Ma Rainey, Ida Cox, Lottie Beamon, Sara Martin, Clara Smith, and Edith Wilson. Some were accompanied by small jazz ensembles,[64] others by keyboard alone.[65]

Bessie Smith emerged as the best of them all, acknowledged even by other singers as the "Empress of the Blues." Born in Chattanooga in 1894, she had been singing in minstrel shows, vaudeville houses, and theaters in the South for more than a decade before

[64] Cf. Clara Smith's performance of "Let's Get Loose" on NW 290, s1 / 7.
[65] Cf. Hattie Hudson's "Doggone My Good-Luck Soul" on NW 290, s1 / 6.

making her first recording in New York in 1923, "Down-Hearted Blues," accompanied by New Orleans–born pianist Clarence Williams. Though the piece begins with a 16-bar verse, its four 12-bar choruses have all the characteristics of traditional blues, in music and text:

> Trouble, trouble, I've had it all my days;
> Trouble, trouble, I've had it all my days;
> It seem like trouble goin'to follow me to my grave.
>
> I ain't never loved but three mens in my life;
> I ain't never loved but three men in my life:
> My father, my brother, the man that wreck my life.

Her singing is supple and highly expressive, based on the style of country blues. Williams accompanies each vocal phrase discreetly, then answers the singer with melodic elaboration in the right hand of the piano—the same melodic echoing between singer and instrumentalist that had become a feature of instrumentally accompanied folk blues.

During her eight-year recording career, in the course of which she cut about 200 discs, Bessie Smith was sometimes accompanied by a keyboard player (often Fletcher Henderson or James P. Johnson), sometimes by a small jazz ensemble, but most often by keyboard and a single horn or violin; some of her best performances were in 1925 with Louis Armstrong.[66] These are in the nature of duos, with voice and instrument sharing the melodic lead in antiphonal fashion. It is here that the connection between blues singing and early jazz playing can best be heard, in similar phrasing, melodic ornamentation, pitch fluctuation, and even tone quality. It is difficult to know if the blues singer is imitating the style of the instrumentalists or vice versa.

White audiences of the 1920s and '30s were less responsive to blues singing than to instrumental and keyboard jazz, and when the Depression cut deeply into the sales of phonograph discs among blacks and the chief financial support of jazz shifted to whites, blues singing went back underground. Even such great blues singers as Joe Turner remained unknown to most whites.[67] In cities with large black populations, Chicago in particular, the blues took on a somewhat different character with the increasing use of electric guitar as the accompanying instrument, the popularity of the saxophone as the "dialogue" instrument, and the frequent employment of

---

[66] *The Smithsonian Collection*, s1 / 4.
[67] Cf. his "Piney Top Blues" on NW 295, s1 / 3.

drums to augment the rhythm section. These urban blues also remained a secret from most whites until the 1950s, which brought the beginnings of rock 'n' roll and a subsequent proliferation of interest in both urban and rural blues.

The singer most closely associated by whites with the singing of blues during the swing era—Billie Holiday—actually devoted herself mostly to the popular songs of Tin Pan Alley. This is not to minimize her talent and success; her singing was profoundly expressive and often moving. But except for bringing to her vocal style some of the flexibility of pitch and vocal embellishment of the blues singing tradition and the same ability to interact with jazz instrumentalists,[68] her career had more to do with the history of popular song in America than with the blues.

A distinctive singing style did emerge out of jazz. Louis Armstrong was the first to use his voice in a way comparable to the playing style of jazz: ornamenting the melody freely, introducing melodic and rhythmic mannerisms matching those of his cornet playing, interacting with the other instrumentalists while he was singing. He was also the first to use scat singing—nonsense syllables rather than words in his vocal choruses—thus bringing the voice even closer to instrumental style by stripping it of an intelligible text. Cab Calloway was his most imaginative immediate successor, and somewhat later a succession of female vocalists developed scat singing styles.[69]

Two separate schools of solo jazz piano emerged in the 1920s. James P. Johnson, born in New Jersey in 1891 and a New Yorker after 1908, made his living as a ragtime pianist while pursuing the study of classical music. His playing encompassed full chords in the right hand (often spanning a tenth) with a more flexible left hand often moving in broken octaves and even larger intervals, giving rise to the name of "stride" piano for this kind of playing. He also introduced more linear elements into his playing than was usual in ragtime, and it is in the suggestion of two or three contrapuntal parts that one begins to hear the influence of early jazz on his style in the early 1920s. This more linear texture superimposed on elements of ragtime appears in some of his early solo recordings, Carolina Shout (1921)[70] and Weeping Blues (1923), for instance. In a handful of pieces recorded with other performers, the piano may be heard playing melodic solo lines and engaging in counter-

[68] Cf. her singing of Vernon Duke's "I Can't Get Started" on NW 295, s1 / 1.
[69] Cf. Ella Fitzgerald's singing of "Robbins Nest" on NW 295, s1 / 7, and Betty Carter's "Thou Swell" on NW 295, s2 / 3.
[70] The Smithsonian Collection, s1 / 4.

point with the other instruments.[71] Never content to pursue a single style of music, he interacted with several Tin Pan Alley songwriters, including George Gershwin, and undertook the composition of large-scale classical pieces: operas, songs, orchestral works. His interpretation of Cole Porter's "What Is This Thing Called Love?," recorded in 1930,[72] demonstrates his characteristic blend of the techniques of stride piano and Tin Pan Alley, and makes an interesting comparison with Gershwin's own piano style.[73] What has emerged is a distinctively New York dialect of jazz piano, drawing on the music of both black and white Americans.

Boogie-woogie, the second style, probably originated in the South and Southwest, though its most important practitioners were in Chicago in the 1920s and '30s. It is a style of playing rather than a genre of composition:

> Boogie-woogie is basically a way of playing the twelve-bar blues on a piano. [It] is a highly percussive style in which the left hand plays a sustained bass figure, usually of one or two measures, usually with eight beats to the bar. Over that continuous pattern the right hand improvises percussive figures that interplay in fascinating and varied polyrhythmic, polymetric patterns.[74]

Though anticipations of the several elements of boogie-woogie may be heard in the playing of ragtime and jazz pianists of the early 1920s, the first phonograph disc in which the style comes together was "The Rocks," made in New York in 1923 by Clay Custer. In Jimmy Blythe's "Chicago Stomp" (1924),[75] the left hand has a steady, broken-octave pattern in eighth notes, which came to be called a "walking bass," grouped into two-bar patterns. The right hand develops seven 12-bar blues choruses over this bass, each based on a somewhat different melodic-rhythmic idea, though the sixth chorus suggests a return to the original material. Some sections of "Suitcase Blues" (1925) by Hersal Thomas demonstrate the other common left-hand pattern in boogie-woogie, a series of steadily drummed chords, usually simple fifths or sixths.[76]

The style was given its name in 1928 with the release of "Pine-

[71] Cf. "Willow Tree," in which he plays in an ensemble of trumpet, clarinet, piano, and organ, on NW 256, s1 / 7.
[72] NW 274, s1 / 3.
[73] Cf. Gershwin's solo piano performance of "Someone to Watch Over Me" on NW 272, s1 / 5.
[74] Martin Williams, liner notes to NW 255, p. 1.
[75] NW 259, s1 / 1.
[76] Cf. his "Suitcase Blues" on NW 259, s1 / 3.

top's Boogie Woogie" by Clarence "Pinetop" Smith.[77] The piece recreates the atmosphere of a black rent party: Smith punctuates his piano playing with exhortations:

> I want all of y'all to know Pinetop's Boogie Woogie.
> I want everybody to dance 'em just like I tell ya.
> Now when I say "hold yourself" I want all of ya git ready to stop.
> And when I say "stop," don't move.
> And when I say "git it," I want all of y'all to do a Boogie Woogie.
> Hold it now. . . . Stop. . . . Boogie woogie!
> That's what I'm talking about.

The infectuous rhythms of his playing made the piece one of the most popular jazz records of the decade.

Other Chicago-based pianists developed individual styles of boogie-woogie. Meade Lux Lewis recorded the largest number of pieces in this genre, between 1927 and 1941. His famous "Honky Tonk Train Blues"[78] introduces astonishing dissonance between the two hands, in the guise of descriptive music; his virtuosity, the independence of the right and left hands, and the rhythmic emphasis on each eighth note ("eight to the bar") may be heard in most of his recordings.[79] Jimmy Yancey, whose first recordings date only from 1939, played in a somewhat more lyric style.[80] In Albert Ammons's "Bass Goin' Crazy,"[81] boogie-woogie is stretched into a piano composition of considerable imagination and complexity, again with harmonic and rhythmic independence between the two hands. The playing of Pete Johnson, with its sustained rhythmic propulsion, begins to approach the substance of early rock 'n' roll.[82]

There were relatively few recordings made of pure boogie-woogie compared to the total number of jazz records released in the 1920s and '30s, and few pianists cultivated the style to the exclusion of any other, but both jazz and popular music drew elements from boogie-woogie throughout the second quarter of the twentieth century.

The best jazz pianists of the 1930s and '40s belonged to neither the stride nor the boogie-woogie school of playing, but rather created individual styles by piecing together elements of both, of other styles of jazz, and of popular music. In fact, the most important

[77] NW 259, s1 / 4.
[78] NW 259, s1 / 6.
[79] Cf. his "Yancey Special" on NW 259, s1 / 7.
[80] Cf. his "The Mellow Blues" on NW 259, s2 / 3.
[81] NW 259, s2 / 2.
[82] Cf. his "Climbin' and Screamin' " on NW 259, s2 / 5.

common denominator of the playing of Fatha Hines,[83] Fats Waller,[84] Art Tatum, and their peers is their reliance on the Tin Pan Alley song repertory as the basis for piano improvisations. Most of their solo playing was done in clubs and bars, usually for white audiences; their playing spawned numerous white imitators;[85] their stories belong as much to the history of Tin Pan Alley as to that of jazz.

Though big-band music dominated the 1930s and much of the '40s, small ensembles featuring solo improvisation were kept alive in small jazz clubs. The most famous of these were in New York, clustered on 52nd Street, but there were others dotted across the country from Boston to San Francisco, New Orleans to Chicago, Miami to Seattle. Many of these clubs had house bands; members of commercial traveling big bands would also sit in, happy for the chance to play a sort of music which was not commercially viable at the time but represented for many jazz musicians and devoted fans the apex of the jazz art.

These groups, whether organized or impromptu, were usually comprised of several horns and a rhythm section. The arrangements of big-band jazz were forgotten; the repertory consisted of 12-bar blues or 32-bar choruses of popular songs, familiar to all participants; a performance consisted of a first chorus in which all of the players joined in, a string of choruses with the players taking turns in improvising solos against the chord changes of the piece, and usually a final chorus bringing the tune back in a more straightforward form.

It was in these small clubs that most of the best solo improvisation of the period took place. Though few live recordings were made of these sessions, we can sample this stream of jazz from the scattering of studio recordings of small ensembles made during the big-band era.

For instance, several of the outstanding players of the early 1930s may be heard in a performance of "I Wish That I Could Shimmy Like My Sister Kate" recorded in 1933.[86] A four-bar introduction leads to a string of five choruses, featuring in turn Red Allen (trumpet), Russell Procope (clarinet), Dickie Wells (trombone), and Coleman Hawkins (tenor saxophone, two choruses). The point is for

[83] Cf. his performance of "Love Me Tonight" on NW 274, s2 / 4.
[84] Cf. his "Honeysuckle Rose" on NW 272, s1 / 7.
[85] A number of these, from Lee Sims through Eddy Duchin to Roger Williams, may be heard on NW 298.
[86] NW 250, s1 / 4.

each player to be given the opportunity to display his individual style, his facility, his musical personality, his imagination in devising and executing a solo line over the same changes. Hawkins, for instance, takes off on flights here and in similar recordings that were not possible in the context of arranged big-band jazz.

"Jungle Love" (1938) by Teddy Wilson and His Orchestra [87] works in just the same way. The first 32-bar chorus is given to Bobby Hackett (trumpet), the second to Johnny Hodges (alto saxophone), the third to Wilson on piano; the first half of the final chorus is split between clarinettist Honey Bear Sedric and Hodges, and the band takes the last half-chorus in a neo-Dixieland style to bring things to a resounding climax.

Not all small-ensemble jazz of the period was totally improvised, however. Red Norvo and his Swing Sextet played for many years at the Hickory House in New York and released a number of discs, in a style combining arranged and improvised jazz. Their version of George Gershwin's "I Got Rhythm" (1936)[88] in an arrangement by Eddie Sauter has a tightly arranged first chorus with suggestions of the antiphonal sectional playing of the big bands; Norvo takes a xylophone solo in the second chorus, against an arranged backing; the third chorus gives brief solos to Herbie Haymer (tenor saxophone), Stew Pletcher (trumpet), and Donald McCook (clarinet); the last chorus pits Norvo against rifflike patterns from the other players. Though there are echoes of big-band style, the sound is much cleaner and the solo playing less encumbered.

The first significant interracial jazz playing took place in the context of small-club jazz. Benny Goodman was at the center of this development. He had been the first white bandleader to feature black soloists: from 1933 onwards, a succession of black vocalists performed and recorded with him—Ethel Waters, Billie Holiday, Ella Fitzgerald, Jimmy Rushing, Mildred Bailey. Black instrumentalists also played with his band, sometimes as featured soloists and occasionally as members of the ensemble: Teddy Wilson, Fletcher Henderson, Lionel Hampton, Cootie Williams, Lester Young, Walter Page. Meanwhile, the first recordings by the Benny Goodman Trio, consisting of Goodman, Teddy Wilson (piano), and Gene Krupa (drums), were released in 1935. The group became a quartet the following year with the addition of Lionel Hampton (vibraphone), and Harry James or Ziggy Elman was sometimes

[87] NW 250, s2 / 3.
[88] NW 250, s1 / 7.

added on trumpet; and in 1939 the Benny Goodman Sextet came into being. Though the personnel varied, their most historic recordings were made with Goodman, Cootie Williams (trumpet), George Auld (tenor saxophone), Count Basie (piano), Charlie Christian (electric guitar), Artie Bernstein (bass), and Jo Jo James (drums)—three white and four black musicians. Typical of their style is "I've Found a New Baby," recorded in January of 1941.[89] The four choruses alternate between ensemble playing decorated by solo breaks and solo choruses taken by Christian, Williams, and Auld. In the first chorus and in the brief coda, the three horns suggest something of the contrapuntal texture of early jazz; the chief emphasis, however, is on a succession of improvised solo choruses.

It was also in the context of small-club jazz that revolutionary musical developments began creeping into jazz in the mid-1940s.

John Birks "Dizzy" Gillespie played trumpet for a number of the best bands of the swing era, beginning with Teddy Hill and His Orchestra at the Savoy Ballroom in Harlem and moving on to Cab Calloway, Benny Carter, Charlie Barnet, Les Hite, Earl Hines, Coleman Hawkins, and Duke Ellington. He built a reputation as a brilliant if sometimes erratic soloist, a good ensemble player, and a talented arranger; gradually his solos began to include harmonic elements not usually heard in jazz, such as chromatically augmented and diminished chords and extensions of the triad to ninth, eleventh, and even thirteenth chords.

When in New York, Gillespie often visited a small jazz club in Harlem, on West 118th Street, run by Henry Minton. The house band, led by Teddy Hill, included Roy Eldridge (trumpet), Dickie Wells (trombone), Chu Berry (saxophone), Kenny Clarke (drums), and Thelonius Monk (piano). In addition to Gillespie, a young saxophone player from Kansas City, Charlie "Bird" Parker, frequented the club.

Parker (born in 1920) came to New York rarely at first, since he played with Jay McShann's band out of Kansas City. But he moved there in 1942 and took a job with Earl Hines's band in the winter of 1943. Gillespie was a member of the band, and the two soon discovered a common interest in incorporating complex and chromatic chords into passages of great speed and virtuosity. They spent many hours practicing in unison, building up facility in playing extremely difficult passages together with remarkable precision. They left Hines in 1944 to join a new band organized by Billy Eckstine, who made Gillespie his musical director and encouraged the

[89] NW 274, s1 / 7.

two to incorporate their emerging new playing style into the fabric of the band.[90]

The first recordings by Gillespie and Parker in which this new style can be heard date from 1945. The essence of what soon came to be called bebop, or simply bop, may be sampled in discs cut by the Dizzy Gillespie All Star Quintet during two sessions in the spring of 1945. "Shaw 'Nuff"[91] consists of five 32-bar choruses based on the chord changes of George Gershwin's "I've Got Rhythm"; the first and fifth choruses are played by Gillespie and Parker in unison; the second features a solo by Parker, the third is given to Gillespie, the fourth to pianist Al Haig. Though the tempo is extremely fast, the solo passages are executed with precision and clarity.

Much of the bebop repertory was based on the chord structures of favorite popular songs, with new melodic lines invented against these changes, usually stressing virtuoso passage work and assymetrical rhythmic patterns. One rarely perceives a conventional melody in bebop performances, and with the fast pace, the virtuosity of most bebop soloists, the breathtaking agility and nervous energy of the best players, bebop was perceived by most listeners as a succession of dazzling technical passages without recognizable melodic contours.

"Ko-Ko"[92] gives an even better idea of the revolutionary character of this new style. A brief introduction features a few bars of solo playing by both Gillespie and Parker and ends with the two playing together, first in thirds and then in unison; rhythmic contours are so jagged and assymetric as to virtually conceal the underlying 4/4 meter; the melodic lines give little hint of a harmonic foundation. Parker then launches into two choruses based on the changes of Ray Noble's "Cherokee," accompanied only by bass, drums, and piano; jazz had never before heard passages of such virtuosity, velocity, and melodic invention. A half-chorus by drummer Max Roach and a slightly shortened version of the introduction end the piece.

The collaboration between Gillespie and Parker was short-lived; they went their seperate ways after a trip together to California in late 1945. Gillespie formed a succession of large bands and small ensembles, and has continued to play until the present day, moving into the role of elder statesman in the style he helped create. Parker's subsequent career was quite different. After some months in a mental hospital in California in 1946–47, he continued to record until 1951; the succeeding years, until his death in 1955, were

[90] For a sample of the band's playing, cf. "Good Jelly Blues" on NW 284, s1/6.
[91] NW 271, s1/3.
[92] NW 271, s1/8.

marred by further deterioration in physical and mental health, permitting only occasional performances, mostly at Birdland, a New York club named after him.

Unlike Gillespie, he played only in small ensembles. Trumpeter Miles Davis played with him in many of his live performances and recording sessions between 1947 and 1951, and the two often managed the same sort of precision playing in unison that had been a trademark of the Gillespie-Parker collaboration. But Parker rarely played at the extremely fast tempos that had marked the earliest bebop style after he broke with Gillespie. His maturing style moved more in the direction of expressive rather than purely virtuosic playing, and though he retained remarkable facility to the end, many of his most memorable performances during the last years of his career were in medium or even slow tempos, usually based on the harmonic patterns of the 12-bar blues or some favorite Tin

Coleman Hawkins and Miles Davis, ca. 1948. (© William P. Gottlieb)

Pan Alley song. "Relaxin' at Camarillo" (1947)[93] might be called a bebop blues: it moves along at a faster tempo than one would expect in a blues. "Parker's Mood" (1948),[94] on the other hand, is a quite traditional blues in tempo, mood, and even melodic line, though transformed into something special by Parker's unmatched melodic invention and phrasing.

In the end, though Parker was involved in the formation of an innovative style of jazz, he is remembered simply for his excellence as a solo improviser and his superb command of his instrument. He is taken by many jazz critics and historians to be the outstanding solo artist in the entire history of jazz, and has been venerated by several generations of jazz enthusiasts. "Bird lives," even three decades after his death.

Bebop spread from its home in Harlem to much of the rest of the jazz world. Bud Powell became the leader of the bebop pianists, adapting the style to the piano, with the right hand playing melodically and rhythmically intricate single-line melodies, accompanied by sparse, jagged, erratic bursts of dissonant chords in the left.[95] Tadd Dameron also developed a bebop style of piano playing, and adapted elements of the new techniques to the band he led during this time;[96] he was probably the most imaginative arranger of music for large band drawing on bebop.[97]

Some of the large bands of the 1940s and early '50s incorporated elements of bebop into their playing. Dizzy Gillespie's own band, between 1946 and 1950, often fused the melodic and rhythmic ideas of bebop with big-band jazz; "Things To Come" (1946),[98] an arrangement for large band by Walter Fuller of Gillespie's small-ensemble "Bebop" of 1945, features five trumpets and five saxophones (playing in unison as sections) sharing the melodic material in the first chorus, a succession of solos by Gillespie and others in interior choruses, and an almost symphonic ending. Woody Herman's bands of the late 1940s continued the tradition of big-band jazz in their instrumentation and some of their repertory, but they contained some of the best white bebop players and sometimes incorporated the sound of this new form of jazz in their performances. "Lemon Drop" (1948)[99] is built on the changes of "I Got Rhythm," used for so many bebop pieces, and has several solos in the new style.

---

[93] NW 271, s1 / 6.
[94] NW 271, s1 / 4.
[95] Cf. his playing on "Un Poco Loco," NW 271, s2 / 2.
[96] Cf. "Jahbero" on NW 271, s2 / 3.
[97] "Dameron Stomp," as played by Harlan Leonard and his Rockets (NW 284, s1 / 2), is a sample of his style of arranging.
[98] NW 271, s1 / 5.
[99] NW 271, s2 / 1.

Charles Mingus (1922–79), who played bass with some of the best bebop soloists, also tried his hand at arrangements for large band based on aspects of this music: his "Mingus Fingers" (1947) for Lionel Hampton and His Orchestra shows off his own virtuosity in an arrangement reflecting the harmonic experimentation and dazzling technique of Charlie Parker and his peers.[100] But the piece is much more than a big-band arrangement seasoned with bebop— it is an imaginative composition, eschewing the usual structural framework of blues or popular song changes, with provocative and adventuresome harmonic patterns of its own and a palette of changing instrumental colors based on novel concepts of voicing chords with mixed brass and reeds.

Woody Herman had several adventuresome arrangers with serious music aspirations. Ralph Burns composed and scored the two-part *Lady McGowan's Dream* for Herman in 1946, then followed with *Summer Sequence* (1946), a four-movement composition requiring both sides of two phonograph discs, poised somewhere between jazz and symphonic style.[101] It was for this band that Stravinsky wrote his *Ebony Concerto* in 1945, incidentally. Claude Thornhill's orchestra played a number of arrangements by Canadian-born Gil Evans, who treated some of the bebop standards— "Robbins' Nest," Charlie Parker's "Donna Lee,"[102] and "Anthropology"—with freedom and imagination, and added several French horns and a tuba to the standard big-band instrumentation.

Even more ambitious was Stan Kenton (1912–79), who became the leader of what was to be called "progressive jazz." Leading a band with five trumpets, five trombones, six reeds, and a rhythm section, he played pieces by composer-arrangers Pete Rugolo and Robert Graettinger. Rugolo's *Egdon Heath* (1954)[103] is in the nature of a tiny tone-poem, making expressive use of Kenton's standard brass-reed instrumentation. Even more ambitious is Graettinger's *City of Glass* (1951), a four-movement piece described by the composer as

> [Deriving] its inspiration from the interplay and counterpoint of the energies and forces that I see and feel in the world around me.[104]

Scored for an orchestra including a large string section and other nonjazz instruments, the piece was released on a 10-inch LP. Crit-

[100] NW 284, s1 / 7.

[101] Three sections are available on NW 216, s1 / 1.

[102] NW 284, s1 / 8.

[103] NW 216, s2 / 1.

[104] As quoted in Robert Badgett Morgan, *The Music and Life of Robert Graettinger* (Urbana: University of Illinois, unpublished D.M.A. thesis, 1974), p. 41.

ical reaction was similar to that which greeted most progressive jazz:

> It is neither jazz nor popular music in any of the several senses in which those categories are generally understood; its only connection with the previous achievement of either the composer or the conductor is the vigorous performance the latter elicits in behalf of the former. As music it seems to me to fall somewhere between Schoenberg and Schillinger. The overall impression is of a muddled modern work ill-defined in purpose and not much closer to a work of art than science fiction.[105]

Composer-performer-educator-author Gunther Schuller was later to coin the term "third stream" for such music—jazz and Western classical music coming together. But though some vital and fascinating music came out of such attempts,[106] the big-band symphonic style proved to be a blind alley, going against the newer emphasis on small ensembles and solo improvisation.

The decades following the emergence of bebop brought a multitude of new jazz performers playing in a wide range of styles. At times the period seemed chaotic, marked more by disparity than conformity of style. But the perspective of time reveals patterns not readily apparent to contemporary observers. Thus it is now possible to isolate a number of features unifying virtually all jazz in the quarter-century following 1945:

a shift from large bands to small ensembles;

greater emphasis on solo improvisation than had been the case during the swing era;

a concern with more complex harmonic, rhythmic, and formal patterns;

the detachment of jazz from dance music;

an equilibrium between black and white musicians, with both races contributing almost equally to the new style of jazz;

a more intellectual approach to jazz on the part of both performers and audience, and the emergence of a new aesthetic.

Dealing with the last point first, jazz may be seen as evolving from a popular art to a form of classical music in the mid-twentieth century.

In the late 1920s and throughout the big-band period, jazz had allied itself with popular song and the several media controlling and profiting from the mass dissemination of music. Most jazz performers catered to popular taste and were cast in the role of enter-

---

[105] Barry Ulanov, in *Metronome* (March, 1953), p. 24.
[106] Cf. Schuller's *Transformation* on NW 216, s2 / 3.

tainers. Only in small-club jam sessions and the few recordings of improvising small-ensemble jazz did players address themselves to other performers and connoisseurs.

Bebop and what came to be called "modern jazz" were played for the gratification of the performers themselves, with virtually no concern for mass appeal. Many jazz musicians furthermore became alienated from the mainstream of American life, adopting idiosyncratic dress and language and often being identified with illegal practices such as drug usage. Their music became difficult and often impenetrable for the casual and uncommitted listener. The jazz world increasingly revolved around a core of the most talented and creative performers, other musicians who admired their playing and aspired to become part of this core themselves, professional critics, and knowledgeable and dedicated fans—a structure mirroring the world of classical music.

All of these elements may be observed in the music and life of Thelonius Sphere Monk (1920–82). Making his way to New York from his birthplace in Rocky Mount, North Carolina, he found jobs as pianist in several bands in the early 1940s, including that of Coleman Hawkins. He gravitated to Henry Minton's club, where bebop took form, then organized and led a succession of small ensembles made up of some of the more innovative younger players of the day: Sonny Rollins, John Coltrane, Milt Jackson, Max Roach. He became a mysterious and withdrawn personality, given to moody behavior and affecting bizarre clothing; his recordings, made mostly between 1947 and 1954, attracted virtually no popular attention, but were cherished and studied by other jazz players and a handful of near-fanatical fans.

*Misterioso* (1948)[107] contains all the components of Monk's style and musical personality. Performed by the Thelonius Monk Quartet (Milt Jackson on vibraphone, Monk on piano, John Simmons on bass, and Shadow Wilson on drums), it is built over a 12-bar blues pattern, though the slow tempo, the asymmetric rhythmic patterns, and the eccentric and dissonant harmonic progressions obscure the form. Four introductory bars of a curious "walking" theme in the piano lead to five choruses; Monk takes the first, third, and fourth, Jackson the second, and both share the last. Monk's solos are marked by jagged and erratic lines in the right hand, often only a single line, punctuated by occasional chords or figured patterns in the left. The bass holds things together with a steady walking pattern while Monk races off into wildly dissonant passages, whole-tone scales, bitonal patterns, and rhythmic phrases

[107] NW 271, s2 / 4.

Thelonius Monk. (Courtesy Retna Ltd., photograph by David Redfern)

often at complete odds with the pulse and phrase structure under-lying the piece. As Gunther Schuller said about another piece by Monk:

It does not describe or portray anything specific, it does not attempt to set a "mood" or the like; it simply states and develops certain musical ideas, in much the way that an abstract painter will work with specific nonobjective patterns.[108]

It was this abstraction and objectivity which led to the coining of the term "cool" for music of this sort.

Another view of Monk's art may be gained from the performance by the Steve Lacy Quartet of his *Introspection*, which had been recorded by Monk in 1947 but virtually forgotten.[109] The style and mood of the performance are faithful to Monk's own way of playing, in the unusual and often dissonant chords implied by the solo lines, the jagged and asymmetrical shape of so many rhythmic phrases, and most of all in the detached, abstract, "cool" manner of playing.

Lennie Tristano, born and trained in Chicago before moving to New York in 1946, played and recorded with a number of the best young white jazz musicians of the post-bebop period, bringing his own personality not only to his own playing,[110] but also to that of a number of players associated with him and influenced by his teaching.[111] Miles Davis, who had played with Charlie Parker at the beginning of his career, began recording with groups under his own name in 1949; his association with arranger Gil Evans produced a series of memorable pieces combining Evans's tight but transparent scoring with the understated and "cool"—but nevertheless brilliant—solo playing of Davis (trumpet), Lee Konitz (alto saxophone), Gerry Mulligan (baritone saxophone), Sonny Rollins (tenor saxophone), and John Coltrane (saxophone). Charles Mingus, who had played with Louis Armstrong, Kid Ory, Red Norvo, Charlie Parker, and Bud Powell, eventually founded his own experimental Jazz Workshop in New York, devoted to the pursuit of noncommercial modern jazz. His own works of the 1950s, including *Pithecanthropus erectus* (1956) and *Eclipse* (1953),[112] are free compositions rather than improvisations, giving further evidence of the incorporation of dissonant and even atonal harmony and counterpoint into modern jazz. Stan Getz, born in Philadelphia in 1927, played saxophone in several big bands of the 1940s, including that of Woody Herman; his "cool" playing in *Early Autumn* (1947) was widely admired and led to performances and recordings with various small groups, with Gerry Mulligan, Dizzy Gil-

[108] "Thelonius Monk," in *Jazz Panorama* (New York: Crowell-Collier, 1962), p. 262.
[109] NW 275, s2 / 2.
[110] Cf. his version of Jerome Kern's "Yesterdays" on NW 216, s1 / 3.
[111] Cf. "Donna Lee," featuring Lee Konitz and Warne Marsh, on NW 242, s1 / 2.
[112] NW 216, s1 / 5.

lespie, Oscar Peterson, and other leading jazzmen of the 1950s and '60s.

Yet another dialect of cool jazz may be heard in the playing of the Modern Jazz Quartet, formed in 1951 by John Lewis (piano), Milt Jackson (vibraphone), Percy Heath (bass), and Kenny Clarke (drums). Their music is disciplined, somewhat detached, free from overt emotionalism or virtuosity for its own sake; several of the group had classical training, and elements of such devices as fugue and variation may be heard in many of their pieces, as well as quotations from classical compositions.[113]

Grouping all of these men together may be disturbing for partisans of any of them, yet a broad overview of the history of jazz must find common features in their music. At the same time it must be admitted that each of them had a more distinctive style than was the case with most jazz musicians of the 1920s and '30s, and this says something about the veneration and cultivation of idiosyncratic styles in the era of modern jazz.

On December 21, 1960, eight jazz musicians led by Ornette Coleman assembled in a New York recording studio. Grouped into two quartets—Coleman (alto saxophone), Don Cherry (trumpet), Scott La Faro (bass), and Billy Higgins (drums) in one; Freddie Hubbard (trumpet), Eric Dolphy (bass clarinet), Charlie Haden (bass), and Ed Blackwell (drums) in the other—they cut an LP album released as *Free Jazz*.[114] The music proceeds with no reference to recognizable tunes or chord changes; the effect is of almost totally free improvisation. As Coleman said:

> The most important thing was for us to play together, all at the same time, wihout getting in each other's way, and also to have room for each player to ad lib alone—and to follow his idea for the duration of the album. When the soloist played something that suggested a musical idea or any direction to me, I played that behind him in my style. He continued his own way in his solo, of course.[115]

In many ways this free jazz was a continuation of the improvisatory small-ensemble jazz that had attracted the most advanced musicians since the emergence of bebop. But in moving away from reliance on structural elements of popular songs, blues, or original pieces, and from any perceivable regular pulse, it ventured into territory new to the genre.

[113] Cf. their "Woody'n You" on NW 242, s1 / 1.
[114] A portion of this disc is available on *The Smithsonian Collection*, s12 / 3.
[115] Liner notes to *Free Jazz*, Atlantic Records S-1364.

Reaction to *Free Jazz*, and to Coleman's other performances and recordings at this time, was by no means universally favorable. Some critics and musicians who had been increasingly distressed with the experimental nature of modern jazz found Coleman's music to be the breaking point:

> I would take issue with Coleman's concept of perfect freedom on the grounds that it is anti-music and anti-art. Art is and always has been the ordering of the disparate and chaotic materials of life into a significant shape of expression. Freedom of Coleman's kind is *not* perfect freedom; indeed, in its way, it is perfect slavery.[116]

Coleman, who was born in Fort Worth in 1930 and had played throughout the South and Southwest in his youth, came to New York in 1958 to play at the Five Spot Cage. Admiration for Charlie Parker helped shape his own style, but by the late 1950s, with such pieces as "Lonely Woman" and "Congeniality," he was stretching the post-bebop style almost beyond recognition:

> [His pieces] use a composed tune to introduce and close the piece, a framework for improvised solos. [They] use the bebop pattern of unison performance of the riff by lead instruments and still rely on an underlying pulse that is less rigid but still apparent and continuous. They differ from bebop jazz in the omission of piano, totally unnecessary in an environment without chord progressions; they stretch phrase lengths into plastic shapes; and they employ improvisations which lack the goal orientation of harmonically directed solos.[117]

*Free Jazz* brought world wide attention to Coleman, who went to Europe in 1965, fueling the fires of European avant-garde jazz. Other milestone LP albums included *Chappaqua Suite* (1967) and *Trouble in the East* (1969); his later playing moved back more into the mainstream of small-ensemble improvised jazz.

Like bebop, free jazz expanded the stylistic boundaries of jazz without becoming a dominant style itself. Few jazzmen embraced its tenets completely, though almost none of them were untouched by it. Its impact may be seen in the music of John Coltrane (1926–67), the dominant solo jazz performer after Charlie Parker's death. After playing in a succession of bands led by some of the leading figures of the 1950s, including Dizzy Gillespie, Johnny Hodges, Thelonius Monk, and Miles Davis, Coltrane made his first strong

---

[116] Gene Lees, "The Compleat Jazz Critic," in *Music 1961* (New York: Down Beat, 1961), p. 14.

[117] Frank Tirro, *Jazz. A History* (New York: W. W. Norton & Company, 1977), pp. 345–46.

personal statement with the LP album *Giant Steps* (1959), containing only pieces of his own composition, played by musicians of his own choosing; the title cut features a string of solo choruses by Coltrane which set a new standard for saxophone improvisation, based on a 16-bar phrase of highly chromatic chords.

Emotional and spiritual involvement were as important to Coltrane's mature style as technical facility and stylistic innovations. He once said:

> You know, I want to be a force for real good. In other words, I know that there are bad forces, forces put here that bring suffering to others and misery to the world, but I want to be the force which is truly for good.[118]

"Alabama" (1963)[119] was written after the death of several black schoolchildren in a racial bombing in that state. *A Love Supreme* (1964), a suite in four parts ("Acknowledge," "Resolution," "Pursuance," and "Psalm"), was a response to the death of Eric Dolphy, who had often played with Coltrane; everything about the album is suffused with a spiritualism unusual for jazz. *Ascension* (1965) moves more in the direction of free collective improvisation. The band, large for the time (two trumpets, five saxophones, piano, drums, two bass players) was supplied with nothing more than fragments of thematic material; Coltrane indicated only the most general shape of the piece by a series of cues while the piece was in progress. With its rich fabric of collective improvisation, the absence of a harmonic framework, and the frequent obscuring of the beat, the piece often resembles a more brilliant and complex version of Coleman's *Free Jazz.*

Sun Ra (born Sonny Bourke), after a short tenure as pianist with Fletcher Henderson's orchestra, organized an ensemble in Chicago in the late 1950s, which moved increasingly to free improvisation. Miles Davis, who seemed little interested in free jazz in its early stages, began experimenting with collective improvisation within prescribed formal boundaries in the late 1960s, and with his *Bitches Brew* (1969) managed one of the first syntheses of free jazz with the electrical instruments associated with rock. Many of the younger players associated with Davis in the 1960s eventually formed groups of their own, playing music of the same general sort—Chick Corea, Wayne Shorter, Herbie Hancock, John McLaughlin, Sam Rivers.

The most determined, imaginative, uncompromising, and productive advocate of free jazz has been Cecil Taylor. Born in

---

[118] Frank Kofsky, *Black Nationalism and the Revolution in Music* (New York: Pathfinder Press, 1970), p. 241.
[119] *The Smithsonian Collection,* s12 / 4.

Cecil Taylor. (Photograph by Marc Brasz)

New York in 1933, classically trained at the New England Conservatory, leader of small improvising ensembles since 1965, he has pursued his own dialect of music without being distracted by the ebb and flow of musical events around him. His first recordings, from 1955, revealed him to be an imaginative adapter of the melodies and chord changes of popular songs, conforming to the general techniques of the day. Little by little he moved away from dependence on tonal harmony or metrical patterns. He drew his ideas from a wide range of music, both classical and vernacular: "Everything I've lived, I am. I'm not afraid of European influences. The point is to use them—as Ellington did—as part of my life as an American Negro."[120] Working alone or with a small ensemble, he built fluid structures from small motifs, bits of precomposed material which took on a shape and a life of their own in the process of performance:

> There is little talking at his rehearsals, and minimal dependence on the extensive notation. Taylor plays a melody; the other musicians pick it up and work with it; and he and his players proceed to the next. In performance, the duration of a piece will depend on the chemistry between the musicians at the moment. The amalgamation of influences—the sonorous images that multiply and clash—in a Taylor presentation combine in a folklorism of the musical past: depending on the background one brings to the music, one may hear Brahms, Liszt, Stravinsky, Bartók, Mahler, Cowell, Charlie Parker, Duke Ellington, Fats Waller, Bud Powell, Lennie Tristano, Thelonius Monk, Horace Silver, and who knows how many others. But they are all transsubstantiated, and the result is never a pastiche. The islets of musical thought are joined in an immense, radiant landscape.[121]

Perhaps the nearest equivalent to Taylor's style in classical music is to be found in certain passages of the *Fourth Symphony* or the *Second String Quartet* of Charles Ives, in which fragments of various pieces rush along with incredible energy in patterns quite out of touch with traditional metrical or harmonic practice.

His first distinctive ensemble was the Cecil Taylor Unit, made up of himself (piano), Jimmy Lyons (alto Saxophone) and Sonny Murray (drums). Expanding the group to include trumpet, saxophone, two basses, drums, and piano, Taylor recorded *Unit Structures* (1966), the first full realization of his mature style, usually ranked with Coleman's *Free Jazz* as a monument of avant-garde jazz.

All later products, including the recent *Idut, Serdab*, and *Holiday en Masque* (all of 1978)[122] and *3 Phasis* of 1979,[123] have grown out of extensions and enrichments of these working methods and aesthetics. At first hearing his music may strike one as chaotic, out of touch with any earlier style of jazz, perhaps indistinguishable in sound from certain contemporary classical pieces. But once one penetrates the external obstacle of a dissonant, asymmetrical,

---

[120] Liner notes to *Looking Ahead*, Contemporary Records S-7562.
[121] Gary Giddens, liner notes to NW 303, pp. i–ii.
[122] NW 201.
[123] NW 303.

uncompromising general vocabulary, individual lines and improvised solos may be heard to unfold according to the same intuitively musical logic that has always characterized the best jazz performance.

Jazz was a dynamic and evolutionary art progressing through a series of stylistic changes until the 1950s. Older performers either adapted to the latest style or dropped out of sight; younger players were not interested in older repertories and styles.

However, jazz began to turn back on itself. There was the New Orleans Revival: older players such as Bunk Johnson and George Lewis were rediscovered and recorded; some younger players, unsympathetic to modern jazz, took up playing in this way. The big-band era seemed to die a natural death, giving way to a new style of small-ensemble playing; yet some of the big bands lingered on, finding audiences still receptive to their repertory, unwilling to adjust their ears to newer sounds. Bebop and then free jazz seemed to be logical evolutions and the best players went along with these newer trends; yet a number of jazz musicians clung to older ways of playing and found many people happy to listen to what they were doing.

Jazz, like classical music in the twentieth century, began living with and competing against its own past. It has been almost a quarter-century since the last major stylistic breakthrough. Jazz, like virtually all music in America, has reached a stylistic plateau, reshaping and refining older elements, marking time until the next, inevitable, stylistic revolution.

# 18

## The Second Wave
## and Its Impact on
## American Composition

A new generation of American composers, emerging in the late 1920s, put aside the notion of writing "American" music and began cultivating an international style. This change in attitude corresponded with the arrival of a second wave of European composers, who visited and in many cases settled in the United States, and it is impossible to separate this new direction in American music from the story of the visitors and immigrants who helped bring it about.

The first wave of European composers, in the late eighteenth and early nineteenth centuries,[1] was made up of competent, versatile musicians of no great distinction in the musical world they left behind. America welcomed Raynor Taylor, Alexander Reinagle, Jean Gehot—but Haydn, Mozart, Cherubini, and Beethoven never set foot in the New World.

The first European composer of international fame to spend time in America was Frederick Delius (1863–1934), at the beginning of his musical career. Sent by his father to manage an orange plantation in Florida in March of 1884, Delius attached himself to Thomas F. Ward, organist of a Catholic church in Jacksonville. By the time he left America in 1886, he was teaching music to the daughters of tobacco growers in Danville, Virginia, and sketching his first compositions. He enrolled at the Leipzig Conservatory in

---

[1] Cf. Chapter IV of the present book for a discussion of these men and their music.

1886, and spent the remainder of his life in Europe. Delius and his music had virtually no impact on the musical life of America. *Florida*, an orchestral suite written shortly after his return from the United States, was not given its first performance in the United States until 1923, when it was played by the Detroit Symphony, and *Appalachia*, based in part on traditional slave songs, was given its American premiere only in 1937, by the New York Philharmonic, under a British music director.

By contrast, Richard Strauss (1864–1949) was a major composer by the time he arrived in New York in 1904, and many of his pieces had already been played by American orchestras. On March 21 of that year he conducted the Wetzler Symphony Orchestra in a program at Carnegie Hall that included *Don Juan, Also sprach Zarathustra*, and the world premiere of *Symphonia domestica*, completed only several months before his arrival. But his stay in America was brief, and his impact on the musical life of the country came chiefly from his compositions, not his presence.

Gustav Mahler (1860–1911) made his debut as principal conductor of the Metropolitan Opera on January 1, 1908 with Richard Wagner's *Tristan und Isolde*. He was appointed conductor of the New York Philharmonic in 1909, holding the post until poor health forced him to retire after the concert of February 21, 1911, his last public appearance on the podium. He was better known in this country—before his arrival—as a conductor than composer. Only two of his symphonies, the fourth and fifth, had ever been heard in America, but his presence sparked a rash of performances. The New York Philharmonic, under his direction, did *Symphony No. 1* (1909) and *No. 4* (1910), as well as songs from *Das Knaben Wunderhorn* and *Lieder eines fahrenden Gesellen*. Damrosch led the New York Symphony in the American premiere of *Symphony No. 2* in 1908; and the publicity surrounding his stay in New York undoubtedly prompted the first American performances of *Symphony No. 3* (Cincinnati, 1913), *Symphony No. 8* (Philadelphia, 1915), and *Das Lied von der Erde* (Philadelphia, 1916).

Sergei Rachmaninoff (1873–1943) had more prolonged contact with the United States. His first public appearance in America was a piano recital at Smith College on November 4, 1909, and on November 28 he premiered his *Piano Concerto No. 3* (written in Moscow between June and October of that year) with Walter Damrosch's New York Symphony. After the revolution in Russia, he divided his time between Switzerland and the United States. The last fifteen years of his life were spent in this country, first in New York and then Los Angeles. The thirtieth anniversary of his first American appearance was celebrated by the New York Philharmonic with a cycle of three concerts featuring him in the triple role of composer, pianist, and conductor. His last American tour was in the winter and spring of 1940 and, shortly before his death in 1943, he became a citizen of the United States.

Thus a significant shift was taking place in the classical music life in America during the first decades of the twentieth century. Performing proficiency was becoming high enough to attract European composers here for performances of their works. American audiences and critics were becoming sophisticated enough to respond intelligently, even to first performances of major compositions by established European composers. And in Ernest Bloch we see a European born and trained musician of considerable talent and reputation choosing a life in America in preference to Europe.

Born in Geneva in 1880, Bloch came to the United States for the first time in 1916, then returned the following year to present a program for the New York Society of the Friends of Music on May 3, 1917 that included two movements of his *Israel Symphony*, *Three Jewish Poems*, *Three Psalms* for solo voices and orchestra, and the first performance of *Schelomo* for cello and orchestra. He stayed in New York, teaching privately and at the Mannes School of Music. In 1920 he became director of the Cleveland Institute of Music, taking American citizenship in 1924. He was later director of the San Francisco Conservatory of Music, then taught at the University of California at Berkeley. Except for professional and personal visits back to Europe, the remainder of his life, until his death in 1959, was spent in America. He was active and visible as a composer, teacher, lecturer. He was the first "American" composer to win the New York Music Critics Award in two different categories, orchestral composition (for his *Concerto Grosso No. 2*) and chamber music (for his *Third String Quartet*).

The first wave of musician-composers to settle in America are discussed in virtually every history of American music. It is assumed that their residency here, the fact that many of their compositions were written after they arrived in the New World, and their impact on American-born composers all qualify them for inclusion in a discussion of American music.

The same things can be said about Bloch. Should he therefore be included in a history of American music?

Bloch was much concerned with his Jewish heritage. His most widely played composition is *Schelomo*, a "Jewish Rhapsody" for cello and orchestra. Other works include *Baal Shem* for violin and orchestra (1941), titled after the Polish founder of the Hassids; a *Sacred Service* for the Reformed Synagogue (1934); a *Suite Hebraïque* for viola and orchestra (1953); *A Voice in the Wilderness* (1937), a symphonic poem; and choral settings of various psalms. Only once did he undertake a piece that deliberately makes musical and programmatic reference to the New World; his *America*, an "epic rhapsody" for orchestra, was the winning work in a competition sponsored by *Musical America* for a new symphonic work "glorifying the ideals of the United States." The piece, which quotes musical material ranging from Indian melodies through popular songs of the nineteenth century, was premiered by the New York Philharmonic on December 20, 1928, then performed in Boston, Philadelphia, Chicago, Cincinnati, Cleveland, Los Angeles, Minneapolis within the next week.

But for the most part, he wrote in a style that borrows melodic ideas from traditional Hebrew music and casts these in the formal and sonic patterns of western European classical music of the eighteenth and nineteenth centuries.

Jewish Americans are just as much a part of the United States as Irish Americans, black Americans, Italian Americans, native Americans, or Americans whose ancestry traces back to the British Isles; and in fact a great deal of the credit for the expansion and improvement of classical music in this country in the early twentieth century must be laid to the influx of talented and dedicated Jewish performers, teachers, composers, critics, and listeners at just this critical time. In writing music that drew on and celebrated his Jewish heritage, Bloch was writing music that spoke to millions of his fellow American citizens. Its reference was to a new America, one coming into existence only in the twentieth century.

Bloch should surely be considered an American composer, but by addressing himself to a specific segment of American culture, he limited the appeal of his music. His attitudes and his career make a fascinating contrast with those of, say, Irving Berlin, George Gershwin, and Aaron Copland, other composers of Jewish ancestry who absorbed elements of older and more broad-based American cultures into their music and who consequently attracted a larger and more varied audience.

The next distinguished European composer to come to the New World, Sergei Prokofiev (1891–1953), arrived in New York on September 18, 1918, fleeing the "intolerable conditions of famine and civil disorder"[2] that raged in his homeland during and immediately after the Russian Revolution. Two months later he offered a

[2] Nicolas Slonimsky, *Music Since 1900* (New York: Charles Scribner's Sons, 1971), p. 301.

program of his own piano compositions in New York, and in the next few years several major new compositions were premiered in this country, most notably his *Piano Concerto No. 3* in 1921 (by the Chicago Symphony Orchestra with Prokofiev as soloist) and his opera *Love for Three Oranges* by the Chicago Opera Company later the same month. But he was only passing through America; as soon as conditions stabilized in Russia, he returned.

The French composer Darius Milhaud (1892–1974) came to America for the first time in 1922 for lectures at Harvard, Princeton, and Columbia universities. In 1940, fleeing the invading German armies, he came to New York, then took a teaching position at Mills College in California. Though he returned to France in 1947, he visited the United States almost annually as a conductor and teacher. Like Bloch, he was an established composer with an established compositional style before he came to these shores. Some rhythmic and instrumental flavoring of American jazz permeates some of his early pieces, such as the ballet *Le Boeuf sur le toit* (1920), but these elements had already entered his musical style before he came here. Many of his compositions were commissioned by American orchestras and were given English titles (*Kentuckiana*, 1949, commissioned by the Louisville Orchestra; *Music for Indiana*, 1966, written for the sesquicentennial of the State of Indiana; *West Point Suite*, 1952, for the sesquicentennial of the United States Military Academy), but neither Milhaud nor music critics ever suggested that his residence in this country brought about any change in his way of writing music, and his position is best summed up by the title of one of his compositions, *A Frenchman in New York*, a symphonic suite first performed by the Boston Pops Orchestra in 1963.

An even more impressive figure came to America for the first time in 1925: Igor Stravinsky (1882–1971), widely accepted as one of the most influential composers of the twentieth century.

This position had already been established before his arrival here, with such pieces as *The Firebird*, *Le Sacre du printemps*, *Petrushka*, *Les Noces*, and *L'Histoire du soldat*. American audiences had known his music for a decade, first through performances of *Petrushka* by the Diaghilev Ballet Troupe during its American tour,[3] then through performances of his ballet scores and other orchestral works by American orchestras. *The Firebird* had been performed in Boston, Chicago, Cincinnati, Cleveland, Detroit, New York, Philadelphia, Rochester, St. Louis, San Francisco, before Stravinsky's first visit to America.

[3] Charles Hamm, ed., *Petrushka*, A Norton Critical Score (New York: W. W. Norton & Company, 1967), pp. 13–18, for a discussion of American audiences' first contact with the music of Stravinsky.

Stravinsky conducted the New York Philharmonic on January 8, 1925 and appeared as soloist with the Boston Symphony in a performance of his new *Piano Concerto* on January 23. Subsequent visits to the United States were frequent, and many of his major works were first performed here: *Apollon musagète* (1928), commissioned by the Elizabeth Sprague Coolidge Foundation and first performed at the Library of Congress; *Symphonie de psaumes* (1930), commissioned by the Boston Symphony Orchestra to celebrate its fiftieth anniversary; *Dumbarton Oaks* (1938), commissioned by Mr. and Mrs. Robert Woods Bliss and named after their estate in Washington, D.C., where it was first performed. He considered Paris his home, and assumed French citizenship in 1934. But his ties with America became closer and, with the outbreak of World War II, he came to this country as the Charles Eliot Norton lecturer at Harvard University for 1939–40. He settled in Los Angeles in 1940 and became a citizen of the United States on December 28, 1945.

Like Milhaud, Stravinsky had heard American syncopated dance music in Paris and had skimmed off features of it in *Piano Rag Music* (1919), *Ragtime* for eleven instruments (1918), and sections of *L'Histoire du soldat* (1918). It is possible to hear rhythmic and melodic fragments in his later works that probably would not have been there had he not listened to American popular music (he was quoted in *Time* magazine in January of 1941 as saying, "I love swings. It is to Harlem I go. It is so sympathetic to watch the Negro boys and girls dancing . . ."); one can hear in his *Symphony in Three Movements* (1946) rhythmic patterns that must have been suggested by bebop. One could make a case that he was an international composer who responded to musical stimuli from several different cultures, that he went through an "American period," and that space should be made for at least this part of his output in histories of American music.

One would be tempted to do just this had matters turned out differently, had his involvement in American life and culture intensified in the last two decades of his life, spent mostly in America. But this was not the case. In the 1950s and '60s he turned sharply away from involvement with things American, musical or otherwise. Stravinsky's musical interests turned to the music of Machaut, Gesualdo, Schoenberg, Webern. He experimented with serialism in *Movements* for piano and orchestra (1948–59), *Canticum sacrum* (1956), and *Threni* (1958). There is nothing in these pieces that points to the music, or the ways of thinking about music, that characterize American as opposed to European culture.

Arnold Schoenberg (1874–1951) came to America in the fall of 1933, to teach a master class at the Malkin Conservatory in Boston. Like most other European composers who settled in the United

States in this decade, his decision to leave Europe was based on the increasingly menacing Nazi presence. Though his name was familiar to other composers, theorists, students of theory and composition—as well as those who read journals devoted to musical happenings in Europe—American audiences were largely unfamiliar with his work. There had been only a scattering of performances of such early compositions as *Chamber Symphony No. 1*, *Five Pieces for Orchestra*, and *Pelleas und Melisande* by American orchestras before his arrival in America, and his chamber and piano works were no better known.

The American League of Composers sponsored a program of his chamber music in New York on November 11, 1933, and the following March he made his debut as a conductor, leading the Boston Symphony Orchestra in *Pelleas und Melisande*. Schoenberg moved to southern California in the fall of 1934, to a colony of other European expatriates. He joined the faculty of the University of Southern California in 1935, then took a position at the University of California in Los Angeles. His first composition written in the New World was a *Suite for Strings* (1934); all of his pieces after Opus 35 were written here, including the *Violin Concerto* (1936), *String Quartet No. 4* (1937), *Piano Concerto* (1942), *A Survivor from Warsaw* (1947), and *Fantasy* for violin and piano (1949). Most of these pieces made use of serial techniques, in a style forged by Schoenberg long before his arrival in America. The United States was a haven for him, where he could continue writing the sort of music he had written before coming here, a place where he could teach younger Americans the traditions of the European classical style that absorbed his entire musical life. He embraced and enjoyed some aspects of life in America, but not its music.

Béla Bartók (1881–1945), the greatest composer of eastern Europe in the first half of the twentieth century, first came to America in December of 1927 on a concert tour, playing his *Piano Concerto No. 1*. He returned in 1940 for the brief remainder of his life. He toured with his wife, offering performances of his *Sonata for Two Pianofortes and Percussion*, then settled in New York, dividing his time between composition (his most notable "American" work was *Concerto for Orchestra* [1943–44] premiered by the Boston Symphony Orchestra on December 1, 1944) and continuing his study of Serbo-Croatian folk music.

Paul Hindemith (1895–1963) came from Germany in 1937, making his first American appearance at the Library of Congress on April 10, 1937, with his *Sonata for Unaccompanied Violin*. After several years of lecturing at colleges and universities and appearing in a number of cities as conductor and performer, he took a teaching position at the University of Buffalo for the spring term of 1940. In the fall he moved to Yale University, where he lectured, taught composition, served as head of the music department, formed and directed a Collegium Musicum. He became an American citizen in 1946, and even though he returned to postwar Europe, he made frequent visits to America in the last two years of his life.

Thus, at one point—the second half of the 1940s—four of the most celebrated European composers of the twentieth century—Stravinsky, Schoenberg, Bartók, and Hindemith—were in the United States. And there were many others of only slightly lesser talent and accomplishments, including Ernst Toch, Bohuslav Martinu, Erich Korngold, Mario Castelnuovo-Tedesco, Bloch, Milhaud, and Rachmaninoff. The presence of these men had a considerable impact on the musical life of the country. Their compositions were more often played and their mere presence prompted a greater interest in contemporary music; they were celebrities who were interviewed, photographed, quoted, and talked about. Perhaps most important, many of them—Hindemith, Milhaud, Schoenberg, Bloch, Martinu—were active and dedicated teachers of theory and composition, willing and eager to pass on to younger Americans their knowledge of the techniques and aesthetics of European classical music.

Roger Sessions, born in Brooklyn in 1896, emerged as the leader of the new wave of American composers who turned once more to Europe and its composers for musical guidance.

Entering Harvard University at the age of fourteen, already a proficient pianist with some youthful compositions behind him, he studied first with Edward Burlingame Hill, and with Horatio Parker at Yale—two relics of the first generation of American composers who looked to European music for their models. When he found a younger and more important teacher, it was Ernest Bloch, over from Europe for only a few years. Sessions became his student and his assistant as well, at the Cleveland Institute of Music from 1921 to 1925. Sessions was in Europe himself for the next eight years—in Paris, Berlin, and Florence—supported by a series of grants.

His first composition to attract attention was *The Black Maskers*, an orchestral suite originally written in 1923 as incidental music to a symbolistic play by Leonid Andreyev; the Cincinnati Symphony Orchestra gave the first concert performance in 1930. It is an astonishing piece. Some sonorities suggest Stravinsky's *Petrushka* and *Le Sacre du printemps*, and there is more than one hint of Debussy. But the piece is essentially original, uncompromising, extravagantly demanding of the orchestra, more contra-

Roger Sessions (left) with his teacher Ernest Bloch in 1923.

puntal than Stravinsky, intensely dissonant in spots, but still more strongly based on tonal language than was the music of Schoenberg at that time.

His *Symphony in E minor* followed. Written in Europe and premiered by the Boston Symphony Orchestra in 1927, it was the first symphony by an American to be performed on concerts of the International Society for Contemporary Music (at the Seventh Festival in Geneva in April of 1929). Working slowly and thoughtfully, he produced pieces only every several years: *Piano Sonata No. 1* appeared in 1930, premiered at the Ninth Festival of the ISCM at Oxford, England; the *Violin Concerto*, completed in 1935, had its first performance in Chicago in January of 1940; *String Quartet No. 1* was completed in 1936.[4] Meanwhile, Sessions had returned to

[4] Available on NW 302, s2, as recorded by the Pro Arte String Quartet in 1945.

America, driven home by the ascension of the Nazi movement. He embarked on what was to be a long career as a teacher of composition, first at the Malkin Conservatory in Boston, and later at Boston University, Princeton, and the University of California at Berkeley.

At a time when most American composers were drawn to either the neoclassical style of Stravinsky or the serial techniques of Schoenberg, Sessions—though admiring both—found his own path elsewhere, in intensely rational, densely contrapuntal, tensely dissonant writing. A former student has this to say about his style:

> In studying this music, one should begin with the shapes of the phrases and the ways in which they are articulated, not with attempts to infer consistent stylistic traits from a mosaic of intervallic and rhythmic relations. Tones and rhythms are best regarded, at first, as means whereby phrases are formed or divided, energy is accrued or expended, harmonic structures are defined or contrasted. From such study one can begin to perceive more clearly the way in which certain harmonic ambiguities or oppositions established in opening phrases may have significance for the larger structure.[5]

A sense of his harmonic and contrapuntal writing may be gleaned from the opening of his *Duo for Violin and Piano* of 1942:

*Duo for Violin and Piano*, by Roger Sessions

---

[5] Andrew Imbrie, article on "Roger Sessions" in John Vinton, ed., *Dictionary of Contemporary Music* (New York: Dutton, 1971), p. 675.

Subsequent works included eight more symphonies (written in 1946, 1957, 1958, 1964, 1966, 1967, 1968, 1978), a concerto for piano, another string quartet (1951), and smaller pieces for orchestra, chamber ensembles, and keyboard, with a sprinkling of vocal works, including a *Mass* for unison voices of 1955. Two large-scale operas occupied much of his attention at two periods of his career: *The Trial of Lucullus*, to a libretto by Brecht, completed in 1947; and *Montezuma*, with a libretto by G. A. Borgese, which he worked on from 1941 until 1963.

With Schoenberg's arrival in America, Sessions became more fascinated with the techniques of serial composition, though he chracteristically modified his own style rather than making an abrupt break with his long-established compositional procedures, adding elements without ever completely embracing the methods of twelve-tone writing. His music remained stern, uncompromising, unassailable. Prizes and awards accumulated, commissions and first performances were readily available, but none of his works entered the standard repertory or became familiar to any but devoted followers and students.

Sessions's late career was climaxed by his setting of Walt Whitman's "When Lilacs Last in the Door-yard Bloom'd," an elegy for Abraham Lincoln. This work for chorus, orchestra, and three soloists (soprano, alto, and baritone) was written in 1970 as a cantata "to the memory of Martin Luther King, Jr., and Robert F. Kennedy." Commissioned by the University of California in celebration of its centennial, it was first performed at Berkeley in 1971 and was given two subsequent performances at Harvard University, then done by both the Chicago and Boston Symphony Orchestras and the San Francisco Symphony.[6]

Throughout his career, Sessions has had a great deal to say about the musical life of America and the role of his music in it. Recurring themes have been the dangers of musical nationalism:

[6] The entire piece is available on NW 296.

I find that two tendencies above all are dangerous to the development of a healthy musical culture in the United States. The first was the type of musical nationalism which was recently so prevalent. The second, which was closely allied with it, was the erection of "accessibility" or "audience appeal" into a kind of dogma—"down with all that is (to use the terms adopted as battle cries) obscure, esoteric, difficult"—let us have only music of "social significance" for the public; the composer must write for "humanity as a whole," not just for himself and his friends and colleagues.[7]

and the desirability of incorporating the musical language and aesthetics of European composers into the experience of Americans:

There are those, to be sure—and all too many of them—who believe that the presence of so many new Americans, of so great distinction, will in some way impair the integrity of our "native culture"—that some especially American quality is threatened by the influx of so-called "foreign ideas." We are told, for instance, that a budding musical culture stands in the gravest danger from the encroachment of so-called "European tradition." Such people, it seems to me, forget, or perhaps misunderstand, two things, First of all they misconceive the nature of tradition itself. Tradition seems, to me, to be nothing more nor less than the accumulation of many generations doing their best. Furthermore, if we examine a little of the history of music or art, we see that no great culture has ever developed on the basis of isolationism or exclusiveness. There can be only one conclusion—America's finding itself means nothing more nor less than the discovery that mankind must be one, and that Americanism is by its very definition inclusive, all-inclusive, not in the smallest degree exclusive, and that loyalty to America means nothing less than a consistent devotion to the human principle in that inclusive sense.[8]

Concerning these attitudes (embraced by most of the composers with whom this chapter is concerned) it must be said that the results have been the creation of a body of music with virtually no audience.

Through the early nineteenth century, almost all classical music performed in the Western world was contemporary; the later nineteenth century was a period of rediscovery of the great music of the past and its gradual introduction into the performing repertory—but, at the same time, the audience for new works continued to be great. In the twentieth century, for the most part, music of

[7] Roger Sessions, *Roger Sessions on Music. Collected Essays*, ed. by Edward T. Cone (Princeton: Princeton University Press, 1979) pp. 163–64.
[8] Sessions, pp. 321–24.

the past dominates classical programs. This is not the place to revive the endless discussions which have sought to uncover the reasons for this repertory reversal and its impact on the performance of contemporary music. Composers have blamed performers and conductors for being unwilling to take chances with repertory; musicians and audiences have blamed composers for writing overly difficult and inaccessible music; critics have blamed everyone but themselves; historians have attempted to plumb the more profound cultural changes of the present century. The situation is not unique to music; similar problems have beset the visual arts and certain types of contemporary literature.

Statistics verify a situation already known to anyone concerned with classical music in the United States. Between 1900 and 1970, the 27 major symphony orchestras of the country played Beethoven's *Symphony No. 5* a total of 538 times; the Philadelphia Orchestra alone offered its listeners 59 performances in this 70-year period.[9] *The Black Maskers*, Roger Sessions's "popular" composition, was played 15 times by these same orchestras between 1923 and 1970. His *Symphony No. 1* received exactly two performances, the premiere by the Boston Symphony in 1926 and another reading by the Philadelphia Orchestra in 1935; *Symphony No. 2* was played 4 times by America's professional orchestras before 1970; none of his other symphonies were heard more than two times.[10] By contrast, Copland's suite drawn from his ballet *Appalachian Spring*, written in a predominantly tonal style and drawing on American folk melodies, was given 53 performances between 1945 (the year of its premier) and 1970, and George Gershwin's *An American in Paris* (1925), poised somewhere between American popular music and nineteenth-century symphonic style, was played 54 times before 1970.

The music of Roger Sessions offers the listener little to grasp at first hearing. It is abstract music, without a program. In the words of the American critic and composer Virgil Thompson, it is music about other music. In harmony, melody, and texture it is fearsomely complex. A thoughtful critic wrote of "When Lilacs Last in the Dooryard Bloom'd":

I found the cantata, like all Sessions' later music, difficult to embrace at first acquaintance. Only after the harmonies of a Sessions score have

[9] These statistics were compiled from Kate Hevner Mueller, *Twenty-Seven American Symphony Orchestras. A History and Analysis of Their Repertoires* (Bloomington: Indiana University Press, 1973).

[10] For another contrast, Brahms's *Symphony No. 4* was played 388 times by these orchestras between 1931 and 1970.

been heard several times, I find, do they begin to make proper sense. What sounded like ever-defeating density of texture is revealed as an energetic, lucid progress of lines, in which the movement of the various themes is clearly perceptible. Even the full-throated lyricism of the melodies is not evident from the start. It takes time to sort out background and foreground, to get one's bearings. When that is done, the scores disclose their merits—so clearly that one is amazed they could ever have been imperfectly perceived. But perseverance is needed; and champions are needed, too, to provide the opportunity for it. Sessions' music is not played as often as it should be; the public gets little chance of overcoming its possible first bafflement.[11]

When Schoenberg and his contemporaries first began writing atonal and then serial music, certain critics maintained that it was merely a matter of time before audiences found this repertory as accessible to the ear as any other music, pointing out that audiences in the past had trouble with the music of Beethoven, Wagner, Debussy, when it was first performed. But music with no clearly perceivable links to the melodic and harmonic language of the eighteenth and nineteenth centuries has continued to baffle listeners; most of Schoenberg's music is as difficult today as it was a half-century ago. Perhaps listeners would learn to respond to it with repeated hearings, but few have been willing to make the effort.

The cultural, historical, and moral issues surrounding this situation are complex, but an inescapable fact remains—certain twentieth-century European composers have produced music that twentieth-century audiences cannot or will not respond to in any positive way. Roger Sessions and his peers based their style and their aesthetics on such music. They have shared its fate.

Concerning Sessions's second point—that Americans should be willing to assimilate European composers and their music—it cannot have escaped even the most casual reader of the present book that the most important theme developed in each of the preceding chapters has been the blending of stylistic elements of two or more sorts of music brought to the United States from elsewhere.

The first classical music brought to this country in the eighteenth century was brought into a void, into a land with no musical traditions. The situation was vastly different in the 1930s, however. There were dozens of professional orchestras, sizable audiences in a number of cities and towns, native-born performers capable of holding their own against European musicians, and a century-old tradition of the composition of classical pieces by

American composers. For several decades, native composers had been moving toward a style that reflected something of America's indigenous music, something of the character of the American people. American audiences were beginning to respond to some of this music.

European composers, fleeing the holocaust in Europe, quite naturally found such music of less interest than the music of their own culture. Stravinsky's reaction was typical:

> I fear that in some ways the American composer is more isolated today than he was in 1925. He has at present a strong tendency to say, "We'll leave all of that *avant garde* stuff to Europe and develop our own musical style, an American way." [But] compared to Webern, for example, most of our simple homespun "American style" is fatuous in expression and in technique the vilest cliché. In the phrase "American music," "American" not only robs emphasis from "music" but it asks for lower standards.[12]

Surely Stravinsky was a composer of greater genius than was Roy Harris, and had a more profound grasp of the techniques, traditions, and aesthetic bases of western European classical composition. Schoenberg had a much firmer grasp of compositional devices than did George Gershwin. Bartók was vastly more skilled and imaginative than John Alden Carpenter. Younger American composers would have been foolish not to learn from these men, to take advantage of their presence in the New World, to benefit from opportunities to know their music. What happened, however, was that American composers in effect started all over again, rather than blending elements of foreign music with the emerging American musical language. In following this path, they also asked their listeners to begin again, to forget earlier attempts at an American style, to attempt to come to terms with a musical language making no reference to cultural, aesthetic, or musical elements of their own country—a musical language, furthermore, that was proving to be extraordinarily difficult for audiences even of the cultures out of which it was growing.

By this act of starting from scratch, classical music in the 1930s, '40s, and '50s took a very different path from that followed by virtually every other musical genre—popular music, jazz, church music, dance music—in which new musical currents were welcomed and absorbed, but were grafted onto what already existed.

[12] Igor Stravinsky and Robert Craft, *Conversations with Igor Stravinsky* (Garden City: Doubleday & Company, 1959) pp. 129–30.

Walter Piston (1894–1976) was perhaps the most successful American classical composer of this time, in terms of performance frequency. Born in Portland Maine, he went with his family to Boston in 1905, where he acquired some skill on the piano and violin. A graduate of the Massachusetts Normal Art School and a professional draftsman, his fascination with music eventually persuaded him to resume his schooling, this time in music at Harvard University, which he entered as a freshman at the age of twenty-six. Several years of study in Paris with Nadia Boulanger followed, and in 1926 he returned to Boston, taking a teaching position at Harvard, where he remained until his retirement in 1960.

Thus his musical training and his musical orientation was toward European music and, like Sessions, he had no inclination to introduce "American" musical elements into his compositions.

> The use of folk-tunes and other Americana, instead of using one's own melodic ideas, is based, I think, on a naively mistaken conception of the nature of musical expression. Ours is a big country and we are a people possessing a multitude of different origins. We already have a large literature of music by native composers. The outstanding characteristic noticeable in this music is its great diversity. If a composer desires to serve the cause of American music he will best do it by remaining true to himself as an individual and not by trying to discover musical formulas for Americanism.[13]

Piston was fortunate in being located in Boston, where Serge Koussevitzky (1874–1951) had assumed the conductorship of the Boston Symphony Orchestra in 1924, a tenure that would last for a quarter-century. Of all conductors in America, Koussevitzky was most active in support of contemporary music, most determined that living composers (including Americans) should have the chance to hear their music.

Piston's *Symphony No. 1*, written in 1927, was premiered by the Boston Symphony that same year. Piston's wider reputation as a composer began with a ballet suite, *The Incredible Flutist*, written the following year. It has been his most widely performed and often-recorded composition, holding a position in his career comparable to *The Black Maskers* by Sessions. And with *Symphony No. 2* of 1943–44, his reputation was firmly established. Premiered by the National Symphony of Washington under Hans Kindler in 1944, it was played later that year by five major orchestras, was awarded the Music Critics' Circle award as the best new composition of the year,

[13] David Ewen, ed., *The Book of Modern Composers* (New York: Alfred A. Knopf, 1950), p. 497.

and was played the following season in Pittsburgh and Rochester. His *Symphony No. 3* of 1947 was awarded the Pulitzer Prize for musical composition, and other performances, awards, and commissions for new works came in a steady stream. He eventually produced eight symphonies, other orchestral works including concertos for violin, piano, oboe, and viola, and a string of chamber works.

Almost all of Piston's music is written in the large forms of the eighteenth and nineteenth centuries—the symphony, concerto, string quartet, various kinds of sonatas and contrapuntal forms. Individual movements can be understood in terms of the formal patterns and procedures of the Baroque, Classical, and Romantic eras of western European music. Harmonies are more complex than those of the nineteenth century, but they still take the triad as their point of reference; tonality is often shifting and temporarily obscured, but still a basic element of larger structures. Thus, it is possible to analyze, and often to hear, Piston's music with reference to the compositional procedures of the previous two centuries. His *String Quartet No. 2* (1935),[14] for instance, begins with a slow canonic introduction establishing the tonal center of A; the first movement is structured in sonata-allegro form, with two clearly contrasting themes and keys, a development, and a recapitulation; the second movement, in extended binary form, is built on a contrasting key center; the final movement, a rondo, returns to the original tonality and ends on a resounding triad. Overlaying these familiar formal patterns are two additional levels of unity: the derivation of almost all thematic material of the three movements from the original motif of the introduction, and pervasive use of contrapuntal development, giving stylistic unity to the several movements.

Perhaps it is Piston's persistent and often audible utilization of formal and harmonic patterns drawn from the music of the past that has made his compositions more accessible to modern audiences than the music of Sessions.

Several American composers found their own way to the musical style of the modern European school before its composers made their way to American soil. Wallingford Riegger (1885–1961) was born into a German-American family in which "discipline, work, and duty, both practical and moral, were at the core of a family life in which love of music and literature was also central."[15] After

---

[14] NW 302, s1. Piston's *Symphony No. 6* is available on NW 286, s1.
[15] Richard F. Goldman, "The Music of Wallingford Riegger," *The Musical Quarterly*, XXXVI (January 1950), p. 41.

study of theory and the cello in New York, Riegger made his way to Germany for further study in Berlin. He did not take up composition seriously until his return to America when, at the age of thirty-five, he wrote a *Trio in B minor* (1919–20) in a conservative Germanic style. Displeased with his own work, Riegger devoted himself to several years of studying the music of Schoenberg and other modern European composers; the orchestral *Rhapsody* (1926) and a *Study in Sonority* (1926–27) for ten violins retained the instrumental writing of the nineteenth century but veered sharply toward free atonality. Within a few years, in his *Suite* for flute of 1929, he was moving in the direction of pitch control by means of a twelve-tone row, and with *Dichotomy* for chamber orchestra (1931–32) he fully embraced serial techniques. His *String Quartet No. 1* (1938–39) takes the final step, with every detail of the composition permeated and controlled by a single row of twelve tones. His style changed in his later years, but is always defined by careful, rational planning of every aspect of composition and a fondness for contrapuntal writing.

Typical is his *Woodwind Quintet* (Opus 51, 1952).[16] Sharp, polyrhythmic atonal staccato chords punctuate cadenzalike solo lines, which are relieved by brief imitative and canonic sections. Without analyzing the score, one cannot relate vertical sonorities to keys or key centers, or sort the horizontal unfolding of material into a succession of movements or sections. There is much of the sound of Stravinsky in the reiterated chords and brief ostinato passages, and much of the playful woodwind mood of Paul Hindemith's *Kleine Kammermusik* of 1922. This is not to suggest that Riegger was an unusually derivative composer, merely to point out that stylistic references are to European rather than American composers.

Adolph Weiss (1891–1971), born in Baltimore of German parents, was a professional bassoonist while still in his teens, in New York, Chicago, and Rochester. Finding his way to Berlin, he became the first American composition student of Arnold Schoenberg. He composed in his own version of the twelve-tone system, though he sometimes used shorter sequences of notes as building materials. Of his various orchestral, chamber, vocal, and keyboard compositions, the most successful—in terms of performances and critical attention—was *American Life* (1928),[17] subtitled "scherzoso Jazzoso," for orchestra. Premiered in New York in 1931 and performed again in June of that year in Paris on a program of American orchestral pieces, it was perceived to "reflect our sentimentality, our nervous energy, and something of our morbid love of the sen-

[16] NW 285, s1 / 2.
[17] NW 228, s2 / 1.

sational."[18] Despite its title, the piece has little to do with American musical materials; there is reference to what the nonblack world thought of as jazz in the 1920s. But in its harmonic patterns and orchestral language, it is closer to the attempts by such European composers as Milhaud, Honegger, Hindemith, Weill, and Křenek to incorporate elements of jazz into symphonic composition. Many touches of Schoenberg's orchestral writing peek through, and one is left with the impression that if Schoenberg himself had ever attempted to write a jazz-influenced piece, it would have sounded very much like this. The piece was not recorded until 1977; a comment in the liner notes could serve as an epitaph for Weiss and many of his contemporaries who chose the same musical directions: "Yet despite high critical esteem and such honors as a Guggenheim Fellowship (1931) and membership in the National Academy of Arts and Letters (1955), little of his music has commanded general attention."[19]

The career and music of Ross Lee Finney, born in Wells, Minnesota in 1906, follow the currents dominating American composition in the third, fourth, and fifth decades of the present century. Between 1927 and 1932 Finney studied with Nadia Boulanger in Paris, with Sessions, and then with Alban Berg in Vienna. His works of the 1930s have been characterized as being in an "eclectic international style";[20] such pieces as a violin concerto, three string quartets, and several sonatas for violin and viola earned him Guggenheim and Pulitzer fellowships.

When serialism began sweeping the land in the 1950s, Finney turned to increasingly complex manipulations of twelve-tone rows. Pitches began to be serialized in his *Violin Sonata No. 2* (1950) and *No. 3* (1953), *Variations on a Theme by Alban Berg* for piano (1952), and *Variations for Orchestra* (1958). The next step was to join various of his European and American peers in experimenting with the serialization of elements other than pitch—duration and structural elements—in such works as *Concerto for Percussion* (1965).

His latest compositions relax such tightly structural manipulation, though he retains elements of serialism. Typical is *Concerto for Alto Saxophone and Orchestra of Wind Instruments* (1974).[21] The structural materials are not a complete twelve-tone row, but rather eight tones, selected to form two diminished triads. Since this chord

[18] Adolph Weiss, in Henry Cowell, ed., *American Composers on American Music* (Stanford University Press, 1933), p. 17.

[19] R. D. Darrell, liner notes for NW 228, p. 4.

[20] Edith Boroff, article on "Ross Lee Finney" in Stanley Sadie, ed., *The New Grove Dictionary of Music and Musicians* (London: Macmillan Publishers Limited, 1980), VI, p. 592.

[21] NW 211, s2 / 1.

suggests an incomplete dominant to the ear, the piece is permeated with horizontal and vertical combinations of tones suggesting strongly dominant harmony—which never resolves.

Among the most successful American serialists in terms of critical acclaim and awards—two Guggenheim fellowships, two Fromm Foundation awards, a citation from the National Institute of Arts and Letters—was Ben Weber (1916–80). Typical of his mature output is a *Sonata da camera* for violin and piano (1950).[22] Like Schoenberg, he often cast his twelve-tone material in classical forms. This piece, rhapsodic, intense, and brooding in character, is shaped into a saraband, a passacaglia, and a rondo. Highly skilled in musical craftsmanship, it is nevertheless indistinguishable in general style and character from other music being written in various parts of the Western world in the post-Schoenbergian era.

Elliott Carter stands somewhat apart in his wider-ranging eclecticism, his fascination with the music of at least one American composer (Charles Ives), and his intellectual confrontation of those aspects of American culture and music that make it unique.

Born in New York City in 1908 and educated at Harvard (where his teachers included Piston) and in France under Nadia Boulanger, he had a thorough exposure to the music of the major European composers of the past and present. But he also investigated the compositions of Ives (whom he knew personally), Ruggles, Copland, Scriabin, Holst, and other writers of the twentieth century whose music was not fashionable in academic circles of the East; he came to know something of the music of several non-Western cultures; and friendship with the young musicologist Stephen Tuttle aroused his interest in older music, as far back as Machaut. An early composition for chorus, "To Music,"[23] set to a poem by Robert Herrick, suggests something of his wide-ranging musical tastes, reflecting both the English madrigal school and the choral music of Paul Hindemith.

His first pieces written after his return to America in 1935 are in what he called a "populist style," reflecting a "political sympathy" with the desire to create a national style.[24] Among these were the ballet suite *Pocahontas* (1938–39); *Three Poems of Robert Frost* for voice and piano (1943); and *The Harmony of the Morning*, for female voices and small orchestra (1944). He deliberately avoided any suggestion of the dodecaphonic music of Schoenberg and Webern, so as to reflect nothing of the "madness that led to Hitler."

[22] NW 281, s1 / 2.
[23] NW 219, s1 / 6.
[24] Elliott Carter, *The Writings of Elliott Carter. An American Composer Looks at Modern Music* (Bloomington and London: Indiana University Press, 1977), p. 347.

A recent photograph of Elliott Carter.

The postwar years brought a "thoroughgoing reassessment of musical materials in the hope of finding a way of expressing what seemed to be more important matters—or at least more personal ones."[25] The *Piano Sonata* (1945) and *Wind Quintet* (1948) were products of this time, and with *Eight Etudes and a Fantasy* for wind quintet (1950) he became even more involved with "the nature of musical ideas," exploring compositional devices based on contrasts of tone colors and attacks. His major concern came to be with complex ways of organizing time within a musical composition:

At the same time, a whole complex of notions about rhythm, meter, and timing became a central preoccupation. In a sense, this was explored according to the principles of "clock," or in this case "metronomic" time, but its relationship to the jazz of the thirties and forties that combined free improvisation with strict time, and with early and non-Western music, as well as that of Alexander Scriabine, Ives, and Conlon Nancar-

[25] Carter, p. 347.

row, made me always look toward ways that could incorporate into "musical time" the methods that interested me.[26]

In the *Cello Sonata* (1948), the piano and cello appear to go off in independent directions at times; coordination comes from inter-locking and superimposed figures.

*Cello Sonata*, by Elliott Carter.

A device seen for the first time in this piece is what the composer calls "metric modulation"—one instrument keeps to a steady rhythmical pattern while the other gradually accelerates or slows down to a new tempo.

Carter's *String Quartet No. 1* (1950–51), a *Sonata* for flute, oboe, cello, and harpsichord (1952), and *Varations* for orchestra (1954–55) involve further attempts to have several instruments move according to individual rhythmic, thematic, and metric patterns, while still coordinated with one another. After a period of reflection and sketching, Carter wrote two pieces in 1959–60 which are among the most impressive compositions by an American of the entire twentieth century.

The *String Quartet No. 2*, premiered in 1959 by the Stanley String Quartet, was awarded the Pulitzer Prize for musical composition,

---

[26] Carter, pp. 348–49.

the New York Critic's Circle Award as the best new piece of the year, and a special UNESCO prize in 1961. As Carter himself describes the piece:

> Each of the four instruments has a repertory of musical characters of its own, while contributing to the total effect in many different capacities, sometimes following, sometimes opposing the leader, usually according to its own capabilities—that is, according to the repertory of expression, continuity, interval, and rhythmic patterns assigned to it. Each is treated as an "individual," usually making an effort to cooperate, especially when this seems helpful in carrying on the musical enterprise.[27]

The *Double Concerto*, first played in 1961, opposed two small orchestras, one with a harpsichord as solo instrument and the other a piano. Rejecting the notion of two simultaneous bodies of music in an uncoordinated relationship to one another, Carter rather created a piece in which

> antiphonal percussion establishes the basic rhythmic oscillations, suggesting the "giant polyrhythms" that underlie the whole structure. Moving inwards, these are gradually associated with the intervallic sets and the combined figures then developed in characteristic gestures by the keyboards in long concertante dialogues that lead towards and away from the work's centre.[28]

Summing up his intentions in these two pieces, Carter says:

> These works depend on a special dimension of time, that of "multiple perspective," in which various contrasting characters are presented simultaneously. Double and sometimes manifold character simultaneities, of course, present, as our human experience often does, certain emotionally charged events as seen in the context of others, producing often a kind of irony, which I am particularly interested in. I have, I think, been trying to make moments of music as rich in reference as I could and to do something that can be done only in music and yet that has rarely been achieved except in opera.[29]

These pieces, and also his *Piano Concerto* (1964–65), *Concerto for Orchestra* (1969), *String Quartet No. 3* (1971), *Duo for Violin and Piano* (1974), and *A Symphony of Three Orchestras* (1976–77, commissioned by the New York Philharmonic for the American Bicen-

---

[27] Carter, p. 353.
[28] Bayan Northcott, "Elliott Carter," *The New Grove Dictionary of Music and Musicians*, III, p. 834.
[29] Carter, p. 356.

tennial Celebration), have been hailed as staggering intellectual and musical achievements.

As do virtually all of the compositions discussed in this chapter, Carter's music has an uncompromising intellectual basis stemming from a conviction that the best music is the product of rational processes. It is ferociously difficult, uncompromisingly so, for performers and audience alike, and has consequently proved to be inaccessible to all but a handful of dedicated performers and listeners. His career underlines the fact that the gulf between audiences and certain types of contemporary composition has grown ever wider in the second half of the twentieth century, despite the work of the most talented and highly praised composers.

Of the next generation of American composers of this persuasion, none has been more acclaimed by critics than Leon Kirchner, born in Brooklyn in 1919. A talented pianist and conductor, he studied with Schoenberg at UCLA, had contact with Bloch at Berkeley, and returned to the East in 1942 to study with Sessions. Though he absorbed elements of the music of these teachers and other major European composers of the day, and though his music has been described as "combin[ing] aspects of Schoenberg without the row, Stravinsky without *ostinati*, Bartók without the folk element, Berg without 'weltschmerz,' and Sessions without excessive intellectual scruples,"[30] these influences were incorporated into a style recognizably his own from early in his career.

The *Piano Concerto No. 1*,[31] composed in 1953 and premiered in 1956 by the New York Philharmonic Society with Kirchner himself as soloist, may be taken as a fair sample of his compositional techniques and expressive goals. The piece is an expansive, grand work that invokes the spirit of the virtuoso concertos of Liszt and Chopin; it is a showpiece for the soloist, sprinkled with passages and cadenzas requiring great technique and showmanship. The first movement unfolds a series of energetic, restless motifs slipping in and out of audible references to tonality; the piano predominates, rarely resting, with the orchestra in a supporting role or joining the piano in contrapuntal statements. After a climax, there is a quieter and slower section, with delicate piano passagework alternating with the orchestra, then a return to the faster tempo of the beginning, a recapitulation in tempo and mood if not in discernible thematic material. A cadenza leads to a soft, slow ending. This movement, with its fast-slow-fast shape, reflects the overall struc-

[30] Alexander Ringer, "Leon Kirchner," *The Musical Quarterly*, XLIII (1957), p. 19.
[31] NW 286, p. 2.

ture of the concerto, suggesting certain of Bartók's mature pieces in which the shape of an individual movement mirrors the structure of the entire work.

Kirchner's slow (second) movement unfolds as a dramatic dialogue between the piano, playing mostly lyric passages, and the orchestra, featuring more emphatic and often recitativelike phrases. Surely the slow movement of Beethoven's *Piano Concerto No. 4* served as a model. The third movement is again fast, more spirited than the first, and sharing with it a fast-slow-fast shape, giving symmetry on several levels to the entire composition.

Thus the entire concerto represents nineteenth-century designs and musical gestures laced with harmonic and melodic idioms of the twentieth.

Kirchner has continued to compose slowly, carefully, and successfully, in terms of critical acclaim. Among his subsequent pieces have been three string quartets (written in 1949, 1958, and 1966), a second piano concerto (1963), various works for voice and for piano, and an opera, *Lily* (1977), based on Saul Bellow's novel *Henderson the Rain King*. Since 1961 he has been at Harvard University as Walter Bigelow Rosen Professor of Music, succeeding Walter Piston in this chair.

Kirchner was one of dozens of American composers turning out symphonic, chamber, and vocal works of highly professional quality during this period. No country in the world can match the quantity and the sustained excellence of American composition in the middle decades of the twentieth century. No doubt the circumstances related above—the presence of so many great composers and teachers—help account for this abundance of riches; the high quality of performance and instrumental teaching, the presence of so many outstanding orchestras of high professional quality, and the massive proliferation of musical instruction at all levels of American education after World War II are also factors. The compositions of William Schuman,[32] David Diamond,[33] Ingolf Dahl,[34] and Vincent Perischetti[35] represent virtually no drop in quality and professionalism from the works of the composers discussed above, and a slightly younger generation—Gunther Schuller,[36] Lukas Foss,[37] Ralph Shapey,[38] Peter Mennin,[39] and many others—benefit-

[32] Cf. the piece for modern dance, *Undertow*, on NW 253, s1.
[33] Cf. his *Symphony No. 4*, on NW 258, s1.
[34] Cf. *Concertino à Tre*, on NW 281, s2 / 2.
[35] Cf. *Pageant* (for concert band), on NW 211, s1 / 1.
[36] Cf. *String Quartet No. 2*, on NW 212, s2.
[37] Cf. *Capriccio for Cello and Piano*, on NW 281, s2 / 1.
[38] Cf. *Configurations* for flute and piano, on NW 254, s2 / 1.
[39] Cf. *Symphony No. 7*, on NW 258, s2.

ted from the experience and teaching of Sessions, Piston, and their peers, and often reveal in their compositions an even more formidable grasp of complex compositional techniques.

Sessions has produced numerous students who have taken their place among the most productive and critically acclaimed composers of the present day. Andrew Imbrie is typical. Born in New York in 1921, he studied with Sessions for some ten years, and also spent a summer with Nadia Boulanger in Paris. He has been a steadily productive composer for several decades, turning out a succession of pieces cast in the forms of European music of the eighteenth and nineteenth centuries—three symphonies, three concertos for piano and orchestra, four string quartets, several operas, and numerous smaller works for smaller combinations of instruments and voices. The music of Sessions and Bartók was most important to him in his formative years; in his own words, he "does not strive to be American like my nationality, nor Scottish like my ancestry."[40] His prose conveys a sense of what his music is all about:

> [*String Quartet No. 4*] is not a serial composition, nor does it adhere to any other formal, precompositional rules. Composing for me is a process of drawing out the consequences of an initial idea. This idea may present itself as contour, resonance, rhythm, gesture, or some combination of these. Once the idea has become specific enough, it begins to generate its own continuation. This is possible because every idea worthy of the name is fraught with potential energy; its components interact so as to create an expectation of forward movement. The energies released by the first forward impulse eventually expend themselves to a point where they create a demand for contrast; yet the character of the new material is very much conditioned by that of the old. Thus the original idea generates not only its own continuation but the nature of its own opposite as well.[41]

The music of this quartet[42] develops in uncompromisingly linear fashion. Though pitches are not organized in systematic serial fashion, the unaided ear cannot distinguish Imbrie's free atonal style from serial writing. One senses a pervasive forward linear propulsion, brought about by the shape and rhythmic design of individual lines; some sense of formal shape emerges from the alternation of smaller sections within movements (the first movement progresses from an *allegro con moto* through an *andantino,*

[40] Philip Ramey, liner notes for NW 212.
[41] Ramey, NW 212.
[42] NW 212, s1.

then back to the original tempo); the musical gestures often suggest the late quartets of Beethoven or Bartók.

Anton Webern (1883–1945), once a student and associate of Arnold Schoenberg, had chosen to remain in Germany and Austria, where he developed a highly distinctive dialect of serial writing. He moved further and further away from any obvious aural dependence on melodic and formal shapes of the nineteenth century. He began organizing not only pitches, but other elements of his compositions as well. Many of the leading composers of postwar Europe turned to Webern as a model. Olivier Messiaen (b. 1908) worked with systematic organization of rhythms as well as pitches in *Mode de valeurs et d'intensities* (1949) and other pieces. Karlheinz Stockhausen (b. 1928), leader of the younger German composers springing from the ashes of the Third Reich, emulated the pointillistic sonorities of Webern in *Kontra-Punkte* (1952–53) and other early works. Pierre Boulez (b. 1925), in *Structures I* for two pianos (1952–53), took a decisive step in the direction of what would soon be called totally organized music—pitches, rhythmic durations, and dynamics were all ordered according to precompositional sequences based on the number twelve (the number of pitches in a chromatic scale).

Milton Babbitt was the first American composer to move in similar directions. Born in St. Louis in 1916, trained as a mathematician, and a student of Roger Sessions in composition, his first pieces were marked by a strong sense of rational, balanced formal structures. As he put it himself:

> I believe in cerebral music—in the application of intellect to relevant matters. I never choose a note unless I know precisely why I want it there and can give several reasons why it and not another.[43]

His compositional attitudes and techniques were honed through study and analysis of music which appealed to his rational mind. His compositions from the late '40s—*Composition for Four Instruments* (1948), *Composition for 12 Instruments* (1948), *Three Compositions* for piano (1947), "Du" for voice and piano (1951)—reveal his preoccupation with intensely rational material. These remained unknown to all but a small circle of fellow composers, students, and performers dedicated to new music; rather than seeing this as

---

[43] Milton Babbitt, "Some Aspects of Twelve-Tone Composition," *The Score and IMA Magazine* XII (June 1955), p. 53.

an unfortunate or negative situation, Babbitt assumed the most defiant stance ever taken by a composer toward his audience:

> Why refuse to recognize the possibility that contemporary music has reached a stage long since attained by other forms of activity? The time has passed when the normally well-educated man without special preparation can understand the most advanced work in, for example, mathematics, philosophy, and physics. Advanced music, to the extent that it reflects the knowledge and originality of the informed composer, scarcely can be expected to appear more intelligible than these arts and sciences to the person whose musical education usually has been even less extensive than his background in other fields.
>
> I dare suggest that the composer would do himself and his music an immediate and eventual service by total, resolute, and voluntary withdrawal from this public world to one of private performance and electronic media, with its very real possibility of complete elimination of the public and social aspects of musical composition. By so doing, the separation between the domains would be defined beyond any possibility of confusion of categories, and the composer would be free to pursue a private life of professional achievement, as opposed to a public life of unprofessional compromise and exhibitionism.[44]

His *Post-Partitions* for piano (1966)[45] epitomizes his compositional methods and attitudes. A sequel to an earlier piece for piano—*Partitions* (1957)—it is based on the same twelve-tone row as the earlier piece; both compositions partition the keyboard into four registers, which are coordinated with four segments of the tone row. Twelve dynamic levels are used, ranging from *pppp* to *ffff*, with the choice of dynamic marking for a given note or group of notes determined by reference to precompositional sequences related to those employed for pitch and register selection. Rhythmic durations and articulation are determined according to similar procedures. Even with these restraints, Babbitt manages to quote material from several piano pieces by Sessions, including his *Piano Sonata No. 1* and a section from *From My Diary*. None of these matters are apparent to a listener, unless he or she has made a careful and detailed study and analysis of the place before listening to it.

Babbitt was a consultant for the David Sarnoff Laboratories in Princeton during the building of the Mark II RCA Music Synthesizer. He thus had access to the first sophisticated electronic music

---

[44] Milton Babbitt, "Who Cares if you Listen?," *High Fidelity*, VIII / 2 (February 1958), pp. 39–40.
[45] NW 209, s2 / 2.

studio in America, and produced a series of electronic pieces in the 1960s including *Composition for Synthesizer* (1961) and *Ensembles for Synthesizer* (1962–64). He was also one of the first American composers to combine live and electronic sounds, in his *Vision and Prayer* for voice and tape (1961) and *Philomel* for the same combination (1964). *Phonemena*, (1969–70)[46] was written for voice and piano in his usual tightly controlled style; in 1974 the instrumental part was synthesized on tape at the Columbia-Princeton Center ("The piano version and the synthesized tape are meant to be musically identical in every respect except timbre").[47]

The career and compositions of George Rochberg can serve to sum up this era in American music.

Born in New Jersey in 1918, Rochberg received a thorough grounding in theory, composition, and aesthetics from his European-born teachers—Hans Weisse, George Szell, Rosario Scalero, Gian-Carlo Menotti. His first pieces—a *Trio* written in 1947, a piece for two pianos and orchestra (1950), *Night Music* (1949), *Symphony No. 1* (1949), *String Quartet No. 1* (1952)—demonstrate a remarkable skill in handling musical materials and his familarity with the music of Stravinsky, Bartók, and Hindemith. A year's study in Italy (1950–51) with Luigi Dallapiccola resulted in closer involvement with dodecaphonic techniques. *12 Bagetelles* for piano (1952) was his first "full-fledged dodecaphonic venture";[48] the next five years brought a string of twelve-tone works "so strong [in] human, if not always technical, identification with Schoenberg that his music strikes one at times as the kind Schoenberg might have written had he been born two generations later."[49] A *Chamber Symphony* (1953), several choral pieces on texts from the Old Testament, *Symphony No. 2* (1955–56), and a *Sonata-Fantasia* for piano (1956) are the most important fruits of this period.

Rochberg's interests turned in other directions, however; like so many of his European and American contemporaries, he became fascinated with the compositional techniques and the sonorities found in the late works of Anton Webern. In a series of pieces beginning with the *Cheltenham Concerto* (1958) and culminating with *String Quartet No. 2* (1959–61), Rochberg incorporated much of the fragmented, pointillistic sonority of the Austrian composer's style into his own work:

[46] NW 209, s1 / 1–2. *Reflections* (1974), for piano and synthesized tape, is available on NW 209, s1 / 4.
[47] Eric Salzman, liner notes for NW 209, p. 3.
[48] Alexander Ringer, "The Music of George Rochberg," *The Musical Quarterly*, LII (1966), p. 412.
[49] Ringer, p. 414.

*String Quartet No. 2 (with Soprano)*, by George Rochberg

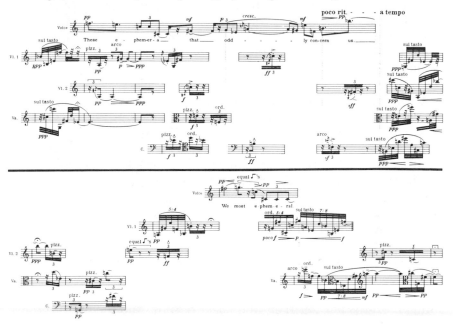

And even though Rochberg never embraced the totally organized techniques of Boulez and Babbitt, he did become concerned for a while with the "use of a basic row in all its possible forms and at many levels of transposition,"[50] and with systematic organization of durations.

As early as 1953, in his *Chamber Symphony*, Rochberg had quoted fragments of another composer's work—Dallapiccola's *Il prigioniero*. In the mid-1960s, extensive quotation from other composers became a dominant component of his style. *Contra mortem et tempus* (1965) draws on bits of pieces by Berio, Boulez, Berg, Varèse, Ives, and Rochberg himself. The middle section of *Music for the Magic Theater* (1965) is essentially a transcription of the adagio movement of Mozart's *Divertimento*, K. 287, combined with quotations from Mahler, Webern, Beethoven, Varèse, Stockhausen, and again Rochberg; *Nach Bach* (1966), a fantasy for harpsichord, is a "parody" of the *Partita No. 6* (E minor) by J. S. Bach.

The 1970s saw Rochberg move even closer to European music of the eighteenth and nineteenth centuries. *String Quartet No. 3* (1972) impressed critics as "approaching Beethoven and Mahler in manner"; the *Violin Concerto* (1975) was largely tonal and triadic, filled

[50] Ringer, p. 419.

with the gestures of the nineteenth century, and was hailed by some as ushering in an era of neoromanticism; and a series of string quartets incorporate sharply contrasting styles within a single piece: one movement may invoke Beethoven, another Mahler, another Berg—not only in musical style, but also in quotation of material.

What is one to make of all this? Surely Rochberg's personality and musical instincts supply a unifying thread to these compositions resulting from his "succession of intensive engagements with many of the major aesthetic issues of his time."[51] And he is far from the first composer to embrace a series of different aesthetic and technical ideals in the course of a lengthy career. But one aesthetic issue which seems not to have engaged Rochberg is the question of how American life and culture differ from that of European countries; and among the various composers who have commanded his attention, none has been American.

American classical composers of this era reached heights never before attained by native-born musicians in compositional skill, technical and analytical understanding of how music of the past and present is put together, and sheer output. And the men whose music is the subject of the present chapter were recognized for their efforts, with fellowships and grants, prizes, critical praise, the esteem of their peers, and teaching positions in America's leading universities and schools of music, allowing them the necessary time and energy to compose.

The nineteenth century had brought a major sociological change to the musical life of Europe and America. Public concerts, and truly public performances of opera, became the chief media for the dissemination of classical music; a dramatic increase in musical literacy made it possible for more people than ever before, from a wider range of economic and social backgrounds, to be involved in the performance of music. The contemporary music of the greatest appeal to this new mass audience was either related to a text or a program—opera, song, instrumental music with a descriptive title or program—or was geared to their own performance abilities. Though music of the past made up a larger part of the repertory as the century progressed, and audiences and performers sometimes grumbled at harmonic innovations of contemporary music, the music of the most talented and important writers of the nineteenth century—Wagner, Verdi, Liszt, Chopin, Schubert, Mendelssohn,

<hr>

[51] Austin Clarkson, "George Rochberg," *The New Grove Dictionary of Music and Musicians*, XVI, p. 81.

Bellini, Schumann, Tchaikovsky, Brahms (to some extent)—was widely performed, and they were fully functioning members of a composer-performer-audience interaction.

Sessions, Piston, Kirchner, Carter, Babbitt, and their peers rejected the notion that a composer should offer audiences some easy accessibility to his music, or that it should be geared to the performance level of nonprofessional musicians.

Their music has become again the almost exclusive property of an elite—not of the nobility and aristocracy, but an intellectual and artistic elite centered not in castles and palaces, but in the leading colleges and universities of the United States.

# 19

## The American Avant-Garde

Everything we do is music.

—John Cage

At just the same time that most American composers were turning to the music of Schoenberg, Stravinsky, Bartók, and Webern for direction, a few of their contemporaries were setting off on a quite different course.

They looked to the twentieth century, rather than the nineteenth or eighteenth, for musical and aesthetic inspiration. Non-Western music was of as much interest to them as that of their own culture. They did not at first constitute a unified school of composition; they were individuals, existing on the fringes of American musical life. For convenience, they will be brought together here as the avant-garde; in retrospect, they had a great deal in common, and their attitudes toward society often approached those of the European avant-garde, though in the end they moved in quite different directions.

The patriarch of these men was Edgard Varèse (1883–1965). Born in Paris, Varèse had conventional training with Giovanni Bolzoni, Vincent d'Indy, Albert Roussel, and Charles Widor. He came to know Claude Debussy, Richard Strauss, and Ferruccio Busoni; he composed a number of orchestral pieces in Paris and Berlin; and his budding reputation took him to Prague in 1914, where he conducted the Czech Philharmonic in a program of contemporary

Edgard Varèse, Santa Fe, 1937.

French music. But the outbreak of World War I put a halt to such activity, and in 1915 he came to the New World.

In 1917 he conducted the Berlioz *Requiem* with such success that a number of wealthy American families, including the Guggenheims, Pulitzers, Vanderbilts, and Whitneys made it possible for him to organize the New Symphony Orchestra, which gave its first programs in Carnegie Hall on April 11–12, 1919. Varèse chose a program of new music, by Bartók, Casella, and Debussy. Neither audiences nor critics—nor sponsors, for that matter—were ready for such fare, and Varèse was forced to relinquish the orchestra, turning instead to composing, organizing concerts of new music, and encouraging other composers. On the grounds that "our official organizations occasionally place on their programs a new work surrounded by established names," but that "such a work is carefully chosen from the most timid and anemic of contemporary production, leaving absolutely unheard the composers who represent the true spirit of our time,"[1] Varèse founded the International Composers' Guild in 1921. In 1922 he became one of the cofounders of the Internationale Komponisten-Gilde in Berlin, and in 1928 he founded the Pan-American Association of Composers.

America first heard his music in the early 1920s, when several of his newest compositions were performed at concerts of the ICG: *Offrandes* (1921), premiered in New York on April 23, 1922; *Hyperprism* (1922), first heard in March of 1923; *Octandre* (1923), done in January of 1924; and *Intégrales* (1924), on March 1, 1925. The first "commercial" performance of one of his pieces came when Leopold Stokowski led the Philadelphia Orchestra in the premiere of his symphonic poem *Amèriques*.

American audiences had never heard anything like this music. And Varèse's rhetoric, on the many occasions when he commented in print on his compositions, did little to dispel the impression that he was headed for uncharted waters. He wrote of *Amèriques*:

> As a boy, the mere word "America" meant all discoveries, all adventures. It meant the unknown. And in this symbolic sense—new worlds on this planet, in outer space, and in the minds of man—I gave the title signifying "Americas" to the first work I wrote in America.[2]

Varèse appended a quotation from the *Hermetic Astronomy* of "Paracelsus the Great, monarch of Arcana" to the title page of his orchestral piece *Arcana*, first played in Philadelphia on April 8, 1927:

> One star exists higher than all the rest. This is the apocalyptic star; the second star is that of the ascendant. The third is that of the elements, and of these there are four, so that six stars are established. Besides these there is still another star, imagination, which begets a new star and a new heaven.

And the piece was described as "probing the arcane essence of the arts, designed as a macrocosmic passacaglia developing through an athematic concatenation of melorhythmic molecules."[3] *Ionization*, written in 1930–31 and "portraying in a recognizably classical sonata form the process of atomic change as electrons are liberated and molecules are ionized, the main subject suggesting a cosmic-ray bombardment,"[4] was first performed on March 6, 1933,

---

[1] Chou Wen-Chung, "Varèse: A Sketch of the Man and his Music," *The Musical Quarterly*, LII 2 (April 1966), p. 154.
[2] Wen-Chung, pp. 151–70.
[3] Nicolas Slonimsky, *Music Since 1900* (New York: Charles Scribner's Sons, 1971), p. 452.
[4] Slonimsky, p. 563.

on a concert of the Pan-American Association of Composers in New York. Speaking in more general terms of his compositional techniques, Varèse in 1936 told of his desire to create music consisting of

the movement of sound-masses, of shifting planes, taking the place of linear counterpoint. When these sound-masses collide, the phenomena of penetration or repulsion will seem to occur. Certain transmutations taking place on certain planes will seem to be projected onto other planes, moving at different speeds and at different angles. We have actually three dimensions in music: horizontal, vertical, and dynamic swelling or decreasing. I shall add a fourth, sound projection—that feeling that sound is leaving us with no hope of being reflected back, a feeling akin to that aroused by beams of light sent forth by a powerful searchlight— for the ear as for the eye, that sense of projection, of a journey into space. In the moving masses you would be conscious of their transmutations when they pass over different layers, when they penetrate certain opacities, or are dilated in certain rarefaction.[5]

He accepted the definition of music by the nineteenth-century Polish philosopher and mathematician Hoëne Wronsky (1778–1853) as "the corporealization of the intelligence that is in sounds,"[6] and began thinking of music as "bodies of intelligent sounds moving freely in space."[7] He came to prefer the term "organized sound" for his music, and often pointed out correspondences between his compositions and certain natural structures:

Conceiving musical form as a *resultant*—the result of a process—I was struck by what seemed to me an analogy between the formation of my compositions and the phenomenon of crystallization. There is an idea, the basis of an internal structure, expanding and split into different shapes or groups of sound constantly changing in shape, direction, and speed, attracted and repulsed by various forces. The form of a work is the consequence of this interaction. Possible musical forms are as limitless as the exterior forms of crystals.[8]

His compositional procedure is to state an idea, to repeat it without change, then to state other ideas in succession; as the piece unfolds, the various bits of material are superimposed in changing combinations, giving a mosaic of sound composed of a finite num-

[5] From a lecture given in 1936, quoted in Elliott Schwartz and Barney Childs, eds., *Contemporary Composers on Contemporary Music* (New York: Holt, Rinehart and Winston, 1967) p. 197.
[6] Schwartz and Childs, p. 199.
[7] Schwartz and Childs, p. 204.
[8] From a lecture given in 1959, quoted in Schwartz and Childs, p. 203.

ber of elements which constantly shift and relate to one another in different patterns. If there is precedent for this technique in European music, it is in some of the late compositions of Claude Debussy.[9]

Varèse was always fond of percussion instruments. *Amèriques,* written for large symphony orchestra, calls for 10 percussion players using a total of 21 different instruments; 8 percussionists play some 40 instruments in *Arcana; Hyperprism* is scored for 8 wind instruments and twice as many percussion, and *Ionization* was the first piece for percussion alone performed in America: 13 performers play 41 different instruments. Most audiences and critics of the day were incapable of hearing any relationships with any known music:

> Varèse's *Arcana* plunged the listener into morasses of sound which seemingly had little relation to music. There was no mercy in its disharmony, no pity in its succession of screaming, clashing, clangorous discords.[10]

Varèse gradually moved beyond the conventional instruments of Western music, always dreaming of the day when new, electronic instruments would open up new fields of sound. As early as 1927, he had discussed with scientists at the Bell Telephone Laboratories the possibility of electronic sound production; *Ecuatorial* (1933–34) made use of two electric instruments built to his specifications by Thérémin; *Déserts* (1949–54) has sections of "electronically organized sound," created on a tape recorder and reworked at the Studio d'Essai of the Radiodiffusion Française, alternating with a small orchestra of wind and percussion instruments; and his *Poème électronique* (1957–58) is a fully electronic piece, created for the Philips Pavillion (designed by Le Corbusier for the Brussel's World's Fair in 1958):

> It is the musical part of a spectacle of sound and light, presented during the Brussels Exposition in the pavilion designed for the Philips Corporation of Holland by Le Corbusier, who was also the author of the visual part. It consisted of moving colored lights, images projected on the walls of the pavilion, and music. The music was distributed by 425 loudspeakers; there were twenty amplifier combinations. It was recorded on a three-track magnetic tape that could be varied in intensity and quality. The loudspeakers were mounted in groups and in what is called "sound

[9] Ronald Lee Byrnside, *Debussy's Second Style* (Urbana: University of Illinois, unpublished doctoral dissertation, 1971).
[10] Oscar Thompson, *Musical America*, April 23, 1927.

routes" to achieve various effects such as that of the music running around the pavilion, as well as coming from different directions, reverberations, etc.

For the first time I heard my music literally projected into space.[11]

Even more spectacular was the projected *Espace*, a sound montage created by broadcasts from different parts of the world, "Voices in the sky, filling all space, crisscrossing, overlapping, penetrating each other, splitting up, superimposing, repulsing each other, colliding, crashing together . . ."[12]

Though he did not live to complete the piece and the technology of the time would not have been capable of producing it, he was until the very end exploring the unknown.

The piece signaling the birth of the American avant-garde was the *Ballet mécanique* by George Antheil. From the moment of its first performance in Paris in 1926, it received as much attention from the press as any single composition of the 1920s, and it was perceived as rooted completely in the twentieth century.

Born in Trenton, New Jersey, on July 8, 1900, Antheil studied at the Philadelphia Conservatory of Music and was a private composition student of Ernest Bloch. Hailed as a brilliant young pianist in Germany and France in the early 1920s, his activity as a performer was soon eclipsed by the furor over his compositions. First came a set of brief sonatas for piano, described by Antheil as "anti-expressive, anti-romantic, coldly mechanical." Many European and American artists and critics were obsessed at just this time with notions of how the various arts might reflect the "Age of the Machine." As one of Antheil's peers wrote of him:

He was not tempered by the sophistication of our larger towns, not ripened under a western sun or made dreamy under a southern moon; no mountains caused him to contemplate the Deity, no chill wind in the north made him austere and pessimistic. It was the factories themselves among which he was born, the exquisite functioning of powerful machines, and all the sleek, ominous, piercing sounds that accompany them, which pounded on his brain and made him seek escape, to transform and interpret. His fellow-citizens, under similar stresses, found outlet chiefly in the movies and jazz. It is in the interpretation of manifest industrialism and of the spirit of popular music that Antheil speaks most naturally and authentically.[13]

[11] From a lecture given in 1959, quoted in Schwartz and Childs, pp. 206–7.
[12] Quoted in Wen-Chung, p. 166.
[13] Randall Thompson, "George Antheil," *Modern Music*, VIII(1931), pp. 17–18.

Antheil himself had a different story of the genesis of these pieces, which included the *Airplane Sonata, Sonata sauvage, Mechanisms,* and *Death of Machines*. He claimed to have dreamed of hearing an orchestra play a piece he had written, a "sort of 'Brotherhood of Man' music, the quadruple essence of nobility and man's greatest spiritual efforts."[14] The following morning he sketched what he could remember of the music, then reworked the material into a piece which he called the *Airplane Sonata* because "as a symbol, the airplane seemed most indicative of that future into which I wanted to escape."[15] The other sonatas followed quickly, and Antheil gave their first public performance in Paris on October 4, 1923 before an audience including Stravinsky, Man Ray, James Joyce, Erik Satie, and Picasso. More convention-bound members of the crowd protested and rioted, and afterwards Antheil always performed with an automatic pistol strapped under his arm—"*I could always shoot myself out.*"[16]

Half a century later, these pieces seem indebted to Stravinsky: they make repeated use of ostinatos, chord culsters often based on several simultaneously sounding tonalities, and frequently changing meters.

*Second Sonata ("The Airplane"),* by George Antheil

But audiences of the 1920s heard them as shockingly new.

The *Ballet mécanique*, written in 1924–25, synthesized and expanded these sonatas into a single composition. Written to accompany an abstract film prepared by the artist Ferdinand Leger,

[14] George Antheil, *Bad Boy of Music* (Garden City and New York: Doubleday, Doran & Company, 1945) p. 22.
[15] Antheil, *Bad Boy of Music*, p. 22.
[16] Antheil, *Bad Boy of Music*, p. 133.

Antheil's "mechanistic" piece was scored for five player pianos, to give the performance an even more impersonal air—the player piano rolls had to be prepared and punched in advance, and thus no live performers were needed at the keyboards. In addition, there were parts for several percussion instruments, including an airplane propeller functioning as a prolonged "pedal point." The young composer thought of the piece as representing a radical break with the past, both in performance forces:

> I have used the sound of airplane propellers *because they are part of the musical sound of our modern life*; they are part of the vast new material of sound, musical sound, as steel and aluminium are now part of the facing material of modern buildings.[17]

and also in the organization of his sound materials:

> It was conceived in a new form, that form specifically being the filling out of a certain time canvas with musical abstraction and sound material composed and contrasted against one another with the thought of time values rather than tonal values. I used time as Picasso might have used the black spaces of his canvas. I did not hesitate, for instance, to repeat one measure one hundred times, I did not hesitate to have absolutely nothing on my piano rolls for sixty-two bars, or indeed to do whatever I pleased with this time canvas as long as each part of it stood up against the other. My ideas were the most abstract of the abstract.[18]

Antheil's provisional title for the piece was *Message to Mars*, since he thought of it as

> a "mechanistic" dance of life, or even a signal of these troubled and war-potential 1924 times placed in a rocket and shot to Mars. My idea was to warn the age in which I was living of the simultaneous beauty and danger of its own unconscious mechanistic philosophy, aesthetic. [It] was streamlined, glistening, cold, often as "musically silent" as interplanetary space, and also often as hot as an electric furnace.[19]

The first performance took place in Paris in the late spring of 1926, in a private home. Several public performances followed, widely covered by the press, prompting an ambitious young American entrepreneur, Donald Friede, to arrange for it to be played in New York's Carnegie Hall.

Friede played up the most sensational aspects of the piece,

---

[17] George Antheil, *Ballet mécanique* (New York: Columbia Records, ML 4956).
[18] Slonimsky, p. 452, from a letter from Vàrese.
[19] Antheil, *Bad Boy of Music*, p. 140.

attracting a capacity crowd to Carnegie Hall on April 10, 1927. The number of pianos was doubled; the player pianos of the first performance were replaced by concert grands, manned by live pianists; the airplane propeller was mounted in the center of the stage; the percussion was augmented. Though Antheil agreed to all this, he afterwards complained that there was too much stress on theatrical effect and the audience left with little idea of the musical content of his piece. He turned down an offer from Sol Hurok to take the piece on tour across America.

Disheartened by what he perceived as a misunderstanding of his goals, Antheil turned to a more conventional musical language, combining elements of neoclassicism and jazz, popular music and folk music. His opera *Transatlantic*, a caricature of a presidential election, was performed in Frankfurt in 1930; other operas, ballet scores, and symphonic, chamber, and vocal works followed. *Ballet mécanique* remained a piece more written about than heard: a performance at the Museum of Modern Art in New York, utilizing the original forces, was mounted in 1935; and the piece became generally available only in the mid-1950s with a recording supervised by the composer, played in its original form but modernized by the substitution of a jet engine for the original propeller.[20]

Conlon Nancarrow used one aspect of the *Ballet mécanique* as the basis for his entire body of mature compositions.

Born in Texarkana, Arkansas on October 27, 1912, Nancarrow pursued his musical education in Cincinnati and Boston, as a trumpet player aspiring to composition. Finding his way to Europe in 1936, he enlisted in the Abraham Lincoln Brigade in Spain, fighting for two years against Franco's forces. Afterwards he settled in Mexico, eventually becoming a citizen of that country. His early compositions, characterized by rhythmic complexity and a certain amount of reliance on the sonorities and rhythms of jazz, remained unperformed, though three were published in the journal *New Music*.[21]

Nancarrow evolved the idea of creating music directly for player piano. A perforated paper roll passes over an induced vacuum, with each perforation activating a mechanism that depresses one of the piano's hammers, causing it to strike a string and thus produce a note. Perforations on the horizontal axis determine pitch, vertical perforations control the time interval between notes. Thus both pitch and rhythm are reduced to linear measurement.

[20] Columbia recording ML 4956 of *Ballet mécanique.*
[21] The issue for October 1951.

589 / The American Avant-Garde

A visit to New York in the late 1940s yielded a machine that would enable him to punch his own piano rolls directly; his first composition for player piano was *Study for Player Piano I* (1948). His chief preoccupation was with rhythm; in addition to jazz—his favorite performers were Earl Hines and Louis Armstrong—he listened avidly to non-Western music, particularly that of Africa and India. The piece was fully composed and written down in standard notation before he began punching his piano roll, but since he was not restricted to what a pianist could play, he was able to create rhythmic complexities and sonorities impossible for a human performer. The climax of the piece requires five staffs for the notation of its ostinato chords marching up and down the keyboard, its full chords in the bass register, and its fragments of frantic running passages in the treble—all happening simultaneously.[22]

Later studies contain rhythmic canons with each voice moving at its own pace, often in complex ratios to other voices. *Study No. 14* has a first voice progressing at a tempo of M.M. 88 and a second entering at M.M. 110; the tempo ratio of 4:5 would be extraordinarily difficult for a person to maintain. *Study No. 36*[23] has tempo indications of M.M. 85, 90, 95, and 100 for the four voices, giving ratios of 17:18:19:20. Other pieces have individual parts or voices accelerate and slow down in the course of the work. *Study No. 27*[24] has one voice moving at a steady tempo throughout, M.M. 220; other voices enter against it in canon, each with its own pattern of increasing and decreasing speeds. At the climax, the central voice is surrounded by eight others, all related by melodic canon but each subjected to tempo differentials of such relationships as 6 percent, 5 percent, 8 percent, and 11 percent. No human performer, or even group of performers, could play these rhythmic patterns with any accuracy.

Nancarrow's music can be played only on the two special Ampico player pianos for which the pieces have been created, one with wooden hammers and the other with steel hammers covered with leather, located in his home in Mexico City. Recordings have been made,[25] but

No recorded image of his compositions ever will reproduce the overwhelming sensation of the raw power and excitement generated when sitting in Nancarrow's sound-proof studio in Mexico City and listening

[22] NW 203, 2 / 5.
[23] NW 203, s2 / 7.
[24] NW 203, s2 / 6.
[25] *Conlon Nancarrow. Studies for Player Piano*, Stereo MS 7222 (Columbia Masterworks); and *Complete Studies for Player Piano. The Music of Conlon Nancarrow. Volume One*, 1750 Arch Records S-1768.

> to his rolls "in the flesh." At best, commercial records so far have been unsuccessful in transmitting the truly extraordinary impact of these sounds to the outside world.[26]

His creative life has proceeded without reference to the musical mainstream of our time, or even to the music of the other composers with whom the present chapter is concerned. He is related to the avant-garde through his attitudes, his determination to forge music out of the contemporary world rather than the past. His pieces are hard, brittle, bright, spectacular—music written for a machine, music for the Age of Machinery. Yet they were conceived, in every detail, by a human brain.

Long before Nancarrow began creating his remarkable pieces and even before Varèse arrived in the New World, Henry Cowell (1897–1965) had begun to find his own way toward some of the musical devices and the ways of thinking about music that were to characterize the avant-garde.

Cowell's credo was stated most succinctly in 1955: "I want to live in the *whole world* of music."[27] From the beginning of his musical life he was exposed to an unusually wide range of materials—European classical music, Irish folk music, Chinese opera, the shape-note music of the rural Midwest, American popular music—and he regarded it all as potential building material and inspiration for his own compositions. When he was in his early teens, he began a series of pieces for piano which explore and expand the sonic range of that instrument. *The Tides of Manaunaum* (1912) uses immense masses of sound, tone clusters encompassing every note in a two-octave range played by the left forearm of the pianist, to represent the surging of tides over bottomless seas. *Advertisements* (1914) has clusters of three and four notes in the right hand, then groups of notes to be played by the clenched fist; against this, the left arm plays larger clusters of sound, then joins the right hand in pounding the piano with the fist. *Aeolian Harp* (1923)[28] asks the pianist to produce sounds directly on the strings of the instrument rather than at the keyboard: depressing a series of three- and four-note chords so as not to activate the hammers, the performer then sweeps the strings with the other hand, producing a chromatic glissando out of which sustaining chords emerge. *The Banshee*

[26] Conlon Nancarrow, *Selected Studies for Player Piano* (Berkeley, California), p. 7 (Critical material by Charles Amirkanian).

[27] Quoted in Stanley Sadie, ed., *The New Grove Dictionary of Music and Musicians* (London: Macmillan Publishers 1980), V, p. 10.

[28] NW 203, s1 / 3.

Henry Cowell and friend. (Courtesy New World Records)

(1925)[29] uses more varied means of obtaining pitches and sounds directly from the strings: the performer stands in the crook of the piano, sweeping his hand across strings to produce glissandos, drawing a finger along a single string for quite a different effect, sustaining chords by sweeping three or four fingers along certain strings, altering all these by using different parts of the hand and the nails to change the attack. The result is a sequence of muted, blurred, mysterious, eerie, wailing sounds that have nothing to do with the usual tone production of the piano.

Cowell experimented with tone clusters in orchestral music in two short pieces written in 1915–16, *Some Music* and *Some More Music*, both of which feature masses of sound built on seconds rather than thirds. At the same time, he was exploring another possible dimension in musical composition, a "physical identity between rhythm and harmony." In the fall of 1914

[29] NW 203, s1 / 1. Cf. also *Piano Piece* (1924) on NW 203, s1 / 3, for a slightly later piece making use of these same devices.

I was already exploring the possibilities inherent in counter-rhythms ...and I was struck with the fact that the lower reaches of the overtone series were expressed by the same ratios I had been using to describe counter-rhythms. Could they be somehow the same?

Experiments with two simultaneous sirens showed that if they are tuned in the relationship 3:2, they will sound the *interval* of a perfect fifth; if they are both slowed down, keeping the same 3:2 relationship, they arrive at a *rhythm* of 3 against 2, heard as gentle bumps but also visible in tiny puffs of air through the holes in the sirens, and so easily confirmed.[30]

Beginning with simple exercises in which an overtone series is built up from a fundamental, Cowell eventually constructed his *Quartet Romantic* (1915–17). Scored for two flutes, violin, and viola, the piece exploits complex simultaneous rhythmic patterns derived from his "rhythm-harmony" calculations:

*Quartet Romantic,* by Henry Cowell

[30] Henry Cowell, preface to *Quartet Romantic. Quartet Euphometric* (New York: C. F. Peters Corp., 1974).

Considered unplayable even by the composer, *Quartet Romantic* was first heard on a recording brought out in 1978,[31] in which each player wore earphones that cut out the sound of the other instruments while feeding a series of click sounds on tape as the means of coordination.

The *Quartet Euphometric* (1916–19), written for the traditional string combination, carries these methods to another dimension:

> The chords are converted into relationships of meters rather than of durations. Thus a triad with the ratio of pitch intervals 2:3:5 would convert to three instrumental lines each in its own meter: one in 2 / 4, one in 3 / 4, and one in 5 / 4. Only occasionally would the bar lines of all voices coincide, creating another kind of rhythmic complexity.[32]

*Vestiges* (1914–20), for large orchestra, incorporates some of the rhythmic complexities of these two quartets into a work for large ensemble, and such later pieces as the *Concerto for Piano and Orchestra* (1928–29) also use intricate patterns growing out of Cowell's "rhythm-harmony" experiments of the 1910s. By 1930 Cowell's eyes were on quite different horizons. With the encouragement and guidance of Charles Seeger (1886–1979), one of the first Americans to embrace the discipline of musicology and a man of tremendous vision, Cowell involved himself more and more in the oral-tradition music of his own country and in the music of other cultures.

Cowell's compositions of the 1920s, '30s, and '40s turn increasingly for their source material to Irish folk music, the hymns and fuging tunes of rural America, and the scales, instruments, and rhythms of various non-Western musics. He wanted his music to be intelligible to persons all over the world. His *String Quartet No. 4* was subtitled the "United Quartet," since he hoped that it would be

> understood equally well by Americans, Europeans, Orientals, or higher primitives; or by anybody from a coal miner to a bank president. The main purpose of it, of course, is not in its technique, but in the message which, of course, is not suitable for expression in words. It may be said that it concerns human and social relationships.
>
> The work is original in spite of its simplicity, because the simplicity is drawn from the whole world, instead of from the European tradition or any other single tradition. Primitive music is represented, not by imi-

[31] NW 285, s1 / 1.
[32] Bruce Archibald, liner notes to NW 218; p. 2. The quartet is on this disc, on s2 / 1.

tating it, nor by taking a specific melody or rhythm from some tribe, but by using at times a three-tone scale and exhausting all the different ways the three tones can appear and by its underlying rhythmic beat—like primitive music, but taken from no specific instance. The Oriental is represented by modes which are constructed as Oriental modes are constructed, without being actual modes used in particular cultures. From Western culture, the archaic is represented by foundational harmonic intervals of fifths, fourths and octaves. The romantic is represented by the emotional outpouring of the melodies. The modern is represented by the use of unresolved discords, by free intervals in two-part counterpoint and by the fact that the whole result is something new—and all that is new is modern.[33]

Other pieces make musical reference to specific cultures: *Irish Suite* (1928), for piano and chamber orchestra; *Symphony No. 13* ("Madras"), written in 1957–58 for tablas, jala-tarang, and orchestra; *Old American Country Set* (1937–39), for orchestra; *Persian Set* (1956–57); *Concerto No. 1 for Koto and Orchestra* (1962).

*New Music*, a quarterly founded by Cowell in October of 1927, was devoted to the publication of scores too experimental to be accepted by commercial publishers; an anthology of writings by American composers, edited by Cowell in 1933, served as a forum for many members of the avant-garde to express their concerns;[34] John Cage and other younger men sought him out as a teacher and were encouraged and assisted by him. He functioned for many decades as a sort of "godfather" of the avant-garde, often serving as a bridge between the most radical music of the day and the more "respected" circles of American music and education into which he had moved himself.

Harry Partch (1901–76) set out to do nothing less than to fashion his own music virtually from scratch.

Before I was twenty, I had tentatively rejected both the intonational system of modern Europe and its concert system, although I did not realize either the ultimate scope or the consequences of that rejection.

The break came first, by intuition; the justification came second, by critical and historical analysis. Sometime between 1923 and 1928 I finally became so dissatisfied with the body of knowledge and usages as ordinarily imparted in the teaching of music that I refused to accept, or develop my own work on the basis of, any part of it. With respect to

---

[33] Henry Cowell, as quoted in Hugo Weisgall, "The Music of Henry Cowell," *The Musical Quarterly*, XLV (1959), pp. 492–93.

[34] Henry Cowell, ed., *American Composers on American Music* (New York: Frederick Ungar Publishing House, 1962).

Harry Partch on the sound stage of the film *The Dreamer that Remains*, San Diego, 1972. (Photograph by Betty Freeman)

current usage this refusal was a rebellion; from the standpoint of my creative work it was the beginning of a new philosophy of music, intuitively arrived at. . . .

I began to write music on the basis of harmonized spoken words, for new instruments and in new scales, and to play it in various parts of the country.[35]

Rejecting equal temperament for just intonation, and rejecting the abstraction that dominated both European and American classical composition as the twentieth century unfolded, Partch imagined a "corporeal" art that would encompass:

Stories sung or chanted, including much folk music.

Poems recited or intoned, including some folk music and some, but not all, popular music.

Dramas, such as the early seventeenth-century Florentine music-dramas, for example.

Music intended specifically for dances which tell a story or describe a situation; both ancient and modern.[36]

[35] Harry Partch, *Genesis of a Music. An Account of a Creative Work, Its Roots and Its Fulfillments* (New York: Da Capo Press, 1974), pp. vi–vii, 4–6, *passim*.
[36] Partch, p. 9.

The first result was a set of *Seventeen Lyrics by Li Po* (1930–33),[37] for intoning voice and adapted viola, a conventional instrument altered by means of a lengthened neck and the placement of bradheads on the fingerboard to serve as frets. The voice sometimes sings on pitch, sometimes speaks; the accompaniment ranges from homorhythmic patterns with the voice, to thick and rhythmically active strummed chords; Partch has taken particular care to prevent musical means from interfering with comprehension of his text. Other pieces for adapted viola and voice followed; several were performed for the New Music Society of San Francisco on February 9, 1932—the first public presentation of his "new" music.

*U.S. Highball* (1943), subtitled "A Musical Account of a Transcontinental Hobo Trip," was Partch's first stage work and introduced several more instruments of his own construction: adapted guitar, with individual frets for each string to create just intonation; kithara, a lyrelike instrument with seventy-two strings; and chromelodeon, an adapted harmonium with new reeds allowing the complex tunings of just intonation. The piece is in "hobo allegro" form:

> The first part is a long and jerky passage by drags (slow freights) to Little America, Wyoming. The second is an adagio dishwashing movement at Little America. The third is a rhythmic allegro, mostly by highway (hitchhiking) to Chicago. The one word, *Chicago*, is the end of the text. Instrumentally, what follows implies a tremendous letdown from the obstinately compulsive exhilaration of *getting* to Chicago. It implies bewilderment and that ever-dominant question in the life of the wanderer—what next?[38]

It should be added that Partch had spent the years between 1935 and 1941 wandering across Depression-ravaged America, as a hobo himself. But a grant from the Guggenheim Foundation in 1943 allowed him to settle down for a bit, and design and construct new instruments: the harmonic canon, with forty-four strings mounted horizontally above a shallow soundbox, played with picks; the diamond marimba and the bass marimba. Each of these gave Partch new timbres and allowed the playing of the forty-three-note scale he had devised for more perfect intonation. Each new instrument called for new techniques, and by now Partch was collecting a small band of students and admirers willing to master new instruments in order to bring his music to performance.

[37] Three of the Li Po settings are on NW 214, s1 / 4–6: "The Intruder," "I Am a Peach Tree" and "A Midnight Farewell."
[38] Partch, p. 321.

"The Street"[39] draws its subject matter from contemporary America, taking the closing passage of Willard Motley's *Knock on Any Door* as its text; the sounds of the harmonic canon and the bass marimba have moved further away from those of traditional Western instruments. As in all of his music, structure grows from his text and his attempts to make it as expressive as possible.

The increasing attention paid to his work in some circles made it possible for Partch to conceive, create, and mount more ambitious compositions. *Oedipus—A Music-Dance Drama* was completed in 1951 and performed at Mills College in March of 1952. Performance forces include four soloists, a chorus of six sopranos, and an accompanying band of more than a dozen of Partch's instruments. Other large stage works followed: the three-section *Plectra and Percussion Dances*; *The Bewitched—A Dance Satire*, choreographed by Alwin Nikolais; *Revelation in the Courthouse Park* (1960), based on *The Bacchae* of Euripides. In the words of a student and colleague,

> In a fully realized Partch production there are spoken words wedded to music without the abstraction typical of singing; there is a dramatic story expressed through action in a theater space not excluding visible actions of performing musicians as well as those of dancer-actor-singers; there is a setting which significantly includes, as sculptural objects, the hand-made instruments themselves. Music functions as part of a many-faceted artwork.[40]

The size of his orchestra was increased as Partch imagined and built new instruments; his last completed piece, *The Dreamer That Remains*—written for the soundtrack of a film by the same name, a portrait of the composer—is scored for fifteen instruments, including the visually spectacular cloud-chamber bowls, suspended pyrex half-globes struck by soft mallets.[41]

Partch and his music lived on the fringes of the musical life of America. The fact that his music could be played only on instruments of his own design meant that none of his pieces was ever performed by established musical organizations. His was an intensely personal and private music, inaccessible and unknown to most Americans. Yet he remained convinced to the end that his "corporeal music" represented one of the truest expressions of indigenous American music.

[39] NW 214, s1 / 8. Three other pieces from this set are on bands 1–3.
[40] Ben Johnston, in John Vinton, *Dictionary of Contemporary Music* (New York: E. P. Dutton, 1974), p. 556.
[41] NW 214, s1 / 9. The text is autobiographical.

Other American composers set out on their own paths. John J. Becker (1886–1961) disowned his early compositions in nineteenth-century Germanic and French styles, turning instead to a highly dissonant music, extensive use of percussion instruments moving in polyrhythmic patterns, and stage works combining music, dance, pantomime, and lights, anticipating the mixed-media events of several decades later. *The Abongo* (1933),[42] for percussion ensemble, is an early attempt by an American composer to create a large-scale piece for percussion alone; the fact that most of the sounds are nonpitched forced him to consider method of organization not dependent on tonality, functional harmony, or serial organization. Ruth Crawford Seeger (1901–53) experimented with differentiated levels of dynamics in the several voices of a composition (in *String Quartet*, 1931), and with the spatial dispersement of performing forces (in her *Three Songs* [1930–32] to texts by Carl Sandburg).[43]

The progress of the American avant-garde is best observed in the career of John Cage, born in Los Angeles in 1912. He confronted each of the musical and aesthetic issues of concern to the composers discussed above, and additional ones as well; his intellectual and musical progress has been recorded in a string of lucid essays; his creative life has encompassed the entire time-span of the movement; and he came to be regarded—in Europe, if not always in his own country—as the American composer of the mid-twentieth century who most successfully forged a style of music unique to the United States.

His early musical life encompassed piano study with local teachers and work in theory and composition with Henry Cowell, Adolph Weiss, and Arnold Schoenberg. His earliest pieces are concerned with manipulating the chromatic scale in systematic ways; in *Composition for 3 Voices* (1934) he set himself the task of

keeping repetitions of individual tones of the three superimposed 25-tone ranges as far apart as possible, even though each voice is obliged to express all 25 tones before introducing a repetition of any one of them.[44]

A job in Los Angeles as rehearsal pianist for a dance company led to a position in Seattle, at the Cornish School, as composer-

---

[42] The piece is available on NW 285, s2 / 1. The best source for information on the composer and his music is Don Gillespie, "John Becker, Musical Crusader of St. Paul," *The Musical Quarterly*, LXII (1976), pp. 195–217.

[43] NW 285, s2 / 2–4. The best source is Charles Seeger, "Ruth Crawford," *American Composers on American Music: A Symposium*, ed. Henry Cowell (Stanford: Stanford University Press, 1933), pp. 110–18.

[44] John Cage, *John Cage* (New York: Henmar Press, 1962), p. 27.

John Cage.

accompanist for the dancer Bonnie Bird. He had begun to write pieces for small groups of percussion instruments and these brought him face to face with the same problem that Varèse, Becker, and others had confronted earlier—the organization of a musical composition made up of unpitched sounds. In 1935, he addressed this matter in a lecture delivered before members of a Seattle arts society:

> Wherever we are, what we hear is mostly noise. When we ignore it, it disturbs us. When we listen to it, we find it fascinating. The sound of a

truck at fifty miles per hour. Static between the stations. Rain. We want to capture and control these sounds, to use them not as sound effects but as musical instruments. If this word "music" is sacred and reserved for eighteenth- and nineteenth-century instruments, we can substitute a more meaningful term: organization of sound. WHEREAS, IN THE PAST, THE POINT OF DISAGREEMENT HAS BEEN BETWEEN DIS-SONANCE AND CONSONANCE, IT WILL BE, IN THE IMMEDIATE FUTURE, BETWEEN NOISE AND SO-CALLED MUSICAL SOUNDS. The composer (organizer of sound) will be faced not only with the entire field of sound but also the entire field of time.[45]

And further on this point:

> Sound has four characteristics: pitch, timbre, loudness, and duration. The opposite and necessary coexistence of sound is silence. Of the four characteristics of sound, only duration involves both sound and silence. Therefore, a structure based on durations (rhythmic phrase, time lengths) is correct (corresponds with the nature of the material).[46]

*First Construction* (*in Metal*) of 1939 is built over a sixteen-measure rhythmic sequence (4–3–2–3–4) stated sixteen times. This underlying structure is not apparent to a listener, but it satisfies the composer's desire for a rational pattern underlying the piece, and may indeed provide coherence at a subconscious level. Other percussion pieces with similar schemes followed: *Second Construction* (1940) and *Third Construction* (1941), both for percussion quintet, and *March* (*Imaginary Landscape No. 2*) of 1942.

Asked to write a piece for the black dancer Syvilla Fort, Cage decided on a percussion composition, but the theater was too small. His solution was to insert various objects, mostly screws and bolts, between certain strings of the piano, to give a variety of pitched and unpitched percussive sounds from the one instrument.

> I soon had a whole new gamut of sounds, which was just what I needed. The piano had become, in effect, a percussion orchestra, under the control of a single player.[47]

After a year in Los Angeles and another in Chicago, Cage settled in New York in early 1942. A program at the Museum of Modern Art, including three of his compositions, brought him to the attention of New York audiences and critics, and he continued to write for and accompany dancers, particularly the innovative Merce

[45] John Cage, "The Future of Music—Credo," in John Cage, *Silence* (Middletown, Connecticut: Wesleyan University Press, 1961), pp. 3–5.

[46] Cage, *Silence*, p. 63.

[47] Calvin Tomkins, a profile of Cage in *The New Yorker*, for November 28, 1964.

Cunningham. This period was climaxed by one of the most successful and remarkable pieces of American music of the entire twentieth century, the *Sonatas and Interludes* for prepared piano written between February of 1946 and March of 1948 and dedicated to the pianist Maro Ajemian, who introduced them. Cage had become deeply involved in Eastern thought and philosophy, and the *Sonatas and Interludes* "are an attempt to express in music the 'permanent emotions' of Indian tradition: the heroic, the erotic, the wondrous, the mirthful, sorrow, fear, anger, and odious and their common tendency toward tranquility."[48] They fell easily on the ears of most listeners; Cecil Smith, writing in the *Musical America*—hardly a bastion of support for radical music—on January 15, 1949, reported:

> The tone of the prepared piano, gentle almost to the point of gentility, is quite enchanting, for Mr. Cage's fabulous ear for timbre and texture has enabled him to achieve gleaming combinations of overtones such as have never been heard in western music.

Despite the complex operations necessary to "prepare" the piano for performance, these pieces were eventually taken up by more and more pianists, until today they are Cage's most frequently performed compositions and are heard as often as any other American keyboard works from the present century.[49]

Rhythmic structures underlie most of the pieces in this set. Typical is *Sonata V*:

> The piece is in a simple AB form.
> The A section is 18 measures long, the B 22½, giving a ratio between the two sections of 4:5. The 18 measures of A divide in half, 9 + 9, the 22½ measures of B are divided 9 + 9 + 4½. Each of the four 9-measure segments of both A and B is further sub divided into 4 + 5 measures, a reflection at a lower level of the 4:5 ratio of the two large sections. At an even lower level, both the 4-measure and the 5-measure segments are divided in half, giving within each 9-measure segment a division of 2 + 2 + 2½ + 2½. Since there are 2 beats to each measure, these smaller segments take up 4 + 4 + 5 + 5 beats, giving a 4:5 ratio at a third level. The final 4½ bars are also constructed of 4 + 5 beats.[50]

But such mathematics were the business of the composer, not the listener, who needed to know none of this in order to enjoy the piece.

To this point, Cage's music had been written down in precise,

---

[48] Cage, *John Cage*, p. 17.
[49] NW 203 contains *Interlude II* and *Sonatas I, V, X*, and *XII*, on s1 / 4–8.
[50] Charles Hamm, liner notes for NW 203, p. 5.

conventional musical notation; in his own words, his concerns were still to "possess sounds (to be able to repeat them)."[51] But all this was soon to change:

> We are faced in life with the unique qualities and characteristics of each occasion. The prepared piano, impressions I had from the work of artist friends, study of Zen Buddhism, ramblings in fields and forests looking for mushrooms, all led me to the enjoyment of things as they come, as they happen, rather than as they are possessed or kept or forced to be.[52]

The impact of this new philosophical attitude may be observed in two pieces written in 1951, *Sixteen Dances* (for four instruments and four percussionists) and *Concerto for Prepared Piano and Chamber Orchestra*. Precompositionally determined rhythmic patterns still form the skeleton of the composition, but individual pitches were selected by a process involving elements of chance. In *Music of Changes* (1951), a lengthy piece for piano, pitch selection involved the *I-Ching*:

> Of the sixty-four elements in a square chart eight times eight (made in this way in order to interpret as sounds the coin oracle of the Chinese *Book of Changes*) thirty-two were sounds, thirty-two silences. The thirty-two sounds were arranged in two squares one above the other, each four by four. Whether the charts were mobile or immobile, all twelve tones were present in any four elements of a given chart, whether a line of the chart was read horizontally or vertically. Once this dodecaphonic requirement was satisfied, noises and repetitions of tones were used with freedom.[53]

*Imaginary Landscape No. 4 (March No. 2)*, also from 1951, uses similar compositional procedures; the performance forces consist of twelve radios, and the performers manipulate the knobs controlling volume and amplitude according to a precisely notated score, so each performance is unique, dependent on what happens to be broadcast during the time of the concert. *Williams Mix* (1952) was constructed for magnetic tape: a variety of natural and artificial sounds was captured on tape, classified into categories, then spliced onto eight simultaneous tracks in a sequence again determined by chance operations involving the *I-Ching*. Soon musical notation had been reduced to a graph, in a series of pieces written in the mid-1950s; in *Aria* (1958), for solo voice, sounds are "roughly

[51] Cage, *Empty Words* (Middletown: Wesleyan University Press, 1979), p. 8.

[52] Cage, *Empty Words*, p. 8.

[53] Cage, *Silence*, pp. 25–26. Two sections of *Music for Changes* are available on NW 214, s2. An extended discussion of the compositional methods used for this piece may be found in the liner notes to this disc, pp. 3–4.

suggested rather than accurately described" by a graph, and "all aspects of a performance (dynamics, etc.) which are not notated may be freely determined by the singer."[54] The sixteen pages of *Music for Piano 4–19* (1953 "may be played as separate pieces or continuously as one piece or." Most notorious was *4'33"* (1952), written for any instrument or combination of instruments but most often performed as a piano solo: no notes are sounded, the composition consisting of whatever sounds come from the audience, or from outside the hall, for the duration of the piece.

In these and other compositions of the 1950s, Cage created a music "free of individual taste and memory and also of the literature and 'traditions' of the art," in which "value judgments are not in the nature of (these) works as regards either composition, performance, or listening" and "the sounds enter the time-space centered within themselves, unimpeded by service to any abstraction."[55] The composer has become an agent setting in motion a sequence of sounds over which he has no control, and in which he has no particular interest. Listeners, including the composer himself, are invited to consider whatever happens. The composer's function has become didactic—to persuade the listener that *any* sound or succession of sounds is potentially interesting or beautiful or meaningful.

It has been suggested that the "radical empiricism" of Cage's music of this period represents the most extreme break in technique and aesthetic in Western music since the Renaissance.[56]

In the summer of 1952, Cage organized a "simultaneous presentation of unrelated events" at Black Mountain College in North Carolina: Cage delivered a lecture, Merce Cunningham danced, Robert Rauschenberg played phonograph discs, David Tudor played the piano, M. C. Richards read poetry, films were projected on the ceiling. This event anticipated the "happenings" and other mixed-media events of the coming decades.

Cage's compositions of this period draw their material from the "real" world. *Imaginary Landscape No. 5* (1952) uses the music contained on any forty-two phonograph discs, transferred to tape, fragmented, and reordered according to chance operations. *Water Music* of the same year asks the performer to create a collage of live sounds—a radio, a deck of cards, whistles, and various aqueous sounds (water poured from pots, whistles blown under water). His intention now was to create art functioning as

[54]Cage, *John Cage*, p. 20.
[55]Cage, *Silence*, p. 69.
[56]Leonard Meyer, "The End of the Renaissance?," in *Music, The Arts And Ideas* (Chicago & London: University of Chicago Press, 1967), pp. 68–86.

an affirmation of life—not an attempt to bring order out of chaos nor to suggest improvements in creation, but simply to wake up to the very life we're living, which is so excellent once one gets one's mind and one's desires out of the way and lets it act of its own accord.[57]

European audiences, critics, and composers heard Cage's new "indeterminate" music in 1954, when he and pianist-composer David Tudor took part in a festival of new music at Donaueschingen, Germany, and also gave programs in France, Italy, England, Switzerland, and Scandinavia. A "25-Year Retrospective Concert of the Music of John Cage" at New York's Town Hall on May 15, 1958, and a commercially released recording of this event—complete with liner notes by Cage, including samples of the notation of many of the pieces performed—made possible the first critical assessment of his role in American music. That summer found him again in Europe, lecturing at Darmstadt, Germany—which, under the leadership of Karlheinz Stockhausen, had become the intellectual center of postwar European experimental music—and performing at the World's Fair in Brussels. In Milan, where he had been invited to work in the new electronic music studio attached to the state radio station, he created the tape piece *Fontana Mix* (1958); he also became a public figure through appearances as an expert on mushrooms on the television quiz program "Lascia o Raddoppia." *Water Walk*, a theater piece, was performed on one of these shows, and upon his return to New York in 1959 it was performed twice on American television—on the "Henry Morgan Show" and on Garry Moore's "I've Got a Secret."

The first important critical attention to his work had come from Henry Cowell in the early 1950s.[58] His first book (*Silence*, 1961) was a series of essays dealing with his musical and aesthetical development over a span of more than two decades. In the first several years of the 1950s, a flood of critical writing concerned with Cage's music appeared.[59]

By this time a group of young American composers based in New York had taken Cage's music and aesthetic as a starting point for their own work. Morton Feldman, born in New York City in 1926, wrote a series of pieces in graphic notation in the early 1950s in which performers are given only general instructions as to what pitches (high, medium, or low) and durations to play. *Projections* (1950–51) for solo cello and *Marginal Intersection* (1951) for orches-

---

[57] Cage, *Silence*, p. 104.

[58] Henry Cowell, "Current Chronicle," *The Musical Quarterly*, XXXVIII (1952), pp. 123 ff.

[59] Cf. article "John Cage," by Charles Hamm in *The New Grove Dictionary of Music and Musicians*, III, pp. 602–3, for a recent bibliography of writings about Cage.

tra came first, then *Projections 2* (1951) for flute, trumpet, violin, cello, and piano. In the latter, the progression through time is indicated by a series of rectangles, each representing four *icti* moving at a rate of 72 pulses per minute; within each, smaller rectangles or squares for each instrument give a general indication of when and for how long to play, though the precise duration of sounds is to be determined by each performer. The vertical placement of these smaller shapes suggests—again in a general way—the pitches to be played. Feldman instructs the players that "Any tone within the ranges indicated may be sounded. The limits of these ranges may be freely chosen by the player."

*Projection 2*, by Morton Feldman

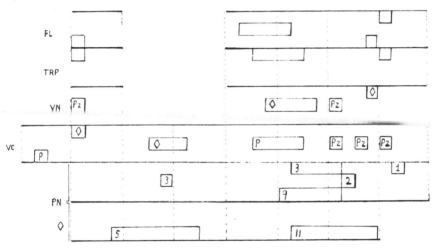

Earle Brown's (b. 1926) first compositions combined serial techniques with the statistical approach to composition proposed by Joseph Schillinger. After coming into contact with Cage and his music, he turned to graphic notation. *Folio* (1952–53), playable on any combination of instruments, uses a series of lines suggesting in a most general way what notes are to be played; *25 Pages* (1953) may be played by any number of pianists—up to twenty-five—in any order or combination; *Indices* (1954), for chamber orchestra, is made up of pitches chosen by a process of random sampling; *Available Forms I* (1961) and *Available Forms II* (1962) are for larger instrumental combinations, with the conductor and/or performers choosing which pages are to be played and in what order.

Early in his career, Christian Wolff, born in Nice (France) in 1934, wrote a series of piano pieces in precise notation exploring a wide range of dynamic and sonorous effects, very sparse in structure. In appearance on the page, and in sound, his *For Piano I* (1952) bears a generic resemblance to Cage's *Music of Changes* and other piano pieces of the early 1950s. But it also looks and sounds like some of the totally organized music written at just this time by Boulez, Stockhausen, and Babbitt. The ear simply cannot distinguish whether the selection of pitches and durations in such a piece has resulted from the application of a rigorously applied intellectual process or from the application of chance procedures. Wolff says of the expressive intent of this music:

> One finds (in new music) a concern for a kind of objectivity, almost ano-nymity,—sound comes into its own. The "music" is a resultant existing simply in the sounds we hear, given no impulse by expressions of self or personality. It is indifferent in motive, originating in no psychology nor in dramatic intentions, nor in literary or pictorial purposes. The final intention is to be free of artistry and taste. But this need not make the work "abstract," for nothing, in the end, is denied. It is simply that personal expression, drama, psychology, and the like are not part of the composer's initial calculation: they are at best gratuitous.
>
> The music has a static quality. It goes in no particular direction. There is no necessary concern with time as a measure of distance from a point

*For 1, 2 or 3 People,* by Christian Wolff

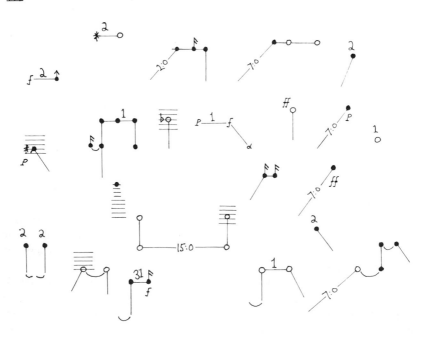

in the past to a point in the future, with linear continuity alone. It is not a matter of getting anywhere, of making progress, or of having come from anywhere in particular. There is neither nostalgia nor anticipation.[60]

Later pieces by Wolff move away from conventional notation and allow indeterminacy in performance. *For Pianist* (1959) offers the performer a general map of territory to be explored, more suggestive than prescriptive. *For 1, 2 or 3 People* (1964) is indeterminate in duration ("There are ten parts, one to a page. A performance can be made of any number of them, repeating none, or of any one, repeated no more than ten times."); pitches, timbres, and durations are only suggested, and a set of symbols indicates to each player how his part is to be coordinated with the others.

When Cage began teaching at the New School for Social Research, in New York, in the late 1950s, he soon found himself at the center of a group of younger people interested in the application of indeterminacy to musical, dramatic, and verbal pieces. Among these were musicians—Toshi Ichiyanagi, John Brooks, Don Heckman, Richard Maxfield—and others more concerned with the visual arts or the written word: Jackson MacLow, Allan Kaprow, Dick Higgins, George Brecht, Al Hansen. The genre of the "happening," which had its beginning in the fall of 1959 with the presentation of Kaprow's *18 Happenings in 6 Parts* at the Reuben Gallery and continued with such works as *The Burning Building* (1959) by Red Grooms, *The American Moon* (1960) by Robert Whitman, and *The Car Crash* (1960) by Jim Dine,[61] was profoundly indebted to Cage. Members of this "New York school" also created smaller events, with verbal descriptions of actions and sounds. *An Anthology* (1963),[62] edited by MacLow and La Monte Young (who had come from California to study with Cage), remains the best monument to this phase of the American avant-garde, which produced such pieces as Brecht's *Comb Music* (1959–62):

For single or multiple performance.
    A comb is held by its spine in one hand, either free or resting on an object.
    The thumb or a finger of the other hand is held with its tip against an

[60]Christian Wolff, "New and Electronic Music," *Audience*, III (1958), pp. 122 and 130.
    [61]For a history of the genre, as well as descriptions and texts of individual happenings, cf. Michael Kirby, *Happenings. An Illustrated Anthology* (New York: E. P. Dutton & Company, 1965); also Richard Kostelanetz, *The Theatre of Mixed Means* (New York: The Dial Press, 1968).
    [62]La Monte Young, ed., *An Anthology* (New York: Heiner Friedrich, 1963).

end prong of the comb, with the edge of the nail overlapping the end of the prong.

The finger is now slowly and uniformly moved so that the prong is inevitably released, and the nail engages the next prong.

This action is repeated until each prong has been used.

Second version:   Sounding comb-prong.

Third version:    Comb prong.

Fourth version:   Comb.  Fourth version:   Prong.

In 1961, some of these men allied themselves with George Maciunas and several foreign artists—Nam June Paik, Robert Filliou, Emmett Williams, Ben Vautier—to form a group called Fluxus, dedicated to the creation and performance of events which "strive for the monostructural and nontheatrical qualities of the simple natural event, a game or a gag. It is the fusion of Spike Jones, vaudeville gags, children's games, and Duchamp."[63] A somewhat similar group grew up in Ann Arbor around the musicians Gordon Mumma, Robert Ashley, George Cacioppo, and the film maker George Manupelli. Calling themselves ONCE, they organized annual festivals of their creations—mostly indeterminate, semitheatrical events, with verbal instructions replacing musical notation—from 1960 to 1965. A more loosely defined group of composers living in California was also responsive to the Cage-led shift toward indeterminate music and the blurring of the boundaries between musical, theatrical, and visual objects: Terry Jennings, Pauline Oliveras, Joseph Byrd, Dennis Johnson, Terry Riley, Ramon Sender, Larry Austin, Morton Subotnick, and others.

Cage's own compositions of this period moved even further from any sort of control imposed on the performer. *Variations I* (1958) consists of six transparent squares with points and lines scattered on each sheet; the performer(s) lay these on top of one another, in any sequence, and take intersections of lines and the position of dots as a stimulus for the production of sounds on any instrument(s) or other sound-producing equipment. *Theatre Piece* (1960) offers its performers—any number of musicians, dancers, singers, or actors, up to eight—a set of "time-brackets within which an action may be made. These actions are from a gamut of twenty nouns and/or verbs chosen by the performer. This gamut changes at given points, so that each part involves a performer in a maximum of 50 to 100 different actions."[64] And *4'33" No. 2* (1962), subtitled *0'0"*, a "solo for any player," allows the performer complete freedom of action, without even a time frame. Cage performed it

[63] Quoted in Michael Nyman, *Experimental Music. Cage and Beyond* (New York: Schirmer Books, 1974), pp. 65–66.

[64] Cage, *John Cage*, p. 42.

himself by sitting on stage at a table, slicing a number of vegetables, placing them in a blender, reducing them to juice, pouring this into a glass, and drinking it—with all of these sounds amplified by contact microphones.

These most radical products of the avant-garde do not in themselves represent a substantial contribution to the musical life of twentieth-century America. In retrospect, their most important function was to help break restrictive and destructive patterns and attitudes, and to suggest alternate ways of creating pieces of music.

A brief examination of several representative pieces written in the 1960s and '70s will underline the extent to which the techniques and aesthetics of the avant-garde were incorporated into the music of an entire generation of American composers.

Robert Erickson—born in Marquette, Michigan in 1917—was a student of both Ernst Krenek and Roger Sessions, and wrote a series of pieces in more or less traditional forms: piano, chamber, vocal, and orchestral works with an atonal and sometimes serial vocabulary. In the late 1950s, however, he was attracted by the new freedoms and expressive potential of avant-garde composition, and in a series of pieces beginning with *Variations for Orchestra* (1957) and *Chamber Concerto* (1960), he explored "expanded notions of instrumental and vocal timbre, increasingly flexible means of rhythmic articulation, and improvisation within controlled limits."[65]

*General Speech* (1969),[66] written for the trombonist Stuart Dempster, underlines how far he progressed away from rational, abstract musical structures. The trombonist is asked to articulate General MacArthur's retirement speech through his instrument. The shape of the piece is thus determined by these words, and the emotional content is shaped by Erickson's interpretation of the text. It must be remembered that opposition to the military policies of the American government was rising to a crescendo at this time; the piece is satirical, not patriotic. The performer is asked to dress in an outfit associated with MacArthur's public image: his familiar hat, with gold wreaths on the brim, and a ribbon-bespangled military jacket. The words and sentiments intended by MacArthur to stir and inspire his audience,

> Duty! Honor! Country! Those three hallowed words reverently dictate what you ought to be, what you can be, what you will be. They are your rallying point to build courage when courage seems to fail. . . .

[65] Harvey Sollberger, liner notes for NW 254, p. 3.
[66] NW 254, s2 / 3.

sound ridiculous as funneled through a trombone by a ludicrous figure on the concert stage.

*Sonata for Microtonal Piano* (1965) by Ben Johnston contains quite a different mix of elements. Born in Macon, Georgia in 1926, Johnston studied with Harry Partch in the early 1950s, was one of the young musicians who made it possible for Partch's music of this period to be heard by learning to perform instruments of his invention,[67] and eventually wrote a perceptive study of Partch's music.[68] Johnston also studied with John Cage and Darius Milhaud, worked at the Columbia-Princeton Electronic Music Studio with Otto Luening and Vladimir Ussachevsky, had been a piano student of John Powell early in his career, and was, at various times, a pianist in a dance band and an accompanist for a dance studio. He was thus exposed to a wide range of musical styles in America in the mid-twentieth century.

One of his compositional concerns has been to "reopen doors closed by the acceptance of the twelve-tone equal-tempered scale as the norm of pitch usage." Pointed in this direction by Partch's work, Johnston has produced both theoretical and creative works concerned with more perfect "acoustical" intonation and smaller divisions of the octave. In his own words, the *Sonata for Microtonal Piano*:

> deploys chains of just-tuned (untempered) triadic intervals over the whole piano range in interlocked consonant patterns. Only seven of the eighty-eight white and black keys of the piano have octave equivalents, one pair encompassing the distance of a double octave and the remaining six pairs separated by almost the entire length of the keyboard. Thus there are eighty-one different pitches, providing a piano with almost no consonant octaves.
>
> Effectively, for the listener, there are three main gradations of consonance/dissonance: (1) smooth, untempered thirds and fifths, which have the least amount of harshness caused by acoustical beats, (2) compounds of these such as sevenths, ninths, elevenths, thirteenths, and fifteenths (which turn out to be slightly sharp double octaves), and (3) chromatic or enharmonic intervals compromising all the even-numbered keyboard distances such as seconds, fourths, sixths, octaves, tenths, twelfths, and fourteenths, and which sound "out of tune."[69]

The composer's description of the piece is fearsomely intellectual, yet the listener is first and most forcefully struck by purely sonic

[67] He may be heard performing several of Partch's compositions on NW 214, s1 / 1, 2 and 8.

[68] "The Corporealism of Harry Partch," *Perspectives of New Music* (Spring-Summer 1975), pp. 210–20.

[69] Liner notes for NW 203, p. 5.

aspects of the sonata—the richness of pitch, the expressiveness of melodies and chords based on intervals strange to Western music, the ever-changing sonorities of the piano sound. The slow movement, for instance, begins with a massive arpeggio sweeping up from the bass, ringing out in a way that would not be possible on a piano tuned in equal temperament; soon a dronelike figure supports a fragment of melody based on microtonal tunings suggestive of music of the Middle East, expressive in a way that would not be possible in traditional Western tuning.

Roger Reynolds' *Blind Men* (1966)[70] is based on fragments of text selected from Herman Melville's *Journal up the Straits, 1856–1857.* Reynolds has added words and phrases of his own, as "both glosses and as phonemic elaborations through correspondences of meaning and sound."[71] Written for a chorus of twenty-four voices and a collection of wind and percussion instruments, the piece alternates three different types of events:

—*Timed Mixtures*, each sixty seconds in length, nonmetrical and not to be conducted. These are blocks of massed, continuous sounds, sometimes for instruments and sometimes for voices; pitches are sometimes notated, sometimes suggested.

—*Measured Sections*, comprising the bulk of the work, combining voices and instruments. These are precisely notated, with barlines and tempo markings; pitches are sometimes indicated with precision, in other places only a general contour is given.

—*Links*, connecting the above. These are instrumental, for a single player or a small collection of instruments, thus contrasting with the massed sounds of the other events. They are unmeasured and indeterminate in length: "events which have natural limitations or conditions on their durations" such as the length of time a player can sustain a note or the time required for a resonating note to fade to silence.

Recognizing that his compositional techniques will inhibit audience comprehension of Melville's words, Reynolds has instructed that posters containing the text be prominently displayed before the performance and/or projected on a screen while the performance is in progress.

*Blind Men* combines organized and notated elements with more indeterminate ones, precise pitches with nonpitched sounds, order with chaos. It is a difficult and complex piece, which must be performed with absolute precision within its prescribed boundaries. Born in Detroit in 1934, Reynolds took a degree in engineering at

---

[70] *Blind Men* has been recorded by the Gregg Smith Singers for Composers Recordings (CRI SD 241).

[71] Quoted from the score (New York: Edition Peters, P6826, n.d.)

the University of Michigan, then studied composition with Ross Lee Finney and Roberto Gerhard before involving himself in the avant-garde activities of the ONCE group in Ann Arbor. Like many of his peers, he moved away from the stance of antiprofessionalism that had been an important dimension of much avant-garde activity, musical and otherwise, in the formative years.

Chou Wen-Chung was born in China (Chefoo, in 1924) and did not come to this country until he was in his twenties. He was traditionally trained at the New England Conservatory and Columbia University, and became fluent in Western music, as a performer and composer. But he never rejected his own heritage; as he wrote early in his career, "I was influenced by the same philosophy that guides every Chinese artist, be he poet, painter, or musician: affinity to nature in conception, allusiveness in expression, and terseness in realization";[72] and private study with Varèse opened to him the possibility of drawing on the melodic and expressive elements of his own music while keeping his compositions within the context of Western music. *Suite for Harp and Wind Quaintet* (1950)[73] is written for European instruments and intended for performance in a concert setting; it draws its melodic material from five Chinese songs; both horizontal and vertical sonorities are heavily dependent on the pentatonic scale; heterophonic techniques are often more apparent than are functional harmonies; and the melodic material is not subjected to the classic Western techniques of expansion and development. Though Chou never embraced "radical empiricism" in as extreme a way as did Cage, some of his compositions of the 1960s and '70s use the *I-Ching* to determine certain parameters of a piece, and he offers his performers some freedom of execution within controlled limits. In addition, he has been an articulate spokesman for the incorporation of non-Western techniques into the compositions of American composers.[74]

Terry Riley's *In C* (1964)[75] was probably the most widely performed avant-garde composition of the 1960s. The score consists of fifty-three melodic figures, ranging from a single note to an extended phrase; it may be performed by any number of instruments, of any sort. One instrument, usually a piano, gives out a steady pulse of octave C's; the other instruments play the first melodic segment whenever they choose, as many times as they please, then move on to the second, the third, and so on until they

[72] Edward Murray, "Chou Wen-Chung," in *The New Grove Dictionary of Music and Musicians*, IV, p. 359.

[73] NW 237, s2 / 1.

[74] Chou Wen-Chung, "Asian Concepts and Twentieth-Century Composers," *Musical Quarterly*, LVII (1971), pp. 211–19.

[75] *In C* is available on Columbia Records, MS 7178.

have worked their way through all fifty-three. The performance ends when the last player has played the last segment for the last time. The effect is of a slowly shifting mass of sound, repetitive and hypnotic. The piece may last for as long as an hour, and is somewhat different in each performance.

La Monte Young, Steve Reich, and Philip Glass also based their works of the 1960s and '70s on the repetition of short phrases, usually in slowly shifting relationships and gradually changing patterns. Each of these men had some significant contact with non-Western music: Riley and Young were students of the classical Indian singer Pandit Pran Nath; Reich studied African drumming in Ghana; Glass studied tabla with Allah Rakha, was associated with Ravi Shankar in creating a film score, and traveled through North Africa and parts of Asia. Their music, which has been labeled "trance music" and "minimal music" by critics grappling to understand it, draws heavily on their understanding of non-Western music and thought; its patterns and gestures are repetitive, hypnotic, and meditative, rather than dynamic and linear.

Young's *The Tortoise, His Dreams and Journeys*, conceived and begun in 1964, assumes a different time reference from that of Western art: a tiny germ of musical material is endlessly repeated and elaborated each day; the entire piece was projected to last for many years, possibly for the lifetime of the composer. Riley's *A Rainbow in Curved Air* (1970) develops a lengthy piece out of a small amount of melodic material, played by the composer himself on the electric organ with the aid of tape loops and studio mixing, overlay, and multiple tracks. Reich's *Come Out* (1967) is based on the recitation of the words "Come out to show them," recorded on several tracks of tape, repeated insistently, and gradually moving out of phase, in the process becoming transformed from intelligible words to nonintelligible sounds. His *Four Organs* (1970) is based on a single chord, and *Drumming* (1971)—for eight small tuned drums, three marimbas, three glockenspiels, piccolo, and solo voices—which lasts for an hour and a half, is based on "one basic rhythmic pattern [which] undergoes changes of phase, position, pitch, and timbre, but all of the performers play this pattern, or some part of it, throughout the entire piece."[76] Glass's opera *Einstein on the Beach* (1976), to a text by Robert Wilson, described by John Rockwell of *The New York Times* as a "mixture of mathematical clarity and mystical allure," brought this music to the attention of the largest public to date when given two performances at the Metropolitan Opera on November 21 and 28, 1976.

[76] Steve Reich, liner notes for *Drumming* (New York and Los Angeles: John Gibson & Multiples, 1971).

A scene from *Einstein on the Beach* by Philip Glass. (Photograph by Ken Howard)

Ever since Henry Cowell strummed, stroked, plucked, and thumped the piano in the 1910s, avant-garde composers have constantly sought to expand the sonic range of traditional instruments. The emergence of a remarkably talented generation of performers in the 1950s and '60s gave new impetus to this trend: Stuart Dempster (trombone), David Tudor (piano), Cathy Berberian (voice), William O. Smith (clarinet), Bertram Turetsky (double bass), and Harvey Sollberger (flute) were only a few of the performers eager to work with composers in enlarging and exploiting the repertory of available sounds. Smith's *Fancies for Clarinet Alone* (1969)[77] will serve to give a sense of what became possible: in the course of the ten sections of the piece, the clarinet explores the extreme ranges of the instrument and a variety of articulations; produces two- and three-note clusters of sound (by humming and playing simultaneously, by employing harmonics, and by a combination of these methods); produces a variety of multiphonics; draws on several different types of vibrato and glissando; and at times manages to combine several of these. Turetsky's performance of *Inflections I* (1969) by Robert Hall Lewis[78] and Sollberger's playing of his own *Sunflowers* (1976)[79] demonstrate the use of similar techniques on the double bass and the flute.

[77] NW 209, s1 / 3.
[78] NW 254, s1 / 3.
[79] NW 254, s1 / 1.

The avant-garde was also involved in the earliest attempts to utilize electrically produced sounds in composition. John Cage, in his several pieces entitled *Imaginary Landscape* written between 1939 and 1943, used electric buzzers, audio oscillators, amplified wire coils, radios, and variable-speed phonograph equipment to obtain a variety of electrically produced sounds. World War II brought magnetic tape; Cage, with Earle Brown, David Tudor, Christian Wolff, and several sound engineers, established the Project of Music for Magnetic Tape in New York around 1950—at just the time that a group of French composers headed by Pierre Schaeffer began experimentation with "musique concrète," compositions created by recording natural and artificial sounds on tape, then cutting and splicing them in the musical equivalent of a collage.

Werner Meyer-Eppler, a German physicist, experimented with the mechanical production of sound as early as 1949 and lectured on the potential of electronic music at the International Summer School for New Music in Darmstadt in 1950. In 1951 a Studio für Elektronische Musik was established by the West German Radio at Cologne. Herbert Eimert and Robert Beyer produced the first compositions of electronically produced sound in 1953; the first public concert of such music took place in Cologne on October 19, 1954, featuring pieces by Eimert, Stockhausen, and others—most of them serial works. This same year, the German periodical *Die Reihe* devoted an entire issue to articles concerned with electronic music. Within a few years, electronic studios had been established at state radio stations in other countries—Japan, Italy, Poland—and composers of many nationalities were attempting to discover the best means of utilizing this new source of sound.[80]

In the United States, the first public demonstration of tape music came in 1952, at Columbia University (by Otto Luening) and at the University of Illinois (the first performance of Cage's *William Mix*). A concert at the Museum of Modern Art in New York on October 28, 1952 included several pieces created on tape by Luening (*Low Speed*, *Invention*, and *Fantasy in Space*) and Vladimir Ussachevsky (*Sonic Contours*). The two combined to produce *Rhapsodic Variations* for tape and orchestra, for the Louisville Orchestra in 1954. Lejaren Hiller began assembling equipment for an electronic studio at the University of Illinois in 1958, and the Columbia-Princeton Electronic Music Centre was formed in January of 1959 around the RCA Mark II Music Synthesizer developed by Harry Olsen and Herbert Belar.

---

[80] For a history of electronic music, cf. Jon H. Appleton and Ronald C. Perera, *The Development and Practice of Electronic Music* (Englewood Cliffs: Prentice-Hall, 1975).

Studios with electronic sound-producing equipment—as opposed to tape studios—thus developed later in the United States than in Europe, and were usually located at universities. Thus many of the first American composers to have access to sophisticated electronic equipment were members of the "university avant-garde," concerned at this time with serialization of the various parameters of a musical composition. When avant-garde composers began having access to electronic equipment, their concerns were so much with indeterminacy and the loosening of controls on performers that purely electronic music was of little interest. More typically, they utilized electronics to produce pieces in which taped sounds are used in conjunctions with live performers,[81] or to create "live electronics"—the use of electrical equipment to amplify, alter, distort, enrich, and intensify sounds produced by live performers. Cage was again a pioneer, with pieces for amplified piano (*Winter Music*, 1957), the use of contact microphones (*Variations II*, 1961), and *Cartridge Music* (1960), in which a variety of sounds is produced through manipulation of phonograph cartridges and amplified through the sound system of these phonograph machines. In the 1960s many younger members of the American avant-garde, including Gordon Mumma, LaMonte Young, Max Neuhaus, Alvin Lucier, Robert Ashley, and David Tudor, experimented with various applications of the concept of live electronics.[82]

John Cage has continued to produce uniquely innovative pieces into the early 1980s, and some second generation avant-gardists have persisted with uncompromising creations reflecting continuing concern with compositional issues first raised in the 1950s and '60s—the "minimalists" and individuals such as Pauline Oliveros, Philip Corner, Nam June Paik, Alvin Lucier, and Malcolm Goldstein.

It is a matter of historical record that the first pieces of European music to make use of aleatoric methods—Karlheinz Stockhausen's *Klavierstuck IX* (1956), *Klavierstuck XI* (1956), and *Zyklus* (1959), Pierre Boulez's *Piano Sonata No. 3* (1956–57) and *Pli selon pli* (1957–62)—were written after Cage and some of his peers had introduced similar concepts into their music, and just after Cage and his music had reached Europe. Composers in eastern Europe in the late 1950s and '60s (Krzysztof Penderecki, Witold Lutosławski, Gyorgy Ligeti) utilized massed clusters of sound, sought to exploit the widest

[81] Cf. Roger Reynolds, *From Behind the Unreasoning Mask* for live performers and tape, on NW 237, s1 / 1.

[82] Cf. Gordon Mumma, "Live-Electronic Music," in Appleton and Perera, Chapter 6, for a history and discussion of this music.

possible range of instrumental sound, and explored the compositional means obtainable through new notational systems—all matters of concern to the American avant-garde in the decades preceding the emergence of this new wave of Polish and Hungarian music. A number of rock musicians involved in the more progressive trends of the 1970s, among them Brian Eno, John Cale, Yoko Ono, David Bowie, Lou Reed, Robert Fripp, and Frank Zappa, had direct ties to the avant-garde. The New York New Wave movement, traceable from the Velvet Underground through the New York Dolls to the Talking Heads, was shaped in part by the New York avant-garde scene. And surely, the free jazz of Ornette Coleman, Cecil Taylor, and Miles Davis draws at least indirectly on avant-garde activity.

The notion that Western classical music went through a dramatic stylistic change in the first years of the twentieth century becomes less tenable as the century approaches its end. We can see, with the perspective of time, that the music of Stravinsky, Schoenberg, Berg, Bartók, Hindemith, Sessions, Prokofiev, Britten, and even Webern represents a continuation and extension of compositional techniques and aesthetic attitudes of the previous century. It was only after World War II that music moved in directions inexplicable in reference to what had come before. Major stylistic breaks in the history of Western music have always necessitated innovations in notation—radically new musical impulses cannot be contained within notational systems devised for another sort of music. Until mid-century, twentieth-century music fit comfortably into the system that had served for several hundred years; from that point on, new notations had to be invented.[83] The American avant-garde initiated these notational innovations, just as they began the approaches to musical composition that have brought a thoroughly new music in the second half of the twentieth century, in America and in the rest of the world.

For the first time, "classical" music in the United States has not been a reflection of what was happening elsewhere, but has become a model for composers in other countries.

[83] Cf. John Cage, ed., *Notations* (New York: Something Else Press, 1969), Erhard Karkoschka, *Notation in New Music* (New York: Alexander Broude, 1972), and Kurt Stone, *Music Notation in the Twentieth Century* (New York: W. W. Norton & Company, 1980).

# 20

## *The Age of Rock*

I believe my music can make the blind see, the lame walk, the deaf and dumb hear and talk, because it inspires and uplifts people. It uplifts the soul, you see everybody's movin', they're happy, it regenerates the heart and makes the liver quiver, the bladder splatter, the knees freeze.

—Little Richard[1]

Rock 'n' roll, which emerged as the dominant form of American popular music in 1955, was understood and enjoyed by a larger cross-section of the racial, ethnic, and cultural groups of the United States than had ever before responded to one type of music.

Worldwide reaction was similar. Rock 'n' roll was heard by responsive audiences in every continent, in virtually every country on the globe not too impoverished for its people to have access to radios and phonograph equipment.

It was perceived, everywhere, as a uniquely American product.

Rock 'n' roll was, first of all, an interracial music.

Performers were both black and white, in roughly equal proportions. Chuck Berry, Little Richard, Fats Domino, the Platters, Sam Cooke, Brook Benton, Lloyd Price, and the Coasters were black; Bill Haley, Elvis Presley, the Everly Brothers, Jerry Lee Lewis, Buddy Holly, and Gene Vincent were white.

*Billboard*, the trade journal of the music industry, had carried

---

[1] *The Rolling Stone Interviews* (New York: Paperback Library, 1971) pp. 376–77.

weekly charts of top-selling phonograph records for some years before 1955. It was assumed that there were three distinct and discrete audiences, each responding to different types of popular music:

a white, middle- and upper-class group, partial to the products of Tin Pan Alley songwriters;

a black audience, responsive to music by black performers, known at this time as "rhythm and blues";

an audience located principally in the South, the Midwest and the West, largely rural (or recently descended from a rural heritage), dedicated to country-western music.

Between 1955 and 1960, a number of rock 'n' roll performers released discs that enjoyed equal popularity with two and even all three of these groups. Some of them—by Elvis Presley, the Everly Brothers, Jerry Lee Lewis, Johnny Horton—not only appeared on all three charts, they became No. 1 hits with all three audiences.

It seems fair to say that rock 'n' roll came as close to being a universal musical language as the country—and the world—had ever known, at least within the age group that responded to such music.

And it was not merely a matter of blacks and whites listening to the same music—they were listening to it together. Alan Freed, a white disc jockey at radio station WWJ in Cleveland who began a show in 1951 featuring music mostly by black performers, organized a live concert in March of 1953; the some 75,000 people who turned out—attempting to get into an auditorium designed for a third of that number—were equally divided between black and white. Similar racially mixed audiences showed up for concerts organized by Freed in Cincinnati, New York, and elsewhere; and when the first rock 'n' roll stars gave live performances, they were confronted with mixed audiences, in all parts of America.

The following sequence of events will serve to underline the interracial nature of rock 'n' roll:

—Two young white songwriters, Jerry Lieber and Mike Stoller, wrote a song entitled "Hound Dog" in 1952 for a black singer, Willie Mae "Big Mama" Thornton.[2] First sung by her in clubs in San Francisco, it was recorded in August on the Peacock label and by the late winter of 1953 had become a No. 1 item on *Billboard*'s rhythm-and-blues charts.

—After being "covered" by several other singers with little commercial success, it was recorded by Elvis Presley for RCA Victor in the winter of 1956. In July it reached the top of the white pop charts in *Billboard*.

[2] NW 261, s2 / 4.

—In August, Presley's disc became the top-selling disc on both the rhythm-and-blues and the country-western charts.

The success of this music with mixed audiences is a reflection of the fact that its style reflects elements of both black and white culture.

The prototype of rock 'n' roll had begun to emerge as early as the 1930s. In order to understand this, it is necessary first to define the rock 'n' roll style of the 1950s.

In any representative sampling of pieces recorded between 1955 and 1958 which were taken by listeners of the time to be unequivocally in the rock 'n' roll style—say "Rock Around the Clock" (1955) or "See You Later, Alligator" (1955) by Bill Haley and the Comets;[3] "Maybellene" (1955)[4] or "Johnny B. Goode" (1958) by Chuck Berry; "Heartbreak Hotel" (1957) or "Hound Dog" (1956) by Elvis Presley; "Whole Lotta Shakin' Going On" (1957) or "Good Golly Miss Molly" (1962)[5] by Jerry Lee Lewis; "Tutti Frutti" (1955) by Little Richard; "That'll Be the Day" (1957) by Buddy Holly and the Crickets;[6] "I Can't Go On" (1955)[7] or "Blue Monday" (1956) by Fats Domino—the following characteristics may be observed:

—Formally, the pieces are shaped in a 12-bar blues structure or some variation on this pattern.

—Instrumentally, there is a rhythm section of drums and bass, sometimes augmented by a piano; one or more amplified or electric guitars function both as melodic and rhythmic instruments; there are usually one or more horns, most commonly an alto saxophone and/or a trumpet. Rock 'n' roll bands had in common a loud but clean sound: all instruments were either naturally loud or amplified, and the small size of the ensemble allowed each to be heard without being lost in a jumble of sound.

—Rhythmically, they are in 4 / 4 or ¢ meter, moving along at a fast, driving pace, suitable to energetic dancing; many early discs were labeled as fox trots. There is a strong emphasis on the first beat of each measure, marked by power strokes from the drummer—Europeans soon called it Big Beat or Beat music—and an emphasis on the second and fourth beats as well, usually by a cymbal or other high-pitched percussion instrument and/or by rhythm guitar.

—Texts are concerned with sex: "rock and roll" was a euphe-

[3] NW 249, s1 / 5.
[4] NW 249, s1 / 6.
[5] NW 249, s2 / 3.
[6] NW 249, s2 / 2.
[7] NW 249, s1 / 8.

mism among blacks for sexual intercourse. A string of episodic verses is interspersed by instrumental choruses; the time restrictions of the 45-rpm phonograph disc—the most important vehicle for the dissemination of this music—imposed a pattern of 3–4 vocal verses alternating with an instrumental chorus or two. In live performance, with no such time restrictions, this pattern was varied with additional vocal verses and many more instrumental choruses. The dominant instrumentalist of a given band would be given the solo verses, whether he was a guitarist, pianist, or saxophonist.

—Rock 'n' roll singers were concerned with a type of vocal projection that would match the raucous, rhythmic sound and mood of the instruments. They shouted, screamed, sobbed, and punctuated their texts with explosive interjections or nonsense syllables.

These stylistic features are drawn from both jazz (the instrumentation and rhythmic propulsion) and blues (the structure and singing style). Thus the term "rhythm and blues," used by *Billboard* as a label for its charts of music by black performers for black audiences between 1949 and 1969, is an apt one.

Once the most important characteristics of early rock 'n' roll have been defined, one can identify similar pieces recorded before the "official" beginning of the genre in 1955, when Bill Haley's "Rock Around the Clock" reached the No. 1 position on the *Billboard* charts.

"Shake, Rattle and Roll," which became a best-selling disc among blacks in early 1954 in a recording by Joe Turner,[8] is a piece of rock 'n' roll in everything save name. "Work with Me, Annie," recorded the same year by the Midnighters, was just as solidly in the mold of what would soon be called rock 'n' roll, as were also a number of rhythm-and-blues hits of the previous year (1953): "Have Mercy, Baby," by Billy Ward and His Dominoes,[9] the above mentioned "Hound Dog" by Big Mama Thornton.[10] Ruth Brown's "Mama, He Treats Your Daughter Mean"[11] is a transitional piece—the 12-bar blues form has been extended to 16 measures through the addition of a fourth phrase; the band is larger and has more the sound of pure jazz, with no guitars; and the tempo is somewhat more leisurely. A recent writer has said of "I'm Your Hootchie Coochie Man," recorded in 1952 by Muddy Waters:[12]

---

[8] NW 249, s1 / 1.
[9] NW 249, s1 / 3.
[10] NW 261, s2 / 4.
[11] NW 261, s2 / 5.
[12] NW 261, s2 / 7.

All the elements of rock are present: whining treble electric-guitar fills around the melody; a slurring, muttering, shouting delivery of the lyrics; rolling drum rhythms underpinned by a near-contrapuntal bass line and a call-and-response riff pattern; a beat that socks away unmercifully. There is even a strong sense of Mick Jaggerish mystical-macho sexism in the lyrics.[13]

"Good Rockin' Tonight," recorded by Wynonie Harris in Cincinnati in 1947,[14] is perfectly defined by the characteristics of rock 'n' roll, and the text even uses the term itself. "Call It Stormy Monday" (1947), featuring the singing and electric guitar playing of T-Bone Walker, needs only a faster tempo and more emphatic drumming to qualify fully as rock 'n' roll. The same is true of many blues recorded as far back as the 1930s in which the singer is accompanied by a small instrumental ensemble playing in a markedly rhythmic style. In fact, in a somewhat broader sense, the entire range of rhythmicized blues of the jazz era, including the "jump blues" featured by many bands (Lionel Hampton's "Hey! Ba-Ba-Re-Bop" of 1945 is a classic example) and even the boogie woogie school of piano playing[15] may be seen as direct ancestors of rock 'n' roll.

All of this music was played by blacks, mostly for black audiences. But some Southern and rural whites were hearing music in a quite similar style in the decades leading up to 1955. Bill Haley's background was in country-western music; beginning with "Rocket 88" in 1951 and continuing through such pieces as "Crazy, Man, Crazy" (1953) and "Happy Baby" (1954), Haley's group performed and recorded a string of rhythmic 12-bar blues pieces approaching the rock 'n' roll style of "Rock Around the Clock." One of Hank Williams's first discs, "Move It On Over" (1949), is in 12-bar blues form with insistent rhythmic drive (including important accents on the second and fourth beats), instrumental choruses featuring an electric guitar, right down to its text filled with sexual innuendoes. The melody of the opening phrase, incidentally, is virtually identical with that of "Rock Around the Clock."

Just as with black music, it is possible to move back into the 1940s and even 1930s in country-western music to find prototypes of this sort of piece. Many of these were the product of the "honky-tonk" culture of the Southwest, the breeding ground of the electric guitar. Others date back even further; "Keep It Clean," recorded in Atlanta in 1930 by the white musicians Rufus and Ben Quillian

---

[13] Don Heckman, liner notes for NW 261.
[14] NW 261, s1 / 8.
[15] Cf. NW 259 for a selection of this music.

and James McCrary,[16] is a rhythmicized blues with a highly suggestive text, a clear anticipation of "Move It On Over" and other later pieces of this genre.

Thus pieces moving in the direction of rock 'n' roll may be found in both rhythm-and-blues and country-western music for a quarter-century before 1955. Most of the elements of this music evolved among black musicians; the 12-bar blues form had its origins in Afro-American music, the rhythmic propulsion has much more to do with black than white music. But, as with ragtime and jazz, it was not simply a matter of white musicians appropriating a style developed by blacks. The rhythmicized blues of country-western music developed its own rhythmic dialect, similar but not identical to that of rhythm-and-blues, colored by the eccentricities of rural white dance music. And the pervasive use of the guitar, which became the basic instrument of the entire rock era, grew out of country-western music.

Whether black or white, virtually all musicians of the early rock 'n' roll period had their musical and cultural roots in the rural South. Rock 'n' roll was not only interracial, it was also Southern. Many of the reactions to this music can best be understood if one keeps these two factors in mind.

The recording industry had sounded an alarm some months before rock 'n' roll hit the nation's headlines in the summer of 1955. *Variety,* the trade journal of the entertainment industry, ran a series of articles in early 1955 calling attention to the fact that rhythm-and-blues discs were grabbing a major share of the white market, and an editorial on February 23, 1955 suggested that the industry should take steps to check this music, which was threatening a "total breakdown of all reticences about sex" with its "leer-ics" resembling "dirty postcards translated into songs."

The commercial success of "Rock Around the Clock" and similar pieces, and the emergence of Elvis Presley in early 1956, brought rock 'n' roll to the forefront of the country's consciousness. The popular press, after virtually ignoring rhythm-and-blues and the first wave of rock 'n' roll, gave intensive and sensational coverage to this "new music" in 1956 and '57. Americans could read about it in *Time:*

> Rock 'n' roll is based on Negro blues, but in a self-conscious style which underlines the primitive qualities of the blues with malice aforethought. Characteristics: an unrelenting, socking syncopation that sounds like a bull whip; a choleric saxophone honking mating-call sounds; an electric

[16] NW 290, s2/2.

guitar turned up so loud that its sound shatters and splits; a vocal group
that shudders and exercises violently to the beat while roughly chanting
either a near-nonsense phrase or a moronic lyric in hillbilly idiom. It
does for music what a motorcycle club at full throttle does for a quiet
Sunday afternoon. The results bear passing resemblance to Hitler mass
meetings.[17]

in *Newsweek*:

Haley gave the downbeat, the brasses blared, and the kids leaped into
the aisles to dance, only to be chased back to their seats by the special
cops. Some of the kids danced, some scuffled, fights broke out, a chair
flew. The fight overflowed into the streets. A 19-year-old was struck over
the head, and a 16-year-old was cut in the ear. Two cars were stoned
and one exuberant teen-ager turned in a false alarm. "It's that jungle
beat that gets 'em all worked up," said Armory manager Arthur (Dutch)
Bergman.[18]

Bill Haley and the Comets. (Courtesy Retna, Ltd., photograph by David
Redfern)

[17] From the issue for June 18, 1956, p. 67.
[18] From the issue for June 18, 1956, p. 47.

and eventually even in the *New York Times*:

> "Rocking" the song as though in a life and death struggle with an invisible antagonist was a tall, thin, flaccid youth who pulled his stringy, blond hair over his eyes and down to his chin. He shook his torso about as the beat of the band seemingly goaded him on. Screams from thousands of young throats billowed toward him. In the pandemonium, youngsters flailed the air with their arms, jumped from their seats, beckoned madly, lovingly, to the tortured figure onstage. The song could scarcely be heard over the footlights. The applause and yells all but raised the roof. Then a Negro quartet raced onstage, adjusted the microphones, and a new tune brought on a new cascade of screams and energetic handwaves.[19]

The press stressed the violence and disorder sometimes accompanying rock 'n' roll concerts and related this to one of the popular topics of the day—juvenile delinquency. There was trouble during concerts by Bill Haley in Washington and Minneapolis; Elvis Presley was mobbed by frenzied fans in Jacksonville; ugly incidents marred performances by Fats Domino and his band in Houston, Newport (Rhode Island), and Fayetteville (North Carolina); twenty-five members of the audience ended up in the hospital after a rock 'n' roll show in Asbury Park's Convention Hall; fifteen persons were injured in incidents outside the Boston Arena following an evening of rock 'n' roll, though police were unable to prove that members of the audience were involved.

Each of these incidents had racial overtones, which the press invariably stressed. Black and white performers were on the same programs; audiences were always mixed, racially; trouble spots were Southern cities, or those in the North with large concentrations of blacks—Washington and Boston, for instance. The implication was that trouble occurred *because* of interracial situations, though incidents usually involved members of the same race, or pitted the audience against police or security guards.

The most overt opposition to rock 'n' roll came from white supremists in the South, who saw the music as part of a plot to "force Negro culture on the South." Asa E. "Ace" Carter, a leader of the North Alabama Citizens Council, described rock 'n' roll as "the basic, heavy-beat music of Negroes. It appeals to the base in man, brings out animalism and vulgarity." Though the "responsible" American press took pains to deplore such attitudes, its own coverage of rock 'n' roll was colored by culturally based innuendoes. The sights and sounds of rock 'n' roll concerts were equated

[19]*New York Times Magazine* for January 12, 1958, p. 16.

with the "jungle" and the "zoo," to remind readers of the African heritage of black performers; the word "hillbilly" was dusted off and used with its old derogatory implications as a label for white rock 'n' rollers. Elvis Presley was portrayed as a near-illiterate, spending his free time at amusement parks and speaking in a corrupt dialect of English:

> "I won 24 Teddy bears at a fair once. People was giving me money to win them one. . . . I wouldn't want no regular spot on no TV program. I don't care nothing whatsoever about singing in no movie. English was what I liked best in high school."[20]

And *Time* ended its first article on rock 'n' roll, in its issue of July 23, 1956, by quoting a writer in the *Denver Post* who had put into words what the editorial staff clearly felt about this music, but was unwilling to say itself: "This hooby-dooby, oop-shoop, ootie ootie, boom boom de-addy boom, scoobledy gobbledy dump—is trash."

The emergence of rock 'n' roll coincided with a period in American history when racial, ethnic, and regional minorities began seeking the equality available to them in theory but long denied in practice; this struggle, and the attempts to contain it, were vividly reflected in the early history of this music.

Though the definition of rock 'n' roll given above serves for much of the repertory of the first several years, the term "rock 'n' roll" soon covered a much wider range of music. For instance, by 1956 virtually any sort of popular music by black performers was taken to be rock 'n' roll.

The history of white acceptance of black musicians predates the advent of rock 'n' roll by many years. The Mills Brothers, a quartet of black singers from Piqua, Ohio, had a million-selling disc as far back as 1930; their "Paper Doll" of 1942 helped bring about the demise of the big bands, and is reputed to have sold more than 10 million discs; their commercial success continued through the 1950s. Almost as successful were the Ink Spots, who cut their first disc in 1937, had their first success in 1941 with "If I Didn't Care," and reached the peak of their careers in 1944 with "Into Each Life Some Rain Must Fall," cofeaturing Ella Fitzgerald. Like most black performers of this era who were widely accepted by whites (Lena Horne, Nat King Cole, Ella Fitzgerald), their repertory was drawn from Tin Pan Alley, and their musical style was close to that of white performers of the era. The penalty for success with whites

[20]*Newsweek* for May 14, 1956, p. 82.

was nonacceptance by blacks, who heard their music as having little to do with black popular music.

The 1940s and early 1950s saw the proliferation of black vocal groups whose products were aimed at black audiences and whose musical style incorporated elements of gospel music: falsetto male singing; exaggerated emotionalism; rhythmic accompaniment, either from instruments or handclapping. In the early 1950s, many whites turned to this new urban black popular music, finding it close enough to their own music to be accessible, while more lively and vital than the products of a dying Tin Pan Alley culture. "Crying in the Chapel," recorded in 1953 by the Orioles,[21] was a No. 1 seller among rhythm-and-blues audiences which also placed high on the "white" charts. Its success with white audiences appears to have more to do with its stylistic indebtedness to white music—it is a straightforward Tin Pan Alley song, consisting of a 32-bar *AABA* chorus, and the Orioles' performance is much *less* rhythmic than the Mills Brothers' "Glow Worm," of the previous year.

Other black groups were performing music more characteristic of the emerging black urban popular style, however. The Clovers made use of more rhythmic exuberance;[22] the Ravens used the full range of the male voice, from low bass to the extraordinary high falsetto of lead singer Maithe Marshall.[23] The Platters had a string of successes with both black and white audiences between 1955 and 1960—"Only You" (1955), "The Great Pretender" (1955), "My Prayer" (1956), "Twilight Time" (1958), "Smoke Gets in Your Eyes" (1958), "Harbor Lights" (1960)—which blend smoothly harmonized vocals, falsetto singing, and subtly rhythmic backings to give a sound heard as distinctly black in style. As a black group with a biracial following, they were accepted as part of the world of rock 'n' roll, despite the great differences between their music and that of Chuck Berry and Little Richard.

The lead singer in these black groups was often accompanied by humming or meaningless syllables. These backgrounds became increasingly rhythmic, in such pieces as "Gee" by the Crows and "Sh-Boom" by the Chords, both released in 1954. Within a few years, these rhythmic, nonsense-syllable backings had become the trademark of a new dialect of black urban music, soon labeled "doo-wop" (or "do-wop"). A classic of the genre is "Get a Job" (1958) by the Silhouettes,[24] which became a best-seller with both white and black audiences. The several verses sketch the vignette of a man

[21] NW 261, s2 / 6.
[22] Cf. their "One Mint Julep" on NW 261, s2 / 3.
[23] Cf. their "Give Me a Simple Prayer" on NW 261, s1 / 9.
[24] NW 249, s2/1.

nagged by his wife (girl friend? mother?) to find a job, with the refrain:

Sha da da da, sha da da da da, ba-dum,   (4 times)
Yip yip yip yip yip yip yip yip
Mm mm mm mm mm mm
Get a job
Sha da da da, sha da da da da.

The rhythmic emphasis of this music, and the fact that it was performed by blacks for mixed audiences, qualified it for inclusion under the umbrella of rock 'n' roll. Thousands of groups were formed in the second half of the 1950s; no rock 'n' roll broadcast or live program was complete without at least one "do-wop" group. Among the most successful were the Flamingos, the Dell-Vikings, the Clovers, the Coasters, the Drifters, Little Anthony and the Imperials. There were all-female groups, like the Shirelles[25] and the Chantels; there were white imitators (the Skyliners, the Fleetwoods, the Safaris). Repertory ranged from "covers" of Tin Pan Alley standards, to new songs in the same style, to an occasional 12-bar blues, to loosely constructed songs with no obvious formal roots in either white or black music. There were sentimental love songs, plenty of humor, a scattering of songs with implied criticism of the social order of America.[26] Mostly they were good-time songs, rhythmic and light-hearted, not nearly as concerned with sex as early rock 'n' roll had been, not as intensely rhythmic and usually not as loud. Many older Americans who had reacted angrily against the first wave of rock 'n' roll found that they could live with, or simply ignore, this sort of music. The most "disturbing" element was that it continued to be biracial.

Country-western audiences had taken to the musical style of early rock 'n' roll, but they accepted their own—Elvis Presley, Jerry Lee Lewis—while rejecting black performers. Not one disc by a black rock 'n' roller, even Chuck Berry or Fats Domino, appeared on *Billboard*'s country-western charts, and the entire "do-wop" movement was by-passed. There developed, rather, a distinctive strain of rock 'n' roll among rural whites. Among these "rockabilly" performers were Carl Perkins ("Blue Suede Shoes," 1956), Eddie Cochran ("Summertime Blues," 1958), Gene Vincent ("Be-Bop-a-Lula," 1956), and Johnny Horton ("The Battle of New Orleans," 1959).[27]

Most successful were the Everly Brothers, with a string of fifteen Top Ten discs between 1957 and 1962 beginning with "Bye Bye

[25] Cf. their "I Met Him on a Sunday" on NW 249, s2 / 5.
[26] Cf. "What About Us?" by the Coasters on NW 249, s2 / 8.
[27] NW 249, s2 / 9.

The Everly Brothers, (Courtesy Warner Brothers)

Love" and including three No. 1 hits—"Wake Up Little Susie" (1957), "All I Have To Do Is Dream" (1958), and "Cathy's Clown" (1960). This music emphasized the features of the early rock 'n' roll style most rooted in white music—the use of guitars as the dominant instrument, the flexible use of 12-bar blues form, singing styles more nasal and less flexible than those of blacks. Curiously, though country-western audiences rejected black rock 'n' rollers and most of the later developments of rock music, blacks responded to these "rockabilly" performers with some enthusiasm.

The established popular music industry was challenged and severely threatened by rock 'n' roll and its great commercial success. The major recording companies—Victor, Columbia, Capitol, Decca, and Mercury—refused at first to go along with it. They were convinced that it was only a fad and they were not comfortable or successful in dealing with its practitioners, the blacks and "hillbillies" who were its first stars. As a result, the five major companies which had accounted for 42 of the 50 top-selling discs in 1954 managed only 17 discs in the top 50 in 1956. They were replaced by a number of small companies, virtually unknown before the onslaught of rock—Sun, Imperial, Chess, Dootone—which recorded black or country-western performers.

The threat of rock 'n' roll went beyond its impact on record sales. Popular music was a large, profitable, and rapidly growing industry in the decade following the end of World War II. *Variety* magazine reported that sales of phonograph discs grossed $215,000,000 in 1953; sales of sheet music versions of popular songs brought many more millions; performance fees and royalties from live and radio performances accounted for tens of millions more. The industry was large and complex, employing thousands of persons—the star singers; instrumentalists in backing orchestras and bands for live performances and recording sessions; songwriters and lyricists; arrangers and copyists; conductors; record producers and A & R men; and people in sales, promotion, and other supporting jobs.

All this was threatened by rock 'n' roll. Since it was an oral music, not written down, performed by a small number of players who had the music in their heads or improvised it on the spot, there was no need for arrangers, studio orchestras, or copyists. Three or four rock 'n' roll musicians could accomplish, without support of any sort, what had taken an entire team of people to bring about in Tin Pan Alley music. It was a simple, efficient, effective system. And it threatened the jobs of many thousands of people.

The industry's first response was an attempt to discredit rock 'n' roll and its performers in its trade journal, *Variety*, and in pronouncements from its union and public relations organization, ASCAP. When it became apparent that rock 'n' roll was taking root in American culture, the industry sensibly decided to embrace it. Within a half-year after the success of Bill Haley's "Rock Around the Clock," the major recording companies were bringing out songs which—while retaining the entire apparatus of Tin Pan Alley— appropriated silly texts, more rhythmic music with a heavier percussion section, and what the industry perceived as other elements of rock 'n' roll.

Perhaps the first piece of this sort was Columbia's release, in late 1955, of "Ooh Bang, Jiggilly Jang" by Doris Day; it had as little to do with rock 'n' roll as its title suggests, and enjoyed only a flicker of success. Much more successful was RCA Victor's "Rock and Roll Waltz," with Kay Starr, offered merely as a novelty song. It reached the No. 1 position on the *Billboard* charts for four weeks in the winter of 1956, the first evidence that the industry was forging a successful alternative to rock 'n' roll.

Other releases of "novelty" songs by the major companies followed, making some reference in text and music to the phonomenon of rock 'n' roll, featuring established singing stars: MGM's "Rock Around Mother Goose" (1955), with Barry Gordon and Art Mooney; Mercury's "Rock Right" (1956) by Georgia Gibbs, of "Your Hit Parade" fame; RCA Victor's "Rockin' Shoes" (1957) by the Ames Brothers. But these did not come close to stemming the tide of legitimate rock 'n' roll, particularly with the emergence of Elvis Presley in 1956.

Virtually the entire rock 'n' roll audience was made up of teen-agers, the first wave of the "baby boom" following World War II. There were not only millions of them, they also had money to pur-chase phonograph discs and transistor radios in affluent postwar America. And they were not likely to respond to recycled singers of their parents' generation. The problem was to locate and promote new singers, young ones, that well-to-do urban teenagers could relate to.

The pattern of the industry's most successful response to rock 'n' roll was set by Pat Boone. Boone fit into the mainstream of urban American culture and he projected the image of a handsome, clean-cut, conservative, mannerly American lad who was a source of pride to his parents and teachers. In 1954, while a student at North Texas Teachers College, he won first prize in both the Ted Mack Amateur Hour and the Arthur Godfrey Talent Scouts Show and was signed to a recording contract by Dot Records. His voice and personality were suited to the Tin Pan Alley repertory, but when rock 'n' roll emerged the year after his first disc, Dot—being a young and aggressive company—decided to capitalize on this turn of events. Many of Boone's releases in 1955 and 1956 were "covers" of rhythm-and-blues and rock 'n' roll hits by black performers: "At My Front Door" by the El Dorados, "Ain't It a Shame" by Fats Domino, "I Almost Lost My Mind" by Ivory Joe Hunter, "Tutti Frutti" and "Long Tall Sally" by Little Richard. These were recorded with the backing of a studio orchestra, sung in a vocal style with only pass-ing resemblance to the delivery of the black and rural Southern rock 'n' rollers; and once he was established as part of the rock 'n' roll scene, Boone began recording older Tin Pan Alley songs ("Love Letters in the Sand," "When the Swallows Come Back to Capis-trano") and new pieces in the same style ("Friendly Persuasion," "April Love"). And his fans accepted everything he did.

Canadian-born Paul Anka had his first hit in 1957 with "Diana." In style and substance, vocal delivery, and instrumental backings, his songs were derived from the Tin Pan Alley tradition. Despite this, he was accepted by substantial portions of the young white audience that had joyfully embraced Bill Haley, Chuck Berry, and Jerry Lee Lewis only several years before.

Boone and Anka were the first of a generation of "Teen Idols"— Frankie Avalon, Steve Lawrence, Fabian, Bobby Vee, Brenda Lee, Annette Funicello (of "The Mickey Mouse Club" fame), Ricky Nel-son, Bobby Rydell. All were white, projected an urban image, offered songs dealing with teenage romance, performed in styles only remotely related to early rock 'n' roll. Media exposure came on such television shows as Ed Sullivan's "Toast of the Town" and—most important—"The American Bandstand," hosted by Dick Clark in Philadelphia and carried by ABC-TV after 1957, with an audience in excess of 20,000,000. Clark, born in Mount Vernon, New York, and educated at Syracuse University, built his show around white, urban, northern and eastern performers. There was no more powerful force in the country for the taming of rock 'n' roll.

By the late 1950s, then, the establishment had regained much of the control of popular music. Predictably, their product had virtually no appeal for black and country-western audiences. The biracial character of early rock 'n' roll had been subdued, and American popular music had largely reverted to its pre-1955 status of three discrete audiences, each with its own performers and repertory.

On May 17, 1954, the United States Supreme Court ruled unanimously that racial segregation in public schools was unconstitutional and ordered integration to proceed with "all deliberate speed." The public high school in Little Rock, Arkansas, was ordered to admit black students in September of 1957; governor Orval Faubus mobilized the state National Guard to prevent this action, whereupon President Eisenhower ordered federal troops to the scene to enforce the court order, and nine black students entered the school on September 25. The year before, blacks in Montgomery, Alabama, led by Martin Luther King, Jr., had boycotted the city's busses and the Supreme Court ruled that segregated seating on public transportation was illegal. The pattern was clear: pressure for racial integration was building up in the country, the federal government was committed to bringing it about, and certain forces were equally determined to resist it. Integration of performers and audiences had occurred quite spontaneously in rock 'n' roll in the mid-1950s, and one could make a case that this music was in the forefront of social reform in America.

Traditional ballads and songs brought to the New World by immigrants from the British Isles, and newer songs in the same mold fashioned on this side of the Atlantic, had been the most important basis for hillbilly and country-western music. Urban, "cultured" Americans had not been responsive to this music, because of its associations with alien layers of American life and because its musical characteristics were derived from music which was strange and crude to their ears. Yet this same music, modified to bring it more in line with their musical taste, was the foundation for a new genre of song emerging in the decade after World War II.

As early as the 1940s, some singers had been attracted to the traditional ballads and songs collected and published by folklorists in various regions of the United States. John Jacob Niles, Richard Dyer-Bennet, Alan Lomax, and Burl Ives were in the forefront of this movement; each came from a literate background, each was college-educated, each learned material chiefly from phonograph records and printed collections of traditional music. They retained tunes and texts with some faithfulness, sang with voices showing more evidence of urban, cultured vocal techniques than the flat, nasal, inexpressive "high country" style of traditional Southern singers and commercial hillbilly artists, and each accompanied himself on an acoustic chord-playing instrument, usually a guitar, fitting simple triadic chords to traditional melodies. They discovered a surprisingly large audience for their products, mostly well-educated Americans looking for an alternative to the cloying, Tin Pan Alley songs comprising the popular song repertory of the day. The simplicity of tune and accompaniment, the directness of traditional texts and their willingness to deal with subject matter excluded from Tin Pan Alley lyrics (death, sex, murder, legend, the supernatural) made them an attractive alternative.

Burl Ives was the most successful, commercially. After attracting a following from his performances at clubs (most notably at the Village Vanguard in New York) and on the radio, he released a series of albums in the late 1940s and early '50s which sold steadily, though not challenging the sales of the top popular singers of the day: *Early American Ballads* for RCA Victor, *Ballads and Folk Songs* for Decca, *The Wayfaring Stranger* and *Return of the Wayfaring Stranger* for Columbia. At the same time, a group calling itself the Weavers, made up of Pete Seeger, Lee Hays, Ronnie Gilbert, and Fred Hellerman, demonstrated that such music had sales potential on single (45 rpm) discs as well; four of their versions of "folk" songs placed on the Top Ten in *Billboard*'s charts, and one ("Goodnight Irene") became a No. 1 hit in 1950. But the "folk" movement was linked with radical political causes. America was in the throes of political repression spearheaded by Senator Joseph McCarthy of Wisconsin, a series of congressional hearings brought unfavorable publicity and blacklisting to many figures in the urban folk movement, and this music disappeared from the commercial charts.[28]

[28] For an account of this movement, cf. Serge Denisoff, *Great Day Coming. Folk Music and the American Left* (Urbana: University of Illinois Press, 1971).

But not for long. Coffeehouses and basement clubs catering to college students and politically liberal urbanites found that their business improved if they employed "folk" musicians. A network of "folk" clubs grew up on the fringes of college campuses and in the larger cities, particularly on the two coasts, and a new crop of singers emerged, mostly young, from well-to-do backgrounds, college-educated, learning their "folk" music from books and discs.

Three musicians in their early twenties—Nick Reynolds, Bob Shane, Dave Guard—billed as the Kingston Trio, made their first public appearance at the Cracked Pot, a small coffeeshop near Stanford University in Palo Alto, then moved on to San Francisco, to the hungry i and the Purple Onion. Engagements at Mr. Kelly's in Chicago and the Blue Angel in New York brought them to the establishment which had become the Mecca for the urban folk movement, the Village Vanguard. Signed to a recording contract by Capitol, their first LP was released in 1958, containing their versions of traditional Anglo-American ballads and songs. Most successful was the American ballad "Tom Dooley," which preserved in oral tradition the details of the murder in North Carolina of a young woman named Laura Foster by Tom Dula, his arrest by Sheriff Jim Grayson, and his consequent execution. Released as a single, "Tom Dooley" became a No. 1 seller, the album itself reached the top of the LP charts (remaining on them for 195 weeks), and the Kingston Trio became a serious rival to the several strains of rock 'n' roll.

The Kingstons shortened the original ballad, smoothed over some of the grisly details, and performed it in their smoothly harmonized style to the accompaniment of acoustic guitars and banjo; a studio orchestra furnishes a discreet background. Country-western audiences wouldn't touch it, but the song, the album, and the Kingstons became one of the great commercial successes of the entire decade with the white urban audience. Their success unleashed a flood of urban folk singers and singing groups seeking to grab a share of this new market.

Peter, Paul, and Mary was the most commercially successful of the groups that followed, with five consecutive Top Ten LPs between 1962 (the year of their debut album) and 1965, and an equal number of Top Ten singles. The three were city-born and college-educated, and the group followed the same path charted by the Kingston Trio—performances in coffeehouses and clubs, a contract with a large record company (Warner Borthers), and a top-selling first album, which remained on the LP charts for 185 weeks. Their repertory included songs from a variety of cultures: "We are a cosmopolitan group. It would be dishonest for us to imi-

Bob Dylan. (Courtesy of Columbia Records, CBS, Inc.)

tate the folk-singing of any particular ethnic group. But our urban background is an asset. We can present in a modern musical form the feelings of many ethnic groups and do it with integrity."[29] Joan Baez made her start as a folk singer while a student at Boston University, built a reputation in clubs in Cambridge, Chicago, and California, and brought out her first LP with Vanguard in 1960.

None of these younger performers had associations with the radical past of the urban folk-song movement, and for the most part avoided ballads and songs with overt political implications. But the arrival on the scene of a young man calling himself Bob Dylan swung things in another direction.

Dylan, born Robert Zimmerman in Duluth, Minnesota, was an admirer and emulator of Woody Guthrie (1912–67). Guthrie's career had been a totally original mix of elements from different layers of American life and culture. Born in Oklahoma, he had begun as a moderately successful hillbilly musician in Texas and California. But his wanderings brought him into contact with the entire spectrum of races and ethnic groups inhabiting the South-

[29] Irwin Stambler, *Encyclopedia of Popular Music* (New York: St. Martin's Press, 1965), p. 182.

west, and both his music and his political thinking took on dimensions alien to the culture which had spawned country-western music. He performed for union meetings and rallies, became involved with politically radical individuals and causes, wrote for the *Daily Worker,* and eventually aligned himself with a group called the Almanack Singers,[30] made up of eastern political radicals. In the late 1930s he recorded a series of songs dealing with the devastating effects of the Great Depression and prolonged drought on much of the Middle West, eventually released as *Dust Bowl Ballads.*[31] Before his death he wrote perhaps a thousand songs, many of them based on traditional tunes, most of them concerned with political and social causes. His songs reached a limited audience: country-western audiences rejected them because of their politics, alien to that segment of American culture; they enjoyed no success whatsoever as urban popular songs, because their musical idiom was too close to that of country-western music. Some would eventually enjoy wider acceptance, but during his lifetime his influence was largely confined to a circle of politically conscious urban Americans.

Dylan arrived in New York in 1960. He visited his idol (terminally ill) and performed in small clubs, imitating Guthrie's vocal style, guitar playing, and harmonica blowing. His repertory consisted of Woody's songs, his own adaptations of traditional songs and ballads, and a sprinkling of pieces he had written himself. He was somewhat of a misfit in the New York folk scene; he sang with a rasping, gravelly voice even less polished than Guthrie's, his guitar strumming appeared to be erratic and casual, his harmonica playing tended to be independent of the rhythm and chords of his guitar accompaniment. As he put it himself in one of his first songs, "Talking New York Blues"—"You sound like a hillbilly. We want folksingers here." But his talent and intensity were obvious to some, including John Hammond, who signed him to a recording contract with Columbia and brought out his first LP album, *Bob Dylan,* in 1961.

Only two songs on this first album were written by Dylan, but his second LP (*The Freewheelin' Bob Dylan*) contained only newly composed songs, as did subsequent releases. His texts deal with a wide range of subjects; many from the mid-1960s are concerned with social injustice ("I Shall Be Free," "Lonesome Death of Hattie Carrol," "Only a Pawn in Their Game"), the threat of war, particularly a nuclear holocaust ("Hard Rain's a-Gonna Fall," "Talking

[30] Cf. their "All I Want" on NW 270, s2 / 7.
[31] One of these, "I Ain't Got No Home in This World Anymore" is on NW 270, s2 / 5.

World War III Blues"), and other social and political issues. Others were concerned with personal relationships ("Don't Think Twice, It's All Right" and "It Ain't Me, Babe"). His lyrics were evocative, with original use of language and striking images:

> Hey! Mister Tambourine Man play a song for me,
> I'm not sleepy and there is no place I'm goin' to.
> Hey! Mister Tambourine Man play a song for me
> In the jingle jangle mornin' I'll come followin' you.

>> Though I know that evenin's empire has returned into sand,
>> Vanished from my hand,
>> Left me blindly here to stand but still not sleepin'!
>> My weariness amazes me
>> I'm branded on my feet.
>> I have no one to meet
>> And the ancient empty street's too dead for dreamin'.[32]

Musically, they were still in the style Dylan had inherited from Guthrie: strophic; accompanied only by his own guitar with interludes played on the harmonica; sung in a voice innocent of any trace of "cultured" vocal training; simple diatonic tunes, sometimes adapted from traditional Anglo-American songs and ballads.

The differences between Dylan and earlier urban folk musicians were that his songs were newly written, not merely arrangements of traditional pieces; his texts were topical, and often concerned with issues of the day; his performance style reflected oral-tradition Anglo-American music rather than urban sophistication.

The urban folk movement swung in directions he pointed out. His own songs were recorded by virtually every folk performer: "Blowin' in the Wind" was brought out by Peter, Paul, and Mary, the Kingston Trio, the Chad Mitchell Trio, the Staple Singers, Odetta, and dozens of other performers. Established folk performers and new ones appearing in the wake of Dylan's breakthrough began writing and performing their own songs, to the exclusion of traditional pieces. And these new songs, like many of Dylan's, were often concerned with issues of the day. Thus the urban folk movement had moved even further away from the traditional music on which it had been based. By 1965, a "folk" performer was anyone singing to the accompaniment of an acoustic guitar or two, whatever the nature of the songs or lyrics. Paul Simon and Art Garfunkel were from Queens; their repertory consisted mostly of songs written by Simon, who had only an occasional and passing interest

---

[32] "Mr. Tambourine Man" (1965), published by Witmark.

in Anglo-American traditional music, and who from the beginning was writing lyrics dealing with the contemporary urban world:

> And the people bowed and prayed
> To the neon god they made.
> And the sign flashed out its warning,
> In the words that it was forming.
> And the signs said, "The words of the prophets are written
>     on the subway walls
> And tenement halls."
> And whisper'd in The Sounds of Silence.[33]

Yet Simon and Garfunkel were accepted as "folk" singers.

The 1960s brought yet another strain of popular song. Berry Gordy, Jr., who had built a modest career as a songwriter for local performers in Detroit while holding down a full-time job at the Ford assembly plant, began producing his own discs in 1959 with a little borrowed money. Drawing talent exclusively from the black population of Detroit, writing many of the songs himself, making tapes in a tiny, poorly equipped studio, and concentrating distribution at first in Detroit and other cities in the Midwest and Northeast with large black populations, Gordy built up three interlocking record companies—Gordy, Tamla, and Motown. In 1961, a disc by the Miracles (headed by singer-songwriter Smokey Robinson) not only reached the No. 1 position on *Billboard*'s rhythm-and-blues charts, it did almost as well with white audiences. A bit later that year, "Please Mr. Postman" by the Marvelettes—five young women in their sensior year at Inkster High School in Detroit—became the first Motown disc to become a top-seller on both the rhythm-and-blues and white pop charts. Both discs sold more than a million copies.

Gordy's unerring ear and instinct for talent led him to sign and record a succession of performers who became central figures in American popular song of the 1960s and '70s. 1961 brought Gladys Knight and the Pips; the Supremes, the Temptations, and Marvin Gaye cut their first discs for Gordy in 1962; Stevie Wonder and Martha and the Vandellas made their debuts in 1963; 1964 brought the Four Tops. By the mid-1960s, more than 10 million discs on the three labels were being sold every year; between 1962 and 1970, 75 percent of all Motown releases placed on *Billboard*'s charts; approximately 10 percent of all Top Twenty songs for the decade of the 1960s were from Motown; the Supremes were third, behind only Elvis Presley and the Beatles, in total No. 1 discs (12) and in

---

[33] "The Sound of Silence" (1964), by Paul Simon.

The Temptations. (Courtesy of Motown Records)

the number of releases placing in the Top Ten (19) in the 1960s. At one point, Motown was the largest-grossing black-owned corporation in the country.

As a result of Gordy's firm control, there was a remarkable stylistic consistency to the Motown repertory. The style had more to do with urban gospel music than with blues, rhythm-and blues, or jazz. There is always a lead singer and a backing group, with echoing (or call-and response) patterns between the two; backing instruments usually include piano, bass, sometimes a few horns, drums, and other percussion instruments, often a tambourine; the singers sometimes accompany themselves with hand clapping. Most songs were written by the team of Brian Holland, Lamont Dozier, and Eddie Holland—second only to John Lennon–Paul McCartney in number of top songs written in the 1960s—or by

Smokey Robinson; texts were almost always concerned with love, poised somewhere between the blatantly sexual themes of early rock 'n' roll and sentimental tone of neo–Tin Pan Alley writers.

Success brought a gradual change in style and image to some Motown performers. Recording techniques became much more sophisticated. The backing orchestra began to include strings (members of the Detroit Symphony Orchestra), flutes and other woodwinds, sometimes even a harp, playing increasingly lush accompaniments. Many Motown artists began singing pieces from the pre-1955 Tin Pan Alley repertory, a trend climaxed by the release of *The Supremes Sing Rodgers and Hart* in 1967. All of this made their music more attractive to certain segments of the white audience. The Supremes in fact had a greater following among whites than blacks, and in 1965 they began appearing on the night-club circuit—the Coconut Grove in Los Angeles, the Eden Roc in Miami Beach, the Copacabana in New York. Just as some country-western performers of the decade had embraced Country Pop, leaving behind ethnic musical styles and much of their original audience in favor of identification with an older, more affluent con-servative white audience, so some Motown singers and groups embraced what could be called Black Pop, which had little to do with either the musical style or the audience which had carried them to fame.

The late 1950s and early '60s thus brought a multiplicity of song styles, none of which gained dominance. By 1963, the pioneers of rock 'n' roll were either dead (Buddy Holly, Gene Vincent), had disappeared from the musical scene for one reason or another (Chuck Berry, Little Richard, Jerry Lee Lewis), or were performing music in other styles (Elvis Presley, Fats Domino). The "teen idols" were still enjoying some success: Steve Lawrence's "Go Away Lit-tle Girl," Bobby Vinton's "Blue Velvet," and Brenda Lee's "Losing You" were top-selling discs in 1963. Urban black music com-manded a large chunk of the market; Motown was enjoying its first hugely successful year in 1963, with such top-selling discs as Stevie Wonder's "Fingertips—Part 2," "Heat Wave" by Martha and the Vandellas, and "You've Really Got a Hold on Me" by the Miracles. The urban folk movement was reaching its peak, and the year brought "Puff the Magic Dragon" by Peter, Paul, and Mary, two new LPs by Joan Baez, *The Freewheelin' Bob Dylan*, a top-selling version of Dylan's "Bowin' in the Wind" by Peter, Paul, and Mary, and continuing sales of a dozen LPs by the Kingston Trio. Music in Tin Pan Alley style was enjoying a revival, with Andy Williams's *Days of Wine and Roses*, the top-selling LP of the entire year, and

Barbra Streisand's first two albums. Even an occasional country-western song showed up on the pop charts.

It was a complex and rather aimless period for American popular song. The audience was fragmented and factionalized, with some listeners confining themselves to one single type of music, others enjoying a variety of styles. There was still a considerable amount of "crossing over," with white urban audiences responding to much music by black performers.

When a new focus came in 1964, it was from abroad.

On February 8, 1964, the "Ed Sullivan Show" brought American audiences their first view of a group from England called the Beatles, which had released its first disc in Great Britain in 1962 ("Love Me Do"). Several of their recordings had reached America in late 1963 and early 1964, and one ("I Want to Hold Your Hand") was at the top of *Billboard*'s chart the week of the Beatles' first television appearance. What happened next made recording history.

The Beatles—Paul McCartney, John Lennon, George Harrison, Ringo Starr—were from Liverpool, a working-class port city which had responded to rhythm-and-blues, rock 'n' roll, and blues with enthusiasm, and which had maintained its taste for rock 'n' roll even when its popularity had waned in America. The Beatles never concealed the fact that American rock 'n' roll was the cornerstone of their style. Voted the best "beat" band in England in 1960, the Beatles based their early repertory on such classics as Chuck Berry's "Roll Over Beethoven" and Little Richard's "Long Tall Sally." Lennon once said:

> Really, I just like rock and roll. I mean these (pointing to a pile of 1950s records) are the records I dug then, I dig them now and I'm still trying to reproduce "Some Other Guy" sometimes or "Be-Bop-A-Lula."[34]

The Beatles gradually introduced their own songs, written by Lennon and McCartney, and while these were rarely in the 12-bar blues form of early rock 'n' roll, they retained other elements of this music. And their performance style clearly drew on several American models: the "big beat" of rock 'n' roll was evident, heavily dominated by drums and bass; amplified and electric guitars made up the core of their sound, both in rhythmic-harmonic accompaniment to singing voices and in solo breaks (mostly by Harrison); falsetto singing was modeled on the technique of black singers; and they stressed group singing by three or four voices in

[34]*Rolling Stone Interviews*, p. 193.

tight harmony, derived from the sound of black American groups of the mid-1950s.

Lennon and McCartney were gifted songwriters, perhaps the most talented of their time, and the Beatles were excellent and dynamic performers. But surely much of their success had to do with the fact that they brought back to America something it had created and then almost forgotten—the essence of early rock 'n' roll.

The suppression of early rock 'n' roll by the American popular music industry in the late 1950s had proven to be a Pyrrhic victory after all.

Within months of the Beatles' success here, other British discs and British performers were pouring into the United States. The most immediately successful were Herman's Hermits and the Dave Clark Five, with 11 and 8 Top Ten American hits during the years of the "British Invasion"—1964 to 1967. The most enduring were the Rolling Stones and the Who; like the Beatles they had begun their careers playing American rock 'n' roll and rhythm-and-blues hits, had incorporated elements of these styles into their own music, and had become the most popular bands among the "mods" of London and other English cities.

Curiously, even though the Beatles and other British groups based their music on early rock 'n' roll, their popularity in America was confined largely to urban whites. The Beatles placed not a single disc on the rhythm-and-blues charts in their entire career, and of the other British groups only the Rolling Stones had some slight appeal to American blacks. Country-western audiences were even more emphatic in their rejection of this music. The Beatles and their peers may have brought much of white urban America together musically, but they did not succeed in recapturing the intercultural appeal of early rock 'n' roll.

Despite the overwhelming commercial success of the Beatles, popular music in America continued to be as volatile as before. At just the time of the Beatles' arrival in this country, there were stirrings from California, which had contributed almost nothing original to American popular music since a dialect of Tin Pan Alley style had grown up in Hollywood during the era of the early sound film.

First came the Beach Boys, from southern California. Their career closely parallels that of the Beatles: formed at the very beginning of the 1960s, they cut their first discs in 1962, and they enjoyed enormous success in the mid-1960s. Their musical roots were in early rock 'n' roll, and they often did songs by Chuck Berry; their style featured falsetto singing, prominent drumming, and close four- and five-part vocal harmonization. It would be tempting to call them America's answer to the Beatles were it not for the fact that their style was formed before the Beatles arrived. Their lyrics were concerned with the "good life" of southern California—surfing, girls, expensive automobiles.

The Byrds were something else. Nominally an urban folk group, their first successful releases were "covers" of songs by Bob Dylan ("Mr. Tambourine Man") and Pete Seeger ("Turn! Turn! Turn!"), in 1965. But their folk instruments, including the twelve-string acoustic guitar of leader Jim McGuinn, were amplified and distorted in the recording studio, giving a percussive, metallic, clanging sound. "Eight Miles High," a song of their own, used such distortion of both the lead guitar and the bass as to make them sound like electronic instruments, and there were whispers that the text—"Eight miles high and falling fast"—had to do with drugs, not the plane trip offered by the Byrds as the inspiration for the lyrics. By now the members of the group had allowed their hair to grow to a considerable length, and they were affecting outlandish clothing. Something strange was happening, and some radio stations, in the first such action since the days of early rock 'n' roll, banned the playing of their music.

To the north, in the Bay Area, the first acts in a drama that was to tear America apart in the late 1960s and early '70s were being played out. Student activism, in the form of the Free Speech Movement led by Mario Savio, cropped up on the campus of the University of California at Berkeley, and the first mass protests against American involvement in Vietnam were orchestrated by the Vietnam Day Committee. Many urban folk musicians, Joan Baez among them, rallied to this new cause through public statements of support and appearances at rallies. Feeling that the university was unresponsive to their concerns, thousands of students (and nonstudents) occupied the administration building, refused to leave, and the country witnessed the first direct and violent confrontation between activist young people and the "establishment" when some 800 of the protesters were arrested.

Across the Bay, San Francisco had been a haven for many members of the "beat generation" of the 1950s, and small communities had sprung up dedicated to the pursuit of an alternate lifestyle. Music and drugs were part of this society from the beginning, first marijuana and jazz, then mild-altering psychedelic drugs and a different sort of music in the 1960s.

In 1965, large numbers of these people began coming together for public celebrations of their way of life. These events, held outdoors in Golden Gate Park or indoors in such places as Longshoremen's Hall, used music as a unifying and spiritual force. The

Charlatans, recently arrived from Virginia City, was the first group associated with such gatherings; they played a rather nondescript mixture of rock 'n' roll and country-western music with a dash of Spanish-American flavor for seasoning, highly amplified to the point of distortion. Virtually all of the audience made use of perception- and time-altering drugs, and the music came into their consciousness as something quite different from the way it was perceived by a "straight" listener.

New "rock palaces" opened to accommodate the swelling number of people wanting to participate in these events. "Light shows"—pulsating and rotating lights, and the projection of slides of violently colorful abstract designs on screens behind the band—helped intensify the experience. Dozens of new bands with curious names—Big Brother and the Holding Company, Quicksilver Messenger Service, Moby Grape, the Jefferson Airplane, the Grateful Dead, County Joe and the Fish—sprang up to satisfy the demand for music at dance palaces, outdoor events, and private gatherings such as those organized by Ken Kesey, novelist and an early exponent of the drug most closely connected with these experiences and this music—LSD, or "acid."

These bands were local, unknown to the rest of the country; none had cut a commercial disc. The popular press first took notice of events in San Francisco in late 1966:

> Every weekend in such immense halls as the Fillmore and the Avalon Ballroom, and college auditoriums like the Pauley Ballroom at Berkeley, the music assaults the ears; strobe lights, pulsating to the beat, blind the eyes and sear the nerves. Psychedelic projections slither across the walls in protoplasmic blobs. Two or three thousand young people jam the floor, many in "ecstatic" dress—men with shoulder-length locks and one earring, cowboy outfits, frock coats, high hats; women in deliberately tatty evening gowns, rescued from some attic, embellished by a tiara and sneakers. Arab kaftans are worn by both sexes, who also affect bead necklaces, the high sign of LSD initiation.[35]

The recording industry began to sense the commercial of yet another dialect of popular music. The Jefferson Airplane assumed a missionary role:

> They were the first to sign a contract with a recording company (RCA Victor), the first to bring out a successful album (*Jefferson Airplane Takes Off*, August 1966), and the first to convert the San Francisco sound-light concert into a travelling show, with the aid of Glenn McKay's Head-

---

[35]*Newsweek* for December 19, 1966.

lights. They were also the first to carry San Francisco rock to *Billboard*'s pop charts; their second album, *Surrealistic Pillow,* was on the LP album charts for fifty-six weeks, rising as high as No. 3, and two singles from the album, "Somebody to Love" and "White Rabbit," made the Top Ten in the singles charts.[36]

Though some of the San Francisco bands attracted fanatical "cult" followings across America and several enjoyed considerable commercial success, their most important impact on popular music came not from their own playing, but from the incorporation of elements of their style by other performers.

Until the mid-1960s, the term "rock 'n' roll" had been used for the loose collection of styles comprising the post–Tin Pan Alley repertory. When the San Francisco groups became nationally known, in late 1966 and particularly in 1967, the term "rock" came into use for their music and other music drawing on elements of their style. Rock is something quite different from rock 'n' roll, and its emergence was the most important stylistic development in American popular music between 1955 and the 1980s.

"Rock Around the Clock" (1955) by Bill Haley and His Comets serves to mark the beginning of rock 'n' roll simply because it was the first piece of its sort to reach the No. 1 position in *Billboard*'s charts and was used as a symbol of what was happening by both proponents and opponents of the style. Likewise the Beatles' *Sargeant Pepper's Lonely Hearts Club Band*, released on June 2, 1967, marks the "official" beginning of rock, for the same reasons: though pieces in this new style had been played and recorded for more than a year, the Beatles' new album became known to virtually everyone with any interest in popular music, brought many of these people their first taste of rock, and was the first No. 1 disc with music clearly and completely in this style.

The Beatles, even when they were at the pinnacle of popular music, continued to absorb ideas and musical styles from various American performers—Bob Dylan, the Everley Brothers, some of the older black rhythm-and-blues musicians. But nothing matched the impact of their first trips to California, which brought them into contact with the emerging drug culture and its electric music.

The albums *Rubber Soul* (1965) and *Revolver* (1966) contain a scattering of songs making use of more varied instrumentation (including an Indian sitar), studio manipulation of sound, and lyrics quite different from those of the teen-oriented love ballads on which their first American success had been built.

[36]Charles Hamm, *Yesterdays—Popular Song in America* (New York: W. W. Norton & Company, 1979), p. 440.

In August of 1966 the Beatles ended their latest American tour in San Francisco; they were never to appear on the stage together again. They are said to have spent some 700 hours in the studio, recording and manipulating the material which became *Sgt. Pepper*. The album is replete with electronic sounds—distorted and filtered instruments and even voices. In addition, taped material of the Beatles themselves, other musicians, natural sounds, and speaking and shouting voices had been spliced, overlaid on multiple tracks, distorted, even run backwards, used as raw material for the creation of a collage of sound impossible to duplicate in live performance. The album was conceived and executed as a whole, not a collection of separate songs; the conceit is of a band concert, for which an audience has gathered, with the opening material reprised near the end. Some of the lyrics suggest the Beatles' earlier style, others are mystic and symbolic, still others apparently make reference to drug usage. The art work on the album cover is colorful, complex, mysterious. The most common word used in connection with the album, one already in use for the music of some of the San Francisco groups, was "psychedelic," suggesting the overriding impact on this music of drug experiences.

1966–68 brought new performers whose orientation from the beginning was more to the electrical style of Californian "acid rock" than to earlier dialects of rock 'n' roll—Jimi Hendrix, Steppenwolf, Creedence Clearwater Revival, and a host of others. In addition, many other performers altered their style to bring it more in line with the new sounds of rock: the Rolling Stones brought out a "psychedelic" album of their own, *Their Satanic Majesties Request* (1967); Cream, a British group headed by guitarist Eric Clapton, released several discs with heavily distorted guitar sounds. Electricity even invaded the folk scene—Bob Dylan had been using an electric guitar since 1965, and the first "psychedelic" years brought electrical, studio songs even from Peter, Paul, and Mary ("The House Song," 1965) and Simon and Garfunkel ("Mrs. Robinson" and the LP *Bookends* of 1968).

Rock differs from rock 'n' roll, then, in its heavy reliance on electricity (amplification, distortion, and mixing of each instrument and voice), its use of studio manipulation of sound, the incorporation of a much wider range of instruments into the sound fabric, its more flexible formal patterns, and its lyrics, which tend to deal with intensely objective matters—the individual and his interaction with the people and events of the contemporary world. Though rock grew out of an American youth culture that was beginning to reject traditional attitudes and values of American society, and though rock music was an inevitable component of rallies and marches giving public evidence of dissent, the lyrics of rock songs are rarely direct political statements but tend rather to mirror internal struggles. Live performance, radio, and the LP disc were the chief means of dissemination, rather than the 45-rpm single with its associations with earlier "pop" music and its time limitations.

The increasing sophistication of rock made it fascinating to many people who had not been attracted to rock 'n' roll or any other sort of popular music. The Beatles' *Sgt. Pepper* album was a watershed; its release in 1967 unleased a flood of critical writing; the popular press began more intensive coverage; even the *New York Times* began offering reviews of rock performances; sociology and other academic disciplines began subjecting the phenomenon of rock to scholarly scrutiny.[37] Theses and dissertations on rock were undertaken. Popular culture was suddenly something to be taken seriously. As Albert Goldman, a college professor turned rock journalist, put it:

My generation had been launched like a flight of rocket-driven missiles straight up into the highest heavens of ambition and aspiration; but just as we reached our apogee, we ran out of gas and came tumbling down on the meadows of our childhood. . . . We were the first generation to feel from our earliest years the powerfully seductive influences of the mass media. Radio came of age with us. The comic-book industry, the music business, juvenile journalism, fashions, fads—the whole teen culture—rose into being as we grew up. . . .

As the years wore on, we began to suffer from a mysterious loss of energy. We were afflicted with cultural anemia. Our painting turned black, our plays absurd. Our composers took to extolling the mystic joys of silence. The high culture, the official culture, the culture we admired, extolled and revered, began to stultify in a dreary atmosphere of middle-class piety. Eventually, the fact became plain. Classic culture and art were destined to dry up and die in the middle of the twentieth century.

Then the great pop bubble began to rise from the lowest depths of our civilization. At first it seemed like a desecration. America's century-old dream of succeeding Europe as the creator and conserver of classic art was being blotted out by the nightmare of the discothèque. Slowly, though, we began to realize that this cultural revolution, this topsy-turvy substitution of the lowest for the highest elements, might have a

[37] Simon Webster Frith, *The Sociology of Rock* (London: Constable, 1978); Charlie Gillett, *The Sound of the City. The Rise of Rock 'n' Roll,* (New York: Dell Publishing Company, 1972); Carl Belz, *The Story of Rock* (New York: Oxford University Press, 1969); Lloyd Grossman, *A Social History of Rock Music* (New York: David McKay Company, 1976); R. Meltzer, *The Aesthetics of Rock* (New York: Something Else Press, 1970); Richard Goldstein, ed., *The Poetry of Rock* (New York: Bantam Books, 1969).

good issue. After all, we were not living in classic times. Our whole civilization had been drastically reshaped. The arts were desperately in need of fresh energies and forms.[38]

Musicians from varied musical backgrounds were being attracted to rock by its growing eclecticism and the freedom of experimentation tolerated by audiences of the late 1960s. Frank Zappa, whose musical taste and talents ranged from rock 'n' roll to jazz to the avant-garde (Varèse was one of his favorite composers), put together a group—the Mothers of Invention—in 1967 which included several players with extensive classical training and experience; their albums, beginning with *Freak Out* in 1967, contained mixtures of hard rock, jazz, and classical styles, music of greater rhythmic and structural complexity than had yet been accepted into popular music. The Velvet Underground, a New York group associated with Andy Warhol in 1966–67, was built around Lou Reed and John Cale, the latter a classically trained violinist and member of avant-garde musical circles. The Beatles came into contact with avant-garde music through Yoko Ono, who later married John Lennon; much of their experimentation with tape came through her. Brian Eno, who had been associated with La Monte Young, was a founding force for a group called Roxy Music.

In England, the Moody Blues brought out a "concept album" in 1967, *Days of Future Passed*, recorded with the London Festival Orchestra. Though it drew most of its stylistic elements from the classical orchestral style of the late nineteenth and early twentieth centuries, it was accepted by rock audience as a legitimate extension of the rock musical vocabulary. Other groups brought out discs drawing heavily on the harmonic, melodic, and instrumental idioms of classical music, leavened with rock rhythms and drumming and some of its characteristic instrumental style, particularly electric guitar solos. Pink Floyd, beginning with the LP *Piper at the Gates of Dawn* (1967), climaxed their career with *Dark Side of the Moon* (1973), which took nine months to record, was premiered in the London Planetarium, and became one of the top-selling LPs ever issued.

Rock also began incorporating elements of jazz and attracting musicians whose orientation was toward this genre. The Electric Flag, built around the white blues musicians Mike Bloomfield and Barry Goldberg, may have been the first "jazz-rock" group, in 1968. Blood, Sweat and Tears, organized by bluesman Al Kooper in 1967, was made up of white, mostly classically trained musicians from

[38] Albert Goldman, *Freakshow* (New York: Atheneum, 1971), pp. vii–x, *passim.*

Blood, Sweat, and Tears. (Courtesy Retna Ltd., photograph by Stephen Morley)

the New York area whose common bond was a love of blues and jazz. Their LP *Blood, Sweat and Tears* (1969) became a top-selling album, and three singles from it each sold a million copies. Their repertory was eclectic, ranging from older blues to songs by other rock musicians to adaptations of classical pieces. The group Chicago was in the same model—white, urban (from the Chicago area), blending elements of big-band jazz with a rock rhythm section.

By the early 1970s, then, the term "rock" had become an umbrella, embracing a bewildering variety of musical styles. The common denominator was the audience, which not only accepted all this music as a single repertory, but which would also listen to Ravi Shankar playing classical Indian music on the sitar, Virgil Fox performing pieces by J.S. Bach, and Joan Baez singing unaccompanied spirituals. Miles Davis and Weather Report, playing avant-garde jazz, were favorites of many rock fans; virtuoso guitarist John McLaughlin and his Mahavishnu Orchestra, playing music that combined elements of jazz, rock, and non-Western music, also belonged. Avant-garde composers Terry Riley and La Monte Young, and even the long-time leader of the American avant-garde, John Cage, found their audiences swelled with long-haired, drug-taking "hippies," the same people who would flock to rock concerts and festivals. The Beatles included a lengthy electronic cut on one of their most successful albums ("Revolution No. 9," on the *White Album*" of 1968), and entire LPs of experimental electronic sound— George Harison's *Wonderwall Music* (1969), Lennon's *Two Virgins* (1969)—were accepted by rock fans.

Like rock 'n' roll a dozen years before, rock managed for a few years to bring together various elements of American music, to draw energy from a wide variety of sources. For a few dizzy years rock promised to become the Great American Music, unifying the most talented musicians and the most receptive audiences from popular music, jazz, classical music, the avant-garde, and rock 'n' roll.

But this did not happen. Just as the tremendous energy of early rock 'n' roll had dissipated within a few years and this remarkably original music had splintered into numerous factions, none with the vitality or universal appeal of the original product, so rock split into a number of dialects in the 1970s. The umbrella collapsed; the political intensity that had unified the rock audience for a half-dozen years was dissipated. Popular music of the 1970s and early '80s came to be marked by the greatest multiplicity of styles in the entire history of the genre.

Some of the groups which had helped establish the stylistic identity of rock continued to perform throughout the decade of the 1970s—Jefferson Airplane / Starship, the Grateful Dead, the Steve Miller Band, the Rolling Stones, the Who—and newer groups appeared with the same instrumentation (lead and rhythm electric guitar, electric bass, drums, keyboard) and essentially the same sound. As this is written, the best-selling LP album for some months is the product of REO Speedwagon, a group indistinguishable in general style from the leading rock groups of a dozen years ago.

But spreading out from this central rock style are dialects with varying points of contact with the mainstream.

"Art rock," taking its lead from the Moody Blues, has made more and more use of sophisticated electronic equipment to achieve orchestral sound; its repertory often draws on classical music, the human voice is downplayed or disappears altogether, characteristic rock rhythms tend to vanish, and the boundaries between popular and classical music are obscured. This has been largely a European phonomenon, led by the English groups Pink Floyd, Emerson, Lake and Palmer, King Crimson, and Roxy Music, and the German Tangerine Dream and Kraftwerk.

"Heavy Metal" groups feature ear-splitting volume, sound so intense as to have a physical effect on listeners. Though Grand Funk Railroad, Black Sabbath, Deep Purple, Ted Nugent, and Aerosmith retain the human voice as a component of their sound, the level of

Billy Joel. (Courtesy Retna Ltd., photograph by Michael Putland)

amplification is so high as to make comprehension of texts virtually impossible, and this music too depends on sheer sound for its effect.

The 1970s also saw the reemergence of the singer-songwriter. Some of the most distinctive music of the decade spotlighted a solo voice, backed by anything from a small rhythm section to a full-blown rock ensemble, usually retaining characteristic rock rhythms in support of the voice and its text. Paul Simon, Carole King, and Joni Mitchell continued from the 1960s, each of the four Beatles brought out solo albums after the breakup of the group, James Taylor and Elton John emerged at the beginning of the '70s, Bruce Springsteen, Billy Joel, and Jackson Browne were among the leaders of a slightly younger generation.

A Southern dialect of rock emerged, more suggestive of early rock 'n' roll than anything the 1960s had produced, making use of the 12-bar blues form and a style of guitar playing that was expressive and virtuostic at the same time, and going back to the earthy lyrics and simple rhythmic propulsion of Jerry Lee Lewis in the 1950s. The Marshall Tucker Band, the Allman Brothers, Lynyrd Skynyrd, and ZZ Top were among the '70s bands with heavy Southern accents.

Rock 'n' roll itself had not completely disappeared, even at the peak of electric rock, and some performers in the '70s contented themselves with smaller bands, less electronics, simpler song forms, and more basic rhythms. Called "pub rock" in England, this trend was partly a reaction against the commercialism and the highly sophisticated equipment of many of the leading rock groups of the mid-1970s, and was a forerunner of "punk rock," which exploded in 1976 with "Anarchy in the U.K." by the Sex Pistols. With its reliance on simple chord patterns, its use of electronic equipment for amplification rather than distortion, the outrageous attire and behavior of performers and audiences, its antiintellectualism, and its political stance squarely on the side of the economically deprived, punk was for England of 1976 what rock 'n' roll had been for America of the mid-1950s. And just as Europe had responded to the *music* of early rock 'n' roll without comprehending the cultural factors which had brought it about, so America sampled punk rock in the late 1970s without having experienced the social and economic deterioration that had brought its birth in Great Britain.

Closely related in style—so close that the distinction is not always obvious—were the "new wave" performers of the late 1970s, stressing basic rock instrumentation, less electronic manipulation, short punchy songs, and more emphasis on lyrics than was possible in the most thunderous electric rock. Elvis Costello, the Clash, and the Police spearheaded this fad in England; American new wave was a bit different, growing first out of the New York avant-garde world of the Velvet Underground and later encompassing the New York Dolls, the Talking Heads, Patti Smith, and then groups from elsewhere in the country—the B-52s, Devo, the Cars, and many others.

The late 1960s and early '70s brought an alternative to Motown, performers initially more oriented toward black listeners than white, with singing styles derived from blues and jazz rather than urban gospel music, and instrumental backings also more suggestive of jazz. Aretha Franklin and James Brown became the biggest stars, though Wilson Pickett, Joe Tex, Booker T. and the MG's, and Otis Redding enjoyed success also. It was this group, more than Motown performers, who were responsible for the term "soul," which in 1969 replaced rhythm-and-blues as *Billboard*'s label for black popular music. Inevitably this dialect of black music attracted white listeners, many of whom gravitated toward it as the distinction between the Motown style and white music diminished.

As Motown moved from Detroit to California and eventually faded, Philadelphia emerged as the center of black urban popular song, largely because of the talents of Leon Huff, Thom Bell, and Kenny Gamble—songwriters, arrangers, producers. The most successful groups were the Delfonics, the O'Jays, the Stylistics, and Harold Melvin and the Blue Notes. The sound was not unlike that of Motown—smooth, richly orchestrated (with strongs and plenty of horns), usually featuring complex interplay between solo voices and small vocal ensembles. But the rhythm section was subtly different, often more varied and prominent than in the Motown style.

Meanwhile groups like Sly and the Family Stone (in "Thank You" of 1970) and the Watts 103rd Street Rhythm Band ("Express Yourself," also 1970) were featuring repetitive bass line, more complex rhythmic relationships among the various voices, suggestions of Latin rhythms. The word "funk" began appearing in titles of songs of this sort: "Funky Chicken" (Willie Henderson, 1970); "Funky Music Sho Nuff Turns Me On" (Edwin Starr, 1971). Soon the subgenre was itself called funk, and such groups as Earth, Wind and Fire, Tavares, Parliament, and the Trammps began identifying themselves with this style.

Suddenly, in the mid-1970s, a number of different elements came together in what appeared to be a consensus style rivaling early rock 'n' roll—disco. The silky orchestral sound of Philadelphia was wedding to the rhythmic impulse of funk, electronic instruments and sophisticated studio techniques were utilized, and, quite unexpectedly, American again had an interracial popular music. Whites, blacks, Hispanics, and the large gay communities of America's largest cities flocked to discotheques to display their dance skills and their wardrobes to the repetitive, hypnotic beat of disco music. Though the style had originated in black music, some whites managed convincing imitations; for the first time since the mid-1950s there was substantial overlap between the white and black charts of popular music. Saturday Night Fever, the album from the soundtrack of the movie of the same name featuring mostly music by the Bee Gees, became the first LP by white performers to appear at the top of the black charts in Billboard. In a worldwide reflection of the same phenomenon, this album became a best-seller in most European and western-oriented countries, and in parts of the Third World as well. No music since the days of Bill Haley and early Elvis Presley had reached a larger and more diverse audience.

But the musical elements of disco were too simplistic to sustain growth or development, and American popular music quickly subsided to its more usual multiplicity of styles and audiences.

The 1970s also brought a sustained revival of the elements of Tin Pan Alley style. The talents of Barbra Streisand had been obvious to followers of the sophisticated New York club style, but her identification with this older strain of American popular music and its largely conservative audiences had insured alienation from young and radical audience through most of the 1960s. But in 1974 she had her first No. 1 hit, with "The Way We Were," and she competed successfully with rock-oriented performers for the remainder of the decade with such songs as "Love Theme from 'A Star Is Born' " (1977) and "You Don't Bring Me Flowers" (1978)—not by changing her repertory or singing style, but from the fact that more and more people looked for an alternative to rock. A number of other singers also achieved popularity with the same type of repertory, not only with white pop audiences (Barry Manilow, Olivia Newton-John, Debbie Boone) but also on the soul charts (Diana Ross, Roberta Flack) and with country-western audiences (Crystal Gayle, Kenny Rogers, Barbara Mandrell).

As America moved into the 1980s, it was apparent that rock music and its constellation of related styles had moved firmly away from pretentions of "serious" music and had gone back to what the popular music of this country has almost always been—music for entertainment, leisure listening, dancing; mass entertainment, pitched in a style making it easily accessible to millions of listeners. It continues to be, as it has been since the Virginia Minstrels arrived in England in 1843, our most successful musical export.

Whether we like it or not, most of the rest of the world regards American popular music and jazz as the most successful and important musical product of the New World.

# Epilogue

In Calcutta, India, in 1976, where I was participating in a conference dealing with "Arts and the People," I heard speaker after speaker urge that ways be found to preserve the traditional arts and crafts of Indian villages, threatened by twentieth-century civilization and in particular by the encroachment of the mass media. Finally another participant, himself an Indian and possibly a Marxist, pointed out that the logical extention of such attitudes would also "protect" village people from other aspects of the modern world—advances in medical treatment, nutrition, agriculture, and the like.

My paper, concerned with American folk and popular music, of course did not touch directly on this debate. My chief point, however, was that the most characteristic and dynamic music to emerge from American culture over the past two centuries invariably resulted from interaction among musicians of several different cultural, racial, national, and ethnic backgrounds. A large part of the history of American music is a history of "contaminated" music; much of the energy characterizing such genres as jazz, country-western music, and the various stages of American popular song results from the stimulation of this "contamination."

I have no quarrel with folklorists and ethnomusicologists, whether Indian or American, whose chief concern is with the "purest" music of their culture. But I choose to view music as a dynamic, ever-changing art, and I see the history of music in our country as retaining a high level of energy and innovation over such a sustained period of time precisely because new vitality has been brought to it periodically by the introduction and integration of music from a succession of different cultures.

This conviction has helped shape the present book. Though I have dealt with a wider range of music than is found in any earlier histories of music in the United States, much has been left out. In fact, one could easily write another book, perhaps of equal length, dealing with the music I have chosen to exclude.

Perhaps I will undertake such a book myself one day.

The pattern of what I have included and excluded is a simple one. With the exception of the music of the American Indian, I have dealt with music which has changed in style and form after being brought to the New World, music which has eventually taken on a different character in America, music which has been subjected to acculturation, or, if you will, "contaminated" music.

I have not dealt with music which did not change in significant ways in the New World, music which remained identified with the national and ethnic groups who brought it to America, music which did not interact with other forms of music.

Thus I have not written of the Moravians, though these people had a remarkably active musical life in settlements in North Carolina and Pennsylvania and a great deal of excellent scholarship has been done in the last several decades on this music and the culture which nourished it,[1] simply because neither European-born nor American-born Moravian composers created pieces significantly different from the European music of the Classical era which was the cornerstone of their music here. I have not dealt with the popular dance music of Slavic, Asian, and Mediterranean peoples who formed ethnic communities in America's cities and towns in the late nineteenth and twentieth centuries, because this music remained unknown to other Americans and had no impact on emerging indigenous styles.[2] I have not discussed the music of the Spanish missions in the Southwest and the traditional music of the oldest Spanish settlements in this area for the same reason.[3] There is nothing in my book about Catholic and Jewish liturgical music, though I am not comfortable with the omission of this

[1] A selection of Moravian music is contained on NW 230.

[2] Samples of various ethnic music of this sort may be found on NW 264 (*Old-Country Music in a New Land: Folk Music of Immigrants from Europe and the Near East*), NW 283 ('*Spiew Juchasa / Song of the Shepherd: Songs of the Slavic Americans*), and NW 244 (*Caliente = Hot: Puerto Rican and Cuban Musical Expression in New York.*

[3] Cf. NW 292 (*Dark and Light in Spanish New Mexico: Music of the Alabados from Cerro, New Mexico: Music of the Bailes from El Rancho, New Mexico.*

material, which has been an important part of the life of so many millions of Americans.

The neglect of these bodies of music, and others whose absence will surely be spotted by critics, if not readers, is in no way a commentary on its quality or its importance to the groups who brought it to the New World and nourished it in their new home. I do not claim that the attitudes which have conditioned my selectivity are the best ones. But they are mine.

There can be no conclusion to a book of this sort. Even though I have offered summaries of the histories of various genres of music from time to time and have often tried to draw generalizations from the body of music with which I have been concerned in one chapter or another, American music is an ever-flowing stream, continually producing new and fascinating pieces and styles. The stream happens to be calm as this book is written, reflecting the general political and social situation of the United States; but inevitably there will be turbulent and more fascinating times again; and inevitably these will produce new forms of music which will be viewed by the rest of the world as typically American and excitingly vital.

# Bibliography

Given the enormous scope of this book, a comprehensive bibliography was out of the question. The choice of what to exclude was often painful; however, there exists a superb, book-length, annotated bibliography of writings on American music which I enthusiastically commend to those in need of a more extensive listing than I was able to include here—David Horn's *The Literature of American Music in Books and Folk Music Collections* (Metuchen: The Scarecrow Press, 1977).

My own bibliography is highly selective, made up of what I judge to be the most important items dealing with the range of topics covered. The majority of these are books, though I have included articles which are clearly major contributions or which cover topics not yet treated in book-length studies. I have given preference to recent, easily available items, but have also included a number of older studies which remain indispensable to a study of American music. I have listed the most recent editions of those works which have been revised and reprinted several times; where both American and foreign editions have appeared, I have listed the American edition in most cases.

The first section lists several important series of books, scores, and monographs concerned with American music, with titles of each item in the series. The bulk of this bibliography, which follows, is organized into the following categories:

1. General Histories of American Music
2. Regional Histories and Studies

3. Period and Genre Histories and Studies
   a. The Music of Colonial and Federal America
   b. The Nineteenth Century
   c. The Twentieth Century
   d. Native Americans and Their Music
   e. Traditional Anglo-American Music; Hillbilly and Country Music
   f. The Music of Black Americans (General)
   g. Blues
   h. Ragtime
   i. Jazz
   j. Popular Song
   k. Sacred Music
   l. Secular Vocal Music: Song and the Musical Stage
4. Individual Composers and Musicians
5. Bibliographical and Reference Works

The general histories of American music are arranged chronologically; the section devoted to individual musicians is ordered alphabetically according to the name of the composer; all other sections are alphabetical by author.

*Music in American Life.* Urbana: University of Illinois Press, 1971–present.

Green, Archie. *Only a Miner: Studies in Recorded Coal-Mining Songs.*

Denisoff, R. Serge. *Great Day Coming: Folk Music and the American Left.*

Bierley, Paul E. *John Philip Sousa: A Descriptive Catalogue of His Works.*

Ohrlin, Glenn. *The Hell-Bound Train: A Cowboy Songbook.*

Gillis, Frank J., and John W. Miner, eds. *Oh, Didn't He Ramble: The Life Story of Lee Collins.*

Foner, Philip S. *American Labor Songs of the Nineteenth Century.*

Malone, Bill C., and Judith McCulloh, eds. *Stars of Country Music: Uncle Dave Macon to Johnny Rodriguez.*

White, John I. *Git Along, Little Dogies: Songs and Songmakers of the American West.*

Paredes, Americo. *A Texas-Mexican Cancionero: Folksongs of the Lower Border.*

Townsend, Charles R. *San Antonio Rose: The Life and Music of Bob Wills.*

Titon, Jeff Todd. *Early Downhome Blues: A Musical and Cultural Analysis.*

Hitchcock, H. Wiley and Vivian Perlis, eds. *An Ives Celebration: Papers and Panels of the Charles Ives Centennial Festival-Conference.*

Epstein, Dena J. *Sinful Tunes and Spirituals: Black Folk Music to the Civil War.*

Ives, Edward D. *Joe Scott, the Woodsman-Songmaker.*

Porterfield, Nolan. *Jimmy Rodgers: The Life and Times of America's Blue Yodeler.*

Wolfe, Richard J. *Early American Music Engraving and Printing: A History of Music Publishing in America from 1787 to 1825.*

Williams, Roger M. *Sing a Sad Song: The Life of Hank Williams.*

Cohen, Norm. *Long Steel Rail: The Railroad in American Folksong.*

Krummel, D. W., Jean Geil, Doris J. Dyen, and Deane L. Root. *Resources of American Music History: A Directory of Source Materials from Colonial Times to World War II.*

Slobin, Mark. *Tenement Songs: The Popular Music of the Jewish Immigrants.*

Randolph, Vance. Norm Cohen, ed. and arr. *Ozark Folksongs.*

*Monographs in American Music.* Brooklyn: Institute for Studies in American Music, 1973–present.

1. Jackson, Richard. *United States Music: Sources of Bibliography and Collective Bibliography.*
3. Mead, Rita H. *Doctoral Dissertations in American Music: A Classified Bibliography.*
4. Crawford, Richard. *American Studies and American Musicology: A Point of View and a Case in Point.*
5. Appel, Richard G. *The Music of the Bay Psalm Book: 9th Edition* (1968).
6. *American Music Before 1865 in Print and on Records: A Biblio-Discography.*
7. Saylor, Bruce. *The Writings of Henry Cowell: A Descriptive Bibliography.*
8. Lowens, Irving. *Music in America and American Music: Two Views of the Scene.*
9. Perlis, Vivian. *Two Men for Modern Music.*
10. Stanislaw, Richard J. *A Checklist of Four-Shape Shape-Note Tunebooks.*
11. Van Solkema, S., ed. *The New Worlds of Edgard Varèse.*

12. Palmer, Robert. *A Tale of Two Cities.*
13. Goldman, Richard F. *Selected Essays and Reviews.*
14. Hitchcock, H. Wiley, ed. *The Phonograph and Our Musical Life: Proceedings of a Centennial Conference.*
15. Inserra, Lorraine, and H. Wiley Hitchcock, eds. *The Music of Henry Ainsworth's Psalter* (Amsterdam, 1612).
16. Manion Martha L. *Writings about Henry Cowell: An Annotated Bibliography.*
17. Spackman, Stephen. *Wallingford Riegger: Two Essays in Musical Biography.*

*Earlier American Music.* H. Wiley Hitchcock, consulting ed. Facsimile scores. New York: Da Capo Press, 1972–present.

1. Paine, John Knowles. *Symphony No. 1.*
2. Parker, Horatio W. *Hora novissima.*
3. Chadwick, George W. *Symphony No. 2.*
4. Chadwick, George W. *Judith: Lyric Drama for Soli, Chorus and Orchestra.*
5. Sankey, Ira D., *et al. Gospel Hymns Nos. 1 to 6.*
6. Belcher, Supply. *The Harmony of Maine.*
7. MacDowell, Edward. *Songs* (Opp. 40, 47, 56, 60).
8. MacDowell, Edward. *Piano Pieces* (Opp. 51, 55, 61, 62).
9. *The American Music Miscellany: A Collection of the Newest and Most Approved Songs* (Northampton, Mass., 1798).
10. Heinrich, Anthony Philip. *The Dawning of Music in Kentucky.*
11. Bray, John, and James Nelson Barker. *The Indian Princess.*
12. Foster, Stephen. *Household Songs.*
13. Foster, Stephen. *The Social Orchestra.*
14. Foster, Stephen. *Minstrel-Show Songs.*
15. Mason, Lowell. *The Boston Handel and Haydn Society Collection of Church Music.*
16. Chadwick, George W. *Songs to Poems by Arlo Bates.*
17. Cheney, Simeon Pease. *The American Singing Book.*
18. Riley, Edward, comp. *Riley's Flute Melodies.*
19. Work, Henry Clay. *Songs.*
20. Billings, William. *The Psalm-Singer's Amusement.*
21. Carr, Benjamin R. *Musical Miscellany in Occasional Numbers.*
22. Ingalls, Jeremiah. *The Christian Harmony.*
23. *The Stoughton Musical Society's Centennial Collection of Sacred Music* (Boston, 1878).

24. Foote, Arthur. *Suite in E Major* and *Serenade in E Major.*
25. Bristow, George F. *Rip Van Winkle.*

*Recent Researches in American Music.* H. Wiley Hitchcock, general ed. Madison: A-R Editions, 1977–present.

1–2. *Anthology of Early American Keyboard Music, 1787–1830.* J. Bunker Clark, ed.
3–4. *The Disappointment: or, The Force of Credulity,* by Andrew Barton. Jerald C. Graue and Judith Layng, eds.
5. *The Philadelphia Sonatas,* by Alexander Reinagle. Robert Hopkins, ed.
6. *The Poor Soldier,* by John O'Keefe and William Shield. William Brasmer and William Osborne, eds.
7. *Selected Compositions,* by James Hewitt. John W. Wagner, ed.

Forthcoming:
   *Pelissier's Columbian Melodies,* by Victor Pelissier. Karl Kroeger, ed.
   *Music for Cello and Piano,* by Arthur Foote. Douglas B. Moore, ed.
   *The Core Repertory of Early American Psalmody.* Richard Crawford, ed.
   *Selected Secular and Sacred Songs,* by Benjamin Carr. Eve R. Meyer, ed.
   *Symphony No. 2, "A Montevideo,"* by Louis Moreau Gottschalk. William E. Korf, ed.
   *String Quartet No. 4,* by George Whitefield Chadwick. Steven Ledbetter, ed.
   *Songs and Choral Music,* by Anthony Philip Heinrich. David Barron, ed.

*Bibliographies in American Music.* Detroit: Information Coordinators, 1974–present.

1. Schwartz, Charles. *George Gershwin: A Selective Bibliography and Discography.*
2. Nathan, Hans. *William Billings: Data and Documents.*
3. Anderson, Donna K. *Charles T. Griffes: An Annotated Bibliography-Discography.*
4. Johnson, H. Earle. *First Performances in America to 1900.*
5. Lowens, Irving. *Haydn in America.*

6. Cipolla, Wilma Reid. *A Catalog of the Works of Arthur Foote, 1853–1937.*
7. Doyle, John G. *Louis Moreau Gottschalk (1829–1869): A Bibliographical Study and Catalog of Works.*

Forthcoming:
Kearns, William. *Horatio Parker: A Bio-Bibliographical Study.*
Freedman, Frederick and James M. Burk: *A Charles Ives Bibliography.*
Phemister, William. *A Bibliography of American Piano Concertos.*
Graber, Kenneth. *William Mason: An Annotated Bibliography.*
Brookhart, Edward. *Music in American Higher Education: An Annotated Historical Bibliography.*
Krohn, Ernst C. *Music Publishing in St. Louis.*
Lowens, Irving. *American Music Criticism: A Bio-Bibliography.*
Lowens, Margery. *MacDowell.*

## 1. GENERAL HISTORIES OF AMERICAN MUSIC

Ritter, Frédéric Louis. *Music in America.* New York: Charles Scribner's Sons, 1883. New ed. 1890.
Mathews, W. S. B., ed. *A Hundred Years of Music in America.* Chicago: G. L. Howe, 1889.
Lavignac, Albert. *Music and Musicians.* New York: Henry Holt and Company, 1899. (Section on music in the United States by H. E. Krehbiel.)
Elson, Louis C. *The National Music of America and its Sources.* Boston: L. C. Page & Company, 1899. New ed., rev. by Arthur Elson, 1924.
Hughes, Rupert. *Contemporary American Composers, Being a Study of the Music of This Country.* Boston: Page, 1900. 2nd ed., 1914.
Krehbiel, H. E. "Music in America," *Famous Composers and their Music,* VI, ed. by Theodore Thomas, John Knowles Paine, and Karl Klauser. New York: Merrill & Baker, 1901.
Elson, Louis C. *The History of American Music.* New York: The Macmillan Company, 1904. Rev. ed., 1915; 2nd rev. ed. by Arthur Elson, 1925.
Hubbard, W. L., ed. *History of American Music.* The American History and Encyclopedia of Music, 8. Toledo: Irving Squire, 1908.
Farwell, Arthur, and W. Dermot Darby. *Music in America.* The Art of Music, 4. New York: The National Society of Music, 1915.
Sonneck, Oscar G. "The History of Music in America," *Miscella-*

neous Studies in the History of Music. New York: The Macmillan Company, 1921.

Howard, John Tasker. *Our American Music: Three Hundred Years of It*. New York: Thomas Y. Crowell Company, 1931. Rev. eds., 1939, 1946, 1954.

Kaufmann, Helen L. *From Jehovah to Jazz: Music in America from Psalmody to the Present Day*. New York: Dodd, Mead, 1937.

Chase, Gilbert. *America's Music, from the Pilgrims to the Present*. New York: McGraw-Hill, 1955. 2nd rev. ed., 1966.

Howard, John Tasker, and George Kent Bellows. *A Short History of Music in America*. New York: Thomas Y. Crowell Company, 1957. 2nd ed., 1967.

Mellers, Wilfrid. *Music in a New Found Land*. New York: Alfred A. Knopf, 1964.

Howard, John Tasker. *Our American Music: a Comprehensive History*. New York: Thomas Y. Crowell, 1964. (This is the 4th rev. ed. of the book, originally published in 1931.)

Marrocco, W. Thomas, and Harold Gleason. *Music in America. An Anthology from the Landing of the Pilgrims to the Close of the Civil War, 1620–1865*. New York: W. W. Norton & Company, 1964.

Rublowsky, John. *Music in America*. New York: Crowell-Collier, 1967.

Edwards, Arthur C., and W. Thomas Marrocco. *Music in the United States*. Dubuque: Brown, 1968.

Hitchcock, H. Wiley. *Music in the United States: A Historical Introduction*. Englewood Cliffs: Prentice-Hall, 1969. 2nd ed., 1974.

Sablosky, Irving. *American Music*. Chicago: University of Chicago Press, 1969.

Boroff, Edith. *Music in Europe and the United States: a History*. Englewood Cliffs: Prentice-Hall, 1971.

Davis, Ronald L. *A History of Music in American Life*. Huntington: Krieger, 1979–80.

Ammer, Christine. *Unsung: A History of Women in American Music*. Westport: Greenwood Press, 1980.

Zuck, Barbara A. *A History of Musical Americanism*. Ann Arbor: UMI Research Press, 1980.

## 2. REGIONAL HISTORIES AND STUDIES

Edwards, George Thornton. *Music and Musicians of Maine*. Portland: The Southworth Press, 1928.

Epstein, Dena J. *Music Publishing in Chicago Before 1871: The Firm of Root & Cady, 1858–1871*. Detroit: Information Coordinators, 1969.

Erskine, John. *The Philharmonic-Symphony Society of New York: Its First Hundred Years.* New York: The Macmillan Company, 1943.

Fisher, William Arms. *Notes on Music in Old Boston.* Boston: Oliver Ditson Company, 1918.

Gerson, Robert A. *Music in Philadelphia.* Philadelphia: Theodore Presser Co., 1940.

Hall, Harry H. *A Johnny Reb Band from Salem: The Pride of Tarheelia.* Raleigh: The North Carolina Confederate Commission, 1963.

Hoogerwerf, Frank W., ed. *Music in Georgia.* New York: Da Capo Press, 1981.

Johnson, H. Earle. *Musical Interludes in Boston, 1795–1830.* New York: Columbia University Press, 1943.

Keefer, Lubov. *Baltimore's Music.* Baltimore: J. H. Furst, 1962.

Kmen, Henry A. *Music in New Orleans: The Formative Years, 1791–1841.* Baton Rouge: Louisiana State University Press, 1966.

Krehbiel, Henry Edward. *The Philharmonic Society of New York: A Memorial.* New York and London: Novello, Ewer & Co., 1892.

Krohn, Ernst C. *Music Publishing in the Middle Western States Before the Civil War.* Detroit: Information Coordinators, 1972.

Mangler, Joyce Ellen. *Rhode Island Music and Musicians, 1733–1850.* Detroit: Information Service, 1965.

Osburn, Mary Hubbell. *Ohio Composers and Musical Authors.* Columbus: F. J. Heer Printing Co., 1942.

Perkins, Charles C., and John S. Dwight. *History of the Handel and Haydn Society of Boston, Massachusetts,* I. Boston: Alfred Mudge & Son, 1883–93.

Pichierri, Louis. *Music in New Hampshire, 1623–1800.* New York: Columbia University Press, 1960.

Shanet, Howard. *Philharmonic: A History of New York's Orchestra.* Garden City: Doubleday & Company, 1975.

Stevens, Harry R. "Folk Music on the Midwestern Frontier, 1788–1825," *Ohio State Archaeological and Historical Quarterly,* LVII / 2 (April, 1948), pp. 126–46.

Stoutamire, Albert. *Music of the Old South: Colony to Confederacy.* Fairleigh Dickinson University Press: 1972.

Swan, Howard. *Music in the Southwest, 1825–1950.* San Marino: Huntington Library, 1952.

## 3. Period and Genre Histories and Studies

### A. THE MUSIC OF COLONIAL AND FEDERAL AMERICA

Appel, Richard G. *The Music of the Bay Psalm Book, 9th Edition*

(*1698*). Brooklyn: Institute for Studies in American Music, 1975.

Billings, William. *Complete Works.* Boston: The American Musicological Society and the Colonial Society of Massachusetts, 1977–81. I: *The New-England Psalm-Singer,* ed. by Karl Kroeger. II: *The Singing Master's Assistant* and *Music in Miniature,* ed. by Hans Hathan.

Brooks, Henry M. *Olden-time Music.* Boston: Ticknor, 1888. Repr., New York: AMS Press, 1973.

Camus, Raoul F. *Military Music of the American Revolution.* Chapel Hill: The University of North Carolina Press, 1976.

Cripe, Helen. *Thomas Jefferson and Music.* Charlottesville: The University of Virginia Press, 1974.

Daniel, Ralph T. *The Anthem in New England Before 1800.* Evanston: Northwestern University Press, 1966.

Fisher, William Arms. *Ye Olde New-England Psalm-Tunes: 1620–1820.* Boston and New York: Oliver Ditson Company, 1930.

Haraszti, Zoltan. *The Enigma of the Bay Psalm Book.* Chicago: University of Chicago Press, 1956.

Hood, George. *A History of Music in New England.* Boston: Wilkins, Carter & Company, 1846.

Howard, John Tasker. *The Music of George Washington's Time.* Washington: United States Washington Bicentennial Commission, 1931.

Lambert, Barbara, ed. *Music in Colonial Massachusetts, 1630–1820.* Boston: The Colonial Society of Massachusetts, 1981.

Lowens, Irving. *Music and Musicians in Early America.* New York: W. W. Norton & Company, 1964.

Maurer, Maurer. "The Library of a Colonial Musician, 1755," *The William and Mary Quarterly,* VII (1950), pp. 39–52.

———. "The 'Professor of Musick' in Colonial America," *Musical Quarterly,* XXXVI (October, 1950), pp. 511–24.

Pratt, Waldo Selden. *The Music of the Pilgrims. A Description of the Psalm-book brought to Plymouth in 1620.* Boston: Oliver Ditson Company, 1921.

Scholes, Percy A. *The Puritans and Music in England and New England.* London: Oxford University Press, 1934.

Silverman, Kenneth. *A Cultural History of the American Revolution.* New York: Thomas Y. Crowell Company, 1976.

Sonneck, O. G. *Early Concert-Life in America (1731–1800).* Leipzig: Breitkopf & Härtel, 1907.

## B. THE NINETEENTH CENTURY

Cooke, George Willis. *John Sullivan Dwight: A Biography.* Hartford: Transcendental Books, 1973.

Disher, Maurice Willson. *Victorian Song; from Dive to Drawing Room*. London: Phoenix House, 1955.

Dwight, John S., ed. *Dwight's Journal of Music: A Paper of Art and Literature. Boston: Oliver Ditson and Company, 1852–81. Repr., Johnson Reprint Corp., 1967.*

Harwell, Richard B. *Confederate Music*. Chapel Hill: University of North Carolina Press, 1950.

Hoffman, Richard. *Some Musical Recollections of Fifty Years*. New York: Scribner, 1910.

Johnson, H. Earle. "The Germania Musical Society," *The Musical Quarterly*, XXXIX (1953), pp. 75–93.

Mussulman, Joseph A. *Music in the Cultured Generation: A Social History of Music in America, 1870–1900*. Evanston: Northwestern University Press, 1971.

Olson, Kenneth E. *Music and Musket: Bands and Bandsmen of the American Civil War*. Westport: Greenwood Press, 1981.

Weichlein, William J. *A Checklist of American Periodicals, 1850–1900*. Detroit: Information Coordinators, 1970.


C. THE TWENTIETH CENTURY

Appleton, Jon H., and Ronald C. Perera, eds. *The Development and Practice of Electronic Music*. Englewood Cliffs: Prentice-Hall, 1975.

Austin, William W. *Music in the 20th Century, from Debussy through Stravinsky*. New York: W. W. Norton & Company, 1966.

Barzun, Jacques. *Music in American Life*. Garden City: Doubleday, 1956.

Basart, Ann Phillips. *Serial Music: A Classified Bibliography of Writings on Twelve-Tone and Electronic Music*. Berkeley: The University of California Press, 1961.

Boretz, Benjamin, and Edward T. Cone. *Perspectives on American Composers*. New York: W. W. Norton & Company, 1971.

Copland, Aaron. *The New Music, 1900–1960*. New York: W. W. Norton & Company, 1968.

Cowell, Henry, ed. *American Composers on American Music*. Palo Alto: Stanford University Press, 1933.

Cross, Lowell. *A Bibliography of Electronic Music*. Toronto: The University of Toronto Press, 1967.

Ewen, David, ed. *The Book of Modern Composers*. New York: Alfred A. Knopf, 1950.

Hanson, Howard. *Music in Contemporary American Civilization*. Lincoln: University of Nebraska Press, 1951.

Howard, John Tasker. *Our Contemporary Composers: American Music in the Twentieth Century*. New York: Crowell, 1941.

Kostelanetz, Richard. *The Theatre of Mixed Means.* New York: Dial Press, 1968.

Lang, Paul Henry, ed. *Problems of Modern Music: The Princeton Seminar in Advanced Musical Studies.* New York: W. W. Norton & Company, 1962.

Mellers, Wilfrid. *Caliban Reborn: Renewal in Twentieth-Century Music.* New York: Harper & Row, 1967.

Mueller, John H. *The American Symphony Orchestra: A Social History of Musical Taste.* Bloomington: Indiana University Press, 1951.

Nyman, Michael. *Experimental Music: Cage and Beyond.* New York: Schirmer, 1975.

Rosenfeld, Paul. *An Hour with American Music.* Philadelphia: Lippincott, 1929.

Salzman, Eric. *Twentieth-Century Music: An Introduction.* Englewood Cliffs: Prentice-Hall, 1974.

Schwartz, Elliott, and Barney Childs, eds. *Contemporary Composers on Contemporary Music.* New York: Holt, Rinehart & Winston, 1967.

Sessions, Roger. *Reflections on the Music Life in the United States.* New York: Merlin Press, 1956.

Slonimsky, Nicolas. *Music Since 1900.* New York: Charles Scribner's Sons, 1971.

Thomson, Virgil. *Twentieth-Century Composers. American Music Since 1910.* New York: Holt, Rinehart & Winston, 1970.

Vinton, John, ed. *Dictionary of Contemporary Music.* New York: Dutton, 1971.

### D. NATIVE AMERICANS AND THEIR MUSIC

Baker, Theodor. *Über die Musik der nordamerikanischen Wilden.* Leipzig: Breitkopf & Härtel, 1882.

Brown, Dee. *Bury My Heart at Wounded Knee.* New York: Holt, Rinehart & Winston, 1971.

Collaer, Paul. *Music of the Americans: an Illustrated Music Ethnology of the Eskimo and American Indian Peoples.* New York: Praeger, 1973.

Collier, John. *Indians of the Americas.* New York: W. W. Norton & Company, 1947.

Curtis, Edward S. *The North American Indian.* Cambridge: Harvard University Press, 1907–30.

Curtis, Natalie. *The Indians' Book.* New York and London: Harper and Brothers Publishers, 1907.

Densmore, Frances. *The American Indians and their Music.* New York: The Womans Press, 1926.

Driver, Harold E. *Indians of North America*. Chicago: University of Chicago Press, 1970.

Fletcher, Alice C. *Indian Story and Song from North America*. Boston: Small, Maynard & Co., 1900.

———. *A Study of Omaha Indian Music*. Cambridge: Peabody Museum of American Archaeology and Ethnology, 1893.

Gilman, Benjamin Ives. *Hopi Songs*. Boston: Houghton Mifflin, 1908.

Herzog, George. "Musical Styles in North America," *Proceedings of the Twenty-third International Congress of Americanists* (1928), pp. 455–58.

Hodge, Frederick Webb, ed. *Handbook of American Indians North of Mexico*. Washington: Smithsonian Institution, 1907–10.

Kroeber, A. L. *Cultural and Natural Areas of Native North America*. Berkeley: University of California Press, 1939.

McAllester, David P. *Peyote Music*. New York: Viking Fund, 1949.

Merriam, Alan P. *Ethmusicology of the Flathead Indians*. Chicago: Aldine, 1967.

Nettl, Bruno. *North American Indian Musical Styles*. Philadelphia: American Folklore Society, 1954.

Roberts, Helen H. *Musical Areas in Aboriginal North America*. New Haven: Yale University Press, 1936.

Underhill, Ruth Murray. *Singing for Power: The Song Magic of the Papago Indians of Southern Arizona*. Berkeley: University of California Press, 1938.

## E. TRADITIONAL ANGLO-AMERICAN MUSIC; HILLBILLY AND COUNTRY MUSIC

Artis, Bob. *Bluegrass*. New York: Hawthorn Books, 1975.

Bailey, Jay. "Historical Origin and Stylistic Developments of the Five-String Banjo," *Journal of American Folklore* LXXXV (1972), pp. 58–65.

Barry, Phillips, Fannie H. Eckstorm, and Mary W. Smyth. *British Ballads from Maine*. New Haven: n.p., 1929.

Bronson, Bertrand Harris. *The Ballad as Song*. Berkeley and Los Angeles: University of California Press, 1969.

———. *The Singing Tradition of Child's Popular Ballads*. Princeton: Princeton University Press, 1976.

———. *The Traditional Tunes of the Child Ballads*. Princeton: Princeton University Press, 1959–71.

Child, Francis James. *The English and Scottish Popular Ballads*. 5 vols. Boston and New York: Houghton, Mifflin Company, 1882–98.

Christeson, R. P. *The Old Time Fiddler's Repertory*. Columbia: University of Missouri Press, 1973.

Coffin, Tristram P. *The British Traditional Ballad in North America*. Philadelphia: The American Folklore Society, 1963.

Combs, Josiah H. *Folk-Songs of the Southern United States (Folk-Songs du midi des Etats-Unis)*. Ed. by D. K. Wilgus. Austin and London: Published for The American Folklore Society by the University of Texas Press, 1967.

Damon, S. Foster. "The History of Square-Dancing," *Proceedings of the American Antiquarian Society*, LXII (April–October, 1952), pp. 63–98.

Davis, Arthur Kyle, Jr. *Traditional Ballads of Virginia*. Cambridge: Harvard University Press, 1929.

Denisoff, Serge. *Great Day Coming. Folk Music and the American Left*. Urbana: University of Illinois Press, 1971.

Epstein, Dena J. "The Folk Banjo: A Documentary History," *Ethnomusicology*, XIX 3 (September 1975), pp. 347–71.

Flanders, Helen Hartness, and George Brown, *Vermont Folk Songs and Ballads*. Brattleboro: n.p., 1931.

Gentry, Linnell. *A History and Encyclopedia of Country, Western, and Gospel Music*. Nashville: Clairmont, 1969.

Green, Douglas B. *Country Roots: The Origins of Country Music*. New York: Hawthorn, 1976.

Guthrie, Woody. *Bound for Glory*. New York: Dutton, 1943.

Haywood, Charles. *Bibliography of North American Folklore and Folksong*. 2nd ed. New York: Dover Publications, 1961.

Jackson, George Pullen. *White Spirituals in the Southern Uplands*. Chapel Hill: University of North Carolina Press, 1933. Repr., New York: Dover Publications, 1965.

Korson, George. *Pennsylvania Songs and Legends*. Philadelphia: n.p., 1949.

Laws, G. Malcolm, Jr. *Native American Balladry*. Philadelphia: The American Folklore Society, 1964.

Lomax, John, and Alan Lomax. *American Ballads and Folk Songs*. New York: The Macmillan Company, 1934.

———. *Cowboy Songs and Other Frontier Ballads*. Rev. and enl. New York: The Macmillan Company, 1945. (1st ed., 1910.)

Malone, Bill C. *Southern Music. American Music*. Lexington: The University Press of Kentucky, 1979.

Nettl, Bruno. *Folk Music in the United States: An Introduction*. 3rd ed. Detroit: Wayne State University Press, 1976.

Patterson, Daniel W. *The Shaker Spiritual*. Princeton: Princeton University Press, 1978.

Price, Steven D. *Old As the Hills: The Story of Bluegrass Music.* New York: The Viking Press, 1975.

Rosenberg, Neil V. "From Sound to Style: The Emergence of Bluegrass," *Journal of American Folklore* LXXX (1967), pp. 143–50.

Sandburg, Carl. *The American Songbag.* New York: Harcourt & Brace, 1927.

Seeger, Mike, and John Cohen. *Old-Time String Band Songbook.* New York: Oak Publications, 1976.

Sharp, Cecil J. *English Folk Songs from the Southern Appalachians.* Ed. by Maud Karpeles. London: Oxford University Press, 1932.

———, and Olive Dame Campbell. *English Folk Songs from the Southern Appalachians.* New York & London: G. P. Putnam's Sons, 1917.

Stambler, Irwin, and Grelun Landon. *Encyclopedia of Folk, Country, and Western Music.* New York: St. Martin's Press, 1969.

Thede, Marion. *The Fiddle Book.* New York: Oak Publications, 1967.

Various authors. *Commercially Disseminated Folk Music: Sources and Resources.* Los Angeles: The John Edwards Memorial Foundation, 1971. (These studies originally appeared in *Western Folklore* XXX/3 [July, 1971]).

Walker, William. *The Southern Harmony.* New Haven: E. W. Miller, 1835. Mod. ed., ed. by Glenn C. Wilcox, Los Angeles: Pro Music-americana, 1966.

White, John I. *Git Along, Little Dogies: Songs and Songmakers of the American West.* Urbana: University of Illinois Press, 1975.

Wilgus, D. K.: *Anglo-American Folksong Scholarship Since 1898.* New Brunswick: Rutgers University Press, 1959.

Winans, Robert B. "The Folk, the Stage, and the Five-String Banjo in the Nineteenth Century," *Journal of American Folklore,* LXXXIX (1976), pp. 407–37.

Wolfe, Charles K. *The Grand Ole Opry: The Early Years.* London: Old Time Music, 1975.

Wyeth, John. *Repository of Sacred Music. Part Second.* Harrisburg: John Wyeth, 1813. Repr., New York: Da Capo Press, 1964.

### F. THE MUSIC OF BLACK AMERICANS (GENERAL)

Allen, William Francis, Charles Pickard Ware, and Lucy McKim Garrison. *Slave Songs of the United States.* New York: A. Simpson & Co., 1867.

Baker, David N., Lida M. Belt, and Herman C. Hudson, eds. *The Black Composer Speaks.* Metuchen: The Scarecrow Press, 1978.

Courlander, Harold. *Negro Folk Music, U.S.A.* New York: Columbia University Press, 1963.

De Lerma, Dominique-Rene. *Bibliography of Black Music. Volume 1: Reference Materials.* Westport: Greenwood Press, 1981.

Du Bois, W. E. Burghardt. *The Souls of Black Folk.* Chicago: McClurg, 1903.

Epstein, Dena J. *Sinful Tunes and Spirituals. Black Folk Music to the Civil War.* Urbana: University of Illinois Press, 1977.

Fenner, Thomas P., with Frederic G. Rathbun and Miss Bessie Cleavland. *Cabin and Plantation Songs as Sung by the Hampton Students.* New York and London: G. P. Putnam's Sonss, 1874.

Herskovits, Melville J. *The Myth of the Negro Past.* New York: Harper & Brothers, 1941.

Huggins, Nathan Irvin. *Harlem Renaissance.* New York: Oxford University Press, 1971.

Jackson, Irene V. *Afro-American Religious Music: A Bibliography and A Catalogue of Gospel Music.* Westport: Greenwood Press, 1979.

Johnson, James Weldon. *Black Manhattan.* New York: Alfred A. Knopg, 1930.

———. *The Book of American Negro Spirituals.* New York: Viking Press, 1925. Vol. 2, 1926.

Jones, A. M. *Studies in African Music.* New York & London: Oxford University Press, 1959.

Jones, LeRoi. *Blues People: Negro Music in White America.* New York: William Morrow & Company, 1963.

Lovell, John. *Black Song: the Forge and the Flame.* New York: The Macmillan Company, 1972.

Marsh, J. B. T. *The Story of the Jubilee Singers; with their Songs:* Boston: Houghton, Osgood and Company, 1880

Nketia, J. H. Kwabena. *The Music of Africa.* New York: W. W. Norton & Company, 1974.

Ramsey, Frederic. *Been Here and Gone.* New Brunswick: Rutgers University Press, 1960.

Ricks, George Robinson. *Some Aspects of the Religious Music of the United States Negro.* New York: Arno Press, 1977.

Roberts, John Storm: *Black Music of Two Worlds.* New York: Praeger Publishers, 1972.

Schoener, Allon, ed. *Harlem on my Mind: Cultural Capital of Black America, 1900–1968.* New York: Random House, 1968.

Seward, Theodore F. *Jubilee Songs: As Sung by the Jubilee Singers of Fisk University.* New York: Biglow & Main, c. 1872.

Southern, Eileen. *Biographical Dictionary of Afro-American and African Musicians.* Westport: Greenwood Press, 1981.

———. *The Music of Black Americans. A History.* New York: W. W. Norton & Company, 1971.

———. *Readings in Black American Music.* New York: W. W. Norton & Company, 1971.

Walton, Ortiz. *Music: Black, White and Blue.* New York: Morrow, 1972.


### G. BLUES

Charters, Samuel. *The Bluesmen.* New York: Oak Publications, 1967.

———. *The Country Blues.* New York: Rinehart, 1959.

———. *The Poetry of the Blues.* New York: Oak Publications, 1963.

———. *Sweet as the Showers of Rain.* New York: Oak Publication, 1977. (Vol. 2 of *The Bluesmen.*)

Cook, Bruce. *Listen to the Blues.* New York: Scribner, 1973.

Ferris, William R. *Blues from the Delta.* Garden City: Anchor Press, 1978.

Godrich, John, and Robert M. W. Dixon. *Blues and Gospel Records, 1902–1942.* London: Storyville, 1969.

Handy, W. C. *Blues: An Anthology.* New York: Boni, 1926. Rev. ed., New York: The Macmillan Company, 1972.

Keil, Charles. *Urban Blues.* Chicago & London: The University of Chicago Press, 1966.

Leadbetter, Mike, and Neil Slaven. *Blues Records, January 1943–December 1966.* New York: Oak Publications, 1969.

Oliver, Paul. *Conversations with the Blues.* New York: Horizon Press, 1965.

———. *The Meaning of the Blues.* New York: Collier, 1963.

———. *The Story of the Blues.* London: Barrie & Rockliff, 1969.

Oster, Harry. *Living Country Blues.* Detroit: Folklore Associates, 1969.

Russell, Tony. *Blacks, Whites, and Blues.* New York: Stein & Day, 1970.

Titon, Jeff Todd. *Early Downhome Blues.* Urbana: The University of Illinois Press, 1977.


### H. RAGTIME

Berlin, Edward A. *Ragtime. A Musical and Cultural History.* Berkeley: University of California Press, 1980.

Blesh, Rudi, and Harriet Janis. *They All Played Ragtime.* New York: Alfred A. Knopf, 1950. Rev. ed., 1959, 1966, 1971.

Jasen, David A. *Recorded Ragtime, 1897–1958.* Hamden: Archon Books, 1973.

————, and Trebor Jay Tichenor. *Rags and Ragtime*. New York: The Seabury Press, 1978.

Schafer, William J., and Johannes Riedel. *The Art of Ragtime; Form and Meaning of an Original Black American Art*. Baton Rouge: Louisiana State University Press, 1973.

Waldo, Terry. *This Is Ragtime*. New York: Hawthorn Books, 1976.

Waterman, Guy. "Ragtime," *Jazz: New Perspectives on the History of Jazz*. Ed. by Nat Hentoff and Albert J. McCarthy. New York: Rinehart, 1959.

## I. JAZZ

Berendt, Joachim. *The Jazz Book: from New Orleans to Rock and Free Jazz*. Trans. by Dan Morgenstern and Helmut and Barbara Bredigkeit. New York: Hill and Wang, 1966.

Blesh, Rudi. *Shining Trumpets: A History of Jazz*. New York: Alfred A. Knopf, 1946. Rev. ed., 1958.

Budds, Michael J. *Jazz in the Sixties*. Iowa City: University of Iowa Press, 1978.

Charters, Samuel B. *Jazz: New Orleans (1885–1963). An Index to the Negro Musicians of New Orleans*. New York: Oak Publications, 1963.

————, and Leonard Kunstadt. *Jazz: A History of the New York Scene*. New York: Doubleday, 1962.

Chilton, John. *Who's Who of Jazz*. Philadelphia: Chilton, 1972.

Feather, Leonard. *The Encyclopedia of Jazz*. New York: Horizon Press, 1955. Rev. ed., 1960.

————. *The Encyclopedia of Jazz in the Sixties*. New York: Horizon Press, 1966.

Finkelstein, Sidney. *Jazz: A People's Music*. New York: Citadel Press, 1964.

Harris, Rex. *The Story of Jazz*. New York: Grosset & Dunlap, 1955.

Hentoff, Nat. *The Jazz Life*. New York: Dial Press, 1961.

Hodeir, Andre. *Jazz. Its Evolution and Essence*. New York: Grove Press, 1956.

Jepsen, Jorgen Grunnet. *Jazz Records: A Discography*. Copenhagen: Knudsen, 1963–70.

Jones, LeRoi. *Black Music*. New York: Morrow, 1967.

Keepnews, Orrin, and Bill Brauer, Jr. *A Pictorial History of Jazz*. New York: Crown, 1966.

Kofsky, Frank. *Black Nationalism and the Revolution in Music*. New York: Pathfinder Press, 1970.

McCarthy, Albert. *Big Band Jazz*. New York: G. P. Putnam's Sons, 1974.

————, Alun Morgan, Paul Oliver, and Max Harrison. *Jazz on*

*Record: a Critical Guide to the First 50 Years, 1917–1967.* New York: Oak Publications, 1968.

Osgood, Henry O. *So This Is Jazz.* Boston: Little, Brown, and Company, 1926.

Ostransky, Leroy. *The Anatomy of Jazz.* Seattle: The Univeristy of Washington Press, 1960.

Pleasants, Henry. *Death of a Music? The Decline of the European Tradition and the Rise of Jazz.* London: Gollancz, 1961.

Ramsey, Frederic, Jr., and Charles Edward Smith. *Jazzmen.* New York: Harcourt, Brace and Company, 1939.

Russell, Ross. *Jazz Style in Kansas City and the Southwest.* Berkeley: The University of California Press, 1971.

Rust, Brian. *Jazz Records, 1897–1942.* 4th rev. and enl. ed. New Rochelle: Arlington House, 1978.

Schuller, Gunther. *Early Jazz. Its Roots and Musical Development.* New York: Oxford University Press, 1968.

Shapiro, Nat, and Nat Hentoff, eds. *Hear Me Talkin' to Ya.* New York: Rinehart & Company, 1955.

Stearns, Marshall W. *The Story of Jazz.* New York: Oxford University Press, 1956.

Stearns, Marshall and Jean. *Jazz Dance. The Story of American Vernacular Dance.* New York: The Macmillan Company, 1968.

Tirro, Frank. *Jazz: A History.* New York: W. W. Norton & Company, 1977.

Whiteman, Paul, and Mary Margaret McBride. *Jazz.* New York, J. H. Sears & Company, 1926.

Williams, Martin, ed. *The Art of Jazz: Essays on the Nature and Development of Jazz.* New York: Oxford University Press, 1959.

————. *Jazz Masters in Transition, 1957–69.* New York: The Macmillan Company, 1970.

————. *Jazz Masters of New Orleans.* New York: Da Capo Press, 1978. (Repr. of 1967 Macmillan ed.)

————. *The Jazz Tradition.* New York: Oxford University Press, 1970.

Wilson, John S. *Jazz: The Transition Years, 1940–1960.* New York: Appleton-Century-Crofts, 1966.

## J. POPULAR SONG

Belz, Carl. *The Story of Rock.* New York: Oxford University Press, 1969.

Burton, Jack. *The Blue Book of Tin Pan Alley.* Watkins Glen: Century House, 1950.

Denisoff, R. Serge. *Sing a Song of Social Significance.* Bowling Green: Bowling Green University Popular Press, 1972.

De Turk, David A., and A. Poulin, eds. *The American Folk Scene: Dimensions of the Folksong Revival.* New York: Dell, 1967.

Eisen, Jonathan, ed. *The Age of Rock: Sounds of the American Cultural Revolution.* New York: Random House, 1969.

Erenberg, Lewis A. *Steppin' Out: New York Nightlife and the Transformation of American Culture, 1890–1930.* Westport: Greenwood Press, 1981.

Ewen, David. *All the Years of American Popular Music.* Englewood Cliffs: Prentice-Hall, 1977.

———. *The Life and Death of Tin Pan Alley; the Golden Age of American Popular Music.* New York: Funk and Wagnalls Company, 1964.

Frith, Simon Webster. *The Sociology of Rock.* London: Constable, 1978.

Gillett, Charlie. *The Sound of the City: The Rise of Rock and Roll.* New York: Dell, 1972.

Grossman, Lloyd. *A Social History of Rock Music.* New York: David McKay Company, 1976.

Hamm, Charles. *Yesterdays: Popular Song in America.* New York: W. W. Norton & Company, 1979.

Heaps, Willard A. and Porter W. *The Singing Sixties. The Spirit of Civil War Days Drawn from the Music of the Times.* Norman: University of Oklahoma Press, 1960.

Hoare, Ian. *The Soul Book.* London: Eyre Methuen, 1975.

Kinkle, Roger D. *The Complete Encyclopedia of Popular Music and Jazz, 1900–1950.* New Rochelle: Arlington House Publishers, 1974.

Marcus, Greil. *Mystery Train: Images of America in Rock and Roll Music.* New York: E. P. Dutton, 1975.

Marks, Edward B. *They All Had Glamour; From the Swedish Nightingale to the Naked Lady.* New York: Julian Messner, 1944.

———. *They All Sang: from Tony Pastor to Rudy Vallée.* New York: Viking Press, 1934.

Mellers, Wilfrid. *Twilight of the Gods: the Beatles in Retrospect.* New York: Alfred A. Knopf, 1965.

Meltzer, R. *The Aesthetics of Rock.* New York: Something Else Press, 1970.

Meyer, Hazel. *The Gold in Tin Pan Alley.* Philadelphia and New York: J. B. Lippincott Company, 1958.

Middleton, Richard. *Pop Music and the Blues.* London: Gollancz, 1972.

Pleasants, Henry. *The Great American Popular Singers.* New York: Simon & Schuster, 1974.

Roberts, John Storm. *The Latin Tinge: The Impact of Latin Ameri-*

*can Music on the United States.* New York: Oxford University Press, 1979.

Rodnitzky, Jerome L. *Minstrels of the Dawn: The Folk-Protest Singer as a Cultural Hero.* Chicago: Nelson-Hall, 1976.

Roxon, Lillian. *Rock Encyclopedia.* New York: Grosset & Dunlap, 1969.

Rublowsky, John. *Popular Music.* New York: Basic Books, 1967.

Rust, Brian. *The American Dance Band Discography, 1917–1942.* New Rochelle: Arlington House, 1975.

———. *The Complete Entertainment Discography, from the Mid-1890's to 1942.* New Rochelle: Arlington House, 1973.

Shapiro, Nat. *Popular Music: An Annotated Index of American Popular Songs.* New York: Adrian Press, 1964–73.

Shaw, Arnold. *Honkers and Shouters: The Rhythm and Blues Years.* New York: The Macmillan Company, 1977.

Spaeth, Sigmund. *A History of Popular Music in America.* New York: Random House, 1948.

Stambler, Irwin. *Encyclopedia of Popular Music.* New York: St. Martin's Press, 1965. Revised ed., *Encyclopedia of Pop, Rock and Soul,* 1975.

Tawa, Nicholas E. *Sweet Songs for Gentle Americans: The Parlor Song in America, 1790–1860.* Bowling Green: Bowling Green Popular Press, 1980.

Whitburn, Joel. *Top Pop Artists & Singles, 1955–1978.* Menomonee Falls: Record Research, 1979. (Whitburn has also compiled and published similar compilations of other repertories: country-western music, LP albums, rhythm-and-blues and soul music, "easy listening" music.)

Whitcomb, Ian. *After the Ball; Pop Music from Rag to Rock.* New York: Simon and Schuster, 1973.

Wilder, Alec. *American Popular Song: The Great Innovators, 1900–1950.* New York: Oxford University Press, 1972.

Witmark, Isidore, and Isaac Goldberg. *The Story of the House of Witmark: From Ragtime to Swingtime.* New York: L. Furman, 1939.

### K. SACRED MUSIC

Benson, Louis F. *The English Hymn.* London: Hodder and Stoughton, 1915.

Davison, Archibald T. *Protestant Church Music in America.* Boston: G. Schirmer, 1933.

Ellinwood, Leonard. *The History of American Church Music.* New York: Morehouse-Gorham Company, 1953.

Foote, Henry Wilder. *Three Centuries of American Hymnody*. Cambridge: Harvard University Press, 1940.

Gould, Nathaniel D. *Church Music in America*. Boston: A. N. Johnson, 1853.

Metcalf, Frank J. *American Writers and Compilers of Sacred Music*. New York and Cincinnati: The Abingdon Press, 1925.

Stevenson, Robert. *Protestant Church Music in America: A Short Survey of Men and Movements from 1564 to the Present*. New York: W. W. Norton & Company, 1966.

Temperley, Nicholas. *The Music of the English Parish Church*. Cambridge: Cambridge University Press, 1979.

Wienandt, Elwyn A., and Robert H. Young. *The Anthem in England and America*. New York: Free Press, 1970.

## L. SECULAR VOCAL MUSIC: SONG AND THE MUSICAL STAGE

Bordman, Gerald. *American Musical Theatre. A Chronicle*. New York: Oxford University Press, 1978.

Burton, Jack. *The Blue Book of Broadway Musicals*. Watkins Glen: Century House, 1952.

———. *The Blue Book of Hollywood Musicals*. Watkins Glen: Century House, 1953.

Davis, Ronald L. *A History of Opera in the American West*. Englewood Cliffs: Prentice-Hall, 1965.

Gagey, Edmond McAdoo. *Ballad Opera*. New York: Columbia University Press, 1937.

Gilbert, Douglas. *American Vaudeville: Its Life and Times*. New York: Whittlesey House, 1940.

Graf, Herbert. *Opera for the People*. Minneapolis: University of Minnesota Press, 1951.

Green, Stanley. *The World of Musical Comedy*. New York: Barnes, 1962.

Kolodin, Irving. *The Metropolitan Opera, 1883–1966: A Candid History*. New York: Alfred A. Knopf, 1967.

Lahee, Henry C. *Grand Opera in America*. Boston: L. C. Page, 1902.

Mates, Julian. *The American Musical Stage Before 1800*. New Brunswick: Rutgers University Press, 1962.

Mattfeld, Julius. *A Handbook of American Operatic Premieres, 1731–1962*. Detroit: Music Information Service, 1963.

———. *A Hundred Years of Grand Opera in New York, 1825–1925*. New York: The New York Public Library, 1927.

Nathan, Hans. "United States of America," pp. 408–60 in Denis Stevens, *A History of Song*. New York: W. W. Norton & Company, 1960.

Root, Deane L. *American Popular Stage Music, 1860–1880*. Ann Arbor: UMI Research Press, 1981.

Sampson, Henry T. *Blacks in Blackface: A Source Book on Early Black Musical Shows*. Metuchen: The Scarecrow Press, 1980.

Smith, Cecil Michener. *Musical Comedy in America*. New York: Theatre Arts Books, 1950.

Sonneck, O. G. *Early Opera in America*. New York: G. Schirmer, 1915.

Toll, Robert C. *Blacking Up; The Minstrel Show in Nineteenth-Century America*. New York: Oxford University Press, 1974.

Upton, William Treat. *Art-Song in America; A Study in the Development of American Music*. Boston: Oliver Ditson Company, 1930.

Wittke, Carl. *Tambo and Bones, a History of the American Minstrel Stage*. Durham: Duke University Press, 1930.

Yerbury, Grace D. *Song in America, From Early Times to About 1850*. Metuchen: Scarecrow Press, 1971.

## 4. Individual Composers and Musicians

### ANTHEIL
Antheil, George. *Bad Boy of Music*. Garden City: Doubleday, 1945.

### ARLEN
Jablonski, Edward. *Harold Arlen: Happy with the Blues*. Garden City: Doubleday, 1961.

### ARMSTRONG
Armstrong, Louis. *Satchmo: My Life in New Orleans*. New York: Prentice-Hall, 1954.

Jones, Max, and John Chilton. *Louis: the Louis Armstrong Story, 1900–1971*. Boston: Little, Brown, 1971.

### BABBITT
Babbitt, Milton. "Some Aspects of Twelve-tone Composition," *The Score and IMA Magazine*, XII (June 1955), pp. 53ff.

———. "Who Cares If You Listen," *High Fidelity*, VIII 2 (February, 1958), pp. 39 ff.

### BARBER
Broder, Nathan. *Samuel Barber*. New York: G. Schirmer, 1954.

### BASIE
Horricks, Raymond. *Count Basie and His Orchestra*. New York: Citadel Press, 1957.

BEIDERBECKE

Sudhalter, Richard M., and Philip R. Evans. *Bix: Man and Legend.* New Rochelle: Arlington House, 1974.

BERLIN

Freedland, Michael. *Irving Berlin.* New York: Stein & Day, 1974.

Woollcott, Alexander. *The Story of Irving Berlin.* New York & London: G. P. Putnam's Sons, 1925.

BILLINGS

McKay, David P., and Richard Crawford. *William Billings of Boston.* Princeton: Princeton University Press, 1975.

Nathan, Hans. *William Billings: Data and Documents.* Detroit: Information Coordinators, 1976.

BIRD

Loring, William C. *The Music of Arthur Bird.* Washington: William C. Loring, 1974.

BLOCH

Sessions, Roger. "Ernest Bloch," *Modern Music,* V (1927), pp. 3 ff.

CAGE

Cage, John. *Silence.* Middletown: Wesleyan University Press, 1961.

———. *Notations.* New York: Something Else Press, 1969.

Kostelanetz, Richard, ed. *John Cage.* New York: Praeger, 1970.

CARTER

Edwards, Allen. *Flawed Words and Stubborn Sounds: A Conversation with Elliott Carter.* New York: W. W. Norton & Company, 1971.

Stone, Else and Kurt, eds. *The Writings of Elliott Carter. An American Composer Looks at Modern Music.* Bloomington: Indiana University Press, 1977.

CARTER FAMILY

Atkins, John. *The Carter Family.* London: Old Time Music, 1973.

CHADWICK

Yellin, Victor. *The Life and Operatic Works of George Whitefield Chadwick.* Ph.D. dissertation, Harvard University, 1957.

COHAN

Cohan, George M. *Twenty Years on Broadway.* New York and London: Harper & Brothers, Publishers, 1924.

COLTRANE

Cole, Bill. *John Coltrane*. New York: Schirmer Books, 1976.


COPLAND

Berger, Arthur. *Aaron Copland*. New York: Oxford University Press, 1953.

Copland, Aaron. *Music and Imagination*. Cambridge: Harvard University Press, 1952.

Smith, Julia. *Aaron Copland: His Work and Contribution to American Music*. New York: Dutton, 1955.


COWELL

Cowell, Henry. *New Musical Resources*. New York: Something Else Press, 1969. (First published in 1930.)


DAVIS

Cole, Bill. *Miles Davis: A Musical Biography*. New York: Morrow, 1974.


DRESSER

Dreiser, Theodore. "My Brother Paul," pp. 76–109 in *Twelve Men*. New York: Boni and Liveright, 1919.


DVOŘÁK

Clapham, John. *Antonín Dvořák. Musician and Craftsman*. New York: St. Martin's Press, 1966.


DYLAN

Gray, Michael. *Song and Dance Man: The Art of Bob Dylan*. New York: Dutton, 1973.

Scaduto, Anthony. *Bob Dylan*. New York: Grosset & Dunlap, 1972.


ELLINGTON

Ellington, Edward Kennedy. *Music Is My Mistress*. Garden City: Doubleday, 1973.


EMMETT

Nathan, Hans. *Dan Emmett and the Rise of Early Negro Minstrelsy*. Norman: University of Oklahoma Press, 1962.


FARWELL

Farwell, Brice, ed. *A Guide to the Music of Arthur Farwell and to the Microfilm Collection of His Work*. Briarcliff Manor: privately printed, 1972.

FOOTE

Foote, Arthur. *Arthur Foote (1853–1937). An Autobiography.* Norwood: Plimpton Press, 1946.

———. "A Bostonian Remembers," *The Musical Quarterly,* XXIII 1 (January, 1937), pp. 37–44.

FOSTER

Austin, William W. *Susanna, Jeanie, and The Old Folks at Home; The Songs of Stephen C. Foster from His Time to Ours.* New York: Macmillan Publishing Co., 1975.

Howard, John Tasker. *Stephen Foster: America's Troubador.* New York: Thomas Crowell, 1953.

Millingan, Harold V. *Stephen Collins Foster.* New York: Schirmer, 1920.

Morneweck, Evelyn Foster. *Chronicles of Stephen Foster's Family.* Pittsburgh: University of Pittsburgh Press, 1944.

Whittlesey, Walter R., and O. G. Sonneck. *Catalogue of First Editions of Stephen Foster.* Washington: Library of Congress, 1915.

FRANKLIN

Grenander, M. E. "Reflections on the String Quartet(s) Attributed to Franklin," *American Quarterly,* XXVII (March, 1975), pp. 73–87.

FRY

Upton, William Treat. *William Henry Fry.* New York: Thomas Crowell, 1954. Repr. Da Capo Press, 1974.

GERSHWIN

Armitage, Merle. *George Gershwin, Man and Legend.* New York: Duell, Sloan and Pearce, 1958.

Jablonski, Edward, and Lawrence D. Stewart. *The Gershwin Years.* Garden City: Doubleday & Company, 1973.

Kimball, Robert, and Alfred Simon. *The Gershwins.* New York: Atheneum, 1973.

Schwartz, Charles. *Gershwin: His Life and Music.* New York: Bobbs-Merrill, 1973.

GILLESPIE

James, Michael. *Dizzy Gillespie.* New York: Barnes, 1961.

GOODMAN

Connor, D. Russell, and Warren W. Hicks. *Benny Goodman on the Record: a Bio-discography.* New Rochelle: Arlington House, 1969.

GOTTSCHALK

Gottschalk, Louis Moreau. *Notes of a Pianist.* Ed. by Jeanne Behrend. New York: Alfred A. Knopf, 1964. (1st ed., 1881.)

Loggins, Vernon. *Where the World Ends: The Life of Louis Moreau Gottschalk.* Baton Rouge: Louisiana State University Press, 1958.

Offergeld, Robert. *The Centennial Catalogue of the Published and Unpublished Compositions of Louis Moreau Gottschalk.* New York: Stereo Review, 1970.


GRATEFUL DEAD

Harrison, Hank. *The Dead Book: A Social History of the Grateful Dead.* New York: Links Books, 1973.


GRIFFES

Maisel, Edward M. *Charles T. Griffes.* New York: Alfred A. Knopf, 1943.


GUTHRIE

Guthrie, Woody. *Bound for Glory.* New York: Dutton, 1968.


HANDY

Handy, W. C. *Father of the Blues.* Ed. Arna Bontemps. New York: The Macmillan Company, 1941.


HARRIGAN AND HART

Kahn, E. J., Jr. *The Merry Partners: The Age and Stage of Harrigan and Hart.* New York: Random House, 1955.


HARRIS, CHARLES

Harris, Charles K. *After the Ball: Forty Years of Melody.* New York: Frank-Maurice, 1926.


HARRIS, ROY

Farwell, Arthur. "Roy Harris," *The Musical Quarterly* XVIII (1932), pp. 18–32.

Slonimsky, Nicholas. "Roy Harris," *The Musical Quarterly*, XXXIII (January 1947), pp. 17–37.


HEINRICH

Upton, William Treat. *Anthony Philip Heinrich: A Nineteenth-Century Composer in America.* New York: Columbia University Press, 1939.

HENDERSON

Allen, Walter C. *Hendersonia: the Music of Fletcher Henderson and his Musicians*. Highland Park: Walter C. Allen, 1973.

HERBERT

Waters, Edward N. *Victor Herbert: a Life in Music*. New York: The Macmillan Company, 1955.

HEWITT

Hewitt, John Hill. *Shadows on the Wall: or, Glimpses of the Past*. Baltimore: Turnbull, 1877. Repr. New York: AMS Press, 1971.

HOLIDAY

Chilton, John. *Billie's Blues: a Survey of Billie Holiday's Career, 1933–1959*. New York: Stein & Day, 1975.

HOLLY

Laing, Dave. *Buddy Holly*. New York: The Macmillan Company, 1971.

HOPKINSON

Hastings, George Everett. *The Life and Works of Francis Hopkinson*. Chicago: University of Chicago Press, 1926.

Sonneck, Oscar G. T. *Francis Hopkinson, The First American Poet-Composer (1737–1791); and James Lyon, Patriot, Preacher, Psalmodist*. Washington: H. L. McQueen, 1905. Repr. New York: Da Capo Press, 1967.

HUTCHINSON

Brink, Carol. *Harps in the Wind. The Story of the Singing Hutchinsons*. New York: The Macmillan Company, 1947.

Hutchinson, John Wallace. *Story of the Hutchinsons (Tribe of Jesse)*. 2 vols. Boston: Lee and Shepard, 1896.

Jordan, Philip D. *Singin' Yankees*. Minneapolis: The University of Minnesota Press, 1946.

IVES

Cowell, Henry and Sidney. *Charles Ives and His Music*. New York: Oxford University Press, 1955.

Ives, Charles. *Essays Before a Sonata, and Other Writings*. Ed. by Howard Boatwright. New York: W. W. Norton & Company, 1962.

———. *Memos*. Ed. by John Kirkpatrick. New York: W. W. Norton & Company, 1972.

Kirkpatrick, John. *A Temporary Mimeographed Catalogue of the Music Manuscripts and Related Materials of Charles Edward Ives, 1874–1954*. New Haven: privately mimeographed, 1960. repr. 1973.

Perlis, Vivian. *Charles Ives Remembered: An Oral History*. New Haven: Yale University Press, 1974.

Rossiter, Frank R. *Charles Ives and His America*. New York: Liveright, 1975.

Wooldridge, David. *From the Steeples and Mountains. A Study of Charles Ives*. New York: Alfred A. Knopf, 1974.

### JEFFERSON AIRPLANE

Gleason, Ralph J. *The Jefferson Airplane and the San Francisco Sound*. New York: Ballantine Books, 1969.

### KERN

Bordman, Gerald. *Jerome Kern: His Life and Music*. New York: Oxford University Press, 1980.

Ewen, David. *The World of Jerome Kern: a Biography*. New York: Holt, 1960.

### KIRCHNER

Ringer, Alexander. "Leon Kirchner," *The Musical Quarterly*, XLIII (1957), pp. 1–20.

### LAW

Crawford, Richard A. *Andrew Law, American Psalmodist*. Evanston: Northwestern University Press, 1968.

### LEDBETTER

Jones, Max, and Albert McCarthy, eds. *A Tribute to Huddie Ledbetter*. London: Jazz Music Books, 1946.

### LIND

Rosenberg, C. G. *Jenny Lind in America*. New York: Stringer & Townsend, 1851.

Shultz, Gladys Denny. *Jenny Lind. The Swedish Nightingale*. Philadelphia & New York: J. B. Lippincott Company, 1962.

### MACDOWELL

Sonneck, O. G. *Catalogue of First Editions of Edward MacDowell*. Washington: Library of Congress, 1917.

Gilman, Lawrence. *Edward MacDowell. A Study*. New York: John Lane Company, 1908.

MacDowell, Edward. *Critical and Historical Essays.* Ed. by W. J. Baltzell. Boston: Arthur P. Schmidt, 1912.

MACON

Rinzler, Ralph, and Norm Cohen. *Uncle Dave Macon: a Bio-discography.* Los Angeles: John Edwards Memorial Foundation, 1970.

MASON

Mason, William. *Memories of a Musical Life.* New York: The Century Company, 1901.

Rich, Arthur Lowndes. *Lowell Mason. "The Father of Singing Among the Children."* Chapel Hill: The University of North Carolina Press, 1946.

Seward, Theodore F. *The Educational Work of Dr. Lowell Mason.* n.p.: n.p., n.d.

MEZZROW

Mezzrow, Milton "Mezz," and Bernard Wolfe. *Really the Blues.* Garden City: Doubleday, 1972.

MORTON

Lomax, Alan. *Mister Jelly Roll: The Fortunes of Jelly Roll Morton.* Berkeley: University of California Press, 1973.

NEVIN

Howard, John Tasker. *Ethelbert Nevin.* New York: Thomas Crowell, 1935.

OLIVER

Allen, Walter C., and Brian A. Rust. *King Joe Oliver.* Belleville: Walter C. Allen, 1955.

PAINE

Howe, M. A. DeWolfe. "John Knowles Paine," *The Musical Quarterly,* XXV 3 (July 1939), pp. 257–67.

Schmidt, John C. *The Life and Works of John Knowles Paine.* Ann Arbor: UMI Research Press, 1980.

PARKER, CHARLIE

Reisner, R. G. *Bird: the Legend of Charlie Parker.* New York: Citadel Press, 1962.

Russell, Ross. *Bird Lives: the High Life and Hard Times of Charlie Parker.* New York: Charterhouse, 1973.

**PARKER, HORATIO**
Chadwick, George W. *Horatio Parker*. New Haven: Yale University Press, 1921.

**PARTCH**
Partch, Harry. *Genesis of a Music*. New York: Da Capo Press, 1974.

**PATTON**
Fahey, John. *Charley Patton*. London: Studio Vista, 1970.

**PISTON**
Carter, Elliott. "Walter Piston," *The Musical Quarterly*, XXXII (1946), pp. 354–75.

**PORTER**
Kimball, Robert. *Cole*. New York: Holt, Rinehart & Winston, 1971.
Schwartz, Charles. *Cole Porter*. New York: Dial Press, 1977.

**PRESLEY**
Hopkins, Jerry. *Elvis: a Biography*. New York: Simon & Schuster, 1971.

**REICH**
Reich, Steve. *Writings about Music*. Halifax: Nova Scotia College of Art and Design, 1974.

**RIEGGER**
Goldman, Richard F. "The Music of Wallingford Riegger," *The Musical Quarterly*, XXVI (January 1950), pp. 39–61.

**ROCHBERG**
Ringer, Alexander. "The Music of George Rochberg," *The Musical Quarterly*, LII (1966), pp. 409–30.

**RODGERS, JIMMIE**
Porterfield, Nolan. *Jimmie Rodgers: The Life and Times of America's Blue Yodeler*. Urbana: University of Illinois Press, 1979.

**RODGERS, RICHARD**
Rodgers, Richard. *Musical Stages: an Autobiography*. New York: Random House, 1975.

**ROOT**
Root, George F. *The Story of a Musical Life*. Cincinnati: John Church Company, 1891.

RUSSELL

Russell, Henry. *Cheer! Boys, Cheer! Memories of Men and Music.* London: J. Macqueen, 1895.

Stephens, John Anthony. *Henry Russell in America: Chutzpah and Huzzah.* D.M.A. thesis (unpublished), the University of Illinois at Urbana-Champaign, 1975.


SCHOENBERG

Newlin, Dika. "Schoenberg in America," *Music Survey,* I (1949), pp. 128 ff, 185 ff.

———. *Schoenberg Remembered.* New York: Pendragon Press, 1980.


SESSIONS

Sessions, Roger. *Roger Sessions on Music. Collected Essays.* Ed. by Edward T. Cone. Princeton: Princeton University Press, 1979.


SHAW

Williams, Thomas. *A Discourse on the Life and Death of Oliver Shaw.* Boston: Charles C. P. Moody, 1851.


SISSLE

Kimball, Robert, and William Bolcom. *Reminiscing with Sissle and Blake.* New York: The Viking Press, 1973.


SMITH

Oliver, Paul. *Bessie Smith.* New York: Barnes, 1961.


STILL

Arvey, Verna, *William Grant Still.* New York: Fischer, 1939.


STRAVINSKY

Craft, Robert. *Stravinsky. Chronicle of a Friendship. 1948–1971.* New York: Alfred A. Knopf, 1972.

Stravinsky, Igor, and Robert Craft. *Conversations with Igor Stravinsky.* Garden City: Doubleday & Company, 1959.


SWAN

Webb, Guy Bedford. *Timothy Swan: Yankee Tunesmith.* D.M.A. thesis, The University of Illinois at Urbana-Champaign, 1972.


THOMAS

Russell, Charles Edwards. *The American Orchestra and Theodore Thomas.* Garden City: Doubleday, Page & Company, 1927.

Thomas, Theodore. *A Musical Autobiography.* 2 vols. Chicago: A. C. McClurg & Co., 1905.

THOMSON

Hoover, Kathleen, and John Cage. *Virgil Thomson. His Life and Music.* New York and London: Thomas Yoseloff, 1959.

Thomson, Virgil. *Virgil Thomson.* New York: Alfred A. Knopf, 1966.

VARÈSE

Ouellette, Fernand. *Edgar Varèse.* New York: Orion Press, 1968.

WARREN

Thomas, Tony. *Harry Warren and the Hollywood Musical.* Secaucus: Citadel Press, 1975.

WATERS

Waters, Ethel. *His Eye Is on the Sparrow: an Autobiography.* Garden City: Doubleday, 1951.

WILLIAMS

Williams, Roger. *Sing a Sad Song: the Life of Hank Williams.* New York: Ballantine Books, 1973.

WILLS

Townsend, Charles R. *San Antonio Rose: The Life and Music of Bob Wills.* Urbana: University of Illinois Press, 1976.

## 5. BIBLIOGRAPHICAL AND REFERENCE WORKS

Adkins, Cecil. *Doctoral Dissertations in Musicology.* 5th ed. Philadelphia: The American Musicological Society, 1971.

————, and Alis Dickinson. *International Index of Doctoral Dissertations and Musicological Works in Progress.* 6th ed. Philadelphia: The American Musicological Society, 1977.

Allen, Daniel. *Bibliography of Discographies, Volume 2: Jazz, 1935–1980.* New York: R. R. Bowker, 1981.

*American Folklore Films and Videotapes: An Index.* Memphis: The Center for Southern Folklore, 1976.

Block, Adrienne Fried, and Carol Neuls-Bates. *Women in American Music: a Bibliography of Music and Literature.* Westport: Greenwood Press, 1979.

Davis, Elizabeth A. *Index to the New World Recorded Anthology of American Music.* New York and London: W. W. Norton & Company, 1981.

DeLarma, Dominique Rene. *Bibliography of Black Music.* Westport: Greenwood Press, 1981.

Grove, Sir George. *Grove's Dictionary of Music and Musicians. American Supplement, Being the 6th Volume of the Complete Work.*

New York: The Macmillan Company, 1944. Edited by Waldo Selden Pratt.

Hartley, Kenneth R. *Bibliography of Theses and Dissertations in Sacred Music*. Detroit: Music Information Service, 1966.

Heintze, James R. "American Music before 1865 in Print and on Records: a Biblio-Discography: *Supplement to Music on Records*," in *Notes*, XXXIV (March 1978), pp. 571–80.

Hitchcock, H. Wiley. *American Music Before 1865 in Print and on Records: A Biblio-Discography*. Brooklyn: Institute for Studies in American Music, 1976.

Hixon, Donald L. *Music in Early America: a Bibliography of Music in Evans*. Metuchen: Scarecrow Press, 1970.

Horn, David. *The Literature of American Music in Books and Folk Music Collections*. Metuchen: The Scarecrow Press, 1977.

Keller, Kate Van Winkle, and Carolyn Rabson, comp. *The National Tune Index*. New York: University Music Editions, 1980.

Krummel, D. W., Jean Geil, Doris J. Dyen, and Deane L. Root. *Resources of American Music History: a Directory of Source Materials from Colonial Times to World War II*. Urbana: University of Illinois Press, 1981.

Lahee, Henry C. *Annals of Music in America*. Boston: Marshall Jones Company, 1922.

Lowens, Irving. *A Bibliography of Songsters Printed in America before 1821*. Worcester: American Antiquarian Society, 1976.

Mattfield, Julius. *A Handbook of American Operatic Premieres, 1731–1962*. Detroit Studies in Music Bibliography, 5. Detroit: Information Service, 1963.

———. *Variety Music Cavalcade, 1620–1960: A Chronology of Vocal and Instrumental Music Popular in the United States*. New York: Prentice-Hall, 1952. Rev. eds., 1962, 1971.

Mead, Rita H. *Doctoral Dissertation in American Music: a Classified Bibliography*. Brooklyn: Institute for Studies in American Music, 1974.

Mueller, Kate Hevner. *Twenty-Seven Major American Symphony Orchestras. A History and Analysis of Their Repertoires*. Bloomington: Indiana University Studies, 1973.

Mugridge, Donald H., and Blanche P. McCrum. *A Guide to the Study of the United States of America*. Washington: Library of Congress, 1960.

Odell, George Clinton Densmore. *Annals of the New York Stage*. 15 vols. New York: Columbia University Press, 1927–49.

Oja, Carol J. *American Music Recordings: A Discography of 20th-Century U.S. Composers*. Brooklyn: Institute for Studies in American Music, 1982.

Rust, Brian. *Guide to Discography*. Westport: Greenwood Press, 1981.

Sadie, Stanley, ed. *The New Grove Dictionary of Music and Musicians*. London: Macmillan Publishers, 1980.

Sonneck, Oscar George Theodore. *A Bibliography of Early Secular American Music (18th Century)*. Washington: The Library of Congress, 1905. Rev. and enl. by William Treat Upton, 1945.

Wolfe, Richard J. *Secular Music in America, 1801–1825: A Bibliography*, 3 vols. New York: The New York Public Library, 1964.

# A Note on New World Records, Recorded Anthology of American Music

In his Introduction, Charles Hamm refers to the numerous resources only recently available for the study of American music; perhaps none is as important as recordings, which have proliferated in the years since 1955 when Gilbert Chase's *America's Music* was first published.

The previous year, both Louisville Orchestra First Edition Records and Composers Recordings, Inc. began their now extensive catalogues of contemporary music; in the mid-sixties, the Nonesuch label began to explore not only contemporary American music, but earlier styles, folk traditions, and an even wider variety of genres.

When *New World Records*, Recorded Anthology of American Music was incorporated in 1975, it set out to do what is probably the broadest, most comprehensive overview of American music ever presented in a single record project. The Anthology comprises everything from concert art to calliope music, marching bands to bebop, film music to field hollers, symphonies to theater songs—music of every genre, spanning well over 200 years of America's history and cultural heritage.

The importance of recordings today cannot be overstated, because recordings have become the primary means by which the public and even many specialists learn music; for better or worse, the disc has effectively replaced the score for many professionals as well as amateurs in music.

And yet, ironically, the repertoire available on disc today is woefully limited and redundant. At this writing, a listener can choose from no less than 39 recorded performances of Beethoven's Fifth Symphony; yet Pulitzer Prize winning symphonic works like Michael Colgrass's *Déjà Vu* or Jacob Druckman's *Windows* have had to wait from several years to nearly a decade for their first (and only) recordings. Records that offer new or unusual repertoire are rarely released by commercial companies and, when they are, they are too often withdrawn from the catalogue.

In such a climate, a small, independent, specialized company like *New World Records* serves multiple and crucial functions. It acts much as a university press for music, offering important research resources, and making available major works which, for one reason or another, are not released or deemed marketable by commercial record companies.

Acknowledgments belong to the many whose contributions make it possible to undertake so ambitious a project. To the late Norman Lloyd and, most especially, to his successor, Howard Klein, Director for Arts of The Rockefeller Foundation, go the credit for having the farsightedness to conceptualize and develop an American music recording project as a fitting Bicentennial celebration.

Gene Bruck and Mario di Bonaventura, followed by William Schuman and Robert Sherman, conducted the initial studies for what would later become *New World Records*. In 1974, Herman Krawitz was asked to organize and head the new company. (He continues to serve as New World's President.) Milton Babbitt and David Hamilton offered invaluable advice as consultants at this early phase, and continue their association with New World to this day.

Krawitz brought together a diverse staff including Andrew Raeburn (Director of Artists & Repertoire, and my predecessor), and Michael Sonino (Art and Literary Director); I served as staff producer and Director of Research, working with a dynamic Editorial Committee of 15 experts in all areas of American music, to put together the Anthology. It was a project involving literally hundreds of renowned specialists, performers, scholars, writers (Charles Hamm among them)—a unique and remarkable confluence of talent.

Elizabeth Ostrow
Vice President
Director of Artists & Repertoire
June 1982

# Discography

*New World Records. Recorded Anthology of American Music.* New York: New World Records, 1976–present.

NW 201. Cecil Taylor
  Recent pieces by a leading Free Jazz ensemble.
NW 202. Songs of the Civil War
  Music sung in homes and around campfires, reflecting the grief and tragedy of both North and South.
NW 203. Sound Forms for Piano
  Experimental piano music by Henry Cowell, Conlon Nancarrow, John Cage, and Ben Johnston.
NW 204. *Loxodonta Africana*
  The jazz sound of Ricky Ford, talented young composer/performer.
NW 205. White Spirituals from *The Sacred Harp*
  Shape-note music from Albama.
NW 206. Malcolm Frager Plays
  Nineteenth-century piano music by Edward MacDowell, John Knowles Paine, Horatio Parker, Ethelbert Nevin, Henry F. Gilbert, Aldolph Foerster, and Henry Huss.
NW 207. Country Music in the Modern Era, 1940s–1970s
  Three decades of country-western music, from Eddy Arnold and Kitty Wells to Merle Haggard and Dolly Parton.
NW 208. Anthony Philip Heinrich and Louis Moreau Gottschalk
  Orchestral compositions by two of America's most important musicians of the mid-nineteenth century.

NW 209. New Music for Virtuosos
Recent music for small ensemble by Milton Babbitt, William O. Smith, Leslie Bassett, and Charles Wuorinen.

NW 210. Salvatore Martirano and Donald Martino
Choral music by Salvatore Martirano and Donald Martino.

NW 211. Winds of Change
Contemporary pieces for wind ensemble, by Vincent Persichetti, Hale Smith, Henry Brandt, Ross Lee Finney, and Robert Russell Bennett.

NW 212. Andrew Imbrie and Gunther Schuller
Recent string quartets by Andrew Imbrie and Gunther Schuller.

NW 213. Works by Arthur Farwell, Preston Ware Orem, Charles Wakefield Cadman
Compositions of the "Indianist" movement, attempts to create an American nationalist music.

NW 214. Harry Partch and John Cage
Experimental and avant-garde music by two of America's most controversial composers of the twentieth century.

NW 215. Follies, Scandals, and Other Diversions
Selections from shows and revues by Ziegfeld, the Schuberts, and others, performed by members of original casts.

NW 216. *Mirage:* Avant-garde and Third-Stream Jazz
Experimental and orchestral jazz by Duke Ellington, Lennie Tristano, Stan Kenton, Charles Mingus, George Russell, Gunther Schuller, Woody Herman, and John Lewis.

NW 217. *Jammin' for the Jackpot*
Big bands and territory bands of the 1930s, by the Casa Loma Orchestra, Chick Webb, Cab Calloway, Bennie Moten, and others.

NW 218. Works by Arthur Shepherd, Henry Cowell, Roy Harris
String quartets of the 1920s and '30s.

NW 219. Choral Music of the twentieth Century
Compositions by Randall Thompson, Elliott Carter, and Seymour Shifrin.

NW 220. *Angels' Visits* and Other Vocal Gems of Victorian America
Songs and hymns of the 1860s and '70s, dealing with the death of children, heaven, and angels.

NW 221. *I Wants to Be a Actor Lady* and Other Hits from Early Musical Comedies
Songs from popular stage shows of the period 1886–1906, with music by George M. Cohan, John Braham, Jerome Kern, Percy Gaunt, Victor Herbert, and others.

NW 222. *Praise the Lord and Pass the Ammunition*

Songs of the First and Second World Wars, in original recordings.

NW 223. *I'm On My Journey Home*
Vocal styles and resources in American folk music, from a variety of times and locales.

NW 224. *Brighten the Corner Where You Are*
Black gospel music and white urban gospel hymnody.

NW 225. *Hills and Home*
Thirty years of bluegrass, from Bill Monroe to the Newgrass Revival.

NW 226. *That's My Rabbit, My Dog Caught It*
Traditional Southern instrumental music from its earliest styles to more recent forms.

NW 227. The Mighty Wurlitzer
Music for movie-palace organs, to accompany silent films.

NW 228. John Alden Carpenter, Henry F. Gilbert, Adolph Weiss, and John Powell
Orchestral pieces of the 1910s and '20s utilizing indigenous musical material in a quest for a national American style.

NW 229. Songs by Samuel Barber and Ned Rorem
A collection featuring songs by two of the most successful American songwriters of the twentieth century.

NW 230. The Flowering of Vocal Music in America: Vol. 1
American vocal music of the early nineteenth century in the continental tradition, by various Moravian composers and Anton P. Heinreich.

NW 231. The Flowering of Vocal Music in America: Vol. 2
Vocal music of the early nineteenth century in the English tradition, by Benjamin Carr, George Jackson, and Oliver Shaw.

NW 232. John Bray and Raynor Taylor
Two extended works for the American musical stage from the early nineteenth century.

NW 233. *Come, Josephone, in My Flying Machine*
Songs of the early twentieth century concerning gadgets, inventions, and developments in transportation and communication.

NW 234. George F. Root: *The Haymakers*
The second part of a mid-nineteenth century secular cantata, offering an idealized view of rural America.

NW 235. *Maple Leaf Rag*
Ragtime in rural America by musicians of the South and Southwest.

NW 236. *Going Down the Valley*
Vocal and instrumental styles in traditional Southern music, by singers and string bands of the hillbilly era.

NW 237. Works by Paul Chihara, Chou Wen-Chung, Earl Kim, and Roger Reynolds
Various styles of post–World War II classical composition.

NW 238. The Vintage Irving Berlin
Selections from Berlin's songs written between the two world wars.

NW 239. *Brave Boys*
Ballads, broadsides, and other traditional music recorded over the past fifteen years among the English-speaking people of New England.

NW 240. *Where Have We Met Before?*
Forgotten songs from Broadway, Hollywood, and Tin Pan Alley.

NW 241. Toward an American Opera (1911–1954)
Excerpts from operas by Victor Herbert, Deems Taylor, Louis Gruenberg, Howard Hanson, Aaron Copland, and Gian Carlo Menotti.

NW 242. *Nica's Dream*
Small jazz groups of the 1950s and '60s, including the Modern Jazz Quartet, Sonny Rollins, Charles Mingus, George Russell, and others.

NW 243. But Yesterday Is Not Today
American art songs by Theodore Chanler, Paul Bowles, John Duke, Israel Citkowitz, Aaron Copland, Roger Sessions, and Robert Helps.

NW 244. Caliente = Hot
Puerto Rican and Cuban popular music in traditional island forms, as played in New York City.

NW 245. *Oh My Little Darling*
A variety of folk-song types—ballads, worksongs, games, and play-party songs.

NW 246. Songs of Earth, Water, Fire, and Sky
Music of the American Indian, of nine native American peoples.

NW 247. *When I Have Sung My Songs*
The American art song between 1900 and 1940, with songs by Edward MacDowell, Mrs. H. H. A. Beach, Horatio Parker, H. T. Burleigh, Richard Hageman, Randall Thompson, and others.

NW 248. *The Music Goes Round and Around*
The golden years of Tin Pan Alley, the 1930s, with songs by Harold Arlen, Richard Rogers, Hoagy Carmichael, and many others.

NW 249. *Shake, Rattle & Roll*
Rock 'n' Roll in the 1950s, from Joe Turner and Bill Haley to the Comets and Gary U.S. Bonds.

NW 250. Little Club Jazz

Small jazz groups of the 1930s, featuring such artists as Red Norvo, Teddy Wilson, and Cootie Williams.

NW 251. *Where Home Is*
Topical songs from nineteenth-century Cincinnati, the crossroads of Western migration and a major musical center of the time.

NW 252. Roots of the Blues
Field recordings made in the South, showing the development of blues from rural worksongs, field hollers, and lining hymns.

NW 253. William Schuman and Morton Gould
Two extended scores for modern dance from the mid-twentieth century.

NW 254. New Music for Virtuosos / 2
Chamber pieces written for virtuoso players, by Harvey Sollberger, Robert Morris, Robert Hall Lewis, Ralph Shapey, Andrew Imbrie, and Robert Erickson.

NW 255. Make a Joyful Noise
Mainstreams and backwaters of American paslmody, 1770–1840, with pieces by William Billings, Supply Belcher, Timothy Swan, Oliver Holden, Daniel Read, and others.

NW 256. *Sweet and Low Blues*
Big bands and territory bands of the 1920s, including those of Erskine Tate, Jabbo Smith, Alphonso Trent, Walter Page, etc.

NW 257. *The Wind Demon*
Mid-nineteenth century virtuoso piano compositions by George Bristow, Louis Moreau Gottschalk, William Mason, Charles Grobe, and others.

NW 258. David Diamond and Peter Mennin
Two major symphonies of the post–World War II era.

NW 259. *Cuttin' the Boogie*
Piano blues and boogie woogie from 1926 to 1941, by Clarence "Pinetop" Smith, Jimmy Blythe, Meade "Lux" Lewis, Albert Ammons, Pete Johnson, and others.

NW 260. *Shuffle Along*
Songs and dance pieces from the famous all-black musical that opened in New York in 1921, featuring music by Noble Sissle and Eubie Blake.

NW 261. *Straighten Up and Fly Right*
Rhythm and blues from the end of the swing era to the beginning of rock 'n' roll, by Lionel Hampton, Nat "King" Cole, T-Bone Walker, Lightnin' Hopkins, Muddy Waters, and many others.

NW 262 / 263. John Knowles Paine: *Mass in D*
A masterpiece of nineteenth-century American choral music, the

first large-scale composition by a native-born composer to be performed successfully in Europe.

NW 264. Old-Country Music in a New Land
Folk music of Russian, Slovakian, Cajun, Italian, British, Syrian, Greek, and Luthuanian immigrants, recorded in America.

NW 265. *Don't Give the Name a Bad Place*
Selections from the American musical stage, 1870–1900, portraying ethnic stereotypes.

NW 266. *The Pride of America*
The Golden Age of the American march, with popular selections from the turn of the century.

NW 267. *The Hand That Holds the Bread*
Post–Civil War songs, tracing the economic and social concerns of rural and urban workers in America.

NW 268. Mrs. H. H. A. Beach and Arthur Foote
Violin sonatas by two turn-of-the-century Americans.

NW 269. *Steppin' on the Gas*
The evolution from ragtime to early jazz, 1913–1927, in performances by such bands as Europe's Society Orchestra, Sam Morgan's Jazz Band, and the New Orleans Rhythm Kings.

NW 270. *Brother, Can You Spare a Dime?*
American song during the Great Depression, from the breadlines of New York to the Dust Bowl of Oklahoma.

NW 271. Bebop
The music of Dizzy Gillespie, Charlie Parker, Thelonius Monk, Bud Powell, Tadd Dameron, and other innovative musicians of the 1940s.

NW 272. . . . and then we wrote . . .
A collection of performances of their own works by some of America's greatest popular composers of the twentieth century, including George Gershwin, Hoagy Carmichael, Stephen Sondheim, and Cole Porter.

NW 273. Charles Tomlinson Griffes
Instrumental and vocal works by America's leading impressionistic composer.

NW 274. *Jive at Five*
The stylemakers of jazz; music by such giants and innovators as Count Basie, Louis Armstrong, Bix Beiderbecke, and Benny Goodman.

NW 275. Introspection
Neglected but important jazz musicians of the 1950s and '60s, among them Steve Lacy, Booker Little, Jaki Byard, and Herbie Nichols.

NW 276. The Birth of Liberty

Music of the American Revolution—ballads, choral works, fife and drum music, and military marches.

NW 277. Aaron Copland
Piano music, 1926–1948, in definitive performances by Copland and Leonard Bernstein.

NW 278. Georgie Sea Island Songs
Field recordings of sacred and secular vocal music preserving close ties with the nineteenth-century folk spiritual.

NW 279. *Yes Sir, That's My Baby*
The golden years of Tin Pan Alley, 1920–1929, in performances of the time by Paul Whiteman, Ruth Etting, Ethel Waters, Gene Austin, Louis Armstrong, and Rudy Vallee.

NW 280. Fugues, Fantasia, and Variation
Nineteenth-century concert organ music by Dudley Buck, Horatio Parker, John Knowles Paine, and George Whiting.

NW 281. Chamber Music
Contemporary music for small ensemble by Lou Harrison, Ben Weber, Lukas Foss, and Ingolf Dahl.

NW 282. The Sousa and Pryor Bands
Original recordings, made between 1901 and 1926, of America's two greatest concert bands.

NW 283. *'Spiew Juchasa / Song of the Shepherd*
Popular songs and dances of Polish Americans and Ukranian Americans, recorded in this country.

NW 284. Jazz in Revolution
Big-band jazz from swing to bebop and beyond, featuring the bands of Stan Kenton, Gerald Wilson, Elliot Lawrence, Billy Eckstine, Lionel Hampton, Claude Thornhill, and Kenny Clarke.

NW 285. Works by Henry Cowell, Ruth Crawford Seeger, Wallingford Riegger, John J. Becker.
Music by composers of the New Music Edition, an early twentieth-century publication of innovative American music.

NW 286. Walter Piston and Leon Kirchner
Orchestral music by two of America's leading classical composers of the post–World War II era.

NW 287. Country Music: South and West
Music by some of the central figures of the hillbilly and early country-western eras, including Jimmie Rodgers, the Carter Family, Gene Autry, Roy Acuff, Bob Wills, and the Sons of the Pioneers.

NW 288 / 289. *The Mother of Us All*
A complete recording of the second operatic collaboration between composer Virgil Thomson and librettist Gertrude Stein.

NW 290. *Let's Get Loose*

Folk and popular blues style through the early 1940s, including country blues, jug bands, vaudeville blues, and Chicago blues bands.

NW291. *Old Mother Hippletoe*

Rural and urban children's songs from a broad cross-section of ethnic and national groups—lullabies, play-party, and story songs.

NW 292. Dark and Light in Spanish New Mexico

Alabados and Bailes from the Spanish peoples of the American Southwest.

NW 293. Come and Trip It

Instrumental dance music popular from the 1780s to the 1920s, including waltzes, polkas, cakewalks, two-steps, and tangos.

NW 294. The Gospel Ship

Baptist hymns and white spirituals from the Southern mountains, recorded in Kentucky, Virginia, and Arkansas.

NW 295. *When Malindy Sings*

An anthology of jazz vocalists, 1938–1961, including Betty Carter, Ella Fitzgerald, Billie Holiday, Jimmy Rushing, and Sarah Vaughan.

NW 296. Roger Sessions: *When Lilacs Last in the Dooryard Bloom'd*

A complete recording of Sessions's setting of Walt Whitman's famous eulogy to Abraham Lincoln.

NW 297. Songs of Love, Luck, Animals, and Magic

Music of the Yurok and Tolowa Indians.

NW 298. *It Had to Be You*

Popular keyboard music from the days of the speakeasy to the TV era, by Zez Confrey, Eddy Duchin, Frankie Carle, Liberace, Roger Williams, and others.

NW 299. Music of the Federal Era

Vocal music, marches, chamber works, and keyboard music from the first decades of the nineteenth century, by such composers as Raynor Taylor, Benjamin Carr, Oliver Shaw, and Victor Pelissier.

NW 300. Songs of the Twentieth Century

Art songs by Charles Ives, Theodore Chanler, Robert Ward, Norman Dello Joio, and Irving Fine.

NW 301. Oku Shareh

Turtle dance songs of San Juan Pueblo.

NW 302. Budapest String Quartet

Major string quartets by Walter Piston and Roger Sessions.

NW 303. Cecil Taylor: *3 Phasis*

A new, extended piece by the Cecil Taylor Unit, created especially for New World Records.

NW 304. Exultation
Contemporary piano music, by Henry Cowell, George Perle, Robert Evett, Samuel Adler, Frederic Goossen, and Wendell Keeney.

NW 305. William Parker: An American Song Recital
Art songs by Ernst Bacon, Robert Evett, Charles Griffes, Lee Hoiby, John Jacob Niles, and Ned Rorem.

NW 306. Parnassus
Contemporary chamber works, by Stefan Wolpe, Mario Davidovsky, Charles Wuorinen, Erik Lundborg, and David Olan.

NW 307. Milton Babbitt and Roger Sessions
More music by these two leading figures of the university avant-garde.

NW 308. Arthur Berger and Stefan Wolpe
Contemporary piano and chamber music.

NW 309. John Corigliano and Samuel Barber
Corigliano's *Concerto for Clarinet* and Barber's *Third Eassy for Orchestra*, his last completed composition.

NW 310/311. The Collected Piano Works of Charles Tomlinson Griffes
All of the major compositions for piano, including several unpublished pieces.

NW 312. The Yankee Brass Band
Mid-nineteenth-century American brass band music from the collections of Walter Dignam, Hosea Ripley, and George Stratton, played on nineteenth-century instruments.

NW 313. Cadenzas and Variations
Sonatas and works for solo violin, by Aaron Copland, Leo Ornstein, Philip Glass, and Richard Wernick.

NW 314/315. *Back in the Saddle Again*
American cowboys songs, in two traditions: field recordings of authentic cowboys such as Glenn Ohrlin, Carl Sprague, and Harry McClintock; and commercial products by Tex Ritter, Gene Autry, and Roy Rogers.

NW 316/317. *Whole Lotta Shaking Going On*
Rock 'n' roll from 1955 to 1958, including original black and white performers, the teen idols, cover versions, and rockabilly singers.

*Folk Music in America.* Ed. by Richard K. Spottswood. Washington: Library of Congress, 1977.

1. Religious Music, Congregational and Ceremonial
2. Songs of Love, Courtship, and Marriage

3. Dance Music, Breakdowns and Waltzes
4. Dance Music, Reels, Polkas, and More
5. Dance Music, Ragtime, Jazz, and More
6. Songs of Migration and Immigration
7. Songs of Complaint and Protest
8. Songs of Labor and Livelihood
9. Songs of Death and Tragedy
10. Songs of War and History
11. Songs of Humor and Hilarity
12. Songs of Local History and Events
13. Songs of Childhood
14. Solo and Display Music
15. Religious Music, Solo and Performance

*The Smithsonian Collection of Classic Country Music.* 8 discs. Selected and annotated by Bill Malone. Washington: Smithsonian Institution, 1981.

*The Smithsonian Collection of Classic Jazz.* 6 discs. Selected and annotated by Martin Williams. Washington: Smithsonian Institution, 1973.

*Anthology of American Folk Music.* Ed. by Harry Smith. New York: Folkways Records, 1952.

FA 2951. Ballads
FA 2952. Social Music
FA 2953. Songs

*Music in America.* Coordinated by Karl Krueger. New York: The Society for the Preservation of the American Musical Heritage, 1958–72.

| | | |
|---|---|---|
| *Bay Psalm Book* (1640) | | MIA 102 |
| Beach, Amy Marcy (Cheney) | *Symphony*, Opus 32 | MIA 139 |
| Billings, William | *Anthems* | MIA 114 |
| Bird, Arthur H. | *Kleine Suite*, Opus 32 | MIA 131 |
| Bristow, George F. | *Arcadian Symphony*, Opus 49 | MIA 135 |
| Bristow, George F. | *Symphony No. 2*, Opus 24 | MIA 143 |
| Buck, Dudley | *Festival Overture* | MIA 141 |
| Carpenter, John Alden | *Sea Drift* | MIA 142 |
| *Catholic Mission Music of California* | | MIA 96 |

| Chadwick, George W. | *Symphony No. 2, Opus 21* | MIA 134 |
|---|---|---|
| Chadwick, George W. | *Symphony No. 3* | MIA 140 |
| *Choral Music of the 18th and 20th Centuries* | | MIA 111 |
| *Choral Music in 20th-Century America* | | MIA 116 |
| Coerne, Louis Adolphe | *Excalibur* | MIA 141 |
| Farwell, Arthur George | *The Gods of the Mountain* | MIA 128 |
| Foote, Arthur William | *Francesca de Rimini* | MIA 127 |
| Foote, Arthur William | *Selected Piano Compositions* | MIA 123 |
| Foote, Arthur William | *Suite for Orchestra, Opus 36* | MIA 122 |
| Fry, William Henry | *Overture to Macbeth* | MIA 132 |
| Gehot, Joseph | *String Quartet, Opus 7* | MIA 101 |
| Gehot, Joseph | *Six String Quartets, Opus 1* | MIA 125 |
| Gilbert, Henry F. B. | *Nocturne for Orchestra* | MIA 141 |
| Gottschalk, Louis Moreau | *Selected Piano Works* | MIA 110 |
| Gualdo, Giovanni | *Trio Sonatas, Opus 2* | MIA 112 |
| Hadley, Henry Kimball | *Salome* | MIA 138 |
| Hadley, Henry Kimball | *Symphony No. 2* | MIA 145 |
| Herbert, Victor | *Hero and Leander* | MIA 121 |
| Hewitt, James | *Sonata for Piano, Opus 5* | MIA 126 |
| Hill, Edward B. | *Stevensoniana Suite No. 1* | MIA 142 |
| MacDowell, Edward A. | *Lamia, Sea Pieces* | MIA 133 |
| MacDowell, Edward A. | *Suite for Orchestra No. 2.* | MIA 137 |
| MacDowell, Edward A. | *Lancelot and Elaine* | MIA 131 |
| MacDowell, Edward A. | *Suite for Orchestra No. 1* | MIA 119 |
| Moller, John Christopher | *String Quartet No. 6.* | MIA 101 |
| Moravian composers | *Eleven Songs* | MIA 98 |
| Paine, John Knowles | *As You Like It (Overture)* | MIA 141 |
| Paine, John Knowles | *Azara (Moorish Dances)* | MIA 132 |
| Paine, John Knowles | *Symphony No. 1* | MIA 103 |
| Paine, John Knowles | *Symphony No. 2* | MIA 120 |
| Parker, Horatio W. | *Vathek* | MIA 138 |
| Parker, Horatio W. | *A Northern Ballad* | MIA 132 |
| Peter, Johann Friedrich | *Six Quintets* | MIA 105 |

| | | |
|---|---|---|
| Read, Daniel | *Anthems from the Columbian Harmonist* | MIA 114 |
| Reinagle, Alexander | *Sonata for Piano*, in E Major | MIA 101 |
| Robertson, Leroy J. | *String Quartet*, in e minor | MIA 115 |
| Still, William Grant | *Afro-American Symphony* | MIA 118 |
| Strong, Templeton | *Second Symphony* (*Sintram*) | MIA 136 |
| Taylor, Raynor | *Rondo for Piano* | MIA 126 |
| Taylor, Raynor | *Six Sonatas for Cello and Continuo* | MIA 108 |
| van der Stucken, Frank | *Rigaudon*, for Orchestra | MIA 132 |
| Wollenhaupt, Hermann A. | *Two Pieces for Piano* | MIA 110 |

*Music*

BILLY THE KID by Aaron Copland. © Copyright 1946 by Aaron Copland. Renewed 1973. Reprinted by permission of Aaron Copland, Copyright Owner, and Boosey & Hawkes, Inc., Sole Publishers. p. 442

"BROOKFIELD" and "WASHINGTON" from *The Complete Works of William Billings.* © 1977 The American Musicological Society and The Colonial Society of Massachusetts. Courtesy of The University Press of Virginia. pp. 144–46

DUO FOR VIOLIN AND PIANO by Roger Sessions. © Copyright: Edward B. Marks Music Corporation. Used by Permission. p. 557

FOR 1, 2, OR 3 PEOPLE by Christian Wolff. Copyright © 1964 by C. F. Peters Corporation. Reprinted by Permission. p. 606

PROJECTION 2 by Morton Feldman. Copyright © 1962 by C. F. Peters Corporation. Reprinted by Permission. p. 605

QUARTET ROMANTIC by Henry Cowell. Copyright © 1974 by C. F. Peters Corporation. Reprinted by Permission. p. 592

SECOND SONATA by George Antheil. © 1931 by George Antheil. Reprinted by Permission of the Estate of George Antheil. p. 586

SONATA NO. 1 FOR PIANO by Charles Ives. Copyright 1954 by Peer International Corporation. Copyright renewed by Peer International Corporation. All Rights Reserved Including the Right of Public Performance for Profit. Used by Permission. pp. 430–31

SONATA III by Alexander Reinagle. © 1978, A–R Editions, Inc. Used by Permission. p. 103

SONATA FOR VIOLINCELLO AND PIANO by Elliott Carter. © 1951, 1953 by Associated Music Publishers. All rights Reserved. International Copyright Secured. Used by Permission. p. 569

STRING QUARTET by George Rochberg. © 1971 Theodore Presser Company. Reproduced by Permission of the Publisher. p. 577

STRING QUARTET NO. 1 by Charles Ives. © Copyright 1961 and 1963 by Peer International Corporation. International Copyright Secured. All Rights Reserved Including the Right of Public Performance for Profit. Used by Permission. pp. 427–28

SWEET GEORGIA BROWN by Ben Bernie, Maceo Pinkard, and Kenneth Casey. © 1925 Warner Bros., Inc. Copyright Renewed. All Rights Reserved, Used by Permission. p. 366

THIRD SYMPHONY by Roy Harris. © 1940 by G. Schirmer, Inc. Renewed 1967. All Rights Reserved. International Copyright Secured. Used by Permission. pp. 443–45

*Lyrics*

"BLUE MOON" by Richard Rodgers and Lorenz Hart. Copyright © 1934, Renewed 1962; Metro-Goldwyn-Mayer Inc. All Rights administered and controlled by Robbins Music Corporation. All Rights Reserved. Used by Permission. p. 360

"BROKEN DOWN TRAMP" words and music by A. P. Carter. © 1938 by Peer International Corp. Copyright Renewed by Peer International Corp. International Copyright Secured. All Rights Reserved, including the Right of Public Performance for Profit. Used by Permission. p. 469

"CAROLINA IN THE MORNING." Courtesy Donaldson Publishing Co. Used by Permission. p. 358

# Index